George W. Clark

The Gospel of Mark

a popular commentary upon a critical basis, especially designed for pastors and

Sunday schools - Vol. 2

George W. Clark

The Gospel of Mark
a popular commentary upon a critical basis, especially designed for pastors and Sunday schools - Vol. 2

ISBN/EAN: 9783337285432

Printed in Europe, USA, Canada, Australia, Japan

Cover: Foto ©Lupo / pixelio.de

More available books at **www.hansebooks.com**

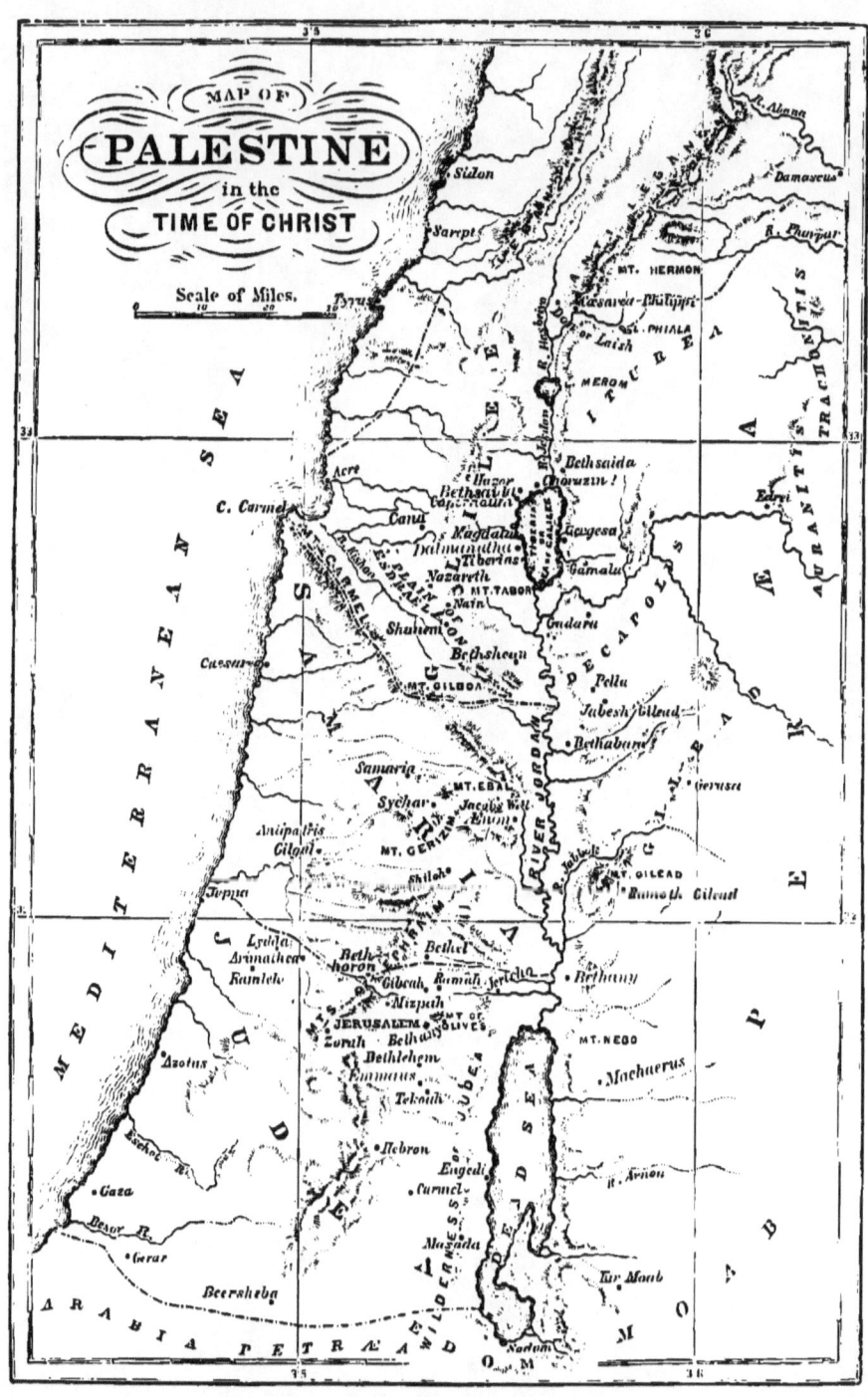

A People's Commentary

THE GOSPEL OF MARK

A POPULAR COMMENTARY UPON A CRITICAL
BASIS, ESPECIALLY DESIGNED FOR PASTORS
AND SUNDAY SCHOOLS ✧✧✧✧✧✧✧✧✧✧✧✧✧

BY

GEO. W. CLARK, D. D.

Author of "A New Harmony of the Gospels," etc.

A NEW AND REVISED EDITION

PHILADELPHIA
AMERICAN BAPTIST PUBLICATION SOCIETY
1420 Chestnut Street
1896

PREFACE.

THIS volume has been prepared under the conviction that no Gospel has been so neglected as that of Mark. But few commentators, either ancient or modern, have given it the attention it deserves. With few exceptions it has been treated as an abridgment of Matthew, or a compilation of Matthew and Luke, or, more lately, as the oldest Gospel and a summary basis of the others. Although the most distinct and graphic of the first three Gospels, it has been generally passed hurriedly over with occasional notes and frequent references to parallel passages in Matthew and Luke. Thus it has been thrown into the background as comparatively unimportant, and readers and students of the Bible, especially of the English Scriptures, have for the most part overlooked its great value and its distinctive character. Such facts show that no commentary, however thorough and exhaustive, on the other Gospels, can do justice to Mark. An attempt is therefore made in this volume to give Notes on Mark, complete in themselves and independent of Notes on Matthew and Luke. At the same time the Chronology and Harmony of the Gospels are kept in view, and thus too the individuality and independence of Mark is the more clearly seen, while catching glimpses of the four sides of the sacred narrative.

The aim has been to give a popular commentary on a critical basis, adapted to Sabbath schools, teachers and scholars, Bible classes and families, and many pastors and preachers. Difficult passages have received attention, and no point on which a commonly intelligent Sabbath-school teacher might wish light has been intentionally passed over. Indeed, many plain questions have been touched upon, because what is clear to one is obscure to another, and from the conviction that we often count too much upon the knowledge of even more intelligent readers. To avoid prolixity, exhortation has been dispensed with, the mere detailing of various views has not generally been attempted, but what has seemed to be the true one stated. Where, however, it seemed necessary, different views have been presented and discussed. The latest results of exegetical and textual criticism, and of recent discovery, have been sought and incorporated in the Notes. And to make all as clear to the eye as possible, a variety of type is used.

The execution of this plan for aiding students of the English Scriptures in studying the Life of Christ as presented by Mark, has necessitated similarity of comment, where thought and expression are similar to those in the other Gospels ; yet variety has been sought, and an independence maintained. This is believed to be a less evil than the troublesome practice of referring to other volumes for what would be, after all, but an imperfect exposition of the sacred text.

Attention is called to the suggestions at the end of each chapter, which are confirmed by references from other portions of Scripture. Almost every verse is thus remarked upon, the whole forming by itself a brief, practical and doctrinal commentary on the Gospel. This is designed to aid teachers in enforcing Sabbath-school lessons, and pastors in expository preaching, and week-day evening lectures.

The division of chapters into verses, first introduced into the English Bible by the Genevan version (A D. 1560), often interferes with the connection of thought, and impedes a quick and intelligent view of many passages. The paragraph form is therefore adopted ; and to aid the eye and facilitate study, subjects have been placed at the head of principal paragraphs or divisions.

Many teachers and advanced scholars prefer to explain Scripture by Scripture. Carefully selected references have therefore been placed in the margin of the text. These, in connection with those given in the Notes and Remarks, are believed to constitute this the most complete reference Mark published.

In preparing this work the author has called to his aid all the helps within his reach, the earlier and later critical and popular Commentaries; Harmonies of the Gospels, Books of Travels, Histories of the Church and of Doctrines; Treatises on the Life of Christ, and Grammatical Authorities on the New Testament. His thanks are specially due to Professor T. J. Conant, D.D., of Brooklyn, N. Y., and Professor H. B. Hackett, D.D., of Rochester Theological Seminary, for facilities in consulting rare and valuable works.

This volume has been prepared with great labor, amid the cares and anxieties of pastoral work, from a deep and abiding conviction of duty to Christ and his cause. The favorable reception given to previous works has encouraged the author to persevere in this; and he hopes, through the blessing of God and the prayers and co-operation of his brethren, to prepare similar works, not only on the remaining Gospels, but upon the whole New Testament. He is, however, deeply conscious that he has not attained to that high standard which has been his aim. But while striving toward it, his earnest prayer is, that God may use this volume in leading many into closer relations to Christ, and into clearer views and a more perfect practice of his word.

BALLSTON SPA, N. Y., *October*, 1872.

REVISED EDITION.

The author has made such changes and corrections as seemed necessary under the present state of exegetical learning and textual criticism.

HIGHTSTOWN, N. J., March, 1896.

INTRODUCTORY REMARKS.

THE SECOND GOSPEL.

It can not be regarded merely fortuitous that the four Gospels have come down to us in a certain order, and that THE GOSPEL ACCORDING TO MARK has been so generally accorded the second place in catalogues, manuscripts, and versions. Thus the Muratorian fragment, as early as A.D. 170, designates the Gospels of Luke and John as the third and fourth, and the imperfect sentence with which it begins points to that of Mark as the second. So also Irenæus, about A.D. 183, who had sat at the feet of Polycarp, the disciple of the Apostle John, mentions the Gospels in the order in which they have since generally appeared. Later still, Origen recognizes the order as chronological. It is very possible that this order was fixed by John himself. Eusebius in his Church History (3, 24) gives an old tradition, that the three Gospels, already extensively known, were laid before John by his friends. He testified to their truth, but said that they passed over the beginning of Christ's public ministry. His friends thereupon requested him to give an account of the period which had been passed over. The tradition is in harmony with the contents and supplemental character of John's Gospel. Some transcribers have indeed put the Gospels of the two Apostles before those of the other two, who were only Evangelists. But this they seem to have done for no better reason than that they regarded the writers of the former to outrank those of the latter. There has doubtless been a Divine providence and design in the order in which the Gospels have been arranged in the Bible. And the importance of this arrangement, I apprehend, is not so much its bearing on the chronology of these sacred narratives, as upon the order in which they should be read and studied.

THE WRITER OF THE SECOND GOSPEL.

The second Gospel has been universally ascribed to Mark, as its author, whom ancient Christian writers with one consent declare to have been "the interpreter of Peter." He was probably the "John whose surname was Mark," mentioned in Acts 12 : 12, 25, the former being his Jewish, and the latter his Roman name; the son of Mary, a Christian matron and Jewish proprietress, residing at Jerusalem, Acts 12 : 12 ; and " a cousin of Barnabas," for so Col. 4 : 10 should be translated. Some without sufficient reasons have supposed two Marks, one the companion of Paul, the other of Peter; while Da Costa even thought to identify the Evangelist with the "devout soldier" sent by Cornelius to Peter, Acts 10 : 7.

Mark appears to have been converted to Christianity through the instrumentality of Peter, who styles him "My son" (1 Pet. 5 : 13); but whether this occurred before or after the resurrection of Jesus is wholly unknown. A tradition reports Mark as one of the seventy, who took offense at our Lord's hard saying (John 6 : 60-66), but this is unsupported and contrary to another, that he was neither a hearer nor a follower of our Lord. More probable is the opinion that he was the young man who followed, and then fled from the betrayed Master, and who is alone mentioned by Mark, and with great minuteness (Mark 14 : 51). But however this may be, we learn that he became an assistant and companion of Paul and Barnabas in their first missionary journey (Acts 13 : 5), but left them at Pamphylia and returned to Jerusalem. He thus became a cause of variance and separation, on their second journey, Acts 15 : 36-40. Barnabas accordingly took Mark with him to Cyprus. Mark, however, recovered the confidence of Paul, and was with him in his first imprisonment at Rome, Col. 4 : 10 ; Philem. 24. After this he was with Peter at Babylon, 2 Pet. 5 : 13. Still later he seems to have been with Timothy at Ephesus, 2 Tim. 4 : 11. Beyond this point the Scriptures are silent concerning him.

Tradition, however, brings Mark with Peter at Rome, but this apparently rests upon a misunderstanding of 1 Pet. 5 : 13, Babylon being wrongly taken as the typical name of Rome (*Eusebius, Eccle. Hist.* ii. 15 ; vi. 14). Thence he is said to have gone to Alexandria, where he became pastor of the church, and where he is said to have suffered martyrdom. But all this is very uncertain.

THE LANGUAGE IN WHICH MARK WROTE.

That Mark wrote in Greek is the decisive testimony of antiquity. Some, indeed, with Cardinal Baronius and Scholz, on the authority of a subscription to the Peshito version and to some Greek manuscripts, have maintained that Latin was the original language. It must be remembered, however, that these postscripts are merely the conjectures of some transcriber; but when written, or by whom, is unknown. The supposition, that because this Gospel was intended for Roman Christians it must therefore have been written in Latin, implies an ignorance of the Roman Christians of that age, who so well understood Greek that Paul wrote to them in

INTRODUCTORY REMARKS.

that language. Some Roman Catholic writers have earnestly maintained a Latin original, in order to strengthen the authority of the Vulgate; and have appealed to a pretended Latin autograph of the Evangelist, preserved in the library of St. Mark at Venice. But this has been found to be merely a part of an ancient Latin manuscript of the four Gospels. If Mark had written in Latin the fact would have been known, and the Gospel seen, in the early ages, and some copies would have doubtless descended to a later period. But no ancient writer mentions either its existence or its loss. Mark's Gospel in Latin is without a single witness, and without any historical foundation.

THE GENUINENESS OF THE SECOND GOSPEL.

All historical testimony unites in support of the common belief that the second Gospel was written by Mark. This appears never to have been called in question till the present century, when Schleiermacher (1832), followed by some other German critics, thought he saw an apparent discrepancy between the orderly Gospel we now possess and that described by Papias of Hierapolis in the first half of the second century. The words of Papias are thus quoted by Eusebius (*Eccle. Hist.* iii. 39): "This is what was related by the elder (that is John, not the Apostle, but a disciple of Jesus); Mark, having become the interpreter of Peter, wrote down accurately whatever he remembered, not indeed as recording in order the things spoken and done by Christ. For he was not himself a hearer or follower of the Lord; but he afterward followed Peter, who gave instructions according to the wants of his hearers, but not as making an orderly narrative of the Lord's discourses or sayings. Mark, however, committed no error in thus writing some things as he remembered them. For he was careful of one thing, to omit nothing of the things he heard, and not to repeat anything among them incorrectly." These words of Papias are somewhat indefinite, referring to what Peter did, and Mark did; to "the discourses of the Lord," and "the things spoken and done by Christ." The language seems to refer to a systematic arrangement, and may have been intended to contrast the Gospel of Mark with that of Matthew (of whom Papias had previously spoken) as an arranged collection especially of our Lord's discourses. It is by no means necessary to make Papias say that Mark's Gospel was only a loose collection of a few narratives without connection or order. Besides, Papias was not a man of the best judgment. Eusebius affirms that he was "a man of very small mind judging from his words," and Papias himself tells us that he depended on oral traditions. While therefore his language must not be used to offset the united testimony of the past, it does most clearly testify in favor of Mark as the author of the second Gospel.

To the testimony of Papias may be added that of Justin Martyr, about the middle of the second century, who quotes Mark 3 : 17 ; of Clement of Alexandria, about A.D. 190, one of the most learned men of his age, who speaks of Mark having composed his Gospel ; and of Irenæus and Tertullian, both of whom speak of this Gospel. There is no need, however, of accumulating testimony. This Gospel has come down to us as one of the undisputed books of the New Testament ; it is named in all the ancient catalogues, and found in the earlier and later manuscripts. It appeared in early versions, the most important of which are the Syriac Peshito, made not later than the close of the second century, the old Latin version, about the middle of the second century, and the Latin Vulgate, made by Jerome near the close of the fourth century. "It is enough," as Alford remarks, " that from the very earliest time the Gospel has been known as that of Mark ; confirmed by the circumstance that *this name belongs to no great and distinguished founder* of the church, to whom it might naturally be ascribed, but to *one, the ascription to whom can hardly be accounted for*, except by its foundation in matter of fact."

GENUINENESS OF MARK 16 : 9–20.

But not so with the last twelve verses of this Gospel. Since the appearance of Griesbach's second edition of the New Testament in Greek (1796), it has become common to regard these verses as not belonging to the original Gospel. Before him, Mill (1707), Bengel (1734), Wetstein (1751), Birch (1788), and Matthæi (1788), defended their genuineness ; and so did even Scholz (1830), a pupil of Griesbach. But a majority of the latest textual critics have given their verdict against the passage. Some with Tischendorf and Meyer pronounce it spurious, or an apocryphal fragment ; others with Tregelles and Alford consider it a later addition by another hand, but to be regarded as an authentic part of the second Gospel ; or with Wordsworth, while defending the passage, reluctantly admit that it may not have been penned by Mark himself.

With Olshausen, Bleek, Ellicott, F. H. Scrivener, J. A. Alexander, and others, I regard these verses as a genuine portion of Mark's Gospel for the following reasons :

FIRST, *External testimony is strong in their favor*. It is found in all the Greek manuscripts of the Gospels, except the two oldest, the Sinaitic and the Vatican. Yet in the latter is this remarkable phenomenon : After ch. 16 : 8, part of the column and the whole of the next are left vacant,—the only vacant column in the New Testament portion of the manuscript, and sufficient to contain the twelve verses. The inference is that the transcriber knew of these verses, and while he did not copy them, for some unknown reason, he left a place for their future insertion. That some copies of this Gospel existed in early times without this passage, may be variously explained. The last leaf of some copy may have been worn away; or torn off by accident, or through hierarchical prejudice against a passage presenting so great unbelief among the Apostles. Or the difficulty of reconciling this portion of Mark with the other Gospels might possibly have led some transcriber to omit it. Such difficulty is noticed by Eusebius and others, which is really of weight for the passage, rather than against it. For, as Dr. George Campbell justly says, "Transcribers sometimes presume to add and alter, in order to remove contradictions, but not, as far as I can remember, in order to make them."

Rev. J. W. Burgon, of Oxford, in his recent able work on The Last Twelve Verses of Mark (pp. 212-242), supposes that this passage constituted one of the lessons for public services, and that some ancient copyist mistook the words "the end," which may have been written after ver. 8, to mark the conclusion of the preceding lesson, for the subscription or the end of the Gospel. And this might easily have occurred if Mark 16: 8 came at the bottom of the left-hand page of a manuscript, the next leaf of which was missing, "the very thing which has happened in respect of one of the manuscripts at Moscow." We have only to suppose the omission of the passage in a single early manuscript, for some reason, and then repeated in others, and we see at once why a note is added in some later manuscripts stating that the verses in question are wanting in some copies; why a short and manifestly spurious ending was prepared by some one, and that both of these endings are found in the Regius manuscript of the eighth or ninth century; and why the section is wanting in some manuscripts of the Armenian version.

But older than any existing Greek manuscript are the most ancient versions. The Syriac Peshito version, which was made during the last half of the second century, and the old Latin version, made about the middle of the second century, both contain these verses. And so also the Curetonian Syriac version, and the Thebaic, made not later than the third century. And let it be remembered that these versions represent Greek manuscripts one and two hundred years older than any now extant. And in the fourth century, to which the Vatican and Sinaitic manuscripts belong, the Latin Vulgate,* made by Jerome, the Gothic, and Memphitic versions, have this portion of Mark's Gospel. And so have several manuscripts of the Armenian version, which was possibly made as early as the fifth century.

To this must be added the testimony of early Christian writers. Justin Martyr (A.D. 151) in his first Apology (c. 45) quotes from verse 20; and Irenæus (A.D. 177-202) in his third book against Heresies (10. 6) quotes verse 19, and thus recognizes this passage as a part of Mark's Gospel.

* As in the oldest manuscript of Jerome's version, Codex Amiatinus.

INTRODUCTORY REMARKS.

The Apostolic Constitutions quote the 17th and 18th verses; and the Apocryphal Acts of Pilate, which is assigned to the third century, contains verses 15-18. Aphraates (Wright's ed., p. 21), of the early Syrian church, in his first Homily (A.D. 337) quotes verses 16-18. The same verses, and also the 20th, are quoted by Ambrose, about A.D. 380. Chrysostom (A.D. 400) refers to the 9th verse, and quotes the 19th and 20th, and says, " This is the end of the Gospel." (Opp. iii. 765, A, B.) Augustine (A.D. 395-430) frequently quotes from this passage, and says that Mark's narrative of the Resurrection was publicly read in the church. Verse 20 is also quoted by Nestorius and Cyril of Alexandria (about A.D. 430).

Eusebius (A.D. 325) is the earliest writer who intimates that the conclusion of Mark's Gospel is wanting in certain manuscripts. In an abridged work on the Apparent Inconsistencies in the Gospels, a certain Marinus is represented as asking concerning a supposed discrepancy between Matthew 28 : 1 and Mark 16 : 9, and Eusebius answers that it admits a twofold solution. He who would reject this whole passage, would say that it is not found in all the copies of Mark's Gospel, that the accurate copies make Mark's narrative end with " For they were afraid " (ver. 8). But another, not daring to reject anything from the text of the Gospels, will hold that both are to be received; and upon this premise Eusebius proceeds to show how the difficulty may be solved. And immediately after he intimates that the difficulty arises from a misconception of the Greek phrase. It must be seen that Eusebius does not himself pronounce against the genuineness of this passage, but rather for it, especially when we add the fact that he elsewhere quotes from it. (*Nov. P. Bib.* iv., pp. 262, 264, 301.)

What Jerome (about A.D. 400), Victor of Antioch (about A.D. 425), Hesychius of Jerusalem (of the sixth or seventh century), and some others, say about certain manuscripts wanting this passage, appears to be but repetitions of what Eusebius had said. " His words," says Rev. J. W. Burgon, " were translated by Jerome, adopted by Hesychius, referred to by Victor, reproduced 'with a difference' in more than one ancient scholion." But Jerome gives these twelve verses a place in his revision of the old Latin version, the Vulgate, and also quotes verses 9 and 14 in his writings. Victor of Antioch also gives the remarkable testimony, that although this passage was not found in many copies, certain persons having supposed it spurious, yet he had found it in very many copies, and in the *authentic Palestinian Gospel of Mark*, and had therefore placed it in his own work (BURGON's *Last Twelve Verses of Mark*, pp. 288-290.) Mr. Burgon* also states (p. 122) that twenty-two later manuscripts contain a

---
* Mr. Burgon (pp. 114-122, 228-231) found by personal examination that Tischendorf, Tregelles, and others had erroneously made some of these manuscripts bear testimony against these verses.

similar comment, while not a single manuscript asserts that these verses are wanting in the more ancient and accurate copies. Hesychius of Jerusalem also, in his "Homily on the Resurrection," which has been erroneously ascribed to Gregory of Nyssa, recognizes the passage as Mark's by appealing to and formally quoting the 19th verse. After such decisive testimony it seems quite needless to seek further from external sources.

SECOND, *Internal evidence, upon the whole, confirms the external, and favors the authorship of Mark.*

(1.) Mark 16 : 8 can not be regarded as an ending, much less an appropriate ending of this Gospel. Leaving out verses 9–20, the eighth verse is manifestly fragmentary, and naturally suggests that something must have followed. Indeed, those critics who regard the present conclusion as ungenuine, generally suppose that the Gospel originally had another. The brief ending found in the Regius manuscript, already referred to, is manifestly of later origin, and is regarded by all as clumsy and spurious. And of any other ending, except the common one, there is absolutely no trace.

(2.) The present conclusion is appropriate. If we turn to verses 19 and 20 we find a fitting close of a Gospel which begins with the announcement of Jesus Christ as "the Son of God," and which throughout represents him as the Mighty Worker. Is not this just the ending we would seek? And we can not separate these verses from the rest, for the whole passage is always found together in manuscripts and versions. Besides, this whole chapter forms a conclusion corresponding with the beginning of the Gospel. They are both brief and summary. In the one Mark proceeds at once to the ministry of John and the baptism of Jesus, and giving the temptation a passing notice, he begins the narrative of our Lord's Galilean ministry. In the other, without relating the scenes of the resurrection, he passes at once to the visit of the women at the empty tomb, where an angel announces to them that their Lord had risen; then notices his appearance to Mary Magdalene, then to two disciples, then to the eleven, and hastens to the last commission and to his ascension.

(3.) The leading thought of this passage is in unison with what precedes. The astonishment, hesitation, and practical unbelief of the women (ver. 8) are in keeping with the unbelief of the disciples (vers. 11, 13, 14), which is only overcome by the appearance of Jesus among them. It seems to have been a design of Mark to show the greatness of their unbelief, and how it was overcome. And this victory over it is appropriately followed by the last commission, in which salvation is promised upon faith, and signs to accompany those who have believed.

(4.) The style has strong resemblances to that of Mark. Such is the vividness of ver. 10. The specifications also in vers. 12, 17–20, in the midst of such brevity, reminds us of Mark. Favorite words, or those quite peculiar to Mark, are found here: such is the word translated *early* in ver. 9, *unbelief* in ver. 14, and *creature* in ver. 15. See also on ver. 17. But it has been objected that Mark's favorite expressions are wanting, and that several words or expressions are used which are not found elsewhere in this Gospel. From these are derived the principal arguments of those who regard this passage as spurious, or as an appendix made by another hand. But such objections and arguments are well answered by Dr. J. A. Broadus (*Baptist Quarterly*, July, 1869, pp. 355–362). He shows that Mark's favorite words, translated *immediately* and *again*, which are wanting here, are also wanting, the former in fifty-four verses, and the latter in forty-three verses, preceding this passage. In regard to words and expressions peculiar to this passage, he makes it appear that their presence is of little weight against the authorship of Mark. And to exhibit the futility of such a process, he takes the twelve verses preceding this passage, and subjects them to a like examination; and finds seventeen words and expressions not elsewhere employed by Mark, which, by a curious coincidence, are the same number that Alford has found in this passage.

In view of these facts I must express the conviction with Bleek, who readily gives full weight to all opposing arguments, that this passage "is genuine and belonged from the beginning to Mark's Gospel."

SOURCES OF THIS GOSPEL.

What were the materials from which this Gospel was composed, is a question which has often been discussed. It is written as by an eyewitness, yet Mark himself saw little or nothing of the things here recorded. The true answer takes us back to the beginning of apostolic preaching. After the ascension of Jesus the Apostles remained at Jerusalem in daily communion. The scenes of Christ's life and his words were deeply impressed on their memory. The promised Spirit was with them to guide them unto all truth. The words and the deeds of Jesus were told over and over again in their conversations and discourses. One may have excelled in relating the conversations of Jesus, another his discourses, and another his mighty works. Thus an early writer makes Peter say: "After midnight has once passed I now of my own accord awake, and sleep no longer comes to me; which happened to me because it was my habit to recall the words of my Lord that I had heard from him." (*Recog. Clem.* 2. 1.) There was thus an oral Gospel before a written one. These recitals of what Jesus said and did were doubtless often committed to writing, especially by the hearers. Accordingly, when Luke wrote, many had undertaken to compose a narrative of these things.

These facts prepare us to receive with favor the early traditions that

Mark wrote under the influence and direction of Peter. The testimony of Papias has already been given. Irenæus calls Mark "the interpreter and attendant of Peter," who "delivered to us, in writing, the things which had been preached by Peter." Origen says that Mark "composed it as Peter directed him." Eusebius says, on the authority of Clement of Alexandria, that the hearers of Peter at Rome besought Mark to commit to writing the substance of his teaching; that the Apostle being informed supernaturally of the work, sanctioned it, and directed that it should be read in the churches. Yet Eusebius elsewhere quotes Clement as saying that Peter neither urged nor hindered it. This may possibly mean that Peter neither helped nor hindered it before its completion, but approved of it afterward. Similar testimony is given by Tertullian, Jerome, and others. Indeed, so well established was this regarded that some did not hesitat to designate this the Gospel according to Peter. Some suppose this fact to be referred to in 2 Pet. 1 : 15, 16.

That Peter had some connection in the preparation of this Gospel may also be inferred: (1.) From the fact that it extends over the exact time intimated by Peter in Acts 1 : 21, 22, and 10 : 36–42. (2.) That scarcely an action or incident of Jesus is related, at which Peter was not present. (3.) The things which would specially impress Peter's mind are related in detail and vividness. For example, the healing of Jairus' daughter, ch. 5 : 39–42; the transfiguration, ch. 9 : 2–27; the denials of Peter, ch. 14 : 54, 66–72. (4.) The modesty of Peter may be noticed in the omission of many things honorable to him; while his failings are frankly and fully recorded. John alone tells us that Peter was the man who boldly drew his sword in defense of his Master. Mark withholds the name of him who displayed such heroism, and simply says, "One of them that stood by." But Peter's sin in denying Christ, Mark relates in such a manner as to fully show his guilt without covering or mitigation. (5.) Taking into account the lengths of the Gospels, he is more frequently mentioned (Simon, Peter, or Simon Peter) than in either Matthew or Luke. At the same time his name appears several times to be modestly omitted, Matt. 15 : 15 and Mark 7 : 17; Luke 22 : 8 and Mark 14 : 13.

From all this I conclude that the sources of Mark's Gospel are to be traced to the oral teachings of the Apostles and especially of Peter; and that Mark, under the guidance of the Holy Spirit, and probably in some way connected with the inspired Apostle, arranged and wrote his Gospel narrative.

ITS RELATION TO THE OTHER GOSPELS.

The Gospel of Mark, however, is not a compilation. From beginning to end are the characteristics of one and the same author. Whatever the sources of information, oral or written, the material was evidently digested in the mind of Mark and it came forth stamped with his individuality. The sacred writers as they were moved by the Holy Spirit retained their individuality and exercised the full powers of their minds.

Neither can we regard this Gospel as a summary of Matthew; nor an epitome of Matthew and Luke. Mark in his topics and incidents generally indeed coincides with one or both. In form and substance he resembles Matthew; in order and arrangement, Luke. But his arrangement is evidently his own, and wherever he is in common with either Evangelist, or with both, he generally enters more into detail, and excels in graphic narration; he has his own characteristics, without the characteristics of the others. All this proves an independent narrator and an independent Gospel.

As little reason also is there for the view of some, that the Gospel of Mark formed the basis out of which Matthew and Luke developed theirs. The large amount of independent narration in the two latter is fatal to such a supposition, and wherever they are in common, each treats his subject independently. Wherever there is verbal agreement, it is principally in reciting the words of Jesus, or of characters introduced.

But Mark holds a somewhat middle ground between Matthew and Luke. The statement of Meyer is quite just, that "in the parts where Mark does not stand with them they two depart furthest from each other, while they essentially agree where Mark forms the middle term." His position in Gospel history (between the other two) is the right one, while as a basis for studying that history he has great advantages. I have said nothing of John's Gospel, because the relation of the others being established, he most remarkably and beautifully supplements the three.

PECULIARITIES OF THE SECOND GOSPEL.

This is peculiarly the Gospel of action. Jesus is presented as the Mighty Worker. His deeds rather than his discourses are given. Compression, and lively detail; precision, and rapid and picturesque description; glowing narrative, and brief, burning words, are marked characteristics. Everywhere Jesus is at work; "in the way," "in the house," "as he sat at meat," in "the synagogue," "by the seaside;" everywhere he is the one who "went about doing good" (Acts 10:38), always ready to be interrupted, always at the service of others, so much so that he had "no leisure even to eat," and even his relatives thought he was "beside himself." In harmony with rapid and life-like narrative, such words as "straightway," "forthwith," "immediately," appear with unusual frequency, the present tense is often used instead of the indefinite past, the first person instead of the third, and incidents are often loosely joined together by merely " and " or " again."

Another peculiarity may be seen in the periods of rest which regularly intervene between the scenes of great activity. " Each fresh advance, each new contest and victory, is preceded by a period of retirement. Thus the Savior at the commencement of his work leaves the obscure abode of his humiliation at Nazareth, that by humble submission to the baptism of John, he might insure his victorious progress. Thence he retires into the wilderness; again and again he repairs into the desert to issue forth anew and to achieve even larger conquests. Even his ascension is presented at the close of our Gospel under the peculiar aspect of Christ retiring in order to conquer, by his power and blessing, the whole world by the instrumentality of his embassadors."—LANGE, *Mark*, p. 4.

Mark is also noted for the many new and precious bits of information which he everywhere throws into his narrative. Zebedee had hired servants (ch. 1 : 20); Levi was the son of Alpheus (2 : 14); James and John were surnamed Boanerges (3 : 17); Jesus is the carpenter (6 : 3); the woman of Canaan a Greek and a Syrophœnician by nation, and Jesus retiring into a house (7 : 24–26); Mary Magdalene dispossessed of seven devils and the first to behold a risen Savior (ch. 16 : 9); and many similar facts.

To Mark also we are principally indebted for what hints we have concerning the gestures and looks of Jesus, chs. 1 : 21; 3 : 5, 34; 9 : 36; 10 : 16, 23, 32, etc. And also for the sighs of Jesus, ch. 7 : 34; 8 : 12; compare ch. 3 : 5. Expressions of tenderness are particularly common, such as " little daughter," " little child," etc. The language is Hebraistic; the exact Aramean, the vernacular, words or expressions of Jesus are often given; the introduction of Latin words and phrases is frequent; all giving life, or minuteness, or interest to the narrative. All these characteristics make the second Gospel peculiarly valuable. It is full of freshness and individuality, reverently and affectionately following the official ministry of Jesus, " recording his positions and looks and gestures, and giving us the very echo of the tones with which he spoke." So that Da Costa has well said, " If any one desires to know an evangelical fact, not only in its main features and grand results, but also in its most minute and more graphic delineation, he must betake himself to Mark." These and other characteristics are brought to view in considering the question :

FOR WHOM WRITTEN?

Mark wrote specially for Gentile Christians. His design was principally to narrate the official life of Jesus Christ, the Son of God. Hence the beginning and the end of the Gospel are brief and summary. He omits the genealogy and all accounts of the early years of both John and

Jesus to which Gentiles would attach less importance than would the Jews. He quotes little from the Old Testament, and makes but few references to the Prophets, because of less interest to Gentiles. He does not even use the word Law, and makes no effort, like Matthew in the "Sermon on the Mount," to show the relation of Jesus to the old dispensation.

Mark also makes those geographical explanations which would be necessary for a Gentile, but not for a Jew. Thus, Judea is a "country," and Jordan is a "river" (1:5); Nazareth is in Galilee (1:9); Bethphage and Bethany are near to Jerusalem (11:1); Jerusalem stands on an elevated position, and the Mount of Olives over-against the temple (13:3).

Similar explanations are given regarding persons. Publicans are spoken of as many, forming a somewhat numerous class (2:15). Simon, who aided the Savior in bearing his cross, was the father of Alexander and Rufus, names, doubtless, familiar to many Gentiles, for whom he immediately wrote, 15:21; Rom. 16:13. Gentiles, too, needed to be told the high position in the Sanhedrim held by Joseph of Arimathea, and he is therefore described as "an honorable counselor," 15:43.

Jewish customs, not familiar to Gentiles, are explained, or referred to. The disciples of John, and the Pharisees, observed stated fasts (2:18); common or defiled hands are explained as unwashen hands; and washing the hands and bathing themselves are described as a Jewish usage for preventing ceremonial uncleanness, 7:1-4. "The preparation" is explained as the day before the Jewish Sabbath, 15:42.

Mark also translates the Hebrew or Aramean expressions coming from the lips of Jesus, which was needed, not for Jewish readers, but for Gentile. Thus *Boanerges* means "sons of thunder" (3:17). *Talitha cumi*, the words addressed to the daughter of Jairus, signifies, "Damsel, I say to thee, arise" (5:41). *Corban* is "a gift" (7:11). *Ephatha* means "be opened" (7:34). *Bartimæus* is explained as "the son of Timæus" (10:46). *Gehenna* or hell is unquenchable fire (9:48). *Abba* means "father" (14:36), and *Golgotha* is interpreted, "place of skull" (15:22). "The first day of the week" is first presented in its Hebraistic form (16:2) according to the usage of the Greek-speaking Jews of Palestine, and then in another form (16:9) which would be more intelligible to Gentile readers. Likewise the two mites, Jewish money, is explained as being equal in value to the Roman farthing (12:42).

Mark also omits some things which might needlessly offend his Gentile readers. For example, "Go not into the way of the Gentiles," etc., recorded by Matthew (10:5, 6); compare Mark 6:7, 8. On the other hand, Mark alone records the words of Jesus, "The Sabbath was made for man, and not man for the Sabbath," 2:27. He alone quotes that part of Isaiah's prophecy, "of all nations," 11:17. He alone gives the admission of the scribe, that love is more than all the whole burnt-offerings and sacrifices, 12 : 33. And he preserves that portion of the last commission, " Go ye into all the world and preach the gospel to every creature," 16 : 15. Other things are likewise omitted, which would chiefly interest the Jews; such as the parable of the king's son, Matt. 22 : 1-14, or the awful denunciation of the scribes and Pharisees in the 23d chapter of Matthew. But the answer regarding tribute, " Render to Cæsar the things that are Cæsar's," (12 : 17), showing his allegiance to constituted authority, was also appropriate for Gentile readers. So Mark also, as well as Matthew, gives the account of the healing of the daughter of the Syrophœnician woman, thereby proving that the sympathies and works of Jesus were not confined by Jewish prejudices.

All these peculiarities indicate very clearly that Mark wrote his Gospel primarily for Gentiles.

WHEN WRITTEN.

The time when Mark wrote his Gospel can not be positively determined. Ecclesiastical tradition is contradictory and untrustworthy. Irenæus says it was written after the death of Peter and Paul ; but according to Papias, and Clement of Alexandria, it was written during Peter's lifetime. If it were important to reconcile these statements, we might say that this Gospel was indeed written during the lifetime of Peter, but completed and published after his death. Later ancient authorities put its date much earlier, as early as A.D. 40 or 43, but without evidence or probability. There is nothing in the New Testament to decide the question. It must have been written before the destruction of Jerusalem, A D. 70, otherwise so remarkable a fulfillment of our Lord's prediction in the thirteenth chapter would have been noticed. On the other hand, the mention of Mark in Col. 4 : 10, as a cousin of Barnabas, as if that were his highest distinction, would indicate that his Gospel was not then published, about A.D. 62, the time when that epistle was written. Mark at this time was with Paul at Rome, Col. 4 : 10 ; Philemon 24. Somewhat later he was with Peter at Babylon, 1 Pet. 5 : 13. There he may have composed his Gospel, or having written it previously, he may have submitted it to Peter for his inspection and approval. When Paul wrote his second epistle to Timothy, during his second imprisonment at Rome, about A.D. 67 or 68, Mark appears to have been in Asia Minor, 2 Tim. 4 : 11. From all this we may conclude that the most probable time of the writing of this Gospel, or at least of its publication, was between A.D. 62 and 68.

PLACE WHERE THIS GOSPEL WAS WRITTEN.

The place is even more uncertain than the time. There is nothing in the Bible to indicate it. The mention of Mark with Peter at Babylon (1 Pet. 5 : 13) gives but the slightest foundation for suggesting that it might have been composed there. Clement of Alexandria, Eusebius, Jerome, etc., mention Rome as the place; but earlier writers, such as Papias and Irenæus, do not speak of it. As for Peter, it is not certain that he ever was at Rome; and if there at all, probably not before the last year of his life. Chrysostom mentions Alexandria, but this is not confirmed by other testimony. Some would combine these views, supposing it published in both cities. Its Latinisms show that Mark understood something of Latin, but prove nothing regarding the place of composition. At most they only strengthen the opinion, already discussed, that the Gospel was written for Gentile, including Roman, readers. The place of writing we must leave where we found it, uncertain. Compare a popular article in THE GALAXY on the question, " Was Peter ever at Rome ?" (Aug. 1872, pp. 231–238).

ARRANGEMENT.

Mark follows a natural and easy arrangement of giving graphic sketches of Christ's mighty deeds, conflicts, and victories. In tracing his growing influence, and the opposition it awakened; his relation to the different classes, scribes and Pharisees, his own countrymen, Herod Antipas, and ecclesiastical leaders at Jerusalem, Mark naturally follows the general order in which events occurred. In Matthew we find grouping and classifying; in Luke historic sequence and order; but in Mark *life-sketches*, developing a series of mighty achievements in overcoming sin and the powers of darkness, the elements of nature, bodily maladies, and death; and these achievements interspersed with seasons of rest and retirement in the wilderness and on the mountain. The principal divisions are :

1. The ministry of John the Baptist; the baptism and temptation of Jesus, ch. 1 : 1–13.

2. Christ's early Galilean ministry, from the imprisonment of John to the appointment of the Twelve. A time of growing popularity, and also of growing opposition, culminating in an organized movement, ch. 1 : 14—3 : 12.

3. Galilean ministry, from the appointment of the Apostles to Christ's departure for the country of Tyre and Sidon. A period of great Pharisaic malignity, marked on the part of Jesus by a change to parabolic instruction; also of great miracles, and great activity of Christ and the Apostles,

INTRODUCTORY REMARKS.   xix

The relation of Jesus to his relatives, to malignant and blasphemous Pharisees, to unbelieving countrymen, and to Herod Antipas, is brought to view, ch. 3 : 13—7 : 23.
  4. Christ's visit to the Gentile world, ch. 7 : 24–30.
  5. Christ's ministry in Decapolis and northern Galilee. The transfiguration, ch. 7 : 31—9 : 29.
  6. Later ministry in Galilee, ch. 9 : 30–50.
  7. Last journey from Galilee through Perea to Jerusalem, ch. 10 : 1–52.
  8. Closing scenes of Christ's public ministry at Jerusalem, chs. 11, 12, 13.
  9. The sufferings and death of Jesus, chs. 14, 15.
  10. Resurrection and ascension, ch. 16.

From this review it is evident that the Gospel according to Mark is a collection of sketches, gathered not at random, but rather arranged in an orderly and chronological narrative, for a definite purpose. This will be farther seen in a careful study of the Gospel itself.

NOTE TO THE REVISED EDITION.

A difference of opinion regarding the genuineness of the last twelve verses of this Gospel still continues. Westcott and Hort, in their critical Greek New Testament (1881), after a full discussion, incline to regard these verses as a fifth narrative of the forty days, by some unknown early author, founded on some tradition of the apostolic age. The Revised version (1881), and the Improved version (1891), both give them separated by themselves, showing that the revisers did not feel justified in omitting them, with the remark, "The two oldest manuscripts and some other documents end this Gospel with ver. 8." The Sinaitic Palimpsest of the Syriac Four Gospels (1882), regarded by some as early as the beginning of the fifth century, and even earlier, omit these verses. The other two Syriac versions and Tatian's Harmony recognize them. A fuller notice cannot be given here. But a quite full examination of the discussion on both sides leaves upon me the impression that these verses are to be regarded as an authentic account, and that they should be retained as a proper conclusion of this Gospel. It is fitting to appeal to them in confirmation of the same truth taught elsewhere.

A FEW WORKS REFERRED TO IN THESE NOTES,

AND ACCESSIBLE TO GENERAL READERS.

ALEXANDER, DR. J. A. Commentary on Mark. Scribner & Co., New York.
ALFORD, DR. HENRY. Critical Commentary. Harper & Brothers, New York.
BENGEL, DR. J. A. Gnomon of New Testament. A New Translation by Professor C. T. Lewis and M. R. Vincent. Perkinpine & Higgins, Philadelphia.
BURGON, J. W. The Last Twelve Verses of Mark. Oxford and London.
CAMPBELL, DR. GEORGE. The Four Gospels. Boston.
COLEMAN, DR. L. Ancient Christianity Exemplified. Lippincott & Co., Philadelphia.
CONANT, DR. T. J. The Gospel by Matthew, Revised with Critical and Philological Notes. Also, The Meaning and Use of *Baptizein*, Philologically and Historically Investigated. American Bible Union, 32 Great Jones Street, New York.
ELLICOTT, DR. C. J. Historical Lectures on the Life of Christ. Gould & Lincoln, Boston.
GILL, DR. JOHN. Commentaries. Philadelphia.
HACKETT, DR. H. B. Illustrations of Scripture. Gould & Lincoln, Boston.
HANNA, DR. WM. Life of Christ. Carters, New York.
HOVEY, DR. A. Miracles ; Scriptural Law of Divorce ; God with Us. Gould & Lincoln, Boston.
KITTO. DR. J. Cyclopædia of Biblical Literature. Third Edition. Edited by Dr. W. L. Alexander. J. B. Lippincott & Co., Philadelphia.
LANGE, DR. J. P. Commentary on the Gospel according to Mark. Translated from the German, with Additions, by Dr. Wm. G. T. Shedd. Scribner & Co., New York.
LYNCH, LIEUT. WILLIAM F. United States Expedition to the Jordan and the Dead Sea. Philadelphia, Baltimore, and London.
MAJOR, DR. J. R. Critical Notes on Mark. London.
MEYER, DR. H. A. W. Critical and Exegetical Commentary. A Translation from the German, to be published by T. & T. Clark, Edinburgh.
NEWMAN, DR. J. P. From Dan to Beersheba. Harper & Brothers, New York.
OLSHAUSEN, DR. H. Commentary, Dr. A. C. Kendrick's Revision. Sheldon & Co., New York.
ROBINSON, DR. E. Biblical Researches in Palestine, etc. Crocker & Brewster, Boston.
RYLE, J. C. Expository Thoughts on Mark. Carters, New York.
SMITH, DR. W. Dictionary of the Bible. American Edition ; revised and edited by Professor H. B. Hackett, D.D. Hurd & Houghton, New York.
STANLEY, DEAN. Sinai and Palestine. Scribner & Co., New York.
STIER, DR. R. Words of the Lord Jesus. Revised American Edition. N. Tibbals & Son, New York.
THOMSON, DR. W. M. The Land and The Book. Harper & Brothers, New York.
TRENCH, PROF. R. C. Notes on Parables ; on Miracles. Appleton & Co., New York.
WILLIAMS, DR. N. M. Notes on Matthew. Gould & Lincoln, Boston.
WILSON, CAPT. C. W. Recovery of Jerusalem. London.
WORDSWORTH, DR. C. The New Testament, with Notes. Scribner & Co., New York.

THE GOSPEL ACCORDING TO MARK.

CHAPTER I.

The ministry of John the Baptist ; the baptism of Jesus.

1. THE beginning of the gospel of Jesus Christ, ᵃ the •Lk. 1. 35 ; John

CHAPTER I.

The inspired narrative, as written and delivered by Mark, is very appropriately inscribed, *The Gospel according to Mark.* The four Gospels present only one divine record, but from four points of view. That of Mark is about to be given. The title is found in many ancient manuscripts, and was doubtless very early applied to this narrative. The word *saint*, so often found in this and other inscriptions, is an addition of a late date, and inconsistent with the style of the book and the simplicity of God's word. In the New Testament, titles are not thus applied to Christians individually as distinguishing epithets.

Mark makes no mention of either the genealogy or birth of Christ, illustrating Jesus in this respect as priest after the order of Melchisedec : "Without father, without mother, without descent; having neither beginning of days, nor end of life; but made like unto the Son of God ; abideth a priest continually," Heb. 7 : 3 ; 5 : 5, 6. He begins his Gospel by describing the preaching and baptism of John, the baptism and temptation of Jesus. Then he proceeds to the ministry of Jesus in Galilee, depicting especially his *works*, which prove him to be the all-powerful incarnate Son of God. Not only this chapter, but also the whole Gospel is in singular harmony with the words of Peter in Acts 10 : 36-38. Indeed it embraces the same extent as that specified by Peter in Acts 1 : 22.

1-8. THE PREACHING AND BAPTISM OF JOHN. Matt. 3 : 1-12 ; Luke 3 : 1-8. The account of Mark is the most concise, but sudden and vivid. The prediction quoted in ver. 2 is not recorded by the other evangelists.

1. **The beginning.** The first three verses are closely connected, and refer to the ministry of John as the forerunner. Hence *the beginning* extends as far as ver. 8, immediately after which Jesus is introduced. To separate this verse from the two following, and make it the title of the whole book, is unnatural and arbitrary. **The gospel.** *The good news*, for so the word means ; the glad tidings of a Savior and of his salvation. *The Gospel of Jesus Christ* here means the good news *concerning* Jesus Christ. Compare Rom. 1 : 3. This *began* to be proclaimed by John. Compare Luke 16 : 16. It should be noted that Mark uses the word *gospel* more frequently than the other evangelists.

Jesus. The personal name of our Lord, the Greek form of Joshua, meaning *Jehovah his help* or *Savior*, and given him by command of the angel of the Lord, because he should " save his people from their sins." Matt. 1 : 21.

Christ. His official name, meaning *anointed*, corresponding to the Hebrew Messiah. Ps. 2 : 2 ; Dan. 9 : 24, 25 ; John 1 : 41 ; 4 : 25. He was the Anointed Prophet, Priest, and King of Spiritual Israel, of the kingdom of God.

The Son of God. *Son of God* or *God's Son*, the article being omitted in the original. Brevity was often studied in titles. Matthew (ch. 1 : 1), who wrote for Jewish Christians, introduces Christ as Son of David in his relation to Israel ; but Mark, who wrote for Gentile believers, presents him at once as Son of God, in the highest sense, divine, partaker of the Godhead, and hence possessed of divine power. The Jew needed to be convinced that Jesus was the Messiah foretold by the prophets ;

2 Son of God ; as it is written in the prophets, Behold I send my messenger before thy face, which shall prepare thy way before thee; the voice of one crying in the wilderness, Prepare ye the way of the
4 Lord ; make his paths straight. ᵇ John did baptize in the wilderness, and preach the baptism of re-

1. 34 ; Heb. 1. 1–3.

ᵇ Mt. 3. 1; Lk. 3. 3; John 3. 26.

the Gentile that he was possessed of divinity, an Almighty Savior, before whom all the pretended divinities of heathendom were evidently spurious. Hence, while Matthew especially gives the fulfillment of prophecies and the words of Jesus, Mark dwells particularly on the acts and power of Jesus.

2. **As it is written.** Though Mark wrote for Gentiles, he did not ignore the old dispensation and the Old Testament Scriptures. He intimates the fulfillment of an ancient prophecy, and the quotation is itself a brief description of John's ministry as the forerunner of Christ. The first three verses of this chapter may be regarded as a superscription of John's ministry. **In the prophets.** Mal. 3 : 1 ; Isa. 40 : 3. The majority of the best manuscripts and versions read "Isaiah the prophet," the name of the principal prophet quoted being mentioned alone, although there is a quotation from Malachi also, which however is really but a development of that of Isaiah. Compare Matt. 27 : 9, and note.

Behold, introduces something wonderful and unexpected. The sense of Malachi is given, not the exact language. **I send forth.** The expression in the original implies a mission of importance. **My messenger.** The Greek word commonly translated *angel*, is here used in its primary and wider sense. John was the messenger of God who was to prepare the way for the Messenger or Angel of the Covenant,—the forerunner of the Messiah. **Prepare thy way.** Fully make ready for thy advent. **Before thy face.** Immediately before thee. **Before thee.** This is not found in the oldest manuscripts.

3. The prediction of Isaiah is also applied to John by Matthew and Luke. John also applied it to himself, John 1 : 23. We have thus an authoritative exposition of its meaning and application. **The voice of one crying.** The voice of a crier, of a herald, exciting attention, but comparatively of short duration. And so was John's ministry. **Wilderness;** denotes an uninclosed, untilled, and thinly inhabited district. The word was applied to mountainous regions, to districts fitted only for pasture, and to tracts of country remote from towns and sparsely settled. **Prepare,** by leveling and straightening the roads, as was customary before Oriental monarchs on their journeys and marches. A different Greek verb is used here from that in the preceding verse. The custom still prevails in the East. The prophecy, which is quoted according to its sense, points to the ministry of John as preparatory, and to him as the precursor of Christ. He went before, rebuking the proud, exposing hypocrites, calling men to repentance, directing their minds to the Messiah, and making ready a people prepared for the Lord, Luke 1 : 16, 17.

John ; means "one whom Jehovah hath graciously given." His name had doubtless reference to his gracious mission. Luke (ch. 1) as an historian gives an account of his birth. His parents were both of the priestly race. He was born in the south of Judea, some suppose Hebron, others Jutta, and lived a Nazarite (Luke 1 : 15; Num. 6 : 1–3) in that wild and thinly settled region, till he began his ministry, Luke 1 : 80. He commenced his ministry in the fifteenth year of Tiberius Cæsar, which was the 779th year of Rome or A. D. 25, probably in the spring or summer. In the autumn commenced a Sabbatical year, the year of our Savior's baptism and the beginning of his ministry, as well as of a good portion of John's ministry. Mark like Matthew introduces John abruptly, as one demanding notice, only in his official work as the Forerunner of Jesus.

4. **John did baptize.** Rather, *John came baptizing . . . preaching, etc.;* in conformity and fulfillment of the prophecies just quoted. The word *baptize* is the Greek word *baptizo* transferred into our language and the termination altered. The literal meaning of the

Greek word is *plunge, immerse*. This is admitted universally among Greek scholars. Alexander de Stourdza, a Greek and one of the most learned men of the present age, says: "The verb *baptizo* has, in fact, but one sole acceptation. It signifies literally and always, to *plunge*. Baptism and immersion are therefore identical; and to say *baptism by aspersion* is as if one should say *immersion by aspersion*, or any other absurdity of the same nature."—*Consid. sur la Doct., etc., p.* 87.

Prof. A. N. Arnold, D.D., for many years a missionary in Greece, says in *The Examiner and Chronicle*, March 16th, 1871:—"The word *baptizo* is used by the modern Greeks, not only in the technical sense, as describing the Christian rite of baptism, but also in its primitive sense of 'to dip, to plunge, to immerse.' . . . The Greeks have continued down to the present day to use the word, as a common and secular one, in no other sense than that in which their fathers used it of old, namely, 'to dip, to immerse.' In a Lexicon of French and Modern Greek published in Athens in 1842, the French word 'immersion' is defined by the three Greek words, 'embapsis, baptisis, katadusis.' The last word is the one commonly used by ancient and modern Greek writers, when they have occasion to describe the act of baptism. Thus when they speak of *trine-immersion*, they always say *treis kataduseis*, and never *tria baptismata*, because they regard the three immersions as constituting only one baptism, in the technical sense of the word. In an English-Greek Lexicon, published in Corfu, in 1827, by a missionary of the London Missionary Society, a zealous defender of infant sprinkling, the first Greek definition of the word 'immerge' is *baptizo*. The lexicographer, however, under an influence which those who knew him can scarcely understand, avoids using the word *baptizo* in defining the very next word, namely, 'immerse.' How it comes to pass that the Greek *baptizo* is an equivalent in English of *immerge*, but not of *immerse*, he has not attempted to explain.

"There is no lack of examples in the Greek literature of the present day, of the use of the verb in question in the same sense, whether used literally or figuratively, in which it was used by Greek authors before it was ever appropriated to designate the Christian rite. In a description of the way of preparing the explosive gun-cotton which made so much noise a quarter of a century ago, the *Minerva*, an Athenian newspaper, says, 'Common cotton, well cleansed, is taken, which being immersed (baptizomenon) for about half a minute in strong nitric acid, is afterwards rinsed in pure water, often changed,' etc. 'Righteousness,' says Coraës, the most renowned of modern Greek writers, 'forbids an honorable man to 'dip (baptizein) his pen in the filth of flattery.' Again the same writer says, 'when any one takes upon him to pronounce judgment upon whole nations, he ought to dip (baptizein) his pen not in ink only, but also in intelligence.' This figurative use of the word is so common that it may be regarded as proverbial. A merciless critic is said to 'dip (baptizein) his pen in gall.' One more example, in which the common and the technical applications of the word are intimately blended, must suffice. It is found in an Athenian paper called *The Age* (Aion): 'The Papists verily believe that they are saved by being sprinkled (rantizomenoi), and not by being baptized (baptizomenoi).'

"In fine, this Greek word has never changed its meaning. Alike in ancient and in modern times, alike in its common and in its ecclesiastical use, its meaning is solely and always, 'to immerse, to dip.'"

Prof. E. A. Sophocles, of Harvard University and a native Greek, in his Greek Lexicon of the Roman and Byzantine Period from B. C. 146 to A. D. 1100, defines *baptizo* to mean *to dip, immerse*, sink, with various metaphorical uses growing directly out of this primary sense. In regard to the religious ordinance he adds: "*There is no evidence that Luke and Paul, and the other writers of the New Testament, put upon this verb* MEANINGS NOT RECOGNIZED BY THE GREEKS." Under the word *baptisma* numerous references are given to the earliest ecclesiastical writers, in proof that baptism was immersion.

It may also be added that the Syriac Peshito version of the second century uses the verb *amad*, to immerse, to translate the Greek *baptizo*. See a learned article in the *Baptist Quarterly* (Jan. 1872, pp. 106-110) by Dr. C. H. Toy, in which he shows that *amad* is never used as a Syriac word in the sense

5 pentance ᶜ for the remission of sins. And there went out unto him all the land of Judæa, and they of Jerusalem ; ᵈ and were all baptized of him in the river of Jordan, ᵉ confessing their sins.

ᶜ Ac. 22. 16.
ᵈ John 1. 25-28; 3. 23-26; Ac. 19. 4, 18.
ᵉ Le. 26. 40.

of "stand," as some have supposed. He not only gives numerous examples of its use in the sense of "immerse," but also shows that the stem of the word exists in Arabic in the same sense. Its figurative use is based on this ground-meaning and always expresses an idea of immersion. See ch. 10 : 38. But it is only with its literal meaning that we have here to do. Compare on Matt. 3 : 6. See also on ch. 6 : 25. For a discussion of the word and subject see Dr. Conant's Baptizein, Carson on Baptism, and kindred works.
In the wilderness; of Judea (Matt. 3 : 1), the eastern portion of Judah; here in the neighborhood of the Jordan north of the Dead Sea. "Baptizing in the wilderness" is explained by the next verse, "In the river Jordan," which flowed through the wilderness. **Preaching.** Proclaiming, announcing publicly. We must not suppose John making set discourses, but announcing his brief messages to the people wherever he found them. **Baptism of repentance;** implying, enjoining, and symbolizing repentance. John's ministry consisted of preaching and baptizing, Matt. 3 : 2-6. He preached repentance as a condition of baptism, and baptism was a symbol of the thorough change of mind denoted by repentance. Since he instituted a new rite which was the distinguishing feature of his ministry, he was called *The Baptist* (Matt. 3 : 1), and his preaching was specially designated as that of baptism; and as his baptism *implied, enjoined, and symbolized* repentance, it was styled the baptism of repentance. **For the remission of sins.** Unto the forgiveness of sins. Baptism had respect to forgiveness as connected with repentance. This forgiveness was through him who was to come, whom the ministry of John was ushering in and proclaiming. This verse states how the gospel of Jesus Christ began in fulfillment of prophecy by the ministry of John.

5. The immediate result of John's ministry. **All the land of Judea.** The country south of Samaria between the Mediterranean and the Jordan. The country is put for its inhabitants. The people come from all parts of Judea. There was a general coming to his baptism. **They of Jerusalem.** According to the best manuscripts, *all they of Jerusalem,* or *all the Jerusalemites.* The people of Jerusalem, as the inhabitants of the capital and holy city, are made prominent. This strong language is peculiar to Mark, and vividly presents, in its concise and popular style, the general coming of the people to John's baptism. We use similar language, as, "everybody is there," meaning a large gathering, or a general coming together. Multitudes came from all parts of the country, and even multitudes from Jerusalem. That Jerusalem was greatly moved is evident not only from this declaration, but from the fact that priests and Levites were sent to him from there (John 1 : 19), and Pharisees and Sadducees came to his baptism, Matt. 3 : 7. Compare John 5 : 35. **And were all baptized.** *All* should be omitted here; it belongs before "They of Jerusalem." See preceding paragraph. The people generally who came were baptized. The Pharisees and Sadducees were exceptions, Matt. 3 : 7-9; 21 : 25, 26. *In the river of Jordan.* Rather, *In the river Jordan.* The Jordan, which means "the descender," well merits its name by passing down an inclined plain, from its several sources in the north to the Dead Sea, broken by a series of rapids. Thus from lake el-Huleh, south to the Sea of Galilee, the distance is only nine miles, yet the fall of the river is about 600 feet; and from the Sea of Galilee to the Dead Sea, a distance of sixty miles, the fall is about 650 feet. In a circuitous route of two hundred miles it rushes over no less than twenty-seven rapids, besides many more of lesser magnitude. Its width varies at different points from seventy-five to two hundred feet, and its depth from three to twelve feet. John was now baptizing in the Jordan, probably at the ford near Jericho, a little north of the Dead Sea. See on verse 9. **Confessing their sins.** Fully con-

A.D. 26.   MARK I.   25

6 And John was ^f clothed with camel's hair, and
with a girdle of a skin about his loins; and he did
7 eat ^g locusts and ^h wild honey. And [he] preached,
saying, There cometh one mightier than I after me,
the latchet of whose shoes I am not worthy to stoop

^f 2 Ki. 1. 8 ; Is. 20.
2 ; Zec. 13. 4 ;
Mt. 3, 4.
^g Lc. 11, 22.
^h Deu. 32, 13 ; 1
Sam. 14. 25-27.

fessing, etc. A free, full, and public acknowledgment of their sins, one of the best tokens of repentance. They professed penitence, and this was not an empty thing, for they made a full confession of sin at their baptism. It could well be called "the baptism of repentance." Confession, too, is a condition of forgiveness, Prov. 28 : 13 ; 1 John 1 : 9.

6. Having spoken of the place, nature, design, and immediate results of John's ministry, Mark proceeds to speak of him in respect to his costume and food, both pointing him out as Christ's forerunner, coming in the spirit and power of Elijah. **Clothed with camel's hair;** that is, with coarse cloth woven from the long shaggy hair of the camel, which was shed every year. Mantles made of this cloth are very common among Arabs of the desert and the shepherds of Palestine. **A girdle of skin.** Rather, *A leathern girdle,* the original being the same as in Matt. 3 : 4. A *girdle* was a regular part of the dress, used in binding the garments, which were loose and flowing, around the loins (Luke 12 : 35), and were of linen, silk, and even of silver or gold. A *leathern* one was very ordinary, and indicates the austerity of John. From Zech. 13 : 4, it would seem that it was common for prophets to wear a coarse outer garment. In 2 Kings 1 : 8, Elijah is described as "a hairy man" (probably referring to his dress, of coarse camel's hair), "and girt with a girdle of leather about his loins." His dress corresponded with his character as a reformer and a stern preacher of repentance to the ten tribes of the kingdom of Israel. Thus in dress, as in his preaching, John was like Elijah. In his *residence* also, for Elijah was of the wild and partially civilized Gilead, and his solitary life was passed in the wilderness, except when his prophetic mission called him elsewhere. **Locusts ;** voracious, winged insects, resembling the grasshopper; *clean* to the Jew, and might be used for food, Lev. 11 : 22. They were used for food by the poorer classes, as is still the case in all Eastern countries

LOCUST.

where they are found. **Wild honey.** Not the *honey dew* or gum which flows from certain trees in Arabia, but the honey made by bees, often found in rocks and in hollow trees, Lev. 20 : 24 ; Deut. 32 : 13 ; Ps. 81 : 16 ; 1 Sam. 14 : 26. It is still found and gathered where John sojourned and came preaching. His simple diet was that of the poorer classes, and his abstemiousness resembled that of Elijah, Matt. 11 : 14, 18.

7. Mark now proceeds to relate what John preached with special reference to him who was to come. Matthew and Luke relate more fully; the former giving his severe denunciations and warnings to the Pharisees and Sadducees; the latter, his answers to the inquiries of several classes, and the popular suspicion that he was the Christ. Mark, however, true to himself, speaks of what John *did,* and just enough of what he said to show that in his preaching also the good news of Jesus Christ began to be proclaimed. As gospel baptism began in John, so also did gospel preaching.

And he preached ; not all of his preaching, nor a summary of it, though all was preparatory to the coming of Christ; but that particular part which referred especially to him, the good news of whose coming and kingdom he was proclaiming. **There cometh.** In announcing the immediate coming of the Messiah he contrasts him with himself. This language he doubtless uttered on several occasions, which is sufficient to account for the variations of the evangelists. That in Luke is

3

8 down and unloose. I indeed have baptized you with water: but he shall baptize you **⸱** with the Holy Spirit. ¹ Joel 2. 28; Ac. 2. 4; 10. 45; 11. 15, 16; 1 Cor. 12. 13.

connected with the suspicions of the people that he was the Christ. **One mightier than I.** *The one mightier,* or *he that is mightier.* John was more than a prophet; none greater had yet arisen (Matt. 11 : 9-11), yet he declares his inferiority to the one he came to herald. **The latchet.** *The strap* which fastened the sandal to the foot. **Shoes.** *Sandals.* They were coverings of the bottom of the feet. On entering a house the sandals were taken off and laid away by the lowest servant, in order that the feet might be washed. Hence the loosing or carrying the sandals became proverbial to express the humblest service. **To stoop down.** The vivid and minute picturing peculiar to Mark. True to himself, Mark seizes that expression of John which is most vivid with action. The meanest slave might unloose the sandals of his master; but he was unworthy to even *stoop down* to do it for him that was coming after him. But he had aroused the Jewish nation to come to his baptism. How great, then, the Messiah! Christ was greater in his person (John 10 : 30), in his authority (John 5 : 27), and in power, John 10 : 41; Matt. 28 : 18.

8. **I indeed have baptized,** rather, *I baptized you,* addressing those already baptized. The contrast is especially between the elements, water and the Holy Spirit, in which they should be baptized. As there is an infinite distance between matter, and the living, personal Spirit of God, so there would be a corresponding difference between the Messiah and his forerunner. **With water—with the Holy Spirit.** *In* instead of *with* in both instances, the preposition *en* (in) being used as in verse 5, "in the river Jordan": *in water—in the Holy Spirit.* "I presume that scarcely any one will deny that our version weakens the force of John's words by translating '*with* water, *with* the Holy Ghost,' instead of '*in* water, *in* the Holy Ghost.' One of the most accurate of recent commentators (Meyer), for instance, in his remark on this verse, says that the preposition here 'is to be understood in accordance with the idea of baptism, that is immersion, not as expressing the instrument *with which,* but as meaning "in," and expressing the element in which the immersion takes place.'"—REV. ALEXANDER MACLAREN, *Sermons,* vol. 2, p. 233 ff. The baptism in the Holy Spirit must not be referred to water baptism in any sense, for Christ never baptized, but his disciples (John 4 : 2); nor to the common influences of the Spirit, which is peculiarly the Spirit's work; but rather to the sending of the Spirit on the day of Pentecost, which was peculiarly Christ's work, John 16 : 7. Our Savior himself evidently pointed to the Pentecostal season, when he said (Acts 1 : 5), "For John truly baptized in water, but ye shall be baptized in the Holy Spirit not many days hence." And Peter looked back to it as the baptism in the Spirit, when he visited Cornelius: "And as I began to speak the Holy Spirit fell on them as on us at the beginning. Then remembered I the word of the Lord, how he said, John indeed baptized in water," etc. Acts 11 : 16; see 10 : 44-46. Add to this, that Paul, in speaking of spiritual gifts, says, "For by one Spirit we were (not "are") all baptized into one body," and it would seem that the baptism in the Holy Spirit, in its widest application must be referred and limited to the miraculous influences of the Spirit, communicated on the day of Pentecost and at other seasons. That it could not refer to the common influences of the Spirit seems evident also from the fact that Jesus, at his ascension, spoke of the baptism in the Spirit as future, yet he had, previous to this, breathed upon his disciples, saying, "Receive ye the Holy Spirit," John 20 : 22.

In the baptism in the Spirit, Christ however showed that he was the dispenser of the Spirit, and that his kingdom would be carried on through the power of the Spirit. It was an evidence that the gospel dispensation had fully commenced, and a pledge that the Comforter would be given to believers in all ages.

The outpouring of the Spirit on the day of Pentecost was in the fullest

9 ᵏ And it came to pass in those days, that Jesus ˡ Mt. 3. 13; Lk. 3. came from Nazareth of Galilee, and was baptized ²¹

sense a baptism. When the sound came from heaven as of a rushing mighty wind, and filled all the house where the disciples were sitting, and tongues as of fire appeared to them, distributed among them, and they were all filled with the Holy Spirit, they were immersed in the divine element. Their souls were penetrated and encompassed on every side by the Spirit, and their bodies by the symbols of the Spirit, which filled all the house. Thus Cyril of Jerusalem, in the fourth century, says, " For as he, who sinks down in the waters and is baptized, is surrounded on all sides by the waters, so also they were completely baptized by the Spirit." Compare on Matt., ch. 3: 11.

Mark omits "and fire," given by Matthew and Luke. But as fire was symbolic of the power of the Spirit, the whole idea is comprehended in the concise expression given by Mark, *in the Holy Spirit*, as also in the prophetic declaration of Jesus just before his ascension, Acts 1 : 5.

9-13. THE BAPTISM OF JESUS. Matt. 3: 13-17; Luke 3: 21-23. Mark introduces Jesus as well as John suddenly, without any reference to their previous history. His account is brief, but lifelike. The baptism of Jesus was the beginning of Christ's public ministry, and the great crowning act of John's ministry. It was that Jesus might be manifested to Israel that John came baptizing in water, John 1: 31-34.

9. In those days; when John was preaching and baptizing in the Jordan. He had probably been exercising his ministry about six months. From Luke 3: 21, it appears that this occurred after the multitudes from Judea and around about Jordan were baptized. The exact time of his baptism is unknown. Tradition very generally places it in the winter. The Basilideans, an ancient sect, who made the baptism of Christ an epoch of the highest importance, fixed it on Jan. 6 or 10. If John commenced his ministry in the spring, as is probable, and Jesus was baptized about six months after, then it occurred in the autumn. It may have been late in the autumn, A.D. 26.

Nazareth. A small city in Lower Galilee, about seventy miles north of Jerusalem, and nearly half-way from the Jordan to the Mediterranean. It was situated on the side of a hill (Luke 4 : 39), not in good repute (John 1 : 46), and mentioned neither in the Old Testament nor by Josephus. It was the residence of Joseph and Mary before the birth of Jesus (Luke 1 : 26, 27), and again after their return from Egypt (Matt. 2 : 23 ; Luke 2 : 39, 51), and from this verse appears to have continued the residence of Jesus until his baptism. Modern Nazareth is one of the better class of Eastern villages, having a population of about 3,000, mostly Latin and Greek Christians. The name *Nazareth* means *a branch*, suggestive of the Branch of prophecy (Isa. 11 : 1 ; Zech. 3 : 8 ; 6 : 12), who, for twenty-seven years or more, made it his residence. Galilee, meaning a *ring* or a *circle*, was probably first given to a small "circuit" among the mountains of Naphtali (Josh. 20 : 7), where were situated the twenty towns given by Solomon to Hiram, king of Tyre, 1 Kings 9 : 11. The name may have contained originally an allusion to one or more of the circular plains of those mountains. It came afterward to be applied to the whole northern portion of Palestine north of Samaria, and which, according to Josephus, was very populous, containing no less than two hundred and forty towns and villages. It was divided into upper or northern, and lower or southern, Galilee.

And was baptized. Jesus was about thirty years old (Luke 3 : 23), the age at which the Levites began their ministry, and the rabbis their teaching. In receiving baptism at the hands of John he not only gave his approval to his ministry and baptism, but also identified himself with his people as their Exemplar, Elder Brother, and Head. Having taken upon himself the form of a servant, and being made in the likeness of men, he commenced his public ministry by placing himself on a level with man, and receiving the baptism of repentance, and thereby the public testimony of his Father's approval.

As Jesus had nothing for which to exercise repentance, his baptism pointed to the vicarious nature of his work. It prefigured not merely his death, burial, and resurrection, Luke 12:50; but also his death to the sins of the people laid upon him, and his life to the righteousness of all who should accept of his atonement. It prefigured sin, as it were, receiving its death and burial with him, and holiness its resurrection and life with him; that thus his people should die with him, be quickened, and rise with him. Col. 2:12, 13; Eph. 2:5; Rom. 6:3, 4, 8; Ps. 40:12.

In Jordan. Probably at the ford near Jericho where John had been baptizing. Here the Israelites under Joshua passed over on dry ground (Josh. 3:17), and twice afterward was it miraculously opened by Elijah and Elisha, 2 Kings 2:8, 14. Tradition also assigns this as the place of our

THE JORDAN. SUPPOSED PLACE OF CHRIST'S BAPTISM.

Savior's baptism, and here pilgrims come and dip themselves, or are dipped by others, in reference to that event. The Latin and Greek pilgrims, however, have each their bathing-place, that of the former being two or three miles up the river from that of the latter.

The prepositions used in connection with the word *baptize*, are in harmony with, and confirmatory of, its meaning, *immerse*. Thus the Greek *en*, *in*, in verses 5 and 8. Here the Greek *eis*, *into*. Literally, *into the Jordan*, the preposition denoting the act of passing into the element in which the rite was performed. Any one without any knowledge of the original can see that neither pour nor sprinkle expresses good sense in this connection. "Was poured by John into the Jordan," or "were all poured by him in the river Jordan" (ver. 5), expresses an absurdity. But only use *dip*, *plunge*, or *immerse*, and the language becomes intelligible at once.

The place, *the Jordan*, also accords

A.D. 26.   MARK I.   29

10 of John in Jordan. ¹ And straightway coming up
out of the water, he saw the heavens opened, and
11 the Spirit like a dove descending upon him: and
there came a voice from heaven, *saying*, ᵐ Thou art
my beloved Son, in whom I am well pleased.

¹ John 1. 32.

ᵐ ch. 9. 7; Ps. 2. 7; Mt. 3. 17; 12. 18; 17. 5; Lk. 9. 35; 2 Pet. 1. 17.

with the meaning of the word, a convenient place for immersing the multitudes that came to him. "If from the general scene we turn to the special locality of the river-banks, the reason of John's selection is at once explained. He came baptizing, that is, signifying to those who came to him, as he plunged them under the rapid torrent, the forgiveness and forsaking of their former sins. . . . Ablutions in the East have always been more or less a part of religious worship, easily performed, and always welcome. Every synagogue was by the side of a stream or spring; every mosque still requires a fountain or basin for lustration in its courts. But John needed more than this. . . . No common spring or tank would meet the necessities of the multitudes who, from Jerusalem and all Judea, and all the region around about Jordan, came to him, confessing their sins! The Jordan, by the very peculiarity of its position, which, as before observed, renders its functions so unlike those of other Eastern streams, now seems to have met with its fit purpose. It was the one river of Palestine, sacred in its recollections, abundant in its waters, and yet, at the same time, the river, not of cities, but of the wilderness; the scene of the preaching of those who dwelt not in king's palaces, nor wore soft clothing. On the banks of the rushing stream the multitudes gathered—the priests and scribes from Jerusalem, down the pass of Adummim; the publicans from Jericho on the south, and the lake of Gennesareth on the north; the soldiers on their way from Damascus to Petra, through the Ghor, in the war with the Arab chief Haroth; the peasants from Galilee with ONE from Nazareth through the opening in the plain of Esdraelon."—DEAN STANLEY, *Sinai and Palestine*, p. 307. See on ver. 5.

10. **Straightway.** A favorite word with Mark, occurring as many times in his Gospel as in all the rest of the New Testament. Jesus did not linger in the water after his baptism, but came immediately out of it, when the Spirit descended, and he received the approval of the Father. **Out of the water.** Not *from*, but *out of* the water, according to the best and highest critical authorities. He went up praying, Luke 3:21. As soon as he had gone up out of the water, reaching the bank of the river, **he saw,** etc. John also witnessed the descent of the Spirit, John 1:32. **The heavens.** The sky. **Opened.** *Rent, cleft, parted*, as by a flash of lightning, Acts 7:56. There was a visible and sudden parting asunder in a certain portion of the sky. **Like a dove.** As a dove, which may refer either to the *shape* or *manner* in which the Spirit descended, probably the former, for Luke (3:22) says "in a bodily shape like (as) a dove." The dove was a fit emblem of the pure, gentle, and peaceful character of Jesus and his work, Isa. 61:1–3; Matt. 10:16; 11:29; 12:21. John (1:32) adds, "And it abode on him." The descent of the Spirit was also the token of the Messiah to John, John 1:33. Thus Jesus received the heavenly anointing, and here the active and official ministry of Jesus begins. Ps. 45:7; Isa. 11:2; 42:1.

11. **A voice from heaven.** From the Father in attesting the Messiahship of Jesus to John, and through him to the people. **My beloved Son.** Not only *my Son* (Ps. 2:7, 12), but *the Beloved*, Isa. 42:1. *Son* was applied to the Messiah, and here not only expresses his Messiahship, but also the close and endearing relation he sustained to the Father, the dignity both of his office and nature. An evidence of his sonship. See on ver. 1. **In whom.** Rather *In thee*, according to the highest critical authority. **Am well pleased.** In all respects as a Son and a Mediator. Compare the repetition of this heavenly testimony, Matt. 17:5; 2 Pet. 1:17.

Thus three persons of the Trinity were manifested at the Savior's baptism. While Jesus was thus honored, the ordinance he had just received was

12 ⁿ And immediately the Spirit driveth him into the ⁿ Mt. 4. 1; Lk. 4.
13 wilderness. And he was there in the wilderness 1; Mt. 4. 11.
forty days, tempted of Satan; and was with the wild
beasts; and the angels ministered unto him.

also honored, by his implicit obedience, the descending Spirit and the approving voice of the Father.
12, 13. THE TEMPTATION OF JESUS, Matt. 4:1-11; Luke 4:1-13. Mark's account is brief and vivid, but passes over the signal temptations of Satan at or near the close of the forty days.
12. **Immediately.** The great manifestations of divine favor and approval are immediately followed by correspondingly great temptations. So it often is. **Driveth him.** *Urged* him on. Translated *send forth* in Matt. 9:38. The Holy Spirit, of which he was full (Luke 4:1), *impelled* him on to the scene of temptation. The second Adam must endure the same trial under which the first Adam fell. Thus his power to overcome the Devil and restore man to his lost state would be manifested. As our great High-Priest, it was necessary also that he should be tempted in all points as we are, so that he might be prepared to sympathize with, intercede for, and help us. See Heb. 2:17, 18; 4:15, 16. **Wilderness.** Possibly the Arabian desert of Sinai, where Moses and Elijah fasted forty days (Deut. 9:9, 18; 1 Kings 19:8); but more probably the wilderness of Judea, adjacent to the Dead Sea and stretching toward Jericho. It is still one of the most dreary and desolate regions of the whole country. The mountain Quarantania, in this wilderness, which tradition has fixed on as the site of the temptation, is described by Robinson as an almost perpendicular wall of rock, twelve or fifteen hundred feet above the plain.
13. **Forty days, tempted.** The most natural meaning of this passage is that Jesus was tempted during the forty days. So also Luke 4:2. The language in Matt. 4:3 does not necessarily indicate the first assault of Satan. The most signal assaults of the tempter, at the close of the forty days, were doubtless those given by Matthew and Luke.
Satan. Satan means *adversary*, the Old Testament name of the chief of fallen spirits and the name uniformly applied to him by Mark. In the New Testament, however, he is somewhat more frequently called the *Devil*, which means a *slanderer*. Both names are descriptive of his character and work, as the opposer and false accuser of God and man. He is also known by the names of Beelzebub, "the prince of devils" (Matt. 12:24); "the prince of the power of the air" (Eph. 2:2), and the "old serpent," Rev. 12:9. That he is a personal agent is evident from the names given him, from the way he is spoken of, and from the acts and attributes ascribed to him, Matt. 4:3, 9; John 8:44; 14:30; 2 Cor. 11:3, 14, 15; Eph. 6:11, 12; 1 Pet. 5:8, 9; 1 John 3:8; Rev. 2:10; 3:9; 20:10.
But how was Jesus tempted? In his human nature, as the second Adam. But being free from all tendency to evil, how could he be tempted? Evidently only from without. Hence temptation approached him through the senses; he was "a hungered," Matt. 4:2. When worn and weak from long abstinence from food, a rare opportunity was afforded Satan to bring against him his strongest and most artful temptations.
Mark takes for granted and implies the victory of Jesus over Satan. The "Son of God," the "beloved Son" of the Father was of course victorious, which was a pledge of the full and final triumph both of himself and all his people, Rom. 8:37.
With the wild beasts. Found only in Mark. A vivid stroke of his pen, completing the idea of the desolateness and wilderness of the region where he was. He was away from human help and ordinary supplies of food. The marshy thickets of cane in the desert near the mouth of the Jordan have always been the favorite retreat of wild beasts. "The actual place of the temptation may have been Kŭrŭntŭl (a corruption of *quadraginta*, 40 days), a part of the desert back of Jericho toward Jerusalem. It is a high mountain cut off from the plain by a wall of rock 1,200 or 1,500 feet high, is frightfully desolate, is infested with

The beginning of Christ's public ministry in Galilee, the calling of Peter, Andrew, James, and John.

14 °NOW after that John was put in prison, Jesus ° Mt. 4. 12.
came into Galilee, ᵖ preaching the Gospel of the ᵖ Mt. 4. 17.

beasts and reptiles, and thus answers fully to Mark's significant intimation (1 : 13) respecting the wildness of the scene."—Dr. Hackett, in *Smith's Dictionary*, *Am. ed.* Jesus was among wild beasts, yet not hurt by them, like Daniel among lions. But are we to suppose that they were a terror to him? Hardly. But rather that, like the first Adam before his fall, he exercised his power over them.

Angels. A race of spiritual beings of a higher nature than man (Ps. 8 : 5), who are the agents of God's Providence, and ministering spirits to the heirs of salvation, Heb. 1 : 14. *Angel* means *messenger*. Mark thus briefly notices three kinds of company, Satan, wild beasts, angels. How widely different, and what a contrast the latter to the two former! **Ministered unto him.** The word translated *ministered* was specially applied to *serving* at table, *supplying* one's wants, and hence here doubtless has reference to providing Jesus with food, and implies that he had fasted. Yet we should not limit it to the low sense of merely supplying his bodily wants, but refer it also to their ministering consolation and heavenly support. Rejoicing in his victory over Satan, they reverently honor him with their ministrations.

14, 15. Jesus begins his Galilean ministry, Matt. 4 : 12-17 ; Luke 4 : 14-31. Between this and the preceding paragraph is an interval of several months. On the return of Jesus from the temptation, John gave renewed testimony to his Messiahship, and pointed him out to Andrew and probably John. Andrew brings Peter to Jesus, John 1 : 29-42. Jesus calls Philip, returns to Galilee ; Philip finds Nathanael, and brings him to Jesus, John 1 : 43-51. Three days after was the marriage of Cana ; then Jesus visits Capernaum, remaining a few days, after which he goes up to Jerusalem to the Passover, and drives the traders out of the temple, John 2 : 1-25. Nicodemus visits him at night ; Jesus leaves Jerusalem, but tarries in Judea, makes disciples, and receives further testimony from John, who was baptizing in Ænon, John 3 : 1-36.

14. **Was put in prison.** The more exact translation is, *was delivered up*, for confinement. He was imprisoned by Herod Antipas, son of Herod the Great, in the castle of Machærus, a fortress on the eastern shore of the Dead Sea. This probably occurred about ten or twelve months after the baptism of Jesus. John's ministry had continued about eighteen months.

Jesus came into Galilee. Luke says that "Jesus returned in the power of the Spirit into Galilee," the same Spirit that had impelled him into the wilderness to be tempted. On this journey he passes through Samaria, and converses with a woman of Sychar, and many Samaritans believe on him, John 4 : 4-42. Arriving in Galilee, he again visits Cana, where he heals the son of a nobleman, lying ill at Capernaum, John 4 : 46-54. It was now probably the latter part of November, or early in December; for it was four months before the harvest (John 4 : 35), the first-fruits of which were presented on the second day of the paschal week.

Thus Jesus commenced his ministry in Judea, following the footsteps of John, who had removed farther north, preaching and baptizing at Ænon. At the latter place John had exercised more direct influence on the inhabitants of Galilee, and upon Herod himself. His labors here having been brought to a sudden end, Jesus at once goes to Galilee and follows him in preaching the kingdom of God. John was thus the precursor of Jesus to the whole of Palestine.

Why the first three evangelists should commence their account of Christ's ministry at the imprisonment of John, we know not. We would suggest : 1. That his full and independent ministry to all Israel did not commence till his forerunner had completed his. 2. That it was the design of God that his principal ministry and the most of it, should be in Galilee (Matt. 4 : 14-16);

15 kingdom of God, and saying, *The time is fulfilled, and 'the kingdom of God is at hand. Repent ye, and believe the Gospel.

q Dan. 9. 25; Gal. 4. 4; Eph. 1. 10.
r Mt. 3. 2; 4. 17.

and that which was a fact in his life, should also be made prominent in his history. 3. It was the design of the first three evangelists to relate particularly his Galilean ministry, of which they were witnesses. It is evident that Matthew was not a witness to his early Judean ministry, since he was called, after its close, from his duties as receiver of customs, Matt. 9:9. Neither probably was Mark, or Peter, under whose direction it is supposed Mark wrote, nor Luke. John, who writes as an eye-witness, was probably present more or less with Jesus in Judea.

Preaching the gospel. Proclaiming as a herald. Mark, who announced in the first sentence of his Gospel, *The beginning of the gospel*, or *good news*, hastens on from the beginning made by John to the full and authoritative proclamation of it by Jesus himself in Galilee.

Kingdom of God. According to some ancient manuscripts, it is simply *the gospel of God kingdom* being omitted. The phrase *kingdom of God* is equivalent to "kingdom of heaven" in Matthew, and to "kingdom of Christ," or simply "kingdom" elsewhere, Eph. 5:5; Heb. 12:28. The prophets had represented the Messiah as a Divine King (Ps. 2:6; Isa. 11:1; Jer. 23:5; Zech. 14:9; Mic. 4:1–4; 5:2), and especially Daniel (2:44; 7:13, 14) who had spoken of "a kingdom which the God of heaven would set up." Hence *kingdom of heaven*, or *of God*, became common among the Jews to denote the kingdom or reign of the Messiah. Their own theocracy was typical of it. They indeed perverted the meaning of prophecy, and expected an earthly and temporal kingdom, the restoration of the throne of David at Jerusalem, and the actual subjugation of all nations. John the Baptist, Jesus and the Apostles, however, rescued the phrase from error, and gave it its full and true meaning. The *kingdom*, *reign*, or *administration* of the Messiah is spiritual in its nature (John 18:36; Rom. 14:17), and is exercised over and has its seat in the hearts of believers, Luke 17:21. It exists on earth (Matt. 13:18, 19, 41, 47), extends to another state of existence (Matt. 13:43; 26:29; Phil. 2:10, 11), and will be fully consummated in a state of glory, 1 Cor. 15:24; Matt. 8:11; 2 Pet. 1:11. It thus embraces the whole mediatorial reign or government of Christ on earth and in heaven, and includes in its subjects all the redeemed in heaven and on earth, Eph. 3:15. *Kingdom of God* and *church* are not identical, though inseparably and closely connected. The churches of Christ are the external manifestation of his kingdom in this world.

15. The time is fulfilled. Words full of meaning, recorded only by Mark. The time, predicted by the prophets, for the appearance of the Messiah, is accomplished. When "the fullness of time" had come God sent forth his Son, Gal. 4:4. Compare Dan. 9:24–27. John had given and finished his testimony; the Father had borne witness, and now Jesus bears witness to himself, John 5:36, 37; 8:17, 18. God now began to speak by his Son, Heb. 1:2. The Jews were expecting the Messiah in fulfillment of prophecy. **The kingdom of God is at hand.** The *reign* of the Messiah has drawn near and has come. On *kingdom*, *etc.*, see preceding verse.

Repent, etc. The coming of the Messiah imposes certain duties and obligations. These were repentance and faith, Acts 20:21. The word *repent* means to *change one's mind*. It expresses an inward change of views and feelings, and implies a sorrow for sin (Matt. 11:21; 2 Cor. 7:10); a turning to God (Acts 3:19; 26:20); and a change of conduct, or outward reformation as the fruits, Matt. 3:8; Acts 26:20. Another word translated repent occurs a few times in the New Testament. It does not, like the more common word, denote a change of mind that is deep, durable, and productive of consequences, but rather a feeling of regret, or remorse, for something done. It is found in Matt. 27:3; 21:29, 32; 2 Cor. 7:8; and Heb. 7:21. **Believe the gospel.** Found only in Mark. Literally, *Believe in the good news*, that is, of the Messiah's advent, and the commencement of his reign, and

A.D. 28. MARK I. 33

16 *Now as he walked by the sea of Galilee, he saw * Mt. 4. 18; Lk. 5.
Simon and Andrew his brother casting a net into the 4.
17 sea; for they were fishers. And Jesus said unto
them, Come ye after me, and I will make you to be-

those things connected with it. Believe what the prophets foretold has come to pass, and believe what is now proclaimed in regard to the kingdom of God. Believe in all that the good news reveals. Notice particularly, that John preached *repentance*, Jesus adds *faith* in the good news. Yet this was but a step in the development of truth. Faith in every age had been required and exercised. They were to believe in the good news of the Messiah and his kingdom, toward which God's ancient people by faith had looked forward. Hab. 2 : 4; Rom. 4 : 3; Heb. 11 : 1—.
The preaching of Jesus was in the synagogues of Galilee, Luke 4 : 15. About this time he visited Nazareth and was rejected by his townsmen, Luke 4 : 16-30.
16-20. PETER, ANDREW, JAMES, AND JOHN CALLED TO BE HIS CONSTANT ATTENDANTS. Matt. 4 : 18-22. Almost exactly like Matthew's account, yet the variations are interesting to notice, and show an independence of narration. Jesus after leaving Nazareth came to Capernaum, making it his residence, Matt. 4 : 13.
16. **As he walked.** Probably in the twilight, or the shades of evening, just as the fishermen were beginning their night's labor. Compare Luke 5 : 5; John 21 : 3.
Sea of Galilee. Called also the Sea of Tiberias, from a city built by Herod Antipas on the southwest shore, and named in honor of the Emperor Tiberius (John 6 : 1; 21 : 1); also the lake of Gennesaret (Luke 5 : 1); and in the Old Testament, the Sea of Chinnereth, from a city and small district on the western shore, Num. 34 : 11; 1 Kings 15 : 20. It is pear-shaped, the broad end being toward the north, the greatest width being six and three-quarter miles; it is twelve and a half miles long, and 165 feet deep. It is surrounded on all sides by hills, from 500 to nearly 2,000 feet high. Its waters are pure and sweet, and abound in fish. The Jordan with a marked current passes through the middle of the lake. It is, according to Lieut. Lynch, 653 feet below the Mediterranean. Many populous towns once stood upon its shores, but they and their commerce are gone. Tiberias and Magdala are the only inhabited spots. It is subject, as in the days of our Savior, to sudden squalls and whirlwinds, owing probably to the high surrounding hills. It was usual for the Jews to call every expanse of water *a sea*. Luke, whose geographical terms are always more distinctive, calls it a *lake*.
Simon. A contraction of *Simeon*, and means *hearkening*. Matthew adds, *called Peter*, a name previously given him (John 1 : 42), but probably not generally applied to him until the twelve were regularly constituted apostles. **Andrew,** an old Greek name meaning a *man*, and shows the influence of Greek in Palestine at that time. Whether he was the older brother is not known. Very little is recorded about him; yet he had the honor of bringing his brother Simon to Jesus, John 1 : 42, 43. Both had been disciples of John. **Casting a net.** Literally, according to the best manuscripts, *casting about*, that is, throwing the net in different directions, in order to inclose the fish. It was a casting-net. They were getting their net in position; commencing their night's labor. Here we see another instance of variation from Matthew, showing the independence of Mark's narrative. **Fishers.** They were fishermen by profession. So Moses and David were called from keeping sheep; Gideon from thrashing wheat; Elisha from the plow. God has honored humble yet honest labor.
17. **Come ye after me.** Literally, *Come hither! behind me*, or *Come after me*, as my disciples, and as my attendants and the proclaimers of my gospel. They had, several months before this, recognized Jesus as the Messiah (John 1 : 41, 42), but had continued to follow their occupation as fishermen. Hence they were, in a measure, prepared to follow Jesus at once. At first they were called to follow him as *disciples*, but now they are expressly called to follow him as his *constant attendants*, ministers, or evangelists, although they

2*

18 come fishers of men. And straightway ¹they for- ¹ Mt. 19. 27; Lk. 5. 11.
sook their nets, and followed him.
19 ᵘ And when he had gone a little farther thence, he ᵘ Mt. 4. 21.
saw James the son of Zebedee, and John his brother,
20 who also were in the ship mending their nets. And
straightway he called them : and they left their
father Zebedee in the ship with the hired servants,
and went after him.

afterward fished sometimes, when near their homes, Luke 5 : 1-11. Their selection among the twelve apostles occurred afterward, ch. 3 : 14 ; Luke 6 : 14-16. Thus their calling was threefold. **Fishers of men.** Preachers of the gospel ; winners of souls to Christ. They were to catch men in the net of Christ's kingdom. Their former secular calling was an emblem of their higher spiritual calling. This language shows that now they were not called merely as disciples, but as preachers, evangelists.
18. They *immediately* leave their nets, though just commencing their night's labor, forsake their calling, and follow Jesus as his constant attendants. Thus by their immediate obedience they show their sincerity and faith. **Their nets.** Rather, *the nets.*
19. **And when he had gone.** Literally, *And going on, advancing*, attended, quite likely, by Andrew and Peter. **James the son of Zebedee.** James was probably the older brother, since he is named first, and also as the son of Zebedee. John was probably the one who, months before this, had gone to the dwelling of Jesus, John 1 : 39. *Zebedee* was a fisherman in very good circumstances, owning a boat, and having laborers with him, ver. 20. His wife was one of those pious women who ministered unto him of their substance (Matt. 27 : 56), and his son John was personally known to the highpriest, to whom also Jesus committed his mother. Such facts show the family to have enjoyed some degree of outward prosperity. **The ship.** A fishing-boat, propelled both by sails and oars. **Mending their nets.** They were repairing *the nets*, getting ready for their night's labor.
20. **Straightway.** The call was immediate, as well as their leaving their occupation and their father. **The hired servants.** The fishermen in the employ of Zebedee, which shows that he had some means, and that he was not left without help. They left, doubtless, a prosperous business to follow Jesus. **Went after him ;** as his constant attendants. The expression is stronger than that of Matthew, who simply says, "followed him." It answers to the call, "Come after me" (ver. 17), "went *behind*," or "after him."
21-28. JESUS TEACHES IN CAPERNAUM, AND HEALS A DEMONIAC, Luke 4 : 31-37. Having spoken of his general teaching in Galilee, and the calling of four disciples to be his constant attendants, Mark proceeds to give a particular instance of his teaching, attested by a wonderful miracle. His account is somewhat fuller than that of Luke.
A few suggestions upon the miracles of Jesus will not be out of place. He performed them in proof of his divine mission, John 2 : 22; 9 : 3-5 ; 10 : 25, 37. The Jews expected the Messiah would work miracles, Matt. 12 : 38 ; Luke 11 : 16, 17; John 7 : 31 ; so also did John the Baptist, Matt. 11 : 3. The miracles of Christ were variously designated. When they were specially regarded as evidences of his divine mission they were called *sēmeia, signs*, ch. 8 : 11 ; John 2 : 11 ; when as the manifestation of supernatural power, they were called *dunameis, mighty works*, corresponding more strictly to the word *miracle* in common English usage, ch. 6 : 2 ; 9 : 39 ; when as extraordinary and portending phenomena, exciting astonishment or terror, they were called *terata, wonders*, John 4 : 48 ; Acts 2 : 22 ; compare Mark 13 : 22 ; and when viewed still more generally and comprehensively, as something completed and to be reflected on—the natural acts and products of his being, they were called *erga*, works, John 7 : 3, 21. In our Common Version, the first of these is translated *signs, miracles, wonders ;* the

Jesus teaches and heals a demoniac and many others at Capernaum.

21. ᵃ AND they went into Capernaum. And straightway on the sabbath day he entered into the syna-   ᵃ Lk. 4. 31; Mt. 4. 13.

second, *mighty works, mighty deeds, wonderful works, miracles;* the third, *wonders;* and the fourth, *deeds.*

To get a full and correct conception of Christ's miracles, they should be viewed in all these aspects. They were not simply the manifestations of a supernatural power, but also the product of that power inherent in our Lord, the natural fruits, the outworkings of his own divine nature; they were not merely adapted to impress the mind deeply and excite astonishment or terror, but they were also the signs, the evidences of himself and of the truth of which he was the embodiment. They were, in fine, the supernatural phenomena produced by his own power in proof of his divine nature. They were not a violation of nature, nor necessarily a suspension of its laws, but rather above nature, so far as we know, or in accordance with laws and principles unknown to us. It is indeed in accordance with nature to expect miracles in connection with a new dispensation. "All the great chapters of nature's history," says Prof. Hitchcock, "begin with them, and if the Christian dispensation were destitute of them, it would be out of harmony with the course of things in the natural world."—*Bib. Sac.*, July, 1863, p. 552.

21. **They.** Jesus and the disciples whom he had called, vers. 16-20. **Went into.** *Enter into* Capernaum as they came from the sea where the four had been called.

Capernaum; was on the western shore of the Sea of Galilee, Matt. 4:18; compare Matt. 14:34 with John 6:17, 21, 24. It is not mentioned in the Old Testament, and only once by Josephus. Its site is unknown. The three most probable spots are:

(1.) *Khan Minyeh*, on the shore, about five miles south-west from where the Jordan enters the lake, and on the northern border of the plain of Gennesaret, where a heap of ruins remains. Near by is the fountain of *Ain et-Tin*. So Robinson, *Biblical Researches,* ii. 403-4, iii. 344-358.

(2.) *Tell Hum*, on a point projecting into the lake, about three miles northeast of Khan Minyeh, where are extensive ruins, and where a synagogue, in a state of fine preservation, has been discovered. But the nearest fountain is said to be about two miles distant. So Dr. Thomson, *Land and Book*, i. 542-548.

(3.) *Ain Mudawarah,* or the Round Fountain, near the south end of the plain of Gennesaret. In this fountain is found the coracine or catfish, which, according to Josephus (*Jewish War,* iii. 10, 8), abounded in the fountain of Capernaum. A considerable stream also flows from it to the lake, which also answers to Josephus' description. So Mr. Tristram, *Land of Israel*, p. 442. The latest travelers are inclined to give the preference to Tell Hum. Still I am not yet fully prepared to say that Khan Minyeh is not the most probable site of Capernaum.

Straightway on the Sabbath-day. He immediately enters upon the work of teaching. Mark very frequently describes events as *straightway* or *immediately* occurring. The Sabbath was doubtless the one following the calling of the four disciples.

Synagogue means *assembly, congregation*, and is applied both to a religious gathering, having certain judicial powers (Luke 8:41; 12:11; 21:12; Acts 9:2), and to the place where the Jews met for their public worship on ordinary occasions, Luke 7:5. The synagogue appears to have been first introduced during the Babylonish captivity, when the people, deprived of their usual rites of worship, assembled on the Sabbath to hear the law read and expounded. Compare Neh. 8:1-8. The times of meeting were on the Sabbath and feast-days; and afterward on the second and fifth days of the week. Each synagogue had its president or ruler (Luke 8:49; 13:14; Acts 18: 8, 17) and elders (Luke 7:3-5), who might chastise (Matt. 10:17; Acts 22:

22 gogue, and taught. ᵇ And they were astonished at his doctrine: ᶜ for he taught them as one that had authority, ᵈ and not as the scribes.
23 ᵉ And there was in their synagogue a man with an

ᵇ ch. 6. 2; Ps. 45. 2; Mt. 7. 28; 13. 54; Lk. 4. 32; John 7. 15, 46.
ᶜ Is. 50. 4; Mt. 5. 20, 28, 32, 44.

ᵈ Mt. 15. 1-9; 23. 2-7.   ᵉ Lk. 4. 33.

19; 26:11) or expel (John 9:34) an offender. In Mark 5:22 and Acts 13:15, the ruler and elders appear to be spoken of indiscriminately as *rulers*. It is, however, uncertain how perfect was the organization of the synagogue in the time of Christ. It was probably changed and developed after the destruction of Jerusalem by the Romans. **Taught.** For his manner of teaching in the synagogue see Luke 4:16-21. The heads of the synagogue were accustomed, after the reading of Scripture, to ask such grave and learned persons as might be present to address the people. Christ and the apostles constantly availed themselves of this privilege.

22. The manner of his teaching and its effect on others. Mark here refers to this particular instance of teaching, yet his remark is applicable to Christ's teaching generally. Thus the same language is used by Matthew, after the Sermon on the Mount, Matt. 7:28, 29. **Astonished.** Struck with wonder, with astonishment. So on other occasions, ch. 6:2; 11:18; Matt. 13:54; Luke 4:32. **At his doctrine.** Rather, *At his teaching;* both in regard to the things taught and the manner of his instruction. **He taught.** He was teaching them. Such was his habitual manner. **As one that had authority.** He taught as the great author and revealer of truth; as the author of the law he expounded it in all of its fullness and spirituality, and enforced it by his personal authority, "Verily I say unto you," Matt. 5:18, 38; 6:2, etc. Compare Matt. 5:22, 28, 32, 34, etc. **Not as the scribes.** The scribes taught with authority, but it was that of tradition and of the ancients; Jesus taught not merely as the expounder, but as one who spoke for God, may, as the Lawgiver himself. They enforced the letter of the law; he brought out the spirit, and spoke as the expounder of his own law, and with the authority of the Christ. The *scribes* were learned men, who preserved, copied, and expounded the law and the traditions,

Ezra 7:6, 12; Neh. 8:1; Matt. 15:1-6. They are called lawyers (ch. 12:28 and Matt. 22:35), and doctors of the law, Luke 5:17, 21. Most of them were Pharisees. It is implied from the language of this verse that they were teachers as well as conservators and copyists of the law. They sat in Moses' seat, but their teaching was strikingly defective, Matt. 23:2, 13, 23.

23. His divine authority is attested by divine power. **With an unclean spirit.** Literally, *in an unclean spirit;* that is, in his possession, in his power, and pervaded by his influence. Luke says (4:33) that he "had a spirit of an unclean devil" or *demon;* one of that inferior order of evil spirits or fallen angels, who are subject to Satan their prince, Matt. 9:34; 25:41; Rev. 12:9. The original Scriptures recognize but one devil, but many demons. See on ver. 13. The one here is called *an unclean spirit* with reference to the moral vileness and wickedness of demons. So they are also called evil spirits, Luke 7:21; 8:2. They were the authors and promoters of wickedness and all uncleanness.

The sacred writers in their account of demoniacal possessions did not speak in mere accommodation to the opinion of the Jews, but stated as matters of fact, that individuals were actually possessed with demons. Demons are spoken of as personal beings, Luke 11:24-26; James 2:19; Rev. 16:14, etc.; Jesus addressed them as persons and they answered as such, verse 25; 5:8; 9:25; they showed a supernatural knowledge of Jesus, Matt. 8:29; Luke 4:34; they requested, and were permitted, to enter a herd of swine, ch. 5:12, 13. Jesus also distinguished between casting out demons and the healing of diseases, verse 32-34; Matt. 8:16; Luke 7:21. A person might be dumb as a result of demoniacal possession, but not every dumb person was possessed with a demon, Mark 7:32; Matt. 9:32, 33. Nowhere is demoniacal possession made identical with any one disease. Yet

24 unclean spirit; and he cried out, saying, Let us
alone; *what have we to do with thee, thou Jesus of
Nazareth? Art thou come to destroy us? I know
25 thee who thou art, ᵍthe Holy One of God. And

ᶠMt. 8. 29.
ᵍPs. 89. 18, 19;
Dan. 9. 24; Lk.
1. 35; Ac. 3. 14;
4. 27, 30.

various mental and bodily disorders are attributed to the agency of the devil or demons, Acts 10: 38; Luke 9: 39, 42. The bodies of individuals are represented as forcibly possessed by a consciousness and will foreign to themselves; so that there appears to have been a double will and a double consciousness, ch. 7: 25, 30; Luke 9: 39; 11: 14. From such passages it is evident that the Scriptures speak of Satan and demons as personal beings, and that they were permitted to take possession of the bodies of men and inflict on them various sufferings. To regard the language of the sacred writers as a mere accommodation, the devil and his angels as mere myths, or the principle of evil, and the possessions as mere diseases, is contrary to the plainest statements and to the uses of language. In the same way all history might be discredited and the actual existence of the principal men of past ages disproved.

To the frequent inquiry, How comes it that similar possessions do not occur at the present day? it may be answered: (1) It cannot be proved that they do not sometimes occur even now. It cannot be said that in many cases of insanity, and in some cases of spiritualism, the malady may not be traced to the direct agency of demons. (2) But admitting that such possessions are not common; yet there was a reason in our Savior's day for the external manifestation of Satan's power. The crisis of the moral history of the world was at hand. The devil was allowed to exercise unusual power in temptation on the souls and bodies of men, in order that Christ might meet him openly and manifest his power in his victory over him. When God was manifested in the flesh, then demons may have been permitted to manifest themselves specially among men. And that demoniacal possessions were more specially limited to that age, is not an unfair inference from both sacred and profane history. For it is a remarkable fact that we have no cases of these possessions in the O. T. and none in the epistles of the N. T.; and

that Josephus speaks of no real possessions except in the generation in which Christ exercised his ministry.

He cried out. The unclean spirit. He had such control of the man that he spoke through him, using his organs of speech. The personality of the demon is distinctly recognized. Neither a disease nor a myth could thus cry out. 24. **Let us alone.** Rather, *hah*, an interjection expressing surprise and displeasure. It is omitted in some of the best ancient manuscripts. **What have we to do with thee?** *What to us and thee in common?* Our relations and our business are wholly different from thine. Wilt thou then disturb us? This form of expression occurs several times in the New Testament. Jesus thus addressed his mother at the marriage in Cana of Galilee. It always implies disapprobation, though sometimes employed in friendly reproof. The demon uses the plural here with reference to fallen spirits as a class of which he was a representative. **Thou.** This is superfluous. **Nazareth.** *Nazarene;* inhabitant of Nazareth. **Art thou come?** or *didst thou come?* Is this the object of thy coming? **To destroy us,** who constitute the kingdom of darkness, of which this one was a representative. The man could not have been included in *us*, for it was the saving of the man, and his own expulsion, that the demon feared. The *destruction* was sending them down to hell, Matt. 8: 29; 10: 28. **I know thee who thou art.** Doubtless by fame and report, but more. He felt the awing influence of so holy a being, filling him with dread; he took him at once to be the Messiah; he believed and trembled, James 2: 19. Compare a similar knowledge in Acts 16: 17. **The Holy One of God.** Not merely morally so, but also officially. The Son of God, the Messiah, the one officially set apart and consecrated to this office and work, John 6: 69. Compare John 10: 36; Rev. 3: 7. Demons knew him to be the Son of God, Luke 4: 41.

25. **Hold thy peace.** *Silence,* a

Jesus [h] rebuked him, saying, Hold thy peace, and [h] ver. 34.
26 come out of him. And when the unclean spirit [i] had [i] ch. 9. 20.
torn him, and cried with a loud voice, he came out
27 of him. And they were all amazed, insomuch that
they questioned among themselves, saying, What
thing is this? [k] what new doctrine is this? for with [k] Mt. 7. 28; Jam.
authority commandeth he even the unclean spirits, 2. 19.
28 and they do obey him. And immediately his fame
spread abroad throughout all the region round about
Galilee.
29 [l] And forthwith, when they were come out of the [l] Mt. 8. 14; Lk. 4.
synagogue, they entered into the house of Simon and 38.
30 Andrew, with James and John. But Simon's wife's
mother lay sick of a fever; and anon they tell him

command with authority and restraining power. The testimony was not with believing confidence; demons were not permitted to give it, Luke 4:41; neither had the time come for so public a promulgation. This Jesus reserved to himself and his followers. **Come out of him.** Two distinct personalities are here recognized. The demon is treated as a person as much as the man. The one was just as much a disease or a principle as the other, no more and no less.

26. The personality of the demon is further evinced by crying out, tearing the man, and coming out of him. Such language would not be used of an epileptic fit, as some would have us believe. **Torn him.** *Tearing* him, *convulsing* him, but not in such a manner as to do him injury, for Luke says (4:35) "he came out of him and hurt him not." Luke also says "the devil had thrown him in the midst." Such paroxysms in connection with casting out demons, showed their malignant and degraded nature (ch. 9:26); and only made the miracle the more impressive.

27. **They were all amazed.** The effect of the miracle is here vividly presented. A general amazement took possession of the people, which led them to discussion and certain conclusions. **Questioning among themselves.** Inquiring and reasoning one with another. **What thing is this?** Rather, *What is this?* What means this strange event, this power over unclean spirits, this commanding and this implicit obedience. **What new doctrine is this?** According to the highest critical authorities this should read: *A new teaching with authority! Even the unclean spirits he commands,* etc. Such a display of superhuman power they regarded as an evidence of a new revelation. It was especially in the manner of teaching, for the commanding the unclean spirits and their obedience is made prominent both here and in Luke 4:36.

28. Further effect of the miracle, which **immediately** followed. **His fame.** The report of him and what he did and taught. **Throughout all the region round about Galilee.** Some suppose this to mean, through all Galilee and into the surrounding districts. But it more strictly means, into the whole surrounding region of Galilee.

This miracle in public is now followed by one in private.

29–34. HEALS PETER'S WIFE'S MOTHER AND MANY OTHERS, Matt. 8:14–17; Luke 4:38–41. Further evidences of his divine mission and doctrine. Mark is the fullest and enters most into detail. The three accounts show the diversity of independent narrators.

29. **Forthwith.** Immediately after leaving the synagogue they enter the house of Simon and Andrew. These latter had formerly resided at Bethsaida (John 1:44), but now had taken up their residence at Capernaum. Mark alone mentions the fact that Jesus was attended by James and John; doubtless also by Andrew and Peter.

30. **Wife's mother.** Mother-in-law. She seems to have resided with Peter. **Simon.** So Mark calls him till he is regularly called to be an apostle, ch. 3:16. This shows the exact-

A.D. 28.　　　　　MARK I.　　　　　39

31 of her. And he came and took her by the hand, and
lifted her up; and immediately the fever left her,
and she ministered unto them.
32 ᵐAnd at even, when the sun did set, they brought　ᵐMt. 8. 16; Lk. 4.
unto him all that were diseased, and them that were　40.
33 possessed with devils. And all the city was gath-
34 ered together at the door. And he healed many

ness of Mark, and is also noticeable since this evangelist is supposed to have written someway under the direction of Peter. From this passage it appears that Peter had a wife. As late as A.D. 57 she was living, and accompanied Peter on a missionary tour, 1 Cor. 9 : 5. The Romish doctrine of clerical celibacy is unauthorized by Scripture, Heb. 13 : 4. **Lay sick of a fever.** She was confined to bed with fever. It was a severe case, for Luke says she was "taken with a great" or "violent fever." Fevers are common in Palestine, and in the vicinity of Capernaum fevers of a malignant type are still prevalent, and especially in the summer and autumn. **Anon.** *Immediately.* Events follow in quick succession. **Tell him of her.** Of her dangerous illness, etc. They also requested him to heal her, Luke 4 : 38.
31. **And he came,** into the room, and to the bed where she lay sick. **Lifted her up;** raised her up from her prostrate position. The idea is not that he lifted her by his own strength merely, but rather that he caused her to rise, assisting her by his hand. It was not necessary to the cure that he should even touch her; but it was often desirable so to do both to strengthen the faith of the one to be healed, and to impress the fact the more deeply on those that witnessed it. **Took her by the hand.** The manner of raising her up. Notice how Mark details each act. Matthew says "touched her hand;" Luke, that he "stood over and rebuked the fever." The differences are not contradictory, but show the independence of the first three evangelists. Jesus did stand over her and rebuke the fever, at the same time placing his hand upon hers, and to raise her up. At his touch the fever departs and he raises her up a well woman. **Immediately.** The third time that this word appears, in the original, in this and the preceding verse. The fever left her instantly, and as an evidence of a full and perfect cure, **she ministered unto them,** she at once attended to her household duties, waited on the table and served them. The fever did not leave her weak and exhausted; she was raised to her full strength and to perfect health.
32. Mark proceeds from these two particular miracles, the one public, the other private, to the statement that his miracle-working power was very largely and wonderfully exercised at that time and place.
Even. Old English for evening. **When the sun did set.** The Jewish Sabbath closed at the setting of the sun, Lev. 23 : 32. It was the cool of the day and therefore the best time for bringing the sick. The news of Christ's presence in the city and of his wonderful cure in the synagogue had had time to spread, and now the people begin to bring their sick. It being the Sabbath also, they may have preferred to wait till its close. **All that were diseased.** A general statement, the worst form of disease being immediately specified. Or the expression may refer to bodily diseases, and distinguished from that produced by the agency of demons. **Possessed with devils.** Possessed with *demons*, an inferior order of evil spirits subject to Satan their prince, Matt. 9 ; 34 ; 25 : 41 ; Rev. 12 : 9. The original Scriptures recognize but one devil, but many demons.
33. **All the city.** The people generally. Recorded only by Mark. The effect of his teaching, and of his wonderful miracle was such, that the people of Capernaum came as it were *en masse* bearing their sick, to see and hear this wonderful teacher and to obtain the benefit of his miraculous power.
34. **He healed many.** Matthew says, he "healed *all* that were sick." This all were *many.* **Divers diseases**

that were sick of divers diseases, and cast out many devils; and ⁿ suffered not the devils to speak, because they knew him.   * ch. 3. 12; Lk. 4. 41; Ac. 16. 17, 18.

First general preaching tour throughout Galilee. A leper healed.

35 And º in the morning, rising up a great while before day, he went out, ᵖ and departed into a solitary place, and there prayed.
36 And Simon and they that were with him followed
37 after him. And when they had found him, they
38 said unto him, All *men* seek for thee. And he said unto them, ᵠ Let us go into the next towns, that I may preach there also: for ʳ therefore came I forth.
39 ˢ And he preached in their synagogues throughout all Galilee, and cast out devils.

º Lk. 4. 42.
ᵖ ch. 6. 46; 14. 32-40; Mt. 6. 6; Lk. 6. 12; 22. 39-46.

ᵠ Lk. 4. 43.
ʳ Is. 61. 1-3; John 16. 28; 17. 4.
ˢ Mt. 4. 23; Lk. 4. 44.

---

and cast out many devils. Here again demoniacal possessions are distinguished from the mere physical maladies unconnected with the agency of demons. **Suffered not the demons to speak.** Recognizing Jesus as the Christ, the demons cried out, "Thou art the Son of God;" but Jesus rebuked them and suffered them not to speak, Luke 4 : 41. Demons were not to be his messengers to proclaim his Messiahship.
35-39. JESUS IN RETIREMENT AT PRAYER. Sought out by his disciples, he goes upon his FIRST GENERAL PREACHING TOUR throughout Galilee. Matt. 4 : 23-25; Luke 4 : 42-44. The retirement of Jesus for prayer is recorded more fully by Mark than by Luke, but omitted by Matthew who, however, relates most fully the first preaching tour throughout Galilee.
35. **In the morning, etc.** This note of time shows that it was the day following the cure of Peter's wife's mother, vers. 30-32. Literally, *very early, by night, rising he went out.* The meaning is that it was the early break of day, when on account of the preponderating darkness it could be called night. Luke (4 : 42) says, *When it was day,* regarding the day as beginning with its early dawn. **He went out.** Of the house of Peter, ver. 29; and of Capernaum, ver. 21. **A solitary place.** A *desert,* uninhabited and unfrequented place near Capernaum. Compare ver. 45. **Prayed.** Thus Jesus prepared for the duties of the day by devoting part of the night to secret prayer. Luke 6 : 12.
36. **They that were with him.** Andrew, James, and John, and possibly others, ver. 29. **Followed after.** Followed eagerly after, in order to find him. They were in earnest and possibly impatient. Pursued him earnestly.
37. **When they had found him.** After looking after or searching for him. **All men seek for thee.** *For* is superfluous. The reason given why he should not continue in solitude, but return and gratify the desires of the multitude in healing their diseases, ver. 32. According to Luke 4 : 42 the people detained him so that he should not depart from them.
38. The reply of Jesus shows that he had other work to do, and that the people and even his disciples understood not the object of his mission. **Let us go.** According to the most ancient manuscripts, *Let us go elsewhere.* This he spoke to his disciples. **The next towns.** The adjacent towns. These were literally *village-cities,* large villages or towns like cities, but without walls. **Preach there also.** Not merely at Capernaum, but in other cities also, Luke 4 : 42. **Therefore came I forth.** Not from Capernaum, but from his Father, John 16 : 28. His mission was to preach the gospel, Luke 4 : 18-21. This the people failed to understand.
39. **Preached, etc.** *He was preaching, etc.* He continued preaching in their synagogues, going throughout all

A.D. 28.   MARK I.   41

40 ¹ And there came a leper to him, beseeching him, ¹ Le. ch. 13, ch.
and kneeling down to him, and saying unto him, If   14; Mt. 8. 2-4;
                                                    Lk. 5. 12-14.

Galilee. This must be the first general preaching tour throughout Galilee recorded in Matt. 4 : 23-25, since according to the first two evangelists, it occurred not long after the calling of the four disciples, Matt. 4 : 18 and Mark 1 : 16. We cannot suppose two such extensive tours throughout Galilee in course of a few weeks. **All Galilee.** Into every part of the province, which was very populous and containing many towns and villages. See on ver. 9. **Cast out devils.** He confirmed and attested his preaching by his miracles, chief among which was his casting out demons. Thus he specially showed his opposition to the kingdom of darkness.

40-45. HEALING OF A LEPER. Matt. 8 : 2-4; Luke 5 : 12-14. Having particularly related the healing of the demoniac, Mark now relates with equal minuteness the cleansing of a leper; the former more closely connected with soul uncleanness, the latter with bodily impurity. Mark's account enters most into detail.

40. **And there came.** While he was in one of the cities of Galilee (Luke 5:12), but what city the evangelists do not tell us. Matthew plainly fixes the miracle immediately after the sermon on the mount, when Jesus descended from the mountain. Some suppose it to have been wrought at Capernaum. But probably not; for Jesus was preaching "throughout all Galilee" (vers. 39; Matt. 4 : 23), commencing from Capernaum (vers. 21 : 35-39; Luke 4 : 31, 44), and the leper was healed, according to Luke, "in one of the cities" of Galilee. Luke would hardly have spoken thus indefinitely of Capernaum.

A leper. Leprosy was a most fearful and foul skin-disease, and in its worse form was the most terrible of all diseases, and absolutely incurable. See Lev. chs. 13, 14; where it is described with certain enactments. It probably began internally, after which it showed itself in swellings, scabs, bright spots, or slight reddish eruptions, grouped in circles, covered with a shiny scale or scab. The disease was not contagious, though it often became hereditary for generations. Its progress was not generally rapid. A leper from birth sometimes lived as many as fifty years; while those afterward infected, sometimes as many as twenty. It was sometimes sent as a special judgment for sin, and hence was called a *plague* or *stroke*, Num. 12 : 10; 2 Kings 5 : 27; 2 Chron. 26 : 20.

Whether this disease is identical with modern leprosy has been much disputed. The latest testimonies favor the belief that, under certain forms, it continues to prevail. Dr. Thomson (*The Land and the Book*, Vol. II., p. 516-520) speaks of it as existing in the East. He saw a number near Jerusalem. "They held up toward me their handless arms, unearthly sounds gurgled through their throats without palates,—in a word, I was horrified. . . . I subsequently visited their habitation, . . . and have made many inquiries into their history. . . . New-born babes of leprous parents are often as pretty and as healthy in appearance as any; but by-and-by its presence and workings become visible in some of the signs described in the 13th chapter of Leviticus. The scab comes on by degrees in different parts of the body; the hair falls from the head and eyebrows; the nails loosen, decay, and drop off; joint after joint of the fingers and toes shrink up, and slowly fall away." Thus slowly the victim dies, and no power of medicine is able to stay the disease or mitigate its tortures.

Leprosy is a striking emblem of sin and its effects. It was indeed regarded as a living death (JOSEPH. *Antiq.* III. 11, 3). The leper was unclean; he was to rend his garments, let his hair hang disheveled, wear garments of mourning as for the dead, and live in exclusion outside the camp or city. Neither Miriam, the sister of Moses, nor King Uzziah, was exempted from this regulation, Num. 12 : 15; 2 Chron. 26 : 21. Not only was he to be excluded from society, while diseased, as if in effect dead; but if cleansed, he was to be cleansed by the same means, as by uncleanness through touching or handling the dead, Num. 19 : 13-20; Lev. 14 : 4-7. Thus sin affects the soul, rendering it unclean, separating it from

41 thou wilt, ⁿthou canst make me clean. And Jesus, ᵘch. 9. 23; Mt. 9. 28, 29.
moved with compassion, ᵛput forth *his* hand, and ᵛ2 Ki. 5. 11.
ʷtouched him, and saith unto him, ˣI will; be thou ʷLe. 13. 44-46
42 clean. And as soon as he had spoken, ʸimmediately ˣGe. 1. 3.
the leprosy departed from him, and he was cleansed. ʸPs. 33. 9.
43 And he straitly charged him, and forthwith sent ᶻch. 5. 43; Mt. 8.
44 him away; and saith unto him, ᶻSee thou say nothing 4; 9. 30.

God, producing spiritual death, unfitting it forever for heaven and the company of the holy, and insuring its eternal banishment, as polluted and abominable. Some, as they look on infancy, reject with horror the thought that sin exists within. But so might any one say, who looked upon the beautiful babe in the arms of a leprous mother. But time brings forth the fearful malady. And so the leprosy of sin manifests itself in every human character as it comes forth from infancy.

In the present instance it was an aggravated case of the disease, for Luke says, "a man full of leprosy;" it covered his whole body from head to foot.

Beseeching him and kneeling down to him. The leper came to Jesus with the most earnest and humble entreaty, and in his respect and reverence fell upon his face, Luke 5 : 12. **If thou wilt, thou canst.** If thou art willing thou art able. The leper had faith in the miraculous power of Jesus, but had a doubt about his willingness to exercise it on such an object as he, on one so unclean. He determined to press his case earnestly, and leave it on the will of Jesus alone, *If thou wilt.* **Make me clean.** Cleanse me, heal my leprosy, and thus remove my uncleanness.

41. **Moved with compassion.** Mark alone describes the Savior's *feelings of pity* upon seeing and hearing the leper. Jesus showed his willingness by stretching forth his hand, and contrary to Jewish law, *touching* him. But Christ was himself the lawgiver and the fulfiller of the law. As it was in harmony with the law of the Sabbath to do good and save life, so was it with the law of leprosy to remove the disease and the defilement. Jesus was also purity itself. He purified, but contracted no uncleanness. Before his power, as symbolized by stretching forth his hand and touching him, the leprosy fled and the leper was cleansed.

I will; be thou clean. Language beautifully and strikingly corresponding to that of the leper. Jesus grants a full and perfect answer to his request.

42. **And as soon as he had spoken,** omitted by the best text. **Immediately.** A favorite word of Mark. The leprosy, the cause of his defilement, went from him, and as a consequence he was cleansed. So Jesus cleanses the sinner by healing the seat of disease.

43. **Straitly charged him.** Sternly charged him. The original expresses strong and earnest emotion, amounting even to sternness, and is quite the opposite of that translated "moved with compassion" in ver. 41. He gave him a strict prohibition, as if on pain of his displeasure. **Sent him away.** The verb in the original is the same as that translated *driveth* in verse 12. He *sent him forth* or *away* from the city, house, or place where they were at that time. The reason will appear in the next verse.

44. **Say nothing to any man.** Jesus frequently gave this prohibition, ch. 5 : 43; 7 : 36. His reasons were various according to circumstances. As a general principle it accorded with his modest and unostentatious bearing, and with the peacefulness and spirituality of his kingdom (Matt. 12 : 16-20), which came not with observation, Luke 17 : 20. Sometimes he would repress, rather than encourage the excitement of the people, who beset him in such crowds as greatly to trouble him (ch. 3 : 9, 20), and to make him a temporal king, John 6 : 15. At other times he doubtless had the good of the persons healed specially in view. In this instance the prohibition was temporary, only binding till he should go and show himself to the priest. He would have him remain silent so as to promptly obey this requirement of the Mosaic law. He would not arouse undue excitement (see next verse); nor would he expose himself or the healed leper

to any man: but go thy way, show thyself to the priest, and offer for thy cleansing those things ᵃ which Moses commanded, for a testimony unto 45 them. ᵇ But he went out, and began to publish it much, and to blaze abroad the matter, insomuch that Jesus could no more openly enter into the city; but was without in desert places: ᶜ and they came to him from every quarter.

ᵃ Le. 13. 2, etc.; 14. 2, etc.; Mt. 5. 17; Lk. 5. 14.
ᵇ Lk. 5. 15.
ᶜ ch. 2. 13.

to the charge of violating the law. Possibly he would have him appear before the priest before any prejudicial report of his cure reached him, which should prevent him acknowledging the cure. **Show thyself to the priest.** At Jerusalem. Possibly the leper, finding himself cleansed, was disposed to remain among his relatives; but Jesus with great earnestness and in an authoritative manner sends him at once to Jerusalem in obedience to the requirement of the law. **Offer for thy cleansing.** Offer because of thy cleansing, which ought to be first recognized by the priest. There were two stages in the ceremonial of purification of the leper, Lev. 14 : 1-32. The purifying ceremonies and offerings were united with confessions of sin and pollution, and with grateful acknowledgment of God's mercy. As the leprosy was a striking type of sin, so these ceremonies were typical of the forgiveness of sin and justification through the blood of Christ and of the anointing of the Holy Spirit for sanctification, Heb. 10 : 21, 22; 1 John 2 : 20. **A testimony unto them.** To the people that he was cured, and that he might safely be re-admitted into society. He had been pronounced unclean by the priest, who alone could pronounce him clean and re-admit him into the congregation.

45. The thoughtless disobedience of the leper and the inconvenience caused thereby to Jesus. **Went out.** From the presence of Jesus. The miracle may have been performed in some house. **Began to publish.** He at once began to herald his cure. He did not realize the importance of keeping silence and obeying Jesus. He gives vent to his joy, forgetful that even the expression of this should be regulated by the word of Jesus. **Blaze abroad the matter.** Rather, *spread abroad the report*, circulate the report of what Jesus had done. **No more.** Rather, *No longer*. **The city;** *a city*, any city. He could no longer **openly enter** any city, because it had become known that he had touched a leper, and he was thus unclean, according to the law, for a season. The crowds of people thus gathered together, and the consequent excitement, would also prematurely make him notorious, and attract the suspicious notice of the authorities. The words **could not** are used in a moral sense, denoting not natural inability, but the indisposition of meeting the difficulties in his way, and of having his own plans defeated. **Desret places;** uninhabited, unfrequented places. **From evrey quarter.** From all places around about. They sought him out, notwithstanding his seclusion.

REMARKS.

1. Jesus is divine, ver. 1; John 5: 18; Rom. 9: 5; Phil. 2: 6; Isa. 9: 6.
2. The new dispensation began with the preaching and baptism of John, and in fulfillment of prophecy, vers. 1-3; Matt. 11: 12, 13; John 5: 35, 40.
3. A preparation is needed for the reception of spiritual blessings, ver. 3; James 4: 8-10; Amos 4: 12.
4. John "prepared the way of the Lord" by the severity of his manners and doctrines; so the terrors of the law prepare the soul through the convicting spirit for the reception of Jesus, vers. 3, 6; Gal. 3: 24; 2 Cor. 5: 11.
5. True repentance is attended with forgiveness of sins and reformation of life. It is in vain to profess repentance or to be baptized without a change of heart and life, ver. 4; Matt. 3: 8, 9; 7: 16, 20; Acts 26: 20.
6. How little dependence can be placed on "popularity." What crowds came to John's preaching and baptism,

yet how few were really converted, ver. 5; Matt. 11 : 16–18 : John 5 : 35.

7. We should ever exalt Christ whether we preach, teach or converse, ver. 7; Acts 5 : 42; 2 Cor. 4 : 5.

8. Christ is the dispenser of the Spirit, and of spiritual gifts, ver. 8; John 16 : 7; Rom. 8 : 9.

9. If Jesus went such a distance to be baptized, and if it became him to fulfill all righteousness, it surely becomes his followers to walk in his ordinances and obey all his commandments, ver. 9; Matt. 3 : 15; John 14 : 15; Acts 2 : 38; 1 Pet. 2 : 21.

10. We should honor that ordinance which received the sanction of the Triune God, vers. 9–11.

11. Christ has obtained complete acceptance of the Father. Heaven is opened to us by the Son, ver. 10; John 1 : 51; 3 : 15; 14 : 6.

12. We should cheerfully follow the leadings of the Spirit, though it be in temptation and trial. Under his influence nothing need to be feared from the tempter, ver. 12; 1 Cor. 10 : 13; James 4 : 7.

13. As Christ's temptation followed his baptism, so great spiritual enjoyments are followed by great trials. Young Christians should especially expect temptation, ver.12; 2 Cor. 12 : 7; 1 John 2 : 14.

14. We need the Spirit in retirement and solitude, since they are often the place and occasion of temptation, ver. 13; Ps. 36 : 4; Prov. 9 : 17; Matt. 6 : 6; Eph. 5 : 12.

15. Angels are interested spectators of our temptations and sorrows, ver. 13; Heb. 1 : 14.

16. Temptations should result in our good, and help fit us for the duties of life, ver. 13; James 1 : 2, 3, 12; 1 Pet. 1 : 6, 7.

17. Repentance and faith are fundamental subjects in all gospel preaching, vers. 14, 15; Acts 20 : 21.

18. True repentance springs from a sense of the mercy of God in Christ. Both John and Jesus preached repentance; for the kingdom of heaven is at hand, ver. 15; Matt. 3 : 2; Acts 5 : 31; Rom. 2 : 4.

19. Improve every opportunity of recommending Jesus and inviting souls to him, vers. 16–20; John 1 : 36, 39, 41, 43, 45.

20. God builds up his kingdom by weak instrumentalities, and thus shows forth his glory, vers. 16, 19; Zech. 4 : 6; 1 Cor. 1 : 26, 27.

21. Ministers should never lose sight of the fact that they are called to be fishers of men, ver. 17; 1 Cor. 9 :22; 2 Cor. 12 : 14; 1 Tim. 4 : 16.

22. Follow Jesus at any cost; prompt obedience is especially pleasing to him, vers. 18, 20; Luke 9 : 57–62.

23. The public services of God's house should not be neglected, ver. 21; Heb. 10 : 25.

24. The true Christian teacher comes with the authority of God and truth, ver. 22; 2 Cor. 5 : 20.

25. A mere intellectual knowledge of Christ is useless. The unclean spirit knew Jesus; devils believe and tremble; they know him as a conqueror, but not as a Savior, vers. 23, 24; James 2 : 19.

26. "Christ scorns the testimony of the demons and obtains the praise of the people."—LANGE. Vers. 25–28, 34.

27. Mark, who especially presents Christ as the Son of God, fittingly records the casting out of the unclean spirit first among the Savior's miracles, vers. 25, 26, 1.

28. Christ's victory over devils foreshadows his complete victory over the kingdom of darkness, vers. 26, 27; 1 John 3 : 8.

29. The displays of Christ's power often produce wonder only, without saving faith, vers. 27, 28; Matt. 9 : 33; 12 : 23; Acts 13 : 41.

30. The compulsory celibacy of the clergy is contrary to Scripture, ver. 30; 1 Cor. 9 : 5; 1 Tim. 3 : 2; Heb. 13 : 4.

31. Christ should be our first resort in times of trouble, ver. 30; Gen. 32 : 11; 2 Kings 19 : 19; Matt. 14 : 12; John 11 : 2; Phil. 4 : 6; James 5 : 14, 15; 1 Pet. 5 : 7.

32. Christ's cures are the most complete. He gives spiritual life and strength as well as the forgiveness of sins, ver. 31; John 1 : 12; 3 : 15.

33. "The love of Jesus is never weary."—QUESNEL. Vers. 32–34; Ps. 78 : 38; 86 : 15; Isa. 40 : 28; Matt. 15 : 32.

34. Early rising and secret prayer are in unison, and will contribute to the health of both body and soul, ver. 35; Ps. 5 : 3; Matt. 6 : 6; Luke 6 : 12; 9 : 28.

35. Go where Jesus is, and seek a blessing on yourselves and others, vers. 36, 37.

A.D. 28.　　　MARK II.　　　45

Jesus heals a paralytic at Capernaum.

1 AND again ^d he entered into Capernaum after *some* days. And it was noised that he was in the house;   ^d Mt. 9. 1; Lk. 5. 18; Prov. 8. 34.
2 and straightway many were gathered together, insomuch that there was no room to receive *them*, no, not so much as about the door; and ^e he preached the word unto them.   ^e Ps. 40. 9.
3 ^f And they come unto him, bringing one sick of   ^f Mt. 9. 2; Lk. 5. 18.

36. Every Christian, like Jesus, should seek to fulfill his mission, ver. 38; John 9 : 4; Matt. 5 : 18-16; 25 : 19 -30.
37. Leprosy is a striking type of sin; ver. 40; Num. 12 : 10-12 ; 2 Kings 5 : 7 ; Isa. 64 : 6.
38. In the leper we have an illustration of the sinner seeking Jesus and saved by him. He *felt* his disease; *despaired* of human help; exercised *faith* in the power of Jesus; and *submitted* to the will of Jesus, and was healed, vers. 40, 41; Luke 15 : 18-21.
39. Jesus is a wonderful and almighty Savior, vers. 41, 42; Isa. 9 : 6; Heb. 7 : 25.
40. There is a time to be silent in regard to Christ, as well as a time to speak of him, vers. 43, 44 ; Eccle. 3 : 7 ; 10 : 10; Matt. 7 : 6; Rom. 10 : 2.

CHAPTER II.

In the preceding chapter Mark graphically pictures the popularity of Christ's ministry in Galilee, and the enthusiasm of the people excited by his miracles and teaching. It was now about three months since he first began his ministry in Galilee, and about fifteen months since his baptism. See note on ch. 1 : 14, 15.
In this chapter Mark traces the growth of the opposition which speedily arose : first, because he claimed power to forgive sins; then, because of his eating and associating with publicans and sinners; again, because of neglecting to fast; and further, because of supposed violation of the Sabbath, one instance of which is recorded in the closing verses of this chapter, and another in the opening verses of the next.
1-12. HEALING OF A PARALYTIC AT CAPERNAUM. Matt. 9:2-8; Luke 5 : 17 -25. Mark is the most minute and graphic; Matthew the most concise.

1. **Again he entered into Capernaum.** This was his return from his first missionary tour throughout Galilee. See notes on ch. 1 : 39, 40. On *Capernaum*, see on ch. 1 : 21. It was the center of his operations to which he often returned from his missionary labors. **After some days.** Literally *after days*, a brief expression in the original very nearly equivalent to our expression, *after some days*. A few days, or several days, had probably elapsed since the healing of the leper, ch. 1 : 40 -45.
It was noised. Literally, *it was heard*. Very probably he returned quietly to Capernaum, without the people knowing it, ch. 1 : 45. **In the house.** *That he is in the house*. The idea is, that he was come into the house and was now there. It was doubtless the house where he resided when in Capernaum, Matt. 4 : 13. The words, therefore, may mean (with ALEXANDER), "It was heard that he had returned home and was now there." His mother and his brethren may have resided there with him.
2. **Many gathered together.** Among them were Pharisees and doctors or teachers of the law from the towns of Galilee and Judæa, and Jerusalem, Luke 5 : 17. How great the curiosity and the desire to see and hear him is shown by the fact that **straightway** so many gathered together and filled the house. **Not so much as about the door.** The place *at the door*. The porch or hall, leading from the street to the open area around which the house was built, could not contain them ; nor yet the house itself. **Preached the word.** Rather, *spoke the word*, of his kingdom, of the new dispensation. Luke (5 : 17) says, " He was teaching."
3. **One sick of the palsy.** One word in the original, which may be rendered *a paralytic*, one palsied, hav-

4 the palsy, which was borne of four. And when they could not come nigh unto him for the press, they uncovered the roof where he was: and when they had broken *it* up, they let down the bed wherein the

---

ing lost the power of muscular motion. **Borne by four.** Each holding a corner of the bed, ver. 4. An instance of the preciseness and definiteness of Mark.

4. They were unable to **come nigh** on account of the multitude who filled both the house and the doorway, ver. 2. Mark implies what Luke states, "they went upon the housetop," by means of stairs or a ladder; or very likely, ascending the stairs within an adjoining house, they pass from its roof to that of the house where Jesus was. "Stairs on the outside of houses are almost unknown in Palestine at present, and would only expose the inmates to violence and pillage."—DR. HACKETT, *Wm. Smith's Dictionary*, p. 1104, note. **Uncovered the roof.** Literally, *unroofing the roof*. They removed that portion of it over Jesus.

UNCOVERING THE ROOF.

Roofs are commonly flat in the East. **Where he was.** Some suppose it an open court, around which an Eastern house was built, in which case they removed the bulwark or parapet which was a safeguard against accident (Deut. 22 : 8); and a light thin covering which projected beyond the parapet over part of the central court. Others think it was a room adjoining the court, and being but a one-story house, the roof was uncovered. Others, regarding the house as more than one story, suppose an upper room, the largest room of the house, where the Jewish rabbies frequently taught, and the roof opened for the bed. **Had broken it up.** Literally, *digging through*, removing the tiles and the earth or plaster which composed the roof. The language seems to imply that it was the actual roof, and not the mere parapet with a thin projection beyond. **They let down.** They *lower* the bed by still holding the four corners, or by means of cords or ropes, Acts 27 : 30 ; 2 Cor. 11 : 33. **Bed.** A light couch or mattress, which could be easily carried, possibly a mere blanket or quilt. "Anciently, however, as at the present time in the East, the common people slept on a light mattress or blanket, with a pillow, perhaps, but without any other appendage. The term 'bed' has this meaning in various passages. It was an article of this description that the paralytic used whom the Savior directed to 'rise, take up his bed and walk' (Mark 2 : 9). It is customary now for those who use such pallets to roll them up in the morning, and lay them aside till they have occasion to spread them out again for the next night's repose."—HACKETT, *Illus. of Scrip.*, p. 113.

Dr. Thomson (*The Land and the Book*, vol. ii., p. 6 ff.) illustrates from modern Arab houses. He supposes those of Capernaum to have been "like those of modern villages in this same region, low, *very low*, with flat roofs, reached by a stairway from the yard or court. Jesus probably stood in the open *lewan* (or reception-room), and the crowd were around him and in front of him. Those who carried the paralytic . . . ascended to the roof, removed so much of it as was necessary, and let down their patient through the aperture. The roof is only a few feet high, and by stooping down and holding the corners of the couch—merely a thickly-padded quilt, as at present in this region—they could let down the

A.D. 28. MARK II. 47

5 sick of the palsy lay. ᵍ When Jesus saw their faith, he said unto the sick of the palsy, Son, ʰ thy sins ⁱ be 6 forgiven thee. But there were certain of the scribes 7 sitting there, and reasoning in their hearts, Why doth this *man* thus ᵏ speak blasphemies? ˡ who can

ᵍ Mt. 8. 10.
ʰ John 5. 14; Ro. 5. 12; 6. 23.
ⁱ Lk. 5. 21; Ac. 13. 38, 39.
ᵏ John 10. 33–36.
ˡ Job 14. 4; Ps. 86.

sick man without any apparatus of ropes or cords to assist them. . . . The whole affair was the extemporaneous device of plain peasants, accustomed to open their roofs, and let down grain, straw, and other articles, as they still do in this country. . . . "I have often seen it done, and have often done it myself to houses in Lebanon; but there is always more dust made than is agreeable. The materials now employed are beams about three feet apart, across which short sticks are arranged close together, and covered with the thickly-matted thorn-bush called *bellan*. Over this is spread a coat of stiff mortar, and then comes the marl or earth which makes the roof. Now it is easy to remove any part of this without injuring the rest. No objection, therefore, would be made on this score by the owners of the house. They had merely to scrape back the earth from a portion of the roof over the *lewan*, take up the thorns and short sticks, and let down the couch between the beams at the very feet of Jesus. The end achieved, they could speedily restore the roof as it was before."

5. **When Jesus saw their faith;** by what they did. It is implied by what follows, that the palsied man also exercised faith; perhaps he directed the men to do what they did. **Son.** Rather, *child*, a title of condescension and kindness, and in this case expressive of an endearing spiritual relation between Jesus and the sick man.

Thy sins be forgiven thee. It seems that disease had awakened in him a sense of guilt; possibly it had come on him on account of some sinful indulgence. Jesus, perceiving his penitence and faith in him as the Messiah, addressed first his spiritual nature, and attended to the deeper and more dangerous disease of sin. Thus he gave peace to the sick man's soul, and taught those who heard, that he came not to remove the *lesser evils* only, but *sin*, the root of all. It also encouraged him that his disease would in due time be healed. In our Savior's miracles there was doubtless a close connection between bodily and spiritual healing. Thus the cleansed Samaritan "glorified God" (Luke 17 : 15); the blind man near Jericho, having received sight, "followed Jesus, and glorified God," Luke 18 : 43. Compare John 5 : 14; 9 : 35–38. In James 5 : 14, 15, a close relation is recognized between the raising of the sick and the forgiving his sins. Jesus, however, did not adopt the Jewish notion that every suffering was caused by some specific sin. Such a notion he elsewhere condemns, John 9 : 3; Luke 13 : 2–5.

6. **Scribes.** See on ch. 1 : 22. They were from those who had come from all parts of the country (Luke 5 : 17); and were doubtless Pharisees, Luke 5 : 21. Certain of these expounders of the law, and spiritual guides of the people, were **sitting there,** possibly in prominent seats (ch. 12 : 38, 39) and near Jesus; and were **reasoning,** deliberately considering and arguing **in their hearts** (Matthew says, *said within themselves*), unconscious that Jesus perceived their thoughts. The reason here appears why Jesus had made the forgiveness of sins so prominent. He knew the feeling it would arouse in the hearts of the Pharisees. It was in accordance with the divine plan, that they should commence an opposition which should culminate in his death. It gave him opportunity also to demonstrate to both his enemies and friends his power to forgive sins.

7. **Why doth this man thus speak blasphemies?** According to the most ancient manuscripts and highest critical authorities this should read, *Why doth this man speak thus? He blasphemes.* *This* and *thus* are here used contemptuously. *This* one, *thus* arrogantly and irreverently. The word translated blaspheme primarily signified to speak evil, slander, revile; and in its scriptural application to God, to speak irreverently, impiously to or of him, also to arrogate to one's self what is the prerogative of God. The latter is the meaning here; for they add, **Who can**

8 forgive sins but God only? And immediately ᵐwhen Jesus perceived in his spirit that they so reasoned within themselves, he said unto them, Why 9 reason ye these things in your hearts? ⁿ Whether is it easier to say to the sick of the palsy, *Thy* sins be forgiven thee; or to say, Arise, and take up thy bed, 10 and ᵒ walk? But that ye may know that ᵖ the Son

ᵖ Is. 7. 14; 9. 6; Gal. 4. 4; Phil. 2. 7, 8.

5; 130. 4; Is. 43. 25; Dan. 9. 9.
ᵐch. 12. 15; Ps. 44. 21; 130. 2; Lk. 6. 8; 9. 47; 11. 17; John 2. 25; 16. 19; Heb. 4. 13; Rev. 2. 23.
ⁿ Mt. 9. 5.
ᵒ Is. 35. 5, 6; John 5. 8.

forgive sins but God only? They justly held that it was God's prerogative to forgive sins; but they failed to see the manifestations of divinity in Christ in his wonderful works and teaching.

8. **Immediately, when Jesus perceived.** *Jesus immediately knowing* or *perceiving.* The knowledge was intuitive; the perception instantaneous. **In his spirit.** As the God-man, by his own omniscient and divine Spirit. Thus he differed from prophets who knew, not from their own spirit, but from the Spirit of God. Here was proof at once that he was Divine, and could forgive sins. "To me it appears manifest, that the intention of the sacred writer was to signify that our Lord, in this case, did not, as others, derive his knowledge from the ordinary and outward methods of discovery, which are open to all men, but from peculiar powers he possessed, independently of everything external. . . . This is a branch of knowledge which was peculiar to the Son of God, whose special prerogative it was, not to need that any should testify concerning man unto him, as of himself he knew what was in man. John 2 : 25."

Why reason ye these things. The *why* is opposed to their *why* in ver. 7; both imply censure. They ask, *Why doth this man,* etc.? He asks, *Why reason ye these things,* etc.? or according to Matthew, "Wherefore think ye evil in your hearts?" The evil was in them and not in him; the evil was in attributing blasphemy to him whose miraculous power showed the justice of his claim; or deeper still, in their caviling and darkened spirits which apprehended neither his person nor doctrine.

9. **Whether is it easier.** *Which is easier.* Notice that Jesus does not ask which is easier to *do;* but which is easier to SAY, etc. To these fault-finding scribes, it would seem easier to pronounce a man's sins forgiven, than to pronounce a palsied man well; for they could see the latter, but not the former. And if there was imposture it would therefore be easier to prove it in respect to that which was physical and seen, than in respect to that which was spiritual and unseen.

10. Jesus proposes to give them evidence adapted to their physical and worldly conceptions. To perform a miracle is as really the work of God as to forgive sins. And Jesus proposes to do the former in proof of his power to do the latter. **That ye may know.** Here do we see the wisdom of Jesus in first pronouncing the man's sins forgiven, and then giving an external proof of his power, thus putting an end to their caviling by the miracle that follows.

The Son of man. A favorite name with Jesus, and yet, with the exception of the expression of the martyr Stephen, who beheld his glorified humanity at the right hand of God (Acts 7 : 56), the name is never applied to him but by himself. It is never applied to any one but Christ in the New Testament. In the first three Gospels, where the external life of Jesus is narrated and his human nature brought out prominently, he more frequently calls himself "the Son of man;" but in the fourth Gospel, where his inner life and divine being are specially brought to view, he styles himself more frequently "the Son of God," or simply "the Son." Daniel (7 : 13), in foretelling Christ's coming with the clouds of heaven, implies that, notwithstanding his exaltation and glory, he would come in the form and likeness of men; for he says that he saw "one like the Son of man." See, also, Rev. 1 : 13; 14 : 14. It was a title of humiliation, though an honor to our race. Jesus applied it pre-eminently to

of man ᵠhath power on earth to forgive sins, (he
11 saith to the sick of the palsy,) I say unto thee, Arise,
and take up thy bed, and go thy way into thine
12 house. And immediately he arose, took up the bed,
and went forth before them all; insomuch that they
were all ʳamazed, and glorified God, saying, ˢWe
never saw it on this fashion.

ᵠ Mic. 7. 18; Lk. 7. 47–49; John 10. 28; 17. 2; Ac. 5. 31; Col. 3. 13.
ʳ Mt. 15. 31; Lk. 5. 26; 7. 16; 17. 15; Ac. 4. 21.
ˢ John 7. 31.

The call of Matthew, and the feast at his house; discourse concerning fasting.

13 ᵗAND he went forth again by the sea side; and all
the multitude resorted unto him, and he taught
them.
14 ᵘAnd as he passed by, he saw Levi the *son* of

ᵗ Mt. 9. 5.

ᵘ Mt. 9. 9; Lk. 5. 27, 28.

---

himself as the Messiah, "as God manifested in the flesh," indicating, notwithstanding his divinity, his *true humanity* and his oneness with the human race. The Jews rightly understood it to mean the Messiah (John 12:34), though they did not enter into the fulness of its meaning. He was the Son of Man in the highest sense (Ps. 8:35; Heb. 2:6–9), possessed of all the attributes and characteristics of our common humanity, a perfect and model man, the representative of the race, the second Adam from heaven, 1 Cor. 15:45, 47.

Hath power. Not delegated *power* or *authority*, but his own as the Messiah, the God-man. The scribes rightly understood Jesus as acting by his own authority, and thereby claiming divine honors for himself, ver. 7. "A mere declaratory absolution they could utter, too, and, no doubt, often did so, but the very manner of our Lord must have evinced that in forgiving, as in teaching, he spoke with authority, and not as the scribes, ch. 1:22."—ALEXANDER. **On earth.** Not only in heaven, but on earth; where sins are committed and forgiven. Jesus has all power in heaven and on earth, ch. 28:18.

11. **I say unto thee, Arise,** etc. Jesus wrought the miracle by his own divine power. Of his first miracle John (2:11) says, he "manifested forth his glory," John 1:14. The apostles often wrought miracles in his name, Acts 3:6; 19:13. It is never said of the miracles of Jesus, as of those of Paul, "God wrought special miracles by the hands of Paul." It was God, in him, manifesting his glory, and hence a proof that he could forgive sins.

12. **And immediately he arose,** took, etc. Rather, according to the highest critical authorities, *And he arose, and immediately taking up,* etc. All eyes were fixed on the paralytic, anxiously awaiting the result. He not only rises, but shows that he is fully restored by immediately taking up his couch and going out openly, **before them all. They were all amazed,** astonished, filled with wonder, and **glorified God,** made him glorious by grateful and adoring praise. There was a general ascription of praise from the *multitude* (Matt. 9:8), the scribes being confounded by the miraculous proof of Christ's power to forgive sins. **On this fashion.** We never saw it *thus.* A palsied man thus healed and sins thus forgiven! Such power they had never seen displayed before.

13–22. THE CALLING OF MATTHEW, AND THE FEAST AT HIS HOUSE. Eating with publicans and sinners. Discourse on fasting. Matt. 9:9–17; Luke 5:27–39. A second ground of Pharisaical opposition to Jesus is here presented in the narrative.

13. **He went forth again,** from Capernaum, ver. 1; ch. 1:16; Matt. 4:12, 18. **By the seaside.** Capernaum was thus near the shore, its suburbs extending to the sea, where was the custom-house. Mark alone tells us that the **multitude resorted unto** Jesus, and he **taught them.** Jesus often taught by the seaside. Luke 5:1; Mark 4:1.

14. **As he passed by.** As he *passed*

5

Alphæus sitting at the receipt of custom, and said unto him, Follow me. And he arose and followed him.

15 ˣ And it came to pass, that, as Jesus sat at meat in his house, many publicans and sinners sat also together with Jesus and his disciples: for there

ˣ Mt. 9. 10; Lk. 5. 29.

along in the way by the shore of the lake. **Levi, the son of Alphæus.** Called *Levi* also in Luke 5 : 27. But in Matt. 9 : 9, we have *Matthew*. The three narratives clearly relate the same circumstances, and point to Levi as identical with Matthew. He probably had two names, like Peter or Paul. Mark and Luke probably designate him by the name by which he was commonly known before his conversion. Matthew probably speaks of himself as he was familiarly known as an apostle; and in ch. 10 : 8, he uses the odious title, *the publican*, which neither of the other evangelists apply to him. *Alphæus*, the father of Levi, is to be distinguished from Alpheus, the father of James the Less, Matt. 10 : 3. In the four apostolic catalogues (Matt. 10 : 2–4; Mark 3 : 16–19; Luke 6 : 14–16; Acts 1 : 13) brothers are usually mentioned in pairs, but Matthew and James the Less are never placed thus together. Alpheus was a common name among the Jews.

Sitting. "The people of this country *sit* at all kinds of work. The carpenter saws, planes, and hews with his hand-adze, sitting on the ground, or upon the plank he is planing. The washerwoman *sits* by the tub; and, in a word, no one stands where it is possible to sit. Shopkeepers always sit; and Levi *sitting* at the receipt of custom is the exact way to state the case."—Dr. Thomson, *The Land and the Book*, vol. i., p. 191. **At the receipt of custom.** The place of receiving custom, which may have been a regular customhouse, or a temporary office. The revenues which Rome derived from conquered countries consisted chiefly of tolls, tithes, harbor duties, tax on public pasture-lands, and duties on mines and salt-works.

Follow me. And he arose, etc. Or, *And rising up*, etc. The obedience was immediate. Like Andrew and Peter (ch. 1 : 16–20; John 1 : 40–42), he had probably before this heard Jesus and recognized him as the Messiah. Like them, he may have been among John's disciples, Luke 3 : 12, 13. Like them, he seems to be called, not as a mere disciple, nor as an apostle (for the apostles were not yet chosen, ch. 3 : 13, 14; Luke 6 : 13), but as one of his constant attendants, a preacher of the *good news*, an evangelist. Like them, *he left all* and followed him, Luke 5 : 28.

15. Mark proceeds to relate two conversations which occurred during a feast at his house. This probably took place soon after his call. Many suppose that a considerable time intervened. See author's Harmony, note on §§ 46, 47, 48. **Sat at meat.** *Reclined at table*, according to the custom of the time, on a couch, resting on the left arm. **His house.** Matthew's. Luke (5 : 29) relates that Matthew made him (Jesus) a great feast in his own house. The guests consisted of publicans, sinners, Jesus and his disciples. "A great company," says Luke (5 : 29). Matthew may have given this entertainment to his late associates and acquaintances, because he was leaving the business, and because he would give them a special opportunity of seeing and hearing Jesus. See last clause of this verse.

Publicans. *Tax-gatherers*, or collectors of revenues and taxes under the Roman government. They consisted of two classes. The first were Roman knights, residing generally at Rome, who levied the revenues of a large district; the second were subordinate collectors, each of whom was required to pay a certain sum to his superior, with the privilege of raising as much more as he pleased for his own profit. This led to extortion and oppression. The latter class were the publicans of the New Testament. Over this class were placed agents in the provinces who superintended the actual business of collecting the revenues. Such an one was probably Zaccheus, who is styled a *chief publican*, Luke 19 : 2. Publicans were under the reproach of being will-

16 were many, and they followed him. And when the scribes and Pharisees saw him eat with publicans and sinners, they said unto his disciples, ʸ How is it that he eateth and drinketh with publicans and sinners? 17 When Jesus heard *it*, he saith unto them, ᶻ They that are whole have no need of the physician, but they that are sick. I came not to call the righteous, but sinners to repentance.

ʸ Mt. 11. 19; Is. 65. 5.

ᶻ Mt. 9. 12, 13; 18. 11; Lk. 5. 31, 32; 19. 10; 1 Tim. 1. 15.

ing tools of oppression, and instruments of a Gentile or heathen power and a foreign despotism. Hence the very name was expressive of a depraved and reckless character. They were classed with harlots (Matt. 21 : 31) and with the heathen, Matt. 18 : 17. The Jews engaged as publicans were practically excommunicated persons, and excluded by their occupation from respectable society, and naturally thrown into that of wicked and disreputable men. This explains the force of the phrase so frequently used in the Gospels, "publicans and **sinners**," companions of the basest and most depraved.

There were many publicans **and they followed him,** attending upon his teaching, Luke 15 : 1. Some may have been disciples of John, Luke 7 : 29. The calling of Matthew also, doubtless had an influence in leading his companions and friends to attend the Savior's ministry.

16. Scribes and Pharisees. Rather, according to the best text, *the scribes of the Pharisees*. On *scribes*, see on ch. 1 : 22. The *Pharisees* were a religious party, which originated about one hundred and fifty years before Christ. Their name means *separatists;* they separated themselves from Levitical and traditional impurity. To join the Pharisaic association, one must agree to set apart all the sacred tithes, and refrain from eating anything that had not been tithed, or about which there was any doubt. As tithes were regarded as holy, so eating and enjoying them were regarded as a deadly sin. A Pharisee must ascertain whether the articles which he purchased had been duly tithed, and have the same certainty in regard to the food he ate, both in his own house and in the houses of others. As publicans and sinners were not careful about this, Pharisees would, of course, not eat with them, for in so doing it was assumed that they partook of food which had not been duly tithed. Neither would they associate with them, for, as excommunicated persons, they regarded them as very heathen, Matt. 18 : 17. It was also binding on them to observe strictly the laws of purity, according to the Mosaic ritual, and the traditions of the elders, Mark 7 : 3. They held strictly to their oral law, or traditions, attaching more importance to them than even to their written law, Matt. 15 : 1–6. They were the formalists of their age and nation, and were too often characterized for their ostentation, self-righteousness, and hypocrisy. They were the most numerous sect among the Jews, and had great influence with the people.

Saw him eat. We are not to suppose Pharisees present at the house of a publican. Being a large feast, they may have observed him through the open hall, or, perhaps, they saw him coming forth from the feast, which gave evidence to them that he had eaten with publicans and sinners.

They said to his disciples. Notice they speak not boldly to him, but broach the subject to his disciples, who may have been going in and out, or, perhaps, coming from the feast.

17. When Jesus heard it. Either he overheard it, or the disciples told him. **Whole.** *Well*, in good health. **Have no need of the physician.** His great mission as a physician was to heal the disease of sin. If any were really righteous as the Pharisees imagined they were, then they did not need his healing power. The fact that these publicans and sinners were notoriously vile and wicked showed how **sick** they were, and how much they needed his attentions.

I came not to call the righteous, but sinners. The article before *righteous* should be omitted. The lan-

18 *And the disciples of John and of the Pharisees used to fast; and they come and say unto him, Why do the disciples of John and of the Pharisees fast,
19 but thy disciples fast not? And Jesus said unto them, Can the children of the bridechamber fast, while the bridegroom is with them? As long as they have the bridegroom with them, they cannot

*Mt. 9. 14; Lk. 5. 33; 18. 12; Gen. 29. 22; Jud. 14. 10, 11; Zech. 13. 7; John 7. 33, 34; 12. 8; Job 32. 19.

guage refers not to the Pharisees, as righteous in their own estimation, but implies rather that there were no absolutely righteous men living. He came not *to call righteous men*, for there were really none such. He came not to call men as unfallen and holy beings, but as sinners, as indeed all are. His mission being to sinners, none should therefore find fault with him for associating with them and trying to save them. The worse they were the more they needed his help. **Repentance** is not found in the oldest manuscripts, and is therefore omitted by the highest critical authorities. It is, however, found in Luke (5 : 32), and is explanatory of our Savior's language as more briefly given by Matthew and Mark. Only sinners needed repentance and his saving power.

18. A third ground of Pharisaic opposition is now presented. Closely connected with the question of eating with publicans and sinners, was that of fasting. The question and discourse on the latter probably took place on the day of Matthew's feast. See below. **The disciples of John.** Had they possessed the spirit of John and obeyed his precepts they would have become the followers of Christ, John 1 : 29-36; 3 : 27-34. But even while John was baptizing some of them showed a spirit of rivalry (John 3 : 26), and much more now after his imprisonment. After his death they still maintained a separate party (Acts 19 : 4, 5), and probably practiced a sort of rigid morality, and in some points resembled the better class of the Pharisees. **Of the Pharisees.** Rather, *the Pharisees,* omitting *of*. Matthew (9 : 14) mentions only the disciples of John, and Luke (5 : 30, 33) only the Pharisees and their scribes, but Mark here happily combines the two as the questioners of Jesus. **Used to fast.** This should be rather translated *were fasting.* The language may describe a practice, indicating what they were wont to do; but it is better and more natural to suppose it to state that they were actually fasting at that time. The contrast between their fasting and the feasting of Jesus and his disciples at the house of Matthew would be specially apparent, and naturally give occasion to the question asked.

Why ... fast. The only stated fast enjoined by Moses was that of the great day of atonement. Lev. 16 : 29. Other fasts were added after the destruction of the first temple, Zech. 7 : 5; 8 : 19; that of the fourth month commemorating the capture of Jerusalem by the Chaldeans, Jer. 52 : 6, 7; that of the fifth month, commemorating the destruction of the temple, Jer. 52 : 12, 13; that of the seventh month, commemorating the murder of Gedaliah, 2 Kings 25 : 25; Jer. 41 : 1, 2; that of the tenth month, commemorating the beginning of the siege of Jerusalem by Nebuchadnezzar, Jer. 52 : 4; that of Esther on the 13th of the twelfth month, commemorating the deliverance of the Jews on that day, Esther 9 : 31; 4 : 16, 17. The Pharisees also observed two weekly fasts (Luke 18 : 12) on the second and fifth day, Monday and Thursday. The number of annual fasts have been increased in the present Jewish calendar to twenty-eight. The disciples of John doubtless observed the stated fasts of the Jews, and imitated their teacher in respect to his rigid habits of fasting; for John came neither eating nor drinking, Matt. 11 : 18. His imprisonment would be an additional motive for fasting. **Thy disciples fast not.** Notice again their want of frankness. They now complain to him of his disciples, just as, in ver. 16, they had complained to his disciples of him. In both cases they show a cowardly and censorious spirit.

19. Jesus replies by presenting three illustrations, showing that it would be unbecoming for his disciples to fast at that time.

20 fast. But the days will come, when the bridegroom shall be taken away from them, and then shall they
21 fast in those days. No man also seweth a piece of new [*or*, raw, *or*, unwrought] cloth on an old garment: else the new piece that filled it up taketh away from the old, and the rent is made worse.
22 And no man putteth new wine into old bottles: else the new wine doth burst the bottles, and the wine is spilled, and the bottles will be marred: but new wine must be put into new bottles.

The first illustration is derived from familiar marriage ceremonies. **Can the children of the bride-chamber.** *The sons*, the male attendants of the bridegroom, who upon the day of marriage (Jud. 14:11) went with him to the house of the bride, in order to bring her home. The language was well fitted to remind the disciples of John, that their master had represented Christ as the **bridegroom** (John 3:29), and the Pharisees, that the prophets, in their predictions of Christ, had used the same figure to illustrate the relation between God and Israel, Ps. 45; Isa. 54:5; 62:5. The form of the question is that used when a negative answer is expected. Could it be expected that the sons of the bride-chamber would fast on a nuptial occasion? By no means. While Jesus the glorious bridegroom is with his disciples, who are represented as his attendants, they **can not fast.** Nothing would be more unsuitable. It became them rather to rejoice. The idea is that a mere usage is not a sufficient reason for fasting. There must be an underlying reason, something that calls for fasting and makes it becoming. The arbitrary appointment of fast-days, such as have been made in the Romish and other formal churches, is contrary to our Savior's teaching.

20. **But the days will come.** The time is coming when the circumstances will be changed, and fasting will be becoming and demanded. **The bridegroom shall be taken away.** Rather, *will* be taken away, as if by violence, the words being a prediction. **Then shall they fast in those days.** According to the oldest manuscripts and the highest critical authorities, *in that day*, referring to the dark day or time of his removal from them.

That would be a special time of mourning, and consequently of fasting. There is no ground here, as Alexander justly remarks, for the doctrine of some Romish writers, that according to the declaration of Jesus, the church after his departure should be a fasting church. His exaltation should fill his followers with hope and joy, rather than doom them to perpetual sorrow, Acts 5:31, 41; John 16:7, 13, 14; Phil. 4:4. The illustration, however, implies that fasting would be proper on suitable occasion. Compare Luke 17:22, where the plural is used, *the days will come*, and in ver. 31 the singular, *in that day.*

21. The second illustration, drawn from the familiar practice of patching, in which he points out what no one of his hearers would think of doing. Mark, more minute than the other evangelists, specifies how the new cloth would be put upon the old garment by the word **seweth. New cloth;** *unfulled cloth*, not yet dressed or fulled, and liable to shrink upon being wet; and hence, if sewed upon an old garment, **taketh away** from it by shrinking, and a worse rent would be made. Such patching an old garment with unfulled cloth would be an act of unheard-of folly. But equally unbecoming and foolish would it be to unite fasting, which is a sign of sorrow, with the joyous work of my disciples, while I, their Lord, am with them. You must not expect, in my kingdom, a mere patching up of the old dispensation, or of the system of observances which you practice; but a complete renovation, and one harmonious and congruous in all its parts.

22. The third illustration, drawn from the common practice and experience in putting up wine in skin bottles. **New wine.** Unfermented. **Old bottles,**

On the Sabbath, the disciples pluck ears of grain.

23 **b** AND it came to pass, that he went through the corn fields on the sabbath day; and his disciples began, as they went, **c** to pluck the ears of corn.

b Mt. 12. 1; Lk. 6. 1.
c Deu. 23. 25.

---

or *skins*. Vessels and bottles of metal, earthen, or glass, were in use among the ancients, and doubtless among the Jews, Jer. 19 : 1; compare Isa. 30 : 14. But bottles or bags, made from the skins of animals, are here meant, which were used by the Greeks, Romans, Egyptians, and other nations, for preserving and transporting liquids, especially wine. They still continue to be used in

SKIN-BOTTLE.

the East. Dr. Hackett saw them wherever he traveled, both in Egypt and Syria. They are made chiefly of goatskins, and commonly retain the figure of the animal, the neck of the animal answering for the neck of the bottle. Dr. Robinson (*Researches*, vol. ii., p. 440) visited a large manufactory of these vessels at Hebron, and thus describes them: "These are merely the skins of goats stripped off whole, except at the neck, the holes at the legs and tail being sewed up."
Doth burst the bottles, that is, the old skins, which have become hard and inelastic, and possibly cracked and rotten, will not expand as the wine ferments. They prove unfit, and burst; thus the bottles are ruined and the wine is lost. **The wine is spilled and the bottles will be marred;** or, according to very ancient manuscripts, *the wine is lost and the bottles*. **But new wine must be put into new bottles,** which are stronger and capable of expansion. This sentence is omitted in some ancient manuscripts. Jesus intimates in this illustration, as well as in the others, that the doctrines and practices of his kingdom are unsuited to the formalism of the Pharisees, and that the new dispensation was not to be mixed up with the old. The gospel, like the new wine, must have its new forms and means for its preservation and propagation.

23-28. THE DISCIPLES PLUCK THE EARS OF GRAIN ON THE SABBATH. A fourth ground of Pharisaic opposition to Jesus is presented: supposed violation of the law of the Sabbath. The Pharisees censure the disciples; Jesus defends them. About a month, probably, intervened between this and the last event. Matthew's feast probably occurred a little before, and the plucking the ears of grain a little after, the second Passover of our Lord's public ministry. Jesus and his disciples may have been returning to Galilee, and a little distance from some village where there was a synagogue. The Passover, A.D. 28, commenced March 29th, Matt. 12 : 1-8; Luke 6 : 1-5. Matthew's account is the fullest. Each evangelist gives evidence of an independent narrative.

23. **And it came to pass.** Mark gives no note of time. Matthew (12 : 1) uses the general expression, *at that time*. Luke gives a definite, but doubtful, note of time, *the second Sabbath after the first*, which was probably the first Sabbath after the second day of the Passover; that is, the first of the seven Sabbaths commonly reckoned between that day and Pentecost. See author's Harmony, note on § 51.
Went through the corn fields. Literally *sown fields;* fields of grain, of wheat or barley. He *went along*, going a short distance to some place, through the standing grain, probably by a footpath which may have bounded the unenclosed field, the grain being within reach. **The Sabbath day.** The weekly day of rest. The name is derived from a Hebrew verb, signifying to *rest* from labor, to *cease* from action. The idea of rest was connected with its origin, Gen. 2 : 2, 3; Ex. 20 : 8-11.

24 And the Pharisees said unto him, Behold, why do they on the sabbath day that which is not lawful?
25 And he said unto them, Have ye never read ᵈ what David did, when he had need, and was an hungered,
26 he, and they that were with him; how he went into the house of God in the days of ᵉ Abiathar, the high priest, and did eat the showbread, ᶠ which is not lawful to eat but for the priests, and gave also to

ᵈ 1 Sam. 21. 6.

ᵉ 1 Sam. 22. 20-22.

ᶠ Ex. 29. 32, 33; Le. 24. 9

His disciples began as they went to pluck the ears of corn. Literally, *His disciples began to make a way plucking the ears.* Wherefore some suppose that Jesus went through the midst of the grain, opening his way right and left; and his disciples followed, making their path by plucking the ears. But this does not necessarily follow; for, (1.) The phrase *to make a way* is found both in the Septuagint and in classic writers, meaning *to make one's journey* (Judges 17: 8), and means here simply to proceed, to go forward. (2.) If the plucking had been for the purpose of making a way through the field, we should have expected Mark to have said *stalks;* but he says *ears,* which evidently had reference to their eating the grain rather than making a path. Mark, indeed, says nothing of eating the grain, but it is implied, and directly affirmed by Matthew (12: 1), and Luke (6: 1). (3.) Plucking was not necessary to make a path, since that could be accomplished by simply walking through the grain. The law allowed them to pluck the grain to appease hunger, but not to apply the sickle to another man's standing grain, Deut. 23 : 25. The custom still prevails in Palestine. "So, also, I have often seen my muleteers, as we passed along the wheat fields, pluck off ears, rub them in their hands, and eat the grains unroasted, just as the apostles are said to have done."—Dr. Thomson, *The Land and the Book,* vol. ii., p. 510. The *disciples* were his personal attendants— probably Andrew, Peter, James, John, Matthew, and others.

24. **Behold.** An exclamation of surprise, directing attention to something strange and unexpected. **Why do they,** etc. Implying censure. It is to be observed that the Pharisees object not to the plucking, but to the time of doing it. It was probably after the offering of the first-fruits—generally a sheaf of barley, at the Passover, as that was the first grain reaped. Had it been before the Passover, doubtless the punctilious Pharisees would have objected on that ground also. **The Sabbath day . . . not lawful.** Unlawful according to their traditions, by which they had loaded this day of rest with grievous restrictions, raising the letter over the spirit, and making formal acts take the place of spiritual observances. According to the rabbins, "he that reaps on the Sabbath, ever so little, is guilty, and plucking ears of grain is a kind of reaping." According to Philo, the rest of the Sabbath extended even to plants, and it was not lawful to cut a plant, a branch, or so much as a leaf.

.25. Jesus replies, first, by referring them to **what David did,** whom they regarded as an eminent servant of God, from which it could be inferred what it was lawful to do under similar circumstances. See 1 Sam. 21 : 1-6. He puts the case strongly and as a matter of surprise that they should not understand and act upon the principle involved, **Have ye never read? **
26. A continuation of the statement of what David and his men did, showing that the letter of the law must give way to the law of necessity; and hence that it was lawful to do works of real necessity, such as appeasing hunger, on the Sabbath. **Into the house of God;** the tabernacle, which was then located at Nob—a place, probably, a little north of Jerusalem and within sight of it, Isa. 10 : 32. Dr. Robinson thought it must be located on the ridge of the Mount of Olives, northeast of the city, but searched in vain for any trace of an ancient site. Mr. J. L. Porter (*Alexander's Kitto Cyclopædia*) very confidently locates it on Sumah, a little, conical hill, about three miles north of Jerusalem, where he found various indications of an ancient town.

27 them which were with him? And he said unto them, ᵍThe sabbath was made for man, and not

ᶠ Ex. 20. 8. 9; 23. 12; Deu. 5. 14.

From the top of the hill Mount Zion is distinctly seen, though Moriah is hid by an intervening ridge. **In the days of Abiathar, the high priest.** But from 1 Sam. 21:1, we find that Ahimelech, the father of Abiathar, was then in office. Various solutions of this discrepancy have been given. (1.) It is possible that Abiathar is mentioned rather than his father, because he was present on the occasion (1 Sam. 22:22), and immediately succeeded his father as high priest, and was familiarly known as such in the *history of David.* Lightfoot says that he was named rather than his father, because he brought the Ephod to David, and by him inquiry was made by Urim and Thummim; that the Jews understood the Urim and Thummim by Abiathar; and hence, to say the thing was done under Abiathar, showed that it was done by divine direction. But the most approved text reads, *when Abiathar was high priest,* hence (2), it is possible that Abiathar was acting as his father's vicar at that time. According to a Jewish rule, "the son of a high priest, deputed by his father in his stead, was called a high priest." Ahimelech and Abiathar may have been hereditary names in the family, and borne by both father and son. There is, at least, some appearance of this, for Abiathar is called the son of Ahimelech in 1 Sam. 22:20, and Ahimelech the son

SHOW-BREAD.

of Abiathar in 2 Sam. 8:17; 1 Chron. 18:16. And Abiathar may have been the more familiar to the Jews, by its connection, through the son, with the history of David. **Did eat the show-bread.** Simply *ate,* there being no emphasis in the original demanding *did.* The *show-bread,* the bread *set forth, exhibited* on a table in the holy place, first in the tabernacle, afterward in the temple. It was *set before* Jehovah (Exod. 25:30), and called in Hebrew *bread of face* or *presence;* that is, of the divine presence, and probably symbolized God's presence with his people, as their sustenance, strength, and support. It consisted of twelve loaves, which were changed every Sabbath, when the old was eaten by the priests, Lev. 24:59. It also seems, from 1 Sam. 21:6, that the bread had just been changed, and hence that David and his men ate it on the Sabbath, which make reference and argument even more pertinent. Thus, Jesus shows, by the example of David, whom all regarded as an eminent servant of God, that things which are unlawful may be done under the law of necessity and self-preservation.

27. At this point Matthew (12:5-7) presents a second and third argument, the one derived from the labors of the priests in the temple on the Sabbath, and the other from the prophet Hosea (6:6), who declares that God desires not mere external observances, but the inward outgushing of kindness and love, which is the true sacrifice in spirit and of the heart.

Passing over these, Mark presents an argument not recorded by either Matthew or Luke, that the Sabbath was designed for the good of man. **The Sabbath was made for man.** At the creation, for his benefit and happiness, Gen. 2:2, 3. For *man,* as connected with the race, whether of one nation or another. It is for his use, and subservient to his highest spiritual good; and therefore the manner of keeping it must ever be in accordance with its design. **Not man for the Sabbath.** The law of the Sabbath is to bend to the highest interests of man, and not the highest interests of man to the Sabbath. The Sabbath must not, by a superstitious observance, be perverted to the exclusion of mercy and necessity. This verse was specially suited to Gentile readers.

28 man for the sabbath: therefore ʰ the Son of man is ʰ Mt. 12. 8. Lord also of the sabbath.

28. The final and crowning argument growing out from the one just stated, and founded upon the relation of the Sabbath to Christ. *Therefore*; rather, *so that*, as a consequence of the great principle he had just uttered. **The Son of man.** The Messiah, indicating, notwithstanding his divinity, his true humanity, his oneness with the human race, and its head. See on ver. 10. **Lord also of the Sabbath.** Since he has come in human nature to redeem man, and all things pertaining to the human race are committed to him as its head, he is emphatically the Lord of the Sabbath, which was made for man's benefit. He is indeed Lord of things in general pertaining to his kingdom, but ALSO of the Sabbath. As mediator, redeemer, and sovereign, he presides over it and controls it. Thus, Jesus asserted before these Pharisees his authority over the Sabbath. His disciples were not to be condemned by their interpretations of the law and their traditions, but were subject to his directions as the Messiah and Lord of the Sabbath.

There is nothing here intimating that Christ abolished the Sabbath. He rather ennobled it, by afterward merging it into the Lord's day, Rev. 1 : 10. The whole argument shows that the day should be kept in a manner best suited to make men holy, and that superstitious observance on the one hand, and neglect of spiritual improvement on the other, are alike censurable and unbecoming.

REMARKS.

1. We should strive to be so useful that, like Jesus, we should be sought after, vers. 1, 2; ch. 6 : 32, 33 ; 7 : 24, 25; Luke 19 : 3.
2. If Christ is in a house or in a church, it will be noised abroad, vers. 1, 2; Acts 2 : 6; 11 : 1 ; Rom. 1 : 8.
3. In doing good we must not confine our efforts to times and places. Jesus preached in private dwellings, in open fields, on the sea-shore, as well as in synagogues and the temple, vers. 2, 13; ch. 4 : 1 ; 14 : 7 ; Gal. 6 : 10; James 4 : 17; Num. 10 : 29.
4. Christians should combine their efforts. What one cannot do, four may accomplish, ver. 3; ch. 6 : 7; Matt. 18 : 16, 19, 20 ; Acts 12 : 25; Eccle. 4 : 12.
5. "We cannot deliver sinners from the maladies of the body, much less from those of the soul ; but we may bring them to Christ for salvation, and we should lose no opportunity and shrink from no self-denial in attempting it."—SCOTT. Vers. 3, 4 ; Matt. 15 : 22 ; 1 Cor. 9 : 22; James 5 : 14, 19, 20 ; Jude 23.
6. Afflictions are often great blessings to the soul, vers. 4, 5; Ps. 119 : 67, 71.
7. Can Jesus apply to thee the endearing name of *son* or *child*, and say, "Thy sins are forgiven," ver. 5 ; Rom. 8 : 14, 17 ; 1 John 3 : 1 ; Ps. 103 : 3; Isa. 40 : 2.
8. Many enjoy the greatest spiritual blessings in vain, and shall receive the greater condemnation, vers. 6–8 ; Luke 4 : 16, 28, 29 ; Matt. 11 : 23, 24 ; John 9 : 41.
9. Christ is the searcher of hearts, and knoweth all things, ver. 8 ; John 2 : 24, 25 ; Rev. 2 : 23.
10. Jesus can forgive sins ; his miracles are a proof of this and of his divinity, vers. 5, 9–11 ; John 10 : 37, 38; Acts 5 . 31 ; Heb. 9 : 26; Isa. 43 : 25.
11. The commands of Christ are all reasonable. He is ready to give grace and strength to do whatever he requires, vers. 11, 12 ; Deut. 33 : 25 ; 2 Cor. 12 : 9; Isa. 41 : 10.
12. The best evidence that our sins are forgiven is the state of our heart and life, a Christ-like disposition, and a Christian walk ; ver. 12 ; Matt. 7 : 20 ; Rom. 8 : 13, 16.
13. Christ calls men to discipleship and service, ver. 14; Acts 13 : 2; Rom. 8 : 30; 9 : 24 ; 2 Tim. 1 : 9 ; 1 Pet. 1 : 15.
14. "True obedience is prompt. Many men of business never become Christians because they will not tear themselves away from its demands."— J. P. WARREN. Ver. 14; ch. 1 : 18 ; Acts 2 : 41; 24 : 25.
15. We may associate with even the openly wicked when we would do them good, ver. 15 ; Acts 17 : 16, 17.

Jesus heals a man with a withered hand on the Sabbath.

III. AND ¹ he entered again into the synagogue. And there was a man there which had a withered hand. ¹ Mt. 12. 9; Lk. 6. 6.

16. Moralists are still offended with Jesus for calling and saving those more openly wicked than themselves, ver. 16.
17. We should never lose sight of Christ as the great physician, ver. 17; Matt. 8 : 17; Jer. 8 : 22.
18. Since all are sinners, all are called upon to repent, ver. 17; Luke 13 : 1–5; Acts 17 : 30; 2 Pet. 3 : 9.
19. Beware of hasty judgments. Prejudice misconstrues the actions of others, vers. 16, 18; Prov. 29 : 20; Acts 23 : 3–5; 1 Cor. 4 : 3.
20. Fasting is good, when rightly observed on proper occasions. Matt. 6 : 16-18; Joel 2 : 12. But when observed as a mere rite, it becomes a yoke of bondage, Rom. 14 : 1, 17 ; 2 Cor. 11 : 20 ; Gal. 2 : 4 ; 4 : 9–11. The Pharisaical spirit is seen in Catholic and formal churches, vers. 19–21.
21. "Where Jesus is the Bridegroom of the soul, there is joy and refreshment."—CRAMER. Ver. 19; John 3 : 29 ; Eph. 5 : 25–27.
22. In Christ's kingdom we must not mix together things essentially different: as uniting church and state ; receiving believers and unbelievers for baptism and into church fellowship ; mingling false doctrines and practices with the true, vers. 21, 22 ; 1 Cor. 10 : 20 ; 2 Cor. 6 ; 14–16 ; Eph. 5 : 11.
23. Beware of raising human rites above divine law ; or of losing sight of the spirit in the letter. These are steps toward formalism and popery, vers. 23, 24 ; Matt. 15 : 3–6 ; Gal. 4 : 10, 11.
24. Learn the value of Scriptural knowledge. The Bible is our rule of faith and practice, vers. 25, 26 ; 2 Pet. 1 : 19–21 ; Ps. 19 : 7–11 ; 119 : 9, 11, 105.
25. Christ has taught us that positive requirements must sometimes yield to the law of necessity, ver. 26.
26. "Since the Sabbath was made for the whole human race, they have a right to its blessings and privileges." It was given man in a state of innocence (Gen. 2 : 3), continued as a merciful provision in his fallen state (Gen. 8 : 10–12 ; Exod. 16 : 23–26 ; Job 1 : 6 ; 2 : 1), confirmed under the law (Exod. 20 : 8), and bequeathed by the Lord of the Sabbath himself at his resurrection, in its greatest and highest glory, as the Lord's day, under the gospel, vers. 27, 28 ; John 20 : 1, 19, 26 ; Acts 20 : 7 ; 1 Cor. 16 : 2 ; Rev. 1 : 10.

CHAPTER III.

In this chapter Mark continues to narrate the increasing opposition to Jesus. A second apparent violation of the Sabbath is related. From threatened persecution Jesus retires ; multitudes follow ; many were healed ; the twelve apostles selected. The concourse of people and the unremitting labors of Jesus continuing, his friends try to restrain him. His enemies, still more incensed, charge him with being in league with Satan, which calls forth a reply in which he warns them against blaspheming the Holy Spirit. The chapter closes with an incident illustrating the relation of Jesus to his relatives and his disciples.

1–6. JESUS HEALS A WITHERED HAND ON THE SABBATH. By precept, example, and miracle, Jesus gives a further exposition of the law of the Sabbath. Opposition takes an organized form, and more directly against him, Matt. 12 : 9–14 ; Luke 6 : 6–11. The three narratives are about equally full, each having some particulars of its own. Mark's is particularly vivid ; the scene seems actually passing before you.

1. **He entered again.** On another occasion. Luke says (6 : 6) "on another Sabbath," probably the next Sabbath after the plucking the ears of grain. Notwithstanding the opposition, he entered **the synagogue.** See on ch. 1 : 21. Some of the oldest manuscripts read, *a synagogue*. Where, is not mentioned. Probably in Galilee and at Capernaum. **His hand.** His right hand, Luke 6 : 6. **Withered.** A passive participle in the original, literally *dried up*, and implying that it was not from his birth, but the effect of disease or a wound. It was similar to that with which Jeroboam was afflicted, 1 Kings 13 : 4–6. It may have been from

A.D. 28. MARK III. 59

2 And ᵏthey watched him, whether he would heal him on the sabbath day; that they might accuse
3 him. And he saith unto the man which had the
4 withered hand, Stand forth. And he saith unto them, Is it lawful to do good on the sabbath days, or to do evil; to save life, or to kill? But they
5 held their peace. And when he had looked round about on them ˡwith anger, ᵐbeing grieved for the hardness of their hearts, he saith unto the man, Stretch forth thine hand. And he stretched it out: and his hand was restored whole as the other.

ᵏ Ps. 37. 32; Is. 29. 20, 21; Jer. 20. 10; Dan. 6. 4.

ˡ Mt. 5. 22; Eph. 4. 26.
ᵐ Ge. 6. 6; Ps. 95. 10; Lk. 19. 41-44.

paralysis; or from a defect in receiving nourishment from the body. It was considered incurable.

2. They. The scribes and Pharisees, Luke 6 : 7. **Watched;** closely, with bad intent. Compare Luke 14 : 1 and Acts 9 : 24, where the same Greek word is used. They were watching him maliciously. The growth of opposition is seen in that they now watch intently for an occasion of censure. They may have thought that he would **heal him on the Sabbath,** from his readiness to do good, and from what he had already taught regarding the Sabbath, ch. 2 : 23-28. **Might accuse him;** not merely to the people but to the local authorities, who were doubtless present and identical with the rulers of the synagogues, ver. 6.

3. Stand forth. *Rise up into the midst.* "Arise and come into the midst."—REVISED VERSION, AM. BIBLE UNION. Doubtless he was called forth to a conspicuous position. Matthew (12 : 10) omits this, but relates that they ask him, "Is it lawful to heal on the Sabbath?" Luke (6 : 8) says that Jesus "knew their thoughts," after which he gave the command, "Rise up," etc. Knowing their thoughts, he called the man forth, when, seeing his intention, they may have asked, "Is it lawful," etc. Jesus makes the misery and the healing of the man conspicuous, yet he performs the cure with a word, ver. 5.

4. Is it lawful to do good, etc.? An answer not only to their thoughts, which he knew (Luke 6 : 8), but also to their question, Matt. 12 : 10. See note on preceding verse. Some take *to do good or to do evil* in a general sense; others in a particular sense, meaning *to benefit or to injure.* The former, I think, is preferable. Jesus first asks in regard to doing good or evil generally on the Sabbath, and then descends to a particular case, **to save life or to kill.** It is not unlikely that Jesus intended some reference, not only to what he was doing, but also to the designs of the scribes and Pharisees against him : Is it lawful to do good and save life on the Sabbath, as I am doing, or to do evil and kill, as you purpose to do to me? The question, however, involved a principle. Doing good and saving life is becoming the Sabbath, rather than doing evil and destroying life, and especially are we to choose the former when there is an alternative between the two. He who neglects to do good or save life when he can do so, is justly held accountable for the loss sustained, Prov. 24 : 11, 12; Ezek. 33 : 6. **They held their peace.** They could say nothing, for it was evident that it was "lawful to do well on the Sabbath," Matt. 12 : 12. They were also self-condemned; they were the Sabbath-breakers. Compare Luke 13 : 14-17; 14 : 2-6.

5. Both Mark and Luke omit at this point the parabolic reference to a sheep fallen in a pit, recorded in Matthew 12 : 11, 12. **And when he had looked round about,** etc. *About* is superfluous. The more literal rendering is the more vivid, *And looking around on them.* Luke (6 : 10) adds the strong word *all.* Mark is noted for his vivid descriptions of our Savior's looks, feelings, and gestures, chs. 1 : 41; 5 : 30, 32; 10 : 23. He here not only refers to his external act, but to his internal feelings, *with anger,* **being grieved.** His *anger* was holy indignation against the sins as manifested in these scribes and Pharisees. Anger, as originally connected with our unfallen nature, is not sinful, and such anger, being without

6 ⁿ And the Pharisees went forth, and straightway ⁿ Mt. 12. 14.
took counsel with º the Herodians against him, how º Mt. 22. 16.
they might destroy him.

Jesus withdraws to the Sea of Galilee; followed by multitudes.

7 BUT Jesus withdrew himself with his disciples to the sea. And a great multitude from Galilee fol-

excess and malignity, was exercised by Jesus in his sinless humanity. The word translated *being grieved* implies sympathy and pity for those in such a miserable and hard-hearted state. Holy anger against sin is consistent with holy grief and compassion for the sinner. **Hardness of heart.** Spiritual dullness and insensibility, John 12 : 40.

Having silenced his opposers, Jesus proceeds at once to perform the miracle. The wisdom of Jesus is seen here, similar to that in the healing of the paralytic, ch. 2 : 8-12; see ch. 2 : 10. He also performs the miracle without any bodily effort, or any word except the command, **Stretch forth thy hand.** His adversaries, therefore, could not charge him with laboring on the Sabbath. Some suppose the miracle performed before uttering a word, and that Jesus commanded him to stretch forth the hand as an evidence of its restoration. It is better, however, to suppose that the healing took place immediately upon Jesus uttering the command and the man making the effort to obey. The faith of the man is thus brought into its natural relation to his obedience and his cure. It is also in harmony with the declaration which follows, **and his hand was restored. Whole as the other** should be omitted according to the best manuscripts. The words are found in Matthew's account, Matt. 12 : 13. The incident affords a good illustration of faith. Christ gave the strength; the man believes, and in obedience to Christ's command stretched forth his hand. So in regard to every divine command we should believe and act; all needed help will be given. Jesus thus showed his power over disease, and gave a practical proof of the correctness of his teachings regarding the Sabbath. It was one of his greatest miracles.

6. The Pharisees, baffled with argument and deprived of legal ground of objection, since the miracle was performed without outward action, are the more incensed, and go out from the synagogue and consult with their political opponents, the Herodians. The **Herodians** were probably a political rather than a religious party, though it is supposed mostly Sadducees in religious sentiment. They were the partisans of the Herodian family, and consequently of the Roman dominion over the country, which was odious to the Jews generally, and especially to the Pharisees. The growing popularity and influence of Jesus with the people of Galilee may have excited the jealousy of the Herodians, whose head-quarters were at Tiberius. His relations to John the Baptist, and occurrences unknown to us, may also have excited their hatred. But it is to be noted that the overtures, though doubtless acceptable to them, came from the Pharisees. They went out and **took counsel,** consulted with the Herodians. They hoped to gain the influence of Herod Antipas against him; possibly by intrigue they would bring some political charge against him, and thus secure his death. What they began to do with the Herodians they afterward fully carried out with Pilate. The intensity of their hatred is shown by their seeking such an alliance, an alliance which was afterward continued, ch. 12 : 13. This is the first organized movement against Jesus of which we have any account.

7-12. JESUS WITHDRAWS TO THE SEA OF GALILEE; HEALS MANY, AND CASTS OUT DEMONS. Matt. 12 : 15-21. Compare Luke 6 : 17-19. Mark enters into details and is very graphic. Matthew is brief, but quotes a prediction from Isaiah.

7. **Jesus withdrew himself.** *Himself* should be omitted as unnecessary. He withdrew from Capernaum,

A.D. 28. MARK III. 61

8 lowed him; ᵖ and from Judæa, and from Jerusalem,   ᵖ Lk. 6. 17.
and from Idumæa, and *from* beyond Jordan, and
they about Tyre and Sidon, a great multitude, when
they had heard what great things he did, came unto
9 him. And he spake to his disciples, that a small
ship should wait on him because of the multitude,

---

or the city where he had just performed the miracle, and indeed from the cities and towns of Galilee generally, **to the sea,** or *unto the sea.* The Sea of Galilee is commonly called simply the sea in the Gospels. This withdrawal was not only to the shore of the lake, but even to the ship upon its waters, ver. 9. It was not from fear, for he had shown himself above fear; but in order that he might prolong his ministry to its appointed length, and properly lay the foundation of his kingdom. He would not permit himself yet to be taken, for his hour had not yet come. So in other instances he withdrew from opposition and violence, John 4 : 1; 7 : 1; 10 : 39, 40; 11 : 54.
And a great multitude. Here begins the most vivid description in the Gospels of the multitudes who attended upon the ministry of Jesus. Two great multitudes are mentioned. The first from Galilee **followed him;** the second from regions outside of Galilee **came unto him** (next verse). To present this plainly to the reader, a semicolon should be put after *followed him,* and a comma after *Judea* (this verse) and after *Jordan* (next verse), as in the text above. The people sided with Jesus and against the Pharisees. It was not really the design of Jesus to withdraw from the people, but from his enemies, whose influence was greatest in the towns. His friends and all who desired had an opportunity of following or coming to him in his retirement. **Galilee.** See on ch. 1 : 9. **Judea;** south of Samaria, bounded by Jordan on the east, the Mediterranean on the west, and the territory of the Arabs on the south. The boundary of the province seems to have been often varied by the addition or abstraction of towns.
8. *Jerusalem* is mentioned, though a part of Judea, from its importance as the religious center of the theocracy. **Idumea** occurs only here in the New Testament, the *Edom* of the Old Testament, Gen. 25 : 30; 36 : 1; Num. 20 ;

20; 1 Sam. 14 : 47; 2 Sam. 8 : 14; Ezek. 36 : 5. It lay southeast of Palestine. It was conquered by the Maccabees (1 Macc. 5 : 65, 68), and incorporated, by submission to the Mosaic law, with the Jewish nation about B.C. 125 (*Joseph. Ant.* xii. 8, 6; xiii. 9, 2). Antipater, father of Herod the Great, was an Idumean by birth. **Beyond Jordan.** On the east of Jordan, often called Perea. **About Tyre and Sidon.** The Jews of that region. Tyre and Sidon were the two principal cities of Phœnicia on the coast of the Mediterranean Sea. Sidon, which means *fishery,* one of the oldest cities of the world, is believed to have been founded by Zidon, the eldest son of Canaan, Gen. 10 : 15; 49 : 13. Its latitude is 33° 34' north, about the same as the middle portions of South Carolina. Tyre, meaning a *rock,* about twenty miles south, was of later date, but grew in importance, and gained an ascendency over Sidon, and became the commercial emporium of Phœnicia. They were the subjects of prophecy and of divine judgments under Nebuchadnezzar and Alexander, Isa. ch. 23; Ezek. chs. 26-28; 29 : 18. The cities that grew up on the ruins of the ancient ones existed in the times of our Savior, Acts 12 : 20; 21 : 3, 7; 27 : 3. Sidon, now called Saida, contains about five thousand inhabitants, and is spoken of as dirty and full of ruins. Tyre, now called Sur, is at present a poor town, and has a population of about three thousand. The great multitude following him from Galilee shows his popularity there, while those coming from the outskirts of Palestine and the borders of the Gentiles show how widely his fame was spread abroad, for **they had heard what great things he did,** especially, what great miracles he was doing. The concourse of people round Jesus seems now to have reached its height.
9. The greatness of the multitude is also presented by the incident here related. **He spake.** With authority,

6

10 lest they should throng him. For he had healed many; insomuch that they pressed upon him for to 11 touch him, as many as had plagues. ᵠAnd unclean spirits, when they saw him, fell down before him, 12 and cried, saying, ʳThou art the Son of God. And ˢhe straitly charged them that they should not make him known.

* ch. 1. 23, 24; Lk. 4. 41.
ʳ ch. 1. 1; Mt. 14. 33.
ˢ ch. 1. 25, 34; Mt. 12. 16.

Jesus chooses the twelve apostles.

13 ᵗAND he goeth up into a mountain, and calleth unto him whom he would: and they came unto him,

ᵗ Mt. 10. 1; Lk. 6. 12; 9. 1, 2.

whether a request or a command. **A ship.** *A small boat*, probably a small fishing boat. **Wait on him.** Be near, in attendance, and at his disposal. It is supposed by some that this little vessel was permanently retained for the use of Jesus. **Multitude.** The crowd, the confused mass of people. **Should throng him.** Press on him. The immediate object was to find a convenient standing or sitting place, where he might escape the pressure of the crowd; but this does not exclude other objects, such as teaching the people from the boat, or going to any part of the lake, or to any place on its shore. The evangelists do not inform us whether Jesus used the vessel at this time; but very probably he did.
10. **For.** The special cause of this great pressure upon Jesus is now given. **He had healed.** Rather, *he healed*, he was at that time healing many. **Insomuch that they pressed upon him.** *So that they rushed, pushed, or pressed upon him.* Their desire was intense, and their efforts to reach him corresponded. **To touch him;** in faith, as the woman with the issue of blood, ch. 5 : 27-34. At their touch in faith, power went out of him and healed them all, Luke 6 : 19. **Plagues.** *Scourges* from God; grievous diseases, regarded as chastisements for sin.
11. **Unclean spirits.** Demons, so called because of their moral vileness and wickedness. See on ch. 1 : 23. Their recognizing Jesus as the Son of God as soon as they saw him, shows that they were not mere diseases, but actual evil spirits possessing the bodies of men. How complete these possessions were may be inferred from the fact that they used the powers and organs of those possessed in seeing, falling down, and crying out, **Thou art the Son of God.** The Messiah, the Son of God in the highest sense, a person of the Godhead, sustaining the relation of eternal sonship with the Father. John 1 : 18; 3 : 16. See on ch. 1 : 24.
12. **He straitly charged them.** Strictly charged them, the demons. Matthew (12 : 16) relates that he also charged those healed of diseases that they should **not make him known** as the Messiah, the Son of God. Demons were unworthy witnesses to his sonship. Their testimony was not that of believing confidence in him as a Savior. Neither had the time come for the proclamation of his character and office. Jesus would avoid all ostentation, and prevent any political movement on the part of the Jews, with their worldly views, to make him king, John 6 : 15. The opposition of the Pharisees was also sufficiently aroused. Just here Matthew (12 : 17-21) points out an ancient prophecy (Isa. 42 : 1-4) signally fulfilled in the unostentatious and noiseless ministry of Jesus; in his gentleness and meekness, and the spirituality of his doctrines.
13-19. JESUS RETIRES TO A MOUNTAIN AND SELECTS THE TWELVE APOSTLES, Luke 6 : 12-16. We must distinguish between their call to discipleship (John 1 : 35-43), their call to be constant attendants, preachers or evangelists (ch. 1 : 16-20), and their selection as apostles here related. After this they were miraculously endowed, and sent out on a mission to the Jews (Matt. 10 : 1-4); see on ch. 6 : 7. The two accounts are very similar. But Luke alone records that Jesus passed the night in prayer, while Mark alone gives the reasons for the appointment of the Twelve.
13. **A mountain.** *The mountain*,

14 And he ordained twelve, that they should be with him, and that he might send them forth to preach, 15 and to have power to heal sicknesses, and to cast

one familiarly so called. There are several mountains on the west side of the Sea of Galilee. Some regard the expression, *the mountain*, to mean the highlands in distinction from the lowlands on the sea-shore. Into *the mountain* is a common expression signifying *in among*, into the region of the mountain. Thus in ch. 13 : 14 and Luke 21 : 21, 66, "flee into the mountains," that is, *in among* the mountains. Luke (6 : 12, 13) says that Jesus went into the mountain to pray and continued all night in prayer, and called his disciples to him when it was day.

Calleth whom he would, in the exercise of his free and unlimited authority. How many we are not told. Probably a number of his followers from whom he selected the twelve. **And they came;** or *went away* from the multitude, or from their employments *to him*.

14. **He ordained twelve.** *He constituted*, or *appointed twelve* of those who went to him. Luke (6 : 13) says, "and of them (or *"from them"*) he chose twelve." The number twelve is significant and frequent in Scripture. It is expressive of fullness, completeness, and strength. Thus there were the twelve tribes of Israel, the twelve stones of the Urim and Thummim on the breastplate of the high-priest (Ex. 28 : 17-21); twelve loaves of show-bread (Lev. 24 : 5-8); the altar and twelve pillars which Moses erected by Mount Sinai (Ex. 24 : 4); the altar of twelve stones, by Elijah (1 Kings 18 : 31); the new Jerusalem with twelve foundation stones, Rev. 21 : 14. The persons thus appointed were called *apostles* (that is, persons *sent forth*, ch. 6 : 30); but more commonly in the Gospels *the twelve* (ch. 4 : 10 ; 6 : 7), or *the twelve disciples* (Matt. 20 : 17), or simply *disciples*, Luke 9 : 12.

The reason of their appointment is given, **that they should be with him,** as constant personal attendants as learners and witnesses. They were to learn by his example as well as by his public and private discourses; they were to be witnesses of his life, death, and resurrection, and thus prepared to carry out his work after his departure. Hence, though named apostles by Jesus himself (Luke 6 : 13), they are so called but once by Matthew (10 : 2), once by Mark (6 : 30), six times by Luke, and not at all by John. They were *disciples* or *learners;* but after the descent of the Holy Spirit, they are called, in the Acts and Epistles, apostles, never disciples. "The characteristics of an apostle were a direct call, a continuous intercourse with Christ, personal observation, the right of preaching universally, the gift of miracles."—BENGEL. A necessary condition of their apostleship was that they had seen the Lord, and were witnesses of him and his resurrection, Acts 1 : 8, 21, 22 ; 1 Cor. 9 : 1 ; Acts 22 : 14, 15. They could therefore have no successors.

Send them out to preach, to proclaim the glad tidings of Christ's kingdom. Thus they went out two by two, ch. 6 : 7 ; and after the ascension they "preached everywhere," ch. 16 : 20. After receiving power on the day of Pentecost, they were to be Christ's witnesses, in Jerusalem, Judea, Samaria, and unto the utmost parts of the earth, Acts 1 : 8.

15. **And** connects this with the preceding verse, which should be separated only by a comma. Jesus would send them forth to preach and to have **power** or *authority* to perform the same miracles that he performed. Their preaching should be attested with the same evidences as his own. And so it was, ch. 6 : 12, 13 ; 16 : 20. **To heal sicknesses** is omitted by several of the oldest manuscripts. The omission makes the casting out of the demons more prominent.

16. FOUR CATALOGUES OF THE APOSTLES are given in the New Testament, which, with their connections, are presented in the following table. See next page.

Thus it appears that each catalogue is divided into three classes, the names of which are never interchanged, and each class headed by a leading name. Thus Peter heads the first class, Philip the second, James the third, and Judas Iscariot stands the last, except in the Acts, where his name is omitted because of his apostasy and death. Notice the connective **And,** by which Mat-

	Matthew 10 : 2.	Mark 3 : 16.	Luke 6 : 14.	Acts 1 : 13.
1	Simon Peter.	Simon Peter,	Simon Peter,	Peter,
2	And Andrew,	And James, son of Zebedee,	And Andrew,	And James,
3	James, son of Zebedee	And John,	And James,	And John,
4	And John.	And Andrew.	And John.	And Andrew.
5	Philip.	And Philip.	And Philip,	Philip,
6	And Bartholomew,	And Bartholomew,	And Bartholomew,	And Thomas,
7	Thomas,	And Matthew,	And Matthew,	Bartholomew,
8	And Matthew.	And Thomas.	And Thomas.	And Matthew.
9	James, son of Alpheus,	And James, son of Alpheus,	James, son of Alpheus,	James, son of Alphens,
10	And Lebbeus Thaddeus,	And Thaddeus,	And Simon Zelotes,	And Simon Zelotes,
11	Simon the Cananite,	And Simon the Cananite,	And Judas, brother of James,	And Judas, brother of James.
12	And Judas Iscariot.	And Judas Iscariot.	And Judas Iscariot.	

thew enumerates the apostles two by two; Mark and Luke one by one; and Luke in the Acts, mixedly. Even such small differences go to show the independent origin of the Gospels.

And Simon he surnamed Peter. Literally, *he placed upon Simon the name Peter*, he added the name, surnamed him. A surname points to authority or sovereignty in the giver and eminence in the receiver, Gen. 17 : 5, 15; 32 : 28; Num. 13 : 16; Acts 4 : 36. Simon is contracted from Simeon, and means *hearkening;* Peter signifies *a stone*, equivalent to the Aramaic *Cephas*, first given him as a surname at his introduction to Jesus, John 1 : 42. Jesus doubtless repeated the surname at this time; Peter was the name by which he was generally, though not always (Acts 15 : 14), designated as an apostle. It was given him in allusion to his hardy character, noted for decision and boldness, and to the conspicuous position he should hold among the apostles, in subordination to Christ, as one of the great foundations of the Church, Eph. 2 : 20; Rev. 21 : 14.

Not only is the name significant, but also its position at the head of the four catalogues of the apostles. He was among the first who recognized Jesus as the Messiah (John 1 : 40-42), and with Andrew, his brother, the first called to be a constant attendant of Jesus, ch. 1 : 16-18. He was spokesman of the apostles, as in Matt. 16 : 16, and the chief speaker on the day of Pentecost. He was also the first to carry the gospel to the Gentiles, Acts ch. 10. Thus Peter may be said to have opened the kingdom of heaven to both Jews and Gentiles. But though prominent and foremost among the apostles, he was not *over* them nor *above* them. That he had no superiority of rank is evident from 1 Pet. 5 : 1, where he describes himself as "a fellow elder," and from the fact that Paul in Gal. 2 : 7-9 speaks of him as one of the "pillars" together with James and John, compares him as an apostle to the circumcision to himself as an apostle to the uncircumcision, and rebukes him as an equal. That the apostles were all equal in rank appears from Matt. 18 : 18; 19 : 27, 28; 20 : 25, 26, 28; 23 : 8; John 20 : 21-23; Acts 1 : 8.

The most we know of Peter is derived from the Gospels and the Acts of the Apostles. The latter book traces him to the Council at Jerusalem. After this he was with Paul at Antioch (Gal. 2 : 11), labored at Corinth (1 Cor. 1 : 2; 3 : 22), and at Babylon, where he wrote his first Epistle, 1 Pet. 5 : 13. According to a tradition which may be considered in the main reliable, he visited Rome in the last year of his life, and suffered martyrdom by crucifixion under the reign of Nero.

17. James the son of Zebedee. The name is the same as Jacob, meaning *supplanter.* It is applied to three

A.D. 28.　　　　　MARK III.　　　　　65

16 out devils.　And ᵘSimon ˣhe surnamed Peter;　ᵘMt. 4. 18; 1 Pet.
17 and ʸJames the *son* of Zebedee, and ˣJohn the brother　1. 1.
　of James; and he surnamed them Boanerges, which　ˣJohn 1. 42.
18 is, ᵃThe sons of thunder: and Andrew, and ᵇPhilip,　ʸMt. 4. 21; Ac. 12. 2.
　and Bartholomew, and Matthew, and ᶜThomas, and　ᵃJohn 13. 23; 1 John 1. 1; 2 John

1. 1; Rev. 1. 1, 9.　　ᵃIs. 58. 1.　　ᵇJohn 1. 43–46.　　ᶜJohn 20. 24–29.

persons in the New Testament. This is James the greater or elder, and is never mentioned in the New Testament apart from John his brother. They were selected with Peter to witness the restoration of Jairus' daughter (ch. 5 : 42), the transfiguration (ch. 9 : 2), and the agony in Gethsemane, ch. 14 : 23. James was the first martyr among the apostles, being slain with the sword by Herod Agrippa I., Acts 12 : 2.

John, whose name means *graciously given by Jehovah*, was, next to Peter, the most noted of the twelve, and characterized by a wonderful mingling of gentleness and firmness. He belonged to a family of influence, as is evident from his acquaintance with the family of the high-priest (John 18 : 15), and was in easy circumstances, since he became responsible for the maintenance of his Lord's mother, John 19 : 26, 27. After the ascension of Jesus he resided at Jerusalem. About A.D. 65 he removed to Ephesus, and for many years labored in Asia Minor. He survived all the apostles, and died at Ephesus about A.D. 100, being then according to Epiphanius ninety-four years old, but according to Jerome a hundred.

Surnamed them Boanerges. Probably a Greek modification of the Aramean pronunciation of the Hebrew *Beni-regesh*, meaning in Hebrew *sons of a tumultuous throng* (Ps. 64 : 2), and in Syriac **sons of thunder.** The exact significance of this surname has been much debated. It is most natural to regard it as an appellation of praise and descriptive of their spiritual character. It is very improbable that the surname bestowed on Peter should be one of praise and that on James and John, as some suppose, an epithet of censure. The application of the surname to the two brothers should not be too limited. It was doubtless descriptive of their vehement and zealous spirit, ch. 9 : 38; 10 : 37; Luke 9 : 54; John 18 : 15, 16; 19 : 26; Acts 4 : 13. Also of their ministerial power. "The thunderbolt is the son of thunder, as it accompanies the crash from the rent clouds."—HILLER. That James should have been the first martyr of the apostles, and that Herod should have singled him out as his first victim when he stretched forth his hand to oppress certain of the church, is best explained by supposing him very earnest and powerful in his preaching and labors as an apostle. The ministerial power of John may be inferred from the fact that he is so frequently associated with Peter in the Acts (3 : 1 ; 8 : 14). John was indeed passively gentle, but positively earnest, stern, and even severe, 1 John 1 : 6; 2 : 4, 22; 3 : 8, 17; 4 : 3, 20. His utterances of truth were solemn and profound, especially respecting the Christ, the Word, in his Gospel and Epistles, and the future in the Apocalypse. This is the only place where this surname is found in the New Testament. That it was not commonly used like the name Peter may be explained by the fact that it was a collective one; they were conjointly named Boanerges.

18. Andrew. In Matthew and Luke (see on ver. 16) Andrew is placed immediately after Peter. But Luke in the Acts, the same as Mark here, places Andrew after James and John. Compare ch. 13 : 8. The separation of the name of Andrew from that of his brother Peter may be explained by the fact that they, like Peter, received a surname from Jesus, that they were illustrious as "sons of thunder," and that they are frequently associated with Peter, as at the transfiguration. See first paragraph on ver. 17.

Andrew was a name of Greek origin, and was in use among the Jews. It is derived from a word that means man, and may have been applied to him on account of his manly spirit. He belonged to Bethsaida (John 1 : 44), and was a disciple of John the Baptist, and had the honor of leading his brother Peter to Christ, John 1 : 40, 41. He resided afterward at Capernaum, ch. 1 :

ᶠJames the *son* of Alphæus, and ᵍThaddæus, and 19 ʰSimon the Canaanite, and Judas Iscariot, which also betrayed him.

ᶠ Ac. 15. 13; Jam. 1. 1.
ᵍ Lk. 6.16; Jude 1.
ʰ Lk. 6. 15; Ac. 1. 13.

29. He appears in connection with feeding the five thousand (John 6 : 8), afterward as the introducer of certain Greeks to Jesus (John 12 : 22), and also with Peter, James, and John, asking concerning the destruction of the temple, Mark 13 : 3. Of his subsequent history and labors nothing is certainly known. Tradition assigns Scythia, Greece, and Thrace as the scenes of his ministry. He is said to have been crucified at Patræ, in Achaia, on a cross in the shape of X, which is therefore called St. Andrew's cross.

Philip. A name of Greek origin, meaning lover of horses. He was a native of Bethsaida, a disciple of John the Baptist, and called by our Lord the day after the naming of Peter, John 1 : 43. He is mentioned in connection with feeding the five thousand; as introducing with Andrew certain Greeks to Jesus; and as asking, after the last supper, "Lord, show us the Father and it sufficeth us," John 6 : 5-7; 12 : 21; 14 : 8-10. Of the labors and death of Philip nothing is certainly known. A tradition says that he preached the gospel in Phrygia, and suffered martyrdom. He doubtless had also a Hebrew name.

Bartholomew. The Hebrew form is Bar-Tholmai, or son of Tholmai, the latter meaning *rich in furrows*, or *cultivated fields*, the whole name implying, as some suppose, rich fruit. It is the patronymic, as is generally supposed, of Nathaniel of Cana of Galilee. In the first three Gospels, Philip and Bartholomew are constantly named together, and Nathaniel is nowhere mentioned; while in the fourth Gospel Philip and Nathaniel are similarly combined, but nothing is said of Bartholomew, John 1 : 45; 21 : 2. According to tradition, he labored in India (Arabia Felix is sometimes called India by the ancients), and was crucified either in Armenia or Celicia.

Matthew was also called Levi the son of Alphæus. See on ch. 2 : 14; Luke 5 : 27. His residence was at Capernaum, and his profession a publican. His great humility is shown by styling himself in his Gospel "Matthew the publican" (Matt. 10 : 3); in his comparative silence in regard to leaving all and following Jesus, and to the great feast he gave at his house, both of which are told us by Luke (5 : 28, 29). His name appears for the last time in the New Testament among the eleven in Acts 1 : 13. Tradition assures us that he preached the gospel for several years in Palestine. Earlier traditions state that he died a natural death, but a later one says that he suffered martyrdom in Ethiopia.

Thomas was also called *Didymus* (John 11 : 16), both meaning *a twin*, the former Aramæan, the latter Greek. He was probably from Galilee. He was impulsive (John 11 : 16), of an inquiring mind (John 14 : 5-6), and slow to be convinced, John 20 : 24-29. Tradition affirms that he preached the gospel in India, and suffered martyrdom.

James the son of Alpheus is also called James the less or the younger, ch. 15 : 40. His father is probably not the same as the father of Matthew, but is generally thought to be identical with Cleophas or Clopas, John 19 : 25. Alphæus and Clopas are but different ways of expressing the same Hebrew name. Some suppose him to be James, the brother or cousin of our Lord (John 19 : 25 ; Luke 24 : 10); and that he had a brother Joses, Matt. 27 : 56.

Thaddeus, the surname of Lebbeus, Matt. 10 : 3. By comparing the four catalogues of the apostles, it appears that he was also called Judas, the *brother* of James, or as some supply, *the son* of James, Luke 6 : 16. He was the "Judas, not Iscariot," John 14 : 22. It has been common to regard Lebbeus and Thaddeus as allied names, being derived from Hebrew or Aramæan words, the former denoting heart and the latter breast, and hence denoting *the hearty, the courageous.* This is, however, doubtful. Judas means *renowned.* Some regard him the author of the Epistle of Jude; but others think that the author of that epistle was Jude the Lord's brother.

Jesus charged by his relations with madness, and by the scribes and Pharisees with being in league with Satan.

20 AND they went into an house. And the multitude cometh together again, ¹ so that they could not ⎫ ch. 6. 31.
21 so much as eat bread. And when his ᵏ friends ᵏ ver. 31.

Simon the Canaanite. Rather, *the Cananite* (Greek *kananaios*), an inhabitant of Cana. Or, more probably, the name corresponds with the Greek *kananites*, a zealot, according to its Hebrew etymology. He is called Simon Zelotes by Luke in his Gospel (6:15), and in the Acts (1:13), probably on account of his former zeal for the law, and possibly as expressive of his character. The name also distinguished him among the apostles from Simon Peter. It has been thought that he took it from having belonged to a political sect known among the Jews as Zealots. This was probably not the case, as the party bearing that name do not appear in Jewish history till after the time of Christ. He is only mentioned in the New Testament in the four catalogues.

19. **Judas Iscariot,** that is, *Judas, man of Karioth*, probably a native of Karioth, a small town in the tribe of Judah, Josh. 15:25. He was probably the only one of the apostles who was not by birth a Galilean. His father's name was Simon, John 6:71. He carried the bag, and appropriated part of the common stock to his own use, John 12:6. The climax of his sins was the betrayal of Jesus, which was speedily followed by suicide. His infamous character doubtless accounts for the position of his name as last on each of the catalogues in the Gospels. **Also.** Besides being an apostle, he **betrayed him,** delivered him up into the power of the authorities. An apostle and *also* a traitor (Luke 6:16), a terrible addition, and fearful guilt. It was a part of infinite wisdom that Christ should have chosen his betrayer among the twelve. God works even through wicked men, as in the case of Balaam. The churches of Christ must not expect absolute purity on earth; some of the chaff must remain among the wheat. The defection of those who have been regarded great in the church will not cause its ruin.

19-30. JESUS CHARGED WITH MADNESS BY HIS RELATIONS, AND WITH BEING IN LEAGUE WITH SATAN BY THE SCRIBES AND PHARISEES. His replies. The blasphemy against the Holy Spirit, Matt. 12:22-37; compare Luke 11:14-23. Mark's account is the shortest, but very life-like. Both Matthew and Mark exhibit striking evidences of independent narratives.

19. **They went into a house.** Rather, *They come*, etc. The meaning probably is that given in the margin of the common version, and long before by Wiclif. *They came home*, that is, to Capernaum (Matt. 9:1), the headquarters and center of their operations. See on ch. 2:1, where house seems to be used in the same sense.

Some time intervened between the selection of the apostles (the account of which ends with the first part of this verse) and the return to Capernaum narrated at the end of the verse. Mark omits the Sermon on the Plain (Luke 6:17-49) and the intervening events Luke 7:1 to 8:3. During this time occurred the second preaching tour throughout Galilee (Luke 8:1-3), which probably occupied two or three months of the summer of A. D. 28. See author's Harmony on §§ 50-58.

20. **The multitude cometh together again.** The gathering and greatness of the crowd is most vividly described. In a former entrance into Capernaum (ch. 2:1, 2), they filled the house so that there was no longer room, even at the door. Afterward the vast multitude thronged him by the seaside, ch. 3:9, 10; now the multitude gathers again, and is so great and constant that **they**—that is, Jesus and his disciples—could not even **eat bread.** They could not find time or opportunity to take their meals, since the throng continued, and people were coming and going all day long.

21. **His friends.** Not his disciples, for they were with him, but his *relations, kindred*. See on ver. 31. **They went out;** from their house or houses where they were living or stopping at

heard *of it*, they went out to lay hold on him: ¹for they said, He is beside himself.

22 And the scribes which came down from Jerusalem said, ᵐ He hath Beelzebub; and, By the prince of the devils casteth he out devils.

¹ John 7. 5; 10. 20.
ᵐ Mt. 12. 24; Lk. 11. 15; Mt. 9. 34; 10. 25; John 7. 20; 8. 48, 52; 10. 20.

Capernaum. To suppose them coming from Nazareth is unnecessary. Jesus may not have remained in the house, but have gone out in the open air to teach and heal. That a table may have been spread in the house is consistent with, though not a necessary inference from, the last clause of the preceding verse. **Lay hold on him.** Seize him, take him, so as to restrain him. **For** introduces the reason. **They said.** His kinsmen who went out to take him; not "it was said," as some suppose. **Beside himself.** *He is out of his mind*, imprudently carried away with earnestness and excitement. "It is designedly ambiguous, inasmuch as the *beside himself* may mean, in a good sense, the being for a season rapt into ecstasy by religious enthusiasm (2 Cor. 5 : 13), as well as in a bad sense, he being permanently insane. In his ecstasy, he is no longer master of himself."—LANGE, *Com. on Mark.*

22. **The scribes.** See on ch. 1 : 22. **Which came down from Jerusalem;** to watch the movements of Jesus. "The expression is too definite to be explained of a mere accidental presence, or a coming down on other business." —J. A. ALEXANDER. Matthew (12: 24) says they were Pharisees. The healing of the impotent man at the pool of Bethesda on the Sabbath (John 5 : 8-10), had a little time before aroused opposition at Jerusalem. The Sanhedrim had doubtless heard of his popularity in Galilee, and of his healing on the Sabbath there, ch. 3 : 1-6. It is not unlikely, therefore, that they sent these scribes who belonged to the strictest party, the Pharisees, to watch and oppose him. So they had once sent a deputation to ask John the Baptist who he was (John 1 : 19); and if they had sent one to John against whom they were making no special opposition, much more would they likely send an embassy into Galilee to watch and question Jesus, whom they were already systematically and malignantly opposing.

Said. The reason of their malicious charge was a most wonderful miracle in healing a blind and dumb demoniac. Matt. 12 : 22-24. The people who witnessed it were filled with astonishment, and in their surprise they asked, "Is this the son of David," the Messiah? The Pharisaic scribes heard it. They could not deny the miracle. They must also acknowledge something more than human power, and in their hatred to Jesus they charge him with being in league with Satan. **He hath Beelzebub.** He is possessed with Satan. Satan is in him or with him, and thus he has power over inferior evil spirits. The other evangelists nowhere state this charge, Matt. 9 : 34; 10 : 35; 12 : 24; Luke 11 : 15. *Beelzebub*, or rather *Beelzebul*, according to the Greek, was a name applied by the Jews to Satan (ver. 23), and immediately explained as **the prince of the devils**, that is, chief ruler, presider over *demons*, see on ch. 1 : 13, 23, 32. The name is variously explained. Thus by some it is supposed that the name Baalzebub, *lord* of flies, the fly-god of Ekron (2 Kings 1 : 2), was changed to Baalzebul or Beelzebul, *lord of dung*, dung-god, expressive of contempt, and applied to Satan as the prince of all idolatry and impurity. But although Lightfoot (Hor. Heb. Matt.12 : 24; Luke 11 : 15) has shown that *Zebul* occurs in the Talmudic writers, in the sense of *dung* and *filth*, and is by them applied in this sense to idols, yet in the Hebrew Scriptures it never occurs in that sense, but means a *habitation*, a *house*. Hence others suppose Beelzebul to mean *lord of the habitation, master of the house*, and thus applied to Satan as the lord of idolatry, or demons, and the kingdom of darkness. Thus Jesus in Matt. 16 : 25 may be regarded as representing himself in contrast, as the true "master of the house." The latter is the better explanation. Satan is the great usurper. The epithet in the mouth of a Jew was one of the most contemptuous he could use. And these wily scribes from Jerusalem, in their hatred, rather than to acknowledge the superhuman power of Jesus to be of

23 ⁿ And he called them *unto him*, and said unto them
24 in parables, How can Satan cast out Satan? And
if a kingdom be divided against itself, that king-
25 dom cannot stand. And if a house be divided
26 against itself, that house cannot stand. And if
Satan rise up against himself, and be divided, he
27 cannot stand, but hath an end. ^o No man can enter
into a strong man's house, and spoil his goods, except he will first bind the strong man; and then he

ⁿ Mt. 12, 25; Judg. 12, 1; 2 Sam. 20. 1, 6.

^o Is. 49, 24; Mt. 12, 29.

God, chose the fearful alternative of ascribing it to the devil.

23. **He called them.** The Pharisees had made this infamous charge not in the hearing of Jesus, but to some of the people. But Jesus knew their words and their thoughts, their malignant feelings and purposes, Matt. 12 : 25 ; compare Luke 11 : 15, 17. **By parables.** By similitudes and comparisons; as *kingdom, house,* strong man, vers. 24-27. Jesus replies, first by showing the absurd ty of the charge: **How can Satan cast out Satan?** How can he fight against himself? To do this he would be self-contradictory, fighting for God and against his own nature and kingdom; he would lose his own distinctive character, and be no longer Satan. The mere asking the questions shows the absurdity and the impossibility of Satan fighting against his own agents and representatives in the world. **Satan** means adversary, see note on ch. 1 : 13.

24. His first illustration is from a **kingdom divided against itself,** a state, a government not merely rent by internal strifes, but fighting against itself, its power, representatives, agents. In such a case that kingdom **cannot stand,** be made to stand, or be established. A kingdom must have unity or it will be destroyed. If it is divided and at war against its own existence it will, such a state of things continuing, be brought to a desolation.

25. The second illustration is from a **house,** a family. **Divided against itself;** divided against its own interests and existence. Similar sayings were doubtless common among the Jews. Thus we "read in the writings of the Jews, *every house in which there is a division, at the end shall come to desolation,* (Derech. Eretz, c. 5.)"—Dr. Gill.

26. So **if Satan rise up against** himself, if I as a representative of Satan, or if Satan through me has risen up against himself, as he is represented by demons in men, and **is divided** against himself, broken into factions and warring against his own interest, **he cannot stand,** he can not be made to stand, **but hath an end** to his power and kingdom. See Matt. 12 : 26, where it is recognized that Satan has a kingdom, but being an usurper, he is never called king. Yet he is called " prince of this world" (John 12 : 31 ; 14 : 30 ; 16 : 11), and "prince of the power of the air," Eph. 2 : 2. Hatred and strife indeed prevail in his kingdom, but there is among the devil and all his subjects a unity in their enmity to God and man, and neither he nor they will deliver any from their cruel tyranny. Should Satan turn against himself he would also have an *end* in the sense that he would cease to be what he is.

27. Mark here passes over an argument, recorded by Matthew (12 : 26, 27), drawn from a similar power which the disciples of the Pharisees professed to exercise in some cases over demons. He comes at once to the final illustration which concludes the argument, showing from the nature of the case that Jesus was the opposer of Satan, and superior to him and all his hosts. **No man.** Some ancient manuscripts begin with *but. But no one.* **Strong man's house.** Not *strong one's house,* referring to Satan as some have supposed, but *strong man's house,* referring to what occurs among men. The illustration is drawn from life. **Spoil his goods.** *Pillage, plunder his goods,* implements, tools, and household stuff. A strong man's house is entered and plundered, not by himself or friends, but by an enemy who is stronger than he, who first binds him, and then *plunders* **his house,** his agents, instruments, tools, furniture, and treasures. Thus Jesus did in cast-

28 will spoil his house. Verily I say unto you, [p] All
sins shall be forgiven unto the sons of men, and
blasphemies wherewith soever they shall blaspheme:
29 [q] but he that shall blaspheme against the Holy Spirit
hath never forgiveness, but is in danger of eternal
30 damnation. Because they said, He hath an unclean
spirit.

[p] Is. 1. 18; 55. 7; Eze. 33. 11; Lk. 12. 10; 1 Tim. 1. 13-15; 1 John 1. 7, 9.
[q] Lk. 12. 10; Ac. 7. 51; Heb. 6. 4; 10. 26, 29; 1 John 5. 16.

ing out demons, who were the agents and instruments of Satan's household. The only conclusion then was, that Satan was overpowered and conquered, cast out and judged, John 12 : 31; 16 : 11; Luke 10 : 18.

28. Jesus now gives the Pharisees a solemn warning against a sin they were in danger of committing. **Verily, I say unto you.** A solemn and authoritative expression often used by our Savior when he was about to utter a momentous truth, or to reveal some new fact to men, ch. 8 : 12; 9 : 1, 41; 10 : 15, 29, etc. **Verily** or *truly* is the translation of the Hebrew *amen* which Jesus often used at the beginning of a sentence to give it force. As emphatically the lawgiver of his people, he could speak with an authority above all other teachers. He is also the *Amen*, the faithful and true witness, Rev. 3 : 14. Jesus first declares that **all sins** in general will be forgiven **the sons of men.** They will not all be committed and hence not all forgiven in a single individual; but all sins committed by the different members of the human race, will be forgiven in different individuals except the one about to be specified. Then he speaks of a particular class of sins, which are the most heinous, namely **blasphemy,** or rather *blasphemies*, those, whatever they may be, wherewith they shall blaspheme. To this class the one unpardonable sin belongs; all others shall find forgiveness in different individuals. It was natural for Jesus to descend from sins in general to blasphemies in particular, and thus reach the deepest and blackest of all sin which could never find forgiveness.

29. **Blaspheme.** The word thus translated primarily means *to speak evil, revile, slander.* Among the heathen, speaking evil of gods was common as well as of men, and but little thought of. But among the Jews, reviling the one true God was regarded as a terrible and capital crime. Hence the word in Scripture when applied to God took upon itself the stronger meaning *to blaspheme*, to speak irreverently and impiously to God, or of God, or of sacred things. As reviling a fellow-man presupposes a malicious purpose, so blasphemy presupposes an impious intention to detract from the glory of God, and to alienate the minds of others from the love and reverence of God. Wherever it is spoken of in Scripture it is also connected with oral utterance. An idea of this sin may be gained from Lev. 24 : 10-16, where the son of an Israelitish woman blasphemed the name of Jehovah, vented against him abuse and imprecations, and he was stoned to death. It was a most heinous sin, and amounted to treason under the theocracy. Another instance is recorded in 2 Kings 18 : 28-35; 19 : 1-6, where Jehovah and his perfections are maliciously reviled. See also Rev. 16 : 10, 11.

We may conceive a gradation of blasphemy, the highest being that against the Holy Spirit, as God convicting, renewing, and sanctifying. Next to this is that against the Son (Matt. 12 : 32), as God manifested in the flesh, engaged in the work of redemption. Then that against the Father, or God, the great original source of love and mercy, or, as Whedon styles him, the original background of Deity. And lowest of all, speaking reproachfully of sacred things.

What, then, is it to **blaspheme against the Holy Spirit?** It can not be mere continued opposition to the gospel, obstinate impenitence, or final unbelief; for this is not specific enough; and besides, on the same principle by which this is regarded unpardonable, every sin might be styled unpardonable if the individual continues to indulge in it. The sin, however, was of a specific kind, and seems to have been willfully maligning and vilifying the Holy Spirit. This seems evident from the context and the accompanying circumstances. The Pharisees had attributed the power of Jesus to Satan, and had used the contemptuous epithet, Beelzebul, and had said, "He has an unclean spirit," ver. 30. They were guilty in this of blasphemy against the Son, especially against his divine nature. Compare Matt. 12 : 32 and note. He warns them, therefore, that but a step further and their sin would be unpardonable. The sin, however, implies a *state of heart*, malignant and willful opposition to the Spirit. Thus the Pharisees, surrounded with abundant evidence that Jesus was the Son of God, exercised a malignant and willful opposition to him, which found vent in abusive and infamous language, constituting blasphemy against the Son, Matt. 12 : 32. So in regard to blasphemy against the Holy Spirit, there must be a knowledge and a full intention. It can be committed, therefore, only where a person is surrounded with the evident manifestations of the Spirit, and under his influence ; where he knows and is convicted that it is the Spirit, and yet in his opposition he maliciously and willfully maligns and traduces the Spirit. Compare 1 Tim. 1 : 13, where we learn that Saul of Tarsus, the *blasphemer*, obtained mercy because he did it ignorantly in unbelief. It is more aggravated than grieving the Spirit, Eph. 4 : 30 ; it is the extreme and highest form of resisting the Spirit, Acts 7 : 51. Compare 1 John 1 : 5 ; Heb. 6 : 4–8 ; 10 : 29 ; 2 Tim. 3 : 8 ; Jude 4, 12, 13.

Yet, since the Spirit brings the truth to the heart in his work of conviction (John 16 : 8–11), and this truth presents Christ, it is difficult to conceive how a person can blaspheme against the Holy Spirit without blaspheming also against the Son. And if this is so, then we get a glimpse at the fact that blasphemy against the Holy Spirit, though the great fatal and unpardonable crime, is generally complicated with other sins, the result of some previous course of sin, and inseparably connected with willful malignity and hardness of heart.

Since God comes to the hearts of men only as the Holy Spirit, sins against the Spirit are the most heinous, being the most directly against God, and blasphemy against him the extreme of all sin. It is an insult which always oversteps that line between God's patience and his wrath, resulting in incorrigible hardness of heart, and in the departure of the Spirit forever. Hence it is a sin which *hath never forgiveness*, both from its nature and the consequent final departure of the Spirit.

Hath never forgiveness. The exact meaning is more clearly brought out by translating, *Hath no forgiveness forever*. The word translated forever is the noun, denoting here eternal duration, *eternity*, and points to the same duration in this clause that its adjective *eternal* does in the next. Thus our Savior makes the strongest assertion possible both negatively and positively : *Hath no forgiveness forever*, **but is in danger** (liable to) **of eternal damnation**, eternal condemnation and consequent punishment ; or according to the most ancient manuscripts and highest critical authorities, *is guilty of eternal sin*, that is, never to be blotted out, one that will be punished eternally.

To the question, *Can this sin be now committed?* it must be answered, Most assuredly. The Holy Spirit is in the world, among the followers of Christ, convicting the world of sin, and of righteousness, and of judgment. He can be thus opposed and blasphemed. He comes in contact with men ; and under the light of the gospel, they have all the knowledge necessary for committing so terrible a sin. The great anxiety of many, however, especially of those under deep convictions of sin, lest they have committed the unpardonable sin, is unnecessary. Their anxiety is an evidence that they have not committed it ; for their convictions show the presence and the striving of the Spirit, who still says, "Come." The spiritually blind and insensible, they who discover no compunctions of conscience and no striving of the Spirit, are the ones to be alarmed. And to all who are trifling with the Spirit, the fact that this sin may be committed should be a warning. Their trifling may grow into a resistance which shall be so intentional, so malicious, and so outspoken, as to constitute this extreme of all sin.

30. Mark gives the reason of Christ's warning against blaspheming the Holy Spirit. It was because the scribes had maliciously said, **He hath an un-**

Christ's mother and brethren.

31 ʳThere came then his brethren and his mother, and, standing without, sent unto him, calling him.

ʳ Mt. 12. 46; Lk. 8. 19; 2 Cor. 5. 16.

clean spirit, which was essentially their meaning when they said, "He hath Beelzebub." They were guilty in this contemptuous language of blaspheming the Son, especially his divine nature (Matt. 12 : 32); and needed only to exercise the same malicious spirit and outspoken opposition against the Holy Spirit, when he should come, in order to blaspheme him. Some suppose that the scribes and Pharisees in uttering such language regarding Jesus and his miracles did really commit blasphemy against the Holy Spirit. But of this Jesus gives no intimation. His discourse immediately after (Matt. 12 : 33-37) is against such a supposition; for why should he exhort them to make their profession and practice agree if they had committed that sin which would put them at once and forever beyond the reach of salvation? Besides, it is not probable that this sin could be committed before the descent of the Spirit on the day of Pentecost. The Jews of Christ's day were evidently not familiar with the doctrine of the Trinity, and hence with the doctrine of the personal Holy Spirit. These doctrines seem not to be prominently nor clearly revealed in the Old Testament. Their germs, however, were there, and many passages are made more intelligible and the better understood now that they are clearly revealed in the New Testament. The coming of the Holy Spirit, and the revelation of him as a manifest fact in the church and the world, took place on the day of Pentecost. The Spirit indeed descended on Jesus, but it was a manifest fact only to John. Jesus breathed the Spirit upon his apostles before his ascension, but it was only a manifest fact to them in enlightening their minds to understand the Scriptures. But to the Jews and to the world at large, the personal Holy Spirit seems to have been not a manifest fact before the day of Pentecost. He could not therefore be intelligently opposed; and without intelligent malicious intention there could be no blasphemy. Compare the ignorance of certain disciples of John, in regard to the Holy Spirit, Acts 19 : 2. See *Article* by the author on this whole subject in Oct. number of the BAPTIST QUARTERLY, 1868, pp. 445-460.

31-35. CHRIST'S MOTHER AND BRETHREN. Who they are in the truest and highest sense. Matt. 12 : 46-50; Luke 8 : 19-21. Luke is the briefest. Matthew and Mark are similar, both presenting some graphic details.

31. **Then.** *Therefore;* supposed by some to indicate the resumption of the narrative from ver. 21, concerning his relatives going out to lay hold on him. It was while he was yet speaking to the people, Matt. 12 : 46. Some of the oldest manuscripts have *and* instead of *therefore:* And his brethren, etc. It should be noted that Mark puts **brethren** first, while Matthew and Luke put **his mother** first. His brethren may have led the way, followed by his mother. As they are mentioned by the three evangelists in connection with his mother, the presumption is that they were his younger brothers, children of Joseph and Mary. Some regard them the children of Joseph by a former marriage. Others take the word *brothers* in the wider Oriental sense to mean near relation, kinsmen, Gen. 14 : 8. See further on, ch. 6 : 3. The description here is vivid. They were **standing without** the circle of the large assemblage of his hearers, who were probably in the open air; **sent unto him** word, a message, passing it doubtless from one individual to another to Jesus, **calling him,** wishing to see him (Luke 8 : 20) and speak to him, Matt. 12 : 46. They could not come near him on account of the multitude, Luke 8 : 19. On account of his continuous teaching his relations had experienced great anxiety, and had gone to lay hold of him, ver. 21. But all this accomplished nothing. Now his mother and brothers, his nearest and dearest relatives, seek to get a hearing. They not only feared that he was injuring himself by overwork and fasting, but they also trembled at the dangers to which he was exposing himself by such plain admonitions. They doubtless wished to caution him,

32 And the multitude sat about him, and they said unto him, Behold, thy mother and thy brethren
33 without seek for thee. And he answered them,
34 saying, Who is my mother, or my brethren? And he looked round about on them which sat about him, and said, Behold my mother and my brethren!
35 For whosoever shall do the will of God, *the same is my brother, and my sister, and mother.

* John 15. 14; 1 John 2. 17.

get him away from the multitude and the present excitement, and shield him from the assaults or designs of those whose enmity he had aroused by his discourse.

Some regard his *friends* or *relations* of verse 21, as *his brethren and his mother* of this verse. Although we might suppose some of his brothers among those who would seize him (ver. 21; John 7:5), yet it is not probable that his mother would have been among them. It is better to suppose two events very near together, the latter growing out of the former, and two companies of relations, the more and the less distant. The first effort, by his general and more remote kinsmen, failed. Jesus continues teaching, and increases in his plainness of speech, and his nearest relatives, his own brothers, and even his mother, try to get his ear in order to get him away from too great toil and threatening danger. Some of his brethren may have been in both companies.

32. **The multitude.** Rather, *A multitude*, or *crowd*. It was because a crowd sat around Jesus that his mother and brethren could not speak to him. **They said to him.** The word was passed from one to another till it reached Jesus. Thus Matthew (12:47) says, "Then one said to him." After **brethren** some ancient manuscripts add *and thy sisters*.

33. Jesus improves the occasion in calling attention to a higher and spiritual relationship, and hence he answers by asking, **Who is my mother?** etc. This was said not to his mother and brethren, but to the multitude, to him and others who had just announced the presence of his mother. There was nothing contemptuous in the language. Jesus did not despise human relationships (John 19:26, 27), but only esteemed the spiritual the more. The language was doubtless intended also as a gentle and indirect reproof to his mother and brethren. He knew better than they what and how long to speak. This and similar language (Luke 2: 48, 49; John 2: 4) shows how groundless is the Roman Catholic doctrine of Immaculate Conception, and of Mary as an object of invocation and worship. She regarded herself by nature a sinner, and needing a Savior, Luke 1: 47. What a contrast to the truth here taught, and the position given Mary in God's word, is the following prayer taken from a Roman Catholic "Key of Heaven," or manual of prayer, p. 26: "O Blessed Virgin, Mother of God; and, by this august quality, worthy of all respect from men and angels; I come to offer thee my most humble homage, and to implore the aid of thy prayers and protection. Thy intercession is most powerful, and thy goodness for mankind on earth is equal to thy influence in heaven. Thou knowest, O blessed Virgin, that I look up to thee as my Mother, my Patroness, my Advocate; I acknowledge, with humble gratitude, that thy virtues singled thee out for the Mother of my Redeemer. I will henceforth honor and serve thee assiduously. Accept, O blessed Virgin, my protestations of fidelity; look favorably on the confidence I have in thee; obtain for me of thy dear Son, a lively faith, a firm hope, a tender, generous, and constant love," etc.

34. **He looked round about**, etc. Here we have the graphic detail of Mark: the *look* of Jesus upon those who sat around him. He looked around upon the whole assemblage. It is the minute description of an eye-witness. Matthew (12: 49) gives not the look, but the *movement* of his hand which he stretched out toward his disciples. The look and the stretched-out hand were both with affectionate regard, as he said, **Behold my mother and my brethren**. These are my

nearest, dearest kindred, and their claims upon me are superior to those of any earthly friends.

35. Jesus explains himself, and shows a reason for his assertion. **For whosoever shall do the will**, etc. Such only are his true disciples, Matt. 7 : 21. Thus they show their spiritual relationship to God the Father, and consequently to him. And this condition extends into the future, *Whosoever shall do the will of God*.

My brother and my sister may be included in the plural *brethren*, vers. 32, 33, 34. **And mother;** a climax, the nearest relationship that any human being can hold to me. Even beyond my beloved and highly favored mother, according to the flesh, is the nearness and dearness of that relationship which exists between me and my followers. Or we may view the enumeration here as a uniting and concentrating human relationships in one, to express and symbolize the highest spiritual between Jesus and his disciples. Jesus does not introduce the word *father*, for he had no human father, and he never speaks of any but God as his Father. And as Joseph is never mentioned in connection with Mary, during Christ's public ministry, it is probable that he was dead.

Jesus thus refused or delayed speaking to his mother and brothers. The whole was an indirect reproof to them for their timidity and over-anxiety on his account.

REMARKS.

1. Jesus did not desist from his work because of opposition, vers. 1, 3; ch. 2 : 24; Luke 13 : 32, 33; John 9 : 4; 1 Pet. 2 : 21.

2. The wicked watch the friends of God in order to ensnare or find fault with them, ver. 2; Ps. 37 : 32; 38 : 12; 62 : 4; Jer. 20 : 10; Luke 14 : 1.

3. Whatever is right may be done openly, ver. 3; John 18 : 20; Acts 26 : 26; Eph. 6 : 19.

4. Deeds of mercy are becoming the Sabbath. But parties, feasting, excursions, and amusements are selfish, and can not be classed with works of mercy, ver. 4; ch. 2 : 25-28; Matt. 12 : 7.

5. There is a righteous anger, a holy indignation, which is lawful and may be exercised on proper occasions, ver. 5; Ps. 31 : 17, 18; Eph. 4 : 26.

6. Indignation against sin is consistent with compassion for the sinner, ver. 5; Luke 13 : 34; 19 : 41-44.

7. In the stretching forth of the withered hand we have an illustration of the act and effort of faith, ver. 5; Eph. 2 : 8; Heb. 11 : 1; James 2 : 17-20.

8. Christ is opposed by all the elements of a wicked world. Wicked men of the most opposite character and aims band together in their hatred to the truth, ver. 6; John 15 : 18-20; Acts 4 : 26; 1 John 3 : 12, 13.

9. We should not expose ourselves to unnecessary danger, in our labors for Christ, ver. 7; Luke 4 : 28-30; John 7 : 1; 10 : 39, 40; 11 : 54.

10. The withdrawal of Jesus from a people is the greatest of calamities, ver. 7; 1 Sam. 4 : 21, 22; Hos. 9 : 12.

11. When compelled to withdraw from one scene of usefulness, we should seek another, vers. 7-9; Luke 4 : 31, 32; John 10 : 40-42; Acts 8 : 5, etc.

12. Conveniences for teaching and preaching should be sought; yet not as an end, but as a means. A ship waited on Jesus, vers. 9, 10; Acts 13 : 5; 16 : 13; 19 : 9; 28 : 30, 31.

13. The wicked often are compelled to own that Jesus is the Christ, and to acknowledge the power of the truth, ver. 11; Acts 8 : 9-13; 14 : 11; 19 : 13.

14. We should not desire the services of the wicked in proclaiming the gospel, ver. 12; Acts 16 : 16-18; 19 : 14; 2 Tim. 1 : 9.

15. Ministers are called of God, but should not hastily be appointed to office. There should be a previous discipleship. The apostles had been disciples, and most, and possibly all of them, disciples also of John, ver. 13; Luke 6 : 12, 13; Acts 13 : 2; 1 Tim. 5 : 22.

16. As among the apostles, so among ministers and Christians generally, God calls into service every variety of talent. Every gift and ability is needed in his kingdom, vers. 16, 19; ch. 11 : 3; 1 Cor. 12 : 4-11.

17. If under our Savior's ministry a Judas was found among his disciples and apostles, we must not think it strange if now unconverted and wicked men are sometimes found in the church and in the ministry, ver. 19; Acts 8 : 18-23; 2 Tim. 4 : 10; 2 Pet. 2 : 1, 12-16; 2 Cor. 11 : 13-15; 2 Tim. 1 : 15.

18. Christian zeal and activity are often misinterpreted, even by professed

Three parables illustrating the mysteries of the kingdom of God.

IV. AND he began again to teach by the sea side: and there was gathered unto him a great multitude, so that he entered into a ship, and sat in the sea; and the whole multitude was by the sea on the land.

(Mt. 13. 1; Lk. 8. 4.

friends of Christ, and called enthusiasm, excitement, or insanity, vers. 20, 21; 2 Cor. 5 : 13; 11 : 26. Compare 2 Kings 9 : 11; Acts 26 : 24, 25.
19. The wicked still blaspheme Christ by slandering and reviling Christians and their religion, ver. 22; Matt. 25 : 45; James 2 : 7.
20. Traducers and blasphemers are guilty of most heinous sins, yet we should try and do them good, vers. 23, 30; 1 Cor. 4 : 13; 1 Tim. 1 : 13.
21. Divisions and dissensions, especially in churches, are most destructive, vers. 23-26; Rom. 16 : 17; 1 Cor. 1 : 10; 3 : 3; 11 : 18, 19.
22. Christians should be known by their opposition to all evil, ver. 27; Rom. 8 : 9; Matt. 12 : 30.
23. How glorious the gospel doctrine of the forgiveness of sins, ver. 28; Isa. 1 : 18; 55 : 6, 7; Acts 13 : 39; 1 John 1 : 7.
24. There is a limit to divine forgiveness, ver. 29; Gen. 6 : 3; Eph. 4 : 19; Heb. 6 : 4-6; 1 John 5 : 16.
25. The Holy Spirit is a personality, and in the highest and fullest sense God, since blasphemy against him is the most heinous sin, ver. 29; Matt. 28 : 19; Acts 5 : 3, 4; Heb. 10 : 15-17.
26. There is no probation after death. The final state of every man is determined in this life, ver. 29; Eccle. 11 : 3; Luke 16 : 26; John 9 : 4; Gal. 6 : 7; Heb. 9 : 27.
27. Christian work is the most important of all; nothing, not even love for our dearest friends, should stand in the way of duty, vers. 31-33; Heb. 6 : 3; Matt. 10 : 37; Luke 12 : 50.
28. How great the honor of being disciples of Jesus. Even the weakest are among his nearest relatives, and enjoy an affection beyond any earthly love, ver. 34; Isa. 49 : 15; Rom. 8 : 17.
29. If we would enjoy this love and honor we must do the will of our Heavenly Father, ver. 35; Matt. 7 : 21; John 15 : 14; 1 John 3 : 2, 10, 14.
30. Let men therefore beware how

they ill-treat the spiritual kindred of Jesus, vers. 34, 35; Ps. 27 : 10; Prov. 23 : 11; Luke 19 : 7, 8.

CHAPTER IV.

Having narrated the opposition of the scribes and Pharisees to Jesus, which had culminated in organized action, and in charging him with being in league with Satan, Mark now narrates a consequent change in our Savior's teaching. He gives three parables which were spoken to the multitude, illustrating the kingdom of God in its planting and growth. The first and third are included, while the second is not included, in the seven given by Matthew.

1-9. THE PARABLE OF THE SOWER. The various receptions that men give to the word of God. The causes and consequences, Matt. 13 : 1-9; Luke 8 : 4-8. Luke's account is the shortest. Mark's is little the longest, very similar to Matthew's, but with some peculiarities of his own.

1. **Began again.** Jesus makes a new beginning. He had taught with great plainness and with great effect; now he begins to teach in parabolic language. **By the seaside.** So he had done on former occasions, ch. 1 : 16; 2 : 13; 3 ; 7. A narrow level beach runs along the edge of the sea. From Matt. 13 : 1 it appears to have been on that day when the Pharisees made their infamous charge that Jesus cast out demons through Beelzebul, the prince of demons; and that he went out of the house, probably where he resided at Capernaum, to the seaside. **Was gathered unto him a great multitude.** Or, more vividly, according to the most ancient manuscripts, *There is gathered to him a very great multitude.* The situation is similar to that described in the preceding chapter, 3 : 9. The crowd is so great that he enters **into a ship,** doubtless the one he commanded to wait on him, ch. 3 : 9.

2 And he taught them many things by parables, ᵘand ᵇch. 12. 38.

He sat in the sea, the boat being a little removed from the shore. Sitting was the usual posture in teaching among the Jews, Matt. 5 : 1 ; Luke 4 : 20. All the multitude was on the land by the sea. They were to, toward the sea, by the seaside. The multitude lined the banks and extended to the very edge of the water, facing the sea and the boat where Jesus was.

2. And he taught them many things, of which he gives a specimen in the parables that follow. But few of the acts or of the words of Jesus are given by the evangelists, John 20 : 30 ; 21 : 25.

Parables. The Greek word thus translated comes from a verb, meaning to throw beside, to compare. Hence a parable in the most comprehensive sense is a placing beside or together, a comparing; and may apply to any illustration from analogy, a comparison, similitude, allegory, figurative or poetical discourse, dark saying or proverb, Num. 23 : 7 ; Job 27 : 1 ; Ps. 49 : 4 ; 78 : 2 ; Matt. 13 : 35. In Luke 4 : 23 it is properly translated proverb. In a more restricted sense the word denotes an illustration of moral and religious truth drawn from events which take place among mankind. The narrative or discourse may be fictitious ; but it must be within the limits of probability, else it becomes a fable. Teaching by parables was common in the East, especially among the Jews, 2 Sam. 12 : 1-14 ; Isa. 5 : 1-5 ; Ezek. 19 : 1-9.

The Parables of Christ were of the more restricted kind, and deserve especial notice. First, they were not fables. Fables illustrate human character and conduct ; the parables of Christ illustrate moral and spiritual truths. Fables are founded upon supposed words and acts of brutes or inanimate things ; the parables of Christ were all founded upon common and familiar incidents in nature and human experience, and all drawn, with one exception, from the present world. None of them was even necessarily fictitious. Facts are better than fiction, and Jesus with his omniscience had before him all events connected with the present and future world. It should also be noted that Jesus never uses the fable. His teaching demanded a higher kind of illustration.

Compare the fables of Jotham (Judges 9 : 8-15) and Joash (2 Kings 14 : 1) with the parables of this chapter.

Second, they were not proverbs. Proverbs are brief sententions sayings, expressing in simple or figurative language the result of human experience or observation. The parables of Christ are more extended, illustrating truth neither obscurely nor briefly, but plainly and in detail. In general it may be said that parables are expounded proverbs, and proverbs are concentrated parables. Compare the proverbs, "Physician heal thyself" (Luke 4 : 25), "A prophet is not without honor, save in his own country," etc. (Matt. 13 : 58), with the parable of the Wicked Husbandmen, ch. 21 : 33-44. Yet many a proverb expanded would be a fable or an allegory.

Third, neither were they allegories. Dr. Trench has well remarked that "the parable differs from the allegory in form rather than in essence." The allegory bears to the parable a relation similar to that which the metaphor bears to the simile or comparison. Thus, "That man is a fox" is a metaphor ; but "That man is like a fox" is a simile or comparison. So "I am the true vine," etc. (John 15 : 1-8) is an allegory ; but "The kingdom of heaven is like the grain of mustard," etc., is a parable. In the parable one thing is compared with another, the two kept separate and standing side by side ; but in the allegory the two are united and mingled together, and the thing which represents is really invested with the attributes and powers of that which is represented. Thus the allegory is self-interpreting ; at least the interpretation is contained within itself. In Bunyan's allegory, the imaginary Christian is invested with the attributes and powers of the real one, and thus the signification is mingled with the fictitious narrative. But the parable, strictly speaking, contains in itself only the types, which illustrate something without and running parallel with them. Thus in the parables of Christ, various facts in the world are made to illustrate great moral and spiritual facts and truths, which are always kept separate and yet are always parallel. Compare the allegories of John 10 : 1-16 ; 15 : 1-8 with the parables of this chapter ; or the parable in

A.D. 28. MARK IV. 77

3 said unto them in his doctrine, Hearken; Behold,
4 there went out a sower to sow: and it came to pass, as he sowed, some fell by the way side, and the
5 fowls of the air came and devoured it up. And some fell on ⟨stony ground, where it had not much earth; and immediately it sprang up, because it had
6 no depth of earth: but when the sun was up, it was scorched; and because it had no root, it withered
7 away. And some fell among thorns, and the thorns
8 grew up, and choked it, and it yielded no fruit. And

* Ezek. 11. 19; 36. 26.

Isa. 3 : 1-7 with the allegory in Ps. 80 : 8-16.

The parables of Christ were thus the illustration of spiritual things by an analogy of facts and incidents in every-day life and human experience. Their design (vers. 10-13), and the right mode of expounding them (14-20), will appear as we proceed.

In his doctrine. *In his teaching.* As he taught he uttered the parable that follows:

3. **Hearken.** Hear! Give attention! The word in this connection is found only in Mark, and was doubtless pronounced loud to quiet the people and call their attention to the parable. **Behold** introduces something specially worthy of notice. **A sower.** Rather, *the sower*, representing the whole class of sowers. The scene was a very familiar one to his hearers. **Went out;** once upon a time from his house, from the village or city. The time is indefinite, but the fact was of common occurrence. Possibly a sower was near at hand in a neighboring field, thus making the parable the more striking and impressive. The sowing season began with October and continued to the end of February. It is not improbable that it was now October.

4. **Some fell.** Or, more literally, *One fell*, one seed or one portion of seed fell. **By the wayside.** Fields were very commonly uninclosed, or separated only by a narrow footpath. The ordinary roads also were not fenced. Hence the seed of the sower was liable to fall beyond the ploughed field upon the hard ground, path, or road, which formed the wayside. **Fowls.** Rather, birds, such as the lark, sparrow, and raven, Luke 12 : 24. **Of the air.** The words are not found in the oldest and best manuscripts.

5. **And some.** Rather, *Another*, seed or portion of seed, *fell*, etc. Just as it is now common to say in graphic discourse, "One here, another there." **Stony ground.** More correctly, *The rocky ground.* Not where stones were numerous, for the soil might be rich and deep; but a rocky surface slightly covered with earth, where it had **not much earth.** "There was the rocky ground of the hillside, protruding here and there through the corn-fields, as elsewhere through the grassy slopes." —Stanley. It would, therefore, soon be warmed and soon parched. The seed would spring up quickly, **immediately.**

6. **When the sun was up.** A vivid description. The grain was quickly up above the surface, and then the sun was above the horizon. **Scorched.** The hot Oriental sun soon scorched them with its beams, evaporating its vital juices; and **because it had no root,** there being no chance for the plant to grow downward, it **withered away,** for want of needful moisture, Luke 8 : 6.

7. **And some.** *Another*, seed or portion of seed, as in ver. 5. **Among thorns.** *Into the midst of,* or, *among the thorns;* where the roots of the thorns remained, not having been carefully extirpated. These **grew up,** rather, *came up* above the surface, and **choked,** strangled, stifled the grain, by pressing upon it, overtopping it, shading it, and exhausting the soil, and thus **it yielded no fruit.** Thorny shrubs and plants abound in Palestine. "The traveler finds them in his path, go where he may. Many of them are small, but grow as high as a man's head. The Rabbinical writers say that there are no less than twenty-two words in the Hebrew Bible denoting thorny and prickly plants."—Dr. Hackett, *Scripture Illustrations,* p. 134.

8. **And other.** *And another,* as in ver. 5. **On good ground.** *Into the*

other fell on good ground, ˣand did yield fruit that sprang up and increased; and brought forth, some
9 thirty, and some sixty, and some an hundred. And he said unto them, He that hath ears to hear, let him hear.
10 ʸAnd when he was alone, they that were about

ˣ John 15. 5; Col. 1. 6.

ʸ Mt. 13. 10; Lk. 8. 9.

good ground, the rich, deep soil; neither hard and beaten, nor rocky, nor infested with thorns, but well prepared for receiving the seed. It therefore **sprang up and increased,** it went through the several stages of development and growth till the fruit was brought to perfection. The gradual process of the seed coming to maturity is brought to view. **Some thirty,** etc. *One thirty, one sixty,* etc., corresponding in style with *one, another* (seed or portion of seed) in this and the preceding verses. Notice also that Mark gives the increasing order, *thirty, sixty,* etc.; Matthew (13 : 8) the decreasing, hundred, sixty, etc.; while Luke (8 : 8) merely mentions the highest number. The independence of the evangelists may thus be incidentally noticed. **Hundred.** Thus Isaac, when sojourning in the land of the Philistines, is said to have sowed and "received in the same year a hundredfold," Gen. 26 : 12. Herodotus mentions two hundredfold as a common yield in the plain of Babylon, and sometimes three. Dr. J. P. Newman (*From Dan to Beersheba,* p. 396) says of the plain of Gennesaret, which may have been near where Jesus was speaking, "Equaling in fertility the Plains of Jericho, it is well watered, and its soil is in part a rich black mould. . . . Were it cultivated with intelligence and taste, it would be the Paradise of Northern Palestine, producing the choicest fruits luxuriantly, and possessing an eternal spring. Even now, notwithstanding its neglected state, it is dotted with magnificent corn-fields and with groves of dwarf palms." Jesus too was familiar with the fertile plain of Esdraelon, directly below Nazareth, which could yield grain enough, if properly cultivated, to support the entire population at present in Palestine.
Dr. Thomson (*Land and Book,* vol. i., p. 115) speaks of this parable as illustrated at the present day in its most minute details : " Behold a sower *went forth* to sow. The expression implies that the sower in the days of our Savior lived in a hamlet or village, as all these farmers now do; that he did not sow near his own house; nor in a garden fenced and walled, for such a field does not furnish all the basis of the parable. There are neither *roads,* nor thorns, nor stony places in such lots. He must go forth into the open country as these have done, where there are no fences; where the path passes through the cultivated land; where thorns grow in clumps all around; where the rocks peep out in places through the scanty soil; and where also, hard by, are patches extremely fertile. Now here we have the whole four within a dozen rods of us. Our horses are actually trampling down the seeds which have fallen by this wayside, and larks and sparrows are busy in picking them up. That man, with his mattock, is digging about places where the rock is too near the surface for the plow, and much that is sown there will wither away. And not a few seeds have fallen among this *bellan,* and will be effectually choked by this most tangled of thorn-bushes. But a large portion falls into really good ground, and four months hence will exhibit every variety of crop up to the richest and heaviest that ever rejoices the heart, even of an American farmer."
9. **He that hath ears,** etc. A call to candid and serious attention. He that can hear, let him now seriously attend and understand the solemn truths taught by this parable. "Now, now, if ever, he that can hear must hear, or incur the penalty of inattention."—J. A. Alexander.
10–12. Reason for speaking in parables, Matt. 13 : 10–17; Luke 8 : 9–10. Matthew, who pays special attention to the discourses of Jesus, is the fullest here.
10. **When he was alone.** Apart or away from the multitude, in private with his disciples, ver. 34. **They that were about him with the twelve.** His believing followers. Matthew (13 : 10) includes all in the term "disciples."

11 him with the twelve asked of him the parable. And he said unto them, Unto you it is given to know the mystery of the kingdom of God: but unto *them that are without, all *these* things are done in parables: 12 ᵃ that 'seeing they may see, and not perceive; and hearing they may hear, and not understand; lest at any time they should be converted, and *their* sins should be forgiven them.'

* 1 Cor. 5. 12; Eph. 1. 9; Col. 4. 5; 1 Thes. 4. 12; 1 Tim. 3. 7.
ᵃ Is 6. 9; Mt. 13. 14; Lk. 8. 10; John 12. 40; Ac. 28. 26; Ro. 11. 8.

Ask of him the parable. In the oldest and best manuscripts the plural is used, *asked him concerning the parables.* The parable just delivered gave occasion for asking not only concerning that parable, but also the design of parables generally. Thus the language here is pregnant, implying the two questions, that in Matthew (13 : 10), " Why speakest thou unto them in parables ? " and that in Luke (8 : 9), " What might this parable be ? " And in the reply of Jesus here recorded, both questions are answered. The inquiries of the disciples imply that this was the first time that Jesus taught the multitude by parabolic discourses. Before this his teaching had been plain and direct, intermingled with occasional similitudes, as in the Sermon on the Mount. But now "without a parable spake he not unto them," ver. 34.

11. Jesus first replies respecting parables generally, as used by him in illustrating the things of his kingdom. He uses them in order that the mysteries of the kingdom might be veiled to the hardened and ill-designing, but illustrated to his believing followers. **To know** is omitted in the oldest and best manuscripts. *Unto you is given the mystery.* Given by the sovereign will and good pleasure of God. Compare Matt. 19 : 11; John 3 : 27; 19 : 11. **Unto you** is emphatic and in contrast to **them that are without**, those who are not my disciples, 1 Cor. 5 : 12. The hardened and ill-designing multitude is here specially referred to. The separation between Christians and the world is brought into view. **Mysteries.** *The secrets*, the truths concerning the kingdom of Christ, hitherto hidden, but now being revealed. Mystery refers not to that which is incomprehensible in its own nature, but to what is unrevealed. See Rom. 16 : 25, 26; 1 Cor. 2 : 7, 8; 15 : 51; 1 Tim. 3 : 16; Eph. 1 : 9, 10. **Kingdom of God.** See on ch. 1 : 14. The great truths of the gospel were intrusted and made known to his followers, not to the opposing scribes and Pharisees. Even what prophets had foretold was a mystery to the worldly-minded multitude, 1 Cor. 2 : 14.

All things are done. All teaching regarding the kingdom of God. It is implied that parables may veil and darken truth to some, while they illustrate it to others.

12. A part of Isa. 6 : 9, 10 is here quoted. Matthew (13 : 14, 15) gives the passage more fully. Both quote with little variation from the Septuagint version, made about two hundred and eighty years before Christ. The hardness of heart exhibited under the preaching of Isaiah, was but a type of that greater hardness which should be shown by the unbelieving Jewish people in the rejection of Christ and his gospel, John 12 : 40; Acts 28 : 26, 27; Rom. 11 : 8. **That** expresses a purpose, and not a mere result. On account of sin they are left to spiritual deafness and blindness. **That seeing they may see** clearly and distinctly the external form, as of the parables, and not perceive the hidden truth and spiritual meaning. And **hearing they may hear** distinctly and clearly the words by which the truths of the gospel are announced, and **not understand** their spiritual meaning. They have faculties and opportunities, but they shall not rightly use them. Though they have moral and intellectual powers, they are righteously given over to their spiritual blindness and deafness.

Lest at any time. Lest, perchance, they see, etc. It was indeed their own voluntary purpose not to see, hear, understand, turn and be saved; but it was God's purpose also on account of their sins and depravity of heart. **They should be con-**

13 And he said unto them, Know ye not this para-
14 ble? and how then will ye know all parables? ᵇ The   ᵇ Mt. 13. 19.
15 sower soweth the word. And these are they by the
way side, where the word is sown; but when they
have heard, ᶜ Satan cometh immediately and taketh   ᶜ 1 Pet. 5. 8.
16 away the word that was sown in their hearts. And
these are they likewise which are sown on stony
ground; who, when they have heard the word, im-

verted, or rather, *should turn*, experiencing that change of heart and life which is necessary to salvation. In all this God did not take away their freedom. He was ready to forgive them if they did but turn, which, however, they would not, and indeed could not do; for they were morally unable, because they were unwilling. Their moral inability was the result of their moral unwillingness, John 5 : 40. **Their sins should be forgiven them.** *Their sins*, omitted by the oldest and best manuscripts. The passage should read, *and it be forgiven them*, or simply, *and be forgiven*. Matthew (13 : 15) retains the original form of the prediction, *should heal them* of their spiritual malady; but Mark gives the sense, for the healing of the disease would be attended with forgiveness.

13–20. INTERPRETATION OF THE PARABLE OF THE SOWER. Matt. 13: 18–23; Luke 8 : 11–15. These three accounts are very similar, yet with the differences of independent narratives. Luke again is shortest, and Mark a little the longest.

13. **Know ye not this parable?** The disciples had asked its meaning, Luke 8 : 9. The question is not one of reproof, but rather of concession to the fact that they needed its explanation in order to understand it and other parables. The question is preparatory to the one that follows, **And how then will ye know**, etc. Without understanding this they could not understand other parables; but knowing this they would have a key to the others. This, therefore, is a model interpretation. Another, that of the tares of the field (Matt. 13 : 36–43), is also given. From these two authoritative expositions, we should learn to avoid the excesses and defects too often exhibited in the interpretation of parables. *All parables;* or rather, *all the parables*, which I shall speak.

14. This parable divides the hearers of the gospel into four classes: the thoughtless, the superficial and fickle, the worldly, and the truly pious. **The sower** represents the Son of man (Matt. 13 : 37), also his ministers and servants, Matt. 25 : 45; 2 Cor. 5 : 20. **Sows the word.** The truths of the gospel. "The seed is the word of God," Luke 8 : 11. See 1 Pet. 1 : 23. The Bible is the great treasure of gospel seed. What a responsibility resting on those who have it!

15. The wayside, or thoughtless hearers. **These are they by the wayside.** These are the ones whose cases are represented by the seed sown by the wayside. The fate of the seed is inseparable from the fate of the man; it can, therefore, truthfully represent the man. **Where the word,** etc. This clause should be connected with the one that follows with *and* rather than **but:** *Where the word is sown, and when they hear.* The sowing and the hearing are thus connected, the one following immediately upon the other. **Satan.** The name means *adversary;* see on ch. 1 : 13. The quickness and activity of Satan is shown by the words, *cometh immediately.* He not only does this himself, but by his agents, wicked men and evil spirits; and also by evil thoughts and desire; and, indeed, by anything which will take away the attention from the truths of the gospel. **Taketh away,** like the birds picking up the grain. **Sown in their hearts;** or rather, with the same meaning, according to the highest critical authorities, *in them.* The heart was indeed the soil on which the seed fell, Matt. 13 : 19.

16. The stony ground, or superficial and fickle hearers. **These are they,** etc. These are the ones whose case is represented by the seed, etc., as in the preceding verse. **Likewise.**

17 mediately receive it with gladness; and have no root in themselves, and so endure but for a time: afterward, when affliction or persecution ariseth for the word's sake, immediately ᵈ they are offended. ᵈ 2 Tim. 1. 15.
18 And these are they which are sown among thorns;
19 such as hear the word, and the cares of this world, ᵉ and the deceitfulness of riches, and the lusts of ᵉ ch. 10. 24; 1 Tim. 6. 9, 17.

In like manner these represent a certain class of hearers. These do not merely learn the word incidentally; not mere passive hearers, but emotional and somewhat thoughtful; they **immediately receive the word with gladness.** Hearing the glad tidings, and thinking upon the pleasures and gains of salvation, they are at once highly pleased and delighted, without counting the cost, Luke 14 : 25–33. Their gladness is not the joy flowing out of repentance. Their emotions are easily aroused, but their heart beneath is hard and unrenewed. There is no deep conviction of sin, no brokenness and contrition of spirit, no change of heart.

17. Have no root in themselves. They are superficial and rootless, wanting in the principles of true religion, such as humility, love, repentance, and faith. They are not "rooted and grounded in love" (Eph. 3 : 17); and are destitute of that hidden life which "is hid with Christ in God," Col. 3 : 3. Hence they are not "rooted and *built up*" in Christ, Col. 2 : 7. They therefore **endure but for a time**; they are *transient, temporary*, or, as the Bible Union version translates, *are only for a time*. They are creatures of excitement, carried away with the novelties, the pleasures, or the sentimental excitements of religion; and hence, as the excitement subsides, they change, and turn back. They experience for a while an emotional and apparent faith (Luke 8 : 13), but believe not with all the heart, Acts 8 : 37.

Afterward, when affliction. Providential dealings and chastisements; affliction and distress. **Persecution.** The word originally means *pursuit*, that is, of an enemy. The evils inflicted by enemies. **For the word's sake.** Because of the word of the kingdom; the doctrines and truths, received with joy and professed for a season. **Immediately.** As suddenly as they received the word at first. **Offended.** They take offense,

become disaffected; their emotions are aroused in an opposite direction, and their profession is renounced. Their disaffection leads them to "fall away" (Luke 8 : 13) from a mere superficial religion and false profession. As the hot sun causes the deeply-rooted plant to grow, while at the same time it withers the rootless grain on rocky places, so tribulation and persecution strengthen and develop the true child of God (Rom. 5 : 3; 8 : 28; 2 Cor. 4 : 17; Rev. 7 : 14), while they offend, discourage, and completely disaffect the false and superficial disciple, Hos. 9 : 10; 2 Tim. 4 : 10. Such hearers are abundant at the present day, among all denominations, and even in the most genuine revivals. It has been estimated that of over twelve hundred thousand persons received as probationers by the Methodist Episcopal Church from 1856 to 1865 inclusive, seven hundred thousand never were received into full membership.

18. The worldly hearers. **And these are they,** etc. According to the highest critical authorities, *And others are they*, etc. Another class of unfruitful hearers are they whose case is represented by the seed sown among the thorns. Their heart is like the plowed but illy prepared field; the soil is rich and deep, but the thorn-roots have not been extirpated. They have conviction of sin, show signs of sorrow and repentance, and pass through an experience similar to that often witnessed in true conversion. But the heart is divided, darling sins are secretly fostered, and the powers of the body and soul are not given to Christ. They are not thoughtless, like those of the first class; nor, like those of the second, do they fail to count the cost, and hence do not participate in their false and fleeting joy. They hear, hear seriously, enter upon a conflict with the world, but fail to conquer. The cause is a heart not consecrated to Jesus.

19. **Cares of this world.** Rather,

4*

other things entering in, choke the word, and it be-
20 cometh unfruitful. And these are they which are sown on good ground; such as hear the word, and receive *it*, and bring forth fruit, some thirtyfold, some sixty, and some an hundred.

Cares of the world; anxious cares about worldly things, which divide the heart between God and the things of this life, James 1 : 6–8. This applies especially to the poor, whose struggles with poverty draw off the mind from God, and also to every one who is so unduly anxious about worldly things (Matt. 6 : 25) as to prevent him from giving up himself to God, and casting his care on him, 1 Pet. 5 : 7. **The deceitfulness of riches,** either obtained or sought, in alluring the heart, and leading it to exercise confidence in wealth; producing self-sufficiency and self-complacency. Hence they take up with a false hope and a mere profession. **The lusts of other things.** *The inordinate desires about other things* in this life, whatever they may be, which will draw away the heart from God. Luke (8 : 14) says, "pleasures of this life." Such are the natural accompaniments of such a course, 1 Tim. 6 : 9, 10. These **entering in,** where the seed had been received in the heart, **choke,** strangle **the word** by their contact and pressure, so that **it becometh unfruitful.** The unfruitfulness of the seed or word of course represents the unfruitfulness of those receiving it. Luke (8 : 14) says, they "bring no fruit unto perfection." They may have much of the outward appearance of the disciple, and even apparent fruits; but these, not coming to perfection, are unfit for use, and as worthless as no fruit at all. In the sight of God they are really destitute of good works.

20. The good-ground hearers, or the truly pious. They hear the word attentively and rightly, and **receive** it into their hearts. According to Matthew (13 : 23) they "understand" its true spiritual import; " in an honest and good heart, keep, or hold fast the word and bring forth fruit with patience," Luke 8 : 15. Their hearts, like the good ground, are prepared for the seed, ready to receive it in such a manner as to retain it and act upon it. All hearts are evil by nature, but in some there is a readiness, through the working of the Spirit and the truth, to hear and accept the gospel. It is heard not thoughtlessly (ver. 15), but seriously; received not superficially (vers. 16, 17), but deeply in the heart; accepted not partially (18, 19), but fully, with the whole heart. There is repentance and faith; a full surrender of the heart to Christ. While the soul acts freely, the Spirit works effectually in connection with the truth, and thus, without infringing upon the will, the heart is prepared by divine grace, John 5 : 40; 6 : 44; 16 : 8; 1 Cor. 2 : 14. **Bring forth fruit.** The distinguishing characteristic of this class. **Thirtyfold, sixty, an hundred.** All bear fruit, but in different degrees, in proportion to their natural endowments of soul, their spiritual culture of heart, their devotedness of life, and their faithfulness in the use of all gospel means, graces, and blessings.

The same classes of hearers are found at the present day, and in every age. The wisdom of our Savior's instructions are thus seen, in their perfect application through all time.

In these verses our Savior has given a *model exposition.* From it we learn to avoid two opposite extremes: first, making every point significant; second, overlooking some points which are really significant. The resemblance in the principal incidents is all that should be generally sought. I would give the following general directions:

First of all, seek carefully the grand design of the parable, and its center of comparison; and then, with the mind fixed on these, explain the principal parts accordingly, without giving too much prominence to minute particulars which serve merely to complete the story. In seeking the *design* of a parable, particular attention must be given to its occasion, connection, introduction and close. The *center of comparison* is that from which all parts of the parable extend in illustrating its grand design. Avoid fanciful interpretations; beware of seeking comparisons which are foreign to the design of the parable,

A.D. 28. MARK IV. 88

21 ⁱAnd he said unto them, Is a candle brought to be put under a ᵍbushel, or under a bed? and not
22 to be set on a candlestick? ʰFor there is nothing

ⁱ Lk. 8. 16; Mt. 5. 15; Lk. 11. 33.
ᵍ Mt. 5. 15.
ʰ Ecc. 12. 14; Mt. 10. 26; Lk. 12. 2.

The interpretation must be natural and easy, not forced and far-fetched. Beware, also, of founding a doctrine or a duty on single phrases, or incidental circumstances.

These principles may be briefly illustrated in the Parable of the Sower, as follows: The *general design* of parables is to illustrate the mysteries of the kingdom of God, vers. 11, 26, 30. The *particular design* of this parable is to illustrate the various receptions men give to the word of God; the causes and consequences are incidentally traced. The *center* of the comparison is the receptivity of the ground to the seed with that of the heart to the word of God. All portions of the parable and its interpretation are in harmony with this grand design and central similitude. The *sower* is the Son of Man, or his representatives, his servants; the *seed* is the word of God; the *ground*, the hearts of men; the seed, with its *results*, as sown on the ground, the various classes of hearers. Now many resemblances might be affirmed which Jesus has not affirmed. Thus, for example, from a *sower* as a *husbandman*, his *going forth*, the *time* and *manner* of his sowing, the *local position* of the wayside. But these would be foreign to the grand design, and very remotely connected, if connected at all, with the center of comparison. So also to refer the wayside hearer to thoughtless childhood; the stony ground to ardent and superficial youth; and the thorny ground to worldly-minded maturity would be fanciful as well as unnatural. For these classes may all be found among persons of the same age. And finally, to conclude that there are but three classes of fruit-bearing Christians corresponding to the thirtyfold, the sixty and the hundred, each bearing no more and no less than the ratio of his class, would obviously be *forced*, and be founding a principle on *single phrases* and *incidental circumstances*.

21–25. ALL OF HIS INSTRUCTIONS DESIGNED TO GIVE LIGHT; HIS HEARERS RESPONSIBLE FOR THEIR MEASURE OF LIGHT. Matt. 13: 12; Luke 8: 16–18. Compare Matt. 5: 15; 7: 2; 10: 26,

where Jesus uses the same language on other occasions. Jesus sometimes repeated great and important truths. See Matt. 6: 9–13 and Luke 11: 2–4; Matt. 16: 21; 17: 22, 23, and 20: 17–19. The same thing has been done by the wisest teachers and by inspired prophets. Compare Ps. 14 and 53; Jer. 10: 12–16 with 51: 15–19.

21. Jesus had told his disciples that it was given them to know the mysteries of the kingdom of God, but not to the unbelieving and hardened multitude, and hence his special reason for speaking in parables at that time, vers. 11, 12. They might possibly infer that these instructions in the great truths of his kingdom were to be kept secret; and that parabolic instruction is, in its very nature, adapted to darken rather than enlighten. Jesus however dispels any such notions by what he now says. It is the nature of all truth to enlighten; if it darkens, the fault is in the hearer, not in the truth. His instructions are all intended to be made public, and the hearer will be made responsible for his manner of receiving it.

Is a candle? *Is the lamp*, the common domestic lamp, brought to be put under a bushel; *the measure*, indicating a familiar household utensil, as the common grain-measure, holding about a peck. Or under a bed? *The couch*, probably that on which people reclined at their meals, which was elevated three or four feet above the floor. The form of the question demands a strong negative answer. The mere putting the question shows the absurdity of bringing a lamp in order to cover it. It should be put on a candlestick, or rather, *on the lamp standard*, the support on which the lamp *is placed*, *in order to give light*. "The lamp, being low, was placed on a support sufficiently high to give light through the room; and this latter would be equally necessary to the candle with its candlestick, as we use the term."—DR. CONANT on Matt. 5: 15. And thus the truths of the gospel are like the lamp, designed not to be covered up, but to be made known, so as to give light to the world.

22. For. Jesus gives the reason of

hid, which shall not be manifested; neither was any thing kept secret, but that it should come 23 abroad. ⁱ If any man have ears to hear, let him hear.

24 And he saith unto them, Take heed what ye hear: ᵏ with what measure ye mete, it shall be measured to you: and unto you that hear shall more be given.

25 ˡ For he that hath, to him shall be given: and he that hath not, from him shall be taken even that which he hath.

ⁱ ver. 9; Mt. 11. 15.

ᵏ Mt. 7. 2; Lk. 6. 38.

ˡ Mt. 13. 12; 25. 29; Lk. 8. 18; 19. 26; John 15. 2-5.

---

his figurative language in the preceding verse in a plain and emphatic declaration. **For there is nothing hid.** If any truth is now hidden by a parable or otherwise it shall be **manifested**, revealed and made known. **Neither was anything kept secret**, nothing has been concealed, intentionally done in secret, **but that it should come abroad**, but in order that it should come into open view, be brought to light. Nothing which had been taught or done in secret was to be withheld, but all is designed to be proclaimed publicly at the proper time. Even their secrecy would help toward their future publicity. And as applied to his parabolic instructions, truth now veiled in parables would be in due time the more manifest through them. That which might seem to hide truth would most beautifully and openly illustrate it. Those who would now withhold the Bible from the people are acting contrary to the design of Christ and of truth.

23. **If any man have ears to hear,** etc. See on ver. 9. The disciples are specially called to attend seriously and earnestly to his instructions, since they were to be the public heralds of his truth. This leads to what follows regarding their responsibility as hearers.

24. **And he said,** etc. Doubtless uttered on the same occasion. **Take heed what ye hear.** See to it, consider carefully, what ye hear from me. Luke says "how ye hear," which is implied in the caution as here given by Mark. **With what measure,** etc. One of the maxims of Jesus applicable to various occasions, Matt. 7 : 2. The general meaning is: As you treat others so shall you be treated. In this instance, as you treat me as a teacher so will I treat you as learners. The measure of careful attention given me will be the measure of instruction given you. What you receive as hearers and disciples will correspond to your ability and diligence. **And unto you that hear.** According to the best authorities, *And there shall be added to you;* you shall receive more instruction, there shall be given you additional truths and increased knowledge.

25. **For.** The reason of what he had just said, given as a general principle. Matthew (13 : 12) gives it earlier in the discourse. But its applicability both there and here, renders it probable that Jesus used it twice on the same occasion. The last clause of the preceding verse prepared the way for its repetition. **He that hath.** He that, having a teachable spirit, has already some knowledge of the gospel and of Christ. Experimental knowledge and love for Christ, an improvement of this knowledge, and a desire for more, are implied in such a state. **To him shall be given** more knowledge. He shall have greater means and facilities in its attainment. **He that hath not;** not having a teachable spirit, has failed to receive and use the instructions of Christ, the truths of the gospel. Hence he has not experimental knowledge and love for Christ, and desires not to know his truth. From such shall be taken away **even that which he hath.** The light, the means and the knowledge which have been proffered him shall be withheld. The possession is explained by Luke (8 : 18), "even that he seemeth to have;" it is only apparent and imaginary. His speculative views and notions shall become more confused and darkened. Judas among the twelve was an example of this class. He who uses and improves the light he has shall obtain more light, Hos. 6 : 3; John 8 : 12;

A.D. 28. MARK IV. 85

26 And he said, ᵐ So is the kingdom of God, as if a   ᵐ Mt. 13. 24.
27 man should cast seed into the ground; and should
sleep and rise, night and day, and the seed should
28 spring ⁿ and grow up, he knoweth not how. ᵒ For   ⁿ Ecc. 8.17; Is. 61. 11; John 3. 8.
the earth bringeth forth fruit of herself; first the   ᵒ Ge. 1. 12.
blade, then the ear, after that the full corn in the
29 ear. But when the fruit is brought forth, immediately ᵖ he putteth in the sickle, because the har-   ᵖ Rev. 14. 15.
vest is come.

---

but he who neglects to do it shall lose it altogether, and be condemned as an unprofitable servant, Matt. 25 : 29, 30.
26-29. PARABLE OF THE SEED GROW-ING SECRETLY. The kingdom of God in the soul and in the world a life and a growth, not dependent on human power; gradual, progressive and com-plete in its development. The parable is an antidote against impatience and despondency. This is the only parable found in Mark alone.
26. The connection and position of this parable are very natural. By the parable of the Sower Jesus had taught the dangers attending the reception of the truth. He had also probably spoken the parable of the Tares (Matt. 13 : 24-30), by which was shown the dangers from the seeds of error sown by Satan and his agents. He had also taught (vers. 21-24) that his followers were to be fellow-laborers with him in proclaiming the truth. He now shows that the seed, the word of God, faith-fully preached, will germinate on the good ground and through an unseen power come to maturity, ready for harvesting.
So is the kingdom of God. Such is the reign or dispensation of the Messiah, in its growth and progress in the world and in the hearts of men. It is like the case of the seed about to be delineated. Notice, it is **a man** and **the seed.** *The seed,* its germination and growth, is the prominent thing in the parable. **Into,** rather, *upon.*
27. **Should sleep and rise, night and day.** Sleeps by night and rises by day as usual. Having sown the seed, he leaves it, attending to other things; pursuing his ordinary course of labor and rest. In the mean time, without any of his aid the seed germinates and grows, **he knoweth not how;** he does not understand the process of its growth; neither does he anxiously

watch it; he lets it alone, assured that it will spring up and grow, though he can not explain it. Human wisdom finds something here into which it cannot penetrate.
28. **The earth bringeth forth fruit of herself.** By the power that God gives. By the hidden processes of life through the power of God. **First the blade,** the *grass,* the small grass-like shoot. "That period of growth in which grains and grasses are alike."—ALEXANDER. **Then the ear.** The head upon the stalk. The period of heading-out when the grains are dis-tinguished from grasses, etc. **After that the full corn,** etc. *Then the full grain;* the kernels full-grown and ripe.
29. **When the fruit is brought forth.** *Gives up, yields, permits.* The spontaneous growth of the fruit con-tinues till it is fully ripe, and then it is ready for the sickle, for men to work in gathering it. **Putteth in the sickle.** *Sendeth forth the sickle.* The reaping is done by himself or by others.

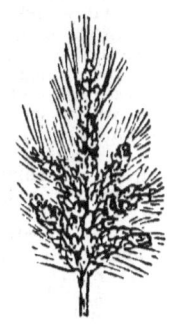

ORIENTAL WHEAT.

INTERPRETATION. The grand *design*

8

30 And he said, ¶ Whereunto shall we liken the kingdom of God? or with what comparison shall we 31 compare it? *It is* like a grain of mustard seed, which, when it is sown in the earth, is less than all

¶ Mt. 13. 31; Lk. 13. 18; Ac. 2. 41; 4. 4; 5. 14; 19. 20.

of this parable is to illustrate the life and the growth of the reign or administration of Christ, in the heart and in the world, independent of human power. Its *center* of comparison is between the regular independent development of the seed and the regular independent development of the life-seed of Christ's kingdom. A *man*, is indefinite, and represents any one who may sow the seed of the kingdom. Christ sowed; but his disciples were to be the principal sowers. Ministers go forth in his stead, 2 Cor. 5:20. It can be said of them that the seed germinates and grows, they *know not how*. *The seed* is the word of God, the truths of the gospel, ver. 14. *The ground* represents the hearts of men. *The seed springing up and growing*, represents the germination and gradual growth of spiritual life, 1 Pet. I:23-25. It does not come suddenly to maturity. The *blade*, the *ear*, and the *full grain*, represent a regular development. It is certainly analogous that John divides believers into three classes (1 John 2:12-14), "little children," "young men," and "fathers." *The earth bringeth forth fruit of herself*, represents the spiritual life springing up and coming to maturity through the power of the Holy Spirit and of truth in the hearts of men, independent of human power. The man *sleeping* at night and *rising* at day, and going about his usual work after sowing the seed, illustrates the assurance the Christian should have in the ultimate success of truth. The great *reaper* is Christ, Rev. 14:14, 15; *his reapers* are the angels, Matt. 13:39. As they did not reap until the fruit was fully ripe, so Christ will call none of his children home until they are fully prepared. *The harvest* represents the end of the world (Matt. 13:40, 41), or death, so far as death is the end of the world to the individual believer. The ministers of the gospel may also be regarded as *reapers*, at last coming with joy and bringing their sheaves with them, Ps. 126:6; John 4:36; 1 Thess. 2:19.
It is altogether aside from the design of this parable to suppose that Jesus intended to encourage slothfulness in any respect. Men are to exercise diligence, prayerfulness, and watchfulness, or religion will not thrive. In this matter we are workers together with God. One plants, another waters, but God gives the increase. The gospel must be preached. It must be heard, understood, believed, and obeyed. But the power which leads men to do this is of God, 1 Cor. 3:6-8. The parable is rather a stimulus to persevering labor. "By such insensible degrees shall the gospel gain ground in the world and ripen to a harvest of glory; and therefore let not my faithful servants be discouraged if the effect of their labors be not so immediately conspicuous as they could desire; a future crop may spring up, and the Son of man will in due time appear to gather it in."—DODDRIDGE.

30-32. PARABLE OF GRAIN OF MUSTARD. The expansive power of truth, Matt. 13:31, 32. Compare Luke 13:18, 19.

30. Having thus by the preceding parable shown the silent and progressive growth of his kingdom in the heart and the world, he proceeds in the same line of thought: **And he said,** using the form of a question for emphasis and for arresting the attention. **Whereunto shall we liken.** According to the oldest and best manuscripts, *How shall we liken*. So also in the next question, instead of **With what comparison,** it should be, *In what parable* (or *comparison*) *shall we place it,* or *set it forth*. Notice that Jesus uses the plural **we,** including his disciples in their work of preaching and teaching. Parables were intended not merely for that occasion, but to be used afterward by preachers and teachers in illustrating the kingdom of God. These questions give great vividness to Mark's narrative.

31. We may well suppose that Jesus paused a moment as if waiting a reply, and then he answers, **Like a grain of mustard seed.** This is popularly described as **less than all the seeds,** etc. It was the smallest of seed-grain

32 the seeds that be in the earth: but when it is sown, it groweth up, and becometh greater than all herbs, and shooteth out great branches; so that the fowls of the air may lodge under the shadow of it.

used in Jewish husbandry, and in proportion to the plant it produces, it was the smallest of all domestic garden-seeds. In Jewish proverbial language it was used to denote the smallest thing, Matt. 17 : 20.

32. **Becometh greater than all herbs;** than all the herbs in the garden, "a tree" (Matt. 13 : 32), or "a great tree" (Luke 13 : 19), of course in a comparative sense. Jesus uses the popular language of the day. **May lodge.** *Can lodge*, light upon, and find shelter in its branches.

The common mustard-plant is not only found in Palestine in a wild state, but is cultivated in gardens. Dr. Thomson (*The Land and the Book*, vol. ii., p. 100) says of the wild mustard, "I have seen this plant on the rich plains of Akka as tall as the horse and his rider." Dr. Hooker (*Hackett's Smith's Dictionary*, p. 2042) also says, "Of the mustard-plants which I saw on the banks of the Jordan, one was ten feet high." Dr. Hackett, while riding across the plain Akka on the way to Mount Carmel, examined an extensive field of this plant. "It was in blossom at the time, full-grown; in some cases, as measured, six, seven, and nine feet high, with a stem or trunk more than an inch thick, throwing out branches on every side. It might well be called a tree, and certainly, in comparison with its tiny seed, 'a great tree.' But still the branches or stems of the branches were not very large, and to the eye did not appear very strong. Can the birds, I said to myself, rest upon them? Are they not too slight and flexible? Will they not bend or break beneath the superadded weight? At that very instant, as I stood and revolved the thought, lo! one of the fowls of heaven stopped in his flight through the air, alighted down upon the branches, which hardly moved beneath the shock, and then began, perched there before my eyes, to warble forth a strain of the richest music."—HACKETT'S *Smith's Dictionary*, p. 2043.

INTERPRETATION. The grand *design* of this parable is to show the expansive and growing power of the gospel under the kingdom or reign of the Messiah. Its *center of comparison* is between the power of growth as exhibited in the mustard-seed and that manifested in gospel truth. The *grain* of mustard represents the word of God, the truth. The *man* that sowed, Christ or one of his servants. The *seed* in the soil *becoming a plant*, the individual believer. The idea of growth and of gradual development is vividly presented. A seed of gospel truth is lodged in the heart, a little word or a single idea. To human view it is indeed small, but it germinates into a new and growing life, begotten " with the word of truth," James 1 : 18. Thus it has pleased God " through the foolishness of preaching to save them that believe," 1 Cor. 1 : 21. The believer now grows in grace, his spiritual strength increases, his graces appear, and his powers are developed, going on from one degree of strength to another, till he becomes a full-grown man in Christ, Eph. 4 : 13. He has now the size, appearance, strength, and activities of a man. But growth includes not only internal development, but also accretion from without, through food, air, water, etc. So the Christian in his growth feeds upon the bread of life. The *birds of the air* are introduced to represent the strength and blessing of this matured and developed state. Christians individually and collectively are indeed a source of blessing and safety to the world, Gen. 18 : 23-33; Deut. 9 : 19, 20; Isa. 1 : 9. See Remark 27.

But this parable also illustrates the power and growth of the gospel generally in the hearts and lives of men. Jesus was indeed "the word," the gospel *seed*, the babe of Bethlehem, the man of sorrows, despised of men, but planted of his own free will by his death, springing up in his resurrection and bearing fruit in the thousands and the millions of his followers, John 12 : 24. This spiritual kingdom commencing with himself, has been constantly augmenting. The gospel from small beginnings has become extensive and

33 ʳAnd with many such parables spake he the word *Mt. 13. 34; John 16. 12; 1 Cor. 3. 1, 2; Heb. 5. 11.
34 unto them, as they were able to hear *it*. But without a parable spake he not unto them. And when they were alone, he expounded all things to his disciples.

Jesus crosses the lake; stills a storm.

35 ˢAND the same day, when the even was come, he ˢMt. 8. 18; Lk. 8. 22.
saith unto them, Let us pass over unto the other
36 side. And when they had sent away the multitude, they took him even as he was in the ship. And

powerful. See a prophecy of this kingdom in Dan. 2 : 44, 45; and compare Dan. 7 : 13, 14; Ezek. 17 : 22–24.

33–34. CONCLUSION OF THE PARABLES; to the multitudes, for so we learn from Matthew, and also that he spoke others the same day to his disciples when alone, Matt. 13 : 34, 35.

The three parables here given by Mark present a broad and connected view of religious truth, respecting the foundation, progress and completion of the kingdom of God, in the hearts and lives of men, and in the world.

33. **And many such parables.** Mark evidently knew of other parables spoken at that time; but he gives these as samples. Matthew gives The Tares, and The Leaven, spoken to the multitude, besides three others spoken to the disciples. **Unto them.** The multitude and his disciples, ver. 34; Matt. 13 : 34. **As they were able to hear.** According to ability or capacity for receiving instruction. " It also includes their being able to hear without being offended,"—LANGE. So the apostles afterward did, adapting their teachings to the capacities of their hearers, 1 Cor. 3 : 1, 2; Heb. 5 : 11–14.

34. **Without a parable spake he not.** On this occasion he confined himself to parables in instructing the multitude. Neither did he explain the parables to them, but to his disciples when they were **alone,** in private. Thus he explained the *sower* and the *tares*, Matt. 13 : 36–43. Compare Matt. 15 : 15–20; Luke 16 : 9–12; John 14 : 5–11; 16 : 20.

35–41. JESUS CROSSES THE LAKE; STILLS THE TEMPEST. Matt. 8 : 18, 23–27; Luke 8 : 22–25. This account given by Mark is the fullest, most graphic, and most definite.

35. As the Sermon on the Mount was followed by a miracle, so was the great parabolic discourse by the seaside. The former was for the enlightenment of all, and the miracle was before all; the latter was specially for those who had ears to hear, his disciples, and the miracle was performed specially for them. That miracle (the leper, Matt. 8 : 2–4) represents man cleansed and saved by the Savior in harmony with the Law; this might be termed an acted parable or dark-saying. In the extremity and darkness of the disciples, Christ appears the solver of their perplexity, and the deliverer from threatening destruction.

The same day when the even was come. *That day*, etc. This fixes this voyage and miracle to the evening and night following the parabolic discourse just given. It was probably about sunsetting. **The other side.** The eastern side of the lake.

36. **When they had sent away,** etc. When the disciples had dismissed the multitude they **took him even as he was in the ship.** That is, without any preparation; Jesus was already in the boat. It appears from Matthew that after discoursing from the boat, he retired awhile to the house, probably where he resided at Capernaum (Matt. 13 : 36); then returned to the boat and possibly discoursed still more; but seeing the multitude continuing (Matt. 8 : 18), he commands to depart to the opposite side, which command was obeyed promptly and in haste. **Little ships.** *Ships* or *boats*, according to the oldest manuscripts and highest critical authorities. These very likely contained some of the multitude, but were separated in the gale.

37. **A great storm of wind.** One

37 there were also with him other little ships. And there arose a great storm of wind, and the waves
38 beat into the ship, so that it was now full. And he was in the hinder part of the ship, asleep on a pillow: and they awake him, and say unto him, Master,
39 ¹ carest thou not that we perish? And he arose, and rebuked the wind, and said unto the sea, Peace,

¹ Is. 40. 27; 1 Pet. 5. 7; Jon. 1. 6.

of those sudden, violent squalls or whirlwinds, attended with some rain, to which the lake is subject. Captain C. W. Wilson (RECOVERY OF JERUSALEM) gives the following graphic description of one of these storms on the Sea of Galilee:

"Sudden storms, such as those mentioned in the New Testament, are by no means uncommon; and I had a good opportunity of watching one of them from the ruins of Gamala on the eastern hills. The morning was delightful; a gentle easterly breeze, and not a cloud in the sky to give warning of what was coming. Suddenly, about midday, there was a sound of distant thunder, and a small cloud, 'no bigger than a man's hand,' was seen rising over the heights of Lubieh, to the west. In a few moments the cloud began to spread, and heavy black masses came rolling down the hills towards the lake, completely obscuring Tabor and Hattin. At this moment the breeze died away; there were a few minutes of perfect calm, during which the sun shone out with intense power, and the surface of the lake was smooth and even as a mirror; Tiberias, Mejdel, and other buildings stood out in sharp relief from the gloom behind; but they were soon lost sight of, as the thunder-gust swept past them, and rapidly advancing across the lake, lifted the placid water into a bright sheet of foam; in another moment it reached the ruins, driving myself and companion to take refuge in a cistern, where, for nearly an hour, we were confined, listening to the rattling peals of thunder and torrents of rain. The effect of half the lake in perfect rest, whilst the other half was in wild confusion, was extremely grand; it would have fared badly with any light craft caught in midlake by the storm; and we could not help thinking of that memorable occasion on which the storm is so graphically described as 'coming down' (Luke 8: 23) upon the lake."

It was now full. *The ship was already becoming filled,* (BIBLE UNION VERSION). It "was covered with the waves," Matt. 8: 24.

38. **He is** emphatic. While all the rest were awake and filled with terror, *he himself* was in **the hinder part,** *the stern* of the vessel, sleeping **on a pillow,** *on the cushion,* which formed part of the furniture of the boat. Alford suggests that the pillow was the cushion used by the rowers, the covering of their seats. **Asleep.** He needed sleep, like other men; especially after such a laboring day, ch. 3: 20 to ch. 4: 35. It was his design also that this storm should be simultaneous with his sleep, so that his disciples should feel their extremity and be the more deeply impressed with his power over the elements. Like Jonah he slept in the midst of the storm; but how differently!—the prophet fleeing from duty, Jesus calmly awaiting the exact moment of duty; the prophet the cause, Jesus the allayer of the storm.

Awake him. They rouse him up, not for his safety, but their own. **Master.** *Teacher.* They recognize him as the great and powerful teacher of Israel. **Carest thou not that we perish?** A mingled prayer and complaint; with mingled fear and faith. The cries of intense anxiety, the exclamations of terror. "Teacher, we are lost! hast thou no concern for us? Canst thou lie sleeping here while we are perishing? Save us from impending ruin!" (Matt. 8: 25.) How great the tempest thus to terrify the disciples, who were accustomed to sailing and fishing on the lake!

39. **And he arose and rebuked.** *Being roused up,* or *woke up fully, he rebuked the wind.* How patiently he bears their murmuring and their little faith, and how quickly he comes to their relief. **Peace, be still.** *Be silent, be hushed,* and remain so. This remarkable command to the sea is given only here. Some infer from the

be still. And the wind ceased, and there was a
40 great calm. And he said unto them, ᵘWhy are ye   ᵘPs. 46. 1, 3; Is. 43. 2.
41 so fearful? How is it that ye have no faith? And
they feared exceedingly, and said one to another,
What manner of man is this, that even ᵛthe wind   ᵛJob 38. 11.
and the sea obey him?

language that Satan and his demons were the cause of the storm, and that they are the objects of rebuke. It may be explained, however, by supposing a strong personification. By thus speaking, Jesus showed that the elements were subject to his bidding. Compare Ps. 106 : 9; 89 : 8, 9. **The wind ceased,** as if weary, tired out, and exhausted. And there was a **great calm,** a great stillness; great in contrast to the violent agitation of both air and water, which had just subsided. Jesus with his disciples in the ship is a beautiful emblem of the church tossed and shaken by the tempests of the world, yet always safe; for Jesus is with her to the end. Compare in contrast, Ezekiel, ch. 27, where Tyre is presented under the figure of a vast ship, built, manned, and freighted by the combined skill, strength, beauty, and riches of all nations; but it is broken by the storm and destroyed.

40. Jesus rebukes the troubled hearts of his disciples. Matthew places this before, and Mark and Luke after, the rebuking of the wind. The language comes in perfectly natural while Jesus is rising up from sleep. A part may have been spoken before and a part after the miracle. Thus as he awoke he may have answered their complaining entreaty, "Why are ye fearful, O ye of little faith?" Matt. 8: 26. Then arising and rebuking the elements, he may have added, "Where is your faith?" (Luke 8: 25;) "Why are you so fearful? How is it that you have no faith?" Their earnest entreaty showed that they had a "little faith;" but as their terror arose from want of confidence in the power of Jesus, and so completely unmanned them, it could be said comparatively that they had **no faith.** Meyer notes the fact that Mark more than the other evangelists makes prominent the weakness of the disciples in knowledge and faith, ch. 6 : 52; 7 : 18; 8 : 18, 33; 9 : 6, 19; 10 : 24, 32; 14 : 40; 16 : 8, 11, 13, 14.

41. **They feared exceedingly.**

Literally, *They feared a great fear,* they were greatly terrified. **What manner of man?** Rather, *Who then is this* who exercises such perfect control over the elements of nature? From Matthew (8 : 27) this seems to be the exclamation of the crew or sailors on board. But here, and also in Luke (8 : 25), it appears that the disciples shared in their feelings and exclamations of amazement. They indeed believed in Jesus as the Messiah, but such an exhibition of power confounded them; not only confirmed their previous knowledge and belief of his greatness, but excited within them wondering thoughts regarding his divine origin, power, etc. Compare the exclamation of the mariners on a similar occasion (Matt. 14 : 33), "Of a truth thou art the Son of God."

REMARKS.

1. Jesus taught by the sea-side. So let us sow the good seed beside all waters. The careless will not come to us; we must go to them, ver. 1; Eccle. 11 : 1; Isa. 32 : 20.

2. Natural objects illustrate spiritual truths; and should be studied for this purpose. "We must translate the book of nature into the book of grace."— THOMAS TAYLOR. Vers. 2, 3. Compare Heb. 8 : 5; 9 : 23; Rev. chs. 21, 22.

3. As the seed was sown on all kinds of ground, so is the truth to be preached to all classes of men, vers. 6-9; ch. 16 : 15; Rev. 22 : 17.

4. We should seek the kernel, not the mere shell of the word, ver. 9; John 6 : 63; 2 Cor. 3 : 6.

5. Whatever is dark to us we should take to Jesus, asking the guidance of the Holy Spirit, vers. 10, 13; John 16 : 13; James 1 : 5.

6. The truths of the gospel are of God, and specially intrusted to Christians, ver. 11; Matt. 16 : 17; 1 Cor. 4 : 1; Heb. 1 : 1, 2.

7. Some persons, though living, are given over to destruction, ver. 12; Rom. 1 : 28; Jer. 6 : 30.

A.D. 28. MARK IV. 91

8. Jesus spoke in parables: *First*, to instruct his followers, ver. 11. *Second*, to justly permit the blindness and destruction of the incorrigible, ver. 12. *Third*, to show how to illustrate spiritual by natural things, vers. 13, 34. *Fourth*, to reprove the Jews without too much exciting their rage, ver. 34; Matt. 21 : 45. *Fifth*, to fulfill prophecy, Matt. 13 : 35.

9. Both the sower and the seed are all-important. Without either, no fruit can be expected, ver. 14; Rom. 10 : 14, 15; 1 Pet. 1 : 25.

10. You may delay to attend to your soul, but Satan will not delay in trying to effect your ruin, ver. 15; 2 Cor. 4 : 3, 4; 1 Pet. 5 : 8; 1 Tim. 5 : 15.

11. In the Spirit's work of renewing the heart, sorrow precedes joy. We have reason to suspect some wrong where nothing but joy attends professed conversion, ver. 16, Luke 15 : 17-23; 18 : 13, 14; John 16 : 8; 2 Cor. 7 : 10.

12. Joy without repentance and a change of heart is delusive and short-lived, vers. 16, 17; Job 20 : 5; Ps. 126 : 5; Prov. 15 : 21; Hos. 6 : 4; James 4 : 9.

13. If we would be the Lord's, the idols of the heart must be destroyed. Property, ease, reputation, and even life itself, if they stand in the way of Jesus, must be sacrificed, vers. 18, 19; Ezek. 14 : 3-5; Matt. 5 : 29, 30; Rom. 8 : 7; James 4 : 4; 1 John 2 : 15.

14. When the word of God is truly received into the heart, the soul is subjected and united to Christ, and brings forth fruit to God, ver. 20; Ps. 126 : 6; John 15 : 4, 7, 8; Gal. 5 : 22-24.

15. If we have received spiritual knowledge it is our duty to impart it to others, ver. 21; Jer. 23 : 28; 1 Pet. 4 : 10.

16. All mysteries of God relating to man will be made known at the proper time, ver. 22; 1 Cor. 2 : 7-10 ; Dan. 12 : 9, 10.

17. We must give account to God for the use of our knowledge, ver. 22; Matt. 25 : 24-30; Luke 12 : 47, 48.

18. You are to hear the truth both for your own good and the good of others, ver. 23; Matt 5 : 16; 1 Thess. 5 : 14; 2 Thess. 3 : 13.

19. Beware and not undervalue the ministry and the preaching of the gospel, ver. 24 ; Rom. 10 : 14 ; 1 Thess. 5 : 20; 2 Tim. 4 : 2.

20. Your eternal interests hang upon how and what you hear, vers. 24, 25 ; ch. 16 : 15, 16 ; Rom. 10 : 17 ; Eph. 1 : 13.

21. The diligent use of religious privileges and opportunities will yield a rich return of blessings upon ourselves, vers. 24, 25 ; Prov. 13 : 4 ; 19 : 15 ; 2 Pet. 3 : 14.

22. There is much beyond our comprehension and control in the work of God in the soul, vers. 26, 27 ; John 1 : 13 ; 3 : 8 ; 1 Cor. 2 : 11.

23. We should do our work faithfully, and then commit the results to God, ver. 27 ; Eccle. 11 : 6 ; 1 Cor. 3 : 7 ; 15 : 10 ; Gal. 6 : 9, 10.

24. The work of grace in the heart is gradual and progressive, from a small beginning to ultimate perfection. We should not therefore despise the day of small things, nor be discouraged if present results come short of our expectation, ver. 28 ; 2 Cor. 3 : 18 ; Zech. 4 : 10 ; Matt. 13 : 33.

25. The Christian shall not die, nor the Christian dispensation close till the respective harvest is ripe, ver. 29 ; Job 7 : 1 ; 14 : 14 ; Matt. 13 : 39-43.

26. In working for God we should expect great endings from small beginnings, vers. 31, 32; Isa. 41 : 14-16 ; 51 : 1-4 ; 60 : 22 ; Dan. 2 : 35, 44, 45.

27. "Those who would have devoured Christianity when it was sown in the earth, are now glad to find protection under its wide-spreading branches," ver. 32.

28. Study to adapt your teaching to those under your instruction. Some truths untimely presented will be only misunderstood and perverted, ver. 33 ; John 16 : 12.

29. Seek to be alone with Jesus ; you will learn all that is necessary respecting his truth and kingdom, ver. 34 ; Prov. 2 : 3-9 ; Matt. 6 : 6 ; 11 : 29.

30. Obedience to Christ often leads into a way of trial, vers. 35-37 ; Luke 9 : 59, 60 ; Acts 20 : 22-24.

31. Jesus was human. He needed sleep like others, ver. 38 ; John 4 : 6 ; 1 Tim. 2 : 5 ; Heb. 2 : 14.

32. Jesus was also divine. He was Lord of the wind and the waves, vers. 39-41 ; John 1 : 1 ; Acts 7 : 59 ; 10 : 36 ; Rom. 9 : 5.

33. Even Christians often distrust Christ in his providence, through a want of faith, yet Jesus deals tenderly with them, vers. 38-40 ; Luke 24 : 25 ; John 20 : 27-29.

At Gerasa, Jesus casts out Legion, who enter and destroy the swine.

V. And ˣ they came over unto the other side of the sea, into the country of the Gadarenes. And when he was come out of the ship, immediately there met

ˣ Mt. 8. 28; 9. 1; Lk. 8. 26.

---

34. In the stilling of the tempest we have a four-fold illustration—of Christ with his people of every age; Christ with his church, against which the gates of hell shall not prevail; Christ with the believer through the voyage of life; and Christ with the repenting sinner, allaying his fears through his word of forgiveness, vers. 36–41; Matt. 28 : 20; Eph. 5 : 25–27; John 10 : 27–30; Luke 7 : 37, 38, 47, 48.

CHAPTER V.

In this chapter Mark relates three more most wonderful miracles illustrating most strikingly that Jesus was the Son of God, ch. 1 : 1. In connection with stilling the tempest (ch. 4 : 35–41) these miracles show the power of Jesus over the elements of nature, the powers of darkness, incurable diseases, and the realm of death.

1–21. HEALING OF THE GADARENE DEMONIAC. After which he returns to the western side of the lake. Matt. 8 : 28 to 9 : 1; Luke 8 : 26–40. The account of Matthew is the briefest; that of Mark the fullest and most vivid. We have here one of the many proofs that Mark's Gospel is not a mere summary of Matthew's, but an independent narrative of an eye-witness.

1. **Other side of the sea.** The eastern side. **Country of the Gadarenes.** According to the highest critical authorities, *country of the Gerasenes;* so also in Luke 8 : 26. But in Matt. 8 : 28 the most approved reading is "country of Gadarenes." It should be added, however, that there is some manuscript authority for reading *Gergesenes* in Mark, and especially in Matthew and Luke. *Gadara,* now *Umkeis,* was a city of Perea, a chief city of Decapolis, about seven or eight miles southeast of the Sea of Galilee. The territory or "*the country*" of Gadara could well extend to the lake. The hill on which the city was located could not, however, have been the scene of the miracle; for it was not near enough to the lake, and besides the swine would have had to run down the mountain, ford the Hieromax (now the *Jermuk*), a river as deep and rapid as the Jordan, and then cross a plain several miles before reaching the sea. *Gerasa,* now *Jerash,* on the eastern boundary of Perea, was a town of Decapolis, about forty miles southeast of the scene of the miracle. Josephus describes it as rich and populous. Most beautiful and extensive ruins now mark its site. A large tract of country adjacent to the city, possibly extending to the Sea of Galilee, may have borne its name. Jerome states that in his day Gilead was called Gerasa. *Gergesa,* according to Origen, was a city that stood on the eastern shore of the Sea of Galilee. Some reference to its ancient inhabitants may possibly have been made by Girgashites in Josh. 3 : 10. Its ruins, now called *Gersa,* may now be seen on the eastern shore of the lake, about midway between the entrance and the outlet of the Jordan. "It is within a few rods of the shore, and an immense mountain rises directly above it, in which are ancient tombs. . . . The lake is so near the base of the mountain, that the swine rushing madly down it could not stop, but would be hurried on into the water and drowned."—DR. THOMSON, *The Land and the Book,* vol. ii., pp. 35, 36. The name as pronounced by the Arabs is very nearly the ancient Gergesa or Gerasa. Hence *the country of the Gerasenes* is best explained as referring to the district of this city on the shore of the lake. The country of Gergesa or Gerasa, probably joined upon that of Gadara; and as the limits of the territory of each city were not very accurately defined, Matthew could call it the country of the Gadarenes, and Mark and Luke the country of the Gerasenes.

2. **When he was come out . . . immediately.** As he came out of the ship, as he landed, immediately the demoniac **met** him. This shows that the miracle was performed near the

him out of the tombs a man with an unclean spirit,
3 who had *his* dwelling among the tombs; and no man
4 could bind him, no, not with chains: because that he had been often bound with fetters and chains, and the chains had been plucked asunder by him, and the fetters broken in pieces: neither could any
5 *man* tame him. And always, night and day, he was in the mountains, and in the tombs, crying, and cutting himself with stones.
6 But when he saw Jesus afar off, he ran and wor-

shore. **Out of the tombs.** The sepulchres of the Hebrews were generally cut out of the solid rock. Caves were also used for this purpose. They are now often resorted to for shelter during the night. And sometimes the wandering Arabs take up their winter abode in them. Compare Judges 6 : 2. A maniac too is sometimes found dwelling in them. **A man.** Matthew says, "two possessed with devils." This, however, is no contradiction, for he who speaks of the two includes the one, and they who speak of the one do not deny that there were two. One of them may have been more prominent and afterward well known to many, and hence may have been only noticed by Mark and Luke. He only may have gone forth publishing the great things done for him, ver. 20; Luke 8 : 39. **With an unclean spirit.** Demonized, in the power and possession of demons. See on ch. 1 : 23.

3. Mark in this and the two following verses describes with great particularity this most terrible case of demoniacal possession recorded in the Gospels. No others are represented as possessing such muscular strength, such abandonment of all society, and such savage and uncontrollable ferocity. **Among the tombs.** Rather, *In the tombs.* Luke (8 : 27) says this possession had been for a long time, and that he wore no clothes. **No man could bind him.** According to the highest critical authorities, *No one could any longer bind him.* His case had been growing worse till he could be no longer confined, binding *even with chains* proving ineffectual.

4. Facts corroborating the last clause of the preceding verse. **Fetters,** or shackles, especially for the feet, though they may be applied to any part of the body. **Chains** specially for binding prisoners. **Plucked asunder.** Torn apart. **Broken in pieces.** Crushed together and thus broken in pieces. **Neither could any man tame him.** No one was able, strong enough, to tame him. No one could subdue him, bring him physically and mentally under his power. Matthew (8 : 28) says that he was "exceeding fierce, so that no man might pass that way."

5. How he spent his time. **Always, night and day.** He was all the time, by night as well as by day. He was sleepless. *In the mountains,* etc. According to the oldest and best manuscripts, *In the tombs and in the mountains.* He did not confine himself to the tombs, which are numerous all along that region, but also wandered outside in the mountains of that vicinity. **Crying.** *Crying out* in a terrible manner, in ferocity, terror, and pain. **Cutting himself with stones,** with the sharp pieces of stones found in tombs and mountains. What a fearful description of demoniacal madness! Wildly roaming in tombs and in solitary places, uttering the oft-repeated scream; and every now and then, as if contending with some foe, rending his own flesh. Under the power of demons he is no longer guided by the law of self-preservation.

6. **Saw Jesus afar off.** Relatively from afar. In the distance, probably from the side of the mountain where were the tombs, ver. 2. **He ran,** it may be, at first with the purpose of assaulting him; but the demons recognized Christ's divine nature, or at least felt his superhuman influence, and **worshipped him,** *bowed down to him, did him reverence.* The word translated *worship* literally means *to kiss the hand to any one* as an expression of reverence and homage. It was especially applied to express the Oriental form of salutation

7 shipped him, and cried with a loud voice, and said, What have I to do with thee, Jesus, *thou* Son of ʸ the most high God? I adjure thee by God, that thou
8 torment me not. For he said unto him, ᶻ Come out
9 of the man, *thou* unclean spirit. And he asked him, What *is* thy name? And he answered, saying, My
10 name *is* Legion: for we are many. And he besought him much that he would not send them away out of the country.

ʸ Ge. 14. 22; Heb. 7. 1; Ac. 16. 17; Jam. 2. 19.
ᶻ 1 John 3. 8; 2 Pet. 2. 4; Jude 6.

of an inferior, by prostration of the face to the ground, kissing at the same time the hand toward the superior. It thus denoted the reverence paid to teachers and the homage paid to kings. When the object of homage was God, it denoted worship, or adoration. When our common version was prepared, the English word *worship*, like the Greek original, was applicable to men as well as to God. Thus in Luke 14 : 10 to "have worship" means to "have honor." Here the word refers to his bowing down, doing the act of reverence; for demons cannot be said in any true sense to worship God. Thus he whom no one could tame prostrates himself in reverence before the Son of God. Demons believe and tremble (James 2 : 19), while unbelieving Jews blaspheme, ch. 3 : 22.

7. In this act of reverence **he cried with a loud voice.** He gave one of his unearthly shrieks, ver. 5. **And said.** Thus the demons speak through the man, so thorough was their control over both his body and soul, **What have I to do with thee.** What is there in common between thee and me? Why interfere with me? Ezra 4 : 3. See on ch. 1 : 24. The use of the singular here may be explained by supposing the chief or commander of these unclean spirits as speaking. **Son of the most high God.** Evidently recognizing his divine nature. Compare on ch. 1 : 1. **I adjure thee.** I charge thee with the most earnest entreaty in the name of God; I conjure thee by God. **That thou torment me not.** The presence of Jesus, sending the demons from the man (see next verse), or sending them into the abyss, or hell (Luke 8 : 31), were each and all a torment to the demon. Matthew (8 : 29) adds "before the time," that is of final doom, Matt. 25 : 41; 2 Pet. 2 : 4; Jude 6.

8. Mark here throws in the reason of this remarkable and importunate adjuration. **For he said,** or *was saying* Jesus had just before this cry commanded the unclean spirit to come out of the man. This itself was a source of torment, and excited the guilty fears of the demon of something more terrible. Demons seem to have been less miserable in human possession than without it. It should be noted that the unclean spirit did not come out immediately upon Christ's command. This was not owing to the strength of the demons, or to any inability in Jesus; but to his wisdom, who permitted the unclean spirit to speak imploringly, tell his name, and the great number under him. Thus the great power of Jesus was the more strikingly manifested to his disciples, and for all time.

9. **Ask him,** the unclean spirit who had spoken through the man, ver. 7. **What is thy name?** Jesus did not ask this for his own information; but to show the miserable condition of the man, and the great combined power of demons, which he was about to overcome. **Legion.** The Roman legion consisted of about six thousand. The word had come to signify any large number with the ideas of order and subordination. It is about equivalent to *host,* and explained by the unclean spirit himself: **for we are many.** One chief, superior one, with inferior ones under him. He gives his name as associated with subordinate spirits. It shows his overwhelming power over the entire nature of the man. That evil spirits go often in companies is to be inferred not only from this, but also from the case of Mary Magdalene, from whom were cast out seven demons, Luke 8 : 2. How many demons there were in this case we have no means of knowing; although the number of the swine, two thousand (ver. 13), may be suggestive of the number of demons.

10. **He besought him much.** Earnest in his entreaty. An unclean

11 Now there was there nigh unto the mountains a
12 great herd of swine feeding. And all the devils besought him, saying, Send us into the swine, that we
13 may enter into them. And forthwith Jesus gave them leave. And the unclean spirits went out, and entered into the swine: and the herd ran violently down a steep place into the sea, (they were about

spirit at prayer! Yet many men are prayerless. **Not send them away out of the country,** where they had been so long, and exercised so much power. That district east of the Sea of Galilee was inhabited with a mingled population of Jews and Gentiles. A country where so many swine were kept, and in which business Jews may have directly or indirectly participated contrary to Mosaic law (Lev. 11 : 7, 8), was pleasing to the demons. Luke (8 : 31) adds "not command them to go into the deep" or *abyss*, the abode of lost spirits, Rev. 9 : 1, 11; 20 : 3.

11. Nigh unto the mountains. Rather, *by the mountain*, on a slope of the mountain, ver. 13. This is entirely consistent with Luke (8 : 32), "on (*in*) the mountain;" and with Matthew (8 : 30), "a good way off from them," a relative expression, which may be applied to a greater or less distance, according to circumstances and the particular feelings of the beholder at the time.

12. The best text has *they*, instead of **all the devils,** and omits **forthwith** in next verse. They do not ask to be made better; but as they must depart from the man, they ask permission to enter the swine.

Send us. They recognize the power of Jesus, as Lord. They do not demand, but entreat him as one who can do with them as he saw fit. Luke (8 : 32) uses the verb "suffer," or permit them to enter. **Swine.** These unclean brutes were congenial with their unclean natures. How they could possess inferior animals is not difficult to imagine, since they so thoroughly possessed the lower and sensual nature of men. They could exert no moral and intellectual influence, as in man; but they could operate through the organs of their bodies, and through their animal and sensual natures.

13. Forthwith Jesus gave them leave. Jesus did not *send* them, but *permitted* them, and the permission was immediate. Why he did this we are not informed. The requests of Satan are sometimes granted (Job 1 : 12; 2 : 6), but always for some good purpose in the end. By giving them this permission it was clearly shown that demons do exist, that those possessed with demons were not simply insane, or suffering from mere bodily disease. It also showed the power and malignity of these fiends of darkness, and their subjection to Christ, who "was manifested that he might destroy the works of the devil," John 3 : 8. Their final and utter overthrow was foreshadowed.

The herd ran violently down a steep place. *Rushed down* the overhanging *steep*. The declivity at the base of the mountain at Gersa is said to be almost perpendicular. "The bluff behind is so steep, and the shore so narrow, that a herd of swine, rushing frantically down, must certainly have been overwhelmed in the sea before they could recover themselves."
—Mr. Tristram, *Land of Israel,* p. 466.

About two thousand. An estimated round number. That so many should at once have rushed into the sea and been drowned shows supernatural power. **Choked.** Strangled in the sea, resulting in their death; Matthew (8 : 32) definitely says, "perished in the waters."

This miracle and that of the withered fig-tree which Jesus cursed (ch. 11 : 12-14, 20) are the only ones which resulted in any destruction of property. Cavillers have seized hold of these in their objections to Christianity. But Christ as the Son of God had a right to send the demons wherever he pleased. The cattle of a thousand hills were also his (Ps. 50 : 10), and he had a right to do what he would with his own, Matt. 20 : 15. "The act was one of sovereign authority attested by the miracle itself, and, so far as we can learn, not disputed by the persons injured, however much they might lament their loss and wish

14 two thousand;) and were choked in the sea. And they that fed the swine fled, and told *it* in the city, and in the country. And they went out to see what
15 it was that was done. And they come to Jesus, and see him that was possessed with the devil, and had the legion, ᵃsitting, and clothed, and in his right
16 mind: and they were afraid. And they that saw *it* told them how it befell to him that was possessed
17 with the devil, and *also* concerning the swine. And ᵇthey began to pray him to depart out of their coasts.

ᵃ Col. 1. 13; 2 Tim. 1. 7.

ᵇ Mt. 8. 34; Ac. 16. 39.

---

to avoid its repetition. There is no more need of any special vindication here than in the case of far more serious inflictions of the same kind by disease or accident."—ALEXANDER. Besides, the permission was our Lord's; the destruction of the swine, the work of demons. Jesus was no more responsible for what the demons did than he is for what wicked men do, whom he permits to live and to hold positions of power in the world. We must believe that Jesus had wise and good reasons for this permission, as for all he ever did or permitted. The owners may have in various ways showed contempt for the Mosaic law, and hence this judgment upon them. This may have been a special providential sermon for the people of that city and vicinity.

14. **The feeders of the swine,** astonished and affrighted at the frenzied destruction of the whole herd in the sea, flee and *report* the catastrophe to the owners **in the city and in the country,** or *fields.* Gersa and vicinity are doubtless meant. From Matt. 8 : 33 it appears that they also told "what was befallen to the possessed with devils." Their haste in fleeing did not give them much time for this. But they doubtless saw and heard the demoniac at the base of the mountain, and from his changed deportment inferred some of the facts of the case. The people at once went out to see for themselves **what it was that was done.** Such a wonderful occurrence would quickly call out a crowd. Matthew (8 : 34) says "the whole city came out to meet Jesus."

15. The mass of people come to Jesus, and **see him that was possessed,** look upon him with surprise and amazement. **And had the legion.** One who had been such a maniac and such a terror to that country. He may have been known by that name in that region. It is not really necessary, however, to suppose this. The order of the original is very striking, " sitting and clothed and in his right mind, him who had the legion." That he who for a long time had been a raving maniac, living like a wild man, and wearing no clothing (Luke 8 : 27) should be calmly **sitting** at the feet of Jesus (Luke 8 : 35) **clothed** like others with raiment, and **in his right mind,** with a sane or sound mind, was indeed a matter of astonishment. Hence **they were afraid,** they were awestruck at such an exhibition of supernatural power, and in the presence of one possessed with greater power than legion.

16. **They that saw it.** Those who had been eye-witnesses; probably those who had come with Jesus across the lake, and possibly other spectators with them not mentioned. The keepers of the swine, who fled and told the owners, doubtless returned with the people, but they were probably not able to relate so particularly the circumstances as those who had been nearer the scene of the miracle. **Told them how,** etc. Gave a detailed account of the two main facts, the healing of the demoniac, and the destruction of the swine. The herdsmen had *reported* the occurrences (ver. 14); now the eye-witnesses relate **how it befell him,** the circumstances, and by whose power they occurred.

17. The effect of the miracle upon the people. Upon seeing and hearing what was done **they began to pray,** *entreat, beseech* **him to depart out of their coasts,** their borders. *Coasts* ordinarily means in Scripture, vicinity, adjacent district, and is well

A.D. 28.   MARK V.   97

18 And when he was come into the ship, ^c he that had been possessed with the devil prayed him that
19 he might be with him. Howbeit Jesus suffered him not, but saith unto him, ^d Go home to thy friends, and tell them how great things the Lord hath done
20 for thee, and hath had compassion on thee. And he departed, and began to publish in Decapolis ^e how great things Jesus had done for him: and all men did marvel.

^c Ps. 116. 12; Lk. 8. 38 · 17. 15–17.

^d Ps. 66, 16; 103. 1-4; Is. 38. 9–20; Jon. 2. 9.

^e Ps. 126. 3.

---

expressed by *borders*. Luke (8 : 37) adds the special reason for this strange request, "for they were taken with great fear." They were not only filled with a superstitious awe at such exhibitions of power (compare Deut. 5 : 25; Luke 5 : 8), but with fear that similar results might attend other miracles. Other owners of swine may have thought their traffic in danger, Acts 19 : 24–31. To what extremes do worldly interests excite men! Worldly gain is valued above the blessings of Jesus. To their minds the loss of the herd of swine more than counterbalanced the cure of the demoniac! Jesus answers their prayer and lets them alone. We do not read of his ever visiting them again.

18. **And when he was come,** etc. *And as he was entering* the ship or boat, the demoniac **prayed him,** *entreated, besought* him, that **he might be with him.** A variety of reasons doubtless united in leading him to make this request. It was the warm expression and desire of gratitude and love. The mean and selfish request and treatment of the Gerasenes doubtless strengthened this feeling and desire. Very likely, too, he might have feared a repossession by the demons after Jesus departed. Matt. 12 : 43–45.

19. **Jesus suffered him not.** The demons pray, and their prayers are granted to their own discomfiture, vers. 10, 12; the Gerasenes pray, and their prayer also is granted by being left to their own destruction; the man who had been healed prays, and behold his petition is not granted, for it was not best, and he had a work to do. **Go home.** Literally, *Go into thy house.* Where is not told, possibly at Gadara. It was somewhere in Decapolis, ver. 20. *To thy friends:* thy relatives, thy kindred. **Tell them.** There is a time to speak and a time to keep silent,

ver. 43, ch. 1 : 44. The proclamation of his miracles often increased the multitude to his great inconvenience, ch. 1 : 45; 2 : 2; 3 : 9, 10. But here Jesus was about to leave the country. The healed man would be a living witness of the goodness and mercy of Jesus to that whole region against the evil reports of herdsmen and swine-owners. A reason for this command may doubtless also be found in the man himself. It was for his good to go to his home and announce the facts of his deliverance. His friends at home needed the spiritual blessings of which he was probably a partaker, and he needed the development which such activity would produce. And nowhere could the great cure be so much appreciated as in his own house. **The Lord.** God, and applicable to Jesus, ch. 16 : 19, 20. The healed man seems to apply it to Jesus, in the next verse. It is quite likely that he had some idea of Christ's divine nature, since the demon had called him the Son of the Most High God, ver. 7. **Had mercy.** Had pity, compassion on thee. He, unworthy, had enjoyed a compassion freely bestowed. He had very probably received spiritual as well as bodily deliverance. Hence he was truly a representative of Jesus to the inhabitants of his country, Matt. 25 : 45. His commission rather implies his belief in Jesus as the Messiah.

20. Obedient to Christ's command, the healed demoniac began to publish what Jesus had done for him, not only to his own house, but in that whole region lying east and south-east of the Sea of Galilee, called **Decapolis,** a name meaning *the ten cities.* After the Roman conquest of Syria, ten cities appear to have been endowed with peculiar privileges, and the country around them called Decapolis. In the enumeration of these cities the learned

9

21 ᶠ AND when Jesus was passed over again by ship unto the other side, much people gathered unto him: and he was nigh unto the sea.

ᶠ Mt. 9. 1; Lk. 8. 40.

Jesus raises to life Jairus' daughter; and heals a woman with an issue of blood.

22 ᵍ And, behold, there cometh one of the rulers of the synagogue, Jairus by name; and when he saw
23 him, he fell at his feet, and besought him greatly, saying, My little daughter lieth at the point of death:

ᵍ Mt. 9. 18; Lk. 8. 41.

are not agreed, which may arise from the same privileges being accorded to other neighboring cities. They are generally reckoned as follows: Damascus, Philadelphia, Raphana, Scythopolis, Gadara, Hippos, Dion, Pella, Gerasa, Canatha. Only one of these, Scythopolis, was in Galilee. The rest were east of the Jordan, and mainly in that part of Palestine occupied by the half-tribe of Manasseh. **All did marvel.** No glorifying God, no conversions, are recorded. The great miracle excited wonder, but led not to repentance and faith. Something more than miracles are needed to reach and savingly benefit the heart. Still the healed demoniac may have accomplished a work preparatory to the future proclamation of the gospel.

21. Jesus having returned **to the other side,** the western side of the sea, **much people,** a great multitude, gathered to him. He was **nigh unto the sea,** by the seaside, probably near Capernaum, Matt. 9:1.

22-43. RAISING OF JAIRUS' DAUGHTER; HEALING OF THE WOMAN WITH THE ISSUE OF BLOOD. Matt. 9:18-26; Luke 8:41-56. Mark again is the fullest and most graphic of the three evangelists. According to Matt. 9:17, 18, these miracles were performed immediately after Christ's discourse on fasting at Matthew's feast. The position of this section then would be just after Mark 2:22 and Luke 5:39. See on ver. 43. For some reason unknown to us Mark and Luke may have deferred this account till after the healing of the demoniac, possibly to bring together these wonderful miracles on opposite sides of the lake, placing last the greatest miracle, the raising of the dead. Or we may suppose that Christ's discourse on fasting (Matt. 9:14-17; Mark 2:18-22;

Luke 5:33-39) finds its position at this point between the healing of the demoniac and the raising of Jairus' daughter. Some suppose that Matthew's feast also (ch. 2:15-22) finds its true position here. But every arrangement is beset with difficulty. Did we know more of the circumstances, all would be plain. See author's Harmony, notes on §§ 46, 47, 48.

22. **And behold, there cometh.** According to the highest critical authorities, *And there cometh.* These words do not necessarily connect this in time with the preceding miracle. The meaning may be, "And on a certain occasion there cometh." Or, taking the last clause of the preceding verse, *On a time he was by the sea, surrounded with crowds, and there cometh.* According to Matthew (9:10, 14, 18) Jesus seems to have been in the house of Matthew, ch. 2:15. But it is not necessary to suppose the whole or even a part of Christ's discourse on fasting to have been delivered in the house; see on ch. 2:16. It may have been given after coming forth from Matthew's feast, in a public place. **One of the rulers of the synagogue.** One of the elders and presiding officers, who convened the assembly, preserved order, invited readers and speakers, Acts 13:15. **Jairus,** probably the Hebrew name Jair (Num. 32:41), meaning *whom Jehovah enlightens.* **And when he saw him.** Literally, *And seeing him.* The use of the present gives vividness to the narrative. It would seem that Jairus did not see him at once, but, making his way through the crowd, he at length saw him and **fell at his feet,** in the posture of reverence and earnest entreaty. The present is still used, *he falleth.*

23. **Besought him greatly.** Be-

I pray thee, come and lay thy hands on her, that she 24 may be healed; and she shall live. And *Jesus* went with him; and much people followed him, and thronged him.

25 And a certain woman, ʰ which had an issue of
26 blood twelve years, and had suffered many things of many physicians, and had spent all that she had, ⁱ and was nothing bettered, but rather grew worse,
27 when she had heard of Jesus, came in the press

ʰ Le. 15. 25; Mt. 9. 20.

ⁱ Ps. 108. 12.

sought him much, the same words in the original as in ver. 10. **My little daughter.** Twelve years of age, ver. 42. An only daughter, Luke 8 : 42. **Lieth at the point of death.** In the last extremity. "She lay a dying," Luke 8 : 42. But Matthew (9 : 18), "is even now dead." The father on reaching Jesus may have first given vent to his fears by the strong statement she "is even now dead," or rather, *has just now died;* and then have explained himself by saying that she was at the point of death or dying. **I pray thee.** Implied in the original, *I beseech thee*, therefore, *in order that thou mayest come*, etc. His strong faith is shown by his leaving his dying daughter to seek the aid of Jesus, and by his earnest entreaty. Yet he seems to have thought that personal contact was necessary, **lay thy hands on her.** His faith was not of so high a type as that of the centurion at Capernaum, Matt. 8 : 8–10. **And she shall live.** According to the highest critical authorities, *and live*, without any punctuation before it, thus: "that she may be healed and live."

24. Jesus immediately complies with the request and goes with Jairus. **Much people,** a great multitude, such as so often attended him, followed and **thronged him,** *was pressing upon him* (ch. 3 : 9), so that, doubtless, he could not walk without difficulty. The time and place of the miracle upon the woman.

25. At this point Matthew, Mark, and Luke relate the healing of a woman having a chronic disease, which according to the law rendered her unclean, Lev. 15 : 25. The details of her grievous disorder are unnecessary. Her hopeless case and the incurableness of her disease are shown in this and the next verse. It was of long continuance, chronic, **twelve years.**

26. **Suffered many things.** *Suffered much* **of many physicians.** There was a medical profession and many practitioners. This woman had probably been possessed of wealth, and had moved in good society, but the expenses of many physicians had reduced her to poverty. She had suffered much not only from her disease, but from their prescriptions. Although she had emphatically spent **all,** yet she was **nothing bettered,** *not at all benefited*, and the hopelessness of her case is indicated by the fact that she **rather grew worse.** How pitiable her condition! excluded from society and suffering from an incurable disease.

27. But having heard of Jesus, the wonderful cures he had wrought, and that he was in the crowd, she had faith in his power to heal her. She approaches him in the **press,** *crowd*, from **behind,** both from a sense of her unworthiness and her uncleanness, and also to escape observation, and **touched his garment,** his mantle, outer garment. And but the fringe of the garment, Matt. 9 : 20; Luke 8 : 44; Lev. 15 : 38. "It is important, though it may be difficult, to realize the situation of this woman, once possessed of health and wealth, and no doubt moving in respectable society, now beggared and diseased, without a hope of human help, and secretly believing in the power of Christ, and him alone, to heal her, yet deterred by some natural misgiving and by shame, perhaps connected with the nature of her malady, from coming with the rest to be publicly recognized and then relieved. However commonplace the case may seem to many, there are some in whose experience, when clearly seen and seriously attended to, it touches a mysterious cord of painful sympathy."—ALEXANDER.

28 behind, and touched his garment. For she said, If I
29 may touch but his clothes, I shall be whole. And straightway the fountain of her blood was dried up; and she felt in *her* body that she was healed of that
30 plague. And Jesus, immediately knowing in himself that ᵏ virtue had gone out of him, turned him about in the press, and said, Who touched my
31 clothes? And his disciples said unto him, Thou seest the multitude thronging thee, and sayest thou,
32 Who touched me? And he looked round about to

ᵏ Lk. 6. 19; 8. 46; 2 Ki. 13. 21.

---

28. The reason of her approaching and touching Christ's garment. **For she said.** She was saying to or within herself, she thought, Matt. 9 : 21. **If I may touch,** if I touch **but his clothes,** only, even his garments, no matter which or what part, **I shall be whole,** healed of my disease. Her faith is vividly presented by revealing the thoughts of her heart. Like Jairus (ver. 23) she thought there must be some contact with Jesus. She believingly and modestly desired to touch only his garments. There may be true faith, and even strong faith, amid much superstition.

29. **Straightway,** etc. The cure in this verse is described as instantaneous and complete. **Was dried up.** The deep-rooted disease was thoroughly cured. **And she knew,** per*ceived* in her body, by the peculiar sensations she experienced, that health was restored, that she was healed of **that plague,** or *scourge*, ch. 3 : 10.

30. **Jesus immediately,** etc. Upon this woman's touch and cure, *immediately Jesus* **turned about in the press,** or *crowd*, **knowing,** *perceiving* in himself that **virtue,** rather *power*, had gone forth from him. He had an inward consciousness of the fact. He knew it intellectually. The words do not imply that the power went out involuntarily. Others touched him, but felt no saving influence, because theirs was not in faith. Her cure was the result and answer of her touch of faith, which reached beyond the fringe of his garment to his divine nature. Compare ch. 6 : 56; Luke 6 : 19. Within that nature there was the inherent power to cure diseases, and a knowledge of all that was going on. He permitted power to go forth to the healing of the woman when her faith was properly exercised. That it went forth without his permission and direction is not required by the language; and at the same time is inconsistent with his divinity, as well as absurd. **Who touched my clothes?** The question implies neither ignorance nor dissimulation in Jesus. It was asked in order to call forth the confession of the woman for her own good and the good of others. Compare Luke 24 : 17-19, where Jesus asks questions of the two on their way to Emmaus, not for his own information, but to draw out a statement of their views and feelings. So a judge asks the prisoner whether he is guilty or not guilty, though he may know the certainty of his guilt. Compare Gen. 3 : 9; 2 Kings 5 : 25.

31. A general denial by the multitude followed. Luke 8 : 45. The question seemed unreasonable, uncalled for. **And his disciples said.** "Peter and they that were with him," Luke 8 : 45. His immediate followers who believed on him. It was much like Peter thus to speak, both for himself and as spokesman for the disciples. Very likely others may have repeated the same exclamation of wonder and surprise, when the multitude was all the time thronging him. But Jesus affirmed that some one had touched him, implying a touch of intention and faith, and not a mere thoughtless and accidental *pressing* of the multitude, for he perceived that power had gone out from him, Luke 8 : 46.

32. **He looked around to see her.** He was not in doubt regarding the object of his search; the very gender implies his knowledge, "to see *her*." Luke (8 : 47) also confirms when he says, "When the woman saw she was not hid." Jesus knew, and now by his look he brings out the confession. Compare his look upon Peter, Luke 22 : 61.

33 see her that had done this thing. But the woman fearing and trembling, knowing what was done in her, came and fell down before him, and told him
34 all the truth. And he said unto her, Daughter, ¹ thy faith hath made thee whole; go in peace, and be whole of thy plague.
35 ᵐ While he yet spake, there came from the ruler of the synagogue's *house certain* which said, Thy daughter is dead: why troublest thou ⁿ the Master
36 any further? As soon as Jesus heard the word that was spoken, he saith unto the ruler of the synagogue,

¹ ch. 10. 52; Mt. 9. 22; Ac. 14. 9.

ᵐ Lk. 8. 49.

ⁿ Mt. 26. 18; John 11. 28, 32.

---

33. The effect of his searching question and look upon the woman. **Fearing and trembling.** The trembling was the result, the outward manifestation, of her fear, which arose from a sense of his greatness and of her own unworthiness; from her stealthy method of obtaining a cure, and his manner of searching her out. In humility and reverence she **fell down**, prostrated herself before him, giving herself up to his power and mercy, and **told him all the truth**, candidly and publicly (Luke 8 : 47) acknowledged what she had done, why she did it, and with what effect. Thus while Jesus permitted her, in her timidity and sense of shame, to receive his saving power secretly, he called out a public acknowledgment after that power had been experienced.

"Nature may shrink back and wish to spare itself the shame of acknowledging its moral pollution, but this weakness must be conquered, and the tide of love and thankfulness permitted to flow out, full and free, to the glory of divine grace. A genuine faith, though untaught, unspoken, and perhaps slightly superstitious, may receive the first blessing; but then it must be spoken, and taught and tested. It can not remain under the soil, but must shoot up into the face of the sky, and live in the light of day."—A. HOVEY, *Miracles of Christ*, p. 168.

34. Having drawn from the woman a proper confession, Jesus now speaks words of comfort, and confirms the miracle. **Daughter.** A term of kindness, like the word "son" in ch. 2 : 5, and doubtless expressive of a spiritual relation sustained to him, 2 Cor. 6 : 18; Heb. 2 : 10. **Thy faith,** etc. According to Matthew (9 : 22) he adds, "Be of good comfort." Jesus makes her faith prominent, though imperfect, as the condition or means of her cure. His divine power had been exerted according to her faith. **Go in peace.** A usual form of parting salutation, especially to inferiors, expressive of friendship and good wishes, Exod. 4 : 18; 1 Sam. 1 : 17; Luke 7 : 50; James 2 : 16. Literally, *Go away into peace*, into a state of serenity and freedom from thy former bodily and spiritual sufferings. He dismisses her with his blessing. **Be whole of thy plague.** The healing is thus publicly and solemnly ratified. The cure should be permanent.

35. **While he yet spake.** How long these moments of delay must have seemed to the anxious Jairus! But in the midst of them, while Jesus was still speaking to the woman, messengers came from the ruler's house announcing the death of his daughter. **Why troublest thou,** etc. It appears that Jairus had come with the knowledge and consent of his family. **Master.** *Teacher*, see ch. 4 : 38.

36. **As soon as Jesus heard,** etc. Rather, *Jesus having overheard* the message, which was spoken as in private to Jairus. Such details show the accuracy of Mark, and give vividness to the narrative. From words of peace and blessing to the woman, Jesus turns to give comfort to Jairus and encourage his faith. **Be not afraid,** as if there was no hope and all were lost. **Only believe** in my power to help you, and save your daughter. According to Luke (8 : 50), Jesus added, "she shall be made whole," *saved*, recovered. He encourages his faith to expect the recovery of his daughter, though somewhat indefinitely. *How*, and really *from what*, Jairus might still be in doubt.

37 Be not afraid, °only believe. And he suffered no man to follow him, P save Peter, and James, and
38 John the brother of James. And he cometh to the house of the ruler of the synagogue, and seeth the tumult, and them that wept and wailed greatly.
39 And when he was come in, he saith unto them, Why make ye this ado, and weep? The damsel is not
40 dead, but q sleepeth. And r they laughed him to scorn. s But when he had put them all out, he

° 2 Chr. 20. 20; John 11. 40; Rom. 4. 18, 24.
P Mt. 17. 1.

q John 11. 11; Ac. 20. 10.
r Ge. 19. 14.
s Ac. 9. 40; 1 Ki. 17. 19, 20; 2 Ki. 4. 33.

37. Only **Peter, James, and John** are now suffered to go with him and Jairus. The multitude and other disciples, doubtless learning that the child was dead, were the more easily prevailed upon to stay from following Jesus. These three formed Christ's innermost circle of disciples. They were afterward selected to be present at his transfiguration (ch. 9 : 2), and his agony in the garden, ch. 14 : 33. Thus were they fitted to be foremost in labors and sufferings, Acts 2 : 14 ; 3 : 3, 4 ; 4 : 3, 13 ; 8 : 14 ; 12 : 2, 3.

38. **He cometh . . . and seeth.** According to the oldest and best manuscripts, *They come . . . and he seeth.* **The tumult,** *a tumult,* an uproar, a noise of loud lamentation, such as commonly attended a funeral. **Wailed greatly,** *howling,* or lamenting much. According to Matt. 9 : 23, the flute-players were performing their doleful music. The custom of mourning for the dead and at funerals is alluded to in such passages as Eccle. 12 : 5 ; Jer. 9 : 17 ; 16 : 6, 7 ; Ezek. 24 : 17 ; Amos 5 : 16. Similar customs still prevail in the East. "It is customary, when a member of a family is about to die, for the friends to assemble around, and watch the ebbing away of life, so as to mark the precise moment when he breathes his last; upon which they set up instantly a united outcry, attended with weeping and often with beating the breast, and tearing out the hair of the head. . . . How exactly, at the moment of the Savior's arrival, did the house of Jairus correspond with the condition of one at the present time in which a death has just taken place! It resounded with the same boisterous expression of grief, for which the nations of the East are still noted. The lamentation must also have commenced at the instant of the child's decease ; for when Jesus arrived he found the mourners present, and singing the death-dirge."—HACKETT, *Illustration of Scripture,* p. 122. In the East burial generally takes place very soon after death. The ancient Jews commonly buried a person the same day that he died. Compare Acts 5 : 5–10.

39. **And when he was come in.** *And coming in* where the mourners were, he at once says to them, **Why make ye this ado,** *this tumult,* clamor, uproar. **The damsel.** Rather, *Little child.* It is interesting to note the several terms by which the daughter is designated, thus : "Little daughter," ver. 23; "daughter," ver. 35; "the little child," vers. 39, 40, 41 ; "damsel," 41, 42; also "an only daughter," Luke 8 : 42 ; "maiden," Luke 8 : 54. In this we discover a pleasing diversity.

Is not dead, but sleepeth. Regard her not as dead, but sleeping, for she is soon to come to life again. Some suppose her death only apparent, that she was in a swoon, or state of unconsciousness like one dead. But according to Luke 8 : 53–55, not only did the mourners *know* that she was dead, but at the command of Jesus *her spirit returned.* Jesus used a similar verb when he said, "Lazarus sleepeth," which he explained to mean death, John 11 : 11, 14. It is true that the verb in the latter passage is the one generally used for describing death as a sleep, Matt. 27 : 52 ; Acts 7 : 60 ; 13 : 36, etc. ; but we find the verb of this passage used also of the dead in 1 Thess. 5 : 10. Jesus also allowed the parents and others to regard the damsel as really dead and raised to life again, Luke 8 : 52, 53, 56. In relation to his power, death was only a sleep from which she should be speedily awakened.

40. The company of mourners was certain that the child was dead, and understanding neither the language nor the power of Jesus, **laughed him to**

taketh the father and the mother of the damsel, and them that were with him, and entereth in where the
41 damsel was lying. And he took the damsel by the hand, and said unto her, Talitha cumi; which is, being interpreted, Damsel, I say unto thee, arise.
42 And straightway the damsel arose, and walked; for she was *of the age* of twelve years. And they were
43 astonished with a great astonishment. And ᵇ he charged them straitly that no man should know it; and commanded that something should be given her to eat.

ᵇ ch. 3. 12; Mt. 8. 4; 9. 30; 12. 16; 17. 9; Lk. 5. 14.

---

scorn, in derision. The crowd of noisy mourners and deriders are put forth. With the consent of the ruler, Jesus orders them to leave, and they depart. He had entered the house (ver. 39), now he enters the room where **the damsel** or *child* was. "Probably the large upper room near the roof, which seems to have been used on such occasions (compare Acts 9: 37, 39)."—ALEXANDER. Only Peter, James, and John (ver. 37), the father and mother now attend Jesus.

41. Suiting his action to his words, Jesus **took** or *seized* the hand of the child. This was not necessary to the miracle, but for the good of those present. Their impression was thus deepened, and the faith of the parents strengthened. **Talitha cumi.** Aramaic, showing that this was the colloquial language of the Jews at that time, which Jesus himself used. The repetition of the exact words gives vividness to the narrative. It is supposed that Mark wrote under the direction of Peter, on whose memory these words were indelibly impressed. As Mark wrote for Gentile and especially Roman readers, he interprets the words into Greek. Compare ch. 3: 17; 7: 11, 34; 14: 36. **Damsel.** A term of endearment in familiar discourse addressed to a girl. **I say unto you.** Not strictly contained in *Talitha cumi*, yet expressing their meaning, and manner of utterance, by making the personal authority of our Lord emphatic. **Arise.** Rouse thee, rise up, arise.

42. **Straightway.** The cure was not gradual, but instantaneous. **Walked.** Thus showing that her cure was complete. Compare Mark 1: 31. **For . . . twelve years.** Reason of the statement that she immediately arose and walked, for she was of suitable age. In tenderness she had been called "little daughter" (ver. 23), and "little child" (see on ver. 39). Notice that the length of the woman's sufferings, who was healed, was also twelve years, ver. 25. **The great astonishment** of the parents and disciples who witnessed it shows that they regarded her as really raised from the dead.

43. Jesus **charged** them strictly that no one should **know** it for wise reasons; see on ch. 1: 44. Possibly to prevent arousing the fanaticism of the people and the greater envy of the Pharisees; for his time had not come. Yet notwithstanding this precaution, Matthew tells us (ch. 9: 26) that the fame went abroad in all that land. There is no contradiction between the evangelists, as some would have us suppose. The death of the child had been announced (ver. 35), but afterward she was alive and well. The mourners and minstrels, who had known of the child's death, and were put forth from the house, must have found out that the child was really restored to life. There were thus ways enough for the report to spread, even though the parents and disciples strictly obeyed Jesus, which they may not have done. This is the first instance of Christ's raising the dead of which we have any account, unless we regard the raising of the widow's son at Nain to have preceded this, Luke 7: 11-17. But aside from questions of harmony, that of the widow's son holds a second and higher place. The ruler's daughter was raised privately, almost immediately after dying; the widow's son publicly and on the way to the grave; and afterward Lazarus, also publicly, from the tomb, having been dead four days, John 11: 39, 45, 46. Thus we have a regular gradation in exhibitions of divine power, which is

at least suggestive of the order in which the events occurred.

The vividness of the narrative is completed by the direction that something should be **given her to eat.** She was not only alive, but well. Jesus was not unmindful of the little things which her parents in their amazement overlooked. These details of what occurred within the house, point to an eye-witness, very probably Peter. Immediately after this miracle Matthew (9 : 27-34) places the healing of two blind men, and the casting out of a dumb spirit.

REMARKS.

1. Jesus is willing to minister not only where people are ready to receive him, but also where they are ready to reject him, vers. 1, 17; John 1 : 11; Rom. 10 : 21; Rev. 3 : 20.

2. Satan and his angels exert an active influence among men, and are prompt in opposing Christ and his kingdom, ver. 2; John 12 : 31; 14 : 30; 1 Pet. 5 : 8, 9.

3. How deplorable the condition of the sinner under the power of sin and Satan! No human means has ever been able to tame him, vers. 3, 4; Jer. 17: 9; 13 : 23; John 3 : 6; Rom. 8 : 3, 4.

4. How terribly cruel, malicious, debasing and unclean are evil spirits! vers. 3-5, 13; Matt. 12 : 43-45.

5. If the condition of men under Satan's power can be so terrible in this world, what must it be at last in hell? vers. 2-5; Matt. 25 : 41.

6. A faith and service of fear are not enough to meet the requirements of God, vers. 6, 7; James 2 : 19; 2 Tim. 1 : 7; 1 John 4 : 18.

7. In vain do the wicked seek peace while they reject the Savior, vers. 6, 7; Jer. 6 : 14; Matt. 15 : 8, 9; Eph. 2 : 14; 1 Thess. 5 : 3; 2 Thess. 1 : 7-9.

8. Jesus is sovereign of the universe, vers. 7, 8; Eccle. 8 : 4; Matt. 28 : 18; Phil. 2 : 9-11; Rev. 19 : 16.

9. How great the number of demons in the world! Even the two demoniacs at Gerasa were possessed with a legion, ver. 9; Eph. 6 : 12; 2 Cor. 4 : 3, 4; Eph. 2 : 1-3.

10. An answered prayer is not always a sign of divine approbation, nor an unanswered one a sign of divine displeasure, vers. 9-13, 18, 19; Ps. 78 : 29; 106 : 14, 15; 2 Cor. 12 : 8.

11. The powers of hell are subject to the word of Jesus; they cannot go beyond his permission, ver. 13; Luke 10 : 18, 19.

12. Jesus may permit our property to be taken from us, either in mercy or judgment, ver. 13 ; Dan. 4 : 34, 35.

13. Multitudes who grovel in the filth of iniquity (like the swine when possessed of the devil) rush madly on in company to their own destruction, ver. 13 : 2 Pet. 2 : 12; Rev. 12 : 12.

14. Many, fearing worldly danger or loss on account of Christ, lose their own souls, vers. 14, 15; Luke 9 : 23-26.

15. Covetousness ruins multitudes, vers. 16, 17; Luke 12 : 15-21; Col. 3 : 5.

16. Christ often answers the prayer, "Depart from us, for we desire not a knowledge of thy ways," and leaves them to perish, vers. 17, 18; Job 21 : 14; 22 : 17.

17. How unhappy would wicked men and demons be in heaven with Christ, whom they so much dread! ver. 17; Rev. 6 : 16.

18. Jesus will not compel repentance. He overcame the tempest in approaching Gerasa, cast out demons on entering the country, but turned back before the opposing will of the wicked inhabitants, vers. 17, 18; Matt. 22 : 3; 23 : 37; John 5 : 40.

19. Jesus knows better than his people where they should go and what they should do, vers. 18, 19; Luke 9 : 57-62.

20. Home has the first claim upon the attention of a Christian, especially of a young convert, ver. 19 ; Ps. 66 : 16; John 1 : 41, 45 ; 4 : 29.

21. Christ often calls into the ministry and to great usefulness those who have been notorious sinners, vers. 19, 20; Gal. 1 : 13-16; 1 Tim. 1 : 12-16.

22. Persevere in doing good. While some may reject the gospel, others will be in readiness to receive it, ver. 21; Acts 13 : 46-49.

23. Influence and wealth are no preventive of sickness and death, ver. 22 ; Luke 16 : 22; Heb. 9 : 27.

24. The earnest prayer of faith shall be answered, vers. 23, 24, 36 ; Luke 7 : 7, 9, 10; James 5 : 15-18.

25. In human diseases and sufferings we see the miseries of sin and the type of the deeper disease of the soul, ver. 25; Gen. 3 : 17-19; Rom. 5 : 12.

26. It is proper in sickness to use medicine and seek physicians, but not

to trust in them rather than God, ver. 26; 2 Chron. 16 : 12, 13.

27. Many sinners, instead of looking to Christ, waste their time and strength on physicians of no value, from whom they suffer many things, and get no better, but rather grow worse, ver. 26; Job 13 : 4; Jer. 6 : 14; 8 : 11, 22.

28. Happy are they whom times of great extremity lead to Jesus, vers. 27, 23; ch. 7 : 26; Acts 12 : 5; Ps. 116 : 3–8.

29. Many press around Christ, but few touch him in faith, ver. 28; ch. 4 : 15–20; John 6 : 67–69.

30. Regeneration is instantaneous. "One touch of real faith can do more for the soul than a hundred self-imposed austerities. One look at Jesus is more efficacious than years of sackcloth and ashes."—RYLE. Ver. 29; John 3 : 3, 15, 36; Acts 2 : 41.

31. Jesus was conscious of his indwelling divinity, and it was through the second person of the Godhead that he performed his miracles, ver. 30; vers. 7, 41; John 1 : 14; 8 : 58; 10 : 36, 37.

32. Sinners in secret may seek and find Jesus, but he demands of them an open profession, and only in so doing will they find the full peace and consolations of the gospel, vers. 32–34; Rom. 10 : 9, 10; Ps. 116 : 13, 14.

33. Faith is a precious grace. It is the appointed means of obtaining pardon and salvation, ver. 34; Rom. 5 : 1; 3 : 26; Heb. 10 : 38.

34. In the darkest hour let the words "Only believe" dispel our fear, ver. 36; Luke 24 : 25, 26; Acts 27 : 33, 34.

35. To wail and howl over our dead is heathenish, but to sorrow in submission and hope is Christian, vers. 38, 39; 1 Thess. 4 : 13.

36. To the Christian death is as a sleep, ver. 39; 1 Cor. 15 : 6, 18; 1 Thess. 4 : 14.

37. The Christian should be nothing daunted, though unbelievers scoff at the word and power of Jesus, ver. 40; Isa. 51 : 7; Acts 26 : 8, 24, 25.

38. Jesus in the house of Jairus displayed that power by which he will raise the dead at the last great day, ver. 41; Hos. 13 : 14; John 6 : 40, 44; 1 Thess. 4 : 4; 1 Cor. 15 : 52.

39. As Christ raised dead bodies, so does he raise dead souls to spiritual life, ver. 41; John 5 : 21; Eph. 2 : 1–7.

40. Jesus is mindful of our smallest necessities, ver. 42 · ch. 6 : 34, 37; Heb. 4 : 15; 13 : 5.

CHAPTER VI.

Mark proceeds to relate the third and last general missionary tour throughout Galilee, which began by a visit to Nazareth, where he was again rejected. This tour is continued in the villages (ver. 6), extended and confirmed by the mission of the twelve (vers. 7-13), ending by retiring to the eastern side of the Sea of Galilee, vers. 30, 31. Herod seems to hear specially of Jesus through the preaching of the twelve; his opinion of Jesus and his beheading of John the Baptist are related, vers. 14–29. The multitude come to Jesus, and even precede him, in his retirement. In compassion he teaches them, and miraculously feeds them (ver. 32–44); dismisses them, and constrains his disciples to return over the sea, while he retires to a mountain for prayer (ver. 45, 46); astonishes his disciples by walking to them on the water, vers. 47–52. Coming to the land of Gennesaret, he exercises most wonderful miraculous power upon those who eagerly sought it.

The chapter affords new proofs and manifestations of Christ's almighty power. It brings into view his relations to his fellow-citizens at Nazareth, and to Herod Antipas, ruler of Galilee. It illustrates the fact that his miracles corresponded very much to the faith exercised, and the reception the people gave him.

1–6. JESUS REVISITS HIS OWN COUNTRY AND IS AGAIN REJECTED. THIRD GENERAL CIRCUIT OF GALILEE. Matt. 13 : 54–58; 9 : 35-38. Many, as Alford, Lange, Van Oosterzee, and Olshausen, regard this visit to Nazareth as identical with that related in Luke 4 : 16–30. But Meyer, Stier, Wieseler, Alexander, Ellicott, and others, for good reasons hold this to be a later visit. The arguments for the former view are: *First*, The same questions asked and the same proverb used on both occasions, Luke 4 : 23 with Matt. 13 : 55-57, and Mark 6 : 2–4. *Second*, It is argued that it is impossible to suppose that Jesus would have *marvelled at their unbelief* (Mark 6 : 6) on a second visit, after such a rejection as that recorded in Luke 4 : 28–30. But on the contrary, in favor of a second and later visit it may be said: *First*, The one related by Luke occurred just before making Capernaum his place of residence, and may be regarded as

Jesus revisits Nazareth, and is rejected. Third circuit of Galilee.

VI. AND ᵃ he went out from thence, and came into his own country; and his disciples follow him. 2 And when the sabbath day was come, he began to teach in the synagogue. And many hearing *him* were astonished, saying, ˣ From whence hath this

ᵃ Mt. 13. 54; Lk. 4. 16.

ˣ John 6. 42; 7. 15.

giving one of the causes of his so doing, Luke 4 : 30, 31; Matt. 4 : 13. But this one, related by Matthew and Mark, occurred according to both of them some time after making Capernaum the center of his operations. Indeed, Matthew really settles the question. For he distinctly refers to two visits to Nazareth, the first (Matt. 4 : 13) being the one just before making Capernaum his residence, and hence parallel with Luke 4 : 18. The second is plainly parallel with this in Mark. *Second*, His healing a few sick (Mark 6 : 5) points to a second visit, for in that related by Luke he could not have healed before his teaching in the synagogue (Luke 4 : 23); nor after, for he fled from their rage, Luke 4 : 30. *Third*, There is a sufficient diversity for holding two distinct visits. In the one Jesus is alone, Luke 4 : 16, 30; in the other he is accompanied by his disciples, Mark 6 : 1. According to Luke he is attacked by the enraged people, and escaping through his supernatural power, he goes to Capernaum; but according to Matthew and Mark he experiences no such attack, but continues awhile performing a few miracles, though marveling at the unbelief of the people, and then goes about the villages teaching. And even the questions asked and the proverb used show that diversity which might be expected on two different occasions. *Fourth*, The accounts themselves are in harmony with the supposition of two distinct visits. The first occurred when he began his labors in Galilee; the second after his fame was spread abroad and his reputation generally established among the people. Hence the envy of his fellow-townsmen showed itself more openly at the first, and was more restrained at the second. That he should have made a second visit is very natural. His first rejection was the result of sudden and heated rage. After giving them time for reflection, and to hear concerning him, he affords them another opportunity. The same persons may not have been in the synagogue on the second as on his first visit. The questions only show that the same envy and wonder existed. The same proverb was equally pertinent. That the people should continue in such unbelief, while thousands had for the year past been almost constantly flocking around Jesus, was indeed a cause for marveling. *Fifth*, The position of the accounts by Matthew and Mark shows a general chronological correspondence, being after the parables by the sea-side. The connection in Matt. 13 : 54 is sufficiently general to allow the supposition of a little time intervening between the parabolic discourse and the visit to Nazareth.

1. **He went out from thence.** From near the Sea of Galilee (ch. 5 : 21), from Capernaum, Matt. 9 : 1. It does not mean from the house of Jairus, for the two members of the sentence would not then correspond. We speak of going out from one house to another, from one city to another, and not from a house to a city or to a neighborhood. So here the statement that Jesus **came into his own country**, that is, Nazareth and its neighborhood, demands that the words *from thence* refer to some other city or neighborhood, namely, Capernaum and vicinity. Nazareth was *his own country*, because his parents had resided there before his birth (Luke 1 : 26, 27; 2 : 4), and he had been brought up there from his infancy (Matt. 2 : 23; Mark 1 : 9; Luke 2 : 39, 41, 51), and was called a Nazarene, Matt. 2 : 23; Mark 1 : 24. **His disciples.** The twelve (ver. 7), and possibly others who were believers and very constant attendants. Mark alone records this fact, that in this visit at Nazareth his disciples attend him.

2. **When the sabbath day was come;** implying that he arrived at Nazareth before the Sabbath. The Sabbath was a fit time to begin his

man these things? and what wisdom *is* this which is given unto him, that even such mighty works are 3 wrought by his hands? Is not this the ʸ carpenter, the son of Mary, ᶻ the brother of James, and Joses, and of Juda, and Simon, and are not his sisters here

ʸ Ps. 22. 6; Is. 49. 7; 53. 2, 3; Mt. 13. 55; Lk. 3. 23; John 6. 42.
ᶻ Mt. 12. 46; Gal. 1. 19.

teaching in the synagogue. Yet **began to teach** does not necessarily imply that this was the first teaching of that visit, but that, beginning to teach on the Sabbath, he was interrupted by the astonished and envious multitude. **Synagogue.** See on ch. 1 : 21. Doubtless both in their stated assembly, and also in the house built for their religious gatherings. How much in keeping with the compassion of Jesus to visit his townsmen again and preach to them the gospel, after their former hasty and ungrateful treatment! Compare Luke 13 : 33–35.

Many hearing him. Or, according to high critical authority, *The many*, the mass, multitude. Doubtless many heard him now who did not on his previous visit. **Astonished.** Struck with amazement that their former humble townsman should speak in such a manner and perform such miracles. But wonder had a hardening effect, as is often the case; they were jealous, envious, and offended, ver. 3; Acts 13 : 41. **From whence hath this man,** etc.? The simple question at the former visit, according to Luke (4 : 22), was: "Is not this Joseph's son?" and had reference simply to his teaching. It is a fair inference from Luke 4 : 23–27, that Jesus wrought no miracles at that time. But here and in Matthew several questions are recorded having reference not only to his **wisdom** but also to **the mighty works wrought by his hands.** Compare ver. 5. The people acknowledge his wisdom and his miracles, but their questions imply that such wisdom and works looked suspicious in one of such humble condition and advantages. They would not accept them as his own, yet they could not account for them. The words **by his hands** seem here to be significant, referring to his manner of performing miracles by laying on of hands, ver. 5. *By his hands,* which so recently were employed in servile and mechanical operations.

3. Is not this the carpenter? Carpenter is here used in the widest sense, one who does all kinds of work in wood. This question seems to imply that Jesus actually worked at the trade of his reputed father. It is true that it may be regarded as the hasty language of the excited populace, and really meaning *carpenter's son*, as Matthew (13 : 55) has it: "Is not this the carpenter's son?" But as Jesus became subject to his parents (Luke 2 : 51), it is a natural inference that he wrought with his father, and hence that he could be called both the "carpenter" and "the carpenter's son." Justin Martyr gives the tradition that Jesus made ploughs and yokes. The reference to *carpenter* was not so much one of contempt as of surprise; for the occupation of carpenter has always been regarded as one of the most respectable manual employments. According to Jewish custom, all the sons, even the rabbis, learned some trade. Paul was a tent-maker, Acts 18 : 3. "The famous Hillel was a hewer of wood, and Carna, a judge in Israel, was a drawer of water."—GILL. His old neighbors regarded Jesus not as an inferior, but as an equal. The evidences of his superiority excited their envy and wonder, and these evidences they would question, and reason away. "We know who he is and what he is. He is the carpenter; his mother and brethren are with us. Whence then has he obtained these things? What is the wisdom given him and the miracles he performs? Surely it is incredible that he is so superior to us, and that he has not been initiated by some one into mysterious doctrines and arts."

The son of Mary. It is probable that Joseph had died before this time, and hence the people of Nazareth mention him as only the son of Mary. In his visit a year before they spoke of him as "Joseph's son," a reference to Joseph as then living, or still remembered, Luke 4 : 22.

Brother of James, and Joses, and of Judah and Simon. Some suppose these to have been his *cousins*; others, that they were his *half-brothers*,

4 with us? And they ᵃ were offended at him. But Jesus said unto them, ᵇ A prophet is not without honor, but in his own country, and among his own

ᵃ Mt. 11. 6.
ᵇ Mt. 13. 57· John 4. 44.

children of Joseph by a former marriage; and others still, his *own brothers*, the younger children of Mary. The latter view appears to me to be the correct one, for:

First. There is nothing in the language or connection of any of those passages, where the brothers of Jesus are mentioned (ch. 3 : 31, 32; 6 : 3; Matt. 12 : 46, 47; 13 : 55, 56; Luke 8 : 19, 20; John 2 : 12; 7 : 3, 5, 10; Acts 1 : 14; 1 Cor. 9 : 5; Gal. 1 : 19), demanding that they should not be regarded as his real literal brothers. The presumption is therefore that they were.

Second. It is not certain from the New Testament that Jesus had any cousins according to the flesh. John 19 : 25 is the only passage on which such an opinion can be grounded. "*His mother's sister*" evidently does not refer to Mary the wife of Cleopas, for we cannot suppose two Marys in one family without any other designation. By comparing Mark 15 : 40, the opinion of several eminent critics seems probable, that Salome is meant. Yet this is uncertain in the light of Matt. 27 : 55; for *many women were there*.

Third. In every instance in the Gospels, except in John ch. 7, the brothers of Jesus are mentioned in connection with his mother; and since *mother* is taken in the literal sense, so brothers should be also. In ch. 3 : 35, the force of our Savior's declaration depends greatly upon the fact that they were literally his brothers. To suppose them to be the sons of Alpheus, who is regarded the same as Cleopas (John 19 : 25), is to suppose them to have been among the apostles.

Fourth. But this could not have been the case; for they did not believe in Jesus till some time after the appointment of the apostles, John 7 : 3, 5, 10. In Acts 1 : 14 they are distinguished from the apostles, and therefore could not have been of them. In Gal. 1 : 19, James, the Lord's brother, does not point necessarily to James the apostle; for that passage may mean, according to Dr. Schaff and others, "But no other of the apostles (besides Peter) did I see, only James, the Lord's brother." The names of our Lord's brothers were very common among the Jews, and therefore it is not strange that we find them among the sons of Alpheus, and the apostles. We have even among the latter two Jameses, two Simons, and two Judases.

Fifth. That they were children of Mary, and not of a former wife of Joseph, appears evident from the fact that with one exception they are always, in the Gospels, associated with her; and also that, if they were elder children of Joseph, then Jesus would not be the heir to David's throne. It has been objected to this view that Jesus (John 19 : 26) committed the keeping of his mother not to these brethren but to the Apostle John. It may be answered that his brethren did not fully believe on him till after his resurrection; and that John, being the most intimate bosom friend of Jesus, could better take his place than any other person. We therefore conclude that the brothers here mentioned by the people of Nazareth were the younger children of Mary, the mother of Jesus. And if brothers are to be taken in the strict literal sense, **sisters** must also be taken in the same sense. See on ch. 3 : 31. From the above examination it appears that the perpetual virginity of the mother of Jesus, as held by many Protestants, and by the Catholic and Greek Church as an article of faith, is without scriptural foundation.

Here with us. The sisters were residing among them as near neighbors, probably married. **Offended in him;** rather *at him*, as an occasion of dissatisfaction and dislike. The meaning is, they took offense at him, who in his humble birth and circumstances was in no way superior to themselves, and yet who now so far excelled them in wisdom and mighty works. They were too proud and envious to receive him as their teacher, much less to regard him as the Messiah. Compare Isa. 53 : 1, 2; John 1 : 11.

4. Jesus does not resent their treatment, but accounts for it by what seems to be a proverbial expression, **a prophet is not without honor,** etc. A

A.D. 28, 29.   MARK VI.   109

5 kin, and in his own house. ᶜAnd he could there do no mighty work, save that he laid his hands upon a
6 few sick folk, and healed *them.* And ᵈhe marvelled because of their unbelief.

ᵉAND he went round about the villages, teaching.

ᶜ ch. 9. 23; Ge. 19. 22; 32. 25; Mt. 13. 58; Heb. 3. 12-19; 4. 6-11.
ᵈ Is. 59. 16.
ᵉ Mt. 9. 35; Lk. 13. 22.

fact in human experience, presenting a general truth, of which the treatment of Jesus in the present instance was an example. A stranger sees the public and spiritual acts of a prophet, and recognizes his heavenly character; but neighbors and acquaintances fix their thoughts upon his earthly relationships, to a partial or total exclusion of his higher excellences, and thus come to a wrong conclusion. Prejudice and rejection are the result. Somewhat similar are the proverbs, "Familiarity breeds contempt;" "Distance lends enchantment to the view." That Jesus as a *prophet* should receive such treatment, was highly unreasonable and wicked on the part of his former neighbors and acquaintances. His wisdom and miracles should have overcome all prejudice and unbelief. In his former visit, according to Luke 4 : 24, Jesus extended this proverb only to a prophet's own country; but at this time, when his brothers and sisters are spoken of, he adds, **among his own kin, and in his own house,** among his relatives, and in his own family, with whom he was brought up from childhood. Later than this we learn that his brothers did not believe on him, John 7 : 3-5. We are not to suppose that his brothers and sisters openly rejected and opposed him; but that they did not fully receive him as the Messiah. As unbelieving or indifferent, the reference to them by the people of Nazareth and the proverbial answer of Jesus is peculiarly pertinent. And here may be an incidental argument for the opinion of a second visit and rejection. During the interval between the two visits, the opinions of his relatives and family were doubtless expressed, and became known. And hence the more reason for their being noticed in the second than in the first.

5. **Could do no mighty work.** The reason was *unbelief,* which is spoken of in the next verse. The want of ability was not in him, but in their want of faith. He had power to perform miracles, but for moral reasons he could not exercise it. As he could not with propriety save without faith, so he could not heal without faith. There was not a physical, but a moral impracticability. We are not, however, to suppose that he refused to perform miracles. The people were too proud and envious to recognize his power by publicly bringing their sick to him, and too unbelieving to expect cures, even if they brought them. Bringing their sick to him would have shown faith in his power; and hence we may conclude that but few brought them.

His power and willingness to heal is shown by the fact that he **laid his hands on a few sick folk and healed them.** A little faith was found among some even in Nazareth.

6. **He marvelled.** In his humanity Jesus exercised all the faculties and acts of the human soul. Thus he grew in wisdom, knew not the day nor the hour (ch. 13 : 32), sorrowed, wept, rejoiced, *wondered.* It was indeed a cause for wonder that Nazareth, where he had lived and had been known as a good and righteous man, should alone of the cities of Galilee be so utterly indifferent to his claims. Everywhere else the crowds flocked around him; here in their unbelief they turn from him and let them alone. Their condition is worse than it was upon his first visit. For rage and open opposition is better than settled lukewarmness and unbelief, Rev. 3 : 15, 16. That they should not have openly opposed him may be explained: (1.) They may have regarded such opposition useless, Jesus having escaped mysteriously from them on his previous visit, Luke 4 : 30. (2.) His general popularity among the people of Galilee. (3.) Their rage had cooled off into sullen indifference, and their hearts had hardened into settled unbelief.

Jesus now leaves Nazareth for ever, and continues on his journey, teaching from town to town, which is very commonly styled his third general preaching circuit of Galilee. Mark presents this briefly and in great simplicity. After the statement concerning the

MARK VI.   A.D. 29.

Jesus endows and sends forth the twelve.

7 ᶠAnd he called *unto him* the twelve, and began to send them forth by two and two; and gave them
8 power over unclean spirits; and commanded them that they should take nothing for *their* journey, save a staff only; ᵍno scrip, no bread, ʰno money in

ᶠ Mt. 10. 1, 5; Lk. 9. 1; ch. 3. 13, 14.
ᵍ 1 Sam. 17. 40.
ʰ 1 Sam. 9. 7; Lk. 9. 3; 10. 4; 22. 35.

---

marveling of Jesus at their unbelief, Mark adds, **And he went round about the villages teaching.** Literally, *And he went about the villages in a circle, teaching.* BIBLE UNION VERSION: "And he went about the surrounding villages, teaching." He continues on in his work of visiting the villages in regular order and teaching the people. It seems very probable that he did not go out of his way in making this visit to Nazareth, but that he took it in its order. It very likely lay among the first in his way, of the villages and towns of that district of Galilee which he was now visiting.

7-13. THE TWELVE ENDOWED WITH MIRACULOUS POWER; INSTRUCTED AND SENT FORTH; THEY GO FORTH, PREACH, AND WORK MIRACLES. Matt. 10 : 1-42; 11 : 1; Luke 9 : 1-6. But little variation is found in the incidents related by the three evangelists; but much in the length of the discourse to the twelve. Matthew, who is ever intent on giving the words of Jesus, presents the discourse very fully; Mark briefly gives that portion which refers to their equipment for the journey, and their conduct toward the people; Luke presents more briefly that portion given by Mark; but his brevity may in part be accounted for by the fact that he gives quite fully Christ's discourse to the seventy (Luke 10 : 2-15), similar to Matt. 9 : 37, 38; 10 : 9-16, which is not found in the other Gospels.

This endowment of the apostles to work miracles and this mission with appropriate instructions, must be distinguished from their selection and appointment as apostles, which is given in ch. 3 : 14; Luke 6 : 13, and was followed by the Sermon on the Plain, Luke 6 : 20-49. We must also distinguish it from their call to be constant attendants, preachers or evangelists, ch. 1 : 16-20; also from their call to become disciples, John 1 : 35-45.

7. **He called unto him the twelve.** Matthew (9 : 36-38) supplies a connecting link. While prosecuting his third general missionary tour, Jesus had compassion on the multitude that attended him, because of their want of religious teachers, and he called unto him the twelve, and **began to send them forth.** He *began* now to do what he had not done before, but for which they had been undergoing a preparation. Mark alone informs us that they were sent forth **by two and two.** Matthew, however, in his catalogue of the apostles (Matt. 10 : 2-4) arranges them in couples, connected by *and.* They were sent out in pairs, for mutual consultation and assistance, Eccle. 4 : 9; for showing their agreement in doctrine and the confirmation of their testimony (ver. 11), as in the mouth of two witnesses every word is established, Matt. 18 : 16. They were now limited in their mission to the Jews, not even permitted to enter a Samaritan village, Matt. 10 : 6. The seventy were sent forth without any such limitation, Luke 10 : 1. Compare Luke 24 : 47; Acts 1 : 8.

He gave them power; or *authority* delegated from Jesus, who possessed it in himself. **Over unclean spirits.** Mark does not add healing of the sick, which they also performed (ver. 13), since he lays emphasis upon casting out demons here and elsewhere (ch. 1 : 34; 3 : 11; 7 : 29) as the greatest miracles of healing. If they could do the greater, it is natural to infer that they could do the less. Power over unclean spirits, the great opponents to Christ's kingdom, was also an evidence that they were truly commissioned to preach the gospel of his kingdom. This mission was preparatory; it also showed progress in their qualifications. They were the more fully empowered by the Holy Spirit for their apostolic work on the day of Pentecost, Luke 24 : 49; Acts 1 : 8.

8. THE PROVISION FOR THEIR JOURNEY is noticed in this and the following verse. They are to rely on God for their

A.D. 29. MARK VI. 111

9 *their* purse: but ʲ *be* shod with sandals; and not put
10 on two coats. And he said unto them, ᵏ In what
place soever ye enter into an house, there ˡ abide till

ʲ Ac. 12. 8.
ᵏ Mt. 10. 11; Lk. 9. 4; 10. 7, 8.
ˡ Lk. 10. 38–42; Ac. 16. 15.

daily supply. **Commanded them.** Charged them as their great leader, their Lord. **That they,** etc. Not the discourse of Jesus, but the substance of what he directed, is given. **For their journey,** or rather *for the way.* **Save a staff only;** which would be of service in a rocky country. According to Matt. 10 : 10 and Luke 9 : 3 (true reading of original) they were forbidden to provide a "staff." This is no discrepancy, but shows the independence of the narratives. If they had a staff they could use it, but they were not to procure one for the journey, nor even take it if not in their hands. The idea is : Make no preparation for the journey, but go just as you are. **No scrip,** *bag,* or *wallet.* Generally made of leather, for carrying provisions; **no bread** in it; **no money,** *copper* coin, in their **purse,** rather *girdle* or belt, which kept their long flowing dress together. The fold of the girdle served as a pocket or purse to carry money. "As I was one day examining the tombs on the western side of the Mount of Olives, a peasant offered his services as a guide, whose costume arrested my attention. He wore a *girdle* around his waist, which had an opening at one end, fitting it to hold money and other valuables, and at the same time carried a *pouch* or *bag,* in which he could store away provisions and other things needed on a journey. Here, beyond a doubt, I saw the articles to which the Savior refers where he speaks of the 'purse and scrip' which wayfarers were accustomed to take with them as a part of their traveling equipment."—Dr. HACKETT, *Illustrations of Scripture,* p. 105. Compare 1 Sam. 17 : 40, where are mentioned a staff, shepherd's crook or club, and a shepherd's bag, into which David put five smooth stones. Dr. Thomson says that shepherds and farmers in the East generally have a bag or wallet, made from the skins of kids, stripped off whole, and tanned by a simple process.

SCRIP OR BAG.

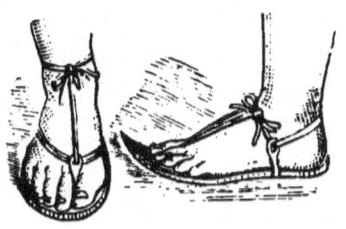

SANDALS.

9. **But be shod with sandals.** What they might have. According to Matt. 10 : 10 they were not to provide themselves with shoes or sandals, that is, they were not to take an extra pair, a common practice on a journey. Thus the seventy (Luke 10 : 4) were forbidden to "carry" sandals. See on ch. 1 : 7. **And not put on,** etc. According to the highest critical authorities this is a direct quotation of our Savior's language : *Put not on two coats,* tunics, under-garments, worn next to the skin, mostly with sleeves, and reaching generally to the knees. They were not to encumber themselves with a change of raiment. "The entire 'outfit' of these first missionaries shows that they were plain fishermen, farmers or shepherds; and to such men there was no extraordinary self-denial in the matter or the mode of their mission. . . . Nor was there any departure from the simple manners of the country (at present) in this. At this day the farmer sets out on excursions quite as extensive, without a para (about a fourth of a cent) in his purse. And the modern Moslem prophet of Tarshiha thus sends forth his apostles over this identical region. Neither do they encumber themselves with two coats. They are accustomed to sleep in the garments they have on during the day, and in this climate such plain people experience no inconvenience from it. They wear a coarse shoe, answering to the sandal of the ancients, but never take two pair of them; and although the staff is an invariable companion of all wayfarers, they are content with *one.*"

10. In this and the next verse Jesus

11 ye depart from that place. ᵐ And whosoever shall not receive you, nor hear you, when ye depart thence, ⁿ shake off the dust under your feet for a testimony against them. Verily I say unto you, ᵒ It shall be more tolerable for Sodom and Gomorrah in the day of judgment, than for that city.

12 And they went out, and preached that men should

ᵐ Mt. 10. 14; Lk. 9, 5; 10. 10, 11.
ⁿ Ne. 5. 13; Ps. 35. 13; Ac. 13. 51; 18. 6.
ᵒ Mt. 11. 22; John 15. 22-24.

gives DIRECTIONS AS TO THEIR CONDUCT TOWARD THE PEOPLE. **In what place soever.** *Wherever,* in whatever city, town or village. **Enter into a house,** as invited and welcomed messengers or preachers. **There abide.** In that house remain. **From that place,** village, town, neighborhood. Similar was the direction to the seventy (Luke 10 : 7), "Go not from house to house." "The reason is very obvious to one acquainted with Oriental customs. When a stranger arrives in a village or encampment, the neighbors, one after another, must invite them to eat with them. There is a strict etiquette about it, involving much ostentation and hypocrisy, and a failure in the due observance of this system of hospitality is violently resented, and often leads to alienations and feuds among neighbors; it also consumes much time, causes unusual distraction of mind, leads to levity, and everyway counteracts the success of a spiritual mission. On these accounts the evangelists were to avoid these feasts: they were sent, not to be honored and feasted; but to call men to repentance, prepare the way of the Lord, and proclaim that the kingdom of heaven was at hand. They were, therefore, first to seek a becoming habitation to lodge in, and there abide till the work in that city was accomplished."— Dr. Thomson, *Land and Book,* I, p. 534.

11. How they should act toward the rejecter of them and their message. **Whosoever shall not receive.** According to the highest critical authorities, *Whatsoever place shall not receive you.* They would be rejected not merely by individuals, but even by whole communities. Thus the Gerasenes (ch. 5 : 17) and a Samaritan village (Luke 9 : 53) rejected Jesus. Going forth from that place when thus rejected, they should **shake off the dust** under their feet **as a testimony** *against them,* or *to them,* as a proof or token that they were as the heathen to them, polluted and devoted to destruction, and hence they were desirous of separating themselves from them forever. Compare on ch. 1 : 44. The Jews were accustomed to shake off the dust of the heathen, when they returned from a foreign country to their own land, by which they renounced all fellowship with Gentiles, and proclaimed that the very dust of those foreign countries was polluting to their own. So Jesus enjoins upon his apostles the same symbolical act toward the Jews who rejected the gospel, intimating thereby that they were no longer to be regarded as God's people, but as the heathen and idolaters. Compare Neh. 5 : 13. Paul shook off the dust of his feet against his persecutors at Antioch in Pisidia (Acts 13 : 51), and shook out his garments against the Jews at Corinth, Acts 18 : 6.

Verily I say, etc. These words to the end of the verse are not found in the oldest and best manuscripts, and were probably added by a later hand from Matt. 10 : 15. **Sodom and** (rather *or,* a variation from the words in Matthew) **Gomorrah.** These cities were types of aggravated sins (Gen. 13 : 13; 18 : 20; Jude 7), and of terrible retribution. Deut. 29 : 23; Isa. 13 : 19; Jer. 49 : 18; Amos 4 : 11; 2 Pet. 2 : 6. Yet their doom would be more endurable than those who should deliberately reject Christ and his message. Their crime and their guilt would thus be greater than the worst of heathens.

After Jesus had instructed and sent forth the twelve, Matthew (11 : 1) relates that he "departed thence to teach and to preach in their cities." In other words, Jesus continued to prosecute his third general missionary tour throughout Galilee. Thus, in this circuit, the twelve by their mission were his assistants in reaching a greater number of places, and in thoroughly compassing the whole region.

12. In this and the next verse Mark gives a BRIEF ACCOUNT OF THIS MISSION.

A.D. 29. MARK VI. 113

13 ᵖ repent ; and they cast out many devils, ᑫ and ᵖ Ac. 2. 38.
anointed with oil many that were sick, and healed ᑫ Jam. 5. 14.
them.

Herod's opinion of Jesus ; beheading of John the Baptist.

14 ʳ AND king Herod heard *of him ;* for his name was ʳ Mt. 14. 1, 2; Lk.
spread abroad: and he said, That John the Baptist 9. 7.
was risen from the dead, and therefore mighty

They went out; "through the towns," or *villages,* Luke 9 : 6. Where is not told us. It seems probable, however, that they went through the southern and south-eastern portion of Galilee, taking in Tiberias and its vicinity. For (1.) Jesus cautioned them against entering a city of the Samaritans (Matt. 10 : 5), which fairly implies that they would at least come near the borders of Samaria. And (2.) Herod appears to have had his attention specially directed to Jesus (ver. 14) by this mission of the twelve. Very likely, therefore, they visited Tiberias, or its vicinity, the capital of Galilee, where Herod resided most of the time. And if he was absent, his officers or courtiers may have sent him the report. **Preached,** announced to the people, individually and collectively, as they had opportunity. **That men should repent.** See on ch. 1 : 15. They preached repentance as a duty. The language *that,* or *in order that,* may also include the idea that they preached in order that men might repent, exercise and experience this deep and thorough change of mind. Thus they announced the same message as that which John the Baptist (ch. 1 : 4) and Christ himself had proclaimed, ch. 1 : 15.

13. Their preaching was attested by miracles. Mark notes specially the fact that they **cast out many devils,** thus showing that as messengers of the Son of God (ch. 1 : 1) they were overcoming the kingdom of Satan. See note on ver. 7. **Anointed with oil,** etc. This method of healing is mentioned only by Mark. It was, however, practiced by the apostles and early Christians (James 5 : 14). Although the Jews used oil in cases of sickness (Luke 10 : 34), it was evidently not used *medicinally* by the apostles, but *symbolically,* as touching with the hand, etc., ch. 7 : 33; 8 : 23; John 9 : 6. The anointing was not the means of healing; but a symbol of the invisible power which effected the cure. It presented to the eye an external or visible connection between the healer and the healed. Thus, as well as by prayer (James 5 : 14), the disciples showed their dependance on Christ. Such anointing was altogether different from the extreme unction of the Roman Catholics, who administer the latter to persons at the point of death, for the remission of sins and the saving of their souls ; but the former was used by the apostles, upon sick persons, for the recovery of their bodily health.

The return of the twelve is recorded in ver. 30. Luke's account of their preaching and healing is even more brief, but comprehensive : "went through the towns, preaching the gospel, and healing everywhere." How long they were out upon this mission is not told us. Some suppose it to have occupied only one or two days ; others extend it to several months. The facts, that Jesus made a considerable circuit after sending them out (Matt. 11 : 1), that they went through the villages teaching (Luke 9 : 6), and that Jesus upon their return invited them to retirement and rest (ver. 31), point to a quite extensive tour, and to considerable time. They probably occupied several weeks, from the latter part of February, or the first part of March, A.D. 29, till early in April. The Passover that year began April 17 ; and it was near, when the five thousand were fed, vers. 32–44; John 6 : 4.

14–29. HEROD'S OPINION OF JESUS. ACCOUNT OF THE RECENT BEHEADING OF JOHN THE BAPTIST. Matt. 14 : 1–12; Luke 9 : 7–9. Mark is fullest. Luke omits the account of John's beheading.

14. **King Herod.** By Matthew and Luke he is called "tetrarch," a Greek word, meaning *a ruler of the fourth part,* and which became a common title for

15 works do show forth themselves in him. said, That it is Elias. And others said, That it is a [s] Others [a] ch. 8. 28; Mt. 16. 14.

---

those who governed any part of a province, subject only to the Roman emperor. Hence in general and popular language, and from courtesy, he is here styled *king*, vers. 22, 26; Matt. 14 : 9. This was Herod Antipas, son of Herod the Great. His dominion comprised Galilee, Samaria and Perea. He first married a daughter of Aretas, king of Arabia Petræa; but afterward took Herodias, his brother Philip's wife. Aretas, indignant at the insult offered his daughter, waged war against Herod and defeated him. This defeat, according to Josephus (Ant. xviii. 5, 2), was regarded by many as a punishment for the murder of John; see quotation in ver. 20. In A.D. 39 he was banished to France, whither Herodias followed him; both died in exile. He was sensual, weak (Matt. 14 : 9), cunning (Luke 13 : 32), unscrupulous (Luke 3 : 19), and superstitious, ver. 20; Luke 9 : 9.

Heard of him. Rather, *heard of it*, the preaching and the miracles of the disciples, and that Jesus had sent them forth; **for his name was spread abroad,** or *had become famous*, by the preaching and miracles of the apostles, as well as his own. It is probable that Herod was at war with Aretas, and making his headquarters at Machærus, a frontier fortress near the Dead Sea, between Perea and Arabia, where John the Baptist was in prison. See on ver. 29. This, in connection with his voluptuous life, will explain why Herod seems not to have heard of Jesus before. "A palace is late in hearing spiritual news."—BENGEL. The murder of John must at least have startled Herod's conscience and made him uneasy, ver. 20, 26. If he had heard before of Jesus, it had produced no impression on his mind; but now the fame of Jesus, the report of his miracles, preaching, and doings, at once arrested his attention, and produced anxiety in his mind, filled with superstition, and tortured by a guilty conscience.

And he said, *was saying*, to his attendants, Matt. 14 : 2. Or according to the preferable text, *And they, some people, were saying*. **John the Baptist,** literally, *the one baptizing*, equivalent to *the Baptist*; he was known by the ordinance he administered; see on ver. 25. **Is risen from the dead;** the imaginings of a guilty conscience. *Dead* refers not to a mere state or condition, but to persons in that state, *from among the dead*. Some suppose that Herod was a Sadducee, from comparing ch. 8 : 15 with Matt. 16 : 6, and that his guilt and fears now made him a cowardly believer in the doctrine of the resurrection. Infidels and skeptics have been known to renounce their unbelief in times of danger. **Therefore mighty works.** *On this account*, because he is risen, *the powers*, that is, superhuman or miraculous powers, *work* or *are active in him*. They are exhibited in him. John did not work miracles (John 10 : 41); but now, Herod reasons, the powers are active in John's person because he has come forth from the dead, having thus acquired new spiritual and miraculous power. His fears may have been excited lest Jesus might become a political rival, or lest his superhuman power might be directed against him. According to Luke (9 : 7) he "was perplexed" because some said that John was risen. This is no contradiction. For he could also make the statement privately as his own opinion. That he should also hear it from others would naturally perplex him. See on ver. 16.

15. The opinions of others concerning Jesus. **Others said.** Others beside Herod, both in and out of his court. The general estimate of the people concerning Jesus is given. Compare similar ones reported a little later in Matt. 16 : 13, 14. **It is Elias.** *Elias* is the Greek form of *Elijah*, whose coming had been foretold by Malachi (4 : 5), and was generally expected by the Jews. "During certain prayers the door of the house was set open, that Elijah might enter and announce the Messiah. . . . So firm was the conviction of his speedy arrival, that when goods were found and no owner appeared to claim them, the common saying was, "Put them by till Elijah comes."—HACKETT'S *Smith's Dictionary*, p. 710. John was indeed the Elijah who was to come, Matt. 11 : 14. See on ch. 9 : 11-13. **That it is a prophet, or as,** etc. *It is a prophet like one of the prophets. Or* is not in the original.

A.D. 29. MARK VI. 115

16 prophet, or as one of the prophets. ¹But when ᵗ Mt. 14. 2.
   Herod heard *thereof*, he said, It is John, whom I beheaded: he is risen from the dead.
17 ᵘ For Herod himself had sent forth and laid hold ᵘ Mt. 14. 3; Lk.
   upon John, and bound him in prison for Herodias' 19, 20.
   sake, his brother Philip's wife: for he had married
18 her. For John had said unto Herod, ˣ It is not law- ˣ Lc. 18. 16; 20. 21
19 ful for thee to have thy brother's wife. Therefore
   Herodias had a quarrel against him, and would have
20 killed him; but she could not: for Herod ʸ feared ʸ Mt. 14. 5; 21. 26.

There were others who were not ready to regard him as the prophet Elijah, but still like one of the old prophets, though not so great as Elijah. Popular opinion thus accorded to Jesus a higher mission; some higher than others, but none so high as that of the Messiah. His Messiahship was perceived by faith, Matt. 16 : 16, 17.

16. A repetition in part of ver. 14. **When Herod heard** the report of Jesus, his miracles, etc. Mark, having briefly related the opinions of others regarding Jesus, now returns to Herod's opinion. "While others were proposing this or that solution of the wonderful phenomena in question, Herod had a theory or an explanation of his own, distinct from all the rest, and suggested by his own guilty memory and conscience."—ALEXANDER. **Whom I beheaded.** *I* is emphatic, made so by his feelings of guilt. It is not to be supposed that he publicly made this confession; but privately, which accords with Matt. 14 : 2, "said unto his servants," attendants, ministers or courtiers. Luke (9 : 9) ends his account here by adding that Herod "desired to see him."

17. With this verse begins the account of the imprisonment and beheading of John. Luke states both the fact and the cause of John's imprisonment in ch. 3 : 19, 20. **For.** This is explanatory of what Mark had just said concerning Herod. Before this, Mark (1 : 14) had only referred to John's imprisonment; now he relates the cause of it and some facts concerning it. **In prison.** In the castle of Machaerus, near the Dead Sea. **For Herodias' sake.** Herodias was grand-daughter of Herod the Great, daughter of Aristobulus, and niece of Herod Antipas. As Jezebel was the foe of the first Elijah (1 Kings 19 : 2), so was Herodias the second. **Brother Philip's wife.**

Not the tetrarch of Iturea (Luke 3 : 1), but another brother, who lived in private life, having been disinherited by his father; and thus uncle to Herodias, whom he married. But she, preferring royalty, left him, and married Herod Antipas, who, to make way for her, divorced his own wife, daughter of Aretas, king of Arabia, supposed to be the one mentioned by Paul in 2 Cor. 11 : 32.

18. **It is not lawful,** etc. For, *first*, she was the wife of Philip, who was still living; *second*, Herod's wife, the daughter of Aretas, was also living; *third*, by marriage Herodias was the sister-in-law of Herod, and by Jewish law a person was forbidden to marry his brother's wife, Lev. 18 : 16; 20 : 21. This incident strikingly illustrates the character of John as a consistent and faithful reprover and preacher of righteousness. He preached as plainly to those in kings' palaces as to the inhabitants of the wilderness (Matt. 3 : 2) or to the self-righteous Pharisees and Sadducees, Matt. 3 : 7. "Violators of the seventh commandment are painfully numerous, and that not merely in the lower classes. They should be rebuked, whatever their social position."—N. M. WILLIAMS. Instead of regarding the reproof of John, and repenting, Herod "added to all this also, that he shut up John in prison," Luke 3 : 20.

19. **Therefore Herodias had a quarrel against him.** Rather, *And Herodias had anger*, or was enraged *against him*. Or simply (Bible Union Version), "was angry with him." **Would have killed him.** Rather, *Wished* or *desired to kill him*. This shows how intense her rage against John. **But she could not.** *And she was not able.* The reason is given in the next verse.

20. **For Herod feared John.** Had him in reverence on account of his

John, knowing that he was a just man and an holy, and observed him; and when he heard him, he did many things, and heard him gladly.
21 ᶻAnd when a convenient day was come, that Herod ᵃon his birthday made a supper to his lords,

ᶻ Mt. 14. 6.
ᵃ Ge. 40. 20; Est. 1. 3, 4.

righteous character. We get a glimpse of the deep impression that John had made and was making on Herod. **Knowing.** John's character was not a matter of supposition, but of knowledge with Herod. **A just man and holy.** A just and holy man. He was just, righteous, upright in his relations toward men; and holy, pious, devoted toward God. **Observed him,** *Watched him closely, kept him in mind,* observing his exemplary life. Compare Luke 2: 19; and in Apocrypha, Tobit 1:11; Sirach 13:12; 39:2, where the Greek word here translated is used. Or the word may mean *kept him,* preserved him from the designs of Herodias. Compare this use of the Greek word in Matt. 9:17; Luke 5:38. It is difficult to decide which meaning here to choose. To me the first seems here a little more natural and fitting. Herod knew that John was a righteous and holy man; and he observed him strictly, noting his life, his acts, words and general conduct, and hearing him did many things and heard him gladly. This also implies that he protected him against the designs of Herodias. **And when he heard him.** *And having heard him,* etc. He did more than merely notice closely his actions and words; **he did many things** which he advised, and he even heard him **gladly,** with relish, with pleasure. He heard him like the stony-ground hearers, receiving the word with joy and outwardly reforming in some things, ch. 4: 16, 17. But instead of **he did many things,** the oldest reading, preferred by the latest critics is, *he was much perplexed,* in doubt and undecided as to what to do; *and he heard him gladly,* John 5:35. Herod was weak and vacillating. The constant influence of Herodias affected his mind; and truth, when it does not harden, softens, so that, after a time, he was even desirous of putting John to death, but feared the people, because they regarded John as a prophet, Matt. 14:5.

Josephus (Ant. xviii. 5, 2), probably aware of no other ground of John's imprisonment and execution, gives only political reasons. I give the passage. Referring to Herod's defeat by Aretas, Josephus says: "Now some of the Jews thought that the destruction of Herod's army came from God, and that very justly, as a punishment of what he did against John that was called the Baptist; for Herod slew him, although he was a good man, and commanded the Jews to exercise virtue, both as to righteousness one toward another, and piety toward God, and so to come to baptism. . . . Now when others came in crowds about him—for they were greatly moved at hearing his words—Herod, who feared lest the great influence John had over the people, might put it into his power and inclination to raise a rebellion (for they seemed ready to do anything he should advise), thought it best, by putting him to death, to prevent any mischief he might cause, and not bring himself into difficulties, by sparing a man who might make him repent of it when it should be too late. Accordingly he was sent a prisoner, out of Herod's suspicious temper, to Machærus, the castle I before mentioned, and was there put to death." There is no difficulty in supposing the reason given by Josephus to be also true; for Herod may have acted from a variety of motives, both political and private. He did fear on account of the popularity of John with the people (Matt. 14:5); and he may have feared lest the people might be aroused against him through the influence of John, on account of his unlawful marriage. The reproof of John and the influence of the malicious Herodias were, however, the private, exciting and immediate grounds of his action.

21. **A convenient day was come** for Herodias to carry out her wily and malicious design. Wine, dissipation, licentiousness, were all favorable to this. **On his birthday.** So Pharaoh celebrated his birthday with great pomp and festivity, Gen. 40:20. This was the festal occasion celebrating his

22 high captains, and chief *estates* of Galilee; and when the daughter of the said Herodias came in, and danced, and pleased Herod and them that sat with him, the king said unto the damsel, Ask of me what-

natural birth. There is no good and sufficient reason for regarding it, as some do, the day commemorating his accession to civil power. **Made a supper** or banquet feast. The *supper* was the chief meal of the day, taken toward or at evening, and often prolonged into the night. This feast doubtless took place at Machærus, where John was imprisoned. See on ver. 27. **To his lords.** *For his grandees*, nobles, princes, officers of state, **high captains,** literally, *commanders of a thousand,* and applied in the New Testament to commanders and military chiefs, Acts 21:31; 25:23. These were doubtless Herod's highest military officers. **Chief estates of Galilee.** *The first* men, *the chief* men of the land generally. Some have inferred from the guests that this celebration took place at Tiberias; but it would not be difficult for his noblemen and courtiers of Galilee to go two or three days' journey to attend at Machærus. The Jews were accustomed to such journeys in attending their feasts. Machærus also was convenient for civil and military officers in Perea.

22. **Daughter of the said Herodias,** whose name, according to Josephus, was *Salome,* a daughter by Philip. She was afterward married to her uncle Philip, the tetrarch of Iturea (Luke 3:1). The earliest and best manuscripts read, *his daughter Herodias.* She was probably also called *Herodias,* as a family name, even as many of the men of the family were called Herod. **Danced.** The sexes did not mingle in the ancient dance. This one performed by Salome seems to have been a mimic or theatrical dance, which was considered below the dignity of persons of rank and character to engage in. It was a sacrifice of decency and maidenly decorum; but the voluptuous Herod, and those with him, all quite likely more or less intoxicated, were **pleased,** doubtless, with the skill and grace of her performance, and with the condescension of a princess in thus honoring the birthday of the king. Many modern dances are equally low, and equally pleasing to the sensual.

DANCING-GIRL.

Dr. Thomson thus describes the Oriental dance: "The whole night will be spent in feasting, singing, dancing and buffoonery, in the open court by the men, and in the *harem,* in equally boisterous games and dances, by the women. These are great occasions for the dancing-girls; and many, not of the 'profession,' take part in the sport. We see little to admire in their performances. They move forward, and backward, and sidewise, now slowly, then rapidly, throwing their arms and heads about at random, and rolling the eye, and *wriggling* the body into various preposterous attitudes, languishing, lascivious, and sometimes indecent; and this is repeated over and over, singly or in pairs or groups. One thing is to be said in their favor: the different sexes do not intermingle in those indecorous sports; and I hope you will not be greatly scandalized if I venture the opinion that the dances spoken of in ancient Biblical times were in most points just such as we have been describing."—*Land and the Book*, vol. ii., p. 345.

Them that sat; or *reclined at table,* according to the custom of the time. Herod is so enraptured with the dancing and condescension of Salome that he makes her a rash offer. **The king . . . the damsel,** or *girl,* appear in marked contrast in connection with his lavish and foolish promise.

23 soever thou wilt, and I will give *it* thee. And he sware unto her, ᵇ Whatsoever thou shalt ask of me, I will give *it* thee, unto the half of my kingdom.
24 And she went forth, and said unto her mother, What shall I ask? And she said, The head of John
25 the Baptist. And she came in straightway with haste unto the king, and asked, saying, I will that thou give me by and by in a charger the head of
26 John the Baptist. ᶜ And the king was exceeding sorry; *yet* for his oath's sake, and for their sakes

ᵇ Est. 5. 3, 6; 7. 2; Prov. 1. 16.

ᶜ Mt. 14. 9; 1 Ki. 13. 29, 30; 2 Chr. 24. 16; Ac. 8. 2.

23. Possibly Salome is at first surprised at the offer, and hesitates. But Herod even confirms his promise by an oath, and, striving to imitate the great Ahasuerus (Esth. 5 : 3), **unto the half of my kingdom,** when he had no supreme power, and hence no half of a kingdom to give. But such were then the ideas of his excited and intoxicated brain. The case of Herod is only one of many examples of Eastern monarchs lavishing gifts on favorite dancers. Such instances show the evils and dangers of sensual excitements and sensual amusements.

24. There seems to have been no secret understanding between the mother and daughter. The latter therefore **went forth** or *out* into the apartment of the women, which was separate from that of the men, to consult with her mother. Herodias, however, like one who was carrying out a preconceived plan, had a ready answer to her daughter's question: **The head,** etc. Not the death only, for that would not have been strictly a gift, but *the head,* which could not be given her without his death.

25. How willing and even eager the daughter was to adopt her mother's advice is seen by the fact that she came into the king *straightway with haste,* and by the boldness and urgency of her request. **I will,** I desire or choose **that thou give me by and by,** rather, *forthwith, immediately,* **in a charger,** etc. *Charger,* in old English, means a large dish; but now a horse used in battle. The Greek word originally meant a board; then, among other applications of the term, a wooden dish, and then a plate, dish or platter of any kind. Here, *on a platter.* **John the Baptist.** John is styled *The Baptist,* as a person well known. The evangelists, without any explanation, thus speak of him, Matt. 3 : 1; 11 : 11; 14 : 2; 16 : 14; 17 : 13; Mark 8 : 28; Luke 7 : 20, 33; 9 : 19. The title was evidently familiar to the Jews. Josephus also says (see quotation in ver. 20) that he was "called," or rather "surnamed the Baptist." He was indeed *the Baptizer,* the institutor of a *new* ordinance, which had special reference to Christ. It was not an offshoot of proselyte baptism, for the latter appears not to have originated till after the destruction of the temple. The earliest mention of it is in the Babylonish Talmud, a Jewish commentary of about the sixth century of the Christian era. Compare the author's "*Notes on Matthew,*" ch. 3 : 1.

26. The unexpected request of Salome produces a sudden change of feelings in Herod. At the time, too, when his highly wrought emotions at the dance were probably subsiding. **And the king was exceeding sorry,** *environed with grief, very sorrowful.* He knows it is wrong; he is concerned for his own popularity among the people; he fears lest the people, who regard John as a prophet, may cause him trouble. "It was reckoned an ill omen with the Romans to take away life on that day they received their own; and therefore carefully abstained on such days from executions."—Dr. Gill, on Matt. 14 : 9. Yet his sorrow was not sufficient to overcome his foolish pride and choose the less of two evils. **Yet for his oath's sake.** *But on account of his oaths.* The plural *oaths* may be equivalent to the singular; or it may refer to the oath, which Herod in his excitement very likely repeated. **And for their sakes,** etc. *And of those reclining at table with him.* A twofold reason is thus given: he must perform his oath, and he must maintain his honor among his guests. Duellists and gamblers act upon a simi-

27 which sat with him, he would not reject her. And immediately the king sent an executioner, and commanded his head to be brought: and he went and
28 beheaded him in the prison, and brought his head in a charger, and gave it to the damsel: and the

lar principle. Herod had doubtless some scruples of conscience in regard to his oath, and one uttered so publicly. He did not wish to be a perjurer, much less to be regarded as one. Neither did he wish to be ridiculed as mean and fickle by his attendants and guests, who doubtless hated John and applauded the king in the generous offer he had made. Pride and shame overcame him. His oath was wicked, because it was uncalled for, and hence taking the Lord's name in vain (Exod. 20 : 7), and because no one has a right to pledge himself beforehand to do what may be wrong. Herod had placed himself in a dilemma, to make choice of two evils—to break a rash, wicked oath, or to commit murder. He should have chosen the former as the less of the two. Compare Lev. 5 : 4–6. But one sin leads to another and even greater, and Herod **would not reject her.** The verb translated *reject* means originally to put away, to set aside, and then to refuse, reject with scorn, also with perfidy. *Would not reject her* with neglect or scorn (*her* including the idea of her request). (ROBINSON.) *Would not deal deceitfully or act perfidiously toward her.* (SOPHOCLES.) To have violated his promise would have been treating her both contemptuously and treacherously. This gives us a still clearer view of Herod's false sense of shame and honor, especially as his drunken guests doubtless applauded the girl's bloody request.

27. **Immediately.** No sooner does Herod decide upon the wicked and bloody act than he orders the execution. **The king sent,** or *sent out*. **An executioner.** The word thus translated means an officer about the person of a general, *one of his body-guard*, who acted, as they often do now in the East, as executioners of capital sentences. The execution by a soldier may be used as a circumstantial argument that Herod was now actually engaged in hostilities with Aretas. **Beheaded him in the prison.** The narrative seems to imply that the prison was near at hand, and the execution performed at once; hence, that the feast was at Machærus. Some suppose that it was at Tiberias, on the shore of the Sea of Galilee; but it would have taken at least two days for the execution of the sentence. Others suppose it took place at Julius or Livias, another place of residence of Antipas, situate not far from Machærus, in the mountains on the eastern side of the Dead Sea. This is less objectionable. But Machærus is more in keeping with the ease and quickness of the execution. It was night, and doubtless late, before the promise of Herod was made, and all was accomplished, we should naturally suppose, by or before the morning's light. See on ver. 21.

It could not have been many months before this that John in prison sent his message to Jesus, Matt. 11 : 2; the reply of Jesus, doubtless, invigorated his faith, preparing him for the last conflict and a martyr's death. He had now been in prison about seventeen months, and it was now about three years from the commencement of his ministry. For the Passover was at hand (John 6 : 4), the third of our Saviour's ministry, which began that year on April 17th, when the report of John's death was brought to Jesus. This report to Jesus was at the same time with the return of the twelve (vers. 29–31; Matt. 14 : 12, 13), that is, late in March or early in April. John was therefore probably beheaded about the time of their going forth on their mission, early in March, A.D. 29. This would give time for Herod to hear of Jesus through the disciples after his execution, and for the disciples to hear of the manner of John's death before their return to Jesus.

28. **Brought his head,** etc. The request was strictly carried out in every particular. It would seem that the head was brought on the platter while the feast lasted, given to this heartless dancing-maid, and by her to her mother, who was the principal actor and guiltiest party in this terrible tragedy. See ver. 22.

29 damsel gave it to her mother. And when his disciples heard *of it*, they came and took up his corpse, and laid it in a tomb.

The twelve return, and report to Jesus. They retire to a desert place; feeding the five thousand.

30 ᵈAND the apostles gathered themselves together unto Jesus, and told him all things, both what they
31 had done, and what they had taught. ᵉAnd he said unto them, Come ye yourselves apart into a desert place, and rest a while. For ᶠthere were many coming and going, and they had no leisure so

ᵈ Lk. 9. 10; John 6. 1.
ᵉ Mt. 14. 13.
ᶠ ch. 3. 20.

---

29. **His disciples.** John's. Matthew (14 : 12) relates that after the burial they went and told Jesus, showing their tender feelings toward John, and their confidence in Jesus as a friend to their master, and as one who would sympathize with them. **Came and took up his corpse.** Where it had been cast after his execution. The place where the castle of Machærus stood was identified in 1806 with ruins of the modern *Mukaur*, east of the Dead Sea, lying on the lofty summit of the long mountain-ridge Attarus, at its northern termination, near the shore of the Zerka Ma'in, and on its south side. The mountain is extremely cragged, precipitous, and here inaccessible on three sides. Large square blocks of stone still show the remains of the ancient walls. See *Seetzen's Reisen*, vol. ii. 330. "It is surrounded by ravines, at some points not less than 175 feet deep. . . . Into one of the deep ravines beneath the fortress the headless body of John (Mark 6 : 29) may have been cast, which his disciples took up and buried, and then went and told Jesus. . . . The crag on which the old fortress stood is said to be visible from Jerusalem."—HACKETT'S *Smith's Dictionary*, p. 1728. **A tomb.** Where is not told. The sepulchers of the Jews were often caverns, or vaults dug sometimes beneath the surface of the ground, but more commonly in the sides of hills, and cut in the solid rocks. The hills of Palestine, of Perea, and Petra abound with these chambers of the dead.

30, 31. THE TWELVE RETURN FROM THEIR MISSION, AND REPORT TO JESUS. Luke 9 : 10. Mark again is the fullest.

30. **The apostles.** The word means *persons sent forth.* Jesus gave this title (Luke 6 : 13) to the twelve when he selected them from among his disciples. This is the only time Mark applies the title to the twelve—appropriately now just returning from their mission. **Gathered themselves together unto Jesus.** From the different places they had visited, and the different ways they had taken. Possibly the news of the death of John the Baptist may have hastened their return. But as they appear to have returned together, it is more probable that Jesus had directed them to come back a little before the approaching Passover. **Told him all things.** Made a detailed report of places visited, how they had been received, and what they had accomplished, what miracles they had wrought, and what doctrines and precepts they had taught. From comparing Matt. 14 : 12, 13, it appears that simultaneously with the apostles' return was the report of John's disciples respecting the death of their master.

31. Jesus had before sought retirement for himself (Luke 5 : 16 ; Matt. 12 : 15 ; ch. 4 : 35) ; now he seeks it for his disciples, returning weary from their mission. **Come ye yourselves apart. Rest a while.** It is proper for Christians to take brief periods of rest from hard and incessant toil. For they could not obtain their needed rest where they were. The people were incessantly **coming and going,** so that they could not find **time to eat** their regular meals. Compare on ch. 3 : 20.

32–44. JESUS RETIRES AND MIRACULOUSLY FEEDS THE MULTITUDE. Matt. 14 : 13–21 ; Luke 9 : 10–17 ; John 6 : 1–14. The great importance of this account and miracle may be inferred from

A.D. 29.   MARK VI.   121

32 much as to eat. ᵍ And they departed into a desert place by ship privately.
33 And the people saw them departing, and many knew him, and ran afoot thither out of all cities, and outwent them, and came together unto him.
34 ʰ And Jesus, when he came out, saw much people, and was moved with compassion toward them, because they were ⁱ as sheep not having a shepherd: and ᵏ he began to teach them many things.

ᵍ Mt. 14. 13.
ʰ Judg. 10. 16; Mt. 9. 36; 14. 14; John 11. 33-35; Heb. 4. 15; 5. 2.
ⁱ Num. 27. 17; 1 Ki. 22. 17; Is. 53. 6; Jer. 50. 6; Eze. 34. 5; Zec. 10. 2.
ᵏ Lk. 9. 11.

---

the fact that all the evangelists relate it. Mark and John are the fullest and enter most into details.

32. As the imprisonment of John formed an era in Christ's ministry when he commenced his active and public labors in Galilee (Matt. 4 : 12), so did the death of John form another era when he extended his labors into northern Galilee and east of the Jordan. Heretofore he had made Capernaum the center of his missionary operations in eastern Galilee. But henceforth making but brief visits to this scene of his former labors, he extends his journeys into Decapolis (ch. 7 : 31) and northern Galilee, going north-west as far as the neighborhood of Tyre and Sidon (ch. 7 : 24), and north-east as far as Cesarea Philippi, ch. 8 : 27.

And they departed from the western side of the Sea of Galilee, probably at or near Capernaum. The reason of their departure was: (1.) The disciples needed rest, ver. 31; (2.) The news of the death of John the Baptist, Matt. 14 : 13; doubtless they were deeply moved; retirement was becoming; (3.) Withdrawing from the jurisdiction of Herod Antipas, who may now have returned to Tiberias and was desirous of seeing Jesus (Luke 9 : 9), to that of the mild Herod Philip (Luke 3 : 1), on the east and north of the Sea of Galilee. These reasons are consistent one with another. **Into a desert place.** Not a barren waste (ver. 39), but an uncultivated and uninhabited region, in the vicinity of eastern Bethsaida, which stood on the north-eastern side of the lake near the Jordan, and which Philip, according to Josephus, advanced to the dignity of a city, and named it *Julias*. See on ver. 45. **By ship,** or transport, a general name for vessels of every grade; here probably a fishing vessel or boat, propelled by both sails and oars. *By the ship* (original) may possibly refer to the vessel provided for him (ch. 3 : 9), and which usually attended him. **Privately.** In private and apart from the people. "He took them and went aside privately," Luke 9 : 10.

33. And the people, etc. According to the oldest manuscripts, *And they saw them departing.* Jesus had withdrawn with his disciples from the people without making known his design of crossing the lake; but they saw him and his disciples embarking covertly, and interpret his design. **Many knew him,** rather, *them.* Though at a little distance, the people knew them by their number and general appearance. They tell the news (Matt. 14 : 13), and the people, seeing from the shore the direction that Jesus was going, follow around the northern end of the lake, **ran afoot thither,** *ran together there on foot,* in opposition to going by *ship,* to the place where they saw that he was about to land. Thus coming **out of all cities,** *from all the cities* of that region, they **outwent them,** or rather, *came before them.* Christ's popularity among the common people, and their eagerness to enjoy his teaching and his miraculous power (John 6 : 2), is here vividly presented. The last clause, **and came together unto him,** is not found in the oldest manuscripts, and is omitted by the highest critical authorities.

34. And Jesus when he came out. Out of the ship, not from the wilderness or his place of solitude, as some have suggested. Jesus and his disciples had enjoyed a little quiet in crossing the lake. Having separated from the multitude, very probably, the evening before, they had taken a night's rest, after which they had embarked early in the morning. This is in harmony with the time indicated in the next verse. **Seeing much people,** in-

11

35 ¹And when the day was now far spent, his disci- | ¹ Mt. 14. 15; Lk.
ples came unto him, and said, This is a desert place, | 9. 12.
36 and now the time *is* far passed: send them away,
that they may go into the country round about, and
into the villages, and buy themselves bread: for
37 they have nothing to eat. He answered and said
unto them, Give ye them to eat. And they say unto
him, ᵐShall we go and buy two hundred ⁿpenny- | ᵐ Num. 11. 13, 22;
38 worth of bread, and give them to eat? He saith | 2 Ki. 4. 43.
                                                    | ⁿ Mt. 18. 28.

stead of being displeased that they should encroach upon his retirement, he was **moved with compassion,** his emotions of pity were deeply excited toward them, **because they were as sheep not having a shepherd,** or *having no shepherd* to feed, guide and take care of them. They were without any spiritual teacher to guide, warn and instruct them, and hence were exposed to all kinds of spiritual danger and destruction from false teachers and spiritual foes. Instead, therefore, of dismissing them, that he and his disciples might enjoy quiet, he **began to teach them many things.** Luke (9 : 11) adds, "and healed them that had need of healing." Matthew (14 : 14) omits reference to his teaching, and simply says, "he healed their sick." John (6 : 3, 4) says that Jesus went up into the mountain or highlands by the shore, and "there sat with his disciples," which was the posture of teaching, Matt. 5 : 1. Also that the Passover was nigh, which began that year, A.D. 29, on April 17th. This also may account in part for the great multitudes present, many of whom were on their way to Jerusalem to keep the feast.

35. **When the day was now far spent.** Much time having passed. The first evening (Matt. 14 : 15), the decline of day, about three o'clock in the afternoon. The second evening (ver. 47) began at sunset. In perfect harmony with Matthew and Mark, Luke (9 : 12) says, "The day began to wear away." Jesus had probably been employed several hours in teaching *many things* (ver. 34), and healing the sick. Hence he must have left the western side of the lake quite early in the morning. See on preceding verse.

His disciples, the apostles (ver. 30), therefore come to him while he is still employed with the multitude. While Jesus was healing the sick, the disciples were doubtless here and there. **This is a desert place.** See on ver. 32. Away from the villages and thoroughfares, no food could be obtained. **The time** (the same word is translated *day* at the beginning of the verse), the day*time* **is far passed,** is far advanced, or far gone; it is now late.

36. **Send them away.** The first reason for *dismissing* the multitude is already given, the lateness of the hour. Another reason was that they might go **into the country round about,** *into the surrounding fields* among the farmers, and **into the villages,** among those who had provisions to sell, and buy for themselves. The third and principal reason is, **for they have nothing to eat.** How they knew this we are not told; but very probably from the general appearance of the people, who had come hurriedly together, and from seeing no provisions on the grounds. Some of the oldest manuscripts finish this verse thus : *and buy themselves something to eat,* which implies that they had nothing to eat.

37. Jesus commands his disciples to give them to eat, declaring that there was no necessity for sending them away, Matt. 14 : 16. This was calculated to excite their expectation and strengthen their faith. Then he asks Philip, in order to try his faith, "Whence shall we buy bread that these may eat?" who answered that **two hundred pennyworth** (two hundred *denaries,* about thirty dollars) would not be sufficient, John 6 : 5-7. The twelve now ask him if they shall go and buy that amount. **Penny,** rather *denary,* a Roman silver coin, worth about fifteen cents.

38. Without directly replying, Jesus asks **How many loaves have ye?** and commands them to go and see. **When they knew.** John tells us

unto them, How many loaves have ye? go and see. And when they knew, they say, ᵒ Five, and two fishes.
39 And he commanded them to make all sit down by
40 companies upon the green grass. And they sat down
41 in ranks, by hundreds, and by fifties. And when he had taken the five loaves and the two fishes, he looked up to heaven, ᵖ and blessed, and brake the loaves, and gave *them* to his disciples to set before them; and the two fishes divided he among
42 them all. And they did all eat, and were filled.

ᵒ ch. 8. 5; Mt. 14. 17; Lk. 9. 13; John 6. 9; Mt. 15. 34.

ᵖ 1 Sam. 9. 13; Mt. 26. 26.

how they knew. Andrew gave the information that a lad had five *barley* loaves, an inferior kind of food, and two *small* fishes, John 6: 8, 9. Loaves were usually made in the form of round cakes, and generally about half an inch in thickness. The language of the four evangelists implies that this was all the provisions on the ground. See especially Matt. 14: 17; Luke 9: 13.

39. With authority Jesus **commanded** the twelve to make the multitude **sit down,** *recline* or *lie down*, the customary posture at table (see on 2: 15), **by companies,** in separate *parties*, or *messes*, for the sake of order and convenience, **upon the green grass,** which now in the spring covered the ground. "The scene of this extraordinary miracle is the noble plain (Butaiha) at the mouth of the Jordan, which during most of the year is now, as then, covered with 'green grass.'"—Dr. J. P. Newman, *From Dan to Beersheba*, p. 395. "This Butaiha belonged to Bethsaida. At this extreme southeast corner of it the mountain shuts down upon the lake bleak and barren. . . . In this little cove the ships (boats) were anchored. On this beautiful sward at the base of the rocky hill the people were seated to receive from the hands of the Son of God the miraculous bread, emblematic of his body, which is the true bread from heaven."—Dr. Thomson, *The Land and the Book*, vol. ii., p. 29. This plain east of the Jordan forms a triangle, the shore of the lake making one side, the Jordan the second, and the eastern mountains the third.

40. The order of Jesus is quickly obeyed. The multitude under the direction of the apostles **sat down,** *lay down* **in ranks,** literally, *in garden-plots* or *beds*, hence in regular groups, *squares* or parallelograms, each consisting of a hundred or fifty. Thus all confusion and all deception was prevented. The multitude could be conveniently served, and easily and accurately counted.

41. **Looked up to heaven,** to the sky which seems to separate us from the place of God's immediate presence. "*Looking up* is a natural and scriptural gesture in addressing God, whom all men, as it were, instinctively regard as dwelling in some special sense above them."—Alexander. Compare 2 Chron. 6: 13; Ps. 123: 1, 2; John 11: 41. **Blessed.** Implored a blessing on the bread (Luke 9: 16) and *praised* God for it. John (6: 11) says "He gave thanks." The latter is included in the former. The word translated *bless* is used in praising God for favors (Luke 1: 64); also in invoking God's blessing. (Luke 2: 34); also in God's conferring favors, Heb. 6: 14; Acts 3: 26. These three senses really met in Jesus. For as a man he praised God and implored his blessing, while, as God, he granted it. So Matthew (15: 36) has *gave thanks*, while Mark (8: 7) has *blessed*. The same diversity is seen in the account of the Lord's Supper. Matthew (26: 26) and Mark (14: 22) have *blessed;* Luke (22: 19) and Paul (1 Cor. 11: 24) have *gave thanks*. **And brake the loaves.** The usual way of preparing bread for eating. The Scriptures speak of breaking bread, but never of cutting it. The thin loaves, or cakes, were very likely brittle. With great minuteness Mark continues, **and gave them to his disciples,** etc. A beautiful illustration and foreshadowing of their future work of bearing the bread of life to perishing sinners. Mark alone says, **the two fishes divided he,** separated into parts, and distributed **among them all.** John (6: 11) comes nearest in detail: "likewise of the fishes, as much as they would."

42. Two facts stated in regard to the

43 And they took up twelve baskets full of the frag-
44 ments, and of the fishes. And they that did eat of the loaves were about five thousand men.

reception of the food. **They did all eat;** *they all ate*, none were passed over. **Were filled.** Their appetites were fully satisfied. These facts were the result of the miracle in multiplying the bread. The broken bread and the divided fishes, like the widow's meal and oil (1 Kings 17 : 16), did not waste nor fail so long as the disciples continued to supply the multitude.

43. **And they took up;** with the additional idea of carrying away with them. While these provisions lasted the disciples were constantly reminded of this wonderful miracle. Jesus had given the command, "Gather up the fragments that remain that nothing be lost" (John 6 : 12), thereby teaching a lesson of prudent economy. They were not to expect a continuation of the miracle. **Twelve baskets full.** The usual Jewish traveling-basket. The number was twelve; thus each apostle filled his basket. The most natural meaning of the original is, that the apostles filled twelve baskets with **the fragments,** the broken pieces of bread, and in addition took up a portion **of the fishes.** This is confirmed by John 6 : 13, "filled twelve baskets with the fragments of the five barley loaves." Mark alone speaks of the relics of the fishes. Thus there remained much more than the original provisions; showing an actual increase of food, and not a supernatural restraining and satisfying of the appetite. Some suppose that the provisions taken up were those broken by Jesus, but undistributed. The most natural supposition, however, is that they had been distributed, or mostly so, and that they were gathered up from the ground where the companies had eaten. John 6 : 12, 13 especially implies this.

44. **About five thousand men.** *About* should be omitted according to the highest critical authorities; it is, however, found in the other Gospels, Matt. 14 : 21; Luke 9 : 14; John 6 : 10. Thus there was one loaf to every thousand men. Matthew adds, "besides women and children," of whom there were doubtless many. It was customary then, as now, in the East, for men to eat alone, reclining, and the women and children by themselves sitting. It was easy to number the men, who were arranged in companies of hundreds and fifties; but not the women and children, who probably sat around promiscuously.

Various attempts have been made by neologists to explain away this miracle, by endeavoring to trace it to natural causes, and even supposing it originally a parable, but by mistake related as an actual occurrence. But all such attempts are manifestly absurd and ridiculous. All of the four narratives clearly convey the idea of superhuman power. They do not tell how that power was exerted, or how the food was increased; but they do clearly tell us that a few loaves and fishes which a lad could carry in his basket, were increased so that thousands satisfied their hunger, and there remained at least twelve times more of fragments than of the original provisions. It is not necessary to suppose creative power; for the laws and the elements of the natural world being under the direction of Jesus, he could bring together at his will all the elements constituting the bread and the fishes. The power in one case was as truly omnipotent as in the other. Similar exhibitions of divine power are recorded in the Old Testament, in giving the manna (Exod. 16 : 4), and in multiplying the widow's oil, 2 Kings 4 : 2-7. Compare the turning of water into wine, John 2 : 9.

In this miracle Jesus also exhibited himself as the bread of life. See the application that Jesus made of it soon after in the synagogue at Capernaum, John 6 : 26-35, 48-58. The multitude was blind to this deep, spiritual import and design; but they felt the force of the miracle as an evidence of the Messiahship of Jesus, and they exclaim, "Of a truth this is the prophet that cometh into the world," John 6 : 14. Possibly a tradition, that the Messiah would rain manna from heaven, may also have had its influence in leading them to this conclusion.

45-56. THE DISCIPLES RETURN ACROSS THE SEA; JESUS WALKS ON THE WATER. Matt. 14 : 22-36; John 6 : 15-21. Mark

Jesus walks upon the water. Miracles in the land of Gennesaret.

45 ᵠAND straightway he constrained his disciples to get into the ship, and to go to the other side before unto Bethsaida, while he sent away the people. ᵠ Mt. 14. 22 ; John 6. 15.

---

as usual enters most into detail, but omits all reference to Peter's walking on the water, which is alone recorded by Matthew, who ever delights in giving the words and sayings of Jesus. John gives a brief but independent account, as of an eye-witness, with several additional particulars. Luke, who passes over very briefly the period of six months, from the Passover A.D. 29 to the Feast of Tabernacles (Luke 9 : 17-51), omits all reference to this voyage and miracle.

45. Straightway after gathering up the fragments, Jesus **constrained** the apostles, compelled or obliged them, by authoritative persuasion and command, to embark in **the ship,** in which they came hither. They dreaded a night passage, but he insisted on their going. Possibly they may have been among the foremost with the multitude to make him king (John 6 : 15); Jesus may have thus quietly thwarted their design by immediately constraining to embark; after which he could the more easily **send away** the people. The distress of that night upon the sea, and the miracle, were, doubtless, what the disciples needed to humble and enlighten them.

To go to the other side before unto Bethsaida. *To go before to* the western Bethsaida, of Galilee, John 12 : 21. The name, which means *a house of fishing,* could easily be applied to two places, especially where fishing was so common a business. Philip (Luke 3 : 1) may have changed the name of the northeastern Bethsaida (see on ver. 32) to Julias, after the daughter of the emperor, because he would distinguish it from the other, and also that its name might more become its dignity. The name could still be applied to the port of the city, a little south at the mouth of the river. Dr. Thomson (*Land and Book,* vol. ii., pp. 9, 29-32) supposes but one place of this name, consisting of two parts, the one on the east and the other on the west bank of the Jordan. He speaks of ruins near the mouth of the river, which indicate a double town. He supposes that the disciples were to go before Jesus to or toward Bethsaida on the other side of the Jordan, expecting Jesus to join them there or somewhere along the coast after dismissing the multitude. But a violent wind beat off the boat, so that they were driven away from near the mouth of the Jordan down toward the plain of Gennesaret. It is possible to harmonize the references to Bethsaida in the Gospels by this supposition. Yet the theory of two towns, one on the north-east and the other on the north-west, seems to me the more probable. For,

First. The north-eastern Bethsaida (Julias) is evidently referred to by Luke (9 : 10), in the vicinity of which the feeding of the five thousand took place; and by Mark, in 8 : 22, where Jesus, on his way to Cæsarea Philippi, healed a blind man. But from this Bethsaida (Luke 9 : 10) Mark, in this verse, says, Jesus constrained his disciples to embark and go before *to the other side* of the sea, the western side, *to Bethsaida.* This marks a place of that name on the western side of the sea. We can hardly suppose Jesus to have meant merely on the other side of the Jordan. *To the other side* was a common expression in reference to the Sea of Galilee, Matt. 8 : 18, 28; 14 : 22; 16 : 5; Mark 4 : 35; 5 : 21; 8 : 13. Compare ver. 53. When Jordan was intended it was distinctly named, ch. 10 : 1; 3 : 8; Matt. 4 : 15, 25 ; 19 : 1.

Second. The association of Bethsaida with Chorazin and Capernaum (between them) by our Lord (Matt. 11 : 21-23 ; Luke 10 : 23-15), points to a place of that name on the western shore of the lake. The natural inference is that these three cities were near together in Galilee.

Third. The comparison of Mark 6 : 45, 53 with John 6 : 17, 21 leads to the same conclusion. The disciples "go before to the other side to Bethsaida" (Mark 6 : 45); were going "over the sea towards or to Capernaum" (John 6 :

46 And when he had sent them away, he departed into a mountain to pray.
47 ʳAnd when even was come, the ship was in the
48 midst of the sea, and he alone on the land. And he saw them toiling in rowing; for the wind was contrary

ʳ Mt. 14. 23; John 6. 16, 17; Is. 64. 11; Jon. 1. 13.

17); passing over, they "came into the land of Gennesaret" (Mark 6: 53); "the ship was at the land whither they went," John 6 : 21. The natural inferences are, that Capernaum and Bethsaida were in the same immediate vicinity; that they were not far from the plain of Gennesaret; that although Jesus and the disciples may not have landed either at Capernaum or Bethsaida, they really did land so near to them that it could be styled "the land whither they went" or "were going." Compare also the fact that the next day after the miracle the multitude came to Capernaum, seeking Jesus, John 6 : 24, 25, 59.

Fourth. Jerome and Eusebius mention together Bethsaida and Capernaum as lying on the shore of the lake; and Epiphanius speaks of them as being not far distant from each other. Wilibald (A.D. 722), who visited this region, went from Magdala to Capernaum; thence to Bethsaida, where there was "a church on the site of the house" of Andrew and Peter; and then to Chorazin. These historical references confirm the conclusion that Bethsaida of Galilee, the birthplace of Andrew, Peter and Philip (John 1 : 45), lay upon the western shore of the lake.

"About half a mile north of Capernaum (*Kahn Minyeh*) is a beautiful little bay, with a broad margin of pearly sand. At its northern extremity are fountains, aqueducts, and half-ruined mills; and scattered round them are the remains of an old town called Tabighah. There is every reason to believe that this is the site of Bethsaida. (Robinson, *Bib. Res.* iii. 358 ff.) No site along the whole shore seems so admirably adapted for a fishing town. Here is a bay sheltered by hills behind, and projecting bluffs on each side, and here is a smooth sandy beach, such as fishermen delight to ground their boats upon. The strand forms a pleasant promenade, and so far answers the description in Mark 1 : 16-20."—Prof. J. L. Porter, *Alexander's Kitto's Cyclo.*, vol. i., p. 357.

46. **When he had sent them away.** Rather, *taken leave of them, bade them farewell.* The Greek verb is translated "bid farewell" in Luke 9 : 61 and Acts 18 : 21; and "took leave" in Acts 18 : 18 and 2 Cor. 2 : 13. Luke 14 : 33 is the only other place in the New Testament where it is found, and there translated "forsake." The meaning here is clear. He took leave of the people, bidding them adieu, while he exercised his authority in dismissing them. The harmony of the evangelists is beautiful. Matthew (14 : 23): "When he had sent away (*dismissed*) the multitude ;" John (6 : 15) : "He departed (*withdrew*) again into a mountain." Mark (vers. 45, 46): "While he sent away (*dismissed*) the people. And when he had *taken leave* of them." Thus his authority, his kind and benignant leave-taking, and his peculiar power of withdrawing when he desired, are brought to view as exercised by him on this occasion. Another reason for sending away the disciples first is also suggested : he could, more easily than they, withdraw from the multitude.

Into a mountain ; the mountain or highlands which rose from the plain and the shore; see on ver. 39; also on 3 : 13. **To pray.** His retirement was not for rest, but for prayer. What was the burden of his prayer is not told us. Doubtless the events of that day and the disciples, the multitude, their desire to make him king (John 6 : 15), and his future labors, formed a part.

47. **When even was come.** The second evening (see on ver. 35), beginning with sunset, continuing from about six till nine o'clock. **The ship . . . in the midst of the sea.** Not necessarily in its center, but out at sea, at some distance from land, in its middle portions. **He alone.** Watching and praying. *Upon the land ;* probably still upon the mountain, which that night formed his closet for secret prayer, Matt. 6 : 6.

48. **And he saw them.** A vivid description peculiar to Mark. It was dark, John 6 : 17; but there was doubt-

unto them: and about the fourth watch of the night he cometh unto them, *walking upon the sea; and 49 †would have passed by them. But when they saw him walking upon the sea, they supposed it had

* Job 9. 8.
† Lk. 24. 28.

less a moon, it being near the Passover, so that the little ship could be seen by the human eye from the mountainous shore. At first the disciples had a prospect of a quick and easy passage; but now the tempest has risen, and Jesus sees them **toiling in rowing**, *tormented, distressed in rowing*, their bodies excited and wearied with the violent exercise, and their minds with anxiety. **For the wind.** "A great wind that blew." John 6 : 18. **Was contrary to them**; blowing from a westerly direction. "My experience in this region enables me to sympathize with the disciples in their long night's contest with the wind. . . . The sun had scarcely set when the wind began to rush down toward the lake, and it continued all night long with constantly increasing violence, so that when we reached the shore next morning the face of the lake was like a huge boiling caldron. The wind howled down every wady from the north-east and east with such fury that no efforts of rowers could have brought a boat to shore at any point along the coast. . . . To understand the causes of these sudden and violent tempests, we must remember that the lake lies low—six hundred feet lower than the ocean; that the vast and naked plateaus of the Jordan rise to a great height, spreading back to the wilds of the Hauran, and upward to snowy Hermon; that the water-courses have cut out profound ravines and wild gorges, converging to the head of this lake, and that these act like gigantic *funnels* to draw down the cold wind from the mountains."—THOMSON, *Land and the Book*, vol. ii., p. 32.

About the fourth watch of the night. About three or four o'clock in the morning. The fourth watch was from three to six o'clock, or sunrise. According to the Roman custom the Jews now divided the night into four watches of about three hours each, ch. 13 : 35. At an earlier period they had divided the night into three equal parts or watches, of about four hours each, called "the first watch" (Lam. 2 : 19),

"the middle watch" (Jud. 7 : 19), "the morning watch," 1 Sam. 11 : 11. At this time, when they were twenty-five or thirty furlongs, more than halfway across (John 6 : 19), **Jesus cometh unto them** still painfully laboring against the adverse wind. **Walking upon the sea.** The silly evasion of those who, to explain away the miracle, would translate "walking on the shore of the sea," is opposed alike to the strict and natural meaning of the words, the evident design and form of the narrative in relating a miracle, and the surprise and terror of the disciples at the sight. How Jesus could have walked on the water we are not informed, whether he suspended the law of gravity in his own case, or counteracted the force of gravity by divine power, or made the waters solid beneath his feet. The second supposition seems to me the most plausible. But he was divine, and the laws of nature were subject to him, of which he could easily make a use wholly unknown to us.

Would have passed by them, had not the disciples been troubled and cried out in fear. Jesus, however, knew that the disciples would see him, and what would be the effect upon them. This was therefore a trial of their faith, and a means of exciting prayer and cries for help. So he remained two days when Mary and Martha sent him word that Lazarus was sick, John 11 : 6. And to the two disciples at Emmaus he made as though he would go further, Luke 24 : 28.

49. **When they saw him walking.** And *they seeing him,* in the act of walking on the water. It is implied that this was when the disciples first saw him, and immediately after. But they did not know him, but **supposed it had been** or *was* **a spirit,** a *ghost* or *specter;* an apparition, indicating approaching evil; and they **cried out;** uttered loud cries, for fear, Matt. 14 : 26; John 6 : 19. Their superstitious feelings were aroused, and they gave vent to their fear in indistinct utterances and incoherent exclamations.

50 been a spirit, and cried out: for they all saw him, and were troubled. And immediately he talked with them, and saith unto them, ᵘBe of good cheer: ᵃ Is. 43. 2; John 20. 19. 21.
51 it is I; be not afraid. And he went up unto them into the ship; and the wind ceased: and they were sore amazed in themselves beyond measure, and
52 wondered. Forˣ they considered not *the miracle* of ˣ ch. 8. 17, 18. the loaves; for their ʸ heart was hardened. ʸ ch. 3. 5; 16. 14.

---

50. For they all saw him. They could not be deceived; if only one had seen him it might have been regarded as the effect of the imagination; but all see the same object. It is also rather implied that they recognized the general form and appearance of Jesus; but as they had left him behind, and regarding it impossible for a human being to walk on the water, they thought they saw a specter. **And were troubled.** Agitated and greatly disturbed, especially with fear at the sight. **Immediately he talked with them.** He no longer continues to pass by them, ver. 48. They are sufficiently tried, and immediately upon their manifesting their terror by crying aloud, Jesus talked with them. The familiar and tender tones of his voice indicate who he is, and tend at once to allay their fears. His words, too, were adapted to dispel their superstitious alarm. **Be of good cheer.** *Take courage.* **It is I,** or *I am he,* whom you know as your Lord and Teacher. **Be not afraid,** *fear not* any danger, since I am here. At this point Matthew relates the incident of Peter's vain desire and attempt to imitate his Master in walking on the water. Why Mark and John should have omitted it, is uncertain, and cannot in this world be known. But this is certain, that only one evangelist under the direction of inspiration recorded it.

51. Immediately after saving the sinking Peter, who obtained permission to come to him (Matt. 14 : 28–31), Jesus **went up** to them into the ship. **And the wind ceased** from blowing, abated. A miracle similar to that recorded in ch. 4 : 39. Their very great astonishment is strongly expressed. **Sore,** *exceedingly* **amazed in themselves beyond measure,** or *vehemently.* This gives us a glimpse at their internal amazement. **And wondered.** A glimpse at their external astonishment, which found expression in exclamations. But many ancient documents omit, *and wondered;* as does also the Improved version. "They were astonished when they found it was Christ, and not a spirit; and they were more amazed at his walking on the sea; and they marvelled still more abundantly when they observed that the wind ceased upon his coming into the ship; their amazement was beyond expression, and therefore a heap of words are made use of to signify it by."—JOHN GILL.

52. The reason of their undue astonishment is given. **For they considered,** etc.; *considered not on the loaves,* understood and comprehended not, so as to infer that he who had exercised such power over the loaves could exercise a similar power over the sea. They did not perceive nor consider that all the elements of nature were under his control, those of water as well as those of bread. The reason of this want of comprehension is given, **for their heart was hardened,** dull, sluggish, insensible, so as not to recognize sufficiently his divine power and nature, and draw just inferences from what they had previously witnessed. The obtuseness of the disciples to us seems amazing; but it may be explained: (1.) Their false Jewish conceptions of the Messiah, in which they had been trained from childhood. (2.) Their comparatively unlettered condition; their minds untrained and unfitted for the higher spiritual conceptions of Christ and his kingdom. (3.) Not being illuminated by the Holy Spirit, Luke 24 : 45, 49; John 20 : 22. It appears to have been in the divine plan that they should not fully apprehend Christ and his kingdom till after his resurrection. Thus the great truths of redemption appeared the more glorious, and the gift of the Spirit the more valuable.

A.D. 29. MARK VI. 129

53 *And when they had passed over, they came into   *Mt. 14. 34–36;
    the land of Gennesaret, and drew to the shore.   Lk. 6. 19.
54 And when they were come out of the ship, straight-
55 way they knew him, and ran through that whole
    region round about, and began to carry about in
    beds those that were sick, where they heard he was.
56 And whithersoever he entered, into villages, or
    cities, or country, they laid the sick in the streets,
    and besought him that *they might touch if it were   *ch. 5. 27, 28; Mt.
    but the border of his garment: and as many as   9. 20; Ac. 19. 12.
    touched him were made whole.

53. **When they had passed over;** the lake, from east to west. Thus they came "to the other side," ver. 45. **Came into** (*to*) **the land of Gennesaret.** A small district of country or plain on the western shore of the sea, about four miles long and two and a half broad, extending southward from *Khan Minyeh*, one of the supposed sites of Capernaum. See on ch. 1 : 21. Its modern name is *el*-Ghuweir, or the "Little Ghor." Josephus graphically describes the wonderful beauty and fertility of this plain. Professor Stanley glowingly says: "The richness of the soil displays itself in magnificent corn-fields; whilst along the shore rises a thick jungle of thorn and oleander, abounding in birds of brilliant colors and various forms; the whole producing an impression such as, to the traveler of modern days, recalls instantly the valley of the Nile." The fine temperature arises from the fact that the plain is almost on a level with the sea, and is therefore more than six hundred feet below the ocean. See on ch. 1 : 16. Gennesaret is probably a corruption of Chinnereth, the name of a fenced city and small district west of the sea, Josh. 19 : 35. Some suppose it to have been the ancient name of Tiberias. From it the lake derived one of its names.

And drew to the shore. Rather, *Came to anchor*, anchored there. They were soon at the end of their voyage after the wind ceased. "And immediately," says John (6 : 21), "they were at the land whither they were going," which would seem to indicate that though they may not have anchored either at Bethsaida (ver. 45) or Capernaum (John 6 : 17), yet these places were not very far out of their way.

54. It would seem from the description that follows that Jesus and his disciples landed at a somewhat retired spot. No name is given the place; the people of the region around bring their sick to Jesus (compare Matt. 14 : 35); villages and towns are mentioned through which he passed. **When they were come out.** Had landed. **Straightway they knew him.** Those that saw him, the men of the place (Matt. 14 : 35), inhabiting the plain and living in that vicinity; they immediately *recognized him.* By his residence at Capernaum, and his public ministry in all the towns and villages of that whole region, he had become generally known.

It was early in the morning (see John 6 : 21 in preceding verse); but anchoring the vessel and embarking would attract the attention of the inhabitants.

55. We have a vivid description in this verse of the excitement among the people of that rural district. **Round about** should be omitted, according to the highest critical authorities. **They ran** through that **whole region,** spreading the news all over the plain (Matt. 14 : 35), and without delay **began to carry about,** some one way and some another, and some missing him and following after, **in beds,** *on* small light *couches* (see on ch. 2 : 4), **those that were sick** to the places **where they heard he was.** It is implied that Jesus passed through that region with but little delay, and that the people directed their course in the direction where he was reported to be. They would therefore *carry about* their sick, this way or that, according to every fresh report; and doubtless, occasionally missing him from wrong information, would follow him from one place to another.

56. **Whithersoever.** *Wherever* he went, the same intense desire for being

healed was manifested immediately upon his coming. **Country;** *the fields* outside of cities and villages, among the farms, ver. 36. **In the streets.** Rather, *in the market-places.* Places of public resort. Any thoroughfare, open place or public square where people met together for business or conversation. In cities they were generally just inside the gates. Their intense earnestness is seen not only in laying their sick in the market-places, but also in that they **besought** him that the sick might touch if it were but **the border** or *fringe* **of his garment.** The fringe was commanded to be worn as a badge of an Israelite, Num. 15 : 38. This gives a vivid view of the faith of the people in Christ's power to heal. There was doubtless some superstition in the people, but faith can exist even with superstition. Their *touch* gave a practical manifestation of their faith, and at the same time kept before them the fact that Jesus was the author of the healing. The effect was more extensive and impressive by keeping a visible connection between the healer and the healed. None touched him in vain. All who did so were **made whole,** restored to health. We get a glimpse here of the many miracles performed by Jesus during his public ministry, ch. 1 : 32-34. One of the **cities** was Capernaum, where those who had been fed the day before, sought and found Jesus; and he delivered them a discourse on the bread of heaven, John 6 : 22-71.

REMARKS.

1. Learn from Jesus to faithfully discharge the religious duties you owe to your friends and kindred, ver. 1; ch. 5 : 19; Luke 4 : 16; 24 : 47.

2. Make repeated efforts to save even the most violent opposers of the gospel, ver. 2; Luke 4 : 28, 29; 13 : 34; Rom. 5 : 6.

3. Many hear the gospel only to admire or wonder, excuse themselves or find fault, and thus perish, ver. 2; Luke 4 : 23; Acts 13 : 41; Heb. 4 : 2.

4. Jesus honored honest labor by engaging in it himself, ver. 3; Luke 2 : 51; Acts 18 : 3.

5. We should not judge others by their outward condition, circumstances and relations, but by what they really show themselves to be, vers. 2, 3; 1 Sam. 16 : 7; Matt. 7 : 20; James 1 : 1-4.

6. Great religious privileges are very generally undervalued. So great is human depravity that even familiarity with them too often breeds contempt, vers. 2-4; John 12 : 37, 38; Rom. 10 : 21.

7. Many would explain the works of Christ and of the Spirit and the power of the gospel by natural causes, and when they fail are offended, ver. 3; Acts 17 : 32.

8. Unbelief is a terrible sin. It robs Jesus of the glory of what he has done, and deprives us of the good he would do, vers. 5, 6; ch. 16 : 16; Matt. 13 : 58; 17 : 17-20.

9. It is often best for Christian laborers to go forth two by two, ver. 7; Luke 10 : 1; Eccle. 4 : 9-12; Acts 3 : 1; 11 : 30; 15 : 39, 40.

10. Christ calls those to preach the gospel who are adapted to the work, and qualifies them with gifts and graces. This, however, does not preclude the necessity of mental discipline, ver. 7; 1 Tim. 3 : 2; 4 : 13; 2 Tim. 2 : 24.

11. Ministers of the gospel should go forth to their work in humble dependence, trusting that he for whom they labor will provide from time to time all that may be necessary, vers. 8 : 9; 1 Cor. 9 : 8-11; 3 John 7.

12. Ministers should not be gossips, but quiet, peaceful, and intent upon their work, ver. 10; 1 Tim 3 : 3; 2 Tim. 2 : 22-25; Tit. 1 : 7-10.

13. The acts as well as the words of God's faithful servants will rise up in judgment against the rejecters of the gospel, ver. 11; Acts 13 : 51.

14. How terrible the doom of those who will not receive nor hear Christ's messengers! Ver. 11; Matt. 25 : 41, 45.

15. Repentance is the sinner's first duty, ver. 12; ch. 1 : 15; Acts 3 : 19.

16. Ministers should strive to do good both to the bodies and souls of men, vers. 12, 13; Acts 3 : 6, 7.

17. How great the power of truth over the conscience! Even the voluptuous Herod feels it, vers. 14, 16, 20, 26; Acts 24 : 25; 26 : 27, 28.

18. Men have been ever ready to suppose Jesus to be what he is not, ver. 15; Matt. 16 : 14; 1 Cor. 1 : 23; John 2 : 22; 4 : 3.

19. A guilty conscience is the sinner's tormentor, ver. 16; Matt. 27 : 3-5; John 8 : 9.

20. The faithful minister should re-

buke sin in high as well as humble places, vers. 17, 18; 1 Kings 21 : 20, 22; Prov. 28 : 23; Gal. 2 : 11, 14.

21. Faithful reprovers must expect the hatred of those who still cling to their sins, vers. 17–19; 1 Kings 22 : 8; John 3 : 20; 2 Tim. 3 : 12.

22. People may go far in external religion, yet be slaves to sin, and miss of salvation, vers. 17–20; ch. 10 : 22; Ps. 106 : 12–14; Ezek. 33 : 31, 32.

23. Woman through grace becomes an angel of mercy, but through sin a demon of wrath, vers. 19, 24; 1 Kings 19 : 2; 21 : 25; Ezek. 7 : 26.

24. The festivities of the world open large and convenient channels to temptation and sin, ver. 21; Dan. 5 : 1–5; James 5 : 5, 6; 2 Pet. 2 : 12–14.

25. Worldly amusements are intoxicating. Dancing led Herod to a rash oath, and then to murder, ver. 22; Job 21 : 11–15.

26. Rash oaths and promises are sinful. No one has a right to make them, ver. 23; Exod. 20 : 7; Lev. 5 : 4–6; 1 Sam. 14 : 24–28; Eccle. 5 : 2.

27. How great the influence of a mother for good or evil, ver. 23, 24; 1 Kings 22 : 52; Prov. 31 : 1; 2 Tim. 1 : 5; 3 : 15.

28. The fear of man leads many into great sorrow and destruction, ver. 26; Prov. 29 : 25.

29. Sin is degrading, progressive and enslaving. Herod and Herodias were at first unlawfully married; at length they imbue their hands in innocent blood, vers. 17–29; 2 Tim. 3 : 13; James 1 : 15.

30. Notoriety has its dangers. By coming in contact with Herod, John was imprisoned and put to death, vers. 14–28; Acts 6 : 8–12; 12 : 1–3.

31. Behold what reward some of God's best servants receive in this world, vers. 27, 28; Acts 7 : 59; 12 : 2; 1 Cor. 4 : 9–13; 2 Tim. 4 : 6–8.

32. They who treat with becoming respect the dead bodies of saints are not forgotten, ver. 29; ch. 14 : 6–9; Acts 8 : 2.

33. We should daily in our prayers give an account of our labors to Jesus, ver. 30; Acts 6 : 4; 2 Cor. 5 : 10.

34. The overworked minister or Christian should seek rest by a change of scenes and labors, ver. 31; ch. 4 : 34.

35. There is no perfect rest in this world, vers. 32, 33; Ps. 55 : 6; Mic. 2 : 10; Heb. 4 : 9.

36. We should never under any circumstances withhold our pity from the spiritually destitute and ignorant, ver. 34; Zech. 7 : 9; Rom. 15 : 3.

37. Jesus will not permit any to seek him in vain, ver. 34; John 6 : 37; 10 : 11; Heb. 13 : 8.

38. Jesus is far more compassionate than it is possible for his people to be, vers. 35–37; Luke 18 : 39–42; Ps. 103 : 11, 13.

39. We can the better do good to the souls of many by first doing their bodies good, vers. 37–39; Heb. 13 : 16.

40. In straitened circumstances, and even in poverty, we should practice Christian benevolence, trusting in Christ, who can make the desert teem with plenty, vers. 37–42; 1 Cor. 16 : 1, 2; Ps. 78 : 19–22; 107 : 35–37; Isa. 32 : 8.

41. Whatever Jesus directs we should do, confiding in his wisdom and power, vers. 37, 42, 43; ch. 3 : 5; Matt. 6 : 33.

42. Christ by example commends to us a due regard to order and system, vers. 39, 40; 1 Cor. 14 : 33, 40; Tit. 1 : 5; Acts 6 : 1–4.

43. Before partaking of food we should give thanks to God and crave his blessing, ver. 41; ch. 8 : 6; Eph. 5 : 20; 1 Tim. 4 : 4, 5.

44. We should be careful and not waste either our temporal or spiritual blessings, ver. 43; ch. 8 : 8; Matt. 7 : 6.

45. The world is a spiritual desert; but Christ is the living bread, and sufficient for all, vers. 41–44; John 6 : 35.

46. Christ's way is the right and best way, but often contrary to the inclinations of his people, ver. 45; ch. 10 : 29; Matt. 16 : 24.

47. Like Jesus, we should be much in prayer, ver. 46; Luke 6 : 12; 9 : 28; 22 : 40; Gal. 4 : 12; James 4 : 2.

48. Jesus never loses sight of his people in this sea of strife; in due time he will come to their relief, ver. 48; 1 Cor. 10 : 13; Ps. 78 : 19–22; Heb. 13 : 5, 6.

49. Jesus tries our faith. That which at first seems threatening with destruction often turns out to be full of mercy, ver. 48–50; Rev. 1 : 17, 18; Isa. 43 : 1, 2; Ps. 119 : 67.

50. Superstition shows that there is something within man that testifies to a world beyond the grave, ver. 49; Luke 24 : 37.

51. When Christ comes among his people and takes possession of the

Discourse on eating with unwashed hands.

VII. THEN [b] came together unto him the Pharisees, and certain of the scribes, which came from Jerusa-
2 lem. And when they saw some of his disciples eat bread with defiled, that is to say, with unwashen,

[b] Mt. 15.1; Lk. 11. 39, 40; Col. 2. 8, 23.

soul, human passions are stilled and opposition banished, ver. 51; Eph. 2 : 4-6.
52. Trials are needed as well as blessings; the storm as well as the bread, ver. 51, 52; Isa. 1 : 3; 2 Cor. 12 : 7; Heb. 12 : 11.
53. Beware lest Christ's blessings only harden your hearts, ver. 52; ch. 16 : 14; Ps. 106 : 13; Heb. 3 : 7-13 ; 4 : 1.
54. Get a spiritual acquaintance with Jesus, so as truly to know him, ver. 54; John 17 : 3; Phil. 3 : 10; 1 John 5 : 13, 20.
55. Be in earnest to bring all you can to Jesus, in order that you may experience his saving power, ver. 55, 56; 1 Cor. 9 : 22; 1 Tim. 4 : 16.
56. Personal faith is necessary to salvation. As many as touched him were made whole, ver. 56; ch. 16 : 16; Rom. 10 : 10.

CHAPTER VII.

At the beginning of this chapter, Mark gives us a fresh glimpse of the organized opposition of the Pharisees against Jesus. See on ch. 3. The scribes and Pharisees make his unceremonious practice of eating with unwashen hands the object of their attack. The authoritative reply of Jesus is given, and his instructions on defilement to the people and to his own disciples. Jesus then prudently withdraws and visits the Gentile world, and performs a miracle upon a Gentile. Returning to the eastern side of the Sea of Galilee, he heals a deaf and dumb man in Decapolis, which is related only by this evangelist.

Between the events of this and the preceding chapter were Christ's discourse at Capernaum (John 6 : 22-71), and the third Passover of his public ministry (April 17th, A.D. 29), which he did not attend, John 6 : 4; 7 : 1. The incidents here related probably took place between the latter part of April and the first part of June.

1-23 ON UNWASHEN HANDS. THE

TRADITION OF THE ELDERS. MORAL AND PHYSICAL DEFILEMENT. To the scribes and Pharisees and to the people; in private to his disciples, Matt. 15 : 1- 20. The account of Mark is in several respects the fullest, and very much what we would expect from one writing under the direction of Peter.
1. **Then.** Rather, *And there.* The connection with the preceding chapter is not close. The natural inference is that Jesus was still in Galilee, yet several days and many incidents could have intervened of which we have here no account. He may have been at Capernaum. **Pharisees.** See on ch. 2 : 16. **Scribes.** See on ch. 1 : 22. They were probably Pharisees. **Came together unto him.** An understanding among themselves and a definite object is here implied. Some suppose that they were a formal deputation, such as once visited John the Baptist, John 1 : 19. This is possibly, though not necessarily, implied. **Who came from Jerusalem.** They most probably belonged there. Disappointed in not seeing Jesus at the Passover (John 6 : 4; 7 : 1), they probably came to Galilee to watch his movements and to conspire against him. They may have been sent by the Sanhedrim, or, at least, they very probably came with the knowledge and approval of that body.
2. **And when they saw;** or, *And seeing some of his disciples eat,* etc. How closely these scribes and Pharisees watch him! They inspect the private acts of his disciples; they discover some of them eating, very likely a little food to satisfy hunger, and not a formal meal, without any previous washing. **With defiled,** literally, *with common,* ceremonially unclean, Acts, 10 : 14, 15, 28; 11 : 8. **That is.** Mark throws in an explanation for his Gentile readers. **With unwashen hands.** Ceremonially impure. There is no reference to personal cleanliness. The disciples were probably as cleanly in their habits as the Pharisees, but re-

A.D. 29. MARK VII. 133

3 hands, they found fault. For the Pharisees, and all the Jews, except they wash *their* hands oft, eat not,

garded the ceremonial washing of hands already clean unnecessary. As the Jews used their hands in eating without knives and forks, it was very necessary that they should be clean. The Pharisees transformed the washing of hands into a religious act, and laid down rules for its performance. The disciples did not follow them in this, but probably washed their hands in a common way, whenever necessary. **They found fault.** The word thus translated is omitted by the oldest manuscripts. It, however, states an implied fact, and has some manuscript support.

3. Mark wrote for Gentile readers, and therefore explains still further the traditional usages of the Jews in regard to washing before eating. Matthew, who wrote specially for Jews, had no need of doing this. **All the Jews.** The Pharisees especially, and indeed the Jews generally, although the Sadducees appear to have been less strict and rigid. **Except they wash their hands oft.** Literally, *Except they wash their hands with the fist;* that is, rubbing them *with the fist*, with the whole hand, and not merely with the fingers, or, more probably, with the clenched hand or fist. "Not merely dipping the fingers or hand in water as a *sign* of ablution, but rubbing the hands together as a ball or fist, in the usual Oriental manner when water is poured over them, 2 Kings 3:11."— DR. ROBINSON, *Lex*. There is, doubtless, some reference to the peculiar manner of ceremonial washing the hands, which the disciples did not observe. There is also an idea of carefulness and thoroughness connected with the expression, and hence the meaning can be generally and popularly expressed, with Alford and others, "*diligently;*" or better, with the Bible Union Version, "*carefully* wash their hands." **Wash.** The word thus translated corresponds well with our word *wash*, and is used with reference to some part of the body, as the face (Matt. 6:17), the feet (John 13: 5, 6, 8, 10, 12, 14), hands, Matt. 15:2. It does not point to any particular mode of washing. A different word is used in the next verse.

Eat not. According to the Talmud: "He who eats bread with unwashen hands is as if he were to commit fornication; and he that despiseth washing of hands shall be rooted out of the world." It is recorded to the praise of Rabbi Akiba, being imprisoned, that he preferred to die, using what little water he had in washing his hands, instead of drinking it.

Holding. Adhering to and practicing. **Tradition.** The oral law which the Jews pretended was handed down from Moses, through Joshua, the judges, and the prophets. At the time of our Saviour it was not reduced to writing. It was afterward compiled in the Mishna, or second law, by Rabbi Jehudah, a Jew of great wealth and influence, in the latter part of the second century. Two commentaries were added, the Gemara of Jerusalem, completed not later than the middle of the fourth century, and the Gemara of Babylon, completed about A.D. 500. These three constitute the Talmud. The Jews attached more importance to their traditions than even to their written law. According to the Talmud: "The words of the scribes are lovelier than the words of the law. . . . The words of the elders are weightier than the words of the prophets." The Pharisees had charged Jesus with violating the written law (ch. 2:24; 3:1–6); now they charge him with violating the tradition of the elders, than which in their estimation nothing could be more authoritative and binding. Yet they come not out frankly against him, but against his disciples, ver. 5. **Elders.** This term was first applied to men of age, elderly men (Gen. 24:2; 50:7), and as persons of ripe age and experience would naturally be called to the management of public affairs (Josh. 24:31), it afterward became an official title, Exod. 3:16; 4:29; 19:7; 24: 1, 9. The office grew out of the patriarchal system. Among the Arabs of the present day the sheikh (the *old man*) is the highest authority in the tribe. Their authority was great, though undefined, Josh. 9:18; 1 Sam. 8:4, 5. They continued during all the political changes of the Jews; under the kings, 1 Kings 12:6; 20:8; during the cap-

12

4 holding the tradition of 'he elders. And *when they come* from the market, except they wash, they eat not. And many other things there be, which they have received to hold, *as* the washing of cups, and

tivity, Jer. 29 : 1; Ezek. 21; and after the return, Ezra 10 : 8, 14. In the time of Christ a portion of the Sanhedrim was chosen from among the elders, ch. 8 : 31; 11 : 27; 14 : 43, 53; 15 : 1. In this verse the term *elders* applies to the *ancients*, the fathers of the nation, to whom it was supposed the oral law had been given. Compare Matt. 5 : 21; Heb. 11 : 2.

4. From the market. Where the whole body was in great danger of being defiled by coming in contact with all classes, many of whom might be unclean. *Market* must not be restricted to a mere place for buying provisions, but denotes a place of general resort for business and conversation. See on ch. 6 : 56.

Except they wash. Rather, *Except they immerse themselves*, or bathe. The Greek word used is *baptizo;* its signification, construction and the connecting circumstances demand the idea of dipping or immersing themselves, thus taking a bath. See on ch. 1 : 4. The learned Lutheran scholar, Dr. Meyer (Commentary on Mark, 5th edition, p. 95), on this verse says that the word "is not to be understood of the washing of the hands, but of immersion, which the word means throughout in the classics and in the New Testament; and therefore here, according to the context, 'to take a bath.' So also Luke 11 : 38." The same is expressed by DeWette, Fritzsche, Winer, Sophocles, and others. Some suppose Mark here to refer to washing by immersion those things which had been purchased and brought from market. But the view just stated is the most natural and better suits the connection and circumstances. Dr. Conant, in his exhaustive treatise on the Meaning and Use of *Baptizein* (sect. iv. 4), says: "In Mark 7 : 3, 4, it is said that the Pharisees 'eat not' (*i. e.* never eat) 'except they wash their hands,' these being always liable to ceremonial defilement; and that when they come from a public place, as the market (the whole body having been exposed), 'except they immerse (baptize) themselves, they eat not.' In the former case the writer uses the appropriate word (*niptein*) for washing any portion of the body; as the *face* (Matt. 6 : 17), the *hands* (Matt. 15 : 2), the *feet* (John 13 : 5). In the latter he uses, in distinction from it, the word *baptizein*, which by constant usage expressed an entire submersion of the object spoken of. As there is no limitation ('they immerse themselves'), the whole body of course is meant."

The usages of the Jews were in harmony with the meaning of this passage. "For 'if the Pharisees touched but the garments of the common people, they were defiled, . . . and needed immersion;' and were obliged to it. Hence when they walked the streets, they walked on the sides of the way, that they might not be defiled by touching the common people." (*Maimonides*, Mish. Chagiga, 2, 7; Hileh. Abot Tumaot, 13, 8).—DR. JOHN GILL.

The means of bathing and the supply of water in tanks (reservoirs) within and around Jerusalem were abundant. Synagogues at the present day in Jerusalem and other parts of the East are furnished with large bathing-rooms. Compare John 13 : 10, "He that is washed," or *bathed*, "needeth not save to wash his feet," referring, doubtless, to *bathing*, especially before partaking of the Passover-meal.

Mark adds that there were **many other** like usages which the Pharisees had received by tradition **to hold,** to adhere to and practice. **Washing.** Literally, *immersion*. Compare Lev. 11 : 32. The word in the Greek is the plural *baptismous*, a noun derived from the verb *baptizo*, and found only three times in the New Testament outside of this verse, ver. 8; Heb. 6 : 2; 9 : 10. The kindred noun *baptisma* is the one generally applied to the rite of baptism. **Cups.** Drinking-vessels. **Pots.** Containing about a pint. The Greek word used is derived from the Latin *sextarius*, denoting a sixth part of some larger measure. Here is another indication that Mark wrote for Roman or Gentile readers. **Brazen vessels.** Of copper or brass, probably small household vessels somewhat larger than the cups

5 pots, brazen vessels, and of tables. ᶜThen the Pharisees and scribes asked him, Why walk not thy disciples according to ᵈthe tradition of the elders, but ᵉeat bread with unwashen hands?
6 He answered and said unto them, Well hath Esaias prophesied of you hypocrites, as it is written, ᶠ'This people honoureth me with *their* lips, but their heart
7 is far from me. Howbeit in vain do they worship me, teaching *for* doctrines the commandments of

ᶜ Mt. 15. 2.

ᵈ Col. 2. 8.

ᵉ Lk. 11. 39, 40.

ᶠ Is. 29. 13; Mt. 15. 8; 1 Sam. 12. 21; Mal. 3. 14; Tit. 3. 9; James 1. 26.

and pots just mentioned. The designation *brazen* rather implies that the cups and pots were of wood, earthen, or of some other metal. In special cases of uncleanness earthen vessels were broken to pieces, Lev. 15 : 12. **Tables.** *Couches,* or *table beds,* on which persons reclined at meat. Often they were raised sofas, but ordinarily they may have been but little more than cushions or rugs, Matt. 9 : 6; Acts 5 : 15. The word is omitted here by some of the most ancient manuscripts; but the evidence for regarding it the true reading preponderates. These couches might be defiled by the leprous, the dead, or others considered unclean, Lev. 15 : 4. It has been thought by some that these couches could not have been immersed. But such was the practice according to ancient Jewish rules; although, in large articles, a cleansing, part by part, was allowed, provided the whole was thus ultimately covered with water. "These were to be washed when they had received any defilement, and that by immersion. Their canon runs thus : 'A bed that is wholly defiled, if he dips it, part by part, it is pure.' Again, 'If he dips the bed in it (the pool of water), although its feet are plunged into the thick clay (at the bottom of the pool), it is clean.' (*Maimonides,* Hilch. Celim. 26, 14; Misn. Mikvaot, 7. 7)."—DR. JOHN GILL.
5. Having explained the traditional usages of the Jews regarding cleansing to his Gentile readers, Mark continues the narrative from ver. 2. **Then.** Simply, *And the Pharisees,* etc., according to the highest critical authorities. **Asked him.** They interrogate, *question* him as if with authority, as censors of his conduct. **Why walk not thy disciples,** etc.? They come not out frankly against Jesus, but cowardly attack his disciples. The authority of their traditions they take for granted. To *live* not according to what they regarded their most sacred rule was to "transgress" it, Matt. 15 : 2. **With unwashen hands.** According to the highest critical authorities, *with common* or *defiled hands.* See on ver. 2.
6. Jesus at once applies a prediction of Isaiah to them. It is a typical prophecy, including both those of the prophet's day and those in our Savior's day. The former were the type of the latter, in whom both the prediction and type centered. **Well.** *Rightly, aptly.* **Esaias,** the Greek form of Isaiah. **Hath Esaias prophesied.** Rather, *Did Isaiah prophesy* long ago. **Of you,** etc. *Concerning you,* showing that the prediction ultimately pointed especially to them. **Hypocrites.** This is the first time he addressed them openly as hypocrites, or *dissemblers,* whose outward professions did not truly indicate their thoughts and feelings. What follows in this verse is a good definition of hypocrites. **As it is written,** or, literally, *has been written,* once written and still on record; a common formula of citing an authoritative divine revelation. Jesus quotes it and appeals to it as a part of the Holy Scriptures; compare ch. 1 : 2; 9 : 12; 14 : 21, 27; Matt. 4 : 4, 6, 7. The quotation is from Isa. 29 : 13, not according to the exact language, but according to the sense of the Hebrew. It seems to be a free quotation from the Septuagint, Greek version of the Old Testament. **This people honoreth me,** etc. They honor me with their professions, with their words and outward observances, but **their heart is far from me,** in their motives, aims and services.
7. **Howbeit.** Rather, *But.* **In vain.** *Empty* is all the honor you give me in your worship, teaching **for doctrines,** *as doctrines* or *precepts,* the command-

8 men.' For laying aside the commandment of God, ye hold the tradition of men, *as* the washing of pots and cups. And many other such like things ye do.
9 And he said unto them, Full well ye reject the commandment of God, that ye may keep your own tradition.
10 For Moses said, ᵍ 'Honour thy father and thy mother;' and, ʰ 'Whoso curseth father or

ᵍ Deu. 5. 16; Mt. 15. 4.
ʰ Le. 20. 9; Pro. 20. 20; Ex. 21. 17.

ments of men. *Doctrines* refer to those things taught as binding upon the conscience, as obligatory. Jesus gives the implied meaning of the passage, and authoritatively applies it to the scribes and Pharisees as religious teachers. They acted the extreme part of hypocrites, in perverting the word of God and adding thereto, and raising mere human precepts to the position, and even above the divine command.

8. For. Jesus gives the reason for this application of prophecy, and shows that it really applies to them. This verse is not found in Matthew. **Laying aside.** *Leaving*, neglecting, disregarding the commandment of God, **ye hold the tradition.** See on ver. 3. **Of men,** in contrast to *God*, whose law you neglect and disregard. This charge of their depreciating and disregarding God's command is preparatory to that of their violating and rejecting that command, in the next verse. **As the washing,** etc.; *immersion*, etc. See on ver. 4. Some of the oldest manuscripts omit these words to the end of the verse; and they are omitted by the Revised and the Improved versions. See ver. 13. **Many other such like things ye do,** some of which have been referred to in vers. 3, 4. The charge is thus made general. "The treatise *Celim*, or, *Of vessels*, in the Mishna, is full of rules concerning the cleanness and uncleanness of almost all things in use with men; and so of what do and what do not stand in need of washing. . . . Their rule is this: 'Vessels made of wood, and of skin, and of bone, if they are plain they are clean, but if they are hollow (or made to hold things) they are liable to pollution.' Which Maimonides explains thus: 'Vessels of wood, and of skin, and of bone, if hollow, receive defilement from the words of the law; but if they are plain, as tables, a seat, a skin on which they eat, they don't receive defilement, but from the words of the scribes.' As this washing of vessels not only concerned such as were for private use, but the vessels of the sanctuary; so it is said, 'after a feast, at the close of a goodday or festival, they dip all the vessels in the sanctuary, because the common people have touched them at the feast in the time of keeping. Wherefore they say, Touch not the table (the shew-bread table), when they show it to them that come up to the feast, that it may not be defiled by touching it; and if after the feast it is found polluted, it must be dipped; and all the vessels are obliged to immersion, except the golden altar and the altar of brass."—DR. JOHN GILL.

9. And he said to them, probably after a brief pause. Matthew brings in this portion first, and the application of the prophecy afterward. The order of Mark seems to me the most natural. **Full well.** The same word translated *well* in verse 6. It is used ironically and disapprovingly here, *Well* do you do it! **Reject.** In comparative contempt, making null and void the commandment of God. Ye do thus in order that ye may **keep,** observe, **your own tradition.** Emphatic language, and in striking contrast to God's commandment, which they rejected. Some suppose that Matthew (15 : 3) gives this verse in an interrogative form. This is possible; the sense being given, and not the exact expression. It is better, however, to regard the pointed question in Matthew as distinct from the exclamation of this verse, and as having preceded it.

10. For. Jesus proceeds to prove his charge against them. He selects a case where their tradition opposed one of the commands of the decalogue, as well as the filial feelings, the consciences and the general customs of men. It was a most striking instance of raising human tradition over the word of God. **Moses said.** God commanded or said through Moses, Matt. 15 : 4. Notice the contrast to *But ye say* of the next verse. The

11 mother, let him die the death:' but ye say, If a man shall say to his father or mother, *It is* ¹ Corban, (that ¹ Mt. 15. 5 ; 23. 18.
is to say, a gift,) by whatsoever thou mightest be
12 profited by me; *he shall be free ;* and ye suffer him no more to do aught for his father or his mother;

quotations are from the fifth commandment (Ex. 20 : 12), and the penalty of cursing or reviling a parent, Ex. 21 : 17. We have here the testimony of Jesus, not only to the divine origin of the decalogue and of the Mosaic law, but also to Moses as an inspired teacher and lawgiver. What Moses *said* was to be received as the *commandment* of God.
Honor thy father, etc., not only in thought, word and deed, but also in providing for them in want and distress, in poverty or old age. **Curseth**, etc. Dishonoring a parent so far as to *curse* or *revile* them. In the preceding clause it is "*thy* father and *thy* mother," thus bringing to every one's mind his personal relation to his own father and mother. In this it is simply "father or mother," the general idea of that sacred relation, which any one by cursing a parent would dishonor and profane.
Let him die the death. A Hebraism in the original; an intensive expression, *let him end with death*, let him be executed, or more freely, *let him surely die.* The severity of the sentence showed the importance of the command and the greatness of the sin in transgressing it.
11. **But ye say**, by your tradition and by your practice in opposition to one of the most solemn and authoritative commands of God. **Corban.** A Hebrew word, which Mark translates for his Gentile readers, **a gift.** It means something *brought near*, or *devoted* to God, as a gift, offering or sacrifice. It was applied to all offerings, whether with blood or without blood, and especially in fulfillment of a vow, Lev. 1 : 2, 10, 14 ; 2 : 1, 4 ; 7 : 13 ; Num. 31 : 50. According to the Mosaic law, persons could devote certain things to God with certain limitations, Lev. 27 : 2-33 ; Num. 30 : 2-15 ; Deut. 23 : 21, 22 ; Jud. 13 : 7. To these regulations were added those of tradition. And so far was it carried that even the pronouncing the word "corban" over one's property absolved him from the obligation of caring for his parents. And even if this was done in the excitement of anger, it was held to be binding. "That such things were permitted and applauded may be proved by certain dicta of the Talmud, and especially by a famous dispute between Rabbi Eliezer and his brethren, in which the very act here described was vindicated by the latter."— J. A. ALEXANDER.
By whatsoever thou mightest be profited by me. Whatever support or advantage thou mightest derive from me, is corban, or let it be corban, devoted to religious purposes. Similar forms of this kind of vow are given in the Talmud. The worst feature in this case was that he was still allowed to use it for his own advantage, though not to the advantage of his parents. If, repenting his rashness, he should assist them, he was regarded as a perjurer, and the user of money devoted to God, and the sacred treasury of the temple could reclaim it. The natural result of this rule was, therefore, both a dishonoring and also a practical cursing of parents. Thus the crime incurred through their tradition corresponded to the two injunctions of the law quoted in the preceding verse. "The words, therefore, *be it corban* or *devoted*, involve an imprecation against himself if he shall ever bestow anything to relieve the necessities of his parents ; as if he should say to them, ' May I incur all the infamy of sacrilege and perjury, if ever ye get a farthing from me ;' than which we can hardly conceive anything spoken by a son to his parents more contemptuous, more unnatural, more barbarous, and consequently more justly termed opprobrious language."—Dr. GEORGE CAMPBELL, on this passage.
He shall be free. This is not in the original. The sentence is unfinished ; the conclusion being left to be inferred by the hearer or reader. The thought may be supplied thus : *Then it is irreclaimably fixed by his vow*, or more simply, *he is bound by his vow*, and so freed from his duty to his parents.
12. **And**, accordingly, **ye suffer him**, etc. ; to do as he desires; that

13 making the word of God of none effect through your tradition, which ye have delivered. And many such like things do ye.

14 ᵏAnd when he had called all the people *unto him*, he said unto them, Hearken unto me every one of 15 *you*, and understand: there is nothing from without a man, that entering into him can defile him: but ˡthe things which come out of him, those are they

ᵏ Pro. 8. 5; Mt. 15. 10.

ˡ Pro. 4. 23.

is, no more to do anything for his parents. But if he should repent his rashness, and should desire to assist them, he must not do it. This accords with the most approved reading of Matt. 15 : 6, he "shall not honor his father and mother." According to Maimonides, if a man should repent of his vow, it might be revoked, or he might be released from it, by one of the wise men or doctors. But this was done, not because it was against the command of God, but at the man's own request, and for the honor of parents. Yet even in such a case the doctors assumed a power and authority above the command of God. It is, however, probable that this last rule was of later date, and the result of this very attack of Jesus upon their traditions. Such an exposure as this should have made them ashamed of so wicked a practice, and may have led to a softening of the requirement.

13. **Making . . . of none effect.** One word in the original, *making void, annulling.* Jesus thus returns in his argument to the charge made in ver. 8, which he had triumphantly sustained. **Which ye have delivered.** *Which ye traditioned,* or *handed down.* The verb in the original corresponds to the noun rendered tradition. The address is to those who came from Jerusalem (ver. 1), identified with the scribes and elders as a class, to whom was intrusted the oral law, and who handed it down to their disciples. These persons had received the traditions from their teachers, and were handing them down with authority. **And many such,** etc. See on ver. 8. This one, Jesus reminds them, is only one example of many like instances of annulling the word of God by their traditions.

14. **And when he had called all the people.** According to the best authorities this should read, *And call-*

ing again the people; the crowd, the multitude. This shows that the preceding incident was somewhat of a private nature. Lange regards it as an examination by the synagogue, in which Christ was separated from the people. This is possible, but not necessarily demanded by the expression. The conversation had been between Jesus and the scribes and Pharisees from Jerusalem (ver. 1), and probably but few, possibly none, of the multitude had heard it. The crowd are engaged among themselves while Jesus attends to these scribes; but now having answered them, he calls the attention of the multitude, and, in the hearing of these learned doctors, he announces a great fact concerning defilement. **Hearken . . . every one;** implying that he had something important to communicate, and of deep interest to *all*. **And understand.** Give diligent attention to the meaning of my words. The scribes and Pharisees tell you of an imaginary and traditional defilement, and ye have heard of a ceremonial defilement (Lev. 11 : 8, 26), but hear and understand from whence real defilement comes, and in what it consists.

15. **There is nothing from without;** food. **That entering into him,** into his mouth as nourishment, Matt. 15 : 11. **Defile him;** make him common, unclean, desecrate him, ver. 2. **The things that come out of him,** out of his mouth and out of his heart (vers. 21–23; Matt. 12 : 34), his words and conduct. This language of Jesus might at first sight seem to conflict with the Mosaic precepts. But things forbidden by the law could produce only ceremonial defilement, which he does not deny. The people, however, were in danger of supposing that there was something in the food forbidden as unclean which would defile, not merely ceremonially, but also

16 that defile the man. ᵐ If any man have ears to hear, let him hear.

17 ⁿ And when he was entered into the house from the people, his disciples asked him concerning

18 the parable. And he saith unto them, Are ye so without understanding also? Do ye not perceive, that whatsoever thing from without entereth into

19 the man, *it* cannot defile him; because it entereth not into his heart, but into the belly, and goeth out

ᵐ Mt. 11. 15.

ⁿ Mt. 15. 15; Jer. 5. 4, 5; John 3. 10; 1 Cor. 3. 2; Heb. 5. 11.

---

morally. Jesus is speaking of real or moral defilement, vers. 21-23. It is not food that really or morally defiles a man; but wickedness in the heart, which comes out in false doctrines and wicked practices. When the ceremonies of the law found their fulfillment in the sufferings and death of Christ, the principle here laid down was of still more general application, Rom. 14 : 14.

16. **If any man have ears to hear.** This verse is omitted by some of the oldest manuscripts.

17. Jesus dismisses or withdraws from the multitude. **Was entered into the house;** possibly the house where he resided when at Capernaum. But literally, *a house*, which may mean simply *within doors.* **The disciples.** The twelve, and possibly others who attended his private instruction, Matthew (15 : 12-14) at this point relates that the disciples inform Jesus of the offense which the Pharisees had taken at what he had said to them, and the reply of Jesus to his disciples. This conversation, which is omitted by Mark, may have taken place as he was entering the house, or just after. **Asked him.** From Matt. 15 : 15 we learn that Peter acted as spokesman of the disciples. Assuming that Mark wrote under the direction of Peter, we have here, as in several other places in this Gospel, a modest suppression of his own name, ch. 6 : 50. **Concerning,** or *of,* **the parable;** the saying in ver. 15. This saying was dark and enigmatical to the disciples, and at the same time figurative. They, therefore, popularly style it a parable, regarding it as containing or illustrating some truth which they did not fully comprehend. See on ch. 4 : 2. The question gives us a view of the spiritual dullness of the disciples and of their low attainments in spiritual knowledge.

18. **Are ye so,** etc. *Are also ye,* my disciples, who have been so highly favored with my instructions, *so,* thus *void of understanding?* Are ye so without comprehension; so lacking in common intelligence as not to perceive the meaning of my remark? This implies that what Jesus had said was perfectly plain and simple. It was a gentle rebuke, and intended to show his disciples their spiritual ignorance. Their difficulty may have arisen from their inability to reconcile the saying of Jesus with the injunctions of the Mosaic law in regard to clean and unclean meats. Jesus now gives them their first lesson on this subject. Peter was afterward taught it on a broader scale, when Cornelius sent for him at Joppa, Acts 10 : 11-16. **Do ye not perceive** that it must be so, that nothing from without, which enters into the man, is able to **defile him,** to make him morally unclean, or unholy? That the question has reference to moral defilement is evident from the next verse.

19. The preceding question required an affirmative answer, and implied both that the truth which he had uttered was plain, and also that the disciples, upon careful consideration, should have apprehended it. **Because.** Jesus now gives the reason why food cannot really defile the man, because it does not affect his moral, spiritual nature, but only his bodily organs. **Heart.** The seat of the emotions and the center of the *inner man,* the soul, as opposed to the stomach and intestines, the digestive organs of the body. **Draught.** *The privy,* drain or sink. **Purging all meats.** Cleansing *all food,* impurities being separated and carried off. The process of digestion is a cleansing one. Whatever is impure is separated from the food and carried off, leaving whatever is nutritious to enter into the

20 into the draught, purging all meats? And he said,
That which cometh out of the man, that defileth the
21 man. °For from within, out of the heart of men,
proceed evil thoughts, adulteries, fornications, mur-
22 ders, thefts, covetousness, wickedness, deceit, lasciviousness, an evil eye, blasphemy, pride, foolish-
23 ness: all these evil things come from within, and
defile the man.

° Ge. 6. 5; 8. 21;
Jer. 17. 9; Mt.
15. 19; 1 Cor. 3.
17; Tit. 1. 15;
Jude 8.

The Syrophenician woman.

24 ᵖAND from thence he arose, and went into the

ᵖ Mt. 15. 21, 22;
Rom. 3. 29; 9. 4;
Phil. 3. 2; Ge. 32.
10; Job 40. 4, 5;
Ps. 145. 19.

blood and to become part of the body. Thus, physically, food is not really defiling; much less can it, through the body, defile the soul.

20. Jesus now states what does defile the man. *That which cometh out,* in a moral sense, from the mouth (Matt. 15: 18), and from the heart or soul (vers. 19, 21), such as he mentions in the two following verses. **That.** Emphatic: *That* is what defiles the man, not food, which never enters into the soul, but only into the stomach and bowels, whence all impurities are cast forth. **The man,** as having a soul or moral nature.

21. **For.** The reason of the statement is given. **From within;** opposite of *from without* (ver. 15), and explained by the more definite expression, **out of the heart of men,** the seat of moral intention and action, the soul. **Proceed.** Come forth. The catalogue of the sins here given is longer than that in Matthew, who mostly follows the order of the second table of the decalogue. There is no discrepancy, however, since the longer includes the shorter, and the shorter does not exclude the longer. Jesus may have even given a longer list, from which each, under the guidance of the Spirit, may have selected such as best suited the narrative and those for whom he wrote. **Evil thoughts.** Emphatically so; not only bad thoughts, but also evil designs. From these, as so many germs in the heart, spring the dark catalogue of sins enumerated in this verse.

Adulteries. Violations of the marriage vow. Notice that this and other sins which follow in the list are in the plural number, suggestive, at least, of the many ways and forms in which they are committed. **Fornications.** Violations of chastity by unmarried persons. Both of these are violations of the seventh commandment, Exod. 20: 14; Matt. 5: 28. **Murders.** This is placed first on Matthew's list, Matt. 15: 19.

22. **Covetousness.** Desires to have more; *greediness of gain* which leads to fraud. The plural is used in the original: *covetous thoughts and purposes,* plans of fraud and extortion. **Wickedness.** Also in the plural: *evil dispositions,* wicked counsels. From this point the singular is used, possibly pointing to particular forms of sin connected with evil dispositions. **Deceit.** Fraud; concealed dishonesty. **Lasciviousness.** Wantonness, lewdness, unbridled lust. **An evil eye.** An envious, grudging, malicious glance, which at once reveals the temper within. Compare Matt. 20: 15; Deut. 15: 9; Prov. 23: 6; 28: 22. **Blasphemy.** Reviling; abusive language against God and man. See on ch. 3: 28. **Pride.** Arrogance, self-exaltation. **Foolishness.** Stupid wickedness, senselessness, folly.

23. Jesus sums up what he had said. **All these evil,** emphatically *wicked* **things,** such as I have mentioned, come forth from within, and **defile,** render **the man,** including his higher spiritual nature, the soul, really, that is, *morally unclean.*

24-30. JESUS VISITS THE NEIGHBORHOOD OF TYRE AND SIDON. THE CANAANITISH WOMAN. Matt. 15: 21-28. Mark, as usual, goes most into detail, yet omits what Matthew (15: 23-25) relates concerning the part the disciples took in the matter. It was probably in the month of May.

24. **And from thence he arose and went.** Or, more literally, *From thence, rising up, he went away,* or de-

borders of Tyre and Sidon; and entered into an house, and would have no man know it. But he 25 could not be hid. For a *certain* woman, whose young daughter had an unclean spirit, heard of him, 26 and came and fell at his feet: (the woman was a Greek, a Syrophenician by nation:) and she besought him that he would cast forth the devil out

parted, from the place where he uttered the preceding discourse, one of the cities or villages in the region of the plain of Gennesaret (ch. 6 : 53–56), and, quite likely, Capernaum, vers. 1, 17; John 6 : 59. Jesus departs from the region where the Pharisaic party was organized (ch. 3 : 6) and intensely aroused against him (ch. 3 : 22; 7 : 1, 2; Matt. 15 : 12), and where Herod Antipas held jurisdiction, Luke 9 : 9. See on ch. 6 : 32. **Into the borders of Tyre and Sidon.** Jesus not only went *to*, but *into* the borders, the *frontier region*, or, according to Matt. 15 : 21, *into the parts* or *region* of Tyre and Sidon. The frontier region or boundary of Phœnicia, adjoining Galilee, is here probably meant. *And Sidon* are wanting in some ancient manuscripts. That he afterward passed northward through Sidon is evident from ver. 31, "*through Sidon.*" This visit to the Gentiles foreshadowed the fact that the gospel was intended for them as well as the Jews. *Tyre and Sidon* were the two principal cities of Phœnicia, on the coast of the Mediterranean Sea. See on ch. 3 : 8. Tyre was about twenty miles south of Sidon, and about one hundred miles in a straight line northwest of Jerusalem. Dr. Thomson supposes that it was Sarepta, about eight miles south of Sidon, where Jesus now was, and where Elijah raised to life the widow's son. Possibly; but the narrative, and especially verse 31, seem to imply that he was farther south.

Jesus here seeks retirement; **he entered into a house,** or within doors (ver. 17), **and would,** *desired,* no one to know it; **but he could not,** rather, *and he was not able* to lie concealed or be hidden. He may have entered the house of one who had previously attended his ministry, or possibly as a traveler or lodger, into a house **of a stranger.** He used every precaution so that no one might know who or where he was. But his fame had reached that region, and both he and his disciples were too well known to escape the notice of those in that region, who had seen him or heard him described.

25. **For** introduces the proof that he could not be hidden, showing the way and means by which he came to be discovered. **A certain woman.** *Certain* is unnecessary. **Young daughter;** rather, *Little daughter,* expressive of tenderness and affection, ch. 5 : 23. **Had an unclean spirit.** Possessed by a demon. See on ch. 1 : 23. **Heard of him.** Of his miracles, his arrival and where he was. **Came** into the house, **and fell at his feet,** an act denoting reverence and earnest entreaty. Her faith in his power is thus at once manifested. His concealment was the first means in its development. Faith led her to him.

26. Mark now more particularly describes the woman as a Gentile, since he was specially writing for Gentiles. **A Greek.** This name had come to be used by the Jews in the broad sense of *Gentile, heathen, idolator.* Yet this woman may have been a descendant of the Greek colonists planted in that region after the conquest of Alexander the Great. **Syrophœnician,** Phœnician of Syria, in distinction from Libophœnician, Phœnician of Libya, in Africa, or Carthaginian. Phœnicia was at first applied to the narrow plain of Tyre and Sidon, which was about twenty-eight miles long, and, on an average, about a mile broad. The name was that given it by the Greeks, and probably derived from the Greek word *palm-tree,* with which that plain may then have abounded. The native name was Canaan, meaning *lowland,* in distinction from the adjoining highlands of Syria, especially those east of the Jordan, and first inhabited by the sons of Canaan, Gen. 10 : 15–19. Phœnicia was afterward applied to a larger district, between the Mediterranean Sea and Mount Lebanon, from Mount Carmel, on the south, to a point about one hundred

27 of her daughter. But Jesus said unto her, Let the children first be filled: for it is not meet to take the
28 children's bread, and to cast *it* unto the dogs. And she answered and said unto him, Yes, Lord: yet the dogs under the table eat of the children's crumbs.

and twenty miles north. But its limits varied at different times. This woman was a Syrophœnician **by nation,** people or birth. She was thus a heathen, and a native of that Phœnicia which belonged to the Roman province of Syria. Mark thus describes her in terms familiar to his Gentile readers, while Matthew (15 : 22), writing for Jewish readers, calls her by their common and familiar appellation, "woman of Canaan."

And she besought him, etc. Jesus was in the house. According to Matthew (15 : 22), she called him in her petition "the Son of David;" thus not only showing some knowledge of the Jewish religion, but also recognizing Jesus as the Messiah, ch. 10 : 47, 48. But Jesus listens in silence and apparently unmoved, Matt. 15 : 23. He now probably goes forth from the house. She follows, crying after him. The disciples, annoyed, beseech him to send her away, granting her request. But Jesus replies that the lost sheep of the house of Israel are the direct object of his personal labors. By this time the woman had come near, and again prostrated herself before him, saying, "Lord, help me," Matt. 15 : 23-25. This interesting portion of the narrative Mark omits. It was more specially adapted to Jewish readers. *Besought* refers specially to her first entreaty. Her second entreaty was, if possible, more earnest, but contained the same request. **The devil.** *The demon,* unclean spirit, ver. 25.

27. But Jesus said to her. *And he said to her,* according to the most approved reading of the original. Notice that Matthew (15 : 26), who related the incident immediately preceding, says, "He answered and said;" but Mark, who omits the intervening incident, says, simply, "He said to her." A beautiful agreement in diversity. In these words of Jesus we have his first and only refusal to perform a miracle, in answer to the request of a sincere and earnest suppliant. Yet the refusal was not absolute, but really contained and implied some things on which a strong faith could rest. **Let the children first be filled.** Suffer the children, the Jews, first to be satisfied. Mark alone mentions these words. The Jews were first to have the gospel and its blessings offered to them. It was not yet time for the Gentiles. The request of the woman was unseasonable. There was, however, hope for her in the future.

For it is not meet, it is not good, proper and right, to take the **children's bread,** that intended and provided for the children, as the Jews were called, and to **cast** or *throw* it to the dogs, as the Gentiles were styled by the Jews. **Dogs.** Literally, *the little dogs,* the domestic dogs in the household, that feed under the table, and not the wild and ferocious dogs which in crowds prowled through the streets and about the country, Rev. 22 : 15. The tribes of Canaan, which remained in the land, were to be servants, the domestic dogs, as it were, of Israel, Josh. 9 : 21; 1 Kings 9 : 20-22. In this saying Jesus would further manifest the faith and humility of the woman; and in the use of this mild and domestic term, he affords a glimpse of his kindness and compassion; and gives her something to take hold of, if her faith and spiritual perception are sufficient.

28. The answer of the woman is a wonderful illustration of faith, turning the most untoward circumstances to a good account. **Yes, Lord;** I admit all that thou hast said; it is not proper and right to take away the children's bread and cast it to dogs; I am indeed one, and would humbly take my place as one; give me but of the crumbs, for the little dogs do indeed eat these as they fall from their master's table. **Yet.** Not a correct translation of the original; rather *for even,* or *for also,* introducing the reason for pressing her suit, based on our Savior's own designation of her, *for even the dogs eat;* or, *for the dogs also eat.* **Crumbs.** Literally, *from the crumbs,* the little bits of food, especially of bread. **Children's.**

29 And he said unto her, For this saying go thy way;
30 the devil is gone out of thy daughter. And when she was come to her house, she found the devil gone out, and her daughter laid upon the bed.

A deaf and dumb man healed.

31 ⁹AND again, departing from the coasts of Tyre and Sidon, he came unto the sea of Galilee, through
32 the midst of the coasts of Decapolis. And ʳ they bring unto him one that was deaf, and had an im-

⁹ Mt. 15. 29.

ʳ Mt. 9. 32; Lk. 11. 14.

Literally, *the little children's.* "*The little children* who often waste the bread. Differing from *the children* (ver. 27), which points to the *right* to the father's bread."— BENGEL. What mingled acuteness and humility is here displayed! She would only take from the crumbs which fall from the little children, accepting and craving the *portion of the dogs,* and that too after all *were filled or satisfied,* ver. 27.

29. **For this saying,** which indicated her strong faith, and showed her to be of spiritual Israel. According to Matthew (15 : 28), Jesus exclaimed, "O woman! great is thy faith." So also he commended the centurion's faith, Matt. 8 : 10. Both of these bright examples were great in comparison to that of any of the more highly favored Jews; and foreshadowed the hearty reception which the gospel would receive from the Gentiles. **Go thy way.** Go, depart, thy request is granted. **The devil is gone out.** *The demon has just gone out.* At the very moment that Jesus said, "Be it unto thee as thou wilt" (Matt. 15 : 28), the demon left the daughter.

30. While Matthew records the instant healing of the daughter, Mark graphically describes the return of the mother to her home, where she **found her daughter laid upon the bed,** a state of quiet and repose in contrast to her previous rage and restlessness. The language also suggests her bodily exhaustion from the constant excitement produced by the possession, and especially from the last paroxysm, ch. 9 : 26. **And the devil gone out.** According to the highest critical authorities, this clause should be at the end of the verse. The order is natural and lifelike. The very first evidence of her daughter's cure, witnessed by the mother on her return, is her quiet resting on the bed, instead of raving and rushing wildly hither and thither, as she had been wont to do. The mother at once examines her, hears the statements of the attendants, finds her in a sound mind, and her body under her own, and not under a foreign will; in other words, that the demon had actually gone out. Thus she found the Savior's declaration verified, and her own strong faith realized.

31-37. JESUS, PASSING THROUGH SIDON, RETURNS THROUGH DECAPOLIS TO THE SEA OF GALILEE. HEALS A DEAF AND DUMB MAN. Matt. 15 : 29-31. The account of Matthew is a general statement of the journey and miracles performed. This of Mark gives the direction and course of the journey, and with great particularity relates a most important miracle. These occurrences probably took place the latter part of May, A.D. 29.

31. **And again departing,** etc. According to the highest critical authorities, this should read: *And again going forth out of the borders of Tyre, he came through Sidon to the Sea of Galilee,* etc. It thus appears that Jesus was within the borders or district of Tyre, for he *went forth out* of that region; that he traveled northward through Sidon; then passed over into Decapolis, on the east of the Jordan, very likely crossing Lebanon by the great road to Cæsarea Philippi; thus approaching the northeastern shore of the Sea of Galilee. **Through the midst of the coasts of Decapolis;** *of the borders or district of Decapolis,* a region of "ten cities" lying east of the Jordan, but not very clearly defined. See on ch. 5 : 20.

32. Jesus had just returned from his only visit, during his ministry, to the Gentile world. Not far from the eastern coast of the Sea of Galilee, he sits upon a mountain, or the highlands of

pediment in his speech; and they beseech him to ^a ch. 8. 23; John 9. 6.
33 put his hand upon him. And he took him aside   ^t ch. 6. 41; John 11. 41; 17. 1.
from the multitude, and put his fingers into his   ^u ch. 8. 12; Is. 53. 3; John 11. 33,
34 ears, and ^t he spit, and touched his tongue; and   35, 33; Heb. 4. 15.
^l looking up to heaven, ^u he sighed, and saith unto

that region (Matt. 15 : 29), and performs miracles. **They;** probably the people of Decapolis. The demoniac of Gadara, after his healing, had gone through this region proclaiming how great things Jesus had done for him (ch. 5 : 20); and thus his fame was spread abroad. **Bring to him one that was deaf.** They conduct him to Jesus. This miracle is related only by Mark; and is important as showing a case of one who was merely diseased or deformed, and not possessed by a demon. That dumbness was sometimes occasioned by a demoniacal possession is evident from ch. 9 : 17, 25; Matt. 9 : 32; 12 : 22; but that all persons diseased in their organs of speech, or of hearing, were not regarded as thus possessed, is evident from this passage. This person was not only deaf, but had an **impediment in his speech;** he *could hardly speak*, or could speak only with difficulty, *a stammerer*. See on ver. 35. There are two kinds of deaf persons: those from birth, who, having never heard sound, cannot speak; and those who in some way having lost their hearing, speak more or less imperfectly. I once knew a man, who, after learning to talk in childhood, became deaf and partially dumb through disease; he stammered and uttered words with great difficulty. The partial dumbness of this person, on whom Jesus wrought the miracle, arose, not so much from his deafness, as from some defect or infirmity in the organs of speech, vers. 33, 35.

The people beseech Jesus **to put his hand upon him,** as he had done in many other cases of healing, expecting thereby a perfect cure. They may have thought this act of Jesus necessary to the result which they desired. Possibly, like Naaman, they wished to witness some outward display, 2 Kings 5 : 11.

33. **And he took him aside from the multitude.** From the crowd, in the presence of only a few witnesses. Why? Various reasons may be assigned. (1.) The people had laid down their way of healing; they needed to be taught that they should leave the way to Jesus. (2.) The people may have gathered to witness a great miracle. But Jesus would make no display; nor satisfy mere curiosity, Matt. 12 : 15-21. (3.) He would withdraw from observation; and produce as little excitement as possible, ch. 6 : 31, 32; 8 : 22, 23. (4.) While he would strengthen their faith, he would not feed their superstition. (5.) For the good of the man himself; that he might have a proper view of Christ's healing power. Jesus showed that he was not limited to any one way of exercising his miraculous power. **And put his fingers,** or *thrust his fingers* **into his ears,** being diseased organs. Jesus could heal without any external acts (ver. 29), but they were doubtless necessary in this case to aid the man's faith. Possibly his soul was also being healed, and these external signs were as speech to him. " He imparted his power first through the eyes and then through the ears."—BENGEL. **He spit and touched his tongue,** the other diseased organ; probably spitting on his finger, he touched the diseased tongue. Jesus also used saliva in two other cases: the blind man at Bethsaida (ch. 8 : 23), and the blind man at Jerusalem, John 9 : 6. Why he should use saliva can only be conjectured. But surely not because of any healing power in it. This may be one way that Jesus teaches us that we are not to enter into the reasons of all his actions; and that when he has appointed any observance, we are humbly to submit, though we may not be able to see why it might not have been different.

In these minute delineations we perceive Mark's vivid manner. See ch. 5 : 42, 43; 7 : 30; 8 : 24, 25. In these examples we seem to get a glimpse of the cures as they were going on. Compare ch. 5 : 8-13.

34. **Looking up,** as to his Father, in earnest desire, not for his own sake, but for the sake of the men and others, whose faith he would strengthen, and whose souls he would benefit, John

35 him, Ephphatha, that is, *be opened. ⁷And straightway his ears were opened, and the string of his tongue was loosed, and he spake plain.
36 And ᶻhe charged them that they should tell no man: but the more he charged them, so much the
37 more a great deal they published *it;* and were beyond measure astonished, saying, He hath done all things well: ᵃhe maketh both the deaf to hear, and the dumb to speak.

*Ge. 1. 3.
ʸPs. 33. 9; Is. 35. 5. 6; Mt. 11. 5.
ᶻch. 5. 43.
ᵃEx. 4. 11.

11 : 41, 42. **To heaven,** *into the sky,* as representing the abode of God. He indeed performed miracles in his own name and by his own authority; but he would not have any regard his power and authority as human; he would specially represent them as divine, and God the source of every blessing. The erroneous and superstitious views of the people in the half-heathen district of Decapolis may have made such a lesson both timely and necessary. **He sighed,** or *groaned.* A mingled sigh of prayer and compassion. The same word in Greek is used in Rom. 8 : 23; 2 Cor. 5 : 2, 4, and translated *groan.* Jesus at one time sighed at the hardness and unbelief of the Pharisees (ch. 8 : 12), and at another groaned when about to raise Lazarus, John 11 : 33, 38. While his looking to heaven would suggest the sigh as a silent prayer, the condition of the man and of the people were such as to call forth his pity. The expression of his compassion in a sigh heavenward, would naturally impress all present with the necessity of looking to God for help. **Ephphatha.** An Aramæan word in the imperative, Isa. 35 : 5. We have here the very word that Jesus used. It also shows what was the colloquial language of the people, as well as our Savior's own vernacular. This is evidently the minute description of an eye-witness. If Mark did not witness it himself, he seems to have given the very words of Peter, under whose direction he is supposed to have written. For his Gentile readers he immediately translates, **be opened.** As he had on former occasions commanded the elements of nature, and demons, so now he commands the organs of the body, that they should be restored to their proper and natural use.

35. **Straightway.** This is wanting in some of the oldest manuscripts. But whether it be regarded as the approved reading or not, the cure was instantaneous. At the command the **ears were opened,** every obstruction was removed, and a healthy action of the organs enjoyed; all before the command was preparatory. There is nothing for, but rather everything against, the supposition of some, that the cure was gradual. **The string of his tongue was loosed.** Rather, *the bond of his tongue,* etc. The word translated *bond* may mean any ligament, impediment, or hindrance, which prevented him from speaking plainly. Some suppose that he was tongue-tied. There was evidently some defect in his organ of speech. His difficulty in speaking was not a mere result of deafness. **He spake plain.** He no longer spoke with difficulty, but in so natural and distinct a manner that he could easily be understood.

36. **He charged them,** etc. Those who brought the man to him, and were near him. See on ch. 1 : 44; 5 : 43. Why he thus charged them does not certainly appear, but of this we may be assured, he had good reasons. It was in keeping with the privacy of the miracle, and with the unostentatiousness of his ministry. It was an impressive way of showing that he did not seek the praise of men. Such admonitions may also have been given for the good of those who should afterward hear or read the account. **But the more he charged them.** The prohibition seemed only to increase their desire to publish it. They were charmed with his humility and modesty. The expression is a strong one: **the more a great deal,** *more abundantly.*

37. **Beyond measure.** *Very superabundantly, superexcessively.* In an extraordinary degree. The word in Greek is found only here, and is of the nature of a double superlative. "The effect of

this great miracle on those who witnessed it was so extraordinary that the writer has to coin a Greek word to express the boundlessness of their amazement."—Dr. J. A. Alexander. **He hath done all things well.** An exclamation of the highest approval and satisfaction. "The exclamation almost reminds us of the history of the creation, where it is said, *all that he had made was very good*, Gen. 1 : 31.— Olshausen. "This work was (may be) properly and worthily compared with that first one of creation; it was the same beneficence which prompted and the same power that wrought it."— Alford. **The deaf . . . The dumb,** referring specially to this case, yet possibly including others. Matthew (15 : 30, 31) relates that many miracles were performed, among which were *the dumb speaking*. The one just healed could popularly be called deaf and dumb, his power of utterance being defective and his speaking difficult, ver. 32.

A mere survey of this miracle shows how futile the attempt of those who would explain miracles by natural causes.—Dr. A. Hovey (*Miracles of Christ*, p. 190) has well put it : "Paulus lays great emphasis on the use of means in the present case. He supposes that Jesus moistened with spittle some kind of powders, and applied them to the tongue, if not to the inner part of the ear. But, if medical science, as he professes to believe, was at so low an ebb in Palestine, how did Jesus, who was a mere man, acquire his great skill ? How is it that he never failed to effect a speedy and perfect cure? Where have lived the successors of this matchless physician ? Or did his skill perish with him ? If so, was it earthborn or heaven-born, natural or supernatural?"

Remarks.

1. Jerusalem was opposed to Jesus. So have always been the seats of formal and false religions, ver. 1 ; ch. 3 : 22 ; Matt. 2 : 3 ; John 5 : 18 ; Gal. 4 : 25.
2. Fault-finders can always find enough to do, ver. 2 ; Acts 6 : 12-14 ; 24 : 5-9 ; 1 Pet. 2 : 14 ; 3 : 16.
3. The Pharisees have their successors at the present day among nominal Christians. "What can we say to the gravity and seriousness with which men argue on behalf of chasubles, albs, tunicles, piscinas, sedalia, credence-tables, rood-screens, and the like, in the present day ? What can we say to the exaggerated attention paid by many to ceremonies, ornaments, gestures and postures, in the worship of God, about which it is enough to say that Scripture is totally silent ? What is it all but Pharisaism over again ? "— Ryle. Vers. 3-5 ; Gal. 4 : 9-11.
4. Formality in worship is hypocrisy, ver. 6 ; 2 Tim. 3 : 5 ; Ezek. 33 : 31, 32.
5. No worship can be acceptable to God, in which the heart is not engaged, ver. 6 ; John 4 : 24 ; Isa. 29 : 13.
6. See that your religion is founded on the word of God, and not on the traditions of men, vers. 7, 8 ; Isa. 8 : 20 ; John 5 : 39 ; Acts 17 : 11 ; Eph. 6 : 17 ; 1 John 4 : 6 ; 1 Tim. 1 : 4.
7. Traditions which merely supplement the word of God are useless ; those which contradict it are impious, vers. 7-9 ; Col. 2 : 8 ; 1 Pet. 1 : 18, 19.
8. God alone has a right to add to his word, vers. 10, 11 ; Deut. 4 : 2 ; 12 : 32 ; Prov. 30 : 6 ; Rev. 22 : 18, 19.
9. Christ came not to make void the law, but to fulfill it, vers. 10-13 ; Matt. 5 : 17 ; Rom. 3 : 31.
10. Children may break the fifth commandment by withholding proper and necessary aid from their parents, vers. 10-12 ; Luke 2 : 51 ; Prov. 28 : 24.
11. It is our duty to hear attentively and understand clearly Christ's teachings. In order to do this we should seek the guidance of the Spirit, vers. 14, 16 ; Prov. 4 : 5 ; John 8 : 12 ; 14 : 26 ; 16 : 13 ; James 1 : 5.
12. "In the New Testament the making distinctions of meats is classed among the works of the devil."— Lange. Ver. 14 ; 1 Tim. 4 : 1-3.
13. It is not evil influences, bad company and the like, but the heart, which is the chief source of human defilement, vers. 15, 21-23 ; Gen. 6 : 5 ; Ps. 14 : 1.
14. Are you seeking of Christ and his Spirit to understand his word ? ver. 17 ; Matt. 13 : 36 ; Luke 24 : 45.
15. Christians are too often inexcusably dull of spiritual understanding, ver. 18 ; Luke 24 : 25 ; Heb. 5 : 12.
16. Men are depraved by nature ; the heart is the seat of sin, vers. 20-23 ; Ps. 14 : 1-3 ; Prov. 4 : 23 ; Jer. 17 : 9.
17. Many evils lie imbedded in the human heart, needing only circum-

Jesus feeds the four thousand.

VIII. IN those days ᵇ the multitude being very great, and having nothing to eat, Jesus called his disciples

ᵇ Mt. 9. 36; 15. 32; ch. 6. 34; Ps. 145. 8; Is. 60. 3, 4; Heb. 2. 17; 4. 15; 5. 2.

stances to develop them. Remember that God looketh into the heart, vers. 21, 22; Gen. 16 : 13; 1 Sam. 16 : 7; Isa. 64 : 6; Jer. 20 : 12; Matt. 6 : 4.

18. True purity depends on the state of the heart, vers. 20–23; Jer. 4 : 14; Rom. 14 : 19; 1 Cor. 8 : 8.

19. Labor and pray for the salvation of children. Nothing but a radical change of heart will suffice, vers. 21, 22; John 3 : 5–7.

20. God often has a people where we little expect it, ver. 24; Matt. 8 : 11; John 10 : 16.

21. In the Syrophœnician woman we have an example of persevering and importunate prayer, vers. 24–29; Gen. 32 : 24–28; Matt. 26 : 39, 42, 44; Luke 18 : 3–8.

22. In going to Jesus for others we should make their cases, as it were, our own, ver. 26; Matt. 15 : 25; Ex. 32 : 31, 32; Rom. 9 : 1–3.

23. Those whom Christ intends to honor the most he often tries the most, vers. 27, 28; Heb. 11 ch.; 1 Pet. 1 : 7.

24. Under all circumstances we should exercise a submissive and unwavering faith in Christ, ver. 28; Heb. 10 : 23; James 1 : 6; 1 Pet. 1 : 9.

25. We should come to God just as we are, poor sinners, ver. 28; Luke 15 : 18, 19; 18 : 13, 14; James 4 : 10.

26. Parents should feel a deep anxiety for their children, that they may be delivered from the power of Satan, ver. 26; Gen. 17 : 18.

27. Most speak and hear; but how many are spiritually deaf and dumb! ver. 32; Ps. 58 : 3–5.

28. Many Christians, afflicted with spiritual impediment of speech, only stammer. Let them take their cases to Jesus, ver. 32; Isa. 32 : 4.

29. We should bring our friends to Jesus, ver. 32; Isa. 35 : 5; John 1 : 42, 45, 46; 6 : 37.

30. Christ and his Spirit is not confined to any one way or instrumentality in regeneration, vers. 33, 34; John 3 : 8.

31. Jesus alone makes the deaf to hear and the dumb to speak, ver. 35; Isa. 35 : 5, 6.

32. Christ's acts were significant;

but superstition often perverts their meaning. Thus in Romish baptism, the priest touches the ears, moistens the tongue with saliva, and lays salt in the mouth, ver. 33; ver. 7.

33. Christ has set us an example of modesty, ver. 36; Matt. 6 : 2; John 8 : 50.

34. Christ has done all things well in his atoning and redeeming work, ver. 37; Heb. 7 : 26–28.

35. Be not merely astonished at the works of Christ; but savingly benefited. Seek his approval, "Well done," ver. 37; Matt. 25 : 21; Heb. 12 : 1, 2.

CHAPTER VIII.

Mark continues his narrative of Jesus in Decapolis, by relating the second miraculous feeding of the multitude. Passing over to the western side of the lake, Jesus suffers further opposition from the Pharisees; returning to the eastern side, he warns the disciples against the doctrines of the Pharisees and of Herod. At Bethsaida Jesus performs a remarkable miracle on a blind man. From thence he goes into the vicinity of Cæsarea Philippi, and there draws forth from Peter in behalf of the twelve the confession that Jesus is the Christ. Jesus reveals more clearly than before the doctrine of his suffering, death and resurrection; rebukes Peter for resisting it; and teaches the duty and necessity of self-denial. It was now probably summer, A.D. 29. By spending his time mostly in the mountainous regions of the north, he not only evaded the opposition of the Pharisees, but also enjoyed a cooler and fresher air.

1–9. FEEDING THE FOUR THOUSAND. Matt. 15 : 32–39. The accounts of the two evangelists are very similar. But Mark is the more vivid and enters somewhat more into detail. It was now quite likely early in June, possibly when the people were going to the feast of Pentecost, or returning. The site of the miracle is not clearly defined. Dr. Ellicott suggests that it was situated about the middle of the eastern coast,

2 *unto him*, and saith unto them, I have compassion on the multitude, because they have now been with
3 me three days, and have nothing to eat: and if I send them away fasting to their own houses, they will faint by the way: for divers of them came from far.
4 And his disciples answered him, From whence can a man satisfy these *men* with bread here in the wil-

on the high ground in the neighborhood of the ravine opposite to Magdala, which is now called Wady Semak, ver. 10; Matt. 15 : 29, 33.
1. In those days. A very indefinite expression of time. Compare ch. 1 : 9. From the connection it appears that it was while he was still in Decapolis, and not long after the healing of the deaf and dumb man, ch. 7 : 36, 37. **The multitude being very great;** or, according to some of the most ancient manuscripts, *There being again a great multitude*, similar to that which had so frequently attended him in Galilee, and especially the one he had fed about two months before in that region, not far distant on the north-eastern shore of the lake. The fame of his great miracles had probably brought the multitude together. It is also possible that many of them were going or returning from the feast of Pentecost, which began, A. D. 29, about June 6th. **His disciples.** Probably the twelve.
2. I have compassion. I am moved with pity for the multitude; so moved in mind as also to produce physical emotion, ch. 6 : 34. The case was more urgent than on the former occasion, *because* **they have now been with me three days,** or rather, *because they continue with me now three days*, according to Jewish reckoning, parts of three days; the third day was now passing. **Have nothing to eat.** If they brought any, it was all consumed; and they were in a wilderness (ver. 4), where no food could be obtained. Compare vers. 1 and 4.
3. And if I send them away, *dismiss them*, as a congregation which he had instructed and healed. *To their own houses*, or homes. It appears that they were **fasting,** eating nothing that day; but whether it was the third day of fasting is uncertain. Quite probably some had gone longer without food than others. **Faint by the way.** Become exhausted and entirely wearied out for want of food and by fatigue on their way home. **For divers of them came from far.** According to the highest critical authorities, *And some of them have come*, or *are*, *from far*. These are not the comment of the historian, but part of the compassionate words of Jesus. How vividly are the wants of the multitude presented, in the wilderness, away from home, and some of them far away, from the borders of Decapolis, and possibly from the regions beyond!
4. From whence. From what source. **Can a man satisfy?** *Will any one be able* to appease the appetite of these men. The location is emphatically referred to: **Here,** and further explained, **in the wilderness,** rather *in a wilderness*. The preposition translated *in* seems rather to mean *on*, or *upon*, suggesting the barren surface of a desert. From what source will one be able to appease the appetite of so great a multitude here on a desert? See on the words, *on the ground*, ver. 6. They could not have forgotten the feeding of the five thousand; yet they seemed not to expect a repetition of the miracle. And why should they? For more than two years Jesus had exercised his ministry, attended with large multitudes; yet, thus far, only once had he miraculously fed them. Compare ver. 14. The disciples were still babes in faith and knowledge, as is frequently illustrated in the Gospels, ch. 7 : 18; 9 : 10, 28, 29; Luke 24 : 25–27. Even putting the worst construction on their question, we find similar examples of weak faith among God's people. The Israelites murmur immediately after their deliverance at the Red Sea (Exod. 15 : 24; 17 : 1–3); and even Moses showed unbelief when God was about to feed Israel with flesh in the wilderness, Num. 11 : 21–23. No reason therefore can be founded on this question for supposing, with certain German interpreters, that this is only another account of the miracle recorded in ch. 6 : 35–44. The questions of

5 derness? ^cAnd he asked them, How many loaves
6 have ye? And they said, Seven. And he commanded the people to sit down on the ground: and he took the seven loaves, and gave thanks, and brake, and gave to his disciples to set before *them;*
7 and they did set *them* before the people. And they had a few small fishes: and ^dhe blessed, and com-
8 manded to set them also before *them.* So they did eat, and were filled: and they took up of the broken

^c ch. 6. 38; Mt. 15. 34.

^d ch. 6. 41; Mt. 14. 19; 1 Ki. 17. 14, 16; 2 Ki. 4. 2, 7.

Jesus in vers. 19, 20, show conclusively that there were two instances of miraculous feeding; and the accounts of the two show marked differences. The journey to the former was from Galilee, probably from Capernaum; to the latter was from Sidon through Decapolis. That was in the spring; this in the summer. The one was in the vicinity of Bethsaida, north-east of the Sea of Galilee; the other was in Decapolis, a few miles farther south. In that the people were principally Jews from the western side of Jordan, who had been with Jesus one day; in this they were a mixed multitude, partly Jews and partly heathen, from the east of Jordan, and had been with Jesus three days. There the number of men was five thousand, who reclined on the grass; here four thousand, who reclined on the ground. In that case there were five loaves; and, after the meal, twelve baskets of fragments; in this there were seven loaves, and, afterward, seven baskets of fragments. Then they used traveling baskets; now provision baskets. With such differences, the attempt to prove but one miracle proves extremely absurd.

5. How many loaves. In the answer Matthew adds, "a few little fishes." But Mark also refers to "a few small fishes," in ver. 7. The disciples seem now to have suspected what Jesus was about to do; for they do not exclaim, as on the former occasion, "What are they among so many?" John 6:9. Their faith certainly had been benefited thereby, for not a word of doubt is expressed. With becoming modesty they neither suggest, nor doubt a miracle. Jesus alone knew when it was proper for him to work one, ver. 12; John 2:4.

6. He commanded the people, doubtless through, or under the direction of the disciples who on the former occasion arranged the people into companies, ch. 6:39, 40. **To sit on the ground.** *To lie down,* according to the Oriental posture in eating. Notice, *on the ground,* instead of *on the grass* at the former miracle. This expression, together with *in a wilderness,* or *desert* (ver. 4), implies a barren surface, either because it was summer and vegetation had dried up, or because it was literally a desert, destitute of vegetation. In any case it shows a striking difference in the locality of the two miracles. **Gave thanks . . . brake,** etc. See on ch. 6:41. A comparison with the account of the former miracle shows what we should naturally expect, a greater conciseness in this.

7. Blessed. *Blessed them.* Invoked God's blessing on the fishes with thanksgiving. See on ch. 6:41. In this instance Mark bestows special attention upon the fishes. Jesus *blesses* them, and commands that they should be **also** set before the people; thus intimating the order in which the two kinds of food were served, and the bountifulness of the feast.

8. So. Rather *And.* **Were filled.** Were fully satisfied. There was not a partial but a full satisfaction of their appetites. At what moment was the miracle performed? We may answer, either with Meyer, "The Lord blessed, and gave the loaves and fishes to the disciples *as they were;* and then, *during their distribution of them,* the miraculous increase took place, so that they broke and distributed enough for all;" or, the increase took place while passing through and from the hands of Jesus, similar to that of the widow's oil (2 Kings 4:5-7), which filled vessel after vessel, and was only stayed when there were no more to fill. But the important point is stated, that the miracle was performed; just when, is comparatively of no consequence.

9 *meat* that was left seven baskets. And they that had eaten were about four thousand: and he sent them away.

The broken meat that was left. *The excess, residue,* or *remnants of fragments,* broken pieces of food. These had been probably distributed, or mostly so, and were gathered up from the ground where the men had eaten. **Baskets.** Grain or provision baskets, and seem to have been larger than the traveling-basket used on the former occasion (ch. 6 : 43), as Paul was let down in one from the wall of Damascus. That the evangelist intended to distinguish the two baskets is evident from vers. 19, 20, where they are both mentioned, and each related to its proper miracle, as here and elsewhere. Thus the seven baskets here may have equaled, or exceeded, the twelve baskets of the former miracle.

9. **About four thousand.** Matthew (15 : 38) adds, "men, besides women and children." This would probably raise the number to about six thousand. This gives us some idea of what the evangelists mean when they speak of great multitudes following Jesus. We see the simplicity and truthfulness of the evangelists in the fact that the provisions of the second miraculous feeding were more, and the number fed less, than in the first. Fiction would rather have made the second miracle apparently, at least, greater than the first. **He sent them away.** *Dismissed* them as an assembly, doubtless with a parting blessing.

Thus in two miracles Jesus presented himself as the bread of life; first to the Jews, and then to the Gentiles as well as the Jews. And it was truly becoming him thus to do. See on ch. 6 : 44.

10-13. A BRIEF VISIT TO GALILEE. CROSSING AND RE-CROSSING THE LAKE. THE PHARISEES SEEK A SIGN. Matt. 15 : 39; 16 : 1-4. Matthew, after his usual manner, gives the words of Jesus more fully. But even here Mark presents more vividly what Jesus did.

SEA OF GALILEE FROM THE NORTH-WEST; MAGDALA AND TIBERIAS.

A.D. 29. MARK VIII. 151

The Pharisees seek a sign; warning against their teaching.

10   AND ᵉ straightway he entered into a ship with   ᵉ Mt. 15. 39.
his disciples, and came into the parts of Dalmanu-
11 tha.   ᶠ And the Pharisees came forth, and began to   ᶠ Mt. 12. 38; 16. 1;
question with him, seeking of him a sign from   John 6. 30.
12 heaven, tempting him.   And ᵍ he sighed deeply in   ᵍ Is. 53. 3.
his spirit, and saith, Why doth this generation seek
after a sign? Verily I say unto you, There shall no

10. **Straightway.** Showing the chronological connection. Both Matthew and Mark place the embarking immediately after dismissing the multitude who had been miraculously fed. **A ship.** Rather, *the ship*, so often mentioned, and which Jesus and his disciples used in going from one point of the lake to another, ch. 3 : 9 ; 4 : 36; 5 : 2.   **Into the parts of Dalmanutha;** *into the regions of*, etc. Matthew says that " Jesus came into the borders (neighborhood) of Magdala." The latter was situated on the west side of the Sea of Galilee, about three miles north of Tiberias, just south of the plain of Gennesaret. The modern village is called Mejdel. About a mile south is a narrow glen, where are copious fountains and ruins of a village. Here, probably, stood Dalmanutha. It does not appear that Jesus landed at either place, but in the vicinity of each. Just south of Magdala high rocks overhang the sea. At the foot of these cliffs, toward Dalmanutha, is the spot where he probably landed. He was thus in the "regions" of the one and in the " borders" of the other. This is an instance of substantial agreement, yet striking independence. Matthew's account may be regarded as the more general of the two. It is very probable that Jesus and his disciples directed their course toward Dalmanutha after landing; they may also have visited Magdala. Here do we see how careful Jesus was to avoid excitement and even observation in Galilee. He lands in a retired place, and very probably at night; and soon returns to the eastern side, ver. 13.

11. **The Pharisees came forth,** or *out;* probably from Dalmanutha, to Jesus, who was in their immediate vicinity. They do not wait for him to come to them, but go out to him. A vivid picture of the alertness of the Pharisees in their opposition to Jesus, and in their endeavors to destroy him. It seems that they had their emissaries and spies abroad. Compare their growing opposition, and repeated attacks, ch. 2 : 6, 18, 24 ; 3 : 6, 22 ; 7 : 1. Matthew (16 : 1) mentions "Sadducees" as leagued with the Pharisees. The latter were the principal leaders of the opposition, and are the only ones mentioned here.   **Began;** at once, as soon as they came out, showing a determination to continue, and an evil design,   **tempting him;** in their unbelief putting him to a test, and trying to induce him to do something which they could use against him.   **To question with him** with a disputatious and caviling spirit and manner. **Seeking,** or requiring, **a sign from heaven,** a miracle from the sky, such as the standing still of the sun and moon in the days of Joshua, or as the thunder and lightning at the giving of the law, and not a sign on the earth, such as his miracles were. Alford mentions that the Jews held that demons and false gods could give signs on earth, but only the true God could give a sign from heaven. A very extraordinary appearance of the rainbow was regarded by some as a sign of the Messiah. Such passages as Dan. 7 : 13 probably also led to the expectation of a sign from heaven. That such an expectation was entertained seems evident from the repeated requests of the Pharisees, Matt. 12 : 38; Luke 11 : 16 ; compare John 2 : 18; 6 : 30. Christ's life was indeed remarkable for such signs, but the Pharisees were blind and could not perceive the signs of the times, Matt. 2 : 2 ; 16 : 2–4 ; Luke 2 : 13, 14 ; Mark 1 : 10, 11 ; 9 : 7; 15 : 32; Matt. 28 : 2–4 ; Acts 1 : 9–11. Of course the Pharisees in their unbelief did not expect from Jesus such a sign.

12. **He sighed deeply in his spirit.** A deep sigh or moan, coming

13 sign be given unto this generation. ᵇ And he left them, and entering into the ship again departed to the other side.   ʰ Mt. 16. 4; Hos. 4. 17; 9. 12.
14 ⁱ Now *the disciples* had forgotten to take bread, neither had they in the ship with them more than   ⁱ Mt. 16. 5–7.
15 one loaf. ᵏ And he charged them, saying, Take heed, beware of the leaven of the Pharisees, and *of*   ᵏ Pro. 19. 27; Mt. 16. 6; Lk. 12. 1.

forth, not only from his physical nature, but also from the depths of his soul. It was a sigh of mingled sorrow and indignation at their unbelief, hypocrisy and crafty opposition. And as he refers to his own resurrection as a sign which should be given them (Matt. 16 : 4), may not a view of his own sufferings and of their continued opposition have contributed to that sigh? Mark alone records it; and here do we see one of those graphic strokes of his pen, by which he presents the looks and gestures of Jesus, and so many little acts of his life.
Why do this generation, etc.? Why do this wicked and faithless generation (Matt. 16 : 4) seek a sign, when they have had so many which they would not receive, and when even a sign from heaven would not satisfy them? There could be no reason or ground for granting such a request. They neither expected it nor deserved it. **Verily I say unto you.** A solemn and authoritative declaration, preceding the utterance of a momentous truth. See on ch. 3 : 28. **No sign shall be given,** such as they demanded. The expression is exceedingly strong in the original, similar in form to a Hebrew oath. Matthew adds, "but the sign of Jonah," which is entirely consistent with the preceding strong assertion. For none of his signs were for such hardened cavilers. Besides, the most emphatic denial of a sign from heaven, did not preclude such a sign as that of Jonah.
13. **And he left them.** Not only *leaving* their company, but also leaving them to themselves. Probably the same day embarking **again in the ship** by which he came, he departed to the eastern side of the lake.
14–21. JESUS CAUTIONS HIS DISCIPLES AGAINST THE LEAVEN OF THE PHARISEES, AND OF HEROD. Matt. 16 : 4–12. Mark goes more into detail, but Matthew alone (16 : 12) states the conclusion, that they understood that he spoke of the *teaching* of the Pharisees and of the Sadducees.
14. **Now.** Rather, *And*, connecting this with what precedes. **Had forgotten,** or, *forgot.* It would seem, from a comparison of this verse with Matt. 16 : 5, that it was after their landing on the eastern side that the disciples forgot to take bread for their further journey into the region beyond, and that they had one loaf remaining after they were over. **More than one loaf.** *But one loaf*, or, *except one loaf.* Mark alone mentions this, showing the vivid recollection of minute circumstances by Peter, under whose direction this evangelist is supposed to have written.
15. We have here an example how Jesus improved the events of daily life for the spiritual advantage of his followers. Their neglect to provide provisions gave him an opportunity of warning them, in parabolic language, against the teachings and influence of the Pharisees and of Herod. While they were absorbed and solicitous about provisions for their journey, Jesus **charged them. Leaven;** a figure of diffusive and assimilating power, generally, though not always, used in Scripture to represent that which is corrupt and evil. Here it denotes the pernicious teaching of the Pharisees, etc., Matt. 16 : 12. Compare Luke 12 : 1. **The leaven of Herod.** The pernicious influence and teachings of Herod and his party. Matthew says nothing of Herod, but adds, "and of the Sadducees." Some, therefore, suppose that Herod and his party were Sadducees, which is not a necessary conclusion. Jesus may have named all three classes, for the influence and teaching of them all were pernicious, formal, worldly, and opposed to Christ. Indeed, leaven could be applied to any false religious teaching. The Herodians were more of a political party than a religious sect, and very likely were, for the most part, Sadducean in religious

16 the leaven of Herod. And they reasoned among themselves, saying, It is ¹ because we have no bread.
17 And when Jesus knew it, he saith unto them, Why reason ye, because ye have no bread? ᵐ Perceive ye not yet, neither understand? Have ye your heart
18 yet hardened? Having eyes, see ye not; and having ears, hear ye not? And do ye not remember?
19 ⁿ When I brake the five loaves among five thousand, how many baskets full of fragments took ye up?
20 They say unto him, Twelve. And ᵒ when the seven among four thousand, how many baskets full of

¹ Mt. 16. 7.

ᵐ ch. 3. 5; 6. 52

ⁿ ch. 6. 43; Mt. 14. 20; Lk. 9. 17; John 6. 13.

ᵒ ver. 8; Mt. 15. 37.

---

sentiment, the wealthiest classes being Sadducees; yet Josephus never intimates nor implies that they were Sadducees; and Herod Antipas, in his opinion that John had risen from the dead (Matt. 14 : 2), seems, in that respect, to entertain Pharisaic sentiment. It should also be noticed that Mark alone (3 : 6) had mentioned the combination of the Pharisees with the Herodians for the purpose of destroying Jesus. It was this sect and this party which exerted the greatest influence against Jesus in Galilee. We may see a special reason in this, and also in the fact that Mark wrote for Gentiles, for mentioning Herod. The admonition, **Take heed and beware,** carefully guard against and avoid, implies that the disciples were more or less under the influence of this leaven. They came constantly in contact with the various Jewish sects and parties, and heard their opinions and utterances, which were adapted to affect their minds, which were still darkened with many carnal views and notions.

16. **They reasoned among themselves.** Talked over the matter, compared their views. And being themselves solicitous regarding provisions, they conclude that Jesus refers to material leaven, and suspect no spiritual meaning. Yet, the saying seemed somewhat dark to them. Was the leaven of the Pharisees unclean to them? or, would the Pharisees, in their hatred, put anything in it injurious or poisonous? Or, did Jesus wish them to have nothing to do with those malignant opposers? But the darkness of the saying only made the meaning the more impressive and striking to the disciples when they understood it.

17. **And when Jesus knew it.** *And Jesus, knowing* what they thought and reasoned among themselves, rebuked them for undue anxiety about bread, which so absorbed their attention as to keep them from perceiving the spiritual import of his words. **Why reason ye?** etc. You surely have no reason for being under such concern because you have no bread, and for thinking that I referred to your neglect in not bringing provisions with you. **Perceive ye not yet** my meaning, nor **understand** or comprehend my language? Have ye your **hearts yet hardened,** stupefied, notwithstanding my miracles and instruction?

18. **Having eyes** and **ears.** Having the powers of seeing and hearing, do ye not exercise them? The language is similar to the quotation from Isaiah, in ch. 4 : 12. And, with memory and reflection, **do ye not remember** what ye were witnesses to not long since in this very region, when large multitudes were miraculously fed? Is there, then, any necessity for your anxiety about bread, and for interpreting my language in a literal sense? By comparing the accounts by the two evangelists, it will be noticed that these questions are more minute in Mark than in Matthew.

19, 20. **When I brake,** etc. Closely connected, and naturally following the preceding question. Their anxiety about bread, which he specially rebuked, showed a want of faith and dulness of spiritual perception. The two kinds of **baskets** are here distinguished in the original, as well as in Matthew (16 : 9, 10), corresponding to those used at the respective miracles. Thus, the *usual Jewish traveling basket* is connected with the five thousand, as in ch. 6 : 43; and the *grain* or *provision basket*, with the four thousand, as in ver. 8. Such a distinction could not have been acci-

21 fragments took ye up? And they said, Seven. And he said unto them, How is it that ᵖ ye do not understand? ᵖ ver. 17; ch. 6. 52.

A blind man healed at Bethsaida Julias.

22 AND he cometh to Bethsaida. And they bring a blind man unto him, and besought him to touch
23 him. And he took the blind man by the hand, and led him ᵠ out of the town; and when ʳ he had spit on his eyes, and put his hands upon him, he asked ᵠ Is. 29. 18. ʳ ch. 7. 33.

---

dental. It shows that the baskets used at the one were really of a different kind from those used at the other. Mark is very lifelike; representing Jesus as drawing forth from his disciples the number of baskets of fragments taken up at each time. He would thus help their faith. With these miracles fresh in their minds, they had no reason for anxiety, or for regarding him as finding fault with them because they had taken no bread.

21. **He said to them,** a common expression with Mark, and giving prominence to this concluding question: **How is it that ye do not understand** that I spoke not to you concerning bread (Matt. 16 : 11), but concerning spiritual leaven? They should have perceived that, even if they had not fully understood his parabolic language. Matthew adds a concluding remark that they then understood that he referred to the *doctrine* or teaching of the Pharisees and of the Sadducees; and we may also add here, of Herod. The teaching of all these classes was carnal and worldly, formal and ceremonial, and alike opposed to Christ, and injurious to all under their influence.

22-26. A BLIND MAN HEALED AT BETHSAIDA JULIAS. This miracle is related by Mark alone; and is the only event of this chapter which is not related, or referred to, by one or more of the other evangelists. We have here an instance of a *gradual* cure, which gives special interest to the miracle.

22. **And he cometh.** According to the highest critical authorities, *And they come,* Jesus and the twelve. On their journey toward Cæsarea Philippi (ver. 27), from the eastern side of the lake, where they landed (ver. 13), they come *into* **Bethsaida**, on the north-eastern extremity of the lake, called Julias by Philip the tetrarch, in honor of the daughter of Augustus. This seems to have been the position of this Bethsaida, and should be distinguished from that on the western side of the lake. See on ch. 6 : 45.

They. The friends or relatives of the blind man **bring** him; and **besought** Jesus to **touch him,** thus specifying the way in which they supposed the cure would be effected. Their faith was contracted. The **blind man** was one who had become so by disease or accident, for he had evidently, at some time in life, seen both trees and men, ver. 24. He probably had heard little or nothing of Jesus. He does not come himself, like Bartimeus at Jericho, ch. 10 : 47. Hence his friends are conspicuous in bringing him, though doubtless he shared their faith.

23. **Led him out of the town,** or *village,* a country town, perhaps, without walls. The Jews were accustomed to call a place that had a synagogue a city, and one that had none a village. Julias was one and a half miles from the lake. Perhaps the landing place was the Bethsaida here meant. Some suppose the place in some way unworthy of such a miracle. But Jesus would avoid observation, and an excited crowd who might follow him on his journey. He would especially avoid anything which might hinder his enemies from carrying out their plans, and accomplishing his decease at Jerusalem. Yet we must not suppose the miracle performed without witnesses. The twelve were doubtless present, for we have no hint of their being left behind; the friends too very probably followed. The blind man saw men as trees walking.

Spit on his eyes, *into* or *in his eyes* . . . **put his hands upon him.** There was no peculiar power or medical virtue in these acts; they were probably intended to assist the man's faith.

24 him if he saw aught. And he looked up, and said,
25 I see men as trees, walking. After that he put *his* hands again upon his eyes, and made him look up: and he was restored, *'and saw every man clearly.
26 And he sent him away to his house, saying, Neither go into the town, 'nor tell *it* to any in the town.

* Phil. 1. 6 ; 2 Pet. 3. 18.
ᵗ ch. 5. 43 ; Mt. 8. 4.

The miracle is remarkable for its external applications similar to that of the deaf and dumb man, ch. 7 : 33. In that Jesus could reach the man through his sight and feeling; in this, through his hearing and feeling. In both he showed that his power was not limited to any prescribed form or manner of working; yet condescended to adapt himself to their infirmity. He put his hands upon him, spit in his eyes, and gradually brought up his faith to the assurance of a full and perfect cure. Our Lord's question **if he saw aught** or *anything*, was an assistance to his faith. He helps him on, as a fond parent helps a child to walk.

24. And the blind man **looked up** and saw according to his faith. **I see men, as trees, walking.** According to most of the oldest manuscripts, *I see the men; for I see them, as trees, walking.* How expressive and vivid the language! *I see the men*, very probably the twelve. An expression of sudden joy at seeing. Then he modifies his language, and explains himself, *for I see them walking*, yet undefined in shape and figure, *as trees*. He sees indistinctly, obscurely, and might suppose the men to be the trees of the hedge by the wayside, did he not observe their motion. In this language we have the evidence that he was not born blind, for he knew how trees appeared. Cheselden says of a child, who, having been born blind, was afterward enabled to see: "When he first saw, he knew not the shape of anything, nor any one thing from another, however different in shape or magnitude." Alford says : "It is a minute mark of truth, that he describes the appearance of persons as he doubtless had often had occasion to do, during the failing of sight which had ended in his blindness."

25. The blind man is now prepared for the exercise of a strong faith so soon as he is made sensible that Jesus would perform the cure. When Jesus therefore again puts his hands on his eyes, at once *he saw clearly;* for such is the reading of the highest critical authorities, instead of **made him look up.** His sight was perfect, his vision was clear. The second and last stage of the cure was instantaneous. **Again** seems to imply that Jesus put his hands on his eyes the first time, yet not necessarily. It may help mark the second stage of the miracle. **He was restored** thoroughly, to a healthy condition, which also implies that he once had enjoyed his sight. **And saw every man clearly,** or *all things distinctly.* This expression is stronger and more definite than *saw clearly* in the preceding clause. In the exercise of his eyes he saw everything within the common range of vision, no longer obscurely, but distinctly. He distinguished men from trees, lights and shades, forms and figures.

The gradual process of the cure distinguishes this miracle from all others ; although it is not entirely without analogy in the healing of the lunatic boy, ch. 9 : 25-27. It must be regarded not only as reflecting the man's faith, but also as an example, illustrating the variety of the divine workings. What is accomplished instantly in one may be gradual in another.

We have an account of several miracles of healing the blind, ch. 10 : 46-52 ; Matt. 9 : 27-31 ; 15 : 29-31 ; John 9 : 1-7, etc. It was also foretold that the Messiah should open the eyes of the blind, Isa. 29 : 18. The natural inference is, that blindness was common. Such is the case at the present day in the East, being caused by the excessive heat and brightness of the sun, by the fine sand driven by the wind, and by the practice of sleeping in the open air.

26. **Sent him away to his house.** It appears from this, and the following clause, that his home was not in Bethsaida. **Neither go into the town,** rather, *Go not even into the village.* The best text ends the verse here, omitting, **nor tell it to any one in the town,**

MARK VIII.

Peter's confession; Jesus foretells his sufferings; rebukes Peter; teaches self-denial.

27 ᵘAND Jesus went out, and his disciples, into the towns of Cæsarea Philippi. And by the way he asked his disciples, saying unto them, ˣWhom do
28 men say that I am? And they answered, John the Baptist: but some *say*, Elias: and others, One of

ᵘ Mt. 16. 13; Lk. 9. 18.

ˣ Mt. 14. 2; John 1. 50.

---

on his way to his house. Thus by taking the blind man out of the village, and by sending him directly home, Jesus succeeded in avoiding undue excitement; and he appears to have passed on in his journey to Cæsarea in comparative seclusion.

27–30. JESUS VISITS THE VICINITY OF CÆSAREA PHILIPPI. CONFESSION OF PETER IN BEHALF OF THE TWELVE. Matt. 16 : 13–20; Luke 9 : 18–21. About at this point, the period of preparation of Christ's last sufferings may be said to commence. He begins to prepare the minds of his disciples by clear views of himself, and by distinct intimations of his sufferings.

27. **And Jesus went out.** Probably from Bethsaida, whither he returned after healing the blind man. Mark appears to be writing a continuous narrative. **Into the towns**, or *villages* **of Cæsarea Philippi**, which was a city three or four miles east of ancient Laish or Dan, situated at the southern ridge of Mount Hermon, upon the side of Mount Panium, adjacent to a cave from which gushes forth a large fountain, one of the sources of the Jordan. In Greece the worship of the silvan Pan was associated with caves and grottoes; hence, the Grecian settlers in Syria dedicated this spot to him, and erected here a shrine, and named the city *Paneas*. It was rebuilt and enlarged by Philip the tetrarch, brother of Herod Antipas, and named Cæsarea; and to distinguish it from Cæsarea on the Mediterranean, it was called Cæsarea Philippi, that is, Philip's Cæsarea. It was a beautiful city, in the midst of the most picturesque scenery, surrounded by a rich and populous country. It was one of the residences of Philip. Agrippa II. (Acts 25 : 3) afterward embellished it, and called it *Neronias*, in honor of Nero. Both of these names have long been disused, and its ancient name, under the Arabic form *Banias*, is now applied to the small village of about forty huts and the surrounding ruin which mark its site. The *villages* of Cæsarea Philippi were those dependent on it and adjacent to it. They are probably spoken of as villages in view of their dependence on the chief town of the district.

By the way; *in the way*, on the road, while Jesus was going among these villages, from one to another. Luke (9 : 18) adds the interesting fact that Jesus "was alone praying," his disciples being with him. Very probably they were going on the way immediately after prayer. It was a fitting time and place to draw from **his disciples**, the twelve, their opinion of him. He therefore asks them, **Whom do men**, "the people," or multitudes who attended his ministry (Luke 9 : 18), **say that I am?** or, *declare me to be*. He thus would first call forth the opinion of the masses, who had followed him and were friendly to him. His enemies had expressed their opinion by words and acts, ch. 3 : 6, 22; 7 : 2.

28. In the answer of the disciples we have a vivid picture of the opinions of the people generally. They did not regard him as the Messiah, but intimately connected with him as a precursor or forerunner. Some, like Herod, thought him to be **John the Baptist** risen from the dead, ch. 6 : 14; some **Elias**, *Elijah*, who was to come, Mal. 4 : 5; and others, **one of the prophets**, as Jeremiah (Matt. 16 : 14), who was regarded as the greatest of the prophets, and expected by some of the Jews as one of the forerunners of the Messiah. The Jews held to the actual coming and the bodily resurrection of these men, and not that the soul of any of them had reappeared in the body of Jesus. We find here the same diversity of views as that described in ch. 6 : 14, 15. Only persons of strong faith had recognized him as the Messiah, Matt. 9 : 27; 15 : 22; John 4 : 42; 6 : 68, 69; 7 : 31.

29 the prophets. And he saith unto them, But whom say ye that I am? And Peter answereth and saith
30 unto him, ʸ Thou art the Christ. ᶻ And he charged them that they should tell no man of him.
31 And ᵃ he began to teach them, that the Son of man must suffer many things, and be rejected of the elders, and *of* the chief priests, and scribes, and be

ʸ Mt. 16. 16; Lk. 9. 20; John 6. 69; 11. 27; 20. 31; Ac. S. 37.
ᶻ Mt. 16. 20; 17. 9; Lk. 9. 21.
ᵃ Mt. 16. 21: Lk. 9. 22; ch. 9. 31;

10. 33; Mt. 17. 22, 23; 20. 17; 26. 2; Lk. 13. 33; 18. 31; 24. 6, 7.

29. Jesus now asks the twelve their opinion of him. **And he saith,** etc. *And he asked them,* according to the highest critical authorities. **Ye** is emphatic, and in contrast to *men* (ver. 27), whose views they had just given. Ye have told me the confused and conflicting views of the people; *but ye, who do ye say* or *declare* me to be? **And Peter answereth;** for the twelve, for Jesus addressed his question to them. Peter appears to have been the spokesman of the apostles, and to have acted somewhat like the chairman of a committee, or the foreman of a jury; ch. 10 : 28; Matt. 15 : 15; Luke 12 : 41; John 6 : 68. Compare Matt. 17 : 24; John 13 : 24. The eleven assent to his declaration of their faith, for they make no other reply. **Thou art.** The language of firm conviction, not merely of united or individual opinion or belief; for he does not answer, *we say* or *believe,* or *I say* or *believe that thou art;* but firmly, confidently, and with all the reverence becoming the announcement of so important a fact. **Thou art the Christ,** *the Messiah,* or *the Anointed,* as the word means, the one foretold by ancient prophets, and styled the Messiah, or Anointed, by David and Daniel. Ps. 2 : 2; Dan. 9 : 25. He was the Son of David, in whom was fulfilled all the types of *anointed* prophets, priests and kings of the old dispensation—the great Prophet, Priest, and King. Luke (9 : 20) gives the answer of Peter briefly and emphatically: "The Christ of God." Matthew (16 : 16) the fullest: "Thou art the Christ, the Son of the living God;" and he adds what Jesus said to Peter, Matt. 16 : 17-19. Mark was not so intent as Matthew in relating the words of Jesus; besides, writing, probably, under Peter's direction, he modestly relates only what was necessary regarding him. See on verse 32. Compare ch. 6 : 50. Mark and Luke give the main and essential proposition of Peter's answer; Matthew's form is more descriptive, and expresses the fullness of their faith.
30. **And he charged them;** strongly, strictly, implying that they would incur his displeasure should they disobey. **Should tell no man of him;** that is, this confession (Luke 9 : 21), "that he is the Christ," Matt. 16 : 20. The time had not yet come for the proclamation that he was the Messiah. He must suffer, die, and rise from the dead, and the Spirit must come. Nothing must be done, either to hasten or delay the designs of his enemies. The people were not yet ready for hearing this truth, neither were the apostles fully prepared for their work.

31-38; ch. 9 : 1. JESUS FORETELLS HIS DEATH AND RESURRECTION; REBUKES PETER; TEACHES THE DUTY AND NECESSITY OF SELF DENIAL. Matt. 16 : 21-28; Luke 9 : 22-27. Luke is the briefest; Mark the most vivid, and the fullest on self-denial.

31. **He began to teach,** etc. From this time (Matt. 16 : 21) Jesus began to teach them that he **must suffer;** the necessity of his sufferings. Before this he had taught them that he was the Christ; now he teaches them that he, the Christ, must suffer. Before, he had given obscure intimations of both his sufferings (Matt. 10 : 38; John 3 : 14) and his resurrection, Matt. 12 : 40; John 2 : 19; but now he speaks plainly, and teaches their necessity. He continued afterward with further particulars, ch. 9 : 9-12; 10 : 32-34. Thus he began also to correct their mistaken and worldly views, and, in a measure, to prepare them for the event when it came, and afterward for the better understanding of both this and of ancient prophecy, Isa. 53 : 4-10; Dan. 9 : 26; Luke 24 : 26, 27, 44, 46. **The Son of Man.** See on ch. 2 : 10. Matthew adds the fact that "he must go unto Jerusalem." **Be rejected of.** By

14

MARK VIII. A.D. 29.

32 killed, and ᵇ after three days rise again. And he spake that saying openly. And Peter took him, 33 and began to rebuke him. But when he had turned about and looked on his disciples, he rebuked Peter, saying, Get thee behind me, Satan: for thou savourest not the things that be of God, but the things that be of men.
34 And when he had called the people *unto him* with his disciples also, he said unto them, ᶜ Whosoever will come after me, let him deny himself, and take

ᵇ John 2. 19-21.

ᶜ ch. 8. 34; 10. 21; Mt. 10. 38; 16. 24; Lk. 9. 23; 14. 27; Ac. 14. 21; 1 Thes. 3. 3; 1 Tim. 3. 12; Tit. 2. 12; 1 Pet. 4. 1, 2.

the Sanhedrim, the highest civil and ecclesiastical court of the Jews, which consisted of seventy-one members, from the three classes immediately named. They denied what Peter and the disciples had confessed; they rejected Jesus as the Messiah, the Son of the living God, Mark 14 : 61-64. **Elders.** See on ch. 7 : 3. **Chief priests.** The heads of the twenty-four classes into which David divided the priests (1 Chron. 24 : 7-18; Luke 1 : 5), the high priest, who was generally president of the Sanhedrim, and his surviving predecessors. **Scribes.** See on ch. 1 : 22. **After three days.** A popular expression equivalent to "the third day" of Matthew 16 : 21, and Luke 9 : 22. The Jews were accustomed to reckon the odd parts of a day as a whole day. Jesus died on Friday afternoon, and rose on Sunday morning; the time intervening was one whole day and parts of two days, which were reckoned as three whole days.
32. **Openly.** Freely, frankly and boldly, without concealment or ambiguity. Mark alone records this. Such views were exceedingly repugnant to Peter and the disciples, with their imperfect views of the Messiah. Doubtless, also, they wounded the pride and aroused the shame of Peter. See on ver. 38. **And Peter took him** aside, as if to speak to him in private. **Began to rebuke him.** He only *began,* for Jesus interrupts him with one of his severest retorts. What Peter said, "Be it far from thee, Lord; this shall not be unto thee," is only recorded by Matthew (16 : 22). Peter, like the Jews generally, probably thought that the Messiah would live for ever, John 12 : 34. It should be noted that while Peter, through Mark, passes over that which would tend to his own honor, he states plainly his own infirmity in rebuking Jesus, and the severe reproof he received in return. The scene is true to life. Extremes often meet in religious experience. Now the bold confessor, and now the unbelieving rebuker and adversary. Peter, highly elated with the position he had just taken in confessing Jesus, and with the approving benediction of Jesus in return (Matt. 16 : 17-19), in his ignorance now gives vent to his impulsive and ardent temperament by chiding, as a friend, with his Master, for indulging such gloomy and unnecessary forebodings. This "is one of the most natural and lifelike incidents recorded in the Scriptures. Affectionate and ardent, but capricious and precipitate, imperfectly instructed even in the great truth which he had avowed in behalf of his brethren and himself, and, no doubt, elated above measure by the praise, or rather blessing which the Lord had just bestowed upon him, although only in his representative capacity, he could not have betrayed his own infirmity in one act more completely than in that recorded here by Mark and Matthew."—J. A. ALEXANDER.
33. **And when he had turned about,** etc. Literally, *And he turning upon, and seeing his disciples.* The meaning seems to be, He instantly turned upon Peter with disapprobation and displeasure, and seeing his other disciples following him and sharing in the feelings of Peter, he **rebuked him,** both for his and their good. Peter's rebuke of his Lord was presumptuous and worldly; Christ's rebuke of Peter was deserved, timely and wise. He thus checked the spirit of insubordination and of worldly ambition in his disciples. Mark alone thus minutely pictures the movements and looks of Jesus in administering this rebuke. These

35 up his cross, and follow me. For ^d whosoever will   ^d John 12. 25. save his life shall lose it; but whosoever shall lose his life for my sake and the gospel's, the same shall 36 save it. For what shall it profit a man, if he shall

---

were indelibly impressed on the memory of Peter. **Get thee behind me, Satan.** Similar to the words used by Jesus to Satan in the wilderness, Matt. 4 : 10. *Begone, out of my sight, Satan.* Satan, meaning *adversary*, is the Hebrew proper name of the devil. He was present with Peter, influencing him to evil. Compare Luke 22 : 3 ; Acts 5 : 3. And Peter, in opposing what Jesus had said, as if untrue, was acting as a representative of Satan. Compare Matt. 4 : 8, 9. Matthew adds the explanatory clause : "Thou art an offence unto me," an aggravation, exceedingly displeasing to God and me. The believing Peter was indeed a foundation stone; but the unbelieving Peter a stone of offence. **For thou savorest,** etc. *For thou thinkest not the things of God, but the things of men.* Thou art not of the mind of God, but of men. Compare Isa. 55 : 8 ; Rom. 8 : 5 ; Col. 3 : 2. His views were carnal and not spiritual. He was thinking of a worldly kingdom, and not of a kingdom which is not of this world. His rebuke of Jesus therefore was in harmony with the views of men, but not with the designs of God.

34. **And when he had called the people with his disciples.** The duties of self-denial and self-sacrifice were of interest to and binding upon all. But the great doctrine of his sufferings was, for the present, intended specially for his disciples. Also should be omitted ; the disciples were already near him. Mark alone speaks of calling the multitude. There is no contradiction to Luke (9 : 18), who represents Jesus alone praying when he began his private interview with his disciples. It is not strange that a crowd should have collected around him in the vicinity of Cæsarea Philippi, as well as elsewhere. Jesus having retired for prayer, the twelve may have first come to him, and then the people may have drawn near. **Whosoever will come after me.** Purposes or desires to come after me as my follower or disciple. **Deny himself.** Renounce himself, abstaining from everything that stands in the way of duty. **Take up his cross,** etc.

A proverbial expression, denoting the self-denials and self-sacrifices, the inner and outer struggles pertaining to the Christian life; and also, doubtless, prophetic of his own ignominious death. He had just told his disciples that he must suffer ; now he teaches them and the people that discipleship also involved sufferings and self-denials. Taking the cross and following Christ are inseparable. Every one has **his** own **cross,** which he must **take** willingly, and **follow** Christ, not the world, or any object of selfish inclination. The language is an allusion to that severest and most disgraceful Roman punishment, in which the malefactor was often compelled to bear his own cross to the place of execution. So Jesus bore it (John 19 : 17). Compare Isaac carrying the *wood* in Gen. 22 : 6. It was, doubtless, very expressive to the disciples when he uttered it, and was well fitted to prepare their mind for trials, as well as for his sufferings and death. Yet that great event served to give an intensity of meaning to this and similar passages, John 12 : 16 ; Rom. 6 : 6 ; Gal. 2 : 20 ; 5 : 24 ; 1 Pet. 4 : 1, 2.

35. As he is to lose his life, so they must be willing to lose theirs. **For whosoever will save his life.** The truth enunciated in this proverbial form of expression shows the necessity and saving results of self-denial and self-sacrifice for Christ, and thus gives a reason for what Jesus had just said in the preceding verse. Whoever purposes to save his natural or temporal life, makes this his great object, and hence rejects me, shall lose his higher spiritual life. **But whosoever shall lose,** etc. But whosoever shall lose his temporal life for my sake and the gospel's, making it secondary and subservient, shall save his life in the higher and spiritual sense. He shall " find " eternal life, Matt. 16 : 25. He shall save both body and soul to a celestial, heavenly life. Compare Paul's language in Phil. 3 : 7, 8, " I have suffered the loss of all things," etc.

36. **For what shall,** etc. *For what will it profit a man.* Further reason for

37 gain the whole world, and lose his own soul ? Or what shall a man give in exchange for his soul ?
38 *Whosoever therefore ᶠ shall be ashamed of me and of my words in this ᵍ adulterous and sinful generation; of him also shall the Son of man be ashamed, ᵇ when he cometh in the glory of his Father with the holy angels.

ᵉ Mt. 10. 33; Lk. 9. 26; 12. 9.
ᶠ Ro. 1. 16; 2 Tim. 1. 8; 2. 12.
ᵍ Is. 57. 3; Mt. 12. 39; 16. 4; John 4. 48; J m. 4. 4.
ʰ Mt. 26. 64.

self-denial in following Christ. The interrogative form makes the statement the more emphatic. It cannot by any means profit him, if he acquire the whole world and all of its enjoyments, etc. **Lose his own soul.** To suffer loss or ruin as a penalty for a fault or crime; hence, *to forfeit his soul* by seeking the world and not following Jesus. The very spirit that Peter had manifested, if followed out, would result in the ruin of the soul. **Soul** is the word translated life in the preceding verse, and here denotes the higher spiritual, immortal nature of man. It cannot mean the life of the body; for a person must lose that, whether he gains the whole world or not; it must refer to the soul and its eternal life. The Greek word has a twofold use, expressing both the natural *life* and the *soul*. Compare Matt. 10 : 28, where the word *soul* is put in contrast to the body. See also ch. 10 : 34; Heb. 10 : 39; James 1 : 21; 5 : 20; 1 Pet. 1 : 9; 2 : 11.

37. The last step in this masterly argument. **Or,** if a man forfeits his soul, what shall be **given in exchange,** *as an exchange*, ransom-price, or equivalent for it? How can he possibly redeem it? The interrogative form makes it especially emphatic. He cannot possibly find an equivalent; the ruin will be irretrievable, and hence perpetual. Compare Ps. 49 : 7, 8. If the soul is lost, all is lost, the man has lost himself (Luke 9 : 25), and cannot even attempt, much less obtain, a ransom. Notice the argument for following Christ in self-denials and taking the cross, ver. 34. Only thus can a person save his soul, ver. 35. All the enjoyments of the world can profit the man nothing who does not thus follow Christ, for he shall forfeit his soul, ver. 36. And if he does forfeit it, he can never redeem it: he is lost forever, ver. 37.

38. An additional reason for following Jesus in self-denial and crosses derived from what his hearers might experience at the judgment. This is partly omitted by Matthew, and briefly given by Luke. **Whosoever therefore.** Rather, *For whoever*. **Ashamed of me,** as his Lord and teacher. **Of my words,** doctrines and precepts, my teachings. Very probably the feelings of pride and shame had, in part, influenced Peter in rebuking Jesus. **Adulterous and sinful generation.** A faithless and wicked people. A perverse and apostate race. In the Old Testament, God is represented as the husband of his chosen people, and hence idolatry and unfaithfulness on the part of the latter are represented as spiritual adultery, Ex. 34 : 15. In their departure from God, in their rejection of Jesus, the God incarnate, their true husband, and in their spiritual idolatry (Ezek. 14 : 3), they were indeed an *adulterous, faithless* generation. See John 12 : 41–43 for an example of some who were ashamed of him before that wicked generation. In contrast, compare Paul, who was not ashamed of him, Rom. 1 : 16. **Of him also shall the Son of man,** whom you now see, **be ashamed,** rightly and justly disowned and rejected by him, **when he cometh in the glory of his Father,** when in contrast to his present humble condition he shall come in the glorious majesty of God the Father, John 17 : 5 ; Heb. 1 : 3; Matt. 24 : 30. **Holy angels,** as distinguished from fallen angels, evil spirits. Luke, who omits "in this adulterous and sinful generation," is fuller here, mentioning three glories, his own, his Father's, and the holy angels'. Jesus evidently refers to his second coming and the judgment, when he shall render to every man according to his works, Matt. 16 : 27; 7 : 21 ; 13 : 40–42 ; 25 : 31, 41.

REMARKS.

1. Jesus pities men in temporal as well as in spiritual poverty. Like him

we should have compassion on the poor and destitute, vers. 1-3; ch. 6:34; Luke 10:30-37; Col. 3:12; 1 John 3:17; James 5:11.

2. Great straits may attend following Jesus. But let us follow on; he will provide, vers. 3-9; Ps. 34:10; Isa. 33:16; Matt. 6:30-34.

3. The people waiting continuously on Jesus three days—a rebuke, an example, and an encouragement to many in our day, vers. 2, 3; Isa. 40:31; Acts 1:12-14.

4. For other thoughts on Feeding the Four Thousand, see on Feeding the Five Thousand, ch. 6:35-46, Remarks 36 to 45.

5. Jesus was soon known wherever he went. So will the Christian be, if he is faithful to Christ, vers. 10, 11; Matt. 5:13-16; Acts 4:13; Acts 28: 3-9, 17, 30, 31.

6. We should seek after light and truth; but beware of a caviling spirit, ver. 11; John 8:6-8; Acts 13:42-46.

7. Wickedness and unbelief are a cause of grief to the Lord Jesus, ver. 12; ch. 7:34; 9:19.

8. Grief over the sins and unbelief of others is an evidence of grace in the heart, ver. 12; Ezek. 9:4; Rom. 9: 1-3; 2 Pet. 2:8.

9. It is a fearful thing when men are left to themselves, and Jesus departs from them, vers. 12, 13; Dan. 12:10; Hos. 9:12; Heb. 10:31.

10. Like Jesus, let us so use those things in which people are most interested, so as to win their attention and turn their minds into profitable channels, ver. 14; John 4:7-15, 31-34; 6:26, 27.

11. False doctrines have an insidious influence. Christians may be affected by those around them, when they little suspect it, ver. 15; Gal. 5:9; Eph. 4: 14; 2 Tim. 4:3; Rev. 2:14, 15.

12. One error may pervert a whole system of doctrine, or affect the whole of one's practice, ver. 15; 1 Cor. 5: 6-8; Gal. 5:9.

13. Guard against superstition and formalism on the one hand, and skepticism and worldliness on the other, ver. 15; Rom. 10:2, 3; Col. 2:8.

14. Christians often suffer much from spiritual ignorance, and dullness of spiritual apprehension, vers. 16-18; 1 Cor. 3:1; Heb. 5:12.

15. Be more anxious about spiritual than bodily nourishment, vers. 16, 17; Luke 10:41, 42; John 6:27.

16. The consideration of past mercies and experiences will strengthen our faith, and help us to understand the word and Providences of God, vers. 18-20; Ps. 77:10-12; Heb. 10:32; 2 Pet. 1:16-18; Rev. 3:3.

17. Sinners are spiritually blind, ver. 22; John 9:39; 2 Cor. 4:4; 1 John 2:11.

18. Christ is not limited in his manner of working and of saving men. Beware, therefore, of limiting his power and spirit. Beware also of ruts, vers. 22, 23; John 3:8; Rom. 11:34; 1 Cor. 12:4-11.

19. Sometimes Jesus confers his favors instantly; at other times, gradually, vers. 23-25.

In conviction, compare Saul of Tarsus with Lydia, Acts 9:3-6; 16:14. In conversion, the Pentecostal converts with the eunuch, Acts 2:41; Acts 8:31-37; also with Paul, Acts 9:9, 11, 17, 18; Apollos, Acts 18:26; and the twelve disciples at Ephesus, Acts 19:1-6.

20. Whoever by faith has caught glimpses of Jesus and spiritual truth, should take courage, vers. 24, 25; ch. 4:26-29; Prov. 4:18; Phil. 1:6. "The blessed experience of the first believing look: a strengthening of faith, which became the transition to perfect sight."—LANGE.

21. A good place for beginning a religious life: at home, in our own family, ver. 26; ch. 5:19.

22. "Happy are those journeys in which time is not wasted on trifles, but redeemed as far as possible for the consideration of spiritual things," ver. 27; Luke 9:57-62; 24:32; Deut. 6:7.

23. Many speculate about Jesus and seem to know much of him, yet fail of saving knowledge, vers. 27, 28; 2 Tim. 3:7; 1 John 2:22.

24. We must both believe in Jesus as the Christ, and confess it, ver. 28; Rom. 10:8-10.

25. There is a time for the utterance of every truth. Seek both the time and the utterance, ver. 30; ch. 9:9; John 16:12; Eccle. 3:7.

26. The atonement was a necessity. If sinners could have been saved without it, they would have been. But "the Son of man must suffer," ver. 31; Luke 24:26; Acts 17:3; Rom. 3:24-26; Gal. 2:21; Heb. 9:22.

27. Unrenewed people generally think their own way better than Christ's. And even Christians may

IX. And he said unto them, ¹Verily I say unto you, That there be some of them that stand here, which shall not taste of death, till they have seen ᵏthe kingdom of God come with power.

¹ Mt. 16. 28; Lk. 9. 27.
ᵏ Mt. 24. 30; 25. 31; Lk. 22. 18.

sometimes thus oppose Jesus, ver. 32; Gal. 3 : 1–4.

28. How much ignorance, pride and conceit may be mingled with love and sincerity in the Christian! vers. 32, 33; 1 Cor. 3 : 1–3; 8 : 2.

29. The minds of men are ever opposed to the mind of God, ver. 33; Rom. 8 : 6–8; Gal. 5 : 21; 1 Pet. 2 : 11, 20, 21; 1 John 2 : 15–17.

30. Learn to exercise charity toward erring disciples, vers. 32, 33; Gal. 6 : 1, 2.

31. Self-renunciation is the soul of true confessing of Christ, ver. 34; Matt. 10 : 38.

32. Through the death of self, we come forth unto eternal life, ver. 35; John 12 : 24–26; Rom. 6 : 5–11; Gal. 2 : 19–21; 5 : 24.

33. Religion must engage the powers and purposes of the soul, or we are lost forever, ver. 35; Luke 14 : 26–33.

34. The soul is of infinite value. If once lost, it can never be retrieved, vers. 36, 37; Luke 9 : 25, 26; 12 : 16–21.

35. How great the danger and how fearful the consequences of being ashamed of Christ! ver. 38; Prov. 29 : 25; 2 Tim. 1 : 8; 2 : 12.

CHAPTER IX.

This chapter is closely connected chronologically and in sentiment with what precedes. The first verse belongs to the preceding context. Having foretold his own death, and taught the necessity of self-denial, Jesus, by his transfiguration, gives three of his chosen disciples a glimpse of his future glory, thus encouraging them, and preparing them for scenes of trial and suffering. This gives rise to a conversation regarding Elijah, in which Jesus points out John the Baptist as the Elijah which was to come. Returning from the mount, they find the nine disciples unable to cast out a demon. Jesus heals the demoniac, and teaches the necessity of a stronger faith, obtained through prayer and fasting. Passing through Galilee, he again predicts his death and resurrection. On their way to Capernaum, the disciples contend for the pre-eminence, which leads Jesus, on their arrival there, to discourse on humility and true greatness; on intolerance and offenses; on purity and peace. The events are evidently narrated chronologically, since both Matthew and Luke present them in the same order.

1. This verse should have been connected with the preceding chapter, like Matt. 16 : 28; and is a good illustration of the arbitrary way in which the Bible has been divided into chapters and verses. Notice Mark's oft-repeated phrase, **And he said unto them,** calling special attention to what follows. **Verily I say,** etc. A most solemn and authoritative declaration. See on ch. 3 : 28. **There be,** etc. *There are some of those standing here.* Of the twelve and of the multitude, all of whom he was addressing, ch. 8 : 34. **Which.** *Who.* **Shall not taste,** etc. A strong negative in the original; death is represented by the figure of a bitter cup or goblet, *shall not die.* **Till they have seen the kingdom of God,** of the Messiah; see on ch. 1 : 14. **Come with power.** *Already come with power,* with the exhibitions of divine and omnipotent power. The kingdom had, indeed, already come or commenced, Luke 17 : 20, 21. The language in Matthew (16 : 28), "Till they shall see the Son of man coming in his kingdom," presents Jesus as the king and divine representative of his kingdom. The fulfillment of this prediction has been variously referred by commentators: 1. To the Transfiguration. 2. To the Resurrection. 3. To the day of Pentecost. 4. To the destruction of Jerusalem. 5. To the progressive establishment of Christ's kingdom, between the effusion of the Holy Spirit on the day of Pentecost and the destruction of Jerusalem. 6. To the second coming of Christ.

The great objection to any of these views appears to be a want of comprehensiveness. They lose sight of a great principle in prophecy, namely, that it often points, not only to the final event itself, but also to types of that event,

The Transfiguration.

2 ¹ AND after six days Jesus taketh *with him* Peter, and James, and John, and leadeth them up into an   ¹ Mt. 17.1; Lk. 9. 28.

thus including a series of events, all ranging under one description, and fulfilled by one prophecy. Thus, the reign of Solomon is a type of the glory and the durability of the reign of Christ, the Son of David, Ps. 72. The return of Israel from their captivity at Babylon is linked in prophecy with the future triumph and glory of spiritual Israel. According to this principle, this prediction was fulfilled to the apostles and disciples in the resurrection (Rom. 1 : 4), to the multitude and people generally in the pentecostal season, and the complete, miraculous establishment of Christianity (Acts 4 : 25–30; 13 : 32–34; 2 Cor. 13 : 4; Ps. 2 : 6), and to the Jewish nation in his providential coming at the destruction of Jerusalem, which was a type of his final coming.

We can hardly refer this prediction to the transfiguration, which occurred only a few days after; for the expression, "*shall not taste of death till,*" implies some distance of time, and not merely length of privilege. Compare 2 Pet. 1 : 15. So, also, it is not absolutely necessary to include in the fulfillment Christ's second coming to judgment; yet, the reference of Jesus to that coming, in the preceding verse (ch. 8 : 38), would naturally suggest that view. Thus, some of those present saw Jesus come as a king in his kingdom, and in this they saw a type and earnest of his final coming. John (John 21 : 22), and probably Philip, survived the destruction of Jerusalem, which occurred about forty years after this.

2–10. THE TRANSFIGURATION. Jesus miraculously presented to three chosen disciples, as a spiritual and glorified Savior, the Redeemer and Lawgiver of his people. An earnest of his future glory and that of his followers, Matt. 17 : 1–9 ; Luke 9 : 28–36.

In the first portion of the narrative Luke is the fullest, but in the latter portion Matthew and Mark. The accounts of the two latter are very similar, but Mark is the more vivid ; he alone records the looking around of the disciples, discovering the sudden vanishing of Moses and Elias ; and the questioning of the disciples among themselves what rising from the dead should mean.

2. **After six days.** Six days after the confession of Peter, related in the preceding chapter. Luke (9 : 28), counting the days of Peter's confession and of the transfiguration, says, less definitely, "about eight days." It was very fitting that Jesus should make some exhibition of his glory as a divine and human Savior, very soon after Peter's confession and his own prediction of his sufferings, and his discourse on self-denial. The specification of time suggests, and indeed implies, some connection or relation between the preceding discourse and the Transfiguration. Why Jesus must suffer death, and how glory should follow, was a mystery to the disciples. Jesus gave them a week to ponder his sayings, and then gave some of them this wonderful exhibition of himself as the Messiah, the Son of God, and the Son of man, the great Lawgiver and Prophet, the great Priest and King, the suffering and the glorified Redeemer. **Taketh with him.** Literally, *Takes along* or *with*, as companions or attendants. **Peter, James and John.** The three specially-favored apostles, and the most intimate bosom friends of Jesus. They alone saw Jesus raise the daughter of Jairus (ch. 5 : 37), and they alone were the witnesses of his agony in the garden, ch. 14 : 33. Now they are chosen to behold his transfigured glory. Peter refers distinctly to this wondrous scene, 2 Pet. 1 : 16–18. John, in a more general manner, says, "We beheld his glory," John 1 : 14.

Leadeth them up into a high mountain apart by themselves. He brings them to the summit of a mountain, to a secluded, solitary place, and there they were alone by themselves. Luke (9 : 28) says that Jesus came to pray, and that the disciples were heavy with sleep. Some therefore suppose that the Transfiguration occurred at night—a very probable supposition ; for night was a very common season with Jesus for prayer (ch. 6 : 46; Luke 6 : 12), and he did not descend

high mountain apart by themselves. And he was
3 transfigured before them; and his raiment became
shining, exceeding ᵐwhite as snow; so as no fuller
4 on earth can white them. And there appeared unto
them Elias with Moses: and they were talking with

ᵐ Dan. 7. 9; Mt. 28. 3; Rev. 1. 12–16; 10. 1.

the mountain till the next day. Besides, the whole scene could be seen to better advantage at night than by day. What *mountain* this was, is wisely concealed from us. Tradition says it was Mount Tabor, the highest peak in Galilee, five miles east of Nazareth, but without foundation; for a fortified town stood on the summit of Tabor, and was garrisoned by the Romans, in the time of Christ. Besides, Jesus was more than fifty miles north of Tabor, in the region of Cæsarea Philippi; and it does not appear that he returned to Galilee till after the Transfiguration, ver. 30. It was, more probably, on one of the summits of Hermon.
"Standing upon the height which overlooks Cæsarea Philippi, I looked around upon the towering ridges which Great Hermon, the Sheikh of the Mountains, as the Arabs call it, projects into the plain. Full of thought that one of these summits on which I gazed had in all probability witnessed the Transfiguration, I had fixed upon one of them which, from its peculiar position, form and elevation, might aptly be spoken of as a 'high mountain apart,' when, casting my eye casually down along its sides as they sloped into the valley, the remains of three ancient villages appeared dotting its base. I remembered how instantly on the descent from the mountain Jesus had found himself in the midst of his disciples and of the multitude, and was pleased at observing that the mountain-top met all the requirements of the Gospel narrative."—DR. WM. HANNA, *Life of Christ,* vol. i., p. 336.
Transfigured before them. He was changed in appearance. Luke (9:29) says "the fashion (or *appearance*) of his countenance was altered," and that this occurred while he was praying. Matthew (17:2) says: "his face did shine as the sun." As faint illustrations, the case of Moses may be used, the skin of whose face shone when he descended from the mount (Exod. 34:29–35), and that of Stephen, whose face shone before the Sanhedrim as the face of an angel, Acts 6:15. In the next verse we learn that the change extended to his raiment. His divine nature shone forth, and its glory enveloped his person. **Before them** implies that this change took place in their presence, and that it was actually seen by them as chosen witnesses. They were witnessing that for which Jesus had brought them hither.
3. **His raiment,** *his garments, clothes,* especially his outer ones, which were visible. Mark specially and most graphically describes the effulgence of his raiment; but speaks less of the glory of his countenance, which is implied in his being transfigured, and indeed by the whole description. **Shining.** "A still more expressive term in the original, applied by Homer to the glistening of polished surfaces, and to the glittering of arms, by Aristotle to the twinkling of the stars, and by Euripides to the flashing of lightning."—J. A. ALEXANDER. Notice how expressive the language, *became shining.* **Exceeding white as snow;** than which nothing could be whiter. Some very ancient manuscripts omit *as snow;* others retain it, and Meyer remarks that if it were an interpolation it would be *as the sun,* after Matt. 17:2. **So as no fuller on earth,** etc. Rather *such, i. e., garments, as no fuller on earth can whiten,* or, according to some ancient manuscripts and high critical authority, *can so whiten.* No fuller can produce such whiteness. It was supernatural. The Romans carried the art of whitening to a high degree. The Jews also gave much attention to it. Linen garments were made to glisten with whiteness. Besides soap (Matt. 3:2) and niter for cleansing (Prov. 25:20; Jer. 2:22), chalk or white earth of some kind was used for whitening, being rubbed into the garments.
4. Glory was not only manifested in and around his person, but heavenly visitors attended him. *And* **there appeared to them,** or *was seen by them.* The disciples actually saw Moses and Elijah. It was no apparition or mere

5 Jesus. And Peter answered and said to Jesus, Master, *it is good for us to be here: and let us make three tabernacles; one for thee, and one for
6 Moses, and one for Elias. For he wist not what to

*Ps. 84. 10; Heb. 12. 22-25; Rev. 1. 17.

appearance, but a glorious reality. **Elias with Moses.** *Elias* is the Greek form of the Hebrew name Elijah. While Matthew and Luke say Moses and Elias; Mark has the peculiar expression above, putting Elias first and adding *with Moses*. This does not imply that Moses was in any subordinate position on this occasion, for in Peter's address to Jesus (ver. 5) Moses is placed before Elijah; but rather that the mind of the evangelist went out naturally to Elijah first, whose appearance had been especially expected by the Jews, ver. 11. Peter, under whose direction Mark wrote, may have at first imagined that the prediction of Malachi (4:5) was now fulfilled, and the thought may have so impressed itself upon his mind that he became accustomed to use this phraseology. It is one of those graphic strokes of Mark's style, which takes us to the mount, and seems to put us in Peter's position. Moses was the representative of the law, and Elijah of the prophets. Luke tells us that they "appeared in glory;" also that the disciples were heavy with sleep; but awaking, saw Jesus in his glory and the two men with him.
It is idle to ask *how* the disciples knew them, since many ways can be conceived how they could come to this knowledge. Jesus may have saluted them by their names; or the conversation may have indicated it; or they may have known them intuitively through the Spirit, etc. In Moses also they saw, in a glorious, visible form, a spirit of the just made perfect, and in Elijah, one in his glorious body. Elijah had been translated nine hundred years before, and Moses died more than fourteen hundred years before, on Mount Nebo, and the Lord "buried him in a valley, in the land of Moab, over against Beth-peor." There is no reason for believing that he had been raised from the dead. He may have appeared in a form assumed by angels on other occasions.
Were talking with Jesus, while they were with him, and were thus engaged when the disciples saw them. The subject of the conversation, as Luke (9:31)

informs us, was his *death*, "his decease (*departure*) which he should accomplish at Jerusalem." They speak of that which the law and prophets had typified and foretold. A becoming theme of such historical personages, and representatives of the Law and Prophets.
5. The effect on the disciples. Peter again appears as spokesman (ch. 8:29), not of the twelve, but of three. **Answering.** The word *answer* is often used in Scripture as a kind of response to some words, circumstance, or occasion which precedes. Thus what Peter had just seen gave the occasion of what he now uttered. His language was a response of his feelings in view of the circumstances around him. See John 2:18; 5:17, as good illustrations of this use of the word. **Said to Jesus.** Addressed him as the principal personage, and the most familiar to him. **Master.** Literally, *Rabbi*, the Hebrew word meaning *Master*. It is worthy of notice that Mark alone gives the original word that Peter uttered in addressing Jesus, while Matt. (17:4) and Luke (9:33) give Greek translations of it. **It is good,** etc. Joy, a holy, spiritual ecstasy pervaded the souls of the disciples. Peter felt delight and a desire for more; but he was not prepared for its continuance, as his confusion and mingled terror showed, ver. 6. To work and suffer was better than to remain there. Their time for rest and glory had not yet come. Peter, in his bewilderment, proposes to erect **three tabernacles,** *booths* or *tents*, doubtless here of branches and leaves of trees, such as could be made in that solitary retreat. Such booths were erected at the feast of Tabernacles. He proposes three booths, though six persons were present. He would have one for each of the glorious personages present, and he and his two fellow-disciples act as servants. In his address he places Jesus first, Moses second, and Elijah last, which shows that the order of the names in the preceding verse do not indicate any superiority in Elijah over Moses.
6. Mark now gives an explanation of this strange request: **For he wist**

7 say; for they were sore afraid. And there was a cloud that overshadowed them: and a voice came out of the cloud, saying, This is my beloved Son:
8 hear him. And suddenly, when they had looked round about, they saw no man any more, save Jesus only with themselves.
9 °And as they came down from the mountain, he charged them that they should tell no man what things they had seen, till the Son of man were risen

° ch. 8. 30; Mt. 16. 20; 17. 9.

not what to say. *For he knew not,* etc. His words came forth without thought or deliberation. He felt he must say something, and he uttered that which came first into his mind. Luke (9:33), presenting a little different side of Peter's bewilderment, says, "not knowing what he said." The cause of this state of mind is given: **For they,** James and John, were affected in the same way as Peter, **were sore afraid,** *greatly terrified;* pervaded and borne down with an intense religious awe at the glory around them. Mark speaks of the first stage of this fear, while Matthew (17:6) describes its climax and overpowering influence when the voice spoke out of the cloud.

7. Two more wondrous events occur, the cloud and the voice. **And there was,** etc. *And there came,* or *became a cloud;* it came into existence. **That overshadowed them,** making a sheltering covering to them. A different covering from what Peter had suggested. Matthew (17:5) says it was a *bright* cloud. It was the symbol of the divine presence, as was the cloud over the tabernacle (Exod. 40:38), the cloud on Mount Sinai (Exod. 24:16, 17), and the cloud in Solomon's temple (1 Kings 8:10, 11). Compare Exod. 16:10; Ezek. 10:4; Rev. 14:14. It was doubtless similar to that at his ascension, Acts 1:9. But who are meant by *them?* Some say Jesus, Moses and Elijah; others, the disciples; and others, still more correctly, I think, all present. See Luke 9:34. **A voice came out of the cloud** from God the Father, as in ch. 1:11, giving the same attestation as that at his baptism. Matthew (17:5) gives the fuller form, having the words, "in whom I am well pleased." The divine testimony is attended by the command which was wanting at his baptism. **Hear ye him.** Attend to his instructions; hear and obey him as the Messiah, the Prophet and Lawgiver of the church. Compare the prediction in Deut. 18: 15-19; Acts 3:22; 7:37. God would now speak through his Son, Heb. 1: 1, 2. He is emphatically the Great Teacher. In these occurrences the disciples were favored with a sign from heaven. Compare 2 Pet. 1:16-18.

8. **And suddenly.** This glorious scene ended abruptly. **When they had looked round about;** *looking around* after those who had been with Jesus. Matthew (17:6) relates that when the disciples heard the voice from the cloud they fell on their face, but Jesus touched them and they recovered from their fear, and looked up. The heavenly messengers departed immediately after the voice, and Jesus at once attends to his overpowered disciples. All took but a moment. **They saw no man,** etc. A strong negative expression. *They no longer saw any one* of those they had previously seen, *but Jesus only* with themselves. They saw **Jesus only,** or *alone,* the one foreshadowed, foretold, and testified to by the law and prophets, and the one now to be heard and obeyed. The old dispensation is passing away: Jesus remains the same, yesterday, to-day and forever.

We have here an open manifestation and declaration of Christ's power and glory. It is not improbable that this was one of the points in his history to which Jesus referred when he said (Matt. 28:18, correctly translated), "All power was given to me in heaven and on earth."

9. **As they came down,** etc. It would seem that they descended immediately, or very soon after the transfiguration. While descending, Jesus charged his disciples **that they should tell,** *relate,* narrate in detail to

10 from the dead. And they kept that saying with themselves, questioning one with another what the rising from the dead should mean.
11 And they asked him, saying, Why say the scribes
12 ᵖ that Elias must first come ? And he answered and told them, Elias verily cometh first, and restoreth all things; and ᑫ how it is written of the Son of man, that he must suffer many things, and ʳ be set at

ᵖ Mal. 4. 5; Mt. 17. 10.
ᑫ Ps. 22. 6; Is. 53. 2, etc.; Dan. 9. 26.
ʳ Lk. 23. 11; Phil. 2. 7.

no man, *no one,* what they saw on the mount. The time had not come for its announcement. The minds of the people and even of the other disciples were not prepared either to receive or use properly such revelations. Even these three privileged disciples were not yet prepared to announce these facts in their proper bearing. They still had carnal views of Christ, and did not yet understand about a crucified, risen and glorified Redeemer. **Till the Son of man,** etc. *Except when the Son of man should have risen from the dead.* Then they would be prepared to announce it, and then would come the time for others to hear it. Notice he says **Son of man.** See on ch. 2 : 10.

10. **And they kept that saying,** or, *word,* the whole charge or command of the preceding verse, **with,** rather *to* **themselves;** they kept it secret. Or, with a different punctuation, which upon the whole seems preferable : *And they kept the saying, questioning among themselves,* etc. They resolutely retained the saying in their minds, pondering it. According to either, it is implied that the disciples obeyed, which is plainly declared in Luke 9 : 36. One thing in that saying gave rise to **questioning** or inquiring among themselves, namely, **what the rising from the dead should mean,** or literally, *is.* Their doubt was not about the resurrection generally, for all the Jews, except the Sadducees, held to a resurrection from the dead (John 11 : 24 ; Acts 23 : 6-8), but about the resurrection of Jesus from the dead. This implied that he must die, and his death formed the great difficulty. The death of Jesus was contrary to their preconceived views of the Messiah, who they expected would live forever, John 12 : 34. They therefore questioned what this rising from the dead was ; whether it was to be taken literally or figuratively ; whether it was plain or parabolic language. It was easy for them to suppose him uttering, as he often did, a dark and figurative saying. What they had seen upon the mount might lead them to infer that as some from the heavenly world, one of them from among the dead, had come to him, so he in some miraculous manner might go among the dead and return.

11-13. **Jesus answers the question concerning Elijah.** Matt. 17 : 10-13. Matthew's account is the fullest.

11. **Why.** The short stay of Elijah, the secrecy of his visit, the prohibition of Jesus not to relate it at present, and his reference to rising from the dead (to them so mysterious, ver, 10), surprised them, and led to this question. **Scribes.** Jewish teachers, learned men in the Scriptures and in the traditions. The scribes taught that Elijah would come personally, settle controverted questions, restore the theocracy, and prepare the people for the coming of the Messiah. Thus Jesus refers to this latter thought in the next verse, "Restoreth all things." The Jews still expect his coming. **Must first come,** before the advent of the Messiah. Yet Jesus had come, and after it Elijah had appeared. Here is another element entering into the reasonings of the three disciples, and leading them to ask the question. They seem to have regarded Mal. 3 : 1-4 ; 4 : 5 as having been just fulfilled on the mount. Yet why did not Elijah stop and do the work he was expected to do ? Or was this appearance of Elijah a precursor of a greater coming of Jesus, which might be indicated by "rising from the dead" ? However that might be, the facts that had just occurred seemed to contradict the teachings of the scribes.

12. **Answered and told.** According to the best critical authorities this verse should begin with simply, *And he said to them.* **Elias verily cometh first.** Rather, *Elijah indeed,* etc. It is true that he comes first, as the scribes teach, and **restoreth all things.** But this coming and reformation were different from what the scribes expected.

13 nought. But I say unto you, That *Elias is indeed come, and they have done unto him whatsoever they listed, as it is written of him.   * Mt. 11. 14; 17. 12; Lk. 1.17.

Healing of a deaf and dumb demoniac.

14 ᶦAND when he came to *his* disciples, he saw a   ᶦ Mt. 17. 14; Lk. 9. 37.

Jesus admits the facts, but would correct false notions. The "restoring all things" was a brief summary of the prophecy concerning Elijah. "He shall prepare the way before me;" "he shall turn the hearts of the fathers to the children," Mal. 3:1; 4:6. This John the Baptist began to do (Luke 1:17; 3:3-14); and this is really done in the dispensation which he came to herald, Acts 3:21-23. The Elijah who was to come was to be a reformer, re-establishing, reducing to order, and bringing things to a proper religious state.

Some interpreters suppose a double coming of Elijah—the first "in spirit and in power," in the person of John the Baptist; the second "literal and in person," at the end of the world, immediately before Christ's second coming. But I cannot see anything in Malachi 4:5, 6 and Matt. 17:11 demanding a second and literal coming. Besides, Jesus in Matt. 17:12 declares that "Elijah has already come." John the Baptist indeed declared that he was not Elijah (John 1:21), that is, in the sense that the Jews used the word, who expected a personal return. But he was the Elijah of prophecy, who was to come, and is distinctly so announced to Zacharias by the angel, Luke 1:17; and also so declared in the next verse and in Matt. 11:14.

And how is it written. This is properly a question in the original. Some place an interrogation at the end of the verse. It is better, with others, to place it thus, *And how is it written of the Son of man?* Concerning his coming and work. The answer is at once briefly given. **That he must suffer,** etc. That is, He comes *in order that* he may suffer. **Be set at nought,** *be treated as nothing, despised,* Isa. 53:3. This prepares the way for what is said regarding Elijah in the next verse. What is true of the Messiah is true also of his forerunner. As they had not properly conceived of the one, so they had not of the other. As the Messiah was to come not for the purpose of worldly splendor and triumph, but for suffering, so the coming and work of Elijah were to be not of a worldly, but of a spiritual character.

13. Having admitted the fact that Elijah must first come before the Messiah, and having pointed to a suffering Messiah as predicted by prophecy, Jesus now declares that Elijah already had come. **That Elias is indeed come,** etc. *That he has also come, and they,* the Jews, the scribes being their spiritual leaders, *did unto him as they* **listed,** *chose,* or *would.* Jesus thus teaches his three disciples that the appearance of Elijah on the mount must not be taken as the fulfillment of Malachi; but that he had already come in the person of one who had suffered. Herod not alone was guilty of John's death; they who were with him at the feast (ch. 6:21) approved of his beheading; the civil and ecclesiastical leaders of the people rejected him, and doubtless rejoiced in his imprisonment and death, Luke 7:30, 33. **As it is written of him;** with reference to his coming (Isa. 40:3; Mal. 3:1); and also to his rejection, for the last chapter of Malachi, as Alexander suggests, implies that "the mission of Elijah would be either a blessing or a curse to those whom it concerned." Matthew (17:13) adds that the disciples then understood that he spake of John the Baptist, Luke 1:17.

14-29. HEALING OF A POSSESSED LUNATIC, WHOM THE DISCIPLES COULD NOT HEAL. Matt. 17:14-21; Luke 9:37-43. This account of Mark is by far the fullest and most vivid. He alone relates the questioning of the scribes, and the amazement of the multitude upon their seeing Jesus (vers. 14-16); also the conversation between Jesus and the father of the demoniac, vers. 21-25. Matthew's account of the miracle is the briefest; yet he is the fullest in his report of the reply of Jesus to the nine on their inability to cast out the demon, ver. 29; Matt. 17:20, 21. Luke omits all reference to this last point.

14. **When he came to his disciples.** To the nine apostles, whom

great multitude about them, and the scribes ques-
15 tioning with them. And straightway all the people,
when they beheld him, were greatly amazed, and
16 running to *him* saluted him. And he asked the
17 scribes, What question ye with them? And "one   *Mt. 17. 14-16;
of the multitude answered and said, Master, I have   Lk. 9. 38.
brought unto thee my son, which hath a dumb

he had left the day before, ver. 2. Possibly other disciples were also present. From Luke 9:37 we learn that it was "the next day when they were come down from the mount." It was probably near the foot of the mountain. See on ver. 2, Dr. Hanna's description. All the three evangelists agree in placing this miracle immediately after the Transfiguration. **A great multitude** with the implied idea of pressing **about them**, the disciples, who were just then objects of curiosity and mingled contempt, because of their inability to heal the demoniac. **The scribes.** Simply **scribes**, who were in the crowd, and gladly used this opportunity of exulting over the weakness of the disciples. **Questioning with them** in a caviling manner, and thus disputing with them. What was the subject of discourse can only be inferred. The scribes very probably were deducing from the failure of the disciples the inability of their Master. How marked the contrast between the glory on the mount, and the scene of misery and unbelief below! There Christ's honor and authority manifested and proclaimed; here the enemies of truth and the devil's kingdom exulting and triumphant.

15. **Were greatly amazed.** Some suppose, from some remains of the divine glory of the Transfiguration on his countenance, as the Israelites were dazzled by the face of Moses when he came down from the mount. But if this had been the case, doubtless something would have been said about it. The great astonishment of the people may be accounted for by the sudden and unexpected appearance of Jesus descending the mountain just at this time, while the scribes were engaged in caviling and disputing with his disciples. His calm, heavenly and awe-inspiring dignity and bearing were adapted also to produce amazement. **Running to him saluted him.** The curious and despising throng be-

came a wondering, eager and welcoming one. They would hasten to repair their error, and disown any part with the caviling scribes, who were still left behind with the disciples.

16. **The scribes.** According to the highest critical authorities this should read simply, *them*, referring specially to the scribes (ver. 14); yet the people (ver. 15) may be included, who had just been ready to take sides with the scribes. If we take the latter view, then the question may be regarded as containing a rebuke for the people also. **What question ye.** What is the point of your debate, the subject of your dispute or contention with them? It was still going on, though broken in upon by the coming of Jesus and the rushing of the people to meet him.

17. Neither the multitude nor the scribes attempt to answer. They feel the rebuke contained in the question, are taken by surprise not only by his coming but also by his question, and are unwilling to engage in a dispute with him. One of the multitude who is more interested than all others **answered** by stating what he had done, which led to questioning the disciples. It thus appears that the disputation, in which the scribes were engaged with the disciples, was connected with demoniacal possessions and the inability of the disciples to cast out the demon. **Master.** *Teacher*. **I have brought.** Rather, *I brought to thee my son*, a while ago, not knowing of thy absence, and I now present him to thee. Matthew (17:14) relates that the man came doing homage to him with bended knees. According to Luke 9:38, the man adds, "for he is mine only child." **A dumb spirit.** Also, "deaf spirit," ver. 25. In Matthew (17:15) the child is described as a lunatic, that is, probably, an epileptic. He was possessed with a demon which caused deafness, dumbness and fits of epilepsy. It was a severe and complicated case. His dumbness consisted

18 spirit; and wheresoever he taketh him, he teareth him; and he foameth, and gnasheth with his teeth, and pineth away: and I spake to thy disciples that 19 they should cast him out; and they could not. He answereth him, and saith, ˣO faithless generation, how long shall I be with you? how long shall I 20 suffer you? Bring him unto me. And they brought him unto him: and ʸwhen he saw him, straightway the spirit tare him; and he fell on the ground, and wallowed foaming.

ˣ Deu. 32. 20; Ps. 78. 6, 8, 22; 95. 10; John 20. 27; Heb. 3. 10.
ʸ ch. 1. 26; Lk. 9. 42.

in his inability to utter articulate sounds, Luke 9:39.
18. The father describes the terrible handling of the child by the demon. **Wheresoever he taketh him.** Wherever he seizes him, as if to destroy him. At any time the demon might exert his frenzied power upon the child, producing sudden and violent paroxysms. **He teareth him.** He throws him into convulsions. **He foameth.** The effect. The child was not only inwardly racked and convulsed, but he foameth at the mouth, **gnasheth** or grinds with his teeth, and **pineth away,** swooning away, his strength becoming entirely exhausted. The accounts of the three evangelists show independence, but no real discrepancy. The father, in Matt. 17:15, says, "for ofttimes he falleth into the fire and oft into the water;" and in Luke 9:39, "hardly departeth from him, bruising him." The three descriptions taken together form a fearful picture of the frenzied paroxysms which were added to his habitual dumbness.
I spake to thy disciples. The nine apostles, since Jesus was absent. **They could not.** An emphatic expression, *They were not strong enough* to cast him out. This lack of power was owing to their weak faith, ver. 29; Matt. 17:20. Jesus had given them power to cast out unclean spirits (ch. 6:7), and doubtless they had exercised this power; but now they falter, and the enemies of truth prevail. The three most favored apostles were also with Jesus; and this case was an extreme one. Their faith was not equal to the exigency. There is some analogy between Israel turning to idolatry while Moses was absent in the mount, and the spiritual weakness of the disciples during our Lord's absence at his transfiguration.
19. **Answereth him;** according to the oldest manuscripts, *them,* the people who had met him, among whom was the father of the child, vers. 15-17. **Faithless generation.** Unbelieving race. In Matthew and Luke, he calls them a "faithless and perverse generation." That generation and race among whom Jesus was laboring were indeed faithless. The scribes were caviling; the multitude was amazed at seeing Jesus; the father acknowledged the weakness of his faith (ver. 22, 24); and the disciples had weak faith, or no faith to heal this one. **How long,** etc. An exclamation, not of impatience of life, nor of continuance with them; but of holy displeasure at their unbelief and hardness of heart. **Suffer you.** *Bear with you,* exercising patience with you, in your unbelief. Compare Exod. 32:19. How great the unbelief of the people in view of the time he had been exercising his ministry, and the wonderful miracles he had performed! Compare John 14:9. And his ministry was drawing to a close. **Bring him unto me.** There is power in me to effect a cure.
20, The vivid description of the terrible paroxysms of the child, the imploring father and the curious multitude, in this and the four verses following, is peculiar to Mark. **They brought him to him.** The order of Jesus is obeyed. He was very probably carried, several being required to do it. **When he saw him,** or *seeing him;* the boy seeing Jesus. The masculine form here, while the noun following, translated *spirit,* is neuter, shows two personal agencies, that of the boy and that of the demon. **Straightway the spirit tare him;** convulsed him. The verb translated *tare* is different from that used in ver. 18, meaning, however, the same thing, and found in ch. 1:26, on which see. The sight of Jesus arouses the infuriated demon. He has great wrath, knowing that his time was short,

A.D. 29.   MARK IX.   171

21   And he asked his father, How long is it ago since
22 this came unto him? And he said, Of a child: and
ofttimes it hath cast him into the fire, and into the
waters, to destroy him: but if thou canst do any
23 thing, have compassion on us, and help us. Jesus
said unto him, ᵃIf thou canst believe, all things *are*
24 possible to him that believeth. And straightway
the father of the child cried out, and said with tears,

ᵃ ch. 11. 23; Mt.
17. 20; Lk. 17.
6; John 11. 40;
Eph. 2. 8; Phil.
1. 29; 2 Thes. 1.
3, 11; Heb. 12. 2.

Rev. 12:12. A further effect was visible: the boy fell upon the ground, and **wallowed,** *rolled himself* about, **foaming** like one with epilepsy.
21. **And he asked his father.** Jesus carefully inquires, not for his own information, but for the trial and strengthening of the father's faith. **Of a child.** A strong expression in the original, equivalent to saying *even from a child,* even from childhood, without exactly fixing the age.
22. **And oft-times,** etc. The father not merely answers the question, but, for exciting the compassion of Jesus, further describes the miserable condition of the child under the power of the demon. **To destroy him.** He regards the demon as an enemy who would kill his only son. **If thou canst do any thing;** showing a weak faith; doubtless too weak at first, but now more weak from the failure of the disciples, and the raving of the demon on approaching Jesus. **Have compassion on us and help us.** A strong and earnest entreaty, *Help us, moved with pity toward us.* Notice he says *us,* joining the life and health of his child with his own. Compare the prayer of the Syrophœnician woman for her daughter, Matt. 15 : 22, 25.
23. **If thou canst believe.** The difficulty is not in my power, but in thy faith. I can help thee if thou canst believe, for **all things,** etc. Or, according to high critical authorities, Jesus quotes the expression of the father, *As it regards, If thou canst? All things,* etc. It is better to regard the quotation not as a question, but as an exclamation. This the revised version of the American Bible Union admirably does, thus: *If thou art able! All things are possible to thee believing.* Be not anxious about my ability; see to thine own faith. All things are possible to one believing. Thus the meaning is essentially the same, whatever reading or rendering may be adopted. Jesus strongly implies and affirms his own ability, but conditions the cure upon the father's faith.
Some commentators very strangely draw an argument for infant baptism from this father's faith for his child. Much better might they argue the salvation of certain individuals on the faith of others! But faith by proxy, either in baptism or salvation, is equally unscriptural, Prov. 9:12; ch. 16:16. We wait to see a single example of either adduced from the word of God. A truth altogether different, however, is taught. In answer to the prayers of Christians the Holy Spirit descends upon a community. Unconverted children and friends are convicted of sin and led to exercise repentance and faith. Thus the prayers and faith of Christians often become the connecting link in a chain of events which result in the salvation of souls.
24. **Straightway . . . cried out.** The effect upon the father was instantaneous and effectual. At once and with earnestness he answers, *cries out,* exclaims with a loud voice. Jesus thus appears first as the helper of the father's faith, which was necessary to granting his request. **With tears** is omitted by the highest critical authorities. So also is **Lord** omitted. **I believe.** I do believe that thou canst cure, and I believe all that thou hast said. I am sensible too that my own faith in this case is poor and defective; **help thou my unbelief,** which still clings to me notwithstanding all that thou hast said. Or, according to the sense, help my deficient faith. Thus the father is brought to a humble confession of his own unbelief. Notice the father uses the same word **help,** as in ver. 22. He had first implored the Savior's help for his son; but now, feeling his own unbelief, and seeing the necessity of **faith** in order to a cure,

25 Lord, I believe; help thou mine unbelief. When Jesus saw that the people came running together, he rebuked the foul spirit, saying unto him, Thou dumb and deaf spirit, I charge thee, come out of
26 him, and enter no more into him. And *the spirit* cried, and rent him sore, and came out of him: and he was as one dead; insomuch that many said, He
27 is dead. But Jesus took him by the hand, and lifted him up; and he arose.
28 ᵃAnd when he was come into the house, his disciples asked him privately, Why could not we cast

ᵃ Mt. 17. 19.

he implores help for himself, and that thus his son may be healed. He desired his unbelief to be helped away; or to be helped against it. In other words, he wanted his infirmity helped, his faith strengthened, and the barrier in the way of his son's cure removed.
25. The prayer of the father was a prayer of faith. Humility and faith went hand in hand. Jesus too helps his faith and heals his son. **The people came running together** *upon* or *to* the spot where Jesus and the demoniac were. Jesus was where a portion of the multitude had run forward to meet him, at a little distance from the main crowd. Many of the people may have also been somewhat scattered. But Jesus, with his unostentatious spirit (Matt. 12 : 16-21), seeing the crowd gathering to the spot, hastens to perform the miracle. Neither would he permit the demon longer to torture the child, nor in his presence to exert his fiendish power before the people. He therefore with authority **rebuked** the **foul,** *unclean* **spirit;** see on ch. 1 :23. **Dumb and deaf spirit.** Jesus thus clearly connects the demon with his deafness and dumbness. It was not a mere disease. **I charge,** or *command.* *I* is emphatic, and in contrast to his disciples. Not my disciples, but I, with my divine authority and power, command you. **Enter no more into him.** The only time that we have it recorded that Jesus gave such a charge to a demon. The unclean spirit would desire repossession, but such an attempt is positively forbidden; the father also is thus assured that the cure was perfect and lasting. This, with ver. 18 and Luke 9 : 39, may together indicate that the demon had been in the habit of departing from the child and then returning. Compare Matt. 12 : 43-45; Luke 11 : 24-26.
26. "'Most unwillingly the evil spirit departs, seeking to destroy that which he can no longer retain,' as Fuller, with wit which is in season and out of season, expresses it, 'like an outgoing tenant that cares not what mischief he does.'"—Trench, *Miracles*, p. 206. The demon **cried,** uttered a shriek of rage and anguish at being compelled to leave. **Rent him sore,** *greatly,* or *sorely.* Convulsed him violently. This shows the terrible malignity and cruelty of the demon. So dreadful was this last paroxysm that the child **was,** *became,* **as one dead.** His bodily powers were entirely exhausted, he swooned, apparently with no breath and life in him. This vivid description is peculiar to Mark. **Many,** or *the many,* the multitude.
27. **But** while most present were ready to pronounce the child dead, Jesus takes him **by the hand and lifted him up,** or *raised him,* and he arises and stands up in restored life and health. This was a second exhibition of his divine power, and was the completion of his miracle. The mere expulsion of the demon without the restoration of the child would not have answered the design of the miracle. Compare elsewhere the reviving power of the Savior's touch, Matt. 17 : 7; Rev. 1 : 7. Luke (9 : 43) adds, that "they were all amazed at the mighty power of God."
28. The conversation of the nine with Jesus regarding their inability to cast out the demon is here very briefly given. Matthew gives it more fully; while Luke omits it entirely. **Into the house;** without the article in the original, and may mean simply *in-doors.* See on 7 : 17. **Why could not we,**

A.D. 29.   MARK IX.   173

29 him out? And he said unto them, This kind can come forth by nothing, but by ᵇprayer and fasting.   ᵇ 1 Cor. 9. 27; Eph. 6. 18.

Jesus again foretells his death and resurrection.

30 AND they departed thence, and passed through Galilee. And he would not that any man should
31 know *it.* ᶜFor he taught his disciples, and said unto them, The Son of man is delivered into the hands of men, and they shall kill him; and after that   ᶜ Mt. 12. 22, 23; Lk. 9. 44.

etc. Implies that they had cast out demons on other occasions; and that they had actually attempted, but failed on this.

29. **This kind;** of evil spirits. Jesus in his reply intimates that there are grades among demons, and that the one which had just been expelled was one of the worst. Compare Matt. 12 : 45; Eph. 6 : 12. **By prayer and fasting.** Some of the oldest manuscripts omit *and fasting.* As yet the disciples were not accustomed to fast (ch. 2 : 18). See Matt. 6 : 18; 9 : 15 for our Lord's instruction on fasting. In Matthew (17 : 20) Jesus tells them that their inability arose from their unbelief. Here nothing is said of their unbelief, but it is implied that they had not prayed and denied themselves sufficiently to exercise the faith necessary for casting out so malignant a demon. But the reply was given for their after guidance.

30-32. JESUS THE SECOND TIME FORETELLS HIS OWN DEATH AND RESURRECTION. Matt. 17 : 22, 23; Luke 9 : 44, 45. The three accounts show independence without discrepancy. That of Mark is somewhat the fullest.

30. **Departed thence;** from the vicinity of Cæsarea Philippi (ch. 8 : 27; Matt. 16 : 13), near the foot of Hermon, where the lunatic child was healed just after the descent of Jesus from the Transfiguration. **Passed through Galilee.** They went on their way through Galilee, traveling in a quiet and private manner toward Capernaum, ver. 33. **And he would not that any man should know it;** that he was thus journeying. He would as far as possible avoid public attention. Matthew (17 : 22) speaks of Jesus abiding in Galilee; and from John 7 : 1-9 we may infer that Jesus, during this whole period, rather sought retirement.

31. A special reason given for this private journeying: **For he taught his disciples;** he was teaching them further respecting his approaching sufferings and death which he had before predicted, ch. 8 : 31. This was the time when he would continue these instructions, and hence he would not be interrupted by the multitude. **Disciples;** probably the twelve, his nearest and most confidential followers, whom he would specially instruct in these doctrines. Some would also include other disciples in Galilee, from whom the seventy were selected. But the privacy of the journey, and the nature of the truths taught, limit it rather to the apostles.

The Son of man is delivered. According to some, this has reference to his betrayal by Judas, a future fact being spoken of as present, as indeed it was present before the mind of Jesus. But it is better to regard this as referring to the fact that Jesus had already been given up by the Father to men, in order that he might suffer and die, Acts 2 : 23. The divine plan of his sufferings and death had formed the topic of discourse on the mount (Luke 9 : 31); and now it is the topic to his nearest circle of disciples. It would seem from Luke 9 : 43, 44, that Jesus began these instructions almost immediately after the healing of the lunatic child; and from Matthew and Mark, that he continued these instructions while journeying in Galilee. According to Matthew (17 : 22) and Luke (9 : 44) Jesus foretells his betrayal. Jesus thus imparts additional information to what he had given immediately after Peter's confession, ch. 8 : 21. He was delivered up by the will and counsel of God, and he was to be betrayed **into the hands of men.** It was thus not a repetition, but a gradual increase in revealing to his disciples the facts of his sufferings. **He shall**

32 he is killed, he shall rise the third day. ᵈBut they understood not that saying, and were afraid to ask him.

Who are the greatest? Intolerant zeal of John. Causes of offense.

33 ᵉ AND he came to Capernaum. And being in the house he asked them, What was it that ye disputed 34 among yourselves by the way? But they held their

ᵈ Lk. 18. 31; 24. 25, 26; John 8. 27, 28; 10. 6; 12. 16; 14. 5-9; 16. 17, 18.

ᵉ Mt. 18. 1; Lk. 9. 46; 22. 24.

rise, from the dead, through his divine power, John 10:18; or, *after three days.*
32. **They understood not that saying.** Luke (9:45) explains by adding, "It was hid from them, that they perceived it not." It was part of the divine plan that they should not yet understand. It is not difficult to conceive how they reasoned. Jesus often spoke in parables and figures (John 16:25, 29), and it was easy to understand him so now. Three of the disciples had seen him transfigured, and might infer that it was not necessary for him to literally die and rise in order to enter upon his full glory. Jesus had taught his followers the necessity of a spiritual crucifixion and death (ch. 8:34-38), and they might infer a similar meaning was to be given to his language concerning himself. See on ver. 10. Yet they were perplexed, and so troubled that Matthew (17:23) says "they were exceeding sorry." "Although they were familiar with the doctrine of atonement, they could not receive the idea that the Messiah was to be himself the atoning victim. Other devout men felt similar difficulties; see Acts 8:32-34."—ANNOTATED PARAGRAPH BIBLE. And true to life it is added, that **they were afraid to ask him,** to question him regarding these things which seemed to be connected with his own death. There is a natural diffidence in speaking to a person regarding near-approaching death. And this diffidence was increased to fear by the awe-inspiring presence and power of Jesus.
33-50. WHO ARE GREATEST IN CHRIST'S KINGDOM. ZEAL OF JOHN. CAUSES OF OFFENSE SHOULD BY ALL MEANS BE AVOIDED. Matt. 17:24-27; 18:1-14; Luke 9:46-50. Mark again is the fullest and most graphic. The three accounts show the diversity of independent narrators, with no real discrepancy.

33. **He came to Capernaum.** Rather, *They came,* etc. Matthew (17:24-27) at this point relates the miracle in providing for the payment of the sacred tribute, which is passed over by Mark, possibly because it made Peter prominent, under whose direction he wrote.
And being in the house. With the idea of *having come* into the house, possibly the house of Peter, ch. 1:29. Capernaum was his residence and the center of his missionary operations in Galilee. He has once more returned, and now he has come into *the house* where he lived when there. This was probably soon after their arrival. **He asked them.** According to Matthew (18:1) the *disciples ask* Jesus. But Luke (9:47), without any reference to questions being asked, says briefly, "Jesus perceiving the thought of their heart, took a child," etc. Jesus probably first asked them concerning their dispute by the way. At first they are silent. But soon after, one or more of them asked Jesus the general question, recorded by Matthew, "Who is the greatest in the kingdom of heaven?" Jesus, perceiving the thought of their heart by the question, as well as by his own supernatural knowledge, takes a child, etc. Such variations show that the evangelists wrote from different points of view, and is really an evidence of their truthfulness.
What was it that ye disputed, *reasoned about,* discussed. Notice that Jesus in his question says not *disputed,* the word in the next verse, but *reasoned about.* **Among themselves,** separate from Jesus; omitted from the text by the highest critical authorities. The idea is, however, implied in the sentence. **By the way** to Capernaum.
34. **They held their peace.** They were silent, doubtless confounded with the question, and ashamed to confess the truth. **For.** Mark gives the reason

peace: for by the way they had disputed among
35 themselves, who *should be* the greatest. And he sat
down, and called the twelve, and saith unto them,
f If any man desire to be first, *the same* shall be last
36 of all, and servant of all. And g he took a child,
and set him in the midst of them: and when he had
37 taken him in his arms, he said unto them, Whosoever shall receive one of such children in my name,
receiveth me: and h whosoever shall receive me, receiveth not me, but him that sent me.

f ch. 10. 43; Mt. 20. 26, 27.
g ch. 10. 16; Mt. 18. 2.

h Mt. 10. 40; Lk. 9. 48.

why Jesus thus inquired of his disciples: **They had disputed among themselves,** with one another, **who should be the greatest,** *who was greatest,* or, more exactly, with the same meaning, *who was greater* than the rest. The Greek comparative here is equivalent to the English superlative. This dispute shows their worldly views of the Messiah's kingdom ; that they still expected his earthly kingdom to be soon established, and that those who were greatest now, would be greatest then. What gave rise to this disputation, we are not told. It is natural to refer to Christ's address to Peter (Matt. 16 : 17-19), and to the privilege accorded the three disciples in being with Jesus on the Mount of Transfiguration and at the raising of the daughter of Jairus. The failure of the nine to cast out the deaf and dumb demon from the child, (ver. 18) may also have had its influence. It is evident from their disputing the point, that they had not understood Jesus on any occasion as pointing out Peter, or any other disciple, as the greatest.
35. **And he sat down,** the usual posture of teaching among the Jews, ch. 4 : 1 ; Matt. 5 : 1 ; Luke 4 : 20. Thus with the solemnity and authority of a divine teacher he **called the twelve.** He would have all the apostles hear this, for even if all were not engaged in this dispute, all had worldly views of Christ's kingdom, and needed instruction. **Desire to be first** in rank and honor, to have the preëminence in position and honor. Whoever has this ambitious spirit **shall be last of all** in honor and **the servant of all,** the lowest of all in position. The word here translated *servant* is not the word for slave, but one that was afterward applied both to ministers (Col. 1 : 25) and to deacons, Phil. 1 : 1. It properly means a *runner,* a *waiter* at table, *an attendant,* and includes an idea of voluntary service. The proud disciple who is debased is made to give Jesus a submissive and willing service, though it be in the lowest place. Hence the language, at least, implies that the path to the highest honors is through humility, Matt. 20 : 27 ; 23 : 12.
36. Jesus teaches humility and true greatness symbolically, by placing a child in their midst. Mark's description is vivid and pathetic. **He took a child and set him,** *stood him up, placed him* **in the midst of them ;** and then *taking him,* or *folding him in his arms,* and having thus treated him with honor and tenderness, *he said to them.* There is an interesting, though unreliable tradition that this child was Ignatius, the martyr, pastor at Antioch from about A.D. 68 to 107. But as Jesus was in the house, possibly of Peter (ver. 33), and the child was doubtless of the household, it may have been the child of Peter, or of one of the other apostles.
37. **Whosoever shall receive ;** cordially to his heart and fellowship. **One such little child.** Not an actual child, but one of these spiritual, humble ones ; one of Christ's little ones, whether a child in years or not. The child was a beautiful symbol of the true disciple who humbly, submissively, and confidently yields himself up to the Savior's will, guidance, and protection. And it must be received **in my name ;** on account of me, because he is my disciple, and sustains a personal relation to me, and from love to me. Here is the reason for receiving one such little one. **Receiveth me,** in one of these little ones as my representative. Christ's disciples are his representatives and one with himself, Matt. 10 : 40 ; 25 : 45. He here shows their nearness to himself

38 ¹And John answered him, saying, Master, we saw one casting out devils in thy name, and he followeth not us; and we forbad him, because he fol-
39 loweth not us. But Jesus said, ᵏForbid him not: ¹for there is no man which shall do a miracle in my
40 name, that can lightly speak evil of me. For ᵐhe
41 that is not against us is on our part. ⁿFor whosoever shall give you a cup of water to drink in my name, because ye belong to Christ, verily I say unto

ⁱ Num. 11. 26-29; Lk. 9. 49.
ᵏ Phil. 1. 18.
¹ 1 Cor. 12. 3.
ᵐ Jos. 24. 15; Mt. 6. 24; 12. 30; 2 Cor. 6. 15, 16; Rev. 3. 15, 16.
ⁿ Mt. 10. 42; 25. 40.

---

and the honor and esteem in which he holds them. And he traces the relation back to the Father. **Receiveth not me** only, **but** especially **him that sent me.** Jesus uses strong language, since he is not only sent by the Father, but is in his divine nature one with the Father. The Father is especially represented in him. Jesus thus taught that his kingdom was spiritual, and that humility and a child-like spirit were essential to true greatness.

38. What Jesus had said respecting the receiving of Christ's little ones led John to refer to a recent occurrence. Having found one who did not accompany the apostles casting out demons, they forbade him. This led Jesus to reply, disapproving their conduct, and warning them against giving offenses. Matthew omits reference to this incident. Luke gives it briefly, but omits the discourse on offenses.

And John answered him. This was the response of his own feelings in view of what Jesus had just said. See on ver. 5. The conscience of John was aroused. He remembers how they had hindered one who confessed the name of Jesus, for good reasons as he then thought, but now he doubts whether they did right. They saw one casting out demons **in thy name,** claiming to do it by thy authority, and uttering thy name in doing it. It appears that this one not merely attempted, as in the case of the sons of Sceva (Acts 19 : 12–16), but actually cast out demons in the name of Jesus. He seems to have been a follower of Jesus, though he did not accompany Jesus and the twelve. **We forbade him.** John very probably took a leading part in this. Compare the proposal of James and John in regard to the village of the Samaritans, that did not receive Jesus, Luke 9 : 54. When this occurred is not told us. **Because he followed not us;** not of our company. Luke (9 : 49) says, "He followeth not with us." Having been commissioned and empowered to cast out demons (ch. 6 : 7), they may have regarded the privilege to have been exclusively theirs. They thought it wrong for one not commissioned by Jesus to exercise the power in his name. Compare a similar spirit exercised by Joshua, Num. 11 : 26–30.

39. Jesus in his answer shows that the man in question could not have been opposed to him, but was evidently acting in his service, and relying upon his power. **Forbid him not.** A general direction; neither forbid him, nor any other one in a similar position. **No man which shall do a miracle.** No one who shall exert miraculous power **in my name,** through my authority, and relying upon me. **Can lightly speak evil of me;** or *readily speak,* etc. He cannot easily or readily speak against him through whom he has his power. It is evident that he is really of Christ's followers, which is brought out in the next verse; hence they should not forbid, or hinder him in any way. Lange very properly observes here, that we should distinguish between forbidding and commanding. They are not to forbid such as seem to be acting in the service of Jesus irregularly, but it does not follow that they are to command it.

40. Jesus clinches the argument by a short proverbial phrase. In his kingdom there is no neutrality in the contest between God and sin. "He that is not with me is against me" (Matt. 12 : 30); and so **he that is not against us** (his disciples are his representatives and one in interest with him) **is on our part,** *for us.*

41. A spirit of toleration and charity should therefore be exercised. The man who was casting out demons was evidently opposing Satan and favoring our side, and all such labors, even the

42 you, he shall not lose his reward. ᵒAnd whosoever shall offend one of *these* little ones that believe in me, it is better for him that a millstone were hanged about his neck, and he were cast into the sea.

43 ᵖAnd if thy hand offend thee [*or*, cause thee to offend], ʳcut it off: ˢit is better for thee to enter into life maimed, than having two hands to go into hell, into the fire that never shall be quenched:

ᵒ Ps. 105. 15; Zec. 2. 8; Mt. 18. 6-9; J.k. 17. 1, 2; Ac. 9. 4. 5; 1 Cor. 8. 9-13; 10. 32, 33.
ᵖ Deu. 13. 6; Mt. 5. 29; 18. 8, 9.
ʳ Ro. 8. 13; Gal. 5. 24; Col. 3. 5; 1 Pet. 4. 1-3.
ˢ Mt. 16. 26; Lk. 9. 24, 25.

most feeble, shall not fail of reward, **for whosoever,** etc. **Give you a cup of water,** representing the smallest favor one may do for another. **In my name,** or, according to some ancient manuscripts, *in that name, that ye are Christ's*. The reward that shall come to the smallest tokens of friendship thus given, is expressed in the strongest language. Not only does he use the solemn and authoritative expression **verily I say unto you** (see on ch. 3 : 28); but a very strong negative, **he shall not lose,** he shall in *no wise* lose his reward. " Even the smallest service done in my name shall not be unrewarded—much more should not so great an one as casting out of devils be prohibited."—ALFORD.

42. Jesus passes to an opposite thought. While the reward is most sure to those doing the least favor to his humblest disciples because they are his, the guilt of those is terrible who shall in any way aim to lead them into error or sin. We can see a connection of thought both with the spirit of contention which the disciples had displayed, and of intolerance which they had exhibited in forbidding one to cast out demons in the name of Jesus. **Whosoever shall offend.** Rather, *Whosoever shall cause one of these little ones to offend*, cause him to fall into sin and error, cause him to become alienated from me. **One of these little ones.** Very likely referring back to the child which he had used symbolically (ver. 36); and meaning, Even one of my true and humble followers. What kind of little ones is explained by the words that follow, *that believe*. **It is better for him.** It is well or profitable for him rather, and hence, better for him. **Millstone.** Strictly this was not the common hand-stone which was turned by women (Matt. 24 : 41); but the larger kind, which was turned by the ass, for the original of the critical Greek text literally means an ass-millstone. Or, it may be more freely translated *upper millstone*, since this was the one turned, while the lower one remained stationary. The common hand upper millstone, being about two feet in diameter and a half foot thick, was well suited as an instrument of punishment for drowning criminals. When, therefore, our Savior speaks of the larger and heavier millstone being hanged about the neck, he uses the most forcible expression, and affirms in the strongest terms. Punishment by drowning was common among the Greeks and Romans, and the Eastern nations, but not among the Jews. Execution by drowning is still practiced in the East. Doubtless persons had been thus punished in the Sea of Galilee. Josephus records that the Galileans, at one time revolting from their commanders, drowned certain persons who were of Herod's party. (Joseph. *Antiq*. xiv. 15, 10).

43-48. Such being the fearful consequences of causes of offense, Jesus teaches the duty of crushing the first beginnings of sin, the causes of offense to themselves and then to others (see ver. 50), and of sacrificing, if it be necessary, what we count most dear. It was perfectly natural for Jesus to trace back these causes of offense to the individual himself. He sins in leading others to sin, and whatever is at the bottom of all this, should be sacrificed at all hazards. **Hand, foot, eye,** the most valuable of our members, and often used proverbially to denote anything peculiarly dear and valuable ; the dearest objects of our desires, the honors, possessions, or enjoyments we most prize. **Offend thee.** Should any of these *cause thee to offend*, be an occasion of falling into sin, and causing others to fall. **Cut it off. Pluck it out.** Mortify and subdue the passions, evil desires, or inclinations which animate the hand, the foot, or the eye,

44 ᵗ where their worm dieth not, and ᵘ the fire is not
45 quenched. And if thy foot offend thee, cut it off:
it is better for thee to enter halt into life, than having two feet to be cast into hell, into the fire that
46 never shall be quenched: where their worm dieth
47 not, and the fire is not quenched. And if thine eye offend thee, pluck it out: it is better for thee to enter into the kingdom of God with one eye, than
48 having two eyes to be cast into hell fire: where their worm dieth not, and ˣ the fire is not quenched.
49 For every one shall be salted with fire, ʸ and every

ᵗ Is. 66. 24.
ᵘ Is. 33. 14; Mt. 3. 12; Rev. 14. 10, 11.

ˣ Mt. 3. 11.
ʸ Le. 2. 13; Eze. 43. 24.

---

let the conflict cost what it may, Col. 3 : 5; Gal. 5 : 24. Whatever become inlets to temptation, or instruments to sin, must be sacrificed or we perish. The repetition of the comparison under different forms gives it strength and intensity. We must do like the surgeon, who cuts off a diseased member in order to save the whole body. **Maimed** or *crippled* from the loss of a hand. **Halt** or *lame* from the loss of a foot. **Life.** Everlasting or eternal life, the state of future blessedness. Thus, in ver. 47 we have instead of life **the kingdom of God,** as consummated in the future world. See on ch. 1 : 14.

Hell. Gehenna. In ver. 48 many manuscripts omit *fire* in the expression, **hell-fire** or Gehenna of fire. *Gehenna,* which is here correctly translated *hell,* is a Greek word derived from two Hebrew words, meaning originally *Valley of Hinnom,* which was west and south of Jerusalem. In its lowest part toward the south-east, the idolatrous Jews sacrificed their children to Moloch, a name of a heathen god worshiped by the Ammonites, into the red-hot arms of whose statue these children were cast alive and burned, 2 Kings 16 : 3; Ps. 106 : 38. On account of the cruel and idolatrous sacrifices that had been offered here, Josiah polluted it (2 Kings 23 : 10); and after that it became the place for casting out and burning all the filth and pollution of the city, and the dead bodies of the worst of criminals. It was apparently in allusion to these detested and abominable fires of idolatrous sacrifices and of the dead bodies of criminals, that the word *Gehenna* became to be used by the Jews to represent the place of future punishment, Isa. 30 : 33; 66 : 24. This appears to have been its use long before the Christian era, and is its only sense throughout the New Testament, where it is found twelve times, namely, Matt. 5 : 22, 29, 30; 10 : 28; 18 : 9; 23 : 15, 33; Mark 9 : 43, 45, 47; Luke 12 : 5; James 3 : 6. That Jesus here spoke emphatically of the future place of torment is also evident from the words that follow, "Into the fire that never shall be quenched. Where their worm dieth not, etc." **Into the fire that never shall be quenched.** *Into the unquenchable fire* that cannot be put out, and hence, "everlasting," Matt. 18 : 9. This phrase is rendered more intense by its repetition; although some of the oldest manuscripts omit it in ver. 45.

Where their worm dieth not, etc. Solemn and terribly sublime from its triple utterance. Some of the highest critical authorities, however, omit it except in ver. 48. Possibly this may have arisen, as Alford suggests, by the copyists, who, finding no such addition to Matt. 18 : 8, omitted vers. 44, 46. **Where.** In hell. The words are taken from Isa. 66 : 24, where the worm is represented as feeding upon the dead bodies of those who have transgressed against the Lord; and here represents the stings of conscience eternally tormenting those that are in hell. **Dieth not.** Literally, *Ends not* its life and its tormenting work. **The fire,** of divine wrath, **is not quenched,** but burns on forever. The sufferings are endless and unceasing.

49. This verse has been regarded as the most difficult in this Gospel, and has received various interpretations. The following I regard the simplest and most natural. **For** introduces the verse as a reason for the solemn declarations in vers. 43-48. **Every one of** the human race. **Shall be salted,** in allusion to burnt-offerings (Ezek. 43 :

50 sacrifice shall be salted with salt. ᵃ Salt *is* good: but if the salt have lost his saltness, wherewith will ye season it? ᵇ Have salt in yourselves, and have peace one with another.

ᵃ Mt. 5. 13; Lk. 14. 34, 35.
ᵇ Eph. 4. 29; Col. 4. 6; Rom. 12. 18; 14. 19; 2 Cor. 13. 11; Heb. 12. 14.

24), **with fire,** either voluntarily with the fire of self-sacrifice and self-denial, as the renouncing and crucifixion of sinful affections and desires; or involuntarily with the fire of hell. For every one must either sacrifice whatever causes him to offend, or be cast into hell. "For this is a fundamental law of sinful humanity: all must enter the fire."—LANGE. **And every sacrifice.** And every one who gives himself up as a sacrifice to God (Rom. 12:1) shall be **salted with the** purifying and preserving **salt** of divine grace. Salt was first commanded for meat-offerings (Lev. 2:13), which were mostly of flour. It was afterward used in burnt sacrifices, Ezek. 43:24; Joseph. *Antiq.* iii. 9, 1. The explanation of Alford, *just as every sacrifice is salted with salt*, is allowable. But the last half of this verse, *and every*, etc., is omitted by some of the best manuscripts.

50. Jesus carries out the figure of the salt. **Salt is good,** for purifying and preserving, 2 Kings 2:19–22. A general statement. Salt may represent divine grace, then the inward principle of divine grace in the heart, and also those who become partakers of divine grace, Matt. 5:13. **But if the salt has lost its saltness** or *becomes saltless*. The Jews believed that salt would, by exposure to the air, become insipid and tasteless. Maundrell, in his travels, found it in this condition. (*Early Travels*, p. 512.) Dr. Thomson saw in the East large quantities of spoiled salt thrown into the street. (*Land and Book*, vol. ii., p. 43.) **Wherewith will ye season it?** Recover the saltness. The interrogative form is equivalent to a strong affirmative. If the salt has lost its saltness it cannot be recovered by any means. If he who professes to be a partaker of divine grace remains, or becomes unholy, there is no other means of purifying him. The remark is hypothetical. Jesus does not say that the preserving and sanctifying power of the gospel would lose its power, although as far as the sinner is concerned it often does; but that if it should, then there would be no other means of restoration and salvation. Neither does he say that the principle of divine grace within Christians will in any case become extinct; but if it should, then their case is hopeless. Jesus would especially direct the minds of his disciples to the necessity of this inward grace and of watching over it. Compare Heb. 6:4; 10:26; 2 Pet. 2:15. Such warnings are part of the means used by the Spirit to keep the elect from entirely falling away.

Have salt in yourselves. In view of what has just been said, see to it that you have the preserving and purifying influences of divine grace and of the Spirit within you. And in thus doing, **have peace one with another.** *Be at peace,* literally, *in one another*, that is, *among yourselves.* Beware and not exercise an ambitious and contentious spirit (ver 23), or an uncharitable zeal (ver. 38); but in accordance with the Spirit, and acting out the principle of divine grace within you, be at peace with one another. Peace is one of the fruits of the Spirit, Gal. 5:22. This last clause, which evidently was spoken with reference to the contention and the uncharitable zeal of the disciples, shows that the whole discourse here given was spoken at this time.

REMARKS.

1. Christ's coming with power, a blessing and joy to his people. This is true both of his spiritual and personal coming, ver. 1; John 14:3, 28; Matt. 25:31–36; Luke 21:28; Heb. 9:28.

2. Jesus manifests greater glory to some of his disciples than to others; but often only to prepare them for greater trials and greater labors, ver. 2; ch. 14:33; John 21:18, 22; Acts 12:2; Rev. 1:9.

3. In the Transfiguration we behold the glory of Jesus now unvailed at the right hand of God, and the future glory of his disciples, vers. 2–4; John 1:14; 17:5; Luke 24:26; Rev. 1:16; Matt. 13:43; Col. 3:4; 1 Pet. 5:1; 1 John 3:2.

4. The glory of the Transfiguration should strengthen our faith. And so should every manifestation of Christ's glory, vers. 2, 3; 2 Pet. 1:16; 2 Tim. 4:17.

5. In Moses we have a representative of departed spirits and a proof of their conscious existence, ver. 4; Job 26:5 ("The departed spirits tremble beneath the waters, and their inhabitants"); Isa. 14:9-12; Luke 16:23; 23:42.

6. In Elijah we have a representation of those who shall be raised in glory, and especially of those who shall be changed at the second coming of Christ, ver. 4; 1 Cor. 15:51, 52; 1 Thess. 4:16, 17.

7. There is a unity in spirit and a fellowship in Christ between the saints of the old and new dispensation, vers. 4, 5; Rom. 3:31; Heb. 10:1; 12:1.

8. We shall know each other in heaven, ver. 5; Luke 23:43; 1 Cor. 13:12.

9. If foretastes of heaven are so glorious, what must heaven itself be? If it was good to be on the mount, how good and blessed will it be to dwell with Jesus and the glorified forever? Ver. 5; Rom. 8:18; 2 Cor. 4:16-18; 5:1-4.

10. Though so ignorant as not to know what to do, and so weak and sinful as to be filled with awe before the divine glory, yet we can safely rest on Jesus, whom God presents to us as our Savior and Teacher, vers. 6, 7; Ps. 2:6, 7, 12; John 10:27, 28; 14:6.

11. The Law and the Prophets gave way to Christ our great Prophet and Lawgiver. Take none other as your guide, and follow human teachers only as they follow him, vers. 7, 8; Acts 3:22, 23; 1 Cor. 11:1; Gal. 1:8, 11, 12.

12. Christ is Lord both of the dead and living, vers. 7, 8; Rom. 14:9; Rev. 1:18; 3:7.

13. Truth should be presented in its proper order and at proper times; milk for babes and strong meat for men, ver. 9; John 16:12; 1 Cor. 3:1, 2.

14. People will do well to be silent, and not try to teach those things which they do not themselves understand, vers. 9, 10. Compare Matt. 16:22, 23.

15. While we seek the aids of the learned to solve the difficulties of Scripture, we should especially apply to Christ for the guidance of his Spirit, ver. 11; John 16:13; James 1:5.

16. Formalists often hold much that is true; but it is truth mingled with error; truth misunderstood and misapplied, vers. 11, 12; Luke 11:42.

17. We need to exercise caution in our interpretation of prophecy. It may be fulfilled in a way and at a time we little expect, vers. 12, 13; Luke 24:24-27.

18. The world will take advantage of Christ's absence from his people, in order to tempt to evil, ver. 14. Compare Exod. 32:1-6.

19. How dependent are Christians on Christ! He often leaves them in great straits to teach them their great need of him, vers. 14-18; Matt. 14:28-31; John 15:5.

20. How early in life does Satan begin to manifest his power in children! Vers. 17, 18, 22; Ps. 58:3.

21. Parents should feel a deep anxiety for those of their children who are spiritually under the power of Satan, and earnestly entreat Christ to come and save them, vers. 17, 18, 22; Eph. 6:4; 2 Tim. 1:5.

22. The faithful labors and believing prayers in behalf of their children shall not be in vain, vers. 22-25; Gen. 17:18-20; James 5:16.

23. Faith and unbelief are often mingled together in the heart, vers. 23, 24; John 11:40.

24. Jesus has complete power over Satan and his kingdom, vers. 19, 25, 26; Luke 10:18; 1 John 3:8.

25. Excessive manifestation of wickedness and of the devil's power often indicate that Christ is near, with victory and salvation, vers. 26, 27; Rev. 12:12; 20:7-10.

26. Unbelief may hinder us from doing what we might for Jesus, ver. 28; Ps. 95:10; Acts 28:23-27; Phil. 4:13.

27. Our faith and our usefulness are increased by prayer and fasting, ver. 29; Acts 10:30; 13:2; 1 Cor. 7:5.

28. Jesus sets us an example of avoiding persecution, when consistent with usefulness and duty, ver. 30; John 7:1; 10:39-42; 11:53, 54.

29. We are not permitted to behold and enjoy the glories of Jesus, without beholding his sufferings, vers. 2, 31; 2 Tim. 2:12; 2 Cor. 12:7.

30. It is well to suspect our own ignorance. Nothing will so blind our eyes as worldliness, prejudice and preconceived notions; and these will make us slow to seek instruction from Jesus, ver. 32; Luke 9:45; John 7:3-5; 8:43, 44.

31. We should avoid doing that which we should be ashamed to acknowledge to Jesus, vers. 33, 34.

32. The Christian must beware of pride and ambition, and of seeking after greatness and pre-eminence. Such a course leads to strife and contention, and is opposed alike to the will, example and teaching of their Lord, ver. 34; Matt. 17 : 3, 4; Prov. 13 : 10; 2 Cor. 12 : 7; Jer. 45 : 5.

33. Christ's standard of greatness is opposed to that of the world. He that does most in Christ's kingdom to serve his fellow-men is the greatest, ver. 35; Matt. 11 : 29; Luke 18 : 14.

34. Moral excellence and greatness is not contentious, but peaceful and loving, and should be diligently sought after and cultivated, vers. 33–36; Matt. 5 : 19; 23 : 11, 12; John 12 : 6; 18 : 42–45; 1 Tim. 6 : 3–5, 9, 11 ; 3 John 9–11.

35. Little children have many characteristics worthy of study and imitation, ver. 36; ch. 10 : 15; Ps. 131 : 1, 2.

36. Child-like humility is essential to, and an evidence of godliness, pleasing to God, and leads to true greatness, vers. 36, 37; Isa. 57 : 15; Luke 18 : 14; James 4 : 6, 10.

37. Christ set us an example of humility, condescension and love, in making the least and the feeblest of his people representatives of himself, ver. 37; Matt. 25 : 45.

38. How close the union between Christ and his people! Ver. 37; Matt. 10 : 40–42; John 17 : 23.

39. Mere party zeal is opposed to the Spirit of Christ. To forbid any to do good in the name of Jesus is to disobey him, vers. 38, 39; 1 Cor. 1 : 11–15; Phil. 1 : 18.

40. No deed, however small, done for Christ, will be forgotten by him, ver. 41; Heb. 6 : 10.

41. The authors of error and the promoters of heresies and wicked divisions, will meet with more fearful punishment than those who have been destroyed by their wicked influence, ver. 42; Mal. 2 : 7–9.

42. It is better to lose our natural life than to cause a Christian to go astray, and thus injure his spiritual life, verse 42; Luke 17 : 1; 2 Thess. 1 : 6; 1 Cor. 3 : 17.

43. Our dearest sins must be renounced and forsaken, and whatever separates between us and God, or we are lost forever, vers. 43–48; Luke : 4 33; Phil. 3 : 7–9.

44. The punishment of the finally impenitent will be terrible and unending, vers. 43–48; Dan. 12 : 2; Matt. 25 : 46; Rom. 2 : 6–10 ; 2 Thess. 1 : 9; Rev. 21 : 8.

45. The punishment of the wicked will consist of the preyings of a guilty conscience on the one hand, and of the wrath of God on the other, ver. 48; Luke 16 : 24, 27, 28.

46. "We must be incorruptible, either in holiness and happiness or in sin and misery; either sacrifices to God's justice, 'salted with fire,' or willing sacrifices to his honor, by the sanctification of his Spirit through the redemption of Christ."—SCOTT. Ver. 49.

47. It is the design of God that Christians should have a saving and preserving influence within them, and endure to the end ; but if they fail of this they have reason to fear that the grace of God is not in them, ver. 50; Phil. 1 : 6; 1 John 2 : 19.

48. Christians are not mere machines; they have something to do in the preservation of their own individual hearts and of one another, ver. 50; Rom. 15 : 1, 2; Phil. 2 : 12, 13; Heb. 4 : 1; 12 : 14–17.

CHAPTER X.

In this chapter we have Mark's summary account of the last journey of Jesus to Jerusalem. Matthew's account (chs. 19, 20) is very similar. Both Matthew and Mark, at this point, appear to pass over in silence several months of our Lord's ministry. From a careful comparison of the accounts of Luke and John, we learn that, soon after the discourse in the preceding chapter, Jesus goes up to the feast of Tabernacles, which began on the 15th of Tishri, or in the year A.D. 29, October 19, John 7 : 2–10 ; Luke 9 : 51—10 : 16. For about two months he exercises his ministry in Judea (Luke 10 : 17—13 : 9), after which he attends the feast of Dedication on the 25th of Chisleu, about the 20th of December, John 10 : 22–39. Then he goes beyond Jordan and exercises his ministry, probably about a month in Perea (John 10 : 40; Luke 13 : 10—17 : 10), after which he goes to Bethany, probably early in February, A.D. 30, and raises Lazarus, John 11 : 7. Compare Luke 13 : 22. After this he withdraws to a city called Ephraim, where he continued a few weeks with his disciples, John 11 : 54.

Jesus goes beyond Jordan; he replies to the Pharisees respecting divorce.

X. AND [b] he arose from thence, and cometh into the coasts of Judæa by the farther side of Jordan. And the people resort unto him again; and, as he was wont, he taught them again.

[b] Mt. 19. 1, 2.

From this point he makes a flying trip through Samaria and Galilee, on his last journey to Jerusalem, Luke 17 : 11. This last journey seems to be recorded in this chapter, and in the account of it Matthew, Mark and Luke coincide. Some, however, with Robinson and others, suppose that Jesus did not return to Galilee, but made a tour from Ephraim over into Perea, and thence to Jerusalem. This is possible; but to me the view above seems the more probable. See NEW HARMONY OF THE GOSPELS, by the author, pp. 257-260, 267.

Jesus now takes his final departure from Galilee, and passes through Perea, where he lays down the Christian law concerning divorce; receives and blesses little children; tests the rich young ruler, and discourses on riches and forsaking all for his sake; foretells his death and resurrection the third time; hears and discourses upon the ambitious request of James and John. After passing to the west of the Jordan he heals Bartimeus, at Jericho. The events probably all occurred in March, A.D. 30.

1-12. JESUS FINALLY LEAVES GALILEE. GOES EAST OF THE JORDAN. REPLIES TO THE PHARISEES' QUESTION CONCERNING DIVORCE. Matt. 19 : 1-12. Compare Luke 17 : 11-19. Matthew is the fullest. The two accounts show the differences of independent narrators. Mark's account is evidently not a mere summary of Matthew's.

1. **And he arose from thence;** from Galilee (ch. 9 : 30), and especially from Capernaum (ch. 9 : 33), which had been the center of his missionary labors in Galilee. This language may be explained : (1.) As taking in at one view the two departures of our Lord from Galilee, that to the feast of Tabernacles and that just previous to his last sufferings. This is possible; and the meaning then would be: Jesus left Galilee, which had been the main scene of his ministry, no more to reside there, nor to exercise his ministry there, except as he should pass through on his last journey to Jerusalem, Luke 17 : 11. To his excursions and labors in Judea and Perea this verse may very briefly and incidentally refer. Thus we may have here the two extremities of a period which Matthew and Mark pass over. (2.) As the last departure from Galilee, without regard to intervening journeys, to which the evangelist passes after finishing the account of our Lord's Galilean ministry in the last chapter. This is a very natural and probable supposition. That six months of Christ's ministry is silently passed over by Matthew and Mark, is quite generally admitted; and it seems better to place the lapse of time between the ninth and tenth chapters of Mark than elsewhere. The reason of this omission by the first two evangelists can only be conjectured. They trace the growing opposition to Jesus through the six months before the feast of Tabernacles. Luke, passing over that period with slight references, traces the same opposition in the succeeding six months, and then the three evangelists join in relating the result— the crucifixion of Jesus. It would seem, also, that Matthew and Mark related principally the Galilean ministry of Jesus, and hence the events in Perea and Judea, related by Luke, would be somewhat foreign to their object.

Into the coasts of Judea; *the borders*, frontiers of Judea. **By** or *through* **the farther side of Jordan.** He passed through the country east of the Jordan, which is called Perea. This, as well as Galilee, was under Herod Antipas. According to the highest critical authorities this verse should read : "He cometh into the borders of Judea and beyond the Jordan." Whatever reading we adopt, the meaning seems to be: He went to the frontiers of Judea by the way of Perea, and not by the near route through Samaria. The expression is brief and general, and seems to imply that he visited and exercised his ministry in both Perea and Judea. **Again.** As on former occa-

2 ᶜAnd the Pharisees came to him, and asked him, Is it lawful for a man to put away *his* wife? tempt-
3 ing him. And he answered and said unto them,
4 What did Moses command you? And they said, ᵈMoses suffered to write a bill of divorcement, and

ᶜ Mt. 19. 3.

ᵈ Deu. 24. 1; Mt. 5. 31; 19. 7.

sions. Some regard this as referring to his previous visit and teaching in Perea, John 10 : 40, 41. When the multitudes again came together to him, he paused in his journey, and as **he was wont** he taught them **again.** They had heard him before.

2. Mark here begins to relate a new mode of opposition to Jesus by the Pharisees. They had found fault with him for violating the law (ch. 2 : 24); and transgressing the tradition of the elders (ch. 7 : 5); had referred his power to Beelzebub (ch. 3 : 22), and had demanded a sign from heaven, ch. 8 : 11 ; Matt. 12 : 38. But in every instance they had met with a most signal failure. Now they seek to entangle him in existing controversies on certain vexed questions, which it would be impossible to answer without displeasing one or another party. This mode of attack was continued up to the very last, ch. 12 : 13–27.

The Pharisees came to him while teaching (ver. 1), thus seeking for an open, public and authoritative expression of view. **Asked him, Is it lawful,** etc. Rather, *Asked him, if it is lawful,* etc. Their first attack is upon divorce, which was a subject of dispute among the Jews. Mark here presents the question in its most general form. Matthew (19 : 3) presents it more definitely. "Is it lawful for a man to put away his wife for every cause?" Moses had directed (Deut. 24 : 1) that a man might put away his wife by giving her a bill of divorcement, if she found "no favor in his sight, because he hath found uncleanness in her." The followers of Rabbi Hillel held that this meant that anything that displeased her husband gave him a right to divorce her. But the followers of Rabbi Shammai held that "uncleanness" referred to unchastity, and therefore denied the right to divorce a wife except for adultery. The Pharisees asked the question, not for information, but **tempting him.** With wrong motives trying him, or putting him to the test. However he might answer he would expose himself to the opposition of one or the other party. Besides, if he should answer in the affirmative, they could charge him with moral laxity; if in the negative, with disregarding the authority of Moses. Very likely also, they wished to call forth a condemnation of Herod Antipas in his married relationship, and thus insure to Jesus an end similar to that of John the Baptist.

3. Jesus answers by appealing to the law of Moses, explaining the reason of its provision concerning divorce, and then drawing an irresistible argument from creation. Matthew presents the argument from creation first, and then from Moses. Neither of them probably gives more than the leading and strong points of the conversation. The wisdom of Jesus is seen in the reply. Without stopping to discuss their nice distinctions, he appeals to their own divine standard. **What did Moses command you?** He also thus sanctions the divine authority of Moses. Compare Luke 10 : 26.

4. The Pharisees reply by giving briefly the law as found in Deut. 24 : 1–3. Though at some point in this conversation they ask, "Why did Moses *command* to give a bill of divorcement?" etc., Matt. 19 : 7; yet they acknowledge, as Jesus taught (Matt. 19 : 8), that Moses only **suffered** or permitted this to be done. "This passage (Deut. 24 : 1–4) presupposes the practice of divorce among the Jews for other causes than adultery, but it does not say a word in commendation of that practice; it only declares that if a husband puts away his wife, and she is united in marriage to another man, he can never take her again to himself. For him at least she had been defiled. Practically, therefore, a husband must look upon his act in giving a bill of divorce as irrevocable. Hence, this provision of the law was a check on the caprice of man, compelling him to weigh the consequences of his proposed act, and teaching him to respect the marriage covenant. 'Moses *suffered* you to put away your wives' (Matt. 19 : 8); he did not

5 to put *her* away. And Jesus answered and said unto them, "For the hardness of your heart he wrote you 6 this precept. But from the beginning of the crea- 7 tion, 'God made them male and female.' 8 'For this cause shall a man leave his father and mother, 8 and cleave to his wife; and they twain shall be one flesh.' So then they are no more twain, but one

• Ne. 9. 16.

ʳ Ge. 1. 27; 5. 2.
ˢ Ge. 2. 24; 1 Cor. 6. 16; Eph. 5. 31.

command it, did not speak of it as right or wise, did not encourage or facilitate it in the least; he merely presupposed the existence of this practice, and, by regulating, suffered it."—A. HOVEY, *Scriptural Law of Divorce*, p. 26. Moses had permitted divorce in such a way as to restrain a bad practice, which had gone so far to annul the original law of marriage, and which still prevails among the Arabs, who, by a word, may dissolve the marriage tie. Josephus, adopting the views of the school of Hillel (see on ver. 2), thus loosely states the law (*Jewish Antiq.* iv. 8, 23) : "He that desires to be divorced from his wife from any cause whatsoever, and many such causes happen among men, let him in writing give assurance that he will never use her as his wife any more ; for by these means she may be at liberty to marry another, although before this bill of divorce was given, she is not permitted so to do."

5. Jesus, having brought them to their own law, now gives the reason of the Mosaic enactment, and expounds the law of marriage. **For the hardness of your hearts,** the depravity and perverseness of men, necessarily resulting in quarreling, putting away of wives, and kindred crimes ; and even in the murder of their wives, if they were not permitted to divorce them. The permitting of divorce under certain restrictions was the less of two evils. **Wrote you this precept,** or *command ;* not a command to divorce, for divorces already existed, but to give a *bill* of divorcement in putting away their wives. Requiring a bill of divorce to be given would lessen the number of divorces. For generally the services of a scribe would be required to write the bill ; the ground also of the separation must be given. These would lead to caution and give time for reflection. It should also be remembered that the enactment of Moses was really a civil one, which was to be enforced by the state. As such it was adapted to the depraved condition of the people. While it permitted, it regulated divorces, and thus restrained and lessened the evil, and prepared the way for bringing the race back to the true idea of marriage.

This throws light upon the Mosaic ritual. It was not intended as a code of perpetual obligation, but was preparatory to something better and higher, when the people were able to bear it, Gal. 3 : 19-25.

6. **But** notwithstanding the permissive command of Moses, **from the beginning of creation,** of the human race, **God made them,** Adam and Eve, **male and female,** man and woman, one human pair. Thus the race was made at their first creation. That **them** refers to the first human pair is evident from the language and from the quotation in the next verse. They were designed one for the other. Thus God showed his will that man and woman should live together in the marriage state, and that polygamy should be excluded.

7, 8. Jesus quotes the prophetic language of Adam (Gen. 2 : 24), showing thereby the strong and close relation of husband and wife. **For this cause.** Because Eve was taken out of Adam, and was bone of his bone and flesh of his flesh (Gen. 2 : 21-24), and hence because male and female was thus made. **Leave his father and mother.** The relation between husband and wife is thus stronger and closer than even that between parent and child. **Cleave.** Shall be joined unto and adhere. **They twain;** rather, *the two*. *The two* is not found in the original Hebrew, but is implied. It is, however, found in the Samaritan Pentateuch, and in the Septuagint version. **One flesh.** They two shall be united in the flesh, one being the part of the other. Having quoted these inspired and prophetic words of Adam, Jesus adds, **So then they are no more twain,** no longer two, **but one flesh,** having a oneness in all their

A.D. 30. MARK X. 185

9 flesh. What therefore God hath joined together, let not man put asunder.
10 And in the house his disciples asked him again of
11 the same *matter*. And he saith unto them, [b] Whosoever shall put away his wife, and marry another,
12 committeth adultery against her: and if a woman shall put away her husband, and be married to another, she committeth adultery.

[b] Mt. 5. 32; 19. 9; Lk. 16. 18; Ro. 7. 3; 1 Cor. 7. 10, 11.

interests and relations pertaining to this world, Eph. 5 : 28–31 ; 1 Cor. 7 : 4. The words, **and cleave to his wife,** are here wanting in some of the best manuscripts; they are in Matt. 19 : 5.
9. The conclusion then is irresistible. **What therefore God.** He is the author. Marriage is of divine origin. **Joined together.** Yoke together, couple, unite. **Let not man,** in contrast to God. *Man* is here used in its broad, generic sense, man as man. The Greek word is not that translated man in ver. 2, where it means husband. The meaning is not merely, Let not the husband, but let not man. Let not human authority in any way oppose the divine. **Put asunder.** Let not man annul the ordinance of God. That relation which was constituted by God, and to which all other relations, even that of parent and child, must yield, can be severed only by him. The relation, however, ceases at death ; for the unity is based on *one flesh* (ver. 7), their united relation in the flesh for this world, ch. 12 : 25; Romans 7 : 2.
Although Jesus was discussing divorces, yet his language is also decisive against polygamy. The *two* are one flesh ; they are no more *two.* The creating one woman for one man showed also God's will in this respect.
10. **In the house.** Hence Jesus and his disciples had withdrawn from the people. Mark alone notices the fact of a confidential interview with his disciples. **Again** has reference to the question of the Pharisees in ver. 2. **Of the same matter,** or, according to the best manuscripts, **of this,** concerning divorces. They wanted more light upon the subject; they did not fully understand Jesus.
11. **He saith unto them.** He appears according to Matthew (19 : 9) to have said the same thing to the Pharisees. He reiterates it to his disciples with the additional reference to women divorcing their husbands (next verse). After hearing this again the disciples probably exclaim, "If the case of the husband be so with his wife, it is not good to marry," to which Jesus replies, Matt. 19: 10–12. Mark is very brief. **Whosoever shall put away his wife.** Mark omits "except for fornication" (Matt. 19 : 9); but this appears to have been the cause plainly understood, Matt. 5 : 32. **Committeth adultery against her,** his former wife. His second marriage is adultery against her, or in the sight of God.
12. **And if a woman,** or, *if she herself puts away* **her husband.** Moses did not permit a woman to divorce her husband. This might possibly refer to desertion by the wife, 1 Sam. 25 : 44 ; 1 Cor. 7 : 12, 13. But the language more probably refers to actual divorce by the wife. This seems to have been introduced from the heathen nations among the Jews. A half century before this, Salome, the sister of Herod the Great, had divorced her husband ; so also afterward did Herodias, and others. (*Jewish Antiq.,* xv. 7, 10 ; xviii. 5, 4.) It must also be remembered that Jesus is here giving a law to his disciples, which in future should guide his followers. It is not necessary therefore to make it square with Jewish practice.
According to our Savior's authoritative instruction, there can be but one ground of divorce, namely, fornication, in the sense of adultery and certain similar monstrous crimes, Lev. 20 : 13, 15, 16 ; 1 Cor. 5 : 1. In the present age, when the laws on marriage and divorce are so lax, it becomes both churches and ministers to follow strictly the principles here laid down by our Lord. Christians should regard no one as really divorced except for one cause.
13–16. LITTLE CHILDREN ARE BROUGHT TO JESUS, AND ARE BLESSED BY HIM. Matt. 19 : 13–15; Luke 18:

Jesus receives and blesses children.

13 ¹AND they brought young children to him, that   ¹ Mt. 19. 13; Lk.
he should touch them: and *his* disciples rebuked   18. 15.
14 those that brought *them*. But when Jesus saw *it*,
he was much displeased, and said unto them, Suffer
the little children to come unto me, and forbid them

15–17. The first three evangelists here unite in relating the same event for the first time since the contention of the disciples in Matt. 18:5; Mark 9:37; Luke 9:48. See note at the beginning of this chapter. In this account Mark is the fullest.

13. **Young children.** Rather, *little children*. The same word in Greek is thus translated in the account of Matthew (19:13), and in the next verse, and is applied to children of different ages. Thus in Mark 5:40, 41 it is applied to a girl about twelve years of age; but in Luke 1:59, 80 to the infant child, Jesus. Compare Luke 2:40; John 4:49, 16:21. But Luke (18:15) in his account uses the word which means a babe or infant, Luke 2:12, 16; Acts 7:19; 2 Tim. 3:15; 1 Pet. 2:2. They were evidently little children of tender age. **They brought;** *bore* them in their arms, or *led* them: the verb in the original may be applied to either mode of bringing them. Who brought them we are not told; probably the fathers and mothers, or those who had charge of them. Jesus may have been about to depart from the place where he was; and hence the parents may have sought his blessing on their children before he left, vers. 10, 17.

That he should touch them. Mark, and also Luke, appears thus to bring out the modest form of their request. Matthew states the full meaning: "That he should put his hands on them and pray." The object of their bringing them was that he might bless them, or invoke the blessing of God upon them. Thus Jacob put his hands upon the two sons of Joseph and blessed them, Gen. 48:14. It seems to have been common among the Jews to put their hands on persons when they prayed for them. Compare ch. 5:23; Luke 4:40. It was also customary with the Jews for the greater to bless the less, Heb. 7:7. **His disciples rebuked those that brought them.** They probably felt that the various duties of Jesus were too urgent for him to turn aside to bless little children. They may have been very much engaged in their conversation with Jesus, and did not wish to be interrupted, feeling that it was more important that they be instructed than that parents and friends be gratified in having their children blessed. They seem also to have thought it unsuitable for little children to be brought to Jesus, either at this time or for this purpose, and hence the reply of Jesus, *Suffer the little children*, etc. How chilling the rebuke of these disciples to fond parents who had doubtless been greatly moved, and drawn by the wise and tender words of Jesus! But they were doomed only to temporary disappointment.

14. **He was much displeased.** He was pained with feelings of grief and indignation at what the disciples had done. Mark alone mentions this displeasure of Jesus. **Suffer the little children.** Note the article: *The little children* that had been brought. Jesus was pleased to have them come to him. He gives the reason: **for of such is the kingdom of God;** for to such as these belongs the kingdom of God. Who are meant by such is evident from ch. 9:42. *These little ones that believe in me*, those who have a child-like spirit, humble, teachable, submissive and obedient. Such indeed are subjects and citizens of the Messiah's kingdom, and entitled to its blessings both for time and eternity. See on ch. 1:14. Next verse confirms this symbolical reference of *children* to the child-like dispositions of the regenerated.

But, while Jesus referred generally to all true believers, as little ones in character, disposition and conduct, he doubtless intended to convey a deep and important spiritual truth in regard to little children themselves; for if he made no reference to them, but only to believers, how could it be a reason for suffering little children to come to him and forbidding them not? To me it seems that Jesus referred to little children in the following respects: *First.* As symbols of true believers, whether young or old, as just explained, and in ch. 9: 36–42. They were the best symbols he could choose from the race, because, though depraved by nature through Adam, yet they are not guilty of actual transgression, and because of their humble and docile dispositions, 1 Cor. 14: 20. Did Jesus use them as symbols? Surely, then, they should suffer them to come and receive his blessing. Hence, *Second.* As the most susceptible to the gospel upon arriving to years of accountability. The age for arriving at this period varies in different individuals. A distinguished medical author says, "The seventh year, and the vicinity of each multiple of seven, is characterized by some great change in the human constitution. Thus the seventh year is that of the second dentition, and the common belief fixes at that age the distinct perception of right and wrong." Children are easily led to Jesus. *Third.* In respect to the multitudes of little children who would enter into this kingdom on earth. Most enter into the kingdom in childhood and youth, and even of those who are converted in later years, the greater part trace their impressions to childhood. The most useful and devoted of Christ's followers have been those who, like Timothy, have *from a child* known the Scriptures. It would not be strange if some or all of these, whom Jesus blessed, were then impressed with the goodness and loveliness of Jesus, and that they early came to him by faith. These *lambs* of the flock, in every age of the gospel dispensation, may most fittingly be included in the *such,* whose is the kingdom of heaven. The disciples, doubtless, thought the kingdom, with its deep and hidden truths, was especially intended for men of full age; but Jesus would correct their false notions, and have children also come to him, for the kingdom of heaven is, in a special sense, intended for and adapted to them. *Fourth.* That the kingdom of heaven, as consummated in glory, would be largely made up of children who died before coming to years of accountability. As their sinfulness is involuntary, so will also be their salvation. Since they were made sinners through Adam, and since Christ made an atonement for Adam's sin, we may reasonably conclude that those who die before committing actual transgression are saved by the blood of Jesus, and that they are regenerated by the Spirit as they enter the unseen world, and thus fitted for the kingdom of heaven. Compare Rom. 5: 12–19. As a further argument for infant salvation, it may be remarked that the Bible addresses, not infants who are incapable of reason and choice, but persons who can reason, understand and choose, and are thus accountable. And also that it lays great stress on the inability of knowing right from wrong, as distinguishing infants from adults, Deut. 1: 39; Isa. 7: 15, 16; Jonah 4: 11; Heb. 5: 14. Compare Gen. 2: 17. Of all who have died, probably not far from one-half have been under five years of age. In view of the large proportion of infants thus saved, in the kingdom of glory, and in reference to them, our Savior could well say, "To such belongs the kingdom of heaven."

To infant baptism there is not the remotest reference. The passage cannot be regarded either as an argument for it, an illustration of it, or as a kernel containing its germ. As well might we infer from it infant communion, or the perpetuity of circumcision. It is really an *argument* against infant baptism; for they were not brought for baptism, and they went away without baptism. The disciples evidently had no knowledge of such an institution; for we cannot suppose they would have rebuked those who brought them, if they had been in the habit of baptizing such little children with the approval of Jesus. If Jesus had intended to institute infant baptism, when could he have had so fit a time as that? Yet he did not institute it. If his saying, "Of such is the kingdom of heaven," was not a sufficient reason for baptizing those children then, why should it be of infants now? The passage *illustrates* the spirit which Christians should exercise toward children. They should pray for them, instruct them, lead them to Jesus. It is a beautiful illustration of children coming to him by faith. The Scriptures do not speak of coming to him by baptism, but by faith. Thus how can it illustrate that which, according to Neander and other eminent church historians, was not an apostolic institution, and which is not recognized in the New Testament? As to the *germ* of infant baptism, bap-

15 not: for ᵏ of such is the kingdom of God. Verily I ᵏ 1 Cor. 14. 20; 1 Pet. 2. 2.
say unto you, ˡ Whosoever shall not receive the ˡ Ps. 131. 1, 2; Mt. 18. 3.
kingdom of God as a little child, he shall not enter
16 therein. And he took them up in his arms, put *his* hands upon them, and blessed them.

Jesus answers the inquiry of a rich young man.

17 ᵐ AND when he was gone forth into the way, ᵐ Mt. 19. 16; 21. 16; Lk. 18. 18.
there came one running, and kneeled to him, and
asked him, Good Master, what shall I do that I may

tismal regeneration was the kernel from which it and infant communion were developed. The notion of a magical charm, and a saving influence connected with the sacraments, gave rise to infant baptism in the North African Church in the third century. It was the development of error, not of truth. Nothing seems more far-fetched than to suppose a reference to an ordinance nowhere intimated in the New Testament, unknown and unpracticed in the apostolic churches, and, by its introducing an unconverted membership, opposed to the spiritual idea of the constitution of a gospel church. We should indeed welcome to baptism all those little children who have come to Jesus by faith; but even to the baptism of these we can see no reference in this passage. See Remark 16 at the end of this chapter.

Neither can this passage be used as an argument for infant church-membership. For it can have no reference to this if it has none to infant baptism.

15. What Jesus has stated concerning the little children leads him to state an important and closely-connected truth. A person cannot belong to the kingdom of God without entering it, and he cannot enter it without a child-like spirit. This solemn truth he introduces with the authoritative expression, **Verily I say unto you.** See on ch. 3 : 28. **Shall not receive the kingdom of God;** in their hearts (Luke 17 : 21), shall not receive Christ and the gospel (ch. 1 : 15), **as a little child,** with the humility, simplicity and confidence of a little child. **He shall not enter therein,** and hence he cannot be saved. We can only enter by receiving Christ, the King, his laws, etc., in a proper spirit. Thus this verse shows that the meek, humble, and child-like disposition implied in the preceding verse is essential to true discipleship.

16. To give emphasis to what he had said, as well as to show his willingness to receive these little children, **he took them up,** rather, *folded them in his arms* (the same word in Greek as in ch. 9 : 36), and **put his hands upon them,** instead of merely touching them, and **blessed them,** pronounced a divine blessing upon them. Thus he abundantly answered the request of those bringing them. Mark alone mentions that condescending act of affection, folding them in his arms.

17-31. THE RICH YOUNG RULER. DISCOURSE ON RICHES AND FORSAKING ALL FOR CHRIST'S SAKE. One thing lacking. This seems to have occurred soon after Christ's blessing the little children, Matt. 19 : 16-30; Luke 18 : 18-30. Mark again is the fullest and most vivid. Luke is the briefest. Matthew (19 : 28), however, records a promise to the twelve not found in the other evangelists.

17. **And when he had gone forth into the way.** *And as he went forth,* or *was going forth,* from the house where he had stopped, and where he taught his disciples (ver. 10) and blessed the little children, **into the way,** on his journey toward Jerusalem, ver. 32. The language indicates a connected narrative, and that Jesus was pursuing a journey. This definite connection is preserved only by Mark; Matthew and Luke agreeing with him in the order of events.

There came one, a man distinguished from the people, not only by his eager and earnest coming to Jesus, but also by his rank; for Luke (18 : 18) says that he was a "ruler," probably of some neighboring synagogue. Mat-

18 inherit eternal life? And Jesus said unto him, Why callest thou me good? there is none good but
19 one, that is, God. Thou knowest the commandments, ᵃ 'Do not commit adultery, Do not kill, Do not steal, Do not bear false witness, Defraud not,
20 Honour thy father and mother.' And he answered

ᵃ Ex. 20. 12-16; Ro. 13. 9.

thew (19:20) speaks of him as a "young man," probably between twenty and forty. He did not come, like many others, "tempting him" (ver. 2), but with reverence and desires to be taught. He was honest but self-righteous. Mark, alone, states the fact that he came **running and kneeled to him**; in haste, in reverence, and earnest desire.
Good Master, *teacher.* A teacher indeed like himself, but one of superior and eminent virtues. **What shall I do,** etc.? A question which a convicted sinner might have asked, as those did upon the day of Pentecost (Acts 2: 37); but which here meant, What work of merit (Matthew says "good thing") must I do in order that I may attain to that goodness which insures eternal life? **Inherit;** *possess* by right, have for my portion. **Eternal life;** an unending blessed existence, everlasting happiness, vers. 21, 30.
18. Jesus *first* replies regarding the epithet, "Good." He reminds him that absolute goodness belongs not to man, but to God. The reply was adapted, on the one hand, to correct the false notion of the young man, who was expecting to arrive at absolute and meritorious goodness, and, on the other, to point him to God as the only source of goodness to man. **Why callest thou me good?** since you regard me as only a virtuous man, an eminent rabbi or teacher. **There is none good but one, that is, God.** God only is absolutely good. "For thou only art holy," Rev. 15:4. Jesus thus makes no reference to his own divinity; but he shows the young man how vain his thought of doing an absolutely good thing. It was the first blow to his self-righteousness.
19. Jesus proceeds to the *second* part of his answer, and attends to the great end which the young man wishes to attain, namely, *eternal life.* **Thou knowest the commandments;** since he was a Jew and a ruler, probably of a synagogue, and instructed in the Scriptures. As if Jesus had said, "Why ask,

What shall I do? Why come to me? Thou knowest what God has already commanded. Jesus thus directs his attention first to the commandments, which pointed out the way of holiness, which is the way of God. Similarly he had answered the young lawyer, in regard to the law, "This do and thou shalt live," Luke 10:28. The law was indeed intended to give life to all who should perfectly obey it, John 12:50; Rom. 7:10. It was fitted to Adam in his state of innocence, and to holy beings. And in our present fallen condition, it is fitted to show men that they are sinners, Rom. 7:7-9. As a wise physician, Jesus would first make this young man feel that he was sick, and hence he preaches to him the law. If he had come a sin-sick soul, he would have proclaimed to him the gospel. Matt. 11:28-30. Jesus quotes as specimens the second table of the decalogue, the duties between man and man, because these are the more easily understood and the more easily tested. The young man may also have laid less stress on these than the other commandments, and may have been remarkably deficient in honor to his parents and in love to his neighbor (ch. 7:9-13; Luke 10:30-35); and then, if he was wanting in performing his duty toward men, surely he was lacking in his duties toward God, 1 John 4:20.
The commandments are not given in their order, but the seventh first, then the sixth, then the eighth, ninth, tenth, and last of all the fifth. Matthew gives the sixth first, and then the seventh; but Luke the same as Mark. The fifth is placed last, very probably because it is a positive command; Matthew also adds, "Thou shalt love thy neighbor as thyself," a positive summary of the second table. Mark alone gives **Defraud not,** by covetousness or any dishonest act; which appears to be a brief summary of the tenth commandment, Exod. 20:17.
20. **Master;** *Teacher.* He does not say, *Good* Teacher, this time. **All**

and said unto him, Master, all these have I observed
21 from my youth. Then Jesus beholding him loved
him, and said unto him, One thing thou lackest: go
thy way, sell whatsoever thou hast, and give to the
poor; and thou shalt have °treasure in heaven: and
22 come, take up the cross, and follow me. And he

° Mt. 6. 19, 20; 19. 21; Lk. 12. 33; 16. 9.

these have I observed, or *kept*. So he honestly thought; and he had doubtless kept them, externally, in outward appearance; but he had no insight into the spiritual nature of the law, as exhibited in the Sermon on the Mount, or he would not have thus spoken, Rom. 7 : 7, 8. **From my youth.** Doubtless from his early youth, or childhood. Like Saul of Tarsus, he was sincere, earnest, circumspect, but intensely self-righteous, Phil. 3 : 4–6. Yet all of his strict external observances did not give him peace of mind. Though self-righteous, he felt an unrest, he felt a need of something more to give him a rightful claim to eternal life.

21. **Then;** rather, *and*. **Beholding him loved him.** With affectionate regard he looked upon one whose open frankness and sincerity contrasted so favorably with the dishonesty and hypocrisy of the scribes and Pharisees. He was also young, amiable, externally moral, sincere, and desirous to know his duty. Jesus seems to have exercised a tender compassion similar to that which pious and devoted ministers often exercise toward inquiring, exemplary, though unconverted youth, 1 John 4 : 10–19.

With this love Jesus proceeds to apply a test which will lay open his heart before him, and reveal to him his idol and his self-love. **One thing thou lackest.** One thing is wanting to thee: the giving up all for Christ. From Matthew we learn that the young man had asked, "What lack I yet?" This is an illustration of the way in which the evangelists drew from the great treasure of facts in the life of our Lord. Doubtless many of their accounts are but summaries of extended conversations and incidents. **Go thy way,** immediately. **Sell . . . . and thou shalt have treasure in heaven,** in place of thy earthly treasures, Matt. 6 : 18, 20. He is thus called upon to part with his possessions, and from the pursuit of riches, and to look forward to heavenly treasures. **Come, and follow me,** as my disciple and personal attendant. The words, **take up the cross,** are wanting in the best text, and should be omitted. Jesus places before him a perfect standard, a life of self-denial, and discipleship of the despised Nazarene. Thus we must understand the command; for what was lacking was *supreme love to God*, not merely selling his earthly possessions. This would not constitute perfection or complete the circle of moral obligation. This was but the type of renouncing his *self-love*, and giving up all for Christ. His selling all in his case was made the test of love to God and of the value he put on eternal life. The young man in keeping the commandments professed to love God supremely; yet Jesus showed him that he loved his possessions more than God. They were his *idol;* and therefore they must be sacrificed. If ambition, love of honor or of pleasure had been his ruling sin, Jesus then would have demanded the sacrifice of these.

The spirit of this command is required of every disciple, Luke 14 : 33. Jesus requires a full surrender of soul, body, talents, influence, property. He does not require us to sell our possessions, impoverish ourselves, and thus unsettle the social system; but he does require us, as his stewards, to use the world as not abusing it, and to give freely as we have the ability, Luke 12 : 33; 1 Tim. 6 : 17, 19. The gospel recognizes and confirms the right of holding property, Acts 5 : 4.

22. Jesus had taken the young man at his word, and pointed out a perfect standard, and by it showed him that,

was sad at that saying, and went away grieved: for he had great possessions.

Jesus discourses on riches, and on forsaking all for his sake.

23 ᵖ And Jesus looked round about, and saith unto his disciples, How hardly shall they that have riches
24 enter into the kingdom of God! And the disciples were astonished at his words. But Jesus answereth again and saith unto them, Children, how hard is it for them ᑫ that trust in riches to enter into the king-
25 dom of God! It is easier for a camel to go through the eye of a needle, than for a rich man to enter

ᵖ Mt. 19. 23; Lk. 18. 24.

ᑫ Job 31. 24; Ps. 52. 7; 62. 10; 1 Tim. 6. 17.

however moral and amiable he had been, he was lacking in the ground principles of righteousness, in supreme love to God and entire consecration to him. **He was sad.** *He became gloomy, sad* **at that saying.** He felt its force; but the requirement was too hard for him, and **he went away grieved,** or *sorrowful,* with the thought of giving up his gay and worldly prospects, or losing eternal life, **for he had great possessions;** "he was very rich," Luke 18:23. He had a struggle and a severe one, he was "very sorrowful" (Luke 18:23), but he could not give up the world. His sorrow showed that Jesus had struck at the idol which stood in the place of God, and which must be renounced and forsaken, or salvation could not be attained. Here was an act of obedience which he could not perform. Here was a turning-point in his history. How solemn that moment! His heart was terribly sad, but sadder still to see him thus leaving the presence of Jesus. Had he renounced his love of wealth, had he gone forth to give up cheerfully his possessions to God and his cause, then as God restored to Abraham Isaac, his son, whom he offered at his command, so Jesus might have said to this young man, "Take back thy possessions, and keep them for me; you have indeed obeyed, and given them to God in your heart; use them to his glory and in the extension of my kingdom." We have no further account of this young man. The words of Jesus may have taken root and borne fruit in after days. It seems pleasant to think that this one, whom Jesus *loved,* and toward whom he may have had purposes of mercy, did afterward repent, and live a life of self-denial in his service. But still we cannot rid ourselves of the thought that this was the decisive time in his existence, when by his decision he lost his soul.

23. Jesus discourses on RICHES, occasioned by the incident which had just occurred. **Jesus looked round.** Mark especially notices the looks and gestures of Jesus, ver. 21; ch. 3:5, 34; 5:32. **How hardly,** etc. With what difficulty shall a rich man become the subject and attain the blessings and honors of the new dispensation, here and hereafter! With what difficulty shall they be saved!

24. **Astonished;** filled with amazement. **Answereth again.** To their thoughts rather than to their words. **Children.** An appellation of affection indicating a desire to comfort and enlighten. This tender answer is preserved only by Mark, and explains our Savior's meaning in the previous declaration. **They that trust in riches.** These words are wanting in some of the best manuscripts. They were very likely omitted by some early transcriber because they were not found in the parallel passages, Matt. 19:23 and Luke 18:24. Riches are apt to produce self-sufficiency, and lead those who have them to fix their hearts upon them, and rely on them. It is only as they renounce their trust in them that they can be saved. But how difficult to do this is seen in the next verse.

25. Jesus now in the most emphatic manner reiterates the extreme difficulty of a rich man entering his kingdom. **It is easier for a camel . . . the eye of a needle.** A strong proverbial expression. Instead of camel,

26 into the kingdom of God. And they were astonished out of measure, saying among themselves,
27 Who then can be saved? And Jesus looking upon them saith, With men *it is* impossible, but not with God: for ʳ with God all things are possible.
28 ˢ Then Peter began to say unto him, Lo, we have

ʳ Job 42. 2; Jer. 32. 17; Mt. 19. 26; Lk. 1. 37.
ˢ Mt. 19. 27; Lk. 18. 28.

some have supposed here a Greek word, meaning *anchor rope*. This supposition, however, is entirely groundless. Others have asserted that *eye of a needle* was used to designate a low gate, through which a camel could not pass unless his load was taken off. The assertion is fanciful and precarious. Such explanations have been invented in order to get rid of the seeming difficulties connected with the plain meaning of this passage. The Arabs have a proverb of an elephant going through a needle's eye. Lightfoot refers to instances in the Talmud of similar proverbial expressions in regard to the elephant. In Matt. 23 : 24 we have the figure of *swallowing a camel*. The passage, therefore, is in harmony with the Oriental modes of conception and proverbial language. Compare also Jer. 13 : 23. It is a hyperbolical proverb, expressing the greatest conceivable difficulty, the greatest human impossibility of a rich man entering Christ's kingdom. In the light of the preceding verse the rich man means one who trusts in riches, and implies the difficulty of renouncing this trust. "It is easier for a camel to go through the eye of a needle than for a rich man to *cast off his trust in riches*."—WESLEY. Humanly speaking, riches and trust in them are inseparable.

26. **Astonished out of measure.** They were before astonished (ver. 24), but now at Christ's emphatic repetition of the same truth, they are *exceedingly*, or *excessively amazed*. **Among themselves.** To one another. **Who then can be saved?** An abrupt question of strong surprise. Quick as thought the disciples *generalized* the class of *the rich*, or of those that *trusted* in riches. They saw that the desire and love of riches were so common among men, and also the trust in them, both of those who had them, and those who were striving to obtain them, as to seemingly render the Savior's declaration of almost universal application, and they exclaim, "Who, then, can be saved?" Their carnal views of a temporal kingdom, in which there would be great power and wealth, doubtless made the declaration of Jesus the more amazing and difficult to their minds.

27. **And Jesus looking upon them,** with compassion, and to give greater force to what he was about to say. See on ver. 23. **With men, impossible.** It is a human impossibility. It is beyond human power for any to be saved, and especially those who are surrounded with the dangers and the difficulties of wealth. **With God all things are possible.** He can break the spirit of covetousness, change the heart, and make the rich humble, believing, self-denying and obedient; so that they shall trust in God, rather than in their possessions, love him supremely, and, consecrating all to his service, act only as stewards, ch. 9 : 23. The answer is general. *All things are possible*, thus including the conversion and salvation of the rich as well as of the poor.

28. **Peter began to say** at once, but only began, in behalf of himself and the other apostles. According to the highest critical authorities **them** should be omitted. **Lo.** *Behold*, look at our case. **We have left all;** when you called us *we left all*, our property and business, *and followed thee*, as personal attendants, ch. 1 : 16-20; ch. 2 : 14. This declaration of Peter was suggested by the command of Jesus to the young man, "Sell whatsoever thou hast," etc. (ver. 21), and his discourse on the difficulty of rich men attaining salvation. We are not to regard it as a *boast*, for that would have called forth a different answer from Jesus. It seems to have been an anxious inquiry regarding themselves, whether they had complied with what was required. They had forsaken all. None of them was rich; yet they had broken many fond ties and made many great sacrifices. James and John, sons of Zebedee, had hired servants, ch. 1 : 20; Matthew was a man of some property, Luke 5 : 29,

29 left all, and have followed thee. And Jesus answered and said, Verily I say unto you, There is no man that hath left house, or brethren, or sisters, or father, or mother, or wife, or children, or lands, for
30 my sake, and the gospel's, ¹ but he shall receive an hundredfold now in this time, houses, and brethren, and sisters, and mothers, and children, and lands, with persecutions; and in the world to come eternal
31 life. ᵃ But many *that are* first shall be last; and the last first.

¹ 2 Chr. 25. 9 ; Lk. 18. 30.

ᵃ Mt. 19. 30 ; 20. 16 ; Lk. 13. 30 ; Ro. 9. 30.

But they had left their occupation and property, renounced the world and entered upon a life of self-denial, and had become disciples of Jesus and his constant attendants. Peter honestly and briefly states this, and wishes to know something of their future lot. Matthew (19 : 27) adds that Peter said further, "What shall we have therefore?" referring to the promise of Jesus, "Thou shalt have treasure in heaven." He wished to know what should befall to them, what should be their portion, and whether they could surely claim the promise to themselves. Peter indeed seems to be looking too much after reward ; and he has low views of Christ's kingdom; but he asks in so much faith, love and devotion, that Jesus graciously answers it without reproof.

29. The answer of Jesus. This answer consists of three parts: First, a special promise to the twelve. This is only given by Matthew (19 : 28); second, a general promise to all believers, vers. 29, 30 ; third, a proverbial fact in regard to the final distribution of rewards. Notice, as Mark omits the portion of the inquiry, "What shall we have therefore?" (Matt. 18 : 27), so does he also omit the first part of Christ's answer.

No man. No one, whether an apostle or not. **That hath left house,** etc. Rather, *That left house*, etc., referring specially to the past, yet by implication to all who should do so in the future. **Brethren or sisters,** etc. The family relations are in the order in which they would be forsaken. The best critical texts omit **or wife,** here and in Matt. 19 : 29, but find the words in Luke 18 : 29. **For my sake and the gospel's.** Not only for his sake while in this world, but also for the sake of *the glad tidings*, even though separated from him. Luke has (18 : 29) "for the kingdom of God's sake." Christ, his truth and his cause, are one. 30. **But he shall receive,** just as surely as that he forsook. **A hundredfold.** A popular expression of a vast proportion. Luke (19 : 30) expresses the same idea by "manifold more." **Now in this time,** in this world, including the time in which they were living, in contrast to **the world to come.** He shall receive many times more real good in this life on earth than all he renounced for Christ, Matt. 5 : 5 ; 1 Cor. 3 : 20–28 ; 1 Tim. 4 : 8. *Brethren,* **sisters, mothers,** etc., spiritual relatives, Rom. 16 : 13 ; 1 Cor. 4 : 14–17 ; 2 Cor. 6 : 13 ; Gal. 4 : 19. "**Wives** are not added, on the ground of propriety."—Bengel. **With persecutions;** with them and in the midst of them. And these were not their least treasure in this life, Matt. 5 : 12 ; Rom. 5 : 3 ; Heb. 12 : 6 ; 1 Pet. 1 : 6. This reference to persecutions, which is recorded only by Mark, shows that the blessings of which Jesus is speaking are chiefly spiritual. In addition to this he shall inherit **eternal life,** an everlasting state of holy and happy existence. Life here means not merely existence, but existence in its right relation to God and truth, hence holy and happy existence. As physical life consists in a certain connection of soul and body, so spiritual life in a certain connection of the soul with God. Thus the reward commences in this world, but has its great realization in the world to come.

31. Jesus now announces in proverbial language a fact in regard to these rewards, which would serve to arouse their zeal, faith and humility, and at the same time check any wrong and worldly spirit. **First.** First in time of their calling, in their own estima-

Jesus a third time foretells his sufferings, death, and resurrection.

32 ˣ AND they were in the way going up to Jerusalem; and Jesus went before them: and they were amazed; and as they followed, they were afraid. ʸ And he took again the twelve, and began to tell 33 them what things should happen unto him, *saying*, Behold, we go up to Jerusalem; and the Son of man

ˣ Mt. 20. 17; Lk. 18. 31.

ʸ ch. 8. 31; 9. 31; Lk. 9. 22; 18. 31; Ac. 13. 27; Ja?. 5. 6.

tion, and in the enjoyment of privileges and blessings. **Shall be last;** in receiving their rewards, in Christ's estimation, and in the scale of final joy and blessedness. Jesus would teach his disciples that God will exercise his sovereign pleasure, not, however, without good reasons, in the distribution of rewards. They must not suppose that because they and others are first in the time of their calling into the kingdom, and in their privileges, that therefore they will be necessarily first in honors and rewards. They are to be faithful and earnest, committing themselves and their own final disposal to him whose right it is to dispose heavenly honors, and who will do it righteously and graciously, ch. 20 : 23 ; Rev. 3 : 21. This truth Jesus illustrated by the parable of the Laborers in the Vineyard, which is recorded only in Matthew, 20 : 1–16.

32–34. JESUS FORETELLS, THE THIRD TIME AND MORE FULLY, HIS SUFFERINGS, DEATH AND RESURRECTION. Matt. 20 : 17–19; Luke 18 : 31-34. Mark is the most copious; Matthew the briefest. The section presents a good illustration of the way in which three independent narrators relate the same event.

32. **In the way.** Compare ver. 17. We have the indications of a continuous journey, though it might be interrupted by discourses and possibly miracles. Jesus seems not to have made his miraculous power prominent in this last journey. At its commencement he wrought cures (Matt. 19 : 2), and also near its close healed the blind men at Jericho, ver. 46. But of other miracles we have no account. **Going up to Jerusalem;** to attend the feast of the Passover. Jesus was probably in Perea near the ford of the Jordan ; possibly he had just passed over into Judea. To have predicted his approaching sufferings, just as he was nearing or entering Judea, would also be most timely. Jerusalem is about four thousand feet higher than the valley of the Jordan. It could well be said that he was *going up* to Jerusalem, 2 Sam. 19 : 34. **Jesus was going before them.** He was at their head, leading them forward and outstripping them. There appears to have been something in his gait, a deep solemnity, a determination and an eagerness which, under the circumstances, **amazed** his disciples. They were struck with awe, and probably filled with dark foreboding, at seeing him press so eagerly forward toward Jerusalem, the seat of his bitterest foes, where the Jews had sought to stone him (John 11 : 8), and the chief priests and Pharisees were counselling to put him to death, John 11 : 53–57. Though reluctant, they **followed** after, but were **afraid** both for him and themselves.

Took again the twelve, apart from the others, who were journeying with them, as on previous occasions, to converse with them confidentially. **Began to tell,** etc. He began again to relate what he had twice before told them (ch. 8 : 31 ; 9 : 31), besides other intimations, ch. 9 : 12; Matt. 10 : 38; 12 : 40; John 2 : 19 ; 3 : 14. But now he speaks more fully. 1. Before he had told them that he must suffer ; now he tells them that he is to suffer at the coming visit at Jerusalem. 2. Before he had foretold in general terms his betrayal ; now he foretells a double betrayal or delivering up : first, to the chief priests, and second, by them to the Gentiles. 3. Before he had foretold his death ; now he more particularly describes his death, especially by crucifixion, ver. 34 ; Matt. 20 : 19.

33. He commences this solemn communication with **Behold,** by which he would call the particular attention of his disciples to what he was about to foretell, to them still strange and surprising. **We go up to Jerusalem.**

shall be delivered unto the chief priests, and unto the scribes; and they shall condemn him to death, 34 and shall deliver him to the Gentiles: ᶻand they shall mock him, and shall scourge him, and shall spit upon him, and shall kill him: and the third day he shall rise again.

ᶻ Ps. 22. 6, 8, 13; Is. 53. 3.

Request of James and John; and our Lord's reply.

35 ᵃAND James and John, the sons of Zebedee, come unto him, saying, Master, we would that thou shouldest do for us whatsoever we shall desire.

ᵃ Mt. 20. 20; Jer. 45. 5; Jas. 4. 3.

More exactly, *We are going*, etc. See on preceding verse. Jerusalem was also morally elevated, John 2:13; Acts 15: 2; Gal. 2:1, 2. **Shall be delivered,** with evil intent. The Greek word is used by classic writers in cases of actual treachery, and is often translated in the Gospels, *betray*, ch. 14:42; Matt. 26:21; Luke 22:48; John 6:64. **Chief priests and scribes.** The Sanhedrim, the highest civil and ecclesiastical court of the Jews. See on ch. 1:22; 8:31. **They shall condemn him to death.** The Sanhedrim could pass sentence of death, but the Roman governor alone had the power of executing the sentence. **Shall deliver him.** The same word in the original as above. Thus Jesus predicts a twofold *delivering up*, or betrayal: first, by one of his own followers; second, by the highest court of his own nation. **To the Gentiles;** for the execution of the sentence. The Greek word for *Gentiles* literally means *nations*, that is, all nations besides the Jews, and is very nearly equivalent to our *heathen*. It is here referred particularly to the Romans, to Pilate and the Roman soldiers, ch. 15:1; Matt. 27:27; John 19:23.

34. This verse describes what the Gentiles would do after Jesus should be delivered to them. This does not exclude the idea of the Jews aiding them in casting contempt upon him and ill-treating him. **Mock him.** See the fulfillment recorded in ch. 15:16-21. **Scourge him.** See ch. 15:15. **Spit upon him.** See ch. 15:19. Crucifixion properly commenced with scourging, yet in the Savior's case, through the brutal cruelty of the soldiery, he was mocked and spit upon. **Shall kill him.** See ch. 15:25. Matthew (20:19) alone records that he definitely foretold at this time that he should be crucified. *The third day*, according to the best text, *after three days*. Compare ch. 8:31 and 9:31. **Shall rise again.** As on the two former announcements of his death, he foretells his resurrection. This was a gleam of light which shone up beyond the intervening darkness. Without his resurrection, his death would have been in vain. Rather, *Will rise again*, exhibiting his own divine power in coming to life, in contrast with the sufferings and death inflicted by men. Although this prediction is so plain to us, yet Luke informs us (18:34) that "they understood none of these things." They may have regarded his language as figurative of great obstacles and difficulties in setting up a temporal kingdom. Or, possibly, his words may have been to them dark and parabolic sayings, which they did not attempt to understand, much less did they desire to understand in their literal sense.

35-45. THE AMBITIOUS REQUEST OF JAMES AND JOHN; THE REPLY OF JESUS. The displeasure of the other ten apostles is excited, which leads Jesus to explain how distinction can only be attained in his kingdom, Matt. 20:20-28. The accounts of Matthew and Mark are about equally full.

35. **James and John.** See on ch. 3:17. According to Mark these two brethren make the request for themselves, which is in entire harmony with Matthew, who says that the mother of Zebedee's children came "with her sons." The mother probably made the request, but the sons doubtless instigated it. **Master, we would.** *Teacher, we wish,* or *desire.* Great importunity. Matthew relates that they "worship-

36 And he said unto them, What would ye that I
37 should do for you? They said unto him, Grant
unto us that we may sit, one on thy right hand, and
38 the other on thy left hand, in thy glory. But Jesus
said unto them, Ye know not what ye ask. Can ye
drink of the cup that I drink of; and be baptized

ped," or fell down with profound reverence before him.
Whatsoever we shall desire, or, rather, *shall ask*. They wish Jesus to pledge himself to grant their request before he heard it. They act as if they were ashamed or afraid to ask it at once. They doubtless remembered the rebuke that had followed the contention about precedence, ch. 9 : 33–37; and also the rebuke they had received when they proposed fire to come down from heaven and consume the Samaritans who would not receive Jesus, Luke 9 : 52–56. Compare Bathsheba's circuitous petition to Solomon for Adonijah, 1 Kings 2 : 20. Compare also Herod's promise and Herodias' request, ch. 6 : 23–25.
36. But Jesus would not promise beforehand, but makes them state their question frankly and plainly. This was not for his own information, for he knew what was in their hearts (John 2 : 25), but for their good. He therefore demands, **What would ye?** etc. *What do you desire me to do for you?*
37. **Grant.** They desire him, as the Messianic King, to give them the two highest places of honor in his kingdom. It was a very improper request made at a very inappropriate time. It showed that they did not understand what Jesus had just told them of his sufferings and death, vers. 33, 34. The promise in Matt. 19 : 28, that the twelve should sit on twelve thrones judging the twelve tribes of Israel, may have suggested the idea of making this request. They thought that he was about to set up his kingdom (Luke 19 : 11), and although they may have foreboded difficulties, yet they looked for a speedy triumph. They had been depressed (ver. 32), but the prediction of a resurrection (ver. 34), which they probably applied to great deliverances, and to the breaking forth of royal power, encouraged them now to seek for the chief positions in that visible kingdom which they thought was about to

be set up with a new and indestructible life.
Thy right hand . . . thy left hand. These were the highest, and next to the highest places of honor in Eastern royal courts. Josephus (vi. 11, 9) speaks of Jonathan sitting on the right hand of Saul, and Abner, the captain of the host, sitting on the left. So in the Sanhedrim, the vice-president sat on the right hand of the president, and the referee or third officer of rank on the left. James and John had, with Peter, been selected for witnessing the raising of Jairus' daughter and the Transfiguration (ch. 5 : 37 ; 9 : 2), and John may have generally occupied a place at table next to Jesus, John 13 : 23. They would occupy the nearest places to Jesus in his **glory**, or the royal splendor of his ambitious kingdom, which they expected would immediately appear, Luke 19 : 11. Matthew says (20 : 21) "in thy kingdom." Little did they think that Jesus would soon be crucified with robbers on his *right and left hand*. How keenly must John have been reminded of their ambitious request as they stood before the cross! John 19 : 26.
38. **Ye know not what ye ask.** You know not what these high positions of honor are, and you little think of the trials and sufferings necessarily connected with attaining them. They understood not the spiritual nature of his kingdom, and that its honors could be attained only through sufferings. **Can ye,** *Are ye able* **to drink of the cup,** rather *drink the cup*, the very cup, **that I drink?** The cup of suffering, especially of internal suffering, is intended, ch. 14 : 34–36 ; John 18 : 11. The *cup* is a common figure in the Bible, sometimes representing joy (Ps. 16 : 5 ; 23 : 5 ; 116 : 13); and sometimes sorrow, Ps. 11 : 6 ; 75 : 8 ; Isa. 51 : 17 ; Jer. 25 : 15 ; Rev. 16 : 19.
Baptized with the baptism that I am baptized with. The reference is not to the ordinance of baptism, but to the overwhelming sufferings which

39 with ᵇ the baptism that I am baptized with? And they say unto him, We can. And Jesus said unto them, ᶜ Ye shall indeed drink of the cup that I drink of; and with the baptism that I am baptized 40 withal shall ye be baptized: but to sit on my right hand and on my left hand is not mine to give; but *it shall be given to them* ᵈ for whom it is prepared.

ᵇ Ps. 42. 7; Lam. 3. 54; Eze. 26. 19.
ᶜ John 17. 14; Ac. 12. 2; Rev. 1. 9.
ᵈ John 17. 24.

Jesus was about to endure. The Greek word *baptizo* means *immerse, plunge, dip,* and figuratively, *whelm* or *overwhelm.* See on ch. 1 : 4. Dr. George Campbell, the distinguished Scotch Presbyterian scholar, translates the phrase, "Can ye undergo an immersion like that which I must undergo?" In the Greek, and, indeed, in all languages, may be found such expressions as these: Plunged in affliction, immersed in suffering, overwhelmed with sorrow. Compare such Scriptural expressions for calamities and sufferings as "All thy waves and billows have gone over me" (Ps. 42: 7); "I am come into deep waters where the floods overflow me" (Ps. 69 : 2); "We went through fire and through water," Ps. 66 : 12. The idea of our Savior's language is, Can ye endure the overwhelming sufferings that I shall endure? Thus, Dr. E. Robinson (*Lexicon of New Testament,* under *baptism*), referring to this passage, explains, "Can ye endure to be overwhelmed with sufferings like those which I must endure?" So also Olshausen on this passage : "The figurative expression, *baptism,* involves at once the idea of a painful submersion (a dying to that which is old) and also a joyful rising (a resurrection in that which is new), as Rom. 6 : 3 ff. shows. Such a path of suffering in order to his being made perfect (Heb. 5 : 8, 9) our Lord declared (Luke 12 : 50) stood yet before himself." Notice that he was even then drinking that cup and undergoing that baptism. As the *cup* which is drunk refers more especially to internal sorrow, so the *baptism* which completely surrounds and covers over, refers more especially to the external sufferings of persecution and crucifixion, or martyrdom, though not excluding, but rather embodying, the mental anguish connected with them.

39. **We can,** or, *We are able.* An expression of mingled sincerity, earnestness and self-confidence; showing, on the one hand, a willingness and a courage to encounter difficulties and endure sufferings, and on the other, a small conception of what those sufferings were. Doubtless they thought of those which would neccesarily arise in assuming kingly power. They were truly Sons of Thunder (ch. 3 : 17), and doubtless felt ready for war and fighting under Jesus against his enemies. Had the position of the two robbers crucified on either side of Jesus arisen to their view, and been offered them, how would they have shrunk from it! **Ye shall indeed drink of the cup;** *drink the cup,* as in ver. 38. You shall indeed be called to pass through such sufferings as I shall endure, and be partakers with me. And so they were in the garden, ch. 14 : 33; Luke 22 : 45; and through the terrible scenes of the crucifixion, ch. 14 : 27, 50; John 19 : 26. They endured not the same but similar sufferings; and the special fulfillment of this prediction may be found in their later history. James was the first martyr among the apostles, and slain with the sword by Herod, A.D. 44, Acts 12: 2. John was the last survivor of the twelve, and by his long life of trials and persecutions for Christ's sake more than equaled the suffering of actual martyrdom. His being scourged by the Jews (Acts 5 : 40), and his banishment by the Romans to Patmos, give us a glimpse of the hatred and persecution which he must have endured. The *cup* and the *baptism* find their fulfillment in these, without having recourse to the tradition that at one time he was plunged into a cask of boiling oil, by which he was refreshed instead of destroyed, and at another, that he drank a cup of poison without injury.

40. **And on my left.** According to the highest critical authorities, *or on the left.* **Is not mine to give,** etc. Rather, *Is not mine to give, but is for those for whom it has been prepared.* It has already been decided, even from the foundation of the world (Matt. 25 : 34;

41 *And when the ten heard *it*, they began to be much displeased with James and John. But Jesus called them *to him*, and saith unto them, ᶠYe know that they which are accounted to rule over the Gentiles exercise lordship over them; and their great ones exercise authority upon them. ᵍBut so shall

* Mt. 20. 24.

ᶠ Lk. 22. 25.

ᵍ ch. 9. 35; Mt. 20. 26, 28; Lk. 9. 48; Ro. 12. 2.

Eph. 1 : 4), who shall enjoy these honors. It was not for Jesus to bestow them then, nor to change the arrangement already made. Neither did it become him to inform them whether it was assigned to them or to others; for it had been prepared according to the principles of the divine government, in which God's sovereignty and man's free agency harmonize. According to those principles, they who enjoy these honors, should also partake of his sufferings (vers. 26–28; 2 Tim. 2 : 12); and, according to them, Jesus, who was one with the Father, should also dispose of the honors of his kingdom, John 5 : 19–23; Luke 22 : 29; Rev. 3 : 21. A very ancient and common interpretation is to take *but* in the sense of *except*, "It is not mine to give *except* to those for whom it is prepared." But this cannot be philologically sustained. Matthew adds "of my Father," pointing to God, the Father, as the Great Author of the arrangements and gifts of redemption, John 3 : 16.

41. **When the ten heard it,** or rather, *hearing it*, what the two brethren had desired and the answer of Jesus. It seems from the language that the ten other apostles not merely heard of it afterward, but were actually present and witnessed the transaction. Very probably they came up while the interview was going on. They may have heard the answer of Jesus, and, by inquiry at once, the request that had just been made. **Much displeased.** They had feelings of mingled grief and indignation. Compare ver. 14. The same emulation which prompted the request of the two now arouses the displeasure of the ten, and needed correcting. Hence the ten only *began* to exercise great displeasure, when Jesus arrested it, by teaching them all a better way.

42. **But.** *And.* **Jesus called them to him;** very probably all the apostles, but especially the ten, who were at least a little apart from Jesus while indulging in their jealous and angry feelings. **They who are ac-** **counted to rule over the Gentiles.** They do not rule, for God only rules; but they *seem* to themselves to rule, and they are *recognized* or *acknowledged* as rulers by others. Compare the similar phrase in Gal. 2 : 9. "Who seemed (were recognized or reputed) to be pillars." **Gentiles.** Heathen nations. See on ver. 33. **Exercise lordship over them.** Lord it over them; ruling in an imperious and oppressive manner, 1 Pet. 5 : 3. **Their great ones.** Their great men, their nobles, chief in rank and power. **Exercise authority;** arbitrarily. The verb in the original is somewhat stronger than the one in the preceding clause. Both verbs, however, represent the power which rulers were accustomed to exercise in coercing or restraining their subjects. But kings were often outstripped in their oppression by the nobles and governors under them. **Them.** The Gentiles.

43. **But so it shall not be,** etc. According to the oldest and best manuscripts, *But not so is it among you;* not so is it in my kingdom which already exists in and among you, Luke 17 : 20, 21. My ministers and great ones are not to exercise civil power or authority over their brethren; neither are they to lord it over God's heritage, 1 Pet. 5 : 3. They are not to seek after greatness by exercising power and authority, but through eminent services and self-denials. **But whosoever will be great.** *But whosoever would become* pre-eminent among you. **Shall be your minister.** Your waiter, attendant, one who ministers to you. The word in the original was applied to one who served or waited on another, principally at table, and who was not a slave. It was afterward applied, among Christians, officially to *deacons*, 1 Tim. 3 : 8. Of its use in the New Testament, Dr. Conant, on Matt. 20 : 26, says: "One who *ministers* to another or others; either in waiting on guests at table (John 2 : 5, 9; compare the verb in Luke 22 : 27); or as a distributor of alms (compare the use

it not be among you: but whosoever will be great among you, shall be your minister: and whosoever of you will be the chiefest, shall be servant of all. 45 For even ᵇ the Son of man came not to be ministered unto, but to minister, and ⁱ to give his life a ransom for many.

ᵇ John 13. 14; Phil. 2. 7.
ⁱ Mt. 20. 28; 1 Tim. 2. 6; Tit. 2. 14.

Healing of blind Bartimæus near Jericho.

46 ᵏ AND they came to Jericho. And as he went out of Jericho with his disciples and a great number of people, blind Bartimæus, the son of Timæus,

ᵏ Mt. 20. 29; Lk. 18. 35.

of the noun and verb in Acts 6:1, 2); or as a magistrate in administering justice (Rom. 13:4); or as an attendant on the person of a sovereign, to execute his commands (Matt. 22:13); or as one who furthers or promotes a thing (*minister of sin*, Gal. 2:17); or as a religious teacher, dispensing knowledge of saving truth (1 Cor. 3:5)." Jesus teaches that they who would become great must in humility engage in a service of love and in doing good.
44. Whosoever will be the chiefest; *would become first* among you. James and John had sought the first and second honors of his kingdom; he now points out the way to become *great* and *first* among his followers. **Servant of all.** The word here translated **servant** was the usual name of a *bondman* or *slave*, and was thus a stronger word than that translated *minister* in the preceding verse, denoting a humbler service. Though it was generally applied to involuntary service, it is often applied, as here, to that which is voluntary, Rom. 6:16; Eph. 6:6; 2 Pet. 1:1. He who would be first, let him engage in the humblest service, and in the most self-denying labors. Compare on ch. 9:35.
45. For even. Jesus illustrates and enforces this precept and principle by his own example. He, the King of his kingdom, the Head of the church, the elder brother, voluntarily entered upon the greatest humiliation and the most humble and self-denying service, Phil. 2:7-11. **Son of man.** The Messiah. See on ch. 2:10. **Came not to be ministered unto.** He took the *form of a servant* when he came into the world to save men (Phil. 2:7). He came not to be waited upon and served by others, but to serve and wait upon others. Compare John 13:4, 5.

This was true of his whole life. But, in addition, at its close he **gave his life a ransom;** his ministration to and for others extended even to the giving up of life; it culminated in becoming obedient unto death, Phil. 2:8. A *ransom* was the price paid to redeem one from death (Exod. 21:30) or from slavery, Lev. 25:51. Men are slaves to sin, dead in trespasses and sin, and condemned to eternal death. Christ came to *give* his life (John 10:18), which was not forfeited by sin, a ransom **for,** *in the stead*, of many. He gave his life in their place as a substitute. His death was a substitution for their death. **Many.** The multitude of the redeemed, Rev. 5:9; 7:4, 9. Many is in contrast to the one life which he gave, Rom. 5:15, 17, 19. Here those are referred to who shall enjoy the efficacy of the ransom, who shall be actually redeemed, ch. 14:24. In 1 Tim. 2:6, *ransom for all* (in behalf of all), the relation of Christ's atonement and death to all men, its sufficiency and its free offer to all, is presented, Rom. 5:18.
46-52. BLIND BARTIMÆUS HEALED NEAR JERICHO. Matt. 20:29-34; Luke 18:35-43. Mark again is the fullest, most vivid, and enters most into details. Matthew is the briefest, yet alone notices that there were two blind men. Luke (18:43) alone records the effect of the miracle on the people.
46. They came to Jericho. As they were pursuing the journey which is related in this chapter. Having crossed the Jordan from Perea, Mark gives vividness to his narrative by saying, "They *come* to," or " into Jericho." *Jericho* signifies the *fragrant place*, and was a city of Benjamin (Josh. 18:21), situate about eighteen miles northeast of Jerusalem, and seven miles west of

the Jordan. It was founded probably after the destruction of Sodom, called "the city of palm-trees" (Deut. 34 : 3), and famous for its roses and balsam. It was the first city in Canaan taken and destroyed by Joshua (Josh. 6 : 24–26), rebuilt five hundred years afterward by Hiel (1 Kings 16 : 24), and became distinguished for its school of the prophets, and as the residence of Elisha, 2 Kings 2 : 18. Meanwhile a new Jericho appears to have been built on a neighboring site, Judg. 3 : 13 ; 2 Sam. 10 : 5; Josephus, Bell. Jud. iv. 8, 2, 3. This seems to have been the city here spoken of. From Josephus and 2 Kings 2: 19-22 we infer that the ancient city stood near Elisha's fountain, supposed to be the one now named Ain-es-Sultan, the plain around which is now strewn with ancient ruins and rubbish. Nearly two miles south of this fountain, and near the place where the road from Jerusalem enters the plain, and on the banks of Wady Kelt, stood the modern city, which Herod the Great adorned with splendid palaces and buildings. It lay in the direct route from Perea to Jerusalem, and was second in importance only to Jerusalem of the cities of Israel ; and was the residence of a chief publican, Zaccheus (Luke 19 : 1), on account of the balsam trade. Ancient ruins now mark its site. Nearly the whole plain is waste and desolate, though the soil is good. Not a single palm-tree is now said to remain of the city of palms. Rihah, a poor, miserable Arab village of two hundred inhabitants, stands on the plain, and is about a mile and a half nearer the Jordan than either the ancient or later Jericho.

As he went out of Jericho. *As he was going out of Jericho*, possibly on some excursion to the immediate vicinity, but probably on his journey toward Jerusalem, ver. 52; 11 : 1. With this Matthew agrees; but Luke says (18 : 35), "As he was come nigh unto Jericho." This is regarded as one of the most difficult points in harmonizing the evangelists. Did we know the full particulars, all would be plain. Some little circumstances not related might remove all apparent discrepancies. In our ignorance of the details of our Savior's visit at Jericho, we may present several ways which have been proposed for harmonizing Luke with Matthew and Mark. See Clark's Harmony, ? 129.

1. There was an *old* and a *new* Jericho.

Jesus may have been leaving the one and approaching the other. The first two evangelists may describe the former act, while Luke describes the latter. 2. There may have been two miracles, one just before entering the city, and one as he was leaving it. Luke mentions the former, and Mark the latter; but Matthew describes both under one account. 3. Some maintain that the Greek verb in Luke, rendered *to come nigh*, may signify *to be near*. See Septuagint, 1 Kings 21 : 2; Deut. 21 : 3; Ruth 2 : 20; 2 Sam. 19 : 42; Jer. 23 : 23. Thus, the language of Luke may mean, while he was yet near the city, including the idea expressed by Matthew and Mark. 4. The language of Mark, "They come to Jericho," may imply that Jesus remained a few days there. Jesus would naturally visit points of interest in the vicinity, for example, the fountain of Elisha, and possibly spend his nights in the country, as he did at Jerusalem. The miracle might have been performed when he was thus going *out of* and returning *to* the city. 5. Bartimæus may have besought Jesus on his entering the city, but for some reason, possibly to test his faith, he was not answered; but at the departure of Jesus on the following morning, with a companion he may have renewed his request and besought Jesus more earnestly, when both obtained a cure. Luke, taking note of the first appeal, may relate the miracle by anticipation. This explanation is as good as any. The second and third are the least satisfactory. No one however need stumble on an apparent discrepancy like this, when we can conceive of so many ways of explaining it.

A great number of people. *A great crowd*, or *multitude*. Jericho would be full of people who were going up to Jerusalem to attend the Passover. The number would be greatly increased by those coming from Galilee by the way of Perea, to avoid passing through Samaria.

Bartimæus. *Bar* is the Aramaic word for *son*. Compare Bartholomew, ch. 3 : 18 ; Barnabas, Acts 4 : 36; Bar-jesus, Acts 13 : 6. The blind man appears to have borne the name of *Son of Timæus*, not so much from any peculiar meaning of the word Timæus, as from his father who bore that name. According to the order of the words in the original, and the highest critical author-

47 sat by the highway side begging. And when he heard that it was Jesus of Nazareth, he began to cry out, and say, Jesus, *thou* son of David, have
48 mercy on me. And many charged him that he should hold his peace: but he cried ¹the more a great deal, *Thou* son of David, have mercy on me.
49 And Jesus stood still, and commanded him to be

¹ Ps. 119. 10; Jer. 29. 13.

---

ities, the passage should read, *The Son of Timæus, Bartimæus, a blind beggar, sat by the way.* It would seem that Bartimæus was well known at Jericho and afterward among Christians. This may explain why Mark and Luke speak of only one blind man, while Matthew speaks of two. The former narrate the miracle performed on the more prominent individual and the one generally known, while they pass unnoticed that performed on the other, who may have been a person of no prominence, and scarcely known, or perhaps an entire stranger in that vicinity. There is no contradiction; for the one does not exclude the two, and the two includes the one. **By the highway side.** By the wayside, probably the road leading to Jerusalem. **Begging.** This should be omitted according to the best authorities.

47. And when he heard that it was, etc. Rather, in the life-like narrative of Mark, *And hearing that it is Jesus the Nazarene.* The great prophet of Nazareth, the miracle-worker, whose name had become familiar to the sick and afflicted of Palestine. He was familiarly, and also contemptuously known as the *Nazarene;* inhabitant of Nazareth, ch. 1 : 24 ; 14 : 67. As soon as he heard who it was, he **began to cry out,** with a loud voice. He addresses him not as Jesus the Nazarene; his faith takes hold of something higher and deeper. In striking contrast he says, **Jesus, thou son of David;** royal descendant of David and successor to his throne, the Messiah, ch. 12 : 35. The angel of the Lord had once applied this title to Joseph, Matt. 1 : 20. It was a popular designation of the Messiah, and by the use of it Bartimæus acknowledged the Messiahship of Jesus. The whole account "affords a striking illustration of the earnest and persevering manner in which spiritual healing is to be sought of the Great Physician, of the certain success of believing application to him, and of the effect that saving mercy has upon its recipient." **Have mercy on me.** Both a confession of misery, unworthiness and helplessness, and an expression of confidence in the ability and willingness of Jesus to help him. This is the essence of prayer.

48. Charged him. *Many rebuked him,* admonished him sternly that he should be silent. They would not have Jesus annoyed or interrupted in his journey; nor did they care to be disturbed with the cries of Bartimæus. They did not probably object to the title *Son of David,* for they were doubtless a part of those who were expecting that the kingdom of God would soon appear (Luke 19: 11), and soon after applied the same title to him, ch. 11 : 10; Matt. 21 : 9. Such cries may have seemed to them ill-timed and discourteous. "Here, it has been often said, is the history of many a soul. When a man is in earnest about his salvation, and begins to cry that his eyes may be opened, that he may walk in his light who is the light of men, when he begins to despise the world and to be careless about riches, he will find infinite hindrances, and these not from professed enemies of the gospel of Christ, but from such as seem, like this multitude, to be with Jesus and on his side. Even they will try to stop his mouth, and to hinder an earnest crying to him."— TRENCH, *Miracles,* pp. 343, 344. But the rebuke of the multitude only aroused his earnestness, for he believed in the ability and willingness of Jesus to heal him. It was a trial of faith, but his faith was not thus to be overcome ; opposition only developed it still more. **He cried the more a great deal;** or rather, *he cried much the more,* or *all the more,* than he did at the first, and on account of opposing obstacles. He repeated again and again his plea for mercy.

49. And Jesus stood still, in his

called. And they call the blind man, saying unto him, Be of good comfort, rise; he calleth thee.
50 And he, casting away his garment, rose, and came
51 to Jesus. And Jesus answered and said unto him, What wilt thou that I should do unto thee? The blind man said unto him, Lord, that I might re-
52 ceive my sight. And Jesus said unto him, Go thy way; ᵐthy faith hath made thee whole. And immediately he received his sight, and followed Jesus in the way.

ᵐ ch. 5. 34; Mt. 9. 22.

journey, at these believing and importunate cries; publicly recognizing the title, Son of David, as applied to himself. **Commanded him to be called.** According to the oldest and best manuscripts, *Jesus stood still and said, Call him.* A graphic description of a wonderful scene. Divine condescension and simplicity mingle in the sublime posture and authoritative command of Jesus. It was not only an honoring of the poor beggar's petition, but also a rebuke to the multitude who would silence his cries.

At once **they call the blind man,** the same ones, no doubt, who had just rebuked him. Now they expect to see a miracle. This was perfectly natural with such a crowd. Popular feelings often swing from one side to the other. The language of the people to Bartimæus is true to life, the more eloquent and affecting from the omission of all conjectures. **Be of good comfort, rise, he calleth thee.** Cheer up, take courage in thy heart, rise from the place where thou art sitting, for, strange and wonderful to say, he calls thee to approach him. These words of the people as well as the next verse are found only in Mark.

50. **Casting away his garment,** throwing aside his upper garment, through eagerness and joy, that it might not hinder him a moment in his movements. This has often been used as an illustration of the way in which the sinner should cast aside whatever would hinder his speedy coming to Jesus, Phil. 3: 7-11. **Rose.** According to the highest critical authorities, *leaped up* in haste and expectation, **and came to Jesus** with the least possible delay.

51. Jesus answered his importunate request by asking him a question. Bartimæus had made a general petition; Jesus would now call forth his particular and special request. **What wilt thou?** etc. Faith seizes hold of particular objects of desire; and the blind man says, **Lord, that I might receive my sight.** *Rabboni, that I may look up,* or *receive sight.* Mark in the original gives the very word which Bartimæus uttered, the Aramaic word, Rabboni, which means *my Master,* or *Lord,* being more reverential than the usual Rabbi, John 20: 16.

52. Jesus now says, **Go thy way,** implying that his request was granted. Matthew alone records (20: 34) that "Jesus moved with compassion touched his eyes," and Luke (18: 42) that he said, "Receive thy sight." His faith was sufficient, for Jesus declares, **Thy faith hath made thee whole,** or *hath saved thee* in respect to bodily blindness, and, as it appears, from spiritual blindness also. Immediately receiving sight, he made a good use of it and **followed Jesus in the way.** Heretofore his blindness had confined him to one place; now, with the freedom of sight, he follows Jesus on his journey with the multitude to Jerusalem. Luke tells us (18: 43), that he followed, "glorifying God," and all the people seeing it, "gave praise to God."

REMARKS.

1. Like Jesus, we should be patient and persevering in doing good, ver. 1; Acts 10: 38; Eccle. 11: 6; Isa. 32: 20.

2. "Every age has its Pharisees whom the devil often uses for the temptation of pastors, and whom God permits to test his people."—OSIANDER. Ver. 2; 2 Pet. 3: 16 Rev. 2: 9.

3. The Bible is our standard of appeal in matters of religion. Jesus appealed to the Old Testament as of divine authority, ver 3; John 5: 39; 2.

Tim. 3 : 16; 1 Cor. 2 : 13; 1 Thess. 2 : 13; 2 Pet. 3 : 2.

4. The spirit as well as the letter of Scripture must be studied and understood. Many misapply or pervert Scripture, or, breaking its spirit, take advantage of the letter in order to ease their own consciences and defend themselves in a course of sin, ver. 4 ; ch. 3 : 2–5 ; 7 : 6–12; Acts 15 : 1, 24; 2 Pet. 3 : 16.

5. On account of the hardness and depravity of the heart, God has given laws which would gradually do away with great moral social evils. Thus, with divorces, polygamy and slavery, ver. 5 ; Matt. 7 : 12 ; Mal. 2 : 15, 16.

6. Frequency of divorce in any country is an evidence of the hardness of heart and wickedness of the people, vers. 5, 11, 12.

7. Because God permits certain practices among many of his true people, we must not, therefore, conclude that they are right, ver. 5 ; Acts 17 : 30.

8. Marriage was instituted by God himself, is most sacred and honorable in all, ministers as well as others, ver. 6 ; Matt. 8 : 14 ; 1 Cor. 9 : 5 ; Heb. 13 : 4.

9. There is no relationship so close and intimate as that of husband and wife, vers. 7, 8 ; 1 Cor. 7 : 10, 11 ; Eph. 5 : 28–31.

10. Since the marriage relation is the closest of all earthly relationships, it should be entered in the fear of the Lord, and the parties entering it should be one in spirit. The Christian should, therefore, seek his companion for life from those who love Jesus, vers. 7, 8 ; 2 Cor. 6 : 14 ; 1 Cor. 7 : 39 ; 1 Pet. 3 : 7.

11. Human governments transgress the law of Christ if they grant divorces, except for one cause, ver. 9.

12. Christ's exposition of the law of marriage reinstates woman in her original rights. In heathen countries she has always been degraded, and generally treated as a slave. Among the Jews she was denied the right of divorcement, while she could be divorced for the most frivolous cause, vers. 11, 12.

13. To love little children and to feel an interest in their spiritual interests is Christ-like. We should bring them to him by prayer and instruction, vers. 13–16 ; Eph. 6 : 4.

14. Children should be encouraged to come to Jesus, who is displeased with any hindrances put in their way,
ver. 14; Deut. 11 : 19; 1 Sam. 2 : 18; 3 : 10; Ps. 8 : 2; Prov. 8 : 17; Matt. 21 : 16.

15. Children who die in infancy are saved by virtue of Christ's sufferings and death, ver. 14 ; Rom. 5 : 12–19 ; 2 Sam. 12 : 23 ; 2 Kings 4 : 26.

16. Infant baptism is of human origin. The testimony of the following eminent Pedobaptist scholars is in point :

"The baptism of the children of Christians, of which no trace is to be found in the New Testament, is not to be regarded as an apostolic institution, . . . but it is an institution of the church, which grew up gradually in the post-apostolic age in connection with the development of church life and the growth of theological doctrine. Concerning infant baptism there is no witness before Tertullian, and it did not become general until after the time of Augustine."—DR. MEYER, *Com. on the Acts*, third edition, p. 329 ff.

"The Scriptural proof for the necessity of infant baptism is untenable. . . . Nor can it in any way be proved that the apostles baptized infants. . . . The testimony of the earliest church history puts it as good as beyond doubt that in the apostolic church infant baptism had no place." —DR. JULIUS MÜLLER, *Dogmatik*, p. 171 ff.

"We have all reason for not deriving infant baptism from apostolic institution."—DR. NEANDER, *Church History* (Torrey's translation), vol. i., p. 310.

"Christian baptism is not to be received, any more than faith, by right of inheritance. This is the great reason why we cannot believe that it was administered in the apostolic age to little children. No positive fact sanctioning the practice can be adduced from the New Testament ; the historical proofs alleged are in no way conclusive."—DE PRESSENSE, *Apostolic Era*, p. 376.

"The passages from Scripture cited in favor of infant baptism, as a usage of the primitive church, are doubtful and prove nothing. Nor do the earliest definite passages in the writings of the fathers afford any absolute proof." —HAGENBACH, *History of Doctrines*, vol. i., p. 200.

It is also a striking fact that all the distinguished fathers of the first five centuries, such as Jerome, Basil the Great, Gregory, Ambrose, Augustine,

Chrysostom, Ephrem Syrus, remained unbaptized till after their conversion, although several of them were dedicated to God from their birth by their pious parents. Origen has been claimed as an exception without proof. He was baptized at an early age, but that it was in infancy does not appear. See *Bibliotheca Sacra*, Jan., 1869, p. 73; *Baptist Quarterly*, Jan., 1869, pp. 32, 33; *Colman's Christian Antiquities*, ch. xiv., § 3, p. 262.

17. It is common for sinners to desire to do some good things to secure their salvation, ver. 17; John 6 : 28 ; Acts 2 : 37; Rom. 9 : 31, 32.

18. God is goodness in himself, and the author of all good. Christ being one with the Father, is also one with him in goodness, ver. 18; 1 Sam. 2 : 2; Ps. 36 : 9; 34 : 8; James 1 : 17; John 1 : 16-18.

19. The law of God is binding on us, and must either be satisfied in us or in Christ. We are condemned by the law, unless justified through faith in Christ, ver. 19; Rom. 3 : 31; 5 : 1; 11 : 6; Gal. 2 : 16; Eph. 2 : 8, 9.

20. We are by nature ignorant of our own hearts, vers. 17-20; Rom. 7 : 7, 8; Rev. 3 : 17.

21. He who thinks he has kept the commands of God, is alike ignorant of himself, of God and his holy law, ver. 20 ; Luke 18 : 11, 12; Rom. 10 : 3; 7 : 9-11; Phil. 3 : 6. Compare 1 Cor. 8 : 2.

22. Jesus exercises a compassionate love toward sinners, especially those that are young and feel an inward need of eternal life, ver. 21; ch. 12 : 34.

23. Christ demands a full surrender of all to him, a complete acquiescence of the human will in the divine, and an entire conformity of human acts to the divine requirement, ver. 21 ; Matt. 5 : 48 ; Prov. 23 : 26; James 2 : 10; Phil. 3 : 7-10.

24. Many think they are willing to do anything that God requires in order to be saved, yet, when told to forsake all, they are unwilling to do it, ver. 22 ; 2 Tim. 4 : 10.

25. The great danger of riches is the love and confidence which men place upon them, ver. 23; 1 Tim. 6 : 10.

26. The rich should feel that they are intrusted with the Lord's money, and should exercise great liberality toward the poor and in support of the gospel. By thus doing, their wealth will be a blessing indeed, vers. 21-25; Matt. 6 : 19, 20; Luke 12 : 33.

27. The poor have reason to be contented and not envy the rich ; nay, to rejoice that they are not exposed to the dangers and temptations of wealth, vers. 23-25; Deut. 31 : 20; 32 : 15; Matt. 13 : 22; Phil. 4 :11 ; 1 Tim. 6 : 8, 9; James 5 : 1-3.

28. The salvation of all, whether rich or poor, which was impossible with men, is rendered possible through Jesus Christ, vers. 26, 27; Rom. 8 : 3, 4 ; Tit. 2 : 11, 12.

29. If we give up all to Christ, we shall receive Christ and all things in return, vers. 28-30; Rom. 8 : 32; 1 Cor. 3 : 21-23.

30. Many, who are first in advantages, are the last to be converted. And many Christians who are first in privileges in this world will, in the world to come, fall far below their less privileged brethren, ver. 31 ; Matt. 8 : 11, 12; Rom. 11 : 11.

31. Jesus goes before us as the Captain of our salvation. Let us fearlessly follow where he leads, ver. 32 ; Heb. 2 : 10; 1 Pet. 2 : 21.

32. How wonderful the grace and compassion of Jesus, as exhibited in his going up to Jerusalem, when he knew what was to befall him there ! How willing was he to suffer! vers. 33, 34; Luke 12 : 50; John 12 : 27, 28; Rom. 5 : 6.

33. "If Jesus cheerfully died for us, it is a small thing to require Christians to live for him."—RYLE. Vers. 33, 34; 1 Cor. 6 : 20 ; 2 Cor. 5 : 14-16.

34. The ignorance of even Christians is often seen in their prayers and desires. If granted, they would prove damaging to their spiritual interests vers. 35, 37; Ps. 72 : 12-20; 2 Cor. 12 : 7-9.

35. We should specially guard against a spirit of worldly ambition. This spirit was thrice strikingly exhibited in the apostles, ver. 35-37; ch. 9 : 34 ; Luke 22 : 24.

36. We must count the cost, if we would seek the highest places in Christ's kingdom, knowing that they are attained only through the deepest humility and suffering, ver. 38 ; Acts 14 : 22; Rom. 8 : 17; 2 Tim. 2 : 11, 12; 2 Cor. 1 : 5-7 ; Col. 1 : 24.

37. We must either be like James, a martyr in act, or like John, a martyr in spirit, ver. 39; ch. 8 : 35.

Our Lord's public entry into Jerusalem.

XI. AND ^a when they came nigh to Jerusalem, unto Bethphage and Bethany, at the mount of Olives, he

^a Mt. 21. 1; Lk. 19. 29; John 12. 12; Ps. 24. 1; Ac. 10. 36.

38. God is a sovereign in his calling and his gifts; yet both are in accordance with infinite wisdom and goodness, ver. 40; Matt. 25 : 34; Heb. 11 : 16.
39. Only a godly jealousy is becoming Christian brethren, ver. 41; 2 Cor. 11 : 2; Rom. 11 : 11.
40. An ambitious and domineering spirit is unbecoming the church of Christ, and should not be exercised among its membership, ver. 42; John 13 : 13–17; Rom. 12 : 10; 2 Cor. 1 : 24; James 3 : 1; 1 Pet. 5 : 3–5; 3 John 9.
41. Humility is a foundation grace, and is necessary to true usefulness, vers. 43, 44; Luke 18 : 14; 1 Pet. 5 : 5.
42. Christ's sufferings and death were vicarious or substitutional, ver. 45; Isa. 53 : 10, 11; Dan. 9 : 24–26; John 10 : 11; 2 Cor. 5 : 21; Gal. 3 : 13, 14; Tit. 2 : 14; Heb. 9 : 28; Rev. 5 : 9.
43. Sinners are blinded by sin. They do not spiritually discern Jesus or his truth, ver. 46; Jer. 5 : 21; John 1 : 5; 1 Cor. 2 : 14; 2 Cor. 3 : 15; 4 : 6.
44. Sinners should call on Jesus to open their blind eyes, ver. 47; Ps. 119: 18; Isa. 42 : 7; Luke 4 : 18; John 8 : 12; 9 : 39; 2 Cor. 3 : 14; Rev. 3 : 18.
45. Sinners should improve present opportunities while Jesus is yet graciously near, and before their blindness becomes forever fixed, ver. 47; Isa. 55 : 6; Ps. 69 : 3; Isa. 44 : 18; Acts 28 : 25–27.
46. They who are seeking spiritual sight will meet with obstacles and opposition from the world; but this should only excite them to greater importunity, lest they fail of a cure, ver. 48; Luke 11 : 5–10; Acts 2 : 40.
47. The sinner has no plea but mercy for the sake of Jesus, ver. 48; Luke 18 : 13.
48. The compassion of Jesus is infinite. He pauses, as it were, to attend to the importunate cry of the sinner, ver. 49; Luke 19 : 5.
49. The seeker after Jesus, as well as the Christian, should come to him with definite requests, ver. 49–51; Acts 8 : 22; Phil. 4 : 6.
50. Jesus will open the eyes of the blind as they send up the prayer of faith, ver. 52; Matt. 21 : 22; Isa. 29 : 18, 19; Acts 9 : 11, 18.
51. They who are made to spiritually see will follow Jesus, ver. 52; Luke 14 : 27; John 15 : 14.
52. The Christian, like blind Bartimæus, does not see Jesus with his bodily eyes, but by faith, vers. 46–52; 1 Pet. 1 : 8.

CHAPTER XI.

Passing over our Savior's visit to the house of Zaccheus, and the parable of the Ten Pounds (Luke 19 : 1–27), the seeking Jesus at Jerusalem and his arrival at Bethany (John 11 : 55–57; 12 : 1, 9–11), Mark begins at once, with this chapter, his account of the last public ministry of Jesus at Jerusalem, and the winding up of his prophetic ministry on earth. The six days whose history is about to be narrated, corresponding with the six days of creation, form an era in all time and eternity; "a world was re-created, and the last fearful efforts of the rulers of its darkness met, quelled and triumphed over for evermore." The public entrance into Jerusalem and the return of Jesus to Bethany to pass the night; the cursing the fig-tree the next morning on his way to Jerusalem, the expelling the traders from the temple, and his departure from the city for the night; the passing the withered fig-tree on the following morning, the discourse occasioned thereby, Christ's authority questioned, and his question regarding the baptism of John, form the incidents of this chapter.

1–11. THE TRIUMPHAL ENTRY OF JESUS INTO JERUSALEM. Matt. 21 : 1–11; Luke 19 : 29–44; John 12 : 12–19. Luke is the fullest, John the briefest. While Mark occupies about the same space as Matthew, he is specially minute and vivid by the use of the present tense, and surpasses the others, throughout the chapter, in his careful specifications of time, ver. 11; compare vers. 12, 19, 20.

1. And when they came nigh. The present tense in the original, *And when they approach*, or *come near to Jeru-*

salem. John says (John 12 : 1), "Jesus, six days before the Passover, came to Bethany." The *six days* may include, or exclude, both the day of his arrival at Bethany and the day of the paschal supper; or it may include one and exclude the other. The expression "*before* the Passover" seems rather to exclude the first day of the festival. If, then, after the Jewish manner, we include the day of arrival, we have: The first day of the Passover was Friday, (commencing Thursday evening), the 15th of Nisan, April 7th, A. D. 30, on which Jesus suffered; six days before was the 9th of Nisan, or Saturday, April 1st. But, since Saturday was the Jewish Sabbath, and Jesus and his company would not have traveled from Jericho on that day, we may suppose that he and his company arrived in the vicinity of Bethany too late to enter Jerusalem before sundown on Friday, the beginning of the Sabbath; and hence they remained near the Mount of Olives, and observed the day quietly in their tents. At the same time Jesus could have gone to Bethany, arriving there at sunset, or a little after, on Friday evening; and after spending the Sabbath with Mary, Martha and Lazarus, he could have rejoined the company on Sunday, and with them entered Jerusalem. It is not necessary to suppose that this procession took place early in the day, ver. 11. **To Jerusalem.** The goal of their journey on their route from Jericho. *Jerusalem*, signifying dwelling or foundation of peace, also known as Jebus (Judg. 19 : 10), and Salem (Ps. 76 : 2 ; Gen. 14 : 18); also as the city of David (2 Sam. 5 : 9), and the holy city (Matt. 4 : 5; 27 : 53), was the capital and most noted city of Palestine. It was built on four hills: Zion on the south, which was the highest, and contained the citadel and palace; Moriah on the east, on which stood the temple; and Acra and Bezetha, north of Zion, and covered with the largest portion of the city. Jerusalem is near the middle of Palestine, about thirty-five miles from the Mediterranean, and about twenty-five from the Jordan and the Dead Sea. Its highest elevation is about 2,600 feet above the former sea, and 3,927 feet above the latter. Seventeen times, is it said, that this city has been taken and pillaged. The modern city is called by the Arabs *El Khuds*, "the holy," and contains about fifteen thousand inhabitants, mostly poor and degraded. **Bethphage and Bethany;** implying that the two places were near to each other. The former name means the *place of figs;* the latter, according to some, *the place of dates*, but according to others, *the place of sorrow*. Bethany, the home of Mary, Martha and Lazarus, was situated less than two miles from Jerusalem, on the eastern slope of the Mount of Olives. At present it is *called El-Azariyeh*, derived from Lazarus, a small village of about twenty families. "It took half an hour to walk over Olivet to Bethany this morning, and the distance from that city, therefore, must be about two miles. The village is small, and appears never to have been large, but it is pleasantly situated near the south-eastern base of the mount, and has many fine trees about and above it."—DR. THOMSON, *The Land and the Book*, vol. ii., p. 599. *Bethphage*, a little nearer Jerusalem than Bethany, was reckoned by the later rabbins as a suburb of Jerusalem. 'About one-third of a mile west of Bethany, and about two hundred yards to the south of the road, is an ancient site. It is separated from Bethany by a low ridge and a deep glen. If this site marks the position of Bethphage, then Jesus, in gaining the top of this low ridge, was just opposite to that place, and could say, "Go into the village over against you." The owner of the ass could see from the village the procession. In the glen and on the adjoining ridges are many fig-trees, reminding us of its name, "house of figs," and of the remarkable incident recorded in ver. 13.'—J. L. PORTER, *Alexander's Kitto's Cyclo.* Bethphage is here placed first, because Mark, having mentioned Jerusalem as the goal of their journey, proceeds to name the places from west to east. But according to Luke (19 : 29), Bethphage would seem to have been reached before Bethany in the journey from Jericho, and hence a little east of Bethany. This may be regarded a popular manner of naming the village nearest to Jerusalem first; or we may suppose that the direct route from Jericho to Jerusalem lay through Bethphage, a little south and west of Bethany, so that those traveling from Jericho, would come to Bethphage first, and could turn off from thence to Bethany, if they desired to visit that place.

2 sendeth forth two of his disciples, and saith unto them, Go your way into the village over against you: and as soon as ye be entered into it, ye shall find a colt tied, whereon never man sat: loose him, and
3 bring *him*. And if any man say unto you, Why do ye this? say ye that the Lord hath need of him; and straightway he will send him hither.

The Mount of Olives. Literally, *The Mount of the Olives*, being descriptive of the olive-trees which grew thereon. Compare 2 Sam. 15 : 30; Neh. 8 : 15; Ezek. 11 : 23; Zech. 14 : 4. It is also called Olivet (Acts 1 : 12), a place set with olives, an olive-yard. This mount is the high ridge east of Jerusalem, and parallel to the city, and separated from it by the valley of the Kidron. The top is notched with three summits, the middle one of which is the highest, being about 2,700 feet above the Mediterranean, 500 feet above the bed of the Kidron, 200 feet above the city, and about half a mile from the city wall. The southern summit, which is lowest, is called the "Mount of Offense," and also "Mount of Corruption," because Solomon and some of the later kings defiled it by idolatrous worship. Three paths lead over the Mount of Olives, the middle one directly to Bethany, which is situated on the eastern slope. The one farther to the south passes a little to the right of that village, and is the road to Jericho. Olive-trees still grow upon the sides of the mount, but less thickly than of old. Other trees are also seen here and there, as the almond, fig, and pomegranate. But on the whole the scene presents a desolate appearance. Gethsemane lay just at the western foot of the mount.
Sendeth forth. The present tense again. The scene is thus presented as actually passing before the mind of the reader. Who the **two disciples** were we are not informed. Some suppose Peter and John. Compare ch. 14 : 13 with Luke 22 : 8.
2. **The village over against you.** Bethphage, Matt. 21 : 1. According to John 12 : 1, 12-15, Jesus had found a young ass after leaving Bethany, which is confirmatory of the view that the village here mentioned was Bethphage. **Ye shall find a colt tied.** Matthew mentions "an ass tied and a colt with her." But Matthew pays special attention to the fulfillment of Messianic prophecy; and he was about to show a remarkable fulfillment of Zech. 9 : 9, where both animals were mentioned; and hence he had occasion to speak of both the ass and the colt, though the latter only was needed. The other evangelists do no violence to the truth. Both Mark and Luke, in adding "whereon never man sat," agree perfectly with the supposition that up to this time the colt had run with its mother; that the mother-ass should have followed is perfectly natural. **Whereon never man sat.** Animals for sacred purposes were selected from those which had been unused by man, ceremonially clean and unblemished, Num. 19 : 2; Deut. 21 : 3; 1 Sam. 6 : 7. Jesus was also born of a virgin (Matt. 1 : 25), and was buried in a new tomb, Luke 23 : 53.
Loose him, and bring him. All was divinely arranged. Such a colt could not be found at any time and place. Jesus knew that he was perfectly welcome to the use of the animal. As the King Messiah, he could claim his service. Compare 1 Sam. 8 : 16. As Jehovah, it was his, Ps. 50 : 10. He was doubtless acquainted with his owner, whose cheerful acquiescence is implied in the narrative.
3. Jesus anticipates an objection which would be made, **Why do ye this?** The answer just needed is given, **The Lord hath need of him.** *Lord* may refer to the Lord Jehovah, or to Jesus as the King Messiah. Compare ch. 1 : 3; 5 : 19; 13 : 20. The two meanings really unite in Jesus; he is truly Jehovah and Christ. Compare Acts 2 : 36. What his owner would understand by the expression is another question from what was the full meaning in the mind of Jesus. They most probably understood that Jesus, as the Messiah, wanted the colt for a temporary service. **Straightway he will send** (literally, *he sends*) **him hither.** The future act of his owner is regarded as present, because it was as certain as if

4 And they went their way, and found the colt tied by the door without in a place where two ways met;
5 and they loose him. And certain of them that stood there said unto them, What do ye, loosing the
6 colt? And they said unto them even as Jesus had
7 commanded: and they let them go. And they brought the colt to Jesus, and cast their garments on him; º and he sat upon him.

º Zec. 9. 9.

it had already occurred. This implies his friendliness to Jesus and his willingness to accommodate him. But in some of the oldest and best manuscripts *again* is found in the last clause, *and straightway he will send him again hither*, a promise that Jesus would return the colt. Some regard this as a very ancient interpolation, designed to soften the seeming violence of the transaction. But certainly such a promise was very natural and lifelike; and *again* may have been omitted by early copyists, who did not understand the statement. It is now regarded as the correct reading by the highest critical authorities. A vivid reminiscence, perhaps by Peter.

4. At this point Matthew shows that the prediction of Zechariah (9 : 9) received a remarkable fulfillment. John (12 : 15) also briefly refers to it. Mark, with more particularity than the other evangelists, tells us where the colt was found, **by the door without,** very probably in front of the house of the owner. **In a place where two ways met.** The word thus translated means literally *a way round*, and was applied to streets of villages and cities, which were seldom straight. *On the street*, possibly the principal one of the village. As this was a small village, and may have had but one street, Alexander explains the word as "meaning the highway upon which the village stood, and by which it was wholly or partially surrounded."

5. **Certain of them that stood there.** Luke (19 : 33) says "the owners." They were probably the man and his sons, the members of the family who were interested in the property. **What do ye?** etc. What is your intention in loosing the colt?

6. The disciples reply as Jesus had **commanded,** or had *said*. Luke (19 : 34) at this point gives the very words, "The Lord hath need of him." Under the divine influence of Jesus they **let them go,** suffered them to unloose the colt and go with it. They were under the influence of Jesus the Messiah, whether they were acquainted with him or not.

7. **They brought.** The present tense in the original, *They bring the colt*. In place of the saddle, they **cast their** outer **garments** or cloaks on him. **He sat upon him.** The ass was used by persons of the highest rank, Judg. 5 : 10 ; 10 : 4. But this was not the king's mule (1 Kings 1 : 33, 38, 44), one kept for the use of royalty; nor the horse, which the Scriptures invariably associate with the idea of war (Ex. 15 : 21 ; Ps. 76 : 6 ; Prov. 21 : 31 ; Jer. 8 : 6), and which the kings of Israel were forbidden to multiply unto themselves, Deut. 17 : 16 ; but the colt of a beast of burden, one used in hard labor, Matt. 21 : 15. The time had come for Jesus to claim and receive Messianic honors, and this he could not well do on foot in a procession. He therefore rides in triumph into Jerusalem, but in a way which was significant, appropriate and suited to the nature of his kingdom. The horse was an animal of pride and war, the ass of humility and peace. Thus Jesus publicly claimed and received honors as the Messiah ; yet not as a proud, worldly monarch, but as the Prince of Peace. The humble, laboring beast also pointed to his humiliation and sufferings connected with his triumphs and victories. His meekness and lowliness in thus entering Jerusalem was in harmony with the nature of his kingdom, and inconsistent with the views of some rationalistic interpreters, that Jesus really designed to head a military movement, deliver the Jews from the Roman yoke and become a temporal monarch. How unfounded the last supposition is, appears from the facts that the multitude was without arms, and that the Roman authorities failed to take any notice of the triumphal procession as in

8 ᵖAnd many spread their garments in the way: and others cut down branches off the trees, and
9 strawed *them* in the way. And they that went before, and they that followed, cried, saying, ᑫHosanna! Blessed *is* he that cometh in the name of the
10 Lord! Blessed *be* the kingdom of our father David, that cometh in the name of the Lord! ʳHosanna in the highest!

ᵖ Mt. 21. 8.

ᑫ Ps. 118. 26; Eze. 34. 23, 24.

ʳ Ps. 148. 1; Is. 9. 6, 7; Jer. 33. 15–17.

---

any degree wrong or disloyal. Jesus probably took the southern road, the direct one from Jericho over the Mount of Olives.

8. Many spread their outer **garments.** As the disciples had spread their outer garments on the beast, so the multitude spread theirs in the way. This was a royal honor. Thus were they spread for Jehu to walk upon, 2 Kings 9:13. Robinson mentions an instance which he saw in Bethlehem, when the people spread their garments under the feet of the English consul, whose aid they were imploring. **Others,** in contrast to the *many* just mentioned, **cut down branches.** According to the highest critical authorities, the word translated *branches* is one that means branches cut for the purpose of being matted into a kind of bed to walk on. The branches thus answered the same purpose as the garments. According to John 12:13, they were palm-branches, the symbols of joy and victory, Lev. 23:40; Rev. 7:9. Instead of **from the trees,** some of the oldest manuscripts read *from the field.* The meaning is really the same, with the additional idea of going out of the highway to procure branches.

9. That went before and they that followed. Probably those who had come out of Jerusalem to meet him (John 12:12, 13) went before him, and the company who had come with him from Jericho followed behind him. They had now reached, according to Luke 19:37, the descent of the Mount of Olives, toward Jerusalem, probably just at the point where the city burst upon the view. Very probably the open ground near the city, including the sides of Olivet, were beginning to be occupied with tents and temporary structures of the multitude, who were assembling from all parts of the country to celebrate the Passover. It has been estimated that about two and a half to three millions attended this great national festival.

Cried, saying. The shouts of welcome and praise doubtless began with the disciples around Jesus and was caught by the multitude before and behind. **Hosanna.** A Hebrew phrase of two words (found in Ps. 118:25), meaning *save now,* and used in joyful acclamation and joyful greeting. It is here an expression of joy and of triumphant gratulation, including an invocation of blessings on Jesus, the royal descendant of David, the King-Messiah. Compare 1 Kings 1:34. "It is no fortuitous coincidence that this same Hebrew verb is the etymon or root of the name *Jesus,* borne by him who came to save his people from their sins, Matt. 1:21."—ALEXANDER. **Blessed is he,** etc. From Ps. 118:26, which was prophetical of the Messiah, and came to be applied to him by the Jews. He was the one that was to come, Matt. 11:3. It was thus a popular welcome to Jesus as the Messiah. The multitude very likely uttered these words responsively, interspersed with hosannas. **Blessed,** *favored* of God with divine and royal honors. **In the name.** By the authority and as the Messiah (the anointed) of Jehovah. According to Jewish tradition the 118th Psalm was one of those sung at the Passover.

10. **Blessed,** etc. According to the highest critical authorities this should read, *Blessed is the coming kingdom of our father David,* omitting **in the name of the Lord.** This first portion of the verse is recorded by Mark alone. In the preceding verse the acclamation was to the Messiah; in this to the Messiah's kingdom as just ushering in upon them. The Jews called David their *father* because the Messiah was his son or descendant. They were looking for the immediate restoration of the throne of David in the Messiah. Compare

11 ᵇAnd Jesus entered into Jerusalem, and into the   ᵇ Mt. 21. 12.
temple. And when he had looked round about
upon all things, and now the eventide was come, he
went out unto Bethany with the twelve.

Luke 1 : 32; 2 Sam. 7 : 16; Isa. 11 : 1-9. They had no conception of the spiritual nature of his kingdom. **Hosanna in the highest.** Variously understood to mean in the highest strains, or in the highest regions, that is, heaven. The latter may mean ratified by God in heaven, or repeated by angels in heaven. The general idea is: Let our hosannas be in the highest degree realized, responded to, and ratified in heaven.

According to Luke 19 : 37 and John 12 : 17, 18, the people met Jesus, with these royal honors, boldly and enthusiastically, because of the miracles they had seen, and especially because of the raising of Lazarus. Luke also adds that certain Pharisees wished Jesus to rebuke the applause; and also that when he came near and beheld the city, he wept over it. While the multitude continue to shout his honors, he weeps over the wicked, the unbelieving, and devoted city.

11. Entered Jerusalem. The goal of his journey. Matthew (21 : 10) describes the effect of this entrance upon the mass of the inhabitants of Jerusalem, and implies that they did not share in the enthusiasm of the multitude. Mark alone adds that Jesus entered **into the temple.** The entrance into the temple recorded in Matt. 21 : 12 is that of the following day, recorded in ver. 15, on which see. He entered the temple as the Messiah, as his Father's house and as his own house, ver. 17. It should also be noted that on the very day that Jesus "the Lamb of God" entered in triumph into Jerusalem, the tenth of Nisan, the paschal lamb was selected for its offering on the fourteenth, Exod. 12 : 3. May we not behold in the events of the day the setting apart of the great and true Paschal Lamb, preparatory to the sacrifice?

Temple. The word here translated temple denotes *sacred*, a sacred, consecrated place, and is applied to the whole sacred inclosure of courts and buildings, including the temple in its strict and proper sense, which is expressed by another word in such passages as ch. 14 : 58; 15 : 38. The temple stood on a rocky eminence, the hill Moriah, on the eastern part of the city, north-east of Zion, from which it was separated by a valley. Here it seems that Abraham was about to offer up Isaac (Gen. 22 : 1, 2), and David interceded for his people at the threshing-floor of Araunah, 2 Sam. 24 : 16-25 ; 2 Chron. 3 : 1. On three sides of this hill walls of huge stone were built up from the bottom, and filled in with cells, or earth, so as to form a large area on which to erect the temple. These walls remain to this day, and in some places, toward the south, are still sixty feet in height. The first temple was built by Solomon, commenced B.C. 1011, and finished B.C. 1004; and was burned down B.C. 588. The second temple was commenced under Zerubbabel B.C. 534, and completed under Ezra B.C. 516. The temple of Herod, which might indeed be styled the third temple, since it was the rebuilding and enlarging of the second, was commenced about fifteen years before the birth of Jesus—about B.C. 20 of our common era, and in a year and a half the temple proper was finished by priests and Levites. The out-buildings and courts required eight years. But some building operations continued long after in progress, and to these the Jews had reference when they said, "Forty and six years was this temple in building," John 2 : 20. According to Josephus, the whole sacred inclosure was a stadium square, or a half-mile in circumference.

The temple proper consisted of two parts: the holy of holies, containing the ark, the lid of which was the mercy-seat; and the holy place, a vail separating it from the holy of holies, where were the golden candlestick, the table of show-bread, and the altar of incense. Before the door of the temple stood the great brazen altar of burnt-offerings, and around the temple was a court or inclosure, into which none but priests might enter. Descending twelve steps was another court, inclosing the former, called the court of Israel, into

The barren fig-tree; cleansing of the temple.

12 ᶫAnd on the morrow, when they were come from
13 Bethany, he was hungry: ᵘ and seeing a fig tree afar off

ᶫ Mt. 21. 18, 19.
ᵘ Lk. 13. 6-9; Jno. 15. 2, 6; 2 Tim. 3. 5; Tit. 1. 16.

which none but male Jews might enter, and in front the court of women. Around these and lower still, was the large outer court, inclosing the whole, paved with variegated stone, and called by some the court of the Gentiles, where Jews and Gentiles might resort, and where were exposed for sale animals and things necessary for the sacrifices and worship of the temple. On the south side of this outer court was a synagogue, where religious services were performed. Here the Jewish doctors might be questioned, and their decisions were heard (Luke 2 : 46); here Jesus taught, and his disciples daily attended with one accord, Acts 2 : 46. Thus each inner inclosure rose, as in terraces, above the outer; and the temple proper was situated on the highest point, toward the north-western corner of the square, and could be seen from the city above the surrounding inclosures.

The front of the temple was on the eastern side, where was its principal entrance, facing the Mount of Olives. It was built of white marble, and stones of stupendous size, some of them twenty-five cubits long, eight cubits high, and twelve cubits thick.

Mark alone records the fact that Jesus **looked around upon all things.** He made a silent and general survey of the temple preparatory to the cleansing of it the next day. It was a silent exercise of his Messianic authority. On this day, most probably, occurred the visit of certain Greeks, who desired to see Jesus, John 12 : 20-36. They were very likely attracted by the triumphal procession. **Now the eventide was come.** *The evening-time* or *evening being now come.* The late or second evening which began with the setting sun is here meant. This marks not the time of our Savior's entrance, but of his departure from the city and temple. Between the two events several hours may have intervened. It is quite possible that Jesus and his disciples did not rejoin the company from Jericho till late in the morning, and hence that the triumphal entry did not occur early in the day. Some suppose it took place in the afternoon. **Bethany.** See on ver. 1. Jesus passed his nights there during this last week, Luke 21 : 37. Mark alone adds **with the twelve,** his constant attendants.

12-14. JESUS RETURNS FROM BETHANY, MONDAY MORNING; CURSES THE BARREN FIG-TREE. Matt. 21 : 18, 19. Mark enters the most into details.

12. **On the morrow,** after the triumphal entry into Jerusalem. Mark is very definite and exact in recording the first three days of this week, vers. 1, 11, 19, 20. Matthew, following the order of thought more than of chronology, groups things that are similar and related to each other. Thus Mark notices Christ's entrance and looking about on Sunday, vers. 1-11; the cursing of the fig-tree and the cleansing of the temple, on Monday, vers. 12-19; the withered fig-tree, and parables in the temple, on Tuesday, ver. 20 ff. But Matthew, after noticing Christ's public entry into Jerusalem, passes at once to notice the cleansing of the temple, Matt. 21 : 11, 12. So also, in relating the cursing of the fig-tree, he passes, without note of time, to its withering, Matt. 21 : 19, 20. **When they were come from** (*out from*) **Bethany.** Matthew states that it was in "the morning," the early morning between daybreak and sunrise. Luke (21 : 38) informs us that the people came early in the morning to hear him. **He was hungry.** It was real hunger. In his haste to enter upon his work he had probably taken no breakfast at Bethany. Some suppose that he had passed the night in the open air, in solitude and prayer. Hunger was a part of his humiliation. Thus he became perfect through sufferings, and able to sympathize with his followers in every trial. Alexander observes that it is necessarily implied that the disciples hungered with Jesus, and that thereby they were prepared to feel the disappointment more sensibly. This may be so; yet it seems more natural to suppose that the hunger of Jesus was at least greater than that of the others. His hunger was marked, and appears to have been intense.

13. **Seeing a fig tree afar off;**

having leaves, he came, if haply he might find any thing thereon: and when he came to it, he found nothing but leaves; for the time of figs was not *yet*.
14 And Jesus answered and said unto it, No man eat fruit of thee hereafter for ever. And his disciples heard *it*.

---

distant from them. The fig-tree was one of the most common and valuable trees of Palestine (Deut. 8 : 8), and was a symbol of peace and plenty, 1 Kings 4 : 25. It grows to a height of about twelve feet, with spreading branches and large dark-green leaves. The fruit is purple when ripe, with sweet pulp and abundance of small seeds. **Having leaves.** Its fruit begins to appear before its leaves shoot forth; hence the leaves gave promise of fruit. The fresh fruit is shaped like a pear, and whether fresh or dried is greatly prized. **If haply he might**, etc. To see whether he should find anything thereon. It was not for his own infor-

FIG-LEAVES AND FRUIT.

mation, but for that of his disciples, and for their good. According to Matthew the tree was by the roadside; it was therefore lawful for travelers to eat of its fruit. **He found nothing but**

leaves; instead of fruit of some size, as might have been expected from its appearance. Dr. Thomson (*Land and Book*, vol. i., p. 538) expresses his belief that a certain kind of fig-tree might have had ripe figs upon it at the Passover (early in April), in the warm, sheltered ravines of Olivet. **For the time of figs,** etc. *For it was not the time* or *season of figs.* The ordinary season of figs had not arrived. The early fig ripened in June, the summer fig in August, and a later fig sometimes hung upon the tree all winter. Mark makes this statement for the information of his foreign readers, to show that it was not too late for figs, and at the same time that the development of the leaves was premature and unnatural. If the season of figs had come, a wayside tree would probably soon be stripped; but if it had not come, then did its leaves show that it was barren. By its leaves the fig-tree gave promise of what it had not. And the curse that follows was pronounced upon it not merely because it was barren, but because it had leaves and yet was barren; its signs were false, its appearance deceptive. It was thus an emblem of the hypocrite, and particularly of the Jewish people, with their high professions, their show of ritual and formal worship, without the fruits of righteousness, Jer. 2 : 21; Luke 13 : 6–9. The Jews alone among the nations professed to be worshipers of Jehovah, but they were barren of fruit.

14. **Answered** the fig-tree, which silently acknowledged its inability to afford fruit, notwithstanding its pretentious appearance. See on ch. 9 : 5. **No man.** *Let no one*, etc. A strong, emphatic, negative wish, expressing the will of Jesus respecting the fig-tree, *Henceforth, forever let no one eat fruit from*

15 ᶻAnd they come to Jerusalem. And Jesus went into the temple, and began to cast out them that sold and bought in the temple; and overthrew the tables of the money changers, and the seats of them

ᶻ Mt. 21. 12; Lk. 19. 45; John 2. 14.

thee. There was no vindictive feeling connected with this expression, nor any implied in the word *cursedst* as used by the disciples in ver. 21. Skeptics have caviled at the destruction of property. But the fig-tree was by the wayside, and probably the property of no one. It belonged, however, to Jesus, in the highest sense, and he could do as he pleased with his own, Matt. 20 : 15. It was barren, and worse than useless; for it might mock the hungry traveler as it had him. It grew, existed and was destroyed, that the work and glory of God might be manifested through it (John 9 : 2–4), that Jesus might show his power as the Messiah over the material world, and that the faith of his disciples might be strengthened, and they prepared for the trials and work before them, John 11 : 4, 15. Jesus knew what he was about to do; all the circumstances occurred according to the divine arrangement. The fig-tree, and its destruction, may also be regarded as a symbol of the spiritual condition and end of the Jewish nation, and of hypocrites in general. The only other destruction of property connected with our Lord's ministry were the swine. See on ch. 5 : 13. It is worthy of notice that he symbolized his judgments on the disobedient and unfruitful with only *one* miracle, and that on a senseless tree; while in numberless miracles for the good of men, he showed forth the mercies and blessings of his salvation. Compare the parable of the fig-tree, Luke 13 : 6; and notice the fact that it is only the fruitless or barren fig-tree that is brought prominently forward in the New Testament, in these two instances, and in each used as a symbol of evil.

His disciples heard it; and were accordingly impressed by it. Mark notices this fact, as he will soon come to the tree again in chronological order.

15–19. JESUS EXPELS THE TRADERS FROM THE TEMPLE, teaches, and goes out of the city for the night, Matt. 21 : 12–16; Luke 19 : 45–48. Compare Luke 21 : 37, 38. Luke is the briefest of all.

Mark's account of casting out the traders is the fullest and most graphic. But Matthew alone records that Jesus then performed miracles, and defended the little children in their joyful acclamations against the murmuring of the chief priests and scribes.

John relates a similar cleansing of the temple at the first Passover of our Lord's ministry, three years before this, John 2 : 14–17. It was appropriate that Jesus should thus exercise his Messianic power, both at the opening and at the close of his public ministry. The Jews expected that the Messiah would correct many abuses, Mal. 3 : 1. That Jesus should have repeated the act is not therefore strange. He was accustomed to repeat some of his most striking sayings, Matt. 6 : 9–13 and Luke 11 : 2–4; Matt. 6 : 25–33 and Luke 12 : 22–31. So, also, he performed similar miracles ; for example, the first and second draught of fishes, Luke 5 : 1–11 and John 21 : 4–6; twice feeding the multitude, ch. 6 : 35–46 and 8 : 1–9. The reason why the first three evangelists omit the first cleansing, is doubtless found in the fact that it took place before the opening of his Galilean ministry, which forms the principal subject of their Gospels. John, however, gives an account of it, because he supplemented the other Gospels, and gives principally the Judean ministry of Jesus, paying special attention to that portion of it before the imprisonment of John the Baptist and the commencement of his ministry in Galilee.

15. They come to Jerusalem. Mark is thus very explicit in fixing this cleansing of the temple the day after our Lord's triumphal entry. Matthew and Luke would seem to fix it a day earlier. But the difference of Matthew can be accounted for from his manner of grouping together miracles, discourses and incidents, without strict regard to chronological order. See on ver. 12. Luke (19 : 45–48) is here very brief, and evidently glances over two or three days in a summary manner.

Temple. The same as in ver. 11, which see. The soul of man is pre-

16 that sold doves; and would not suffer that any man 17 should carry *any* vessel through the temple. And he taught, saying unto them, Is it not written, 'My house shall be called of all nations the house of prayer? But ye have made it a den of thieves.'

eminently the temple of God, 1 Cor. 3:16. The cleansing of the one naturally suggests the cleansing of the other. In both his Messianic power is displayed. **Cast out them that sold,** etc. In the court of the Gentiles was the temple-market, where animals, oil, wine and other things necessary for sacrifices and temple worship were sold. This was a convenience for those who came to worship. But what was intended at first for an accommodation became a source of gain and extortion, of noise and confusion. Jesus casts out these profane intruders; they were doubtless filled with awe before him. His moral power and spiritual authority, as the Messiah, ruled them into submission, and they flee before him. "Jerome regards this expulsion of a multitude by one humble individual as the most wonderful of the miracles, and supposes that a flame and starry ray darted from the eyes of the Savior, and that the majesty of the Godhead was radiant in his countenance."—P. SCHAFF, D.D. **Money-changers.** These changed at a premium, often a very exorbitant one, the current coin of the day, which was regarded as profane, for the Jewish half-shekel, the yearly temple tribute. See Matt. 17:24. Some made donations to the treasury (Luke 21:1, 2); and others who came to the Passover probably paid their tribute, which became due in the month Adar, answering to parts of February and March. The Jews of Palestine, and especially those who were dispersed abroad, were under the necessity of exchanging the Greek and Roman coin, which they used for the common purposes of trade, but not for their sacred purposes. Money-changers were a convenience and a necessity; but they were dishonest in their exactions, practiced extortion, and violated the law, Deut. 23:19, 20. Jesus overturned also the seats of the sellers of **doves.** The poor were allowed to offer doves in sacrifice, instead of a lamb, Lev. 5:7; 12:8; 14:22; Luke 2:24.

16. **And would not suffer,** etc. This statement is recorded only by Mark, and shows that Jesus remained there for some time. **Carry any vessel through.** *Carry a vessel* or an *implement through* the sacred inclosure; make a thoroughfare of it. Reference is made to any vessel or implement connected with their traffic, or borne by any one through the outer portion of the temple, from one part of the city to another. Making any part of the temple such a thoroughfare was a profanation. According to the Talmud, the rabbins also forbade it. But Jesus defended what he did, not by human authority, but by the divine authority of Scripture, ver. 17.

17. **Taught them** the design of God's house, and to what an extent they had perverted that design; thus giving a reason why he had used his Messianic authority in purging the temple. He quotes freely the predictions of Isaiah (Isa. 56:7) and Jeremiah (7:11), uniting them together without doing injustice to their meaning. **Is it not written?** Jesus appeals to the Holy Scriptures, as of divine authority. **My house.** The temple is represented as God's earthly dwelling-place. **The house of prayer.** Rather, *A house,* etc. Prayer is the principal part of worship, 1 Kings 8:33, 35, 38, etc. **Of all nations.** *For all the nations,* not for the Jews alone, but also for Gentiles, whoever may resort to it for worship. The principal idea which Jesus wished to enforce was that his house was a house of prayer, since both Matthew and Luke omit "for all nations." Mark wrote for Gentiles, and elsewhere lays stress on the universality of the gospel, ch. 16:15; which may help explain the additional clause. Luke, indeed, wrote for all, but his account here is very brief.

Ye have made it a den of thieves. More correctly, *Ye have made it,* or, according to some ancient manuscripts, *Ye made it a den of robbers.* In contrast to *a house of prayer* is

A.D. 30. MARK XI. 215

18 And ʸ the scribes and chief priests heard it, and sought how they might destroy him: for they feared him, because ᶻ all the people was astonished at his doctrine.
19 And when even was come, he went out of the city.
20 ᵃ And in the morning, as they passed by, they saw

ʸ Mt. 21. 45, 46; Lk. 19. 47.
ᶻ ch. 1. 22; Mt. 7. 28; Lk. 4. 32.

ᵃ Mt. 21. 19.

---

a den, cave, or cavern, where robbers often resort, *a den of robbers*. The word here translated thieves means robbers, those who seize what does not belong to them, openly and by violence, and is stronger than the Greek word for thief, which means one who takes what is another's, by fraud, and in secret. The latter word is always translated thief, in our common version; but the former is unfortunately translated thief eleven times, and correctly, robber, only four times, John 19 : 1, 8; 18 : 40; 2 Cor. 11 : 26. These two words are used together in John 10 : 1, 10, where their meanings may be compared. Jesus thus rebukes their open dishonesty and extortion, which presents a marked difference from his former cleansing the temple, when he reproved the unbecoming introduction of worldly business, John 2 : 16. The court, where Gentiles might pray, they had turned into a place of dishonest gain and open fraud. This quotation was also a reproof of the contempt thus cast upon Gentile proselytes.

Thus began to be fulfilled the prophecy of Malachi (3 : 1-3.) Jesus, the Lord Messiah, suddenly came into the temple, and began the work of purification. According to the prophecy of John the Baptist (Matt. 3 : 12,) his "fan was in his hand," and he wielded it in separating the precious from the vile, and in reforming the abuses of his house. Compare Isa. 4 : 2-4.

18. At this point Matthew records the healing of the blind and lame, the children crying hosanna, the displeasure and the murmuring of the Pharisees, and the reply of Jesus. **The scribes and chief priests,** members of the Sanhedrim, **heard it,** the application of prophecy in ver. 17, and were offended by it. The act of Jesus in purging the temple, as well as his teaching, indicated his prophetic and Messianic power and authority, and excited the fear and jealousy of the Jewish leaders. **Sought,** cautiously and deliberately, ch. 14 : 1. **How they might destroy him.** They had counseled before to destroy him, but the *how* troubled them, John 11 : 53-57. Here do we see the reason of their various artifices to entrap Jesus the next day, vers. 27-33; ch. 12. They saw that their own influence, authority and gains were endangered by the works and teaching of Jesus, and they would put him out of the way. **For they feared him;** personally, as a miracle-worker and a powerful teacher, and also in his popular influence with the people. They saw that he was necessarily opposed to them. They therefore carefully devise plots against him. **All the people.** All the crowd or multitude. **Astonished.** Struck with surprise and admiration. **At his doctrine.** *At his teaching*, its matter, manner, authority, and its accompanying exhibitions of divine power.

19. **And when the even was come.** According to the best text, *And whenever it became late,* at evening, about the setting of the sun, *they* went out of the city, probably to Bethany, ver. 11. This states the custom of Jesus and his disciples during these days, as in Luke 21 : 37. Thus ended the day of Christ's undisturbed works and teachings. The Jewish leaders, however, were exasperated. A day of conflict was to follow.

20-26. GOING AGAIN INTO JERUSALEM. THE WITHERED FIG-TREE. Matt. 20 : 20-22. Mark is the fuller and the more life-like, not only in detailing the facts about the tree, but also the discourse occasioned by it.

20. **And in the morning.** Early in the morning; the people came early to hear him in the temple, Luke 21 : 38. Mark with great exactness fixes this incident about to be related upon the morning (Tuesday) after the cursing of the fig-tree. Matthew was intent in telling the principal facts concerning the fig-tree, and does not mark definitely the time of each part of the his-

21 the fig tree dried up from the roots. And Peter
calling to remembrance saith unto him, Master,
behold, the fig tree which thou cursedst is withered
22 away. And Jesus answering saith unto them,
23 Have faith in God. For ᵇ verily I say unto you,
That whosoever shall say unto this mountain, Be
thou removed, and be thou cast into the sea; and
shall not doubt in his heart, but shall believe that
those things which he saith shall come to pass; he

ᵇ Mt. 17. 20; 21.
21; Lk. 17. 6; 1
Cor. 13. 2.

tory. In rapid and vivid discourse, days and even weeks are sometimes passed over unnoticed. **As they passed by** from Bethany or the place on Olivet (Luke 21 : 37) where they lodged during the night; they were without doubt upon the same road as the morning before ver. 12. **They saw the fig tree.** They appear to have seen it now for the first time since the previous morning. In the dusk or darkness of the preceding evening they could not well have observed it. **Dried up from the roots.** Wonderfully dried up, not merely in its tender branches and limbs, but in its trunk, and down to its very roots. Very likely it was stripped of its leaves, and presented the appearance of a thoroughly blasted tree, dead in root and branch. In contrast to its former show of leaves, it presented a marked appearance, and specially attracted attention. From Matthew (21 : 19) we learn that the withering began immediately after the words of Jesus, "Let no fruit grow," etc. Mark, in perfect harmony, says nothing about the time of its withering, but notes the time when the disciples first discovered it.

21. **Peter calling to remembrance.** This is one of the special references to Peter in this Gospel which confirms the common opinion that Mark wrote it under his direction. **Master;** or *Rabbi*, the very word Peter used, a title of great respect given to a teacher, equivalent to Master, or My Master. **Behold.** An exclamation of surprise, calling attention to something strange and unexpected. **The fig tree which thou cursedst.** This is the only place where Jesus is spoken of as cursing the fig-tree, or indeed any object. He cursed the tree, only in the sense of devoting it to death, which he had a perfect right to do as Lord of both animate and inani-

mate creation. He expressed the will of God concerning it. As there was no sin in him, we must separate all that is vindictive or sinful from the human conception of cursing. See ver. 14. Matthew gives the exclamation of the disciples, expressing wonder at the sudden withering, but passes over this observation of Peter.

22. Jesus answers in a way best suited to benefit his disciples. **Have faith in God.** A strong expression. Hold a steadfast trust and confidence in God. Here do we get one of the designs of this miracle, and the immediate design so far as his disciples were concerned. He would strengthen their faith and prepare them for the trials before them.

23. Jesus proceeds to teach them that through faith they might perform even greater miracles. **This mountain.** Probably the Mount of Olives, over which they were passing. It is implied that Jesus could have removed this mountain as well as have dried up the fig-tree. Compare Zech. 14 : 4. **Be thou removed,** or *taken up.* **The sea.** A general expression, the Dead Sea, the Sea of Galilee, or the Mediterranean Sea, being several miles distant. The kind of faith Jesus describes: First, the negative side, **shall not doubt in his heart,** without hesitation or wavering. Second, the positive side, **shall believe . . . shall come to pass.** More exactly, *shall believe that what he says comes to pass;* shall so believe that the answer is a present reality, indeed *granted,* and as certain as if already accomplished. The result, **he shall,** etc. According to the highest critical authorities, *he shall have it,* Acts 3 : 6; 9 : 34.

The exercise of faith in miracles, as well as in prayer, must be in accordance with the will of God. Indeed, true faith is so far in harmony with that will

24 shall have whatsoever he saith. Therefore I say unto you, °What things soever ye desire, when ye pray, believe that ye receive *them*, and ye shall have *them*.

25 And when ye stand praying, ᵈforgive, if ye have aught against any: that your Father also which is
26 in heaven may forgive you your trespasses. But ᵉif

° Mt. 7. 7; Lk. 11. 9; John 14. 13; 15. 7; 16. 24; Jam. 1. 5, 6.
ᵈ Eph. 4. 32; Col. 3. 13.
ᵉ Mt. 18. 35; Jam. 2. 13.

---

that it really asks nothing contrary to it. The mountain may symbolize any great and apparently insurmountable difficulty. Faith is also attended with works, James 2 : 18. And by works the man of faith often in a measure answers his own prayers. He meets these mountains of difficulties with an earnest, active faith, and they disappear before him while he labors on. See on ch. 9 : 29; Matt. 17 : 20.

24. **Therefore,** *For this reason*, that faith is essential in obtaining divine help, and to encourage you, *I say to you*. **Whatsoever things ye desire,** *ask*, **when ye pray.** True prayer is inspired by God, and hence will be according to his will (1 John 5 : 14), and in the name of Christ (John 14 : 13), and will be answered either in kind or in equivalent, 2 Cor. 12 : 8, 9. The promise here given is not to the presumptuous, the arrogant and self-confident, but to those who exercise simple and childlike faith in their Heavenly Father, with entire submission to his all-wise and infinitely benevolent will, Matt. 18 : 4. **Believe that ye receive them.** According to the best critical authorities, *Believe that ye received them*, that your request was granted while in the very act of prayer. In the preceding verse the answer of prayer is vividly regarded as a present fact; in this, as a past fact attending the prayer itself. Thus Daniel prayed for the restoration of Jerusalem; and Gabriel informs him, "At the beginning of thy supplication the commandment came forth," that is, "the commandment to restore and build Jerusalem," Dan. 9 : 3, 23, 25. While in the act of prayer his request was granted, and the blessing sought was received, though many years were required for its accomplishment. So the Christian parent interceding for the soul of a wayward child, may have the full assurance of faith that his prayer is answered. The conflict between light and darkness in his child's heart may still go on, but his own heart rests in an abiding faith. He believes that he has received the blessing in answer to prayer, and he calmly waits the issue in God's own time, which to him is as certain as if already accomplished.

The promise of this verse is not limited to miracles in connection with prayer and faith. It relates to *all things whatever ye ask, when ye pray* (Bible Union Version). This faith in God which Jesus was enforcing upon his disciples, was something that they needed at all times and under all circumstances. They especially needed it under the great trials of that week of conflict, suffering and darkness.

25. Jesus adds another condition of effectual prayer, perhaps to guard them from making a wrong use of the withering of the fig-tree. They were not to harbor a spirit of imprecation against those that opposed them (Luke 9 : 54), but a spirit of forgiveness. Mark alone records the command in this place. Matthew records an earlier utterance of it, and Luke an earlier intimation of it, Matt. 6 : 14; Luke 6 : 37.

Stand praying. A common posture in prayer, Luke 18 : 11, 13. **Forgive, if ye have aught,** any ill-will, or any cause of complaint, just or unjust. **That your Father also . . . may forgive.** That is, exercise the spirit of forgiveness as an essential condition, in order that God may forgive you. It is no arbitrary condition, but so inseparable from right feeling that God conducts himself toward us according to the spirit we cherish, Ps. 18 : 25, 26. Judgment without mercy is for him who shows no mercy. **Trespasses.** The figure of a *lapse*, *fall* or *false step*. Sin, in one sense, is a fall from the straight line of moral rectitude.

26. Some of the oldest manuscripts omit this verse; others retain it. Its position here is natural and possible. **But if ye do not forgive.** The preceding verse states the positive side, this the negative. If we will not

19

ye do not forgive, neither will your Father which is in heaven forgive your trespasses.

The authority of Jesus questioned; his question in reply, respecting the authority of John the Baptist.

27 AND they come again to Jerusalem. ᵇAnd as he was walking in the temple, there come to him the
28 chief priests, and the scribes, and the elders, and say unto him, By what authority doest thou these things? and who gave thee this authority to do these things?
29 And Jesus answered and said unto them, I will also ask of you one question, and answer me, and I will tell you by what authority I do these things.

ᵇ Mt. 21. 23; Lk. 20. 1; Ex. 2. 14; Ac. 4. 7; 7. 27; Prov. 26. 4, 5; Col. 4. 6.

---

exercise mercy toward our fellow-men, whose offenses against us are comparatively trifling, how can we expect forgiveness from God, against whom we are so great sinners? Matt. 18 : 23–35. The spirit of forgiveness is essential to acceptable prayer, and an evidence of forgiven sin.

27–33. THE AUTHORITY OF JESUS QUESTIONED BY THE SANHEDRIM. Matt. 21 : 23–27; Luke 20 : 1–8. The three accounts are very similar. Mark is the most vivid; Luke begins indefinitely; Matthew adds the parable of the Two Sons.

27. **Come again into Jerusalem.** Tuesday morning, ver. 20. Luke says: "On one of those days, as he taught the people in the temple and preached the gospel." **As he was walking in the temple;** in the courts of the sacred inclosure. At home in his Father's house, as the Messiah and the Lord of the temple. **The chief priests and the scribes and the elders.** Members of the three classes composing the Sanhedrim, the highest ecclesiastical council of the Jews. In reference to these classes, see on ch. 1 : 22; 7 : 3; 8 : 31. They were evidently the leading members of the Sanhedrim, though it does not appear that they came as an official and formal deputation, similar to that which had been sent to John the Baptist, John 1 : 19–28.

28. **By what authority.** Not only *by what,* but also *by what kind* of authority, divine or human, Messianic or prophetic. **These things.** Cleansing the temple, performing miracles and teaching. **Who gave thee?** Who, with authority, gave thee this authority? The Sanhedrim authorized teachers in the temple and tried false prophets, but Jesus had not been authorized by them. Hence their two questions, implying that his authority was not of God. The Mosaic law had given directions for the discovery, rejection and death of false prophets (Deut. 13 : 1–5; 18 : 20–22); these questions in themselves were therefore entirely proper for any Jews, and especially for the members of the Sanhedrim to ask. John had asked a somewhat similar question, Matt. 11 : 3. But they now ask with wrong motives, wishing to entrap him and find occasion to destroy him (Luke 19 : 47), and to draw forth some such declaration as that he was the Son of God, and charge him with blasphemy, ch. 14 : 61–64. The questions were also really needless; for the works and doctrines of Jesus were evidences that he was the Messiah, and that he came from God, John 3 : 2; 10 : 24, 25, 37, 38; 12 : 37. Jesus, therefore, was not called upon under such circumstances to answer their questions. We have here the first direct assault of the authorities of the temple and of the great Jewish council upon Jesus.

29. Jesus does not evade them, but he brings them to the consideration of a fundamental fact in this discussion, the admission of which would lead to an irresistible conclusion, John 5 : 33–36; 10 : 41. He might have appealed to the raising of Lazarus, and his other miracles; but since these Jewish rulers

30 The baptism of John, was *it* from heaven, or of
31 men? answer me. And they reasoned with themselves, saying, If we shall say, From heaven; he
32 will say, Why then did ye not believe him? But if we shall say, Of men; they feared the people: for ¹all *men* counted John, that he was a prophet indeed.
33 And they answered and said unto Jesus, We cannot tell. And Jesus answering saith unto them, Neither do I tell you by what authority I do these things.

¹ ch. 1. 5; 6. 20; Mt. 3. 5; 14. 5.

---

came with wicked designs, and were not even deserving an answer, he adopts a different mode of reply, one which both answers and confounds them. The reference to John, whom Jesus had declared to be his forerunner (the Elijah that was to come, Matt. 11 : 14), and by whom he had been baptized, was indeed a suggestive answer that he was from God, the Messiah, since John had declared him so to be, John 1 : 26, 29, 32-34. Jesus could appeal to these declarations. At the same time he defeats their designs, and extorts from them an unwilling and hypocritical confession that they are unable and incompetent to judge.

30. **The baptism of John.** The whole ministration of John, of which baptism formed a very prominent part. **From heaven, or of** (*from*) **men.** Did John act by the authority of God, or by his own? Was he a true prophet or a false one? This was a fundamental question, really involving the question they asked. If they acknowledged John as a prophet, they must also acknowledge Jesus. Mark alone gives the demand or challenge, **Answer me,** giving greater life to the narrative.

31. **They reasoned with** (rather *among*) **themselves.** They saw that the question was a legitimate one, but it troubled them. They consulted and deliberated as to what answer they should give, and what might be the effect of the different replies suggested. **Why then did ye not believe him?** Why did you not become his followers, and believe when he testified of me as the Messiah. To acknowledge that John was a true prophet would be to condemn themselves for rejecting both John and Jesus.

32. **But if we say, Of men.** Rather, according to oldest and best manuscripts, *But shall we say from men?*

The interrogative form makes it the more emphatic. Mark abruptly gives their language in his own words, **they feared the people.** They would have preferred to have said, From men; but they feared to brave popular opinion, and perhaps a popular tumult. "All the people will stone us," Luke 20 : 6. This was the grand motive of their silence. **Accounted; esteemed, regarded. A prophet indeed.** Really a prophet.

33. Against all the evidence they had seen of John's prophetic office, and doubtless against their own convictions, they answer, **We cannot tell,** literally, *We do not know.* This answer was falsehood, and hypocritical was their confession of ignorance. **Neither do I tell you.** One of our Savior's brief answers replete with meaning. If you are unable or unwilling to judge of John and his teaching, you are equally so in regard to me. If you dare not deny his divine commission, you should acknowledge mine. Your real unwillingness to acknowledge, according to the convictions of your own consciences, that John was a true prophet, merits from me a corresponding unwillingness to give you any more evidence in regard to myself than that you already have.

Matthew (21 : 28-32) adds the parable of the Two Sons, in the application of which Jesus administers a severe rebuke to these Jewish rulers for their treatment of John and his preaching.

REMARKS.

1. Jesus is omniscient. All events, persons and things are within the circle of his knowledge, vers. 1, 2; John 2 : 24, 25; 16 : 30; 21 : 17.

2. Jesus has a right to all things, and

can use them as he pleases, ver. 2; Col. 1 : 16, 17; Ps. 50 : 10–12.

3. Whatever Jesus requires, whether it be in word, in labor, or in property, let it be promptly and cheerfully given, vers. 3–6; Isa. 1 : 19; Acts 4 : 19, 20, 32.

4. Persons, animals and things are received, employed and required in Christ's service, ver. 3; Num. 22 : 28–33; 1 Cor. 1 : 26–29.

5. Poverty is no sin in itself, and of it none need be ashamed, vers. 2, 3; Matt. 8 : 20; Acts 3 : 6.

6. We should do our part in honoring Jesus, our Prophet and King, thankful to engage in any service, however humble, vers. 4–10; Isa. 52 : 7; Zeph. 3 : 14–17; Hos. 4 : 6.

7. Jesus had often sought retirement (Matt. 12 : 15–21); but now for wise purposes he makes his coming to Jerusalem most public. It was meet that his sufferings and death should be before angels and men, vers. 7–11; John 3 : 14; Acts 2 : 22–24; 10 : 39.

8. Jesus was meek and lowly even in his triumphal entrance into Jerusalem. How unbecoming, then, are pride, avarice and ambition in his followers under any circumstances! Ver. 7; Phil. 2 : 3–5; Eph. 4 : 1, 2; James 3 : 13–18.

9. The true glory of Christ's kingdom is not in outward display, but in righteousness and salvation, vers. 7–10; Heb. 1 : 8, 9; 5 : 9; Rev. 7 : 9–14.

10. "The coming of Christ to establish his kingdom among men is the most joyful event in the world's history. It repeats itself in all the triumphs of truth over error, of right over wrong; in the spread of Christianity through the earth; in revivals of religion; in whatever manifests the divine power of the gospel."—REV. I. P. WARREN. Ver. 10; Acts 4 : 31–33; Rom. 1 : 16; Heb. 1 : 6–9.

11. Whenever we visit the city or town we should seek the house of God rather than the place of amusement, ver. 11; Ps. 65 : 4; 84 : 1, 2; 122 : 1.

12. Jesus knows what are the cravings of appetite. "He was hungry," ver. 12; John 4 : 6, 7; Heb. 4 : 15.

13. It is not enough that we have an outward profession and an appearance of fruitfulness; we must *bear* fruit, if we would meet our Lord's approval, vers. 13, 14; Gen. 3 : 7, 11; Matt. 7 : 20–23.

14. They who fail to bring forth fruit to Christ shall forever be given over to barrenness and death, ver. 14; Matt. 23 : 25–28; 1 Cor. 16 : 22.

15. The followers of Christ should exercise great zeal in removing every thing erroneous and injurious from his house and worship. They should do it wisely, in the name of Christ, and according to his word, vers. 15, 16; 1 Tim. 3 : 15; Rev. 2 : 20.

16. "To carry the world into the worship of God, and serve self under the pretence of serving him, is a hypocrisy which he will not fail to detect and to punish."—REV. I. P. WARREN. Vers. 15, 16; Mal. 3 : 1, 2; 1 Cor. 3 : 16, 17; 2 Thess. 2 : 8.

17. God's house is emphatically a house of prayer, and anything inconsistent with prayer is unbecoming it, or his people, ver. 17; Jer. 7 : 8–11; 1 Cor. 3 : 16, 17.

18. Formal and hypocritical churches are dens of robbers. They take from the people the blessings of the gospel, and leave them to perish, ver. 17; Isa. 1 : 21–23; Matt. 23 : 15, 25.

19. Faithfulness in duty will arouse opposition, ver. 18; Acts 28 : 17; 2 Tim. 3 : 12; 4 : 16.

20. "Even the vegetable creation is dependent on Christ. There is not a plant or flower in the garden, not a tree by the wayside, in the orchard, the field or the forest, but will wither away if not supported by him." — FAMILY BIBLE, Am. Tract Society, N. Y. Ver. 20; John 1 : 1; Col. 1 : 17.

21. Jesus is the Lion as well as the Lamb. In him are exhibited both the severity and goodness of God, ver. 21; Rom. 11 : 22; Rev. 5 : 5; 17 : 14.

22. Faith and true prayer go together; and so do prayer and submission to God's will, vers. 23, 24; ch. 14 : 36; Heb. 11 : 16; James 1 : 6.

23. The miracles of Christ should strengthen our faith and encourage our prayers, since he is our Intercessor, and through him we can do all things, vers. 22, 23; John 14 : 12–14; Phil. 4 : 13; Heb. 7 : 25.

24. The answer to the prayer of faith is certain and immediate, although not always manifest at once, ver. 24; Isa. 65 : 24.

25. Faith and the spirit of forgiveness are two conditions of acceptable prayer, vers. 24, 25; Matt. 6 : 12–15; 17 : 20.

26. The servants of Christ must expect opposition, and that their autho-

Parable of the vineyard let out to wicked husbandmen.

XII. And ¹ he began to speak unto them by parables. A *certain* man ² planted a vineyard, and set an hedge about *it*, and digged *a place for* the winefat, and built a tower, and let it out to husbandmen, and

¹ Mt. 21. 33; Lk. 20. 9.
² Jer. 2. 21; Rom. 3. 1, 2; 9. 4, 5; 11. 17, 24.

rity will be questioned by the enemies of truth, ver. 27; John 15 : 20, 21.

27. Persons of high ecclesiastical office and authority may be spiritually blinded, vers. 27, 28; Matt. 23 : 24; Rev. 3 : 17, 18.

28. Religious teachers should be called of God and appointed to their work, vers. 28, 29; Acts 13 : 2, 3; Heb. 5 : 4.

29. The envious and unbelieving will throw discredit on those who work for God, vers. 28, 29; Ex. 2 : 14; Acts 6 : 10-12; 17 : 5.

30. Analogical arguments and interrogative answers to the cavils of skeptics are often the most effectual, vers. 29, 30.

31. Formalists and wicked opposers of Christ will feign ignorance, and will lie, rather than injure their popularity, or confess the truth which they dislike, vers. 31-33; Acts 4 : 15-18; 6 : 10-14.

32. An honest spirit in religious matters will overcome obstacles, and sooner or later come out on the side of truth, vers. 31, 32; John 7 : 17; 8 : 31, 32, 43.

33. They who do not honestly seek after truth must expect to be left in error, ver. 33; Isa. 29 : 15, 16; Matt. 13 : 12; 2 Thess. 2 : 11, 12.

CHAPTER XII.

In this chapter, Mark continues the account of the conflict on Tuesday of the Passion Week between Jesus and the ecclesiastical leaders of the Jews. Having foiled them in their demand for his authority and credentials, Jesus shows their guilt and terrible doom by the parable of the Vineyard let out to Wicked Husbandmen. Gladly would they have laid hands on him, but they were restrained from fear of the people. They, therefore, resort to artifice, hoping to entrap him and in some way render him obnoxious either to the Romans or to the people. First, certain Pharisees and Herodians are sent to inquire concerning paying tribute to Cæsar; but his answer excites admiration and astonishment. Next, Sadducees come and ask a perplexing question regarding the resurrection; but they are put to silence. Then a scribe asks regarding the first commandment, but Jesus answers so discreetly that none of his opposers had heart to interrogate him further. Jesus then puts a question concerning the Messiah, which is unanswered; and follows it by warning the people against their covetous and hypocritical teachers. Thus ends Mark's account of Tuesday's conflict. The evangelist closes the chapter by adding the incident of the Widow's Mite.

1-12. THE PARABLE OF THE WICKED HUSBANDMEN. Matt. 21 : 33-46; Luke 20 : 9-19. The fearful guilt of the Jewish people in persecuting the prophets and murdering the Messiah, and their terrible doom. Mark is fresh and vivid, somewhat the fullest in the parable itself; but Matthew excels in giving the application, in which Mark is the briefest of all.

1. **He began,** etc. It is here implied that Jesus spoke other parables at this time, although this alone is recorded by Mark. Matthew gives three: the Two Sons, this parable and the Marriage of the King's Son, Matt. 21 : 28 —22 : 14. All of these were specially applicable to the Jewish leaders in their rejection of the Messiah. But this is the central one, and deals most pointedly with the murderous rejecters of Jesus. Hence Mark appropriately selected this. **Unto them.** The chief priest, scribes and elders, ch. 11 : 27. So, also, Matthew, "the chief priest and elders of the people," 21 : 23. But Luke (20 : 9) says "the people." The evangelists write according to their different stand-points. All these classes were among his auditors. It was specially intended for the scribes, chief priests and elders; but he intended that the people should also hear it, for it was a matter of great concern to them. We have here a beautiful illustration of

2 went into a far country. And at the season he sent to the husbandmen a servant, that he might receive from the husbandmen of the fruit of the vineyard. 3 And they caught *him*, and beat him, and sent *him*

diversity and harmony in the independent accounts of the evangelists. **By parables.** *In parables.* See on ch. 4 : 2.

A certain man. Simply, *A man.* **A vineyard.** A simile often used in Scripture, Ps. 80 : 8-16 ; Isa. 27 : 2-7. See especially Isa. 5 : 1-7, which bears a close resemblance to this parable. The Jewish leaders were familiar with these passages, and were thus somewhat prepared to understand the parable, ver. 12. The Jews planted their vineyards most commonly on the sides of hills and mountains, Exod. 15 : 17 ; 2 Chron. 26 : 10 ; Jer. 31 : 5. **See a hedge about it.** Set a fence about it, probably a thick row of thornbushes, the best protection against man and beast. Sometimes a vineyard was surrounded with both a hedge and a wall, Isa. 5 : 5.

Digged . . . the wine-fat. Simply, *Dug the wine-vat,* the lower receptacle. A wine-press consisted of this lower vat for receiving the juice, and an upper vat for treading the grapes. Dr. Hackett (*Illustrations of Scripture,* p. 165) thus describes the wine-press as ordinarily used at the present day : " A hollow place, usually a rock, is scooped out, considerably deeper at one end than the other. The grapes are put into this trough, and two or more persons, with naked feet and legs, descend into it, where they jump up and down, crushing the fruit as they trample on it, while to enliven their labor they often sing at the same time. The juice flows into the lower part of the excavation. . . . The place for treading out the grapes is sometimes dug in the ground, lined, probably, with a coating of stone or brick. The expression in Matt. 21 : 33, *and he digged a wine-press* in his vineyard, may allude to such an excavation. . . . Dr. Robinson describes a wine-press which he saw at Hebleh, near the site of Antipatris (Acts 23 : 31), which was hewn out of a rock and divided into two parts. The upper and more shallow part was the place where the grapes were put, the lower and deeper one was the place for receiving the liquor pressed out of them. It was the work, no doubt, of the ancient Hebrews or Philistines."

A tower. A watch-tower from which the whole vineyard and its surroundings might be seen. In it a watchman kept guard against thieves, especially during the season of ripe grapes. Watch-towers are still common in Palestine, built of stone, circular in shape, though sometimes square, and generally fifteen or twenty feet high, yet occasionally rising to forty or fifty feet. "Those which I examined had a small door near the ground, and a level space on the top, where a man could sit and command a view of the plantation." —Dr. Hackett, *Scrip. Illus.,* p. 172. Compare Luke 14 : 28. **Let it out to husbandmen.** Tillers of the ground, who in this instance turned their attention to keeping a vineyard. From Sol. Song 8 : 11 and Isa. 7 : 23 we may infer that a most valuable vineyard of a thousand vines yielded a rent of a thousand shekels of silver, or about five hundred dollars. In this instance the husbandmen were to give a portion of the fruits as the rent, ver. 2; Luke 20 : 10. Vineyards were very productive, but required great labor and care in digging, planting, propping, pruning, gathering grapes, and making wine. **Went into a far country.** Rather *went abroad.* Nothing is said whether it was far or near. Luke adds, "for a long time."

2. **At the season.** The time of vintage. The general vintage was in September. The "first ripe grapes" were gathered somewhat earlier. Num. 13 : 20. **Of the fruit ;** that portion of the product which belonged to him as rent. The vineyard was let out on shares.

3. All the three evangelists show in their accounts of this parable that the husbandmen treated the servants worse and worse. The ground thought is the same in all ; but Mark is the most particular in describing the gradation of their crimes. Instead of cheerfully and honestly giving the servant the portion

A.D. 30.   MARK XII.   225

4 away empty. And again he sent unto them ¹an-
other servant; and at him they cast stones, and
wounded *him* in the head, and sent *him* away shame-
5 fully handled. And again he sent another; and
him they killed, and many others; beating some,
6 and killing some. Having yet therefore one son,
his wellbeloved, he sent him also ᵐlast unto them,
7 saying, They will reverence my son. But those husbandmen said among themselves, This is the heir;
come, let us kill him, and the inheritance shall be
8 ours. And they took him, and killed *him*, and cast
9 *him* out of the vineyard. What shall therefore the
lord of the vineyard do? he will come and destroy
the husbandmen, and will give the vineyard unto

¹ 2 Chr. 36. 15.

ᵐ Heb. 1. 1; Ps. 2. 2, 7; 22. 12, 16.

of fruit which was due the owner, **they caught him** (rather *took him*) **and beat him** severely with rods or with their fists, and sent him away empty.

4. The husbandmen treated the second servant worse than the first: **At him they cast stones,** a common way of putting to death among the Jews (Deut. 21:21; Josh. 7:25; Acts 7:58), but in this case not resulting in death, as the immediate connection shows. It was a contemptuous act of violence, resulting in a severe wound, **wounded him in the head,** almost fatally. **Shamefully handled,** treated with dishonor, outraged, shamefully treated. According to some most ancient manuscripts, this verse should read, "And again he sent unto them another servant; and they wounded him in the head and treated him shamefully." Mark's manner and the form of the discourse at this point favor the fuller expression. The beating and sending away empty of the preceding verse are in this naturally followed by the wounding in the head with stones and sending away shamefully treated.

5. The climax of ill-treatment attains its height in this verse. The third servant is killed. **And many others.** Briefly expressed, meaning, And in like manner they maltreated many other servants. Thus the three servants just specified were only selections from many examples.

6. The owner perseveres with wonderful patience in his peaceful endeavors to obtain from these lawless husbandmen his due. Having exhausted every resource, having sent every servant that could have any influence, he now sends his *beloved son*. Mark alone records that it was his **one son,** his *one beloved son.* **They will reverence,** etc. They will so respect and revere my son as to heed what he says, and pay the rent.

7. **The heir.** The one to whom the vineyard would at length belong. **Come, let us kill him.** Compare the similar language of the sons of Jacob concerning their brother Joseph, Gen. 37:20. **The inheritance shall be ours.** Thus, in opposition to the great clemency and wonderful patience of the owner, these wicked men consulted among themselves and plotted against him. When the only son and heir was destroyed, they thought to hold the vineyard as their own. The parable presents an extreme case. But it is not necessary to regard it unlifelike or fictitious. Doubtless his hearers could recall similar agreements violently broken. In the unsettled state of the country, we can conceive that an atrocious case, as the one here presented, could have happened.

8. They put their fiendish plans into execution. **Killed him and cast him out of the vineyard,** which seems to mean both killing and contemptuous treatment of his dead body. But both Matthew (21:39) and Luke (20:15) put the casting out before the killing. Compare 1 Kings 21:13. It would seem, therefore, that no great stress is to be put on the order of the words, other than that the heartless and inhuman cruelty of the murder is thus exhibited.

9. **What shall therefore,** etc. Rather, *What will therefore the lord of the*

vineyard do? Not merely what *would* he do, nor what *can* he do, but, such being the terrible state of things, what *will* he do? There seems to be some transition, or at least a reference, from the parable to the things signified among the Jewish people. **He will come and destroy the husbandmen,** etc. Isa. 5 : 4, 5. According to Matthew (21 : 41) the Jewish rulers give this answer, and thus pass sentence upon themselves. But here and in Luke (20 : 16) Jesus seems to answer the question himself. It is not impossible, however, to regard the answer even here, as given by some one of the chief priests, elders or scribes. But it is better to suppose that Jesus repeated the answer, to give it emphasis and his approval. And as he repeated it, the people seemed to have caught the meaning of the parable, for, according to Luke (20 : 16), they exclaimed, *God forbid!* or rather, May it not be! Far be it! Let it never happen!

The parable being completed, it is best at this point to consider its meaning. Its *grand design* was to shadow forth the rejection of the Jewish people on account of their rejection of the prophets, and especially of the Messiah. Verses 1-7 referred to the past; verse 8 and onward was prophetic. The *center of comparison* is found in the ungrateful and cruel treatment of the servants and son on the one hand; and the righteous judgment upon the husbandmen, on the other. The *man* or *lord* of the vineyard represents God the Father; the *husbandmen*, the Jewish people, as is evident from Matt. 21 : 43, "The kingdom of God shall be taken from you, and given to a nation bringing forth the fruits in their seasons." The chief priests and Pharisees, being both the civil and religious leaders, representatives and rulers of the people, could very truly regard the parable as against them, ch. 12 : 12. The *vineyard* cannot here represent, as in Isa. 5 : 1, the Jewish people, for they are already represented by the husbandmen; but rather, the religious blessings and privileges intrusted to them as a people; the *true religion* as revealed in the word of God, Rom. 9 : 4, 5.

The minute details in regard to the vineyard need not be pressed closely. The *planting* may be said to have occurred under Moses and Joshua, Ps. 80 : 8. The *hedge*, "the middle wall of partition" between Jews and Gentiles, Eph. 2 : 14. It has been noted by commentators that Palestine is geographically hedged around, east by the river Jordan, south by the desert and mountainous country of Idumæa, west by the Mediterranean, and north by the mountains of Lebanon. Compare Ps. 125 : 2; Zech. 2 : 5. The *wine-press* may represent the services, ordinances and ceremonies in which the people could engage for the glory of God and their own spiritual advantage; the *tower*, the office of the watchman, Isa. 62 : 6. The *letting it out to husbandmen* may refer to the solemn covenants between God and the people, as at the giving of the law, Ex. 20 : 19; 24 : 7, 8. The householder *going to another country* can also be used to represent the withholdment of such open revelations as upon Sinai, and the speaking face to face with Moses, Deut. 34 : 10-12. The *fruit* represents the wise improvement of their gifts and blessings, the bringing to God not only the service of their lips, but also their hearts (Isa. 5 : 4; 29 : 13); the tithes, offerings, prayers, and labors, Mal. 3 : 8-10; Rom. 7 : 4.

The *servants* sent by the householder represent the prophets. A period of about three hundred and eight years intervened between the death of Moses and the call of Samuel to be a prophet. Though there were prophets during the Judges, yet the more conspicuous prophets began with Samuel, continuing till Malachi, and ending with John the Baptist, Matt. 11 : 13. The treatment they received accords well with the language of the parable. Thus, the children of Israel preferred a king to Samuel in his old age, 1 Sam. 8 : 6-8; 12 : 12, 13. Elijah was persecuted by Ahab, 1 Kings 18 : 10-12. Isaiah, according to Jewish tradition, was sawn asunder by King Manasseh. Zechariah, the son of Jehoiada, was stoned to death, 2 Chron. 24 : 20-22. Jeremiah was imprisoned (Jer. 37 : 15) and, according to tradition, was stoned by the exiles in Egypt. Compare also 1 Kings 22 : 26-28; 2 Chron. 36 : 16; Neh. 9 : 26; Matt. 27 : 37; Acts 7 : 52; Heb. 11 : 36-38.

The *son* represents Christ, who was sent after a long series of revelations and prophets, Heb. 1 : 1, 2. He is the only-begotten and well-beloved Son, the Son of God in the highest sense, ch. 1 : 11; John 1 : 14; Heb. 1 : 3-9. He

A.D. 30. MARK XII. 225

10 others. And have ye not read this Scripture; ᵃ 'The ᵇ Ps. 118. 22, 23.
stone which the builders rejected is become the

is the "*heir* of all things," Heb. 1 : 2. Thus, in parabolic language, Jesus answers the question of the chief priests and elders, in ch. 11 : 28. He had done "these things" by the authority of the Son. The language, *They will reverence my son*, presents the human side, as it would seem to men, to intelligent creatures who had no knowledge of the future. It was their duty to reverence the Son of God. It was reasonable to suppose that they would have reverenced their long-expected Messiah. God's foreknowledge of their wicked conduct did not affect their freedom and their duty. They acted without compulsion. The *killing of the son* points to the crucifixion, ch. 15: 24 ; Acts 3 : 13-15. And as the son was *cast out of the vineyard*, so Jesus "suffered without the gate," Heb. 13 : 12, 13 ; Mark 15 : 20-23. Compare 1 Kings 21 : 13 ; Acts 7 : 58. The *reason* for killing the son, *that the enheritance may be ours*, must not be pressed too closely. The very nature of sin is robbery ; the sinner robs God, and would usurp his place and authority. So the Jewish people, in rejecting Christ, wanted their own way, and were determined to have it. They were robbers, murderers, and usurpers. John 11 : 47-53 throws light on their feelings and motives a little time before uttering this parable. They feared lest *all* should *believe on him*, and they would lose their power and position ; they also feared, or professed to fear, lest the people should make him king, and the *Romans come and take away* their *place* and *nation*.

Thus far the parable represents the patience and forbearance of God in sending his servants, the prophets, and last, his Son. What more could he have done? Isa. 5 : 4, 5. After receiving such ungrateful and cruel treatment from their hands, what was left but to punish ? Isa. 5 : 5, 6.

The *coming of the Lord of the vineyard*, and the *destruction* of these husbandmen, represent the coming of God in judgment upon the Jewish nation, in the destruction of Jerusalem, when "their house was left unto them desolate" (Luke 13 : 35), and they suffered "affliction such as was not from the beginning of the creation," ch. 13 : 19. At Jerusalem alone, it is said, 1,100,000 perished by the sword, famine and pestilence. Besides, 97,000 were sold as slaves, and vast multitudes perished in other parts of Judea. Compare Matt. 23 : 34-36. *The giving the vineyard unto others* represents the rejection of the Jews and the calling of the Gentiles, Rom. 9 : 30, 31 ; 11 : 9, 10.

10. Jesus further rivets the application of the parable by quoting an ancient prophecy, and thereby intimating, at the same time, that the son who had been left dead would come to life again and be the Head of the people of God. **Have ye not read this scripture ?** You surely have read it. The scripture quoted is Ps. 118 : 22, and in the words of the Septuagint version. The Jews applied it to the Messiah ; from it (vers. 25, 26) the multitude had derived their hosannas at the public entry of Jesus into Jerusalem, ch. 11 : 9, 10. As the multitude had applied this Psalm to Jesus, so Jesus now applies it to himself as the Christ. **The stone,** in the figurative language of prophecy, was Christ. This is regarded as a typical prophecy, some referring its typical fulfillment to David, who was disallowed and rejected by Saul and the ruling men of the nation, and yet was chosen to be king of Israel ; others refer it to Zerubbabel (Zech. 3 : 8, 9 ; 4 : 7) ; and others still to Mordecai ; its special and complete fulfillment was in Christ. Compare on Matt. 1 : 22, 23. **The builders** were the Jews, John 19 : 15. **Rejected.** *Disapproved, disallowed.* They did not allow the claims of Jesus. **Head of the corner.** The head-stone, or corner-stone ; the stone that lies at the foundation of the building, where the two walls come together, binding them firmly, and giving the building its strength and support. Thus Christ is the support of the spiritual building, the "holy temple in the Lord." Eph. 2 : 20-22 ; 1 Cor. 3 : 11. Though the Jews rejected Jesus, yet God has made him the head-stone of his spiritual temple (Acts 4 : 10, 11) ; uniting both Jews and Gentiles in himself, Gal. 3 : 28. He is highly exalted as a Prince and Savior, Acts 2 : 33-36 ; 5 : 29-31 ; Phil. 2 : 9-11. Compare 1 Pet. 2 : 7, where the prophecy is quoted with a similar application.

226　　　　　　　　MARK XII.　　　　　　A.D. 30.

11 head of the corner. This was the Lord's doing, and it is marvellous in our eyes'?
12 º And they sought to lay hold on him, but feared the people: for they knew that he had spoken the parable against them: and they left him, and went their way.

º ch. 11. 18; Mt. 21. 45, 46; John 7. 25, 30, 44.

Concerning the payment of tribute to Cæsar.

13 ᴾ AND they send unto him certain of the Pharisees and of the Herodians, to catch him in *his* words.
14 And when they were come, they say unto him, Master, we know that thou art true, and carest for

ᴾ Mt. 22. 15; Lk. 20. 20; Ps. 56. 5, 6; Heb. 12. 3.

---

11. **This was the Lord's doing.** *This is from the Lord,* namely, that the stone which was disallowed should become the head-stone of the corner, and it is **marvellous,** *wonderful,* in our eyes. A wonderful display of wisdom, grace, mercy and power in its accomplishment. Matthew adds a further application: the kingdom of God taken from them and given to a nation bringing forth fruit; and, with Luke, presents the stone as a stumbling-stone, and also as a stone of retribution, Matt. 21 : 43, 44; Luke 20 : 18.
12. The effect of the parable upon the chief priests, scribes and elders. They had already resolved to kill Jesus (John 11 : 53), and now, perceiving that he had spoken the **parable against them,** with direct reference to them, and with a prophetic allusion to them, they are enraged, and seek some means whereby they may **lay hold of him;** but they fear the **people,** who regarded him as a divinely commissioned teacher, Matt. 21 : 46; John 7 : 49; 12 : 19. Seeing that they could accomplish nothing, either by word or by open violence, **they left him,** thus ending the direct conflict between Jesus and the rulers on that day; **and went their way,** to plot against him privately, oppose him indirectly, and by some means accomplish their purpose, Matt. 22 : 15. At this point Matthew gives the parable of the Marriage of the King's Son.

13–17. THE CUNNING ATTACK OF THE PHARISEES AND HERODIANS, AND THEIR DEFEAT. CONCERNING PAYING TRIBUTE TO CÆSAR. Matt. 22 : 15–22; Luke 20 : 20–26. The three accounts are very similar, with the usual differences of independent narrators.

13. **They send.** The rulers who had a little before left him. Matthew mentions the Pharisees, who were the leaders of the opposition, and probably formed the principal ones of those who had questioned his authority. **Certain of the Pharisees,** their disciples, pupils and followers, young and unknown persons, Matt. 22 : 16. Luke (20 : 20) says "sent forth spies which should feign themselves just men." **And of the Herodians.** See on ch. 3 : 6. Enemies meet in their common hatred to Jesus. The Pharisees hated and opposed the Herodians, but they hated Jesus so much more that they could unite with them in their opposition to him. The Herodians probably united with the Pharisees from political and selfish motives. Herod Antipas was desirous of obtaining the title of king from the Roman emperor; and if his friends could rid Palestine of one who opposed Roman dominion and aspired to be king of the Jews, it might work to Herod's advantage.

To catch him in his words; *to ensnare* or *entrap him with a word,* supposing that he must answer either *yes* or *no* to their question in ver. 14. They thought that by the utterance of a single word in answer, he must fatally involve himself in his relations either to the government or the people. Their object was to find a civil or ecclesiastical accusation against him. Supposing that he would probably give a negative answer, they thought thereby to "deliver him unto the governor," Luke 20 : 20.

14. **Master, we know,** etc. *Teacher, we know.* They affirm what is true, but hypocritically. Nicodemus used similar language, but sincerely. They

no man: for thou regardest not the person of men, but teachest the way of God in truth: Is it lawful 15 to give tribute to Cæsar, or not? Shall we give, ᵠ Jer. 18. 18. or shall we not give? But he, knowing their hypocrisy, said unto them, Why tempt ye me? Bring

came to Jesus not as Pharisees or Herodians, but as just men, hoping by their words to hide their character and purpose, and by flattering Jesus to put him off his guard and lead him into the snare set for him. They pretended to acknowledge him to be all that he claimed, and to be ready to abide by his decisions, since they would be absolutely true and just, independent of the influence and authority of men. **Carest for no man.** A strong expression in the original. Thou art entirely independent, being influenced neither by the censure nor the applause of any one. **Thou regardest not the person of men.** Thou art not influenced by rank or position, not even by Cæsar himself, in thy decisions, but art perfectly impartial, Lev. 19 : 15. **The way of God.** The way that God has marked out for men to walk in, Ps. 27 : 11. **In truth.** Truly, as it is, without any addition or diminution.

Is it lawful, is it right for us as Jews, the chosen people of God, Luke 20 : 22. The question is not whether it was advisable, but whether it was lawful for them, who acknowledged God as their King. **To give tribute.** The Roman poll-tax imposed on all males from fourteen, and on females from twelve to sixty. **Cæsar.** The family name of Julius Cæsar, the first Roman emperor, and applied to his successors, whether of his family or not, as a designation of their office, and a representation of Roman power. The Cæsar then reigning was the Emperor Tiberius. **Or not?** The question was so put as to require, as they thought, the answer, either yes or no. They would rather have him answer in the negative, for then they would "deliver him into the power and authority of the governor" as a seditious person, Luke 20 : 20. But if he answered in the affirmative, then they would accuse him before the people as opposed to the law of God. The Herodians, as friends of Herod, and hence of the Roman supremacy, were in favor of paying tribute. The Pharisees generally espoused the popular Jewish sentiment, that paying tribute to a foreign power was a badge of servitude, and even contrary to the law of Moses. Thus Judas, the Gaulonite (Acts 5 : 35), had raised an insurrection in opposition to levying this tax, holding that it was unlawful, and even rebellion against God for the Jews to pay tribute and submit to a foreign power. These sentiments were extensively promulgated; and the Jewish people, who were very restless under the Roman yoke, quite generally espoused, or sympathized in them. This was, however, a fanatical view of the law, since the Jews were nowhere forbidden to pay tribute to a foreign conqueror. They were only forbidden to set a stranger over them as king, Deut. 17 : 15. They had, at different times, paid heavy tribute to Syria and Babylon.

15. Mark alone gives the vivid addition, **Shall we give, or shall we not give?** by which the Pharisees and Herodians would push Jesus to an immediate answer, yes or no. They thought they had brought him to a point where he must speak out, either as a rebel against Cæsar, or a traitor to God, whose prophet or son he professed to be. **But he, knowing their hypocrisy,** their dissimulation and false pretenses, that they were assuming a character and disposition which did not belong to them. "Feigning themselves to be just men," Luke 20 : 20. **Why tempt ye me?** Why entice me to say something which you can use against me? Why do you try to draw me into a snare, so as to entrap me? Then, instead of answering as they expected, he calls for a coin in which the Roman tax was paid, so that he might address the eye as well as the ear. **A penny;** a dinary, a Roman silver coin, worth about fifteen cents. It was a current maxim of Jewish teachers, that "wherever a king's coin is current, there his sovereignty is acknowledged." It was an evidence of the Roman dominion over the land,

16 me a penny, that I may see *it*. And they brought
it. And he saith unto them, Whose *is* this image
and superscription? And they said unto him,
17 Cæsar's. And Jesus answering said unto them,
Render to Cæsar the things that are Cæsar's, and to
God the things that are God's. And they marvelled at him.

ʳ Mt. 4. 10; 17, 25-27; Ac. 5. 29.

that Roman currency was used; and, by using it, the Jews acknowledged their subjection to the Roman power.

ROMAN DENARIUS.

Jesus also adds, **that I may see it,** as if he would for the first time handle and examine the coin. But he was about to teach an object-lesson from it, and he wishes to see it so as to direct attention specially to it.

16. **They brought it.** We may conceive of Jesus receiving it, and for a moment looking at it and holding it in his hand, thus riveting attention and exciting expectation; and then asking, **Whose is this image and superscription?** or *inscription*. The *image* was probably the likeness of the Roman emperor, Tiberius Cæsar. The *inscription* was the motto of the coin, the title of the emperor, declarative of his sovereignty. The image showed that it was not a Jewish, but a foreign coin, for the Jews put no images on their coins, though they put inscriptions on them. **Cæsar's.** Both the coin and their answer showed that they were peacefully submitting to Cæsar's government, and enjoying his protection.

17. Everything is now ready for the answer of Jesus. **Render.** *Pay off.* The idea is not *rendering a gift*, but rendering what is *due*. **The things that are Cæsar's.** Render to Cæsar whatever is due to him, what rightfully belongs to him; if you are under his government, obey him and pay him fully for his protection, so long as you violate no divine obligation. He does not discuss a political question, nor the right or wrong of Roman supremacy; but taking their condition as it really was, the Roman power peacefully acknowledged and its protection enjoyed, he teaches that they should pay toward its support, and render to it whatever was rightfully its due. Paul expands this idea in Rom. 13 : 1-7. The Jews themselves taught that a king ought to have his dues, whether he was a king of the Jews or of the Gentiles. **The things that are God's.** And since in the highest sense you are under God's government, preserved, protected, and supported by him, render to him whatever is due to him as your God and King—your obedience and the whole circle of religious duty. The two precepts are in harmony, and the one really flowing out of the other. As love to our neighbor is in harmony with, and flows from, love to God, so rendering all rightful obedience to human government is in harmony with, and springs from, discharging our full obligation to God, 1 Tim. 2 : 1, 2 ; 1 Pet. 2 : 13-16. There is no reference, much less any sanction of union of church and state.

"Man is the coinage, and bears the image of God, Gen. 1 : 27; 9 : 6; Acts 17 : 29; James 3 : 9. . . . We owe, then, *ourselves* to God ; and this solemn duty is implied, of going ourselves to him, with all that we have and are. The answer also gives them the real reason why they were now under subjection to Cæsar, namely, because they had fallen from their allegiance to God," 2 Chron. 12 : 5-8.—ALFORD.

They marvelled at him. They wondered at a reply so unexpected, so apt and true, and at his wisdom in escaping their snare. He maintained both the rights of government and the rights of God, and in such a manner that neither party could accuse him. The wisdom of his reply may well command our admiration. He laid down a great moral principle, which is applicable in every age of the world, and

Concerning the resurrection.

18 ᵃThen come unto him the Sadducees, ᵇwhich say there is no resurrection; and they asked him, say-
19 ing, Master, ᶜMoses wrote unto us, If a man's brother die, and leave *his* wife *behind him*, and leave no children, that his brother should take his wife, and
20 ᵈraise up seed unto his brother. Now there were seven brethren: and the first took a wife, and dying
21 left no seed. And the second took her, and died,

ᵃ Mt. 22. 23; Lk. 20. 27.
ᵇ Ac. 23. 8; 1 Cor. 15. 12-14; 2 Tim. 2. 18.
ᶜ Deu. 25. 5.
ᵈ Ru. 1. 11, 13.

which, if properly carried out, will conduce to the highest good of man and to the glory of God. No wonder that his interrogators " could not take hold of his words and held their peace" (Luke 20 : 26); that they " left him and went their way " (Matt. 22 : 22), sensible of overwhelming defeat.

18–27. THE QUESTION OF THE SADDUCEES CONCERNING THE RESURRECTION. THE REPLY OF JESUS. Matt. 22 : 23–33; Luke 20 : 27–40. Luke is the fullest; Matthew the briefest. Mark holds a middle place, but exhibits his usual descriptive style. This attack of the Sadducees was less artful and insidious than the preceding one of the Pharisees and Herodians. Their question was most frivolous, and their design seems to have been to throw contempt, not merely on the doctrine of the resurrection, which they denied, but especially upon Jesus, by any answer he might give.

18. Then come unto him. Rather, *And there come to him.* There is no note of time. Matthew says, " On the same day," or *that day*, on which the Pharisees and Herodians were baffled and put to silence; probably a short time after. **The Sadducees.** Simply, *Sadducees*, there being no article in the original. The Sadducees were a Jewish sect, and were so called either from *righteousness*, the meaning of their name, or from Zadok, some distinguished individual (1 Kings 1 : 32; 2 Chron. 31 : 10), or, as some suppose, the founder of the sect about B. C. 260. They were opposed to the Pharisees, and rightly rejected tradition, and that God gave it, the oral law, to Moses; but they unhappily denied the resurrection and the existence of angels and spirits, Acts 23 : 8. They also laid special stress on the freedom of the will, while the Pharisees held strongly to the doctrine of providence. The opinion that the Sadducees held to only the five books of Moses is now given up. As a sect they disappear from history after the first century. They were mostly men of rank, wealth, and education; but the Pharisees were more numerous, and had greater influence with the people.

The word **resurrection**, as used in this and the following verses, appears to have a somewhat broader signification than merely rising from the dead, including not only the life that ensues, but also the life of the soul previous to the reunion of soul and body. Thus it is very nearly equivalent to future life, the rising from the dead being the central hinge around which that life turns. Compare the language in verse 23, " In the resurrection, therefore, when they shall rise."

19. Master. *Teacher,* ver. 14. They also approach him with apparent regard as a prophet or religious teacher. **Moses wrote unto us.** Rejecting all human tradition, they acknowledge the writings of Moses as authority, and as pre-eminent authority. The law which they cite is found in Deut. 25 : 5, 6, and was designed to prevent any family of Israel from becoming extinct. The case stated in the following verses was very likely fictitious, and took for granted that if there was a resurrection, the present relations of life must continue in the future state. The Sadducees thought thus to show from the law the manifest absurdity of the doctrine. It may have been a favorite argument of theirs with the Pharisees, and illustrates the manner of their opposition. **Seed unto his brother;** the first born was regarded as the offspring of his deceased brother.

20, 21, 22. Having quoted the law, they now state the case formally and

neither left he any seed: and the third likewise. 22 And the seven had her, and left no seed. Last of 23 all the woman died also. In the resurrection therefore, when they shall rise, whose wife shall she be of them? For the seven had her to wife. 24 And Jesus answering said unto them, ˣ Do ye not therefore err, because ye know not the Scriptures, 25 neither the power of God? For when they shall rise from the dead, they neither marry, nor are given in marriage; but ʸ are as the angels which are

ˣ Ps. 17. 15; 49. 14, 15; 119. 130; Is. 26. 19; Dan. 12. 2; Hos. 13. 14; Jno. 5. 39; 20. 9.
ʸ 1 Cor. 15. 42, 49, 52.

with great particularity. They doubtless made it as ludicrous as possible. **The seven had her;** *the seven took her.* The Sadducees speak of it as an actual fact, especially according to Matt. 22: 25, "There was with us." Some suppose it founded on the apocryphal book of Tobit 3: 7, 8, "Sara the daughter of Raguel was also reproached by her father's maids, because she had been married to seven husbands." It may have been a long-disputed problem never before solved. In the case of two husbands the rabbins taught that the wife would belong to the first in the next world. But here were seven. What would the great teacher say to that?

23. **In the resurrection.** In the resurrection state or life; the state of being into which the resurrection issues. **When they,** the seven brothers and wife, **shall rise,** as the Pharisees and others say. Some ancient manuscripts omit this phrase; so also the later critics. **Whose wife should she be?** The Pharisees appear to have held that the relationships of this life would continue in the future state. And with no other conception of the doctrine the Sadducees foresaw a certain conflict between these seven brothers. All, then, cannot have her, but only one; yet none has a claim upon her above the rest. Whose wife, then? They see here, as they suppose, an insurmountable difficulty to supposing a resurrection life. It would be a state of confusion, with interests and relationships which could never be justly settled. And besides, as this case grew out of a Mosaic enactment, it was evident, as they thought, that Moses never intended to reveal a resurrection and a future life. Their object was not to have their question solved, but rather to puzzle Jesus, or to draw forth some expression which they could use against him. They could not expect him to deny the resurrection; for he had raised Lazarus from the dead, and had repeatedly inculcated the doctrine. He was doubtless known to side with the Pharisees in this respect. But they hoped to bring him into conflict with the law of Moses, or induce him to utter that which they could construe into blasphemy, or turn into ridicule.

24. Jesus answers them differently from what they expected. He at once points out the error underlying their question: first showing their mistake through ignorance, and then expounding a passage in point from the law. **Do ye not therefore err?** Do ye not go astray or wander from the truth on this account, namely, your two-fold ignorance of Scripture and the power of God? Mark alone puts this in form of a question, but equal to a strong affirmative declaration. **Because ye know not the Scriptures;** ye do not understand them in their deep spiritual import, especially in regard to a future existence. Jesus refers to the Old Testament as the authoritative word of God. **Neither the power of God;** which can and will remove all obstacles in way of a future life, as taught in his word. Since God is omnipotent, the dead can be raised; and they will be raised since God has taught that they shall be. The same two-fold ignorance and unbelief lie at the foundation of the principal objections to the doctrine of the resurrection at the present day, Acts 26: 8; Rom. 4: 17; 1 Cor. 6: 14; 15: 34–36.

25. **For.** Jesus proceeds to show their ignorance, as charged against them in the preceding verse. **When they shall rise;** when people shall rise at the last great day. In that state which is ushered in by the resurrection.

26 in heaven. And as touching the dead, that they rise: have ye not read in the book of Moses, how in the bush God spake unto him, saying, "I am the God of Abraham, and the God of Isaac, and the *Ex. 3. 6, 16; Ac. 7. 32; Heb. 11. 16.

From the dead. The expression, *from among the dead*, may point to the glorified condition of the saints. From Luke 20:35, we learn that the reference is to the resurrection state of the righteous. The resurrection of both righteous and wicked is taught elsewhere, John 5:28, 29. All the Jews except the Sadducees held to the resurrection of all mankind. **Neither marry.** With reference to males. **Nor given in marriage.** With reference to females, who, among the Jews, were given in marriage by their fathers. **But are as the angels;** rather *as angels*, omitting the article; not constituted for the marriage relation. Their existence, relations and state will be similar to those of angels; not earthly, sensual and mortal, but heavenly, spiritual and immortal. "Neither can they die any more; for they are equal unto the angels, and are the children (*sons*) of God," Luke 20:36. Being themselves immortal, they are not dependent on the marriage relation for the preservation of their species. As no such relation exists among angels, so it will not exist among the saints in heaven. As the righteous will be as angels; the wicked will be as fallen angels or demons.

26. **And as touching** (*And concerning*) **the dead, that they rise.** The *dead* here refers not merely to the bodies of those who have died, but to their disembodied spirits—with reference, indeed, to their being reunited to their bodies and raised. The Hebrew had a distinct word, *rapha*, which refers to that part of man which survives death, and was a distinct name for that separate existence, Job 26:5; Ps. 88:10; Prov. 2:18; 9:18; 21:16; Isa. 14:9; 26:14, 19. **Have ye not read,** in proof of the resurrection, and of the future life which it implies. **In the book of Moses,** the five books taken as a whole, the law from which the Sadducees had just quoted. **How in the bush.** Rather, *At the bush*, at the passage relating to the burning bush, Ex. 3:1 ff. *Bush* denotes the section in the Pentateuch where the quotation about to be given is found. Jesus aptly appeals to Moses inasmuch as the Sadducees had just drawn their argument from Moses. Some affirm, and others deny, that the Sadducees rejected all the other parts of the Holy Scriptures but the five books of Moses. The true statement seems to be, that they rejected all tradition, and received only the written law, and that they held that the five books of Moses should be greatly preferred above the rest of the Old Testament, and regarded as the only ultimate standard of appeal for all doctrine. We thus see another reason why Jesus appeals to Moses, since they regarded his writings of the highest authority. He, however, implies, according to Luke, that he might have appealed to the strong testimonies of other Scripture (Isa. 26:19; Ezek. 37:1-14; Dan. 12:2); "*Even* Moses showed," Luke 20:37.

I am the God of Abraham, etc., Ex. 3:6. The living and eternal God, bearing a personal relation, as the living God, to Abraham and to Isaac and to Jacob, which supposes that those patriarchs were still bearing a living and personal relation to him as his servants, and also implies he will not suffer them always to remain under the power of the grave, but will, in due time, raise them to a glorified life. Jehovah is the **I am,** the ever-faithful, the unchangeable, the living and eternal God. He was the personal God of the patriarchs. That he continued this personal relation implies their continued existence. Since he declares, "*I am* the God of Abraham," etc., their God absolutely and without reference to time, that is, eternally, their immortality is implied. And since he was the God of their whole existence, body and soul, it is implied that, though the relation between their bodies and souls be suspended for a time, they will be reunited ere long in an endless existence.

It does not follow that these inferences and truths thus brought out were plain on the surface of this declaration to Moses, or that they would ever in this world have been clearly

27 God of Jacob'? He is not the God of the dead, but the God of the living. Ye therefore do greatly err.

The great commandment.

28 ᵃAnd one of the scribes came, and having heard them reasoning together, and perceiving that he had answered them well, asked him, Which is the first • Mt. 22. 31.

---

seen or thoroughly understood without revelation. It is enough to know that Jesus has authoritatively brought them to light, and that when thus revealed they come with the beauty and the internal testimony of truth. They came home to the hearts of the Sadducees and others, who heard Jesus, with convincing power, ver. 28; Matt. 22 : 33, 34. The various objections, therefore, against our Lord's interpretation of this passage are of no force. Christ's words are authority, and these words of his bear along with them their own evidences of truth.

27. Not the God of the dead ; in the sense of *extinct*, as the Sadducees used the word *dead*. God is not the God of the non-existent. He can bear no relation to a nonentity. **But the God of the living ;** of those who continue to live. He can only bear a relation to the living. The souls of the patriarchs, their essential being, were still living; their bodies, the less important part, had indeed died, yet still existed in matter, and the fact that Jehovah was God of the living was a pledge that this suspension of bodily existence was only temporary. The additional idea of a covenant-keeping God is fitting here, since "*I am the God of Abraham,*" etc., may briefly express the blessing pertaining to a covenant relation to God. Compare Deut. 26: 16; Isa. 41: 10; Zech. 13: 9; Heb. 11: 16. Abraham, Isaac, and Jacob must be living; for the blessings and promises of this covenant can only be enjoyed by the living; and the full enjoyment of them must be in connection with the most perfect life and the highest state of being, their glorified and immortal bodily existence. Mark alone states the concluding application, **Ye therefore do greatly err,** or, according to the highest critical authorities, *Ye greatly err,* in your interpretation of Scripture, and in rejecting the doctrine of the resurrection.

Mark does not stop to describe the effect of this reasoning upon the hearers, but only incidentally remarks in the next verse that the scribes perceived that Jesus "had answered them well." Luke records of the Sadducees, "After that they durst not ask him any question." And Matthew states that the multitude "were astonished at his doctrine." The Sadducees were put to silence. The scribes could not but admire, and the multitude were astonished at the light thrown upon a doctrine about which they had confused and gross conceptions.

28–34. JESUS REPLIES TO A SCRIBE CONCERNING THE GREAT COMMANDMENT OF THE LAW. Matt. 22 : 34–40. Compare Luke 10 : 25–29. Matthew's account is the briefer and more general; Mark's the fuller and the more particular; he alone records the reply of the scribe, and the final reply of Jesus, vers. 32–34.

28. One of the scribes. See on ch. 1 : 22. Matthew (22 : 35) says, "One of them," that is, of the Pharisees, "a lawyer," one learned in the law. The scribes were mostly Pharisees, and this one acted as speaker for those assembled there. They would gladly have seen Jesus ensnared by the Sadducees; but the latter had been so thoroughly routed and put to silence, that it caused much pleasant emotion among the scribes and Pharisees. **Perceiving that he had answered them well,** rightly and aptly, admirably. Matthew says that he "asked, tempting him," which shows the design of the assembled Pharisees, for whom this scribe spoke, and very likely his own design till he heard Christ's reply to the Sadducees. Mark presents him simply as an individual, and thus separated from the party to which he belonged. Individually he was pleased with what Jesus had just said, and privately he desired to know the opinion of Jesus upon the question he proposed.

29 commandment of all? And Jesus answered him, The first of all the commandments is, ᵇ 'Hear, O Israel; The Lord our God is one Lord: and thou 30 shalt love the Lord thy God with all thy heart, and with all thy soul, and with all thy mind, and with all thy strength': this is the first commandment.
31 And the second is like, *namely* this, ᶜ 'Thou shalt love thy neighbour as thyself.' There is none other commandment greater than these.

ᵇ Deu. 6. 4, 5; Lk. 10. 27.

ᶜ Lev. 19. 18; Mt. 22. 39; Ro. 13. 9; Gal. 5. 14; Jam. 2. 8.

In the question itself there was nothing malicious, as in that regarding the tribute; only in the use that might be made of the answer. **Which is the first commandment of all?** *What kind of commandment, or What commandment is first of all?* The principal and chief in importance. There seems to be some reference to the quality as well as to the preeminence of the command. The scribes made numerous distinctions and classifications of the law, dividing the commandments, six hundred and thirteen in number, into greater and less, giving preference to the letter rather than to the spirit, and to the ceremonial rather than the moral. The Jewish doctors were by no means agreed as to which precept was pre-eminent; some contending for the law of sacrifices, others for that of circumcision, others for that of meats, washing, phylacteries, etc. As a rule among them, the law of the Sabbath was to give way to the law of circumcision, John 7: 22. This was one of the *strifes* about the law, Tit. 3: 9. On a question which had been long discussed, doubtless the scribe felt a curiosity to know the opinion of Jesus.

29. Jesus replies by giving the great law of love, first, to God; second, to men. He gives not any one precept of the decalogue, but a comprehensive summary found in Deut. 6: 5 and Lev. 19: 18. The first passage was a part of the Scripture on the Jewish phylacteries, the quotation of which may have made the well-disposed scribe even better disposed. That he felt its spiritual import to some extent appears in ver. 33. **Hear, O Israel.** This is also a quotation from the passage which the Jew repeated morning and evening, every day, and was a precept held in great esteem. **The Lord our God.** This is the foundation of all the commandments. Out of this relation grows directly or indirectly all moral duties. Or, *the Lord,* Jehovah, *is our God, the Lord is one,* in contrast to the false gods which the heathen worshiped.

30. **Thy God.** Hence you should love him. Whatever be the thoughts or desires of men, Jehovah is *their* God, and this fact should call forth their supreme love. **Heart.** Desires, feelings and affections. **Soul.** Sentiments, passions and vital bodily powers. **Mind.** Will and intellectual powers. **Strength.** Might, ability. We must not expect here the nice distinctions of philosophical language. Whatever be the exact differences in these four terms, they together express the whole man with all his affections and powers, in the inner and outer life. The command equals, Thou shalt love God supremely. **This is the first commandment,** in order and in importance. Some of the oldest manuscripts omit these words. According to Matthew, "This is the great and first commandment," in its nature, order, rank and importance; involving a principle lying at the foundation of all goodness and of every proper affection.

31. Jesus had really answered the question of the scribe; but he would not have him stop there, nor consider other commands unimportant. **And the second is like, namely this.** Of the same kind, a part of the great law of love. Some of the oldest manuscripts read, *Second is this;* second in importance, second great command. As the first command is a summary of the first table of the law, of the duties we owe to God; so the second is a summary of the second table, the duties we owe to men. Supreme love to God involves indirectly proper love to our fellow-men; and a right love toward men presupposes and springs from true

32 And the scribe said unto him, Well, Master, thou hast said the truth: for there is one God; ᵈ and
33 there is none other but he: and to love him with all the heart, and with all the understanding, and with all the soul, and with all the strength, and to love *his* neighbour as himself, ᵉ is more than all whole

ᵈ Deu. 4. 39; Is. 45. 6, 14; 46. 9.

ᵉ 1 Sam. 15. 22; Pro. 21. 3; Hos. 6. 6; Mic. 6. 6–8.

love to God, Rom. 13 : 9 ; 1 John 4 : 20, 21. The two commands are thus alike in nature, springing from the same source, yet they are distinct. **Thy neighbor.** Thy fellow-man. See Luke 10 : 29–37. **As thyself.** The Scriptures forbid *selfishness*, but not *self-love*. Self-love is an original principle in our nature, and, though the Scriptures do not command it, they take for granted and imply that men ought to exercise a proper love for themselves. It is not subject to the caprices of the will, as Alexander remarks, and is therefore wisely made the standard of men's love to one another. The command here is the inner life and principle of the golden rule. "God loves me as he loves thee ; and thee as he does me ; therefore I ought to love thee, my neighbor, as myself ; and thou me as thyself; for our love ought to correspond to God's love." —BENGEL. This answer of Jesus showed the Pharisees that their conduct toward him was a transgression of this law of love.

None other commandment greater than these; since they comprehend the substance of true religion. Thus Jesus gives pre-eminence to the law of love. "Of all our Savior's wise and happy answers to insidious or puzzling questions, this is the most exquisitely beautiful, because so unambiguous, so simple, so exactly corresponding to the form of the question, so evasive of its trifling and unprofitable element, so exhaustive and demonstrative of what was really important in it, and therefore so unchangeably instructive and so practically useful to the end of time."—J. A. ALEXANDER.

32. Mark alone records the effect of our Lord's answer upon the scribe. It came home to his heart with convincing power. Doubtless he never before saw so plainly the deep, spiritual truths of these commands. Entering into our Lord's reply, he cannot but express his approval and even admiration : **Well, Master;** rightly, admirably, Teacher. **The truth ;** in accordance with truth, *truly*. **For there is one God.** According to the highest critical authorities, *That he is one;* one in himself. The unity of God is thus affirmed. **And there is none other.** He is the only God. Hence he should have supreme and undivided affection, as the scribe goes on to say in the next verse. Compare 1 John 4 : 8. This reply is not merely a quotation from Moses, or a repetition of our Savior's answer, but a brief exposition and comment upon the great law of love.

33. In enumerating the parts of man which should be wholly devoted in love to God, Jesus had said *mind*, ver. 30. The scribe uses an equivalent, very nearly, **understanding,** discerning and intellectual power. **Is more than,** etc. Is more important, more valuable and more acceptable to God than all outward and ritual observances, Ps. 15 : 22 ; Ps. 51 : 16–19 ; Hos. 6 : 6. Under the law the rites and ceremonies not only were in harmony with the great law of love, but also that law was their very life. Without it they were worthless. The spirit of the true worshiper is presented in Ps. 66 : 13–16. **All whole burnt offerings and sacrifices.** Rather, *All the whole burnt-offerings*, etc. The whole burnt-offerings were the most costly kind of sacrifices, and were entirely consumed, typifying the whole work of expiation. "The meaning of the whole burnt-offering was that which is the original idea of all sacrifice, the offering of the sacrificer of himself, soul and body, to God ; the submission of his will to the will of God. It typified our Lord's offering (as especially in the Temptation and the Agony), the perfect sacrifice of his own human will to the will of his Father. As that offering could only be accepted from one either sinless or already purified from sin, therefore the burnt-offering was always preceded by a sin-offering, Ex. 29 : 36–38 ; Lev. 8 : 14; 9 : 8; 16 : 3, 5." *Sacrifices* here points to the *victims* of animal or bloody sacrifices, part of which was burned,

34 burnt offerings and sacrifices. And when Jesus saw that he answered discreetly, he said unto him, Thou art not far from the kingdom of God. ᶠAnd no man after that durst ask him *any question*.

ᶠ Mt. 22. 46; Rom. 3. 19.

The Christ the Son of David.

35 ᵍAnd Jesus answered and said, while he taught in the temple, How say the scribes that Christ is the

ᵍ Mt. 22. 41; Lk. 20. 41; 2 Sam. 23. 2; Ps. 110. 1.

and part eaten, Lev. 4 : 1-17 ; 1 Cor. 10 : 18. These whole burnt-offerings and sacrifices were the most important part of ritual observances, and may well stand in concise and popular expression as representing all of them. They may be regarded not only as typifying Christ, but as emblems of the spiritual sacrifices which we should offer to God, Ps. 51 : 17; Heb. 13 : 16; 1 Pet. 2 : 5.

34. The approving reply of Jesus. **Discreetly ;** *understandingly, intelligently.* He answered as one having understanding and right views of religion. He looked through externals to the fundamental principles of both the Law and Gospel, and of "the kingdom of God." **Not far from the kingdom of God.** He stood at its very door, and almost in the position of a true follower. The reference is principally to intellectual perceptions of truth. He apprehended the spiritual duties and service of God's kingdom, and needed but the moral disposition to be within it. He had discernment of moral duty, but he wanted practical and saving faith. There are many such in every Christian community. "If thou art not far off, enter; better otherwise to have been far off."—BENGEL.

This closes the attacks to which Jesus was subject, on Tuesday of the Passion-Week, in the temple. All his opposers are silenced, and the last one who represented them is almost brought into the position of his own disciples. The effect upon their minds is briefly yet pointedly expressed. **And no man after that durst ask him;** *No one any longer dared to question him,* in any captious manner; in order to tempt or try him in any way. They felt their own inferiority, and stood in awe of him.

35–37. JESUS CONFOUNDS THE PHARISEES WITH A QUESTION CONCERNING THE PARENTAGE OF THE CHRIST.

Matt. 22 : 41–46 ; Luke 20 : 41–44. Matthew is the fullest and most lifelike; Luke the briefest; Mark holds an intermediate position, yet shows his characteristic style by the additional statements, that this incident occurred " while he taught in the temple;" and that "the great multitude heard him gladly," vers. 35, 37.

Jesus had thus far been acting on the defensive ; but now he turns to the offensive, and convicts the scribes and Pharisees with ignorance and false views of the Messiah, which opens the way for his warning and denunciations against them in vers. 38–40. They had disputed his claims as a spiritual Messiah, and, by repeated efforts, had vainly tried to prove him a base pretender ; he now turns and shows the incongruity of their view of a worldly Messiah with the prophetic idea of him. He had silenced their *questioning,* ver. 34 ; now, as Alford aptly remarks, he silences their *answering* also.

35. **Answered.** Responded not so much to the words as to the feelings of the scribes and Pharisees. See on this word in ch. 9 : 5. They were greatly agitated on the subject of the Messiahship and Jesus. Though he had shown himself their superior in argument, power and authority, yet in their opposition to the truth they would not accept him as their teacher, much less as their Messiah. They would rather point out and dwell upon every conceivable objection, and very likely upon his humble condition and lineage. **While he taught in the temple.** *While teaching* the people (ver. 37) in one of the courts or halls of the temple. Thus Jesus triumphs over and humbles his opposers in the presence of the multitude. Mark alone brings out this point prominently.

How say the scribes ? Authoritatively as religious teachers. The scribes were generally Pharisees, ver.

36 son of David ? For David himself said by the Holy Ghost, 'The Lord said to my Lord, Sit thou on my right hand, till I make thine enemies thy footstool.' 37 David therefore himself calleth him Lord; and whence is he then his son ?

28. According to Matthew (22 : 42) Jesus asked the Pharisees, "What think ye of Christ? Whose son is he?" and they answered, "The son of David." As Jesus was addressing the multitude as well as the Pharisees, it is natural to conceive of him as giving emphasis to the answer of the Pharisees by incorporating it in a question, "How say the scribes, that the Christ is the son of David?" **Christ.** Rather *The Christ*, the Greek equivalent to the Hebrew *The Messiah*, meaning *anointed*. See on ch. 1 : 1. **Son of David** was a common title of the Messiah. See on ch. 10 : 47.

36. **For** introduces the reason for the question just asked. But according to some of the highest authorities, *for* should be omitted. **By the Holy Ghost.** *In the Holy Spirit;* in union with him and under his control; pervaded by his influence and under his guidance. Luke says (20 : 42), "David saith in the book of Psalms," which, in connection with the accounts here and in Matthew, is strong though incidental allusion to the inspiration of that book.

Jesus quotes from Ps. 110 : 1. This passage is said to be more frequently quoted or referred to in the New Testament than any other in the Old Testament. The Psalm from which it is quoted was written by David, after Zion became the seat of the theocracy (2 Sam. 6 : 16, 17), and not long after the promises made to David in 2 Sam. 7 : 11-16 and 1 Chron. 17 : 9-14. The application of the Psalm, and of the language here quoted, to the Messiah, is taken for granted by Jesus, is silently acknowledged by the Pharisees, and was the common interpretation among the Jews at the time of Christ and long after. Acts 2 : 34.

The Lord. Jehovah. **To my Lord.** The Messiah, as the Jews understood the words to refer, and as our Savior applied them. Thus David spoke of the Messiah as his Lord, his superior and sovereign. **Sit.** An appropriate posture of a sovereign (Ps. 29 : 10), especially of one who was about to use his enemies as a footstool. **On my right hand.** On the throne beside me, not merely as a position of honor, but as a partner of my sovereignty and power, Ps. 110 : 2, 3. See on ch. 10 : 37. **Till I make,** etc. *Till* does not limit the time of his reign, but only carries the thought to a certain point, without going beyond it. Compare Gen. 28 : 15; Ps. 112 : 8. Paul, in 1 Cor. 15 : 24-28, reveals to us some things that shall take place after Christ has subjugated his enemies. **Thine enemies thy footstool.** Emphatic in the original, *a footstool of thy feet*. So in the Hebrew, *a stool for thy feet*. This implies their utter and ignominious defeat and their most abject subjugation. The foot was often put on the neck of the vanquished, Josh. 10 : 24, 25; Ps. 47 : 3. This prophecy plainly pointed to the divine nature of the Messiah; for only thus could he be spoken of as *Lord*, by Israel's greatest king, and as occupying such an exalted position and exercising such power.

37. **Therefore** should be omitted, according to the highest critical authorities. **David himself;** in contrast to the scribes, who merely spoke of him as his son. **Calleth him Lord.** Applies to him the solemn, reverential and lofty title of Lord. **Whence is he then his son ?** If David acknowledged him as his superior and sovereign, from what source, by what means is he his son, and hence his inferior? The question could only be answered by acknowledging the divinity and humanity of Christ. It is thus answered in Rom. 1 : 3, 4. But the Jews, especially the scribes and Pharisees, in their worldly views of the Messiah, had lost the doctrine of his divinity, and only held to his humanity as a royal descendant of David. If the scribes had truly understood the character of the Christ, they could have said, As man, he is David's son; but as God, David's Lord. This closes the oral conflict between Jesus and his ene-

Warning against the scribes.

38 AND the common people heard him gladly. And ᵇ he said unto them in his doctrine, ¹ Beware of the scribes, which love to go in long clothing, and
39 ᵏ love salutations in the marketplaces, and the chief seats in the synagogues, and the uppermost rooms

ᵇ Lk. 20. 45; ch. 4. 2.
¹ Mt. 23. 7; Lk. 20. 46, 47.
ᵏ Lk. 11. 43.

---

mies. They were so thoroughly entangled and discomfited, that they feared both to ask and also to answer questions, Matt. 22 : 46. They felt their inferiority to him in wisdom and knowledge, and in debate; and they found it necessary to have recourse to some other means for overcoming his influence and putting him to death.

Mark describes his influence on the **common people** or *great multitude*, who at that season visited the temple and gathered to hear him. **Heard him gladly;** with great pleasure. And so have they ever heard him, 1 Cor. 4 : 26-28.

38-40. DENUNCIATION OF THE SCRIBES. From the last public discourse of Jesus to the Jews, Matt. 23 : 1-39; Luke 20 : 45-47. Matthew, who wrote specially for Jewish Christians, gives a full report of this discourse. But Mark, writing for Gentile Christians, gives but a brief denunciation of the scribes, whom he had named prominently among his opposers, ver. 35. And Luke, writing for the race, is equally brief, and agrees almost verbally with Mark.

38. **Said ... in his doctrine;** *in his teaching,* implying that what follows is but a portion of what he then taught. There is a seeming reference to a fuller discourse as given by Matthew. **Unto them.** "To the multitude and to his disciples," Matt. 23 : 1. "In the audience of all the people, he said unto his disciples," Luke 20 : 45. Here we have a good illustration of three independent statements of the same thing.

Beware. Be on your guard against. **The scribes,** the class that opposed him, and who had just been confounded by his question. **Which love.** Jesus states their ruling passion: their love of display and honor and " to be seen of men," Matt. 23 : 5. Since this verse is so near the one in which Jesus pronounced a scribe not far from the kingdom of God (ver. 34), some suppose the language to refer to only a part of the scribes, those who love, etc. This is indeed allowable, but not necessary. Jesus had afterward arraigned the scribes generally, ver. 35; besides, what is here affirmed was true of the scribes as a class, although there were doubtless exceptions. Compare the woes pronounced upon them, Matt. 23 : 13-29. **To go in long clothing;** *to go about in long* flowing *robes,* such as were worn by priests and kings, and by persons of rank and distinction. The reference is undoubtedly to their walking about the streets and public places in their long robes of office and rank. **Salutations,** deferential and complimentary *greetings,* which were performed in a formal and ceremonious manner. **In the marketplaces;** where the people were accustomed to resort. See on ch. 6 : 56; 7 : 4. They loved these greetings in the most public places.

39. **Chief seats in the synagogues.** *The first seats,* the foremost row, nearest the reading-desk and the ark where the sacred books were kept. See on ch. 1 : 21. **The uppermost rooms at the feasts.** *Rooms* is here

RECLINING AT TABLE.

in the obsolete sense of *place, position,* the uppermost *places* at the feast. Literally, *the first reclining-places at the feasts,* the most honorable position,

40 at feasts: ¹ which devour widows' houses, and for a ᶦ Mt. 23. 14; Lk. 20. 47.
pretence make long prayers: these shall receive
greater damnation.

The widow's mites.

41 ᵐ And Jesus sat over against the treasury, and be- ᵐ Lk. 21. 1.
held how the people cast ⁿ money ᵒ into the treasury.   ⁿ See Mt. 10. 9.
 ᵒ 2 Ki. 12. 9.

which was the middle place of the couch on which they reclined at table. Or, according to others, the couches were ordinarily arranged on three sides of a square, the fourth being left open for the servants to wait on the tables. The couch on the right was called the highest, the others, respectively, the middle, and the lowest couch. Compare Luke 14 : 7–10. *Feasts;* dinners or suppers. The chief meal among the Jews was taken toward evening, and often prolonged into the night. This verse shows how the scribes loved positions of honor.

40. Jesus in this verse points to other traits of the scribes; their dishonest and voracious avarice, and their hypocritical external piety. **Devour widows' houses.** Like cunning yet ferocious beasts, they devoured the substance of widows, who were the most defenseless of the people, and the most deserving of sympathy and kindness. *Houses* is here used for *possessions, property.* They influenced widows to give them of their property, as an act of piety, or to bequeath it to them. As spiritual advisers, and sometimes as the executor of their wills and the guardian of their children, they could rob widows of their property. Pious women were accustomed to contribute to the support of religious teachers, Luke 8 : 2, 3. "What words can better describe the corrupt practices of the so-called priesthood of Rome, than these of our Lord?"—ALFORD. **For a pretence, make long prayers.** For a show, praying long. As a pretext. They made religion a mask in order to gain the confidence and the property of even the most helpless. Some of the rabbins would pray nine hours a day. **Greater damnation.** A more abundant *condemnation,* implying a most terrible punishment as a consequence. For the double sin of hypocrisy and fraudulent injustice, they should meet a terrible doom.

41–44. THE WIDOW'S MITES. Luke 21 : 1–4. Mark's account is fuller and more picturesque. How fitting this incident just here, after the description of the scribes as devouring widows' houses!
41. **And Jesus sat.** According to the best critical authorities, *And sitting.* This was the posture of teaching (ch. 4 : 1), and may indicate that posture during and after concluding his last discourse to the Jews. With this well agrees Luke 21 : 1. "And he looked up." Some suppose that after finishing his discussions with the scribes, and his discourses in the temple, he sat down wearied, and rested himself opposite the treasury. Like a king he sits in his own temple. **The treasury,** according to the rabbins, was a name applied to thirteen brazen chests, which stood in the second court of the temple or the court of the women, each chest bearing an inscription denoting the object of the contribution. These chests were called trumpets, either from their shape or the shape of the opening into which the money was cast. The contributions were made for various purposes connected with the temple services, and one chest is said to have been devoted to offerings for educating poor children of good families.
Beheld. He looked at them attentively. So now Jesus surveys the offerings of his people. See Remark 41, at the end of the chapter. **How the people** of all classes and conditions. We may suppose that the people generally cast in their voluntary offerings. This is said to have been the custom before the Passover. **Cast.** The present tense is used in the Greek, representing the scene as actually passing. **Money.** Literally *brass* or *copper.* But brass, the compound of copper and zinc, appears not to have been known among the ancients; bronze, compounded of tin and copper, was extensively used, and is sometimes desig-

42 And many that were rich cast in much. And there came a certain poor widow, and she threw in two
43 mites, which make a farthing. And he called *unto him* his disciples, and saith unto them, Verily I say unto you, That ᵖ this poor widow hath cast more in,
44 than all they which have cast into the treasury: for all *they* did cast in of their abundance; ᵠ but she of her want did cast in all that she had, ʳ *even* all her living.

ᵖ Mt. 10. 42; 2 Cor. 8. 1-3, 12.
ᵠ ch. 14. 8.
ʳ Deu. 24. 6; 1 John 3. 17.

nated by the word here translated brass. But copper is said to have been the first metal that was wrought, and was early used for money, and seems to be generally intended by the word in the New Testament. The word also seems to have been used as a general term for money, with reference doubtless to coins of the lowest value. **Many ... rich cast in much.** Probably not copper alone, but also silver. It would seem that observers could see what each one gave.

42. **And there came,** etc. Rather, *And one poor widow came.* Alone and lonely, she arrests the attention of observers; possibly calling forth sympathy from a few; but Jesus regards her with admiration, while the multitude of donors pass her unnoticed or with indifference. Perhaps one of those widows, whose property had been devoured by some hypocritical scribe. **Threw in two mites.** She cast in *two,* when she might have reserved one for her own use. This shows how her whole heart was for giving all to God. A *mite* was equal to about two mills, and was the smallest coin current in Palestine, Luke 12 : 59. Mark explains to his Roman readers that two mites are equal to a **farthing** (Matt. 5 : 26), or two-fifths of a cent. In the Græco-Roman coinage of Palestine the mite and farthing were the two smallest coins.

43. Jesus called his disciples, who were near at hand, and directed their attention to this poor widow, and especially to her gift. He commenced with the solemn and authoritative declaration, **Verily I say unto you,** with which he announced new and momentous truths. **More than they all,** in proportion to her means and in the sacrifice that she made. This Jesus explains in the next verse. The motives of the contributors are not taken into comparison, but only their gifts. Yet the motive of the poor widow, in her circumstances and with our Lord's commendation, can be easily inferred. It was in her case a free-will offering to God. How it was in the cases of the others cannot be so decidedly known; for some doubtless from proper motives cast in their gifts. Yet from the character of the leading classes, very justly represented by the scribes (vers. 38-40), it may be presumed that a majority of those casting in much, did it not so much from love to God as from love of human praise.

44. **For all,** particularly the rich, with whom the poor widow is contrasted in vers. 41, 42. **Of their abundance;** *out of* their excess, superabundance, overflow. But she, in contrast, **of her want,** *out of* her deficiency, poverty. The two expressions, **all that she had,** and **even all her living,** or rather, *her whole living,* explain each other. She gave all the money she had at that time, and all she had to live upon, at least for that day. Luke (21 : 4) more briefly says, "All the living that she had." She would fast in order to give. She felt what she gave, they did not; to her it was real self-denial, but not to them. In love she devoted all to God, with strong faith in his providential care.

Some very improperly apply the term mite, or widow's mite, to their trifling contributions. At the lowest estimate a person contributes "the widow's mite," only as he gives a whole day's income. And that in most cases would not reach the poor widow's self-denial, for she gave "out of her want."

REMARKS.

1. God, who bestows all our gifts and blessings, has a right to our service, vers. 1, 2; James 1 : 17; 1 Pet. 4 : 7-11.

2. God's dealings with the Jewish

nation an illustration of his goodness, patience, long-suffering and judgments toward wicked nations and individuals, vers. 1-8; Ps. 81 : 13-16; Ezek. 39:23; Heb. 1 : 1, 2; Jer. 7 : 25.

3. The history of the Jewish people is an argument for human depravity, vers. 2-8; Jer. 17 : 9; Acts 7 : 51, 52; 1 Thess. 2 : 15, 16; Rom. 8 : 7, 8.

4. A church should be of God's planting, separated from the world, with tower and every part well manned, and bringing forth fruit unto God, vers. 1, 2; Eph. 2 : 19-22; 4 : 20-23; 5 : 7; Rom. 12 : 6-8; 1 Cor. 3 : 8, 9; 2 Cor. 6 : 16-18; John 15 : 16; Col. 1 : 10.

5. The greater the privileges, if unimproved, the greater the guilt, and the more awful the condemnation, ver. 9; Matt. 23 : 34-38; Luke 12 : 45-48.

6. They who obstinately reject the offers and privileges of the gospel shall have them forever taken from them, ver. 9; Prov. 1 : 24-32.

7. Let those to whom Christ has become a stone of stumbling beware lest he become a stone of condemnation and unutterable ruin, ver. 9; Luke 2 : 34; 2 Cor. 2 : 16.

8. Christ the rock on which are built our hopes, joys and full salvation, ver. 10; 1 Cor. 10 : 4; 1 Pet. 2 : 8; Matt. 16 : 18; Heb. 5 : 9; 12 : 2.

9. Christ is triumphant; and so will his cause and people be, however dark and foreboding their circumstances, vers. 10, 11; Eph. 4 : 8; Rom. 8 : 37-39; Luke 12 : 32.

10. Many have had their consciences aroused, but continue impenitent; and in many an aroused conscience only begets greater hatred and wickedness, ver. 12; 2 Cor. 2 : 16; Acts 13 : 45.

11. Those who are now offended at God's faithful servants for preaching the truth would have joined with the scribes against Jesus, ver. 12; John 15 : 18-21.

12. How great the opposition of the wicked to Christ! Enemies unite in conspiring against him; play the hypocrite and act as his friends; acknowledge the truth and his true character with evil intent, vers. 13, 14; Ps. 2 : 2; 12 : 2; 55 : 21.

13. Hypocrisy and deceit in religion will not escape the detection of Christ, nor his withering curse, ver. 15; Isa. 29 : 15, 16; Heb. 4 : 13.

14. Let us beware of partial views of truth and duty, failing neither to recognize our duties to government nor to God, vers. 15-17; Dan. 6 : 3, 10.

15. The distinction made by Jesus between duties to God and to government shows that the two are in harmony, yet not to be mingled together. The church and state should be distinct yet harmonious, vers. 16, 17; Rom. 13 : 7; 1 Pet. 2 : 13-17.

16. Civil government is an ordinance of God, and all of its lawful requirements ought to be obeyed. The best citizen will make the best Christian, ver. 17; Rom. 13 : 1-5; Acts 4 : 19; Dan. 4 : 27; 3 : 16-18.

17. "Nothing is more likely to ensnare ministers than bringing them to meddle with controversies about civil rights, and to settle landmarks between the prince and the subjects, which it is fit should be done, while it is not at all fit that they should do it."—MATTHEW HENRY. Vers. 14-17; 2 Tim. 2 : 4.

18. Men in every lawful station have their rights, and should receive all due honor, ver. 17; 1 Pet. 2 : 13-17.

19. If there come a collision between human and divine law, the Christian's duty is plain : he must obey God rather than man. "Julian was an unbelieving emperor, an apostate, a wicked man, and an idolator. Yet Christian men served as soldiers under him. . . . When the emperor wished them to worship idols or burn incense to them, they preferred honoring God before him. But when he said, ' Draw out in order of battle, march against that nation,' they obeyed. They made a distinction between their eternal Master, and their temporal; yet they were submissive to their temporal master for their eternal Master's sake."—AUGUSTINE. Ver. 17; Dan. 3 : 16-18; 6 : 10; Acts 4 : 19, 20.

20. As in the days of our Savior, so ever since have infidels and opposers of Christ been shifting their ground of attack, vers. 13, 18, 28; ch. 11 : 28.

21. The object of infidels and opposers to Christ is often only to entangle Christians with difficulties. Press them with plain facts and evidences of Christianity, vers. 20-23; Acts 13 : 8-11.

22. Beware of imaginary difficulties in the doctrine of a future life, and of drawing certain conclusions in respect to it from analogies of the present life, vers. 18-24; 1 Cor. 15 : 39-41, 51-54; 1 John 3 : 2.

23. Thorough and experimental knowledge of Scripture, and just conceptions of the power of God, are preventives of error in regard to the doctrines of revealed truth, ver. 24; Job 26: 14; Ps. 62: 11; John 5: 39; Acts 17: 11; 26: 8; 1 Cor. 1: 25; 2 Tim. 3: 15.
24. Christ and the Scriptures clearly teach the existence of angels, ver. 25; Matt. 13: 41; 24: 31, 36; Ps. 8: 5; Heb. 2: 7, 9.
25. We may reason analogically from the condition of angels in regard to our future state, ver. 25; Jud. 13: 17–20; 2 Sam. 14: 20; Ps. 103: 20; Heb. 12: 22; Rev. 12: 7; 22: 8, 9.
26. There is to be a resurrection of the body from the dead, ver. 26; John 5: 28, 29; 1 Thess. 4: 16, 17.
27. There is a conscious existence between death and the resurrection, ver. 26; Job 19: 26, 27, clearly and correctly rendered by Dr. Conant, *Without my flesh I shall see God*, that is, separated from my body, in my disembodied state after death, Luke 16: 22, 23; 23: 43; 2 Cor. 5: 8; Phil. 1: 21–23.
28. The resurrection is so important in man's future existence, and essential to his glorified state, that the Scriptures associate it with his whole future life and immortality. "Without the body man has not his whole full life."—NAST. Ver. 26; Luke 20: 36; Rom. 8: 11, 23; 2 Cor. 5: 4; 2 Tim. 1: 10.
29. In the establishment and defense of any doctrine, our first appeal should be to Scripture, ver. 26; Isa. 8: 20.
30. Seek not the mere letter of Scripture, but its deep and spiritual meaning, vers. 26, 27; John 16: 13; 1 Cor. 2: 10–16; 2 Cor. 3: 6.
31. The essence of true religion is holy love, vers. 28–31; Rom. 5: 5; 13: 8, 10; 1 Cor. 13: 1–3, 13; 1 John 4: 21.
32. The duties we owe to God and man do not conflict, but rather confirm and support each other, vers. 29–31; Matt. 22: 40; Rom. 13: 10.
33. The ordinances and external duties of religion have their place and are important, but they should only be the expressions of an inward and more important service, ver. 33; Rom. 10: 9, 10; 14: 17; 1 Cor. 11: 2, 23.
34. How far a person can go in religion, and not be a true disciple! Ver. 34; ch. 10: 20, 21; John 12: 42, 43.
35. Many wonder at the wisdom of Christ, and feel the force of his doctrines, without being savingly benefited, ver. 34; Acts 13: 41.
36. What think you concerning the Christ? of his nature, character, work? What is he to thee? Vers. 35–37; Rom. 9: 5; 1 Cor. 1: 23, 24; 15: 25; Heb. 12: 2, 3.
37. Jesus recognized the old Testament Scriptures as written by inspiration of God, ver. 36; Luke 24: 25–27.
38. The doctrine of Christ's humanity and divinity is taught in Scripture, and explains difficulties which would be otherwise insuperable, vers. 36, 37; Matt. 1: 23; John 1: 1, 14; Phil. 2: 6; 1 Tim. 2: 5; Heb. 2: 14–17.
39. A religion that seeks a mere outward appearance, and has for its motive the applause of men, is not only destitute of the power of godliness, but an enemy to it and its graces, vers. 38, 39; Matt. 6: 1, 5, 16; 2 Tim. 3: 2–5; 2 Pet. 2: 3; 3 John 9.
40. A love of human honors and flattering titles is unbecoming a follower of Jesus, vers. 38, 39; Phil. 2: 5; 1 Pet. 5: 5; 1 John 2: 15.
41. Jesus beholds and estimates our offerings, vers. 41–44; Matt. 6: 19, 20; 10: 8; Acts 20: 35; 2 Cor. 8: 12.

"Jesus unseen—but who all hearts can see,
Still sits and overlooks the treasury!
Cast in your offerings where his cause invites,
Ye rich your talents, and ye poor your mites.
Render to God the things that are his due,
He gave his Son, who gave himself for you."
MONTGOMERY.

CHAPTER XIII.

Jesus, having closed his ministry to the people, leaves the temple, and continues it with his disciples. In this chapter we have a remarkable prophetic discourse, which has been variously explained and justly considered one of the most important and difficult in the New Testament. It is given most fully by Matthew, chapters twenty-four and twenty-five, which see and compare notes; also, Author's "Harmony of the Gospels," § 154.

Three events appear to be foretold in this chapter: the destruction of the temple and Jerusalem by the Romans; the second coming of Christ; and the end of the world. The great difficulty is to understand the relation of the

Jesus foretells the destruction of Jerusalem, and his second coming.

XIII. AND ¹ as he went out of the temple, one of his disciples saith unto him, Master, see what manner ¹ Mt. 24. 1; Lk. 21. 5.

several portions of this prophecy to these topics, and their relation to one another. Some hold that they are successively presented, and that the transitions from one to another are clearly marked. They are not, however, agreed as to where the transitions are. Others suppose a blending of topics, in which the destruction of Jerusalem is made typical of the end of the world, and that this, like many of the prophecies of the Old Testament, has successive fulfillments. So far as need be these points will be discussed in the notes that follow. 1 suggest the following synopsis:
I. The Occasion of the Inquiry and Discourse: Jesus foretelling the destruction of the temple, vers. 1, 2.
II. The Inquiry: When shall these things be? And what the sign when they are about to be accomplished? Vers. 3, 4.
The disciples conceived of the destruction of Jerusalem, the coming of Christ, and the end of the world, as simultaneous, or nearly so.
III. The Reply, vers. 5-37.
1. Jesus cautions them against expecting his coming before the gospel is preached in all the world, vers. 5-13. This includes cautions:
a. Against being deceived by false Christs, vers. 5, 6.
b. Against being troubled about wars and calamities, which are not indicative of the end, but are only the beginning of sorrows, vers. 7, 8.
c. Against themselves in persecution; persecution itself would tend to forward the gospel, which must first be preached to all nations, vers. 9, 10.
Not to premeditate, but to depend on the Holy Spirit in making their defenses before their enemies. He that endureth to the end shall be saved, vers. 11-13.
2. The destruction of Jerusalem, with directions as to what they should then do, and a caution against expecting him then, vers. 14-23.
a. The abomination of desolation betokening the destruction of Jerusalem, ver. 14.

b. The disciples are instructed to make a precipitate flight, vers. 15, 16.
c. The unparalleled sufferings of that time, vers. 17-19.
d. Those days shortened far the sake of believers, ver. 20.
e. Cautions against the Christs of that day, for they will be but pretenders, vers. 21-23.
3. The *signs* and the *time* of his coming, vers. 24-27.
a. Terrific phenomena and changes in nature after the Jewish people have endured their full measure of suffering, vers. 24, 25.
b. The Son of man coming in the clouds of heaven, ver. 26.
4. Attendant circumstances of his coming, ver. 27.
5. Returning somewhat in his discourse, he teaches, by an illustration from the fig-tree, how to judge concerning the time of those things which should occur in that generation, and were more certain than the established order of nature, vers. 28-31.
6. But of the time of his coming, that is known only to the Father. Watchfulness is therefore necessary, and enforced by a case of a porter left in charge of his master's house, vers. 32-37.
Jesus speaks of the time of his coming without special reference to the destruction of Jerusalem, whether soon after or long after that event. "That day and hour" (ver. 32), the time of his coming, is, however, in contrast to "these things" (ver. 30), the calamities attending the destruction of Jerusalem We can thus see the reason why the early disciples expected a speedy return of our Lord, 1 Thess. 4 : 15 ; 2 Thess. 2 : 1-4.
1, 2. JESUS LEAVES THE TEMPLE AND FORETELLS ITS DESTRUCTION. Matt. 24 : 1, 2; Luke 21 : 5, 6. Luke omits the fact that Jesus now left the temple. Mark is the most definite in his statement.
1. **As he went out of the temple,** taking his final departure ; more clearly expressed by Matthew (24 : 1), "And Jesus went out and departed

A.D. 30. MARK XIII. 243

2 of stones and what buildings *are here!* And Jesus answering said unto him, Seest thou these great buildings? *There shall not be left one stone upon another, that shall not be thrown down.
3 And as he sat upon the mount of Olives over against the temple, Peter and James and John and

<small>a Lk. 19. 44.</small>

from the temple." It was now toward evening, Tuesday, April 4th. *Temple here* is the whole sacred inclosure. See on ch. 11 : 11. **One of his disciples,** very probably Peter, who frequently acted as spokesman for the apostles, Matt. 16 : 16 ; John 6 : 68. Hence Matthew could say "his disciples." Mark alone vividly gives the exclamation, **Master** (*Teacher*), **see what manner of stones and what buildings,** *what manner of buildings!* The lamentation over Jerusalem, and the denunciation against her (Matt. 23: 37, 38), may have led the disciples to turn his attention to the magnificence of the temple, as if to plead for its preservation. Josephus describes the temple as built of white marble, its face toward the east, covered over with plates of gold, appearing in the distance like a mountain covered with snow, with its gilding dazzling as the rays of the sun. Some of its stones were forty-five cubits long, five high, and six broad. (Joseph. *Jewish War*, v. 5. 6; vi. 4. 1.) Dr. Robinson speaks of immense stones still remaining in the wall, one of which measures 24 feet long, 6 feet broad, and 3 feet high. Similar stones are found in Baalbek, Lebanon, measuring 63 and 64 feet each.
2. **And Jesus answered,** etc. According to the highest critical authorities, *And Jesus said to him,* a phrase so often used by Mark, ch. 1 : 17; 4 : 21, 24. 26, 30, 35, etc. **Seest thou,** etc. The question fixed their whole attention for the moment on the great buildings of the temple, and prepared them for what he was about to say. Notice that he speaks both of the building and the stones, ver. 1.
There shall not be left one stone upon another. This was fulfilled forty years afterward, A.D. 70. Josephus relates that Titus tried in vain to save the temple. The Jews themselves first set fire to its porticoes; after which one of the Roman soldiers, without any command, threw a burning firebrand into the golden window, and soon the holy house was in flames. Titus ordered the fire to be extinguished, but his command was not obeyed. The soldiers were furious, and nothing could restrain them. Thus, even against the will of Cæsar, the temple was completely destroyed, and the prophecy was fulfilled. After the city was taken, Titus gave orders to demolish the entire city and temple, except three towers and part of the western wall. The rest of the wall was laid so completely even with the ground by those who dug it up from the foundation that there was nothing left to make those believe that came thither that it had ever been inhabited. (Josephus, *Jew. War*, vi. 4. 5–7; vii. 1.) Later still, Terentius Rufus, an officer in the army of Titus, ordered the site of the temple to be furrowed with a plowshare. Thus nothing was left but parts of the massive foundations, which still remain, Mic. 3 : 12 ; Jer. 26 : 18.
3, 4. **The inquiry,** Matt. 24 : 3 ; Luke 21 : 7. Luke omits the fact that this occurred on the Mount of Olives. Mark alone mentions the names of those making the inquiry.
3. **And as he sat upon the Mount of Olives.** Having gone to the mount, on his way to Bethany, and sitting down there. Concerning this mount, see on ch. 11 : 1. Mark alone states that he sat **over against the temple.** "I went out of the city, and ascended to the top of the Mount of Olives. . . . Crossing the upper bridge over the Kedron, I followed the middle path which leads over the hill, a little to the left of the garden of Gethsemane. When about half way up the ascent I found myself, apparently, off against the level of Jerusalem. Hence Mark is perfectly exact when he represents the Savior as being 'over against the temple, as he sat upon the Mount of Olives,' and foretold the doom of the devoted city."—Dr. Hackett, *Illustrations of Scripture,* p. 281. It is a remarkable fact that the

4 Andrew asked him privately ˣTell us, when shall these things be ? and what *shall be* the sign when all these things shall be fulfilled ?   ˣ Mt. 24. 3; Lk. 21. 7.
5 And Jesus answering them began to say, ʸTake   ʸ Jer. 29. 8; Eph. 5. 6; 1 Thes. 2. 3.
6 heed lest any *man* deceive you: for many shall come in my name, saying, I am *Christ;* and shall deceive

siege of Jerusalem began on this mount, and at the Passover, the time of this prophecy. (Joseph. *Jewish War,* v. 2. 3; vi. 9. 3.) Mark alone mentions **Peter, James, John and Andrew** as the inquirers, ch. 1 : 16–20 ; 3 : 16–18. Matthew says "the disciples." The four asked for the rest, or possibly were the only earnest seekers. **Privately.** They very probably came first to Jesus and asked him, the rest coming up and hearing the discourse.

4. **When shall these things be,** which he had predicted respecting the destruction of the temple, ver. 2. **What shall be the sign ?** *What is or will be the sign?* **When all these things,** which his prediction involved. They conceived of the destruction of Jerusalem, the coming of Christ, and the end of the world or the present dispensation, as closely connected. Hence in these two questions we have the three in Matthew, (1.) "When shall these things be ?" (2.) "What is the sign of thy coming ; and (3) of the end of the world ?" **Shall be,** *about to be* **fulfilled,** or *accomplished.* If the temple was to be destroyed, they would naturally expect his glorious coming immediately, when, after destroying his enemies, he would establish a magnificent and religious kingdom, Luke 24 : 21 ; Acts 1 : 6. Such brief revelations of such great and terrible events arouse their desire for more definite information. Hence they ask for the *time* of "these things," and the *sign* or tokens of "all these things."

5–37. OUR LORD'S REPLY. Jesus wisely says nothing about a temporal kingdom, but describes more minutely the destruction of Jerusalem and the signs and manner of his second glorious coming, with certain cautions against the errors to which they would be exposed, Matt. 24 : 4–51 ; Luke 21 : 8–36. Matthew is the fullest, and, in addition to what is parallel in this chapter and in Luke, gives the parables of the Ten Virgins and the Talents. Yet Mark is in some places more vivid and circumstantial. Notice the repeated exhortation, "Take heed," vers. 5, 9, 23, 33, The command not to premeditate (ver. 11) is not given by Matthew, though the thought is presented by Luke (21 : 14, 15).

5–13. JESUS BEGINS HIS REPLY BY CAUTIONING THEM AGAINST EXPECTING HIM BEFORE THE GOSPEL IS PREACHED IN ALL THE WORLD. Matt. 24 : 4–14; Luke 21 : 8–18.

5. In this and the following verse Jesus cautions them against false Christs. A false Christ is one who assumes to take the place or act the part of the Messiah. **Began to say,** which Dr. J. A. Alexander aptly says "is something more than *said,* and seems here to imply that what he said was not restricted to a single topic, that he first spoke of one thing and proceeded to another. This is the more probable because our Lord, instead of beginning with the signs or premonitions of his second coming, as many seem to think he does, and as the twelve may have expected, begins by telling them what was not to be so reckoned, although apt to be mistaken for the signs in question." **Take heed.** Be on your guard. Often repeated in this chapter. See preceding paragraph on vers. 5–37. **Lest any man deceive you.** Lest any one lead you astray. This shows the cautionary and admonitory nature of the first portion of this discourse, and indeed the general nature of the whole discourse.

6. A reason for giving the preceding warning. **In my name.** Not in the name of Jesus, but of the Messiah, claiming to be him, or to represent him. **I am Christ;** rather, *I am he.* "I am the Christ," Matt. 24 : 5. There were many such. Josephus, a Jew not converted to Christianity, but an eye-witness of the calamities attending the destruction of Jerusalem, and, to a considerable extent, an actor in them, has, in his account of the Jewish War, given a striking comment, and delineated the

A.D. 30.   MARK XIII.   245

7 many. And when ye shall hear of wars and rumours of wars, *be ye not troubled: for *such things* must needs be; but the end *shall* not *be* yet. For
8 nation shall rise against nation, and kingdom against kingdom: and there shall be earthquakes in divers places, and there shall be famines and troubles. *These *are* the beginnings of sorrows.

* Pro. 3. 25.

* Mt. 24. 8.

wonderful fulfillment of the first portion of this chapter. He speaks of the land being overrun with magicians, seducers, and impostors, who drew the people after them into the wilderness, promising to show them signs and wonders. Thus Theudas, not the one mentioned Acts 5 : 36, but a later one, persuaded a large body of people to follow him to the Jordan, promising to divide the river, as Elijah and Elisha had done of old. But he was taken prisoner before arriving there, and beheaded. An Egyptian also pretended to be a prophet (Acts 21 : 38), and deluded thirty thousand men. (Joseph. *Antiq.* xx. 5. 1; 8. 6; *Jewish War*, ii. 13. 4, 5.) After the destruction of Jerusalem, Bar Cochba and Jonathan appeared, and almost every age since has witnessed false Christs, some of whom have claimed, in one sense or another, to be our Lord himself.

7. In this and the verse that follows Jesus cautions them against being troubled with wars and various calamities which should come upon the earth and the Jewish nation, supposing them to be indicative of the end, when they were but the beginning of sorrows. **Hear of wars and rumors of wars.** These wars must be such as to be a terror to Christians, threatening their nation and their homes. The *wars* are to be regarded as certain and actual to them. But the *rumors of wars* would naturally be exaggerated, confused, and frightful, and hence more terrible than war itself. There were numerous agitations and insurrections in the Roman empire previous to the destruction of Jerusalem, in which much blood was shed. Also in Rome itself four emperors, Nero, Galba, Otho, and Vitellius, came to violent deaths in eighteen months. Alford refers to the *three threats of war against the Jews* by Caligula, Claudius, and Nero. When this prediction was made it was a time of peace throughout the Roman empire.

Be ye not troubled, etc. Be not confused, agitated, filled with alarm. The reason is given; such things must take place, but the end of the world **is not yet.** Some suppose *end of tribulations* is here meant; but it is more natural to refer it to the end of the world, or the present state of things, since that is one of the main points of his discourse. Besides, as Lange remarks, "the end of the calamities is the end of the world," 1 Pet. 4 : 7. When it is remembered how often Christians have regarded wars and great national commotions as signs of the coming of Christ and the end of the world, it may be seen how wise and necessary was this caution of our Savior. These things must take place; they are in the divine plan, but the end is not yet; therefore be not troubled, but patient, hopeful, and tranquil.

8. **For.** The calamities mentioned in the preceding verse, and the reason for not being troubled enlarged upon. **Nation shall rise against nation, and kingdom,** etc. Race against race, and kingdom against kingdom. In the preceding verse, Jesus says they shall *hear;* now he states what will certainly take place. There shall be great national struggles, and political revolutions. "There were serious disturbances, (1) which gave rise to the complaint against and deposition of Flaccus, and Philo's work against him (A.D. 38), in which the Jews as a nation were the especial objects of persecution; (2) at Seleucia, about the same time (Josephus, *Antiq.* xviii. 9. 8, 9), in which more than fifty thousand Jews were killed; (3) at Jamnia, a city on the coast of Judea, near Joppa. Many other such national tumults are recorded by Josephus."—ALFORD. The reference here, however, must not be confined merely to the Jewish people.

Earthquakes. A great earthquake occurred in Crete about A.D. 46; at Rome in 51; in Phrygia in 53; in Laodicea in 60; in Campania in 58; at Jerusalem in 67 (Joseph. *Jewish War*,

9 But ᵇtake heed to yourselves: for they shall de- ᵇ Mt. 10. 17, 18; 24. 9; Rev. 2. 10.
liver you up to councils; and in the synagogues ye
shall be beaten; and ye shall be brought before
rulers and kings for my sake, for a testimony against
10 them. And ᶜthe Gospel must first be published ᶜ Mt. 24. 14.
among all nations.

iv. 4. 5.) Pompeii was visited with two disastrous earthquakes about 63.

Famines. Historians speak of several famines, in different parts of the world, which happened in the reign of Claudius (A.D. 41–54), one of which was particularly severe in Judea, about 44–47. (Joseph. *Antiq.* xx. 2. 5; 5. 2.) Compare Acts 11 : 28. Suetonius and Tacitus speak of famines about this time. There was also a famine in Judea in the third year of Nero's reign, about A.D. 56.

Troubles. *Commotions*, tumults. Mark alone gives this, and it is omitted by some of the oldest manuscripts. Josephus records many insurrections and tumults. The threat of Caligula to put his image in the temple caused a great commotion. **The beginnings of sorrows.** Not the end, as too many will be ready to imagine, but the beginning of *throes* or *birth-pangs;* often applied to intense sufferings which precede a change for better or worse. Rom. 8 : 22; 1 Thess. 5 : 3. The death-pangs of the present state, and the birth-pangs of Christ's glorious kingdom, Acts 3 : 21; Rom. 8 : 18–23.

9. Jesus cautions them in regard to their own conduct in persecution. Persecution will tend to forward the gospel, which is to be preached to all nations. **But take heed to yourselves.** Care not for other matters, *but look to yourselves* (2 John 8), in order to guard against and avoid dangers which shall be close upon you. They would be in danger of becoming offended, disaffected toward the cause of Christ (Matt. 24 : 10); or their love might wax cold (Matt. 24 : 12); or they might trust in themselves instead of trusting in the Spirit, ver. 11.

Councils; not to *the council* (ch. 14 : 55), or Sanhedrim, which was the supreme national court of the Jews; but to *councils* (without the article), the lower courts, Matt. 10 : 17. Some suppose them to be the *courts of seven* established in every city, in conformity to Deut. 16 : 18, and explained by Josephus (*Antiq.* iv. 8. 14). Others, that they were the tribunals connected with the synagogues, commonly known as "the council of three," who could punish by scourging. Both may be intended; this, however, is unimportant, since the idea simply is that they should be arraigned before courts of justice.

In the synagogues, etc. The most literal rendering is, *Ye shall be beaten into the synagogues*, which some adopt. After the trial and condemnation in the councils, they would be led into the synagogues or public assemblies to be beaten. But fanaticism would not wait; they will be scourged on the way thither. But a common and I think preferable construction makes the words mean, *Into the synagogues ye shall be taken and beaten*. Scourging was actually inflicted in the assemblies for public worship. Compare Acts 5 : 40; 2 Cor. 11 : 24.

Ye shall be brought, as criminals. **Rulers.** *Governors.* **For a testimony,** respecting Christ and the truth. **Against them,** *to them*, the governors and kings. Thus by means of persecution many in authority would hear the gospel. Paul gave his testimony to King Agrippa (Acts 26 : 1) and to Cæsar, 2 Tim. 4 : 16. Compare Acts 4 : 8; 16 : 20; 22 :30. Persecution in the early church resulted in the furtherance of the gospel, Acts 8 :4; Phil. 1 :12.

10. **The gospel must first be published,** etc.; *first be preached among all the nations*, before the end, ver. 7; Matt. 24 : 14. And suffering and preaching will go together. This was really the case, so far as the world was then known, in the apostolic age, and before the destruction of Jerusalem, Rom. 1 : 5, 8; 10 : 18; 15 : 24; Col. 1 : 6, 23; 2 Tim. 4 : 17. The gospel had been preached as far as Scythia on the north, Ethiopia on the south, India to the east, and Spain to the west. So before the end of this dispensation the gospel shall be made known to all nations. "The universal promulga-

11 ᵈ But when they shall lead *you*, and deliver you up, take no thought beforehand what ye shall speak, neither do ye premeditate: but whatsoever shall be given you in that hour, that speak ye: for it is not
12 ye that speak, ᵉ but the Holy Spirit. Now ᶠ the brother shall betray the brother to death, and the father the son; and children shall rise up against *their* parents, and shall cause them to be put to
13 death. ᵍ And ye shall be hated of all *men* for my name's sake. But ʰ he that shall endure unto the end, the same shall be saved.

ᵈ Mt. 10. 19; Lk. 12. 11; 21. 14.

ᵉ Ac. 2. 4; 4. 8, 31.
ᶠ Mic. 7. 6; Mt. 10. 21; 24. 10; Lk. 21. 16.
ᵍ Mt. 24. 9; Lk. 21. 17; John 15. 18; 17. 14.
ʰ Dan. 12. 12; Mt. 10. 22; 24. 13; Rev. 2. 10.

tion of the gospel is the true sign of the end, both in the (narrow and restricted) sense in which the disciples put the question, and in the (wider and universal) sense which, in the Savior's mind, it really involved."—JUDGE JONES. The end of the Jewish state and the destruction of Jerusalem are typical of the end of the world, or the gospel dispensation.

11. Jesus cautions them against trusting in themselves instead of the Holy Spirit in their defense before councils, governors and kings, ver. 9. Compare Matt. 10 : 19, 20. **Shall lead you and deliver you up.** Rather, *lead you, delivering you up;* or, with the Bible Union version, "Lead you away to deliver you up." **Take no thought beforehand.** *Take not thought,* etc. Be not unduly solicitous, be not anxious, Matt. 6 : 25. **Neither do ye premeditate.** This is omitted by the best text. Words shall be given you in that hour, when you shall be arraigned. **That speak ye** in your defense. See Acts 4 : 8-12. The command is to speak only what should be given them; and the reason is, **For it is not ye that speak,** etc. They should be specially and completely under the control of the *Holy Spirit,* so that they would be as instruments in his hands. It should be noted that this command has no reference to preaching generally without any forethought or previous preparation. It cannot be used to support such practice. Read the direction of Paul to Timothy, "Give attendance to reading," etc., 1 Tim. 4 : 13, 16.

12. **Now.** *And.* Jesus enlarges upon the persecutions, which would be so severe that even the tenderest relations of life would not form a barrier. Brother would **betray,** *deliver up* (the same word so translated in the preceding verse) to the magistrate brother; the father, the child; and even children would rise up against parents. The result of such judicial proceedings would be death. Early church history shows the fulfillment of these predictions.

13. The climax of hatred; universal, *by all;* and founded on their relation to Christ, **for my name's sake.** On account of their attachment to me, and because they bear my name. Here do we see why Christians have been hated and persecuted beyond the adherents of any other sect. "Concerning this sect we know that everywhere it is spoken against," Acts 28 : 22. "The friendship of the world is enmity with God," James 4 : 4. See also 1 Pet. 2 : 12; 3 : 16; 4 : 14. Christianity is exclusive, and therefore Christians are hated by both Jews and Gentiles. It proclaimed salvation through Jesus alone. The Jewish theocracy was superseded by a spiritual kingdom, and all that was indestructible and essential to man's duty in the law was incorporated in the gospel. The Jew would, of course, hate a system destructive of his own, and one which shut him out of salvation except through a hearty reception of faith in its doctrines. Pagans tolerated each other; their systems of religion were local and limited in their claims, confined to tribes, nations, and countries. They could even worship each other's gods. But they could not tolerate Christianity, which proclaimed itself a universal religion; and exclusive, in that it was the only true religion; and exterminating, in that it condemned all idolatry, and waged war with all other religions as embraced in the kingdom of darkness. Pagans, therefore, hated Christians, and regarded them, in the

14 ᶦBut when ye shall see the abomination of desolation, ᵏspoken of by Daniel the prophet, standing ˡwhere it ought not, (ᵐlet him that readeth understand,) then ⁿ let them that be in Judæa flee to the

ᶦ Mt. 24. 15; Lk. 21. 20.
ᵏ Dan. 9. 27.
ˡ Lam. 1. 10; Eze. 44. 9.
ᵐ Pro. 22. 3.
ⁿ Lk. 21. 21.

language of Tacitus, the Roman historian, as exercising "enmity to the human race." The doctrines and claims of the gospel, which are so repugnant to the human heart, aroused the hatred not only of the Jews and pagans, but of all other opposers not included in these two classes.

Jesus adds a comforting assurance, and encourages them with the prospect of final triumph. **But he that endureth,** perseveres and continues faithful **unto the end** of life, which is practically the end of the world to the individual, **shall be saved,** fully, finally and eternally. "The end" to every believer is the end of life, 1 Cor. 1 : 8; Heb. 3 : 6, 14; 6 : 11; Rev. 2 : 10, 26. He shall be saved from sin and all its consequences, temporal and eternal, physical and spiritual. "'Enduring to the end' is the proper evidence of the reality and solidity of the Christian profession ; 'drawing back unto perdition' exposes the want of foundation."—P. SCHAFF. It is, however, worthy of notice that not a single Christian, so far as is known, perished in the destruction of Jerusalem. They escaped to Pella, beyond the Jordan, where they remained in safety till after the fall of the city. See on ver. 14. Their deliverance may be taken as an illustration and type of the deliverance of all God's people at the end of the world and at the judgment. Luke (21: 19), who omits this sentence, gives another in keeping with it, "In your patience possess ye your souls."

14–23. Jesus now proceeds to speak definitely of the DESTRUCTION OF JERUSALEM, and to answer the first question of the disciples, with directions as to what they should then do, and with a caution, or hint, that THEY ARE NOT TO EXPECT THE SECOND COMING OF CHRIST AT THAT TIME, Matt. 24 : 15–28 ; Luke 21 : 20–24.

14. **Abomination of desolation.** Spoken of through Daniel the prophet, Dan. 9 : 27; compare Dan. 11 : 31 ; 12 : 11. These words were supposed by the Alexandrine Jews to refer to an idol statue of Jupiter Olympius, erected in the temple by Antiochus Epiphanes (B.C. 168), when for three years and a half the Jews were deprived of their civil and religious liberties. See Apocrypha, 1 Macc. 1 : 54 ; 6 : 7 ; 2 Macc. 6 : 2. Josephus (*Antiq.* x. 11. 7) seems to refer this prophecy to the destruction of Jerusalem. The *abomination* in the original Hebrew refers to things unclean and revolting, and especially to objects of abhorrence connected with idols and idolatry. The *desolation* is especially applied to the wasting devastations of war. The *abomination of desolation* thus naturally refers to the profanations connected with the devastations of heathen conquest, and points unmistakably to the destruction of Jerusalem and the temple by Titus. But what particular thing or event in this destruction is here meant ? Some refer it to the eagles, which the Romans carried as standards, worshiped as idols, and hence were an abomination to the Jews. The standards in the hands of the Roman legions besieging the holy city foreshadowed its conquest and destruction. This view is supported by the fact that the Roman army under Cestius Gallus, after taking a portion of the city, A.D. 66, withdrew, and thus gave time to the Christians to escape before the city was closely invested by Vespasian, A.D. 68. The expression of Luke (21 ; 20), who wrote especially for Gentile readers, also favors it : "When ye shall see Jerusalem encompassed with armies, then know that the desolation thereof is nigh." Others, however, think that "the abomination of desolation" points especially to the murders committed in the temple by the party of the zealots, who occupied it at the very time that the Roman general, Cestius, approached the city and assaulted it. Such pollutions and tragedies in the temple must have deeply impressed Jewish Christians, and, in connection with the threatening armies and conquest of the Romans, must have deepened the conviction that the end of the city and its temple was nigh. Still, I think that the quotation from Luke above, shows that the language

15 mountains: and let him that is on the housetop not go down into the house, neither enter *therein*, to
16 take any thing out of his house: and let him that is in the field not turn back again for to take up his garment.
17 ° But woe to them that are with child, and to them that give suck in those days! And pray ye
18

° Lk. 21. 23; 23. 29.

here refers to this first approach and attack of the Roman armies, with their idolatrous ensigns, ready to desolate Jerusalem. **Spoken of by Daniel the prophet.** This clause is found in Matthew, but should be omitted here, according to the best critical authorities. **Standing where it ought not,** because the place was holy, as Matthew expresses it. Some would refer this language to the whole of Palestine; but this is too general. Nor is it necessary to limit it to the temple; for it may properly be applied to the holy city and its precincts, Matt. 4 : 5.

Let him that readeth understand; consider, give heed to, and note it. This is a parenthetical clause, uttered probably by our Savior, being an admonition to any who should read this prediction of Daniel. Possibly there is some reference to the words of the angel to Daniel, "Know therefore and understand," Dan. 9 : 25. Many suppose the clause to have been thrown in by the evangelist, intimating the near approach of this sign. But why should he throw it in for his Roman readers? And why should Matthew use the same language if it were not a part of the discourse of Jesus? Matt. 24 : 15. The omission by Luke (21 : 20) may be explained by the fact that he was writing for Gentile readers, giving a brief synopsis of the discourse, and that he gives the admonitory and significant clause, "Then know that the desolation thereof is nigh." The disciples are instructed to make a precipitate flight **then,** when they should see this sign of approaching destruction. **Them which be in Judea.** In the country, towns, and cities of Judea. **Mountains.** The mountainous regions and highlands, where there were caves affording a safe retreat. By a singular providence the Roman general Cestius, after taking a portion of the city, with good prospects of capturing the whole, withdrew without any apparently good reason. This gave the Christians an opportunity to escape, which they did, over the mountainous region to Pella, and other places east of the Jordan, where the country was at peace with the Romans. Pella was on the northern border of Perea. According to Eusebius, the historian, the Christians were divinely directed to flee thither. Compare Gen. 19 : 15-23.

15. They were to flee with all possible haste, and not descend into their houses to collect their goods. **Housetop.** Literally, *Upon the house.* The houses in Palestine were flat-roofed, and communicated with each other, so that a person might proceed to the city walls and escape without coming down into the street. Persons would naturally go to the housetop to view an invading army. Roofs were also used for sleep, retirement, prayer or recreation, Luke 12 : 3. Jesus, however, may have referred to escaping by a stairway leading from the court to the roof, without entering the house. The stairway landed "outside the house, but within the exterior court. It would not be either agreeable or safe to have the stairs land outside the inclosure altogether, and it is rarely done, except in mountain villages and where roofs are little used." —*The Land and the Book,* vol. i., p. 52.

16. Their precipitate flight is also illustrated and further enforced. He that is **in the field,** and consequently dressed for the field, must not turn back to get that upper **garment** or cloak which he would only need for a journey. He must escape without his full dress, or garment at home.

17. **Woe unto them . . . with child.** An exclamation of pity, with reference to both Jewish and Christian females. The sufferings of both would be greatly increased. Flight would be far more difficult, or impossible.

18. **And pray.** Thus teaching them to depend entirely upon God, and to

19 that your flight be not in the winter. ᵖ For *in* those days shall be affliction, such as was not from the beginning of the creation which God created unto
20 this time, neither shall be. And except that the Lord had shortened those days, no flesh should be saved: but for the elect's sake, whom he hath chosen, he hath shortened the days.

ᵖ Dan. 9. 26; 12. 1; Joel 2. 2; Mt. 24. 21.

seek from him the facilities needed. The correct text reads, *Pray ye that it be not*, referring to the flight, and things attending it. **Winter.** When storms are frequent, and roads are bad; a season unfavorable for traveling, and especially for a hasty flight. Dr. Thomson says that it is not easy to exaggerate the hardships, and even dangers, which traveling parties encounter at this season of the year. Heavy falls of snow often occur during January and February. Such was the case in 1854, when twenty-five persons are said to have perished from the cold at Nazareth. Cestius (ver. 14) withdrew from Jerusalem early in November, A.D. 66. The final siege under Titus took place in the spring and summer, A.D. 70. Matthew (24:20, correctly translated) adds "nor on a Sabbath."

19. Jesus foretells the unparalleled judgments and sufferings of the time. **Affliction;** those days will be a scene of affliction, or distress. Or, those days will be affliction itself. According to Josephus, eleven hundred thousand perished during the siege at Jerusalem by the sword, pestilence and famine. The city was full of people, attending the Passover festival, when the last siege under Titus commenced. Thousands had come from remote parts of the earth, not only to attend the festival, but to assist in the defense of their religion, country, liberties, city and temple. Ninety thousand were taken prisoners, and sold into perpetual bondage. Besides, during the war nearly three hundred thousand Jews perished elsewhere, in addition to a vast multitude who died in caves, woods, common-sewers, banishment and various ways, of whom no computation could be made. Some suppose that Josephus greatly exaggerated the number of sufferers. Tacitus gives six hundred thousand as the number within the city at the time of the siege. Nothing is more common than to overestimate large gatherings. But making all proper allowance, a vast multitude perished, in whose sufferings our Lord's strong language found a literal fulfillment. **From the beginning of the creation,** the things created, Mark's strong language answering to "the world" in Matthew. The sufferings of the Jews, for so short a time (the final siege lasted five months), and for so confined a space, exceeds anything in the known history of the world. The prediction in Deut. 28: 53-57 was literally fulfilled. The language of Josephus is noteworthy: "I shall, therefore, speak my mind here at once briefly, that neither did any other city ever suffer such miseries, nor did any age ever breed a generation more fruitful in wickedness than was this, from the beginning of the world." And again: "The multitude of those that therein perished exceeded all the destructions that either men or God ever brought upon the world." (*Jewish War*, v. 10. 5; and vi. 9. 4.) When Professor Gellert was sneeringly asked by the skeptical Frederick the Great, "What do you think of *Christ?*" he aptly replied, "What does your Majesty think of the destruction of Jerusalem?"

20. Jesus intimates that **those days** of judgment and distress shall be shortened for the sake of those among the Jews who were and should be his chosen followers. **No flesh be saved.** No one of the Jewish nation. The whole nation would have perished. **For the elect's sake.** 1 Pet. 1:1. For the sake of those whom God had chosen from among the Jews to be his people. Compare Gen. 18:23-33. **He hath shortened the days;** rather, *he shortened the days*, in his divine purpose, which would therefore become an actual fact in history. The time from the first siege under Cestius to the destruction of the city by Titus was four years. The final siege lasted

21 [q]And then if any man shall say to you, Lo, here
22 *is* Christ; or, Lo, *he is* there; believe *him* not: for
false Christs and false prophets shall rise, and shall
show signs and wonders, to seduce, if *it were* possi-
23 ble, even the elect. But [r]take ye heed: behold, I
have foretold you all things.

[q] Mt. 24. 23; Lk. 17. 23; 21. 8.

[r] 2 Pet. 3. 17.

only about five months. It commenced in April, A.D. 70. The daily sacrifice ceased for want of priests to offer it on the twenty-third of June, and from that day to the fourteenth of July the last death-struggle took place. Then followed plunder and destruction, till the whole city was reduced to ashes, except the three great towers on the western wall. Titus recognized divine help in taking the city, and confessed, "We have indeed had God for our assistant in this war, and it was no other than God who ejected the Jews out of these fortifications; for what could the hands of men or any machines do toward overthrowing these towers?" (Josephus, *Jewish War*, vi. 9. 1.) Alford, and others, notice several things which may be regarded as providential causes in shortening the siege: (1.) Herod Agrippa had begun to fortify the walls of Jerusalem, and make them, as Josephus says, "too strong for all human power to demolish;" but was stopped by orders from Claudius, A.D. 42 or 43. (2.) The Jews, being divided into factions among themselves, had totally neglected to prepare to withstand a siege. (3.) The magazines of grain and other provisions, which, according to Josephus, "would have been sufficient for a siege of many years," were burnt just before the arrival of Titus. (4.) Titus arrived suddenly, and the Jews voluntarily abandoned parts of the fortification." (Josephus, *Antiq.* xix. 7. 2; *Jewish War*, v. 1. 4; vi. 8. 4.)

21. In this, and the two following verses, Jesus cautions his disciples against false Christs and false prophets which should arise in those days. **Then;** at the time of these sufferings, or immediately after. **Lo, here is Christ,** *the Christ*, the Messiah. **Believe him not.** *Believe not* what he says. Jesus was not to come in this manner, ver. 26. Neither was he then to come personally, vers. 24–27. There was danger that some Jewish Christians might expect Christ to come to deliver the city from destruction. At the most there would be only an invisible and impersonal coming then, which would be in judgments upon the unbelieving race and their wicked city.

22. Jesus further affirms that there will be **false Christs,** those who pretend to be the Messiah; and **false prophets,** false teachers, who should **show signs and wonders,** work false miracles. They would, like Simon Magus (Acts 8:10), lead many to regard them as illustrious instruments of God's power. **If possible,** implying that it is impossible, John 10:28, 29. **Seduce . . . even the elect.** Lead them astray; seduce them from Christ and the truth. Compare Acts 21:38; 2 Thess. 2:9–12; 1 John 2:18; Rev. 16:13, 14.

These impostors were numerous before and after the destruction of the city. Felix (A.D. 53–60) put down false prophets and false Messiahs. According to Josephus, they persuaded many "to follow them into the wilderness, and pretended that they would exhibit manifest wonders and signs, that should be wrought by the providence of God." They deluded the people under pretense of divine inspiration." So, also, during the siege a great number of false prophets proclaimed that the people "should wait deliverance from God;" and just before the burning of the temple, one of them made a public proclamation that "God commanded them to get upon the temple, and that they should receive miraculous signs of deliverance." (Joseph. *Antiq.* xx. 8. 6; *Jewish War*, ii. 13. 4; vi. 5. 2.) And long after this, about A.D. 135, a false Messiah arose, who called himself Bar Cochevas, or son of a star, from the star prophesied by Balaam. He performed tricks of legerdemain, deluded multitudes, among whom were three of the greatest rabbis, and raised an insurrection against the Roman government, which was put down with great bloodshed.

23. **But take ye heed.** An emphatic admonition in the original. *Do*

24 *But in those days, after that tribulation, the sun shall be darkened, and the moon shall not give her
25 light, and the stars of heaven shall fall, and the
26 powers that are in heaven shall be shaken. ᵗAnd then shall they see the Son of man coming in the

*Dan. 7. 10; Zeph. 1. 15; Mt. 24. 29; Lk. 21. 25.
ᵗ ch. 14. 62; Dan. 7. 13, 14; Mt. 16. 27; 24. 30; Ac. 1. 11; 1 Thes. 4.

16; 2 Thes. 1. 7, 10; Rev. 1. 7.

ye see to it, be on your guard. **Behold is not in the original**, according to the highest critical authorities. **I have foretold all** these things. **Things is not in the original**. To be forewarned was to be forearmed. As I have affectionately exercised the caution to foretell these dangers, so do you exercise a like caution in guarding against them. Mark here passes over something regarding the manner of Christ's coming, Matt. 24 : 26–28.

24–27. JESUS NOW PASSES TO THE SIGNS AND THE TIME OF HIS COMING. Matt. 24 : 29–31; Luke 21 : 25–28. Mark is the briefest; Matthew the most definite; Luke the most indefinite.

24. **But in those days.** Indefinite, and may be many or few—a long or a short time. **After that tribulation.** *That* refers back to the preceding discourse; *those* points toward the last events. *That tribulation* or *affliction* is not necessarily limited to the destruction of Jerusalem by Titus, but may also refer to the trials connected with the dispersion of the Jews. The language in Matthew, "the tribulation of those days," seems to refer to these sufferings, extending till "the fullness of the Gentiles come in." About A.D. 135, Jerusalem was captured again, in consequence of an insurrection under Bar Cochevas, which brought most terrible sufferings upon the Jews, who were utterly driven out from the land of their fathers. (See on ver. 22.) A temple of Jupiter was then erected on the site of the Lord's house. Afterward, A.D. 635, the mosque of Omar was built upon the same site. If we may conceive of Daniel's prophecy, concerning the abomination that made desolate, having repeated fulfillments, we might place its final reference to this last event, and also suppose it to mark the commencement of his periods of 1260, 1290, and 1335 years. The distress of the Jews still continues, and Jerusalem is still trodden under foot by the Gentiles. Let it be noted that *those days*, as presented by Mark, comes *after* that tribulation. **The sun shall be darkened and the moon**, etc. This language may be taken figuratively to mean great calamities and revolutions among the nations of the earth, after the manner of Hebrew prophecies, Isa. 13 : 10; Ezek. 32 : 7; Joel 3 : 15. Wordsworth applies it to the church: "The solar light of Christ's truth shall be dimmed, the lunar orb of the church shall be obscured by heresy and unbelief, and some who once shone brightly as stars in the firmament of the church shall fall from their place." All this is true; but it is doubtful whether all of these, and similar passages from the Old Testament, are to be taken figuratively. It is better to take this language of our Lord literally, especially as what follows in regard to his coming must be taken literally. See on ver. 26. The meaning is, that terrific phenomena and changes in nature shall occur in those days after the Jewish people shall have endured their measure of suffering. There shall be darkness, as during the crucifixion of our Savior (ch. 15 : 33) and in the plague of Egypt (Exod. 10 : 22, 23); appearances of falling stars (ver. 25), or the shooting of meteors; and the **powers** and the forces of nature, the elements of the heavens, shall be **shaken**, agitated and convulsed like the waves of the sea, Heb. 12 : 26. **The powers that are in heaven** are referred by some to the sun, moon and stars; but as these had just been mentioned, it is better to understand the words as above.

26. Jesus here speaks of his second coming. The coming of Christ is spoken of elsewhere as actual and visible, Acts 1 : 9, 11; 1 Thess. 4 : 16; 2 Thess. 1 : 8; 2 Pet. 3 : 10, 12; Jude 14; Rev. 1 : 7. In harmony with these plain declarations, I take this passage in its natural and literal meaning, and can see no sufficient reason for departing from it. **Then,** when these wonder-

27 clouds with great power and glory. And then shall he send his angels, and shall gather together his elect from the four winds, from the uttermost part of the earth to the uttermost part of heaven.
28 ⁿNow learn a parable of the fig tree; When her branch is yet tender, and putteth forth leaves, ye
29 know that summer is near: so ye in like manner, when ye shall see these things come to pass, ˣknow
30 that it is nigh, even at the doors. Verily I say unto you, that this generation shall not pass, till all these

ⁿ Mt. 24. 32; Lk. 21. 29.

ˣ Eze. 12. 25; Rev. 22. 20.

ful phenomena shall have been seen, vers. 24, 25. Mark omits the statement, that all the tribes of the earth shall mourn, which Matthew gives, ch. 24 : 30. **Son of man**, the Messiah, now in humiliation, then in his exaltation; see on ch. 2 : 10. **Coming in the clouds.** *In clouds*, without the article. As he ascended, Acts 1 : 9. Not merely in ordinary clouds, but such as anciently attended the divine presence, Exod. 16 : 10; 19 : 18; Dan. 7 : 13. **With great power,** with the actual possession of it; **and glory,** a visible display of his power and majesty, Ps. 68 : 17; Acts 7 : 55.
27. Jesus foretells the attendant circumstances of his coming.
Then shall he send his angels. Angels are elsewhere described as attending Christ at his coming and active at the judgment, Matt. 13 : 41, 49. They shall **gather together** to him, as their great and common center, **his elect**, his chosen followers, 2 Thess. 2 : 1; 1 Thess. 4 : 16, 17. **From the four winds.** From every quarter, and from the remotest places under heaven, Deut. 4 : 32; Ezek. 37 : 9. **From the uttermost part,** etc. A strong expression, *From end of earth to end of heaven.* From the whole visible creation, wherever the elect are found. This gathering will be for safety, for the enjoyment of Christ's presence, and for glorious rewards. Then will follow the gathering of the wicked for punishment. Compare Rev. 20 : 4, 5, 12-15. See at this point Luke 21 : 28.
28-31. Returning somewhat in his discourse, JESUS TEACHES, BY AN ILLUSTRATION FROM THE FIG-TREE, HOW TO JUDGE CONCERNING THE TIME OF THOSE THINGS, WHICH SHOULD OCCUR IN THAT GENERATION, and were more certain than the established order of nature, Matt. 24 : 32-35; Luke 21 : 29-33. The three accounts present very slight differences. See the analysis at the beginning of this chapter, 5 and 6.
28. **Now learn a parable of,** etc. Rather, from the fig-tree learn the parable which illustrates the circumstances and signs preceding "these things;" learn the illustration which the fig-tree affords. Fig-trees abounded on the Mount of Olives, where Jesus was now discoursing. **Is yet tender;** rather, *is already become tender.* **Ye know that summer is near.** "On my first arrival in the southern part of Syria, near the end of March, most of the fruit-trees were clothed with foliage and in blossom. The fig-tree, on the contrary, was much behind them in this respect; for the leaves of this tree do not make their appearance till comparatively late in the season. . . . As the spring is so far advanced before the leaves of the fig-tree begin to appear (the early fruit, indeed, comes first), a person may be sure when he beholds this sign, that summer is at hand."— DR. HACKETT, *Illustrations of Scripture,* p. 141. See on ch. 11 : 13.
29. **Ye shall see these things come to pass,** or *coming to pass;* which he had told them in his discourse, particularly those described, verses 7, 8, 14. **It or He is nigh,** either subject being admissible. Especially the destruction of Jerusalem, foretold to the Jews, in Matt. 23 : 36-38, and referred to by the words *these things* in the fourth verse of this chapter. The illustration can also be applied to the coming of Christ and the end of the world. If they, or his followers, to whom he spoke through them, should observe the signs described in verses 24, 25, then they would know that his coming and the end are at hand.
30. **This generation.** That present generation. **All these things.**

31 things be done. Heaven and earth shall pass away: but ⁷ my words shall not pass away. ⁷ Is. 40. 8
32 But of that day and *that* hour knoweth no man, no, not the angels which are in heaven, neither the

The *these things* of verse 4, connected with the destruction of Jerusalem. *All these things* are in contrast to *that day* in ver. 32, which refers exclusively to the coming of Christ. Thus Jesus passes, in verses 30, 32, from one event to the other, the former being typical of the latter.

Another explanation makes *this generation* to mean those who know and observe these signs, the generation of his followers who shall be living when these signs occur. In which case it could apply to both the fall of Jerusalem as a type, and Christ's coming to judgment as an antitype.

Others maintain that, according to Hellenistic Greek, *this generation* may mean *this race*, or *family of people*. According to which view our Savior says, This race or Jewish people shall not pass away till all these things just foretold be accomplished. The first view is preferable. The destruction of Jerusalem occurred about forty years afterward, within the lifetime of many then living. If, however, we give a double or extended meaning to *these things*, we must give a corresponding extended meaning to *this generation.* **Be done.** *Are accomplished* or *done*. To say with some, " are in course of fulfillment, or begin to be fulfilled," is grammatically incorrect.

31. Jesus had just announced the preceding declaration with the authoritative and solemn clause, "Verily I say unto you." He now affirms most emphatically that his words shall be certainly accomplished. **Heaven and earth shall pass away.** Even these which have been so generally regarded as firm and unchangeable, Ps. 89 : 37 ; Jer. 33 : 25. Even these shall be changed, and give place to the new heaven and new earth, 2 Pet. 3 : 11-13. This is in harmony with the deductions of science. **My words,** in general, and what I have spoken at this time. **Shall not pass away.** Cannot at any time prove to be false, or fail of their accomplishment. They are infallible, and more certain than the established order of nature, Isa. 40 : 8; 51 : 6 ; 1 Pet. 1 : 24, 25.

32-37. CONCERNING THE TIME OF HIS SECOND COMING ; THE CONSEQUENT NECESSITY OF WATCHING. Matt. 24 : 36-51 ; Luke 21 : 34-36. There is very little in common in these three accounts. Each evangelist, in this portion of the discourse, seems to have seized upon points, similar but different. Luke omits reference to the time of his coming, but gives exhortations to watchfulness. The accounts of Matthew and Mark, when taken together, show the different illustrations by which Jesus enforced the necessity and duty of watching. In Matthew we have the case of the thief, the faithful servant and his reward, and the unfaithful servant and his punishment. In Mark, the case of the porter and the servants. Luke guards against the heart, without parabolic illustration.

32. **But of that day and that hour.** *But of that day or hour ;* the exact time of his second coming. The expression *that day or hour* is emphatic, and in contrast to *these things* in ver. 30. He has just been speaking particularly of the time of those things, the destruction of Jerusalem and the temple, which had first led to their questions and to this discourse. Now he turns to that other day, the time of his coming, concerning which they had also asked. **Knoweth no man,** etc. *Knoweth no one, not even the angels,* who, being in the presence of God and constantly doing his bidding, might be supposed to know. **Neither the Son.** This is given by Mark alone. Jesus spoke in respect to his human nature. As a man he increased in wisdom and acquired knowledge (Luke 2 : 52), and was ignorant of the exact time of his coming. His human soul was necessarily finite and progressive. He exercised human emotion (John 11 : 35), prayed (Luke 6 : 12), and depended on divine influence, John 3 : 34 ; Luke 22 : 42-44. As "the Son," in his mediatorial character, he was in a state of voluntary humiliation (Phil. 2 : 7), and of subjection to the Father (Heb. 5 : 5-8 ; 10 : 5-7). The progress of his manhood must have been correspondingly limited. Hence, though mysteri-

33 Son, but the Father. ¹Take ye heed, watch and
34 pray: for ye know not when the time is. ᵃ *For the
Son of man is* as a man taking a far journey, who
left his house, and gave authority to his servants,
and to every man his work, and commanded the

¹ Mt. 24. 42; 25.
13; Lk. 12. 40;
21. 34; Ro. 13.
11; 1 Thes. 5. 6.
ᵃ Mt. 24. 45; 25.
14, 15; Lk. 19. 12.

ous, our faith should not be staggered because he neither knew the time nor was he commissioned to make it known.
The following paragraph on this verse from Dr. A. Hovey's recent work, *God with Us*, is worth pondering:
"This language appears at first sight to deny that Christ knew in any sense, even in his higher nature, the time of the last day. But what if Jesus, acting as mediator between God and man, must apprehend by the faculties of his human soul, as well as by his higher nature, whatever he taught? And what if the powers of his human soul, though strengthened by the grace of the Holy Spirit given without measure, had thus far been in quest of more profitable truth, and had not so much as craved a knowledge of the date in question? So that speaking, as he ever did, in his mediatorial capacity, Christ had not a knowledge of that hour? It is surely conceivable that such was the law of his action, and that, while the fact of his higher nature, being truly God, and therefore omniscient, was revealed to the faculties of his human soul, and could therefore be affirmed by him as a theanthropic being, the particulars of that omniscience were only apprehended by his human faculties in part, even as they were needed for his Messianic work. In a certain sense, to be sure, his knowledge was unrestricted, infinite—even as Peter felt when he exclaimed, 'Lord, thou knowest all things, thou knowest that I love thee,' and as Christ was assured when he said, 'The Father loveth the Son, and showeth to him all things which he himself doeth.' His higher nature was omniscient, but the lower was not. Yet even this, the lower, was never, it may be confidently affirmed, in ignorance of what pertained to the work of any hour or moment of the Savior's life. The divine was ever in communication with the human, giving it light for every emergency; and the human was ever absorbed in its proper work, untroubled about envious questions or events in the distant future."

But the Father. God only knew the time, and hence Jesus could only have known it in his divinity. It was one of those things which God had appointed by his own authority, and was not intended for men to know, Acts 1: 7. This verse is a strong statement that the time was kept a profound secret in the counsels of God.
33. Watchfulness enforced from this uncertainty of the time of his coming. **Watch.** Be awake and on your guard against danger. **For ye know not**, etc. Ignorance of the time, a reason for watchfulness. The same reason will apply to death and the judgments which are coming on the earth. We should watch since we know not when their time is.
34. Jesus enforces constant watchfulness from the case of a porter left in charge of his master's house. **For the Son of man is.** These words added by our translators are unnecessary. The thought is easily supplied. The time and the consequent necessity of watching are as in the case of a man, etc. **Taking a far journey.** *Away from his people*, or absent in foreign lands. The idea of distance is indefinite: it may have been near or far off. **Who left . . . and gave.** *Having left . . . and given.* **And after servants** should be omitted, according to the highest critical authorities. **To every man.** *To each one* of his servants. They had authority according to their various stations to manage his affairs while absent, and with this authority was individual work or labor. This may remind us of the parable of the Talents given by Matthew (ch. 25: 14–30). To the **porter**, or doorkeeper, was the special injunction **to watch,** to be vigilant, and on the lookout for his return. The porter's office required him to be watching for any approaching the house and to receive them in a becoming manner. The *porter* aptly represents the ministers of the gospel, who are Christ's watchmen to his churches, Heb. 13: 17; Ezek. 33: 7; 2 Tim. 2: 15; 1 Pet. 5: 2–4.

35 porter to watch. ᵇ Watch ye therefore: for ye know not when the master of the house cometh, at even, or at midnight, or at the cockcrowing, or in the 36 morning: ᶜ lest coming suddenly he find you sleep- 37 ing. ᵈ And what I say unto you I say unto all, Watch.

ᵇ Mt. 24. 42, 44.

ᶜ Pro. 24. 33, 34; Eph. 5. 14.
ᵈ Lk. 12. 41–44.

35. Watch ye therefore, as this porter should watch, for ye are porters in my house, and for the same reason, that ye know not when I, **the master of the house,** may come. The application of the illustration is brief and vivid. The disciples are at once addressed as if they were porters, left in charge of their Master's house. **At even.** According to the Roman custom, the Jews now divided the night into four watches of about three hours each. Jesus in popular language refers to these divisions of the night. *At evening*, from sunset to nine o'clock; **at midnight,** from nine to twelve; **at the cockcrowing,** from twelve to three; **in the morning,** from three to sunrise. See on ch. 6 : 48.

36. Jesus intimates an additional reason. He had enforced watchfulness from their ignorance of the time; and with this still in mind he adds the thought of his coming **suddenly.** That he will come suddenly is recorded by Matthew (24 : 44). **Sleeping,** negligent and inactive, disobedient to his command, and unprepared to meet him.

37. Jesus makes the command general. **Unto you;** my apostles. **Unto all,** believers, to all my followers of every age. **Watch.** Be awake, be vigilant. The great practical lesson of this discourse.

Matthew in the twenty-fifth chapter continues this discourse, giving the parables of the Ten Virgins, and the Talents, and closing with a graphic description of the final judgment.

REMARKS.

1. Earthly temples, however costly, are of no religious worth without spiritual worship. They are doomed if the Lord has departed from them, vers. 1, 2; 1 Sam. 4 : 21; Jer. 7 : 3, 4, 14.

2. The true glory of a church does not consist in its house of worship or its outward arrangements, but in the faith and piety of its members, vers. 1, 2; Eph. 5 : 27; Rev. 3 : 7–10, 14–18.

3. Earthly structures are temporal; God's cause and truth are eternal, ver. 2; Sam. 2 : 15–17; Ezek. 21 : 27; Matt. 16 : 18; 2 Cor. 4 : 18; 1 Pet. 1 : 23–25.

4. In the study of prophecy we should seek the guidance of Christ and his Spirit, and not go beyond the word of the Lord, vers. 3, 4, 14; Luke 24 : 15–27, 45; 2 Pet. 1 : 19; Rev. 1 : 3.

5. We should guard against false leaders, and trust only in Jesus as the true Messiah, vers. 5, 6; Jer. 29 : 8, 9; Acts 20 : 30; Eph. 5 : 6; Col. 2 : 8; 2 Thess. 2 : 3.

6. National convulsions, conflicts, and disasters, while they are the beginning of sorrows to the wicked, are instrumental in advancing, purifying and consummating Christ's kingdom, vers. 7, 8; Hag. 2 : 6, 7; Rom. 8 : 19–23.

7. Persecutions, defections from the faith, false teachers, and decrease of love amid abounding iniquity, are to be expected, and should lead us to trust in Christ, and persevere unto the end, vers. 9–13; Heb. 10 : 39; James 5 : 7–11; 1 Pet. 4 : 12, 13; Rev. 2 : 10.

8. The gospel, if received, is a witness of the power of God unto salvation; but if rejected, it is a witness of the righteousness and justice of God in final condemnation, ver. 9; ch. 16 : 16; Acts 10 : 36; 2 Cor. 2 : 16; 1 John 5 : 9–12.

9. Missionary operations are but carrying out the will of Christ, ver. 10; ch. 16 : 15.

10. Christians should count the cost and expect the hatred and opposition of the wicked, vers. 11–13; John 15 : 17–21; Gal. 4 : 29.

11. The word of God is not bound though they who preach it are persecuted, imprisoned and put to death, vers. 10–12; 2 Tim. 2 : 9, 19.

12. The most dangerous temptations and the bitterest opposition often come from unconverted relatives. "Faith and love unite even strangers; unbelief

and hate break the closest ties of nature."—QUESNEL. Ver. 12; Matt. 10 : 35, 36.

13. Through much tribulation we must enter into the kingdom of God. Patient perseverance will be crowned with final salvation, ver. 13; Acts 14 : 22; Heb. 3 : 14; Rev. 2 : 10.

14. We should mark in history the abomination of desolation and the destruction of Jerusalem, and behold in them a testimony to the truth of Christ, ver. 14; Rev. 1 : 2, 3; John 14 : 29.

15. We should live in constant readiness, so that if called to escape dangers which may threaten Christians or the church, we may do so at once, vers. 14–16; Gen. 19 : 17; Prov. 22 : 3; Luke 17 : 31, 32.

16. In connection with prayer, it is not only right, but also our duty to use means for our own personal safety, vers. 14–16; Gen. 32 : 13–20; Acts 27 : 22–25, 31, 43, 44.

17. It is right to pray that the seasons and the weather may be favorable to us in all Christian enterprises and undertakings, ver. 18; James 5 : 17, 18.

18. The judgments of nations in this world foreshadow the judgment of individuals in the world to come, vers. 17–19.

19. Christians are the salt of the earth, on whose account the calamities of men and nations are limited and restrained, ver. 20; Gen. 18 : 23–33; Isa. 1 : 9.

20. We are not to believe a teacher merely because he can produce great phenomena. The sorcery of ancient times, the witchcraft and spiritualism of modern days, have done this, vers. 21, 22; Lev. 19 : 31; 20 : 6; Isa. 8 : 19, 20; Acts 8 : 9–12; 13 : 8; 1 John 4 : 1.

21. Let us give special heed to the prophetic words and warnings of the Lord Jesus, the faithful and true witness, ver. 23; Rev. 1 : 5; 3 : 14; 1 Thess. 5 : 6.

22. Though heaven and earth be visited with fearful phenomena, foreboding the coming of Christ, yet amid the sorrows of the nations, Christians may rejoice and feel secure, vers. 24–27; Luke 21 : 28; 2 Tim. 2 : 19.

23. The safety of believers is in Christ. Not one of them, at his second coming, shall be forgotten; not one be lost, ver. 27; 1 Thess. 4 : 14–17; 2 Pet. 2 : 9; 3 : 13.

24. Let us be as wise in perceiving the signs of the spiritual world as of the natural, and be prepared for the coming of the Lord either in death, judgments, or the clouds of heaven, vers. 28, 29; Matt. 16 : 1–3.

25. Nothing can be more certain than the coming of Christ, and the fulfillment of his word, vers. 30, 31; Isa. 54 : 10; Luke 16 : 17; 1 Pet. 1 : 24, 25; 2 Pet. 1 : 19; 3 : 9, 10.

26. It is best for us to be ignorant of the time both of our death and of Christ's coming, ver. 32; Acts 1 : 7.

27. Watchfulness is a trait of a faithful disciple, and will be gloriously rewarded, vers. 35–37; 1 Thess. 5 : 5–7; Rev. 2 : 7, 11, 17, 26; 3 : 5, 12, 21.

28. We should watch, pray and work till Jesus comes. "Would you have my Master find me idle?" was a frequent saying of Calvin, toward the end of life, when his friends would have him work less on account of his health. Vers. 34–37; 2 Pet. 3 : 11–14.

CHAPTER XIV.

With the last chapter Mark closes his account of the *prophetic* ministry of Jesus. In this he proceeds to the *sacrificial* work of Jesus. The conspiracy of the Jewish rulers against him; the anointing at Bethany, and the engagement of Judas to betray him; the preparation for the Passover, its actual celebration, the pointing out the traitor, and the institution of the Lord's Supper; his departure to the Mount of Olives, and his predictions concerning the scattering of the Twelve and the fall of Peter; his agony in Gethsemane and his betrayal; his arraignment before Caiaphas and the Sanhedrim, and the three denials of Peter, form the topics of the chapter.

1, 2. THE JEWISH RULERS CONSPIRE TO KILL JESUS. Matt. 26 : 1–5; Luke 22 : 1, 2. Matthew is the fullest, and, in addition to the other accounts, relates our Lord's final and definite announcement of his crucifixion. Luke is briefest and most indefinite.

1. **After two days.** Equivalent indeed to two days before the Passover, but also pointing from the close of the preceding discourse, which was spoken late on Tuesday, or early on Wednesday, that is, in the evening after the sunset of Tuesday. It must be remem-

The Jewish rulers conspire against Jesus ; the anointing at Bethany ; Judas engages to betray Jesus.

XIV. AFTER ᵃtwo days was *the feast of* the passover, and of unleavened bread. And the chief priests and the scribes sought how they might take him by 2 craft, and put *him* to death; but they said, Not on the feast day, lest there be an uproar of the people.

ᵃ Mt. 26. 2; Lk. 22. 1; John 12. 2; 11. 55; 13. 1.

---

bered that the Jews reckoned the day as beginning at sunset. **The feast of the passover, and of unleavened bread.** Rather, *The passover and the feast of unleavened bread*, the whole occupying eight days, and sometimes called the "feast of the passover" (Luke 2 : 41), and sometimes "the feast of unleavened bread," Luke 22 ; 1.

The *Passover* was instituted in commemoration of God's *passing over* (for this is the meaning of the word) or *sparing* the Hebrews when he destroyed the first-born of the Egyptians. On the tenth day of the month Abib (Exod. 13 : 4), or, as it was afterward called, Nisan (Esth. 3 : 7), answering most nearly to our month of April, a male lamb or kid, without blemish, was selected. On the fourteenth day of Nisan, it was slain in the temple, between the two evenings of three and six o'clock. In the evening, the beginning of the fifteenth day, the paschal supper was eaten by not less than ten nor more than twenty persons. Bitter herbs and unleavened bread were to be eaten with it, and all was done orginally with haste, standing, with loins girt, their feet shod, and their staff in hand. The standing posture and the apparent readiness for a journey was at length discontinued. The Jewish year was reckoned from this month, and John marks the various stages of Christ's public ministry by the Passover, John 2 : 13, 23; 4 : 45; 5 : 1; 6 : 4; 11 : 55. The civil commencement of their year began six months later.

In the New Testament, the word *passover* is applied to the paschal lamb (ver. 12; Luke 22 : 7); to *the paschal supper*, including the lamb (vers. 12, 14; Matt. 26 : 17; Luke 22 : 11, 15; Heb. 11 : 28); and to the *paschal festival* of unleavened bread, Luke 2 : 41; 22 : 1; John 2 : 13; 6 : 4, etc. Here the word more strictly refers to the paschal supper.

For further on the Passover see on ver. 18.

With the paschal supper began *the feast of unleavened bread*, which lasted seven days. See Exod. 12 : 1–20, 34, 39; Lev. 23 : 5–8; Num. 9 : 1–5; Deut. 16 : 3. See further on ver. 12.

The chief priests and scribes. Members of the Sanhedrim, the highest court of the Jews. See on ch. 1 : 22 and on ch. 8 : 31. These, as Matthew tells us, assembled in the court of the high-priest, who was Caiaphas, and consulted together. **Sought how,** by what means, **they might take him by craft,** *deceit* or *fraud*. They had witnessed his power and had been overcome by him, both before and in the view of the people. They were afraid to undertake it openly, lest he should be rescued by the people, or they should be still more humiliated in the presence of the people. Their only hope of seizing him and putting him to death was by fraud. Judas had not yet made his proposal. **Put him to death;** as an official act. This occurred probably in the night after Tuesday or morning of Wednesday, April 5th.

2. **But they said.** According to the best manuscripts, *For they said.* We see the need of craft and of deferring the execution of their plans. **Not on the feast day.** Rather, *Not at the feast*, the whole festival of seven days, during which time the vast multitude, amounting sometimes to two millions, were gathered at Jerusalem. They were afraid of an **uproar** or *tumult* of the people; they say nothing of the sacredness of the feast. That they regarded such result very probable, is seen from a more exact translation, *lest there shall be an uproar.* They hoped to carry out their plans the better after the feast, when the people had gone. But this determination of the Sanhedrim was changed by

A.D. 30.   MARK XIV.   259

3 *And being in Bethany in the house of Simon the leper, as he sat at meat, there came a woman having an alabaster box of ointment of spikenard very precious; and she brake the box, and poured it on

*Mt. 26. 6; John 12. 1, 3; see Lk. 7. 37.

the treacherous proposal of Judas, as will be presently related.
3–9. THE SUPPER AND THE ANOINTING AT BETHANY. Matt. 26 : 6–13 ; John 12 : 2–8. The three evangelists evidently relate the same event, with merely the variations of independent narrators. The anointing related in Luke 7 : 36–50 is altogether different from this in time, place, and circumstances. That took place much earlier, in Galilee, probably in the vicinity of Nain; this at Bethany, just before the Crucifixion. The one at the house of Simon the Pharisee; the other at the house of Simon the leper. That both were named Simon is not strange in a country where that name was very common. There were even two Simons among the apostles, ch. 3 : 16–19.
3. In Bethany. See on ch. 11 : 1. The *time* of this supper has been much discussed. From John 12 : 1 it appears that Jesus came to Bethany six days before the Passover, on Friday, about sunset (see on ch. 11 : 1), and from Luke 21 : 37 we learn that during the week Jesus was wont to spend the days in the city, and the nights at or near Bethany. Hence, the supper might have occurred upon any one of these evenings. According to John, it seems more natural to place it about twenty-four hours after his arrival, on the evening of Saturday, a common time for supper. But, according to Matthew and Mark, it would seem that it could not have occurred earlier than two days before the Passover. They both relate the supper as the occasion which led to the treachery of Judas, ver. 10. The language in Matt. 26 : 14, *then went Judas,* connects his visit to the chief priests immediately with the supper. As the Sanhedrim had, two days before the Passover, probably Wednesday morning, resolved not to put Jesus to death till after the feast, this visit of Judas must have occurred later on Wednesday, or early on Thursday. The supper, then, might have taken place on the evening of Tuesday, after his final discourse in the temple, and on the Mount of Olives, or on Wednesday evening, after spending the day in retirement in Bethany. The latter seems the more natural conclusion, when we remember how much Jesus did on Tuesday, and that Wednesday appears to have been spent in quiet among his friends. See Author's HARMONY, note on § 158.
Simon the leper. Who had probably been healed by Jesus. He was, perhaps, a relative of Lazarus, and a near neighbor, or both families may have occupied the same house. Hence, Martha serves and Lazarus is a guest, John 12 : 2. One tradition makes him the father of Lazarus, another the husband of Martha. This is, however, all uncertain. **As he sat at meat.** *As he was reclining* on a couch *at table.*
A woman. John calls her Mary, the well-known sister of Martha and Lazarus. Matthew and Mark speak indefinitely, as they make no special reference to the family of Lazarus. The same characteristics are here observable as in the incident recorded in Luke 10 : 38, 41. Martha serves; Mary comes in to be by her Lord, and to show her devotion to him.
Alabaster box. One word in the original, meaning *alabaster,* and well expressed here by *alabaster vase* or *box.* The same word is translated simply *box* near the end of this verse. Alabaster was a variety of gypsum, white and semi-transparent, very costly, and used for making vases and vials for ointments. It was considered by the ancients the best for preserving them. Layard found vases of white alabaster among the ruins of Nineveh, which were used for holding ointments or cosmetics. The general shape of these boxes or vases was large at the bottom, with a long, narrow neck. It was probably the neck of a flask which the woman **broke,** or *crushed,* an act expressive of her feelings that she would devote it all to her Lord, reserving nothing for herself. **Ointment of spikenard,** *of pure spikenard* of the finest quality ; an aromatic oil or ointment, probably produced from the *jatamansee* plant in India, and is still very highly valued. The quantity was a

MARK XIV. A.D. 30.

4 his head. And there were some that had indignation within themselves, and said, Why was this 5 waste of the ointment made? For it might have been sold for more than three hundred ᵍpence, and have been given to the poor. And they murmured 6 against her. And Jesus said, Let her alone; why trouble ye her? She hath wrought a good work on

ᵍ Mt. 18. 28; Ecc. 4. 4; Phil. 2. 14.

---

pound, John 12 : 3. **Very precious.** Very costly. **Poured it on his head.** A distinction conferred on

CRUSES AND VASES.

guests of honor, Luke 7 : 46. John says she anointed his *feet*. She anointed both his head and feet, which was the very highest honor. There is no contradiction, but only variety of statement between the evangelists. Matthew and Mark notice only the first act, anointing the head; John dwells upon the final and longest, and on her part the most humble and devoted act, the anointing the feet and wiping them with her hair. See on ver. 8.

4. **There were some.** Matthew says, "The disciples;" but John, pointing out the leader and instigator, says, "One of his disciples, Judas Iscariot." We have here a beautiful illustration of the independent and truthful statements of the three evangelists. The three accounts taken together are lifelike. The suggestion of Judas is caught up and inconsiderately repeated by the rest. The murmuring spreads and becomes general. **Had indignation within themselves.** *Were much displeased among themselves.* They had the feeling of disapprobation, bordering on resentment.

Why was this waste? The quality and costliness of the ointment was at once discovered by the peculiar richness of the odor which instantly filled the room.

5. **For.** The reason or ground of their objection is given.

For more than three hundred pence, or *denaries.* The denary was a Roman silver coin worth about fifteen cents. The sum here named was about forty-five dollars, and about a laborer's wages for a whole year. See Matt. 20 : 2. **Given to the poor.** A good reason under ordinary circumstances, and, doubtless, uttered honestly by all except Judas, who desired the money for his own use rather than for the poor, John 12 : 6. Yet under this guise of charity the others were led to join with him. But this selfish instigator soon after sold the life of his Master for thirty shekels, about a third of this amount, the price of a slave, Exod. 21 : 32. **Murmured at her,** with the idea also of *to her.* They gave vent to their struggling and somewhat restrained feelings of displeasure.

6. **And Jesus said.** Matthew (26 : 10) says, "When Jesus understood it," or rather, *And Jesus knowing it,* which implies that the murmuring and the reproof of the disciples were intended for the woman, and not for the ear of Jesus, who was the recipient of such honor. Their disapprobation would naturally trouble and confuse her. But Jesus takes up her defense against their complainings, and the avaricious and thievish spirit of Judas. **Wrought a good work.** A work distinguished for its moral beauty, fitness, and grace; literally a *beautiful work.* She had com-

7 me. For ʰ ye have the poor with you always, and whensoever ye will ye may do them good: but me 8 ye have not always. She hath done what she could: she is come aforehand to anoint my body to the 9 burying. Verily I say unto you, Wheresoever this Gospel shall be preached throughout the whole world, *this* also that she hath done shall be spoken of ⁱ for a memorial of her.

ʰ Deu. 15. 11; 2 Cor. 10. 18.

ⁱ Ps. 112. 6; 1 Sam. 2. 30.

---

mitted no offense, but had given a proper expression to her grateful and reverential love, in bringing so costly an offering. Jesus goes on in the next two verses to show why it was such a work.

7. The poor always . . . me not always. They would ever have opportunities of doing good to the poor; but their opportunity to honor him would be short and soon gone. The next verse shows that such an opportunity would never occur again. The words, **Whensoever ye will ye may do them good,** are found only in Mark, and make the contrast the more vivid. An extraordinary offering was fitting an extraordinary opportunity. "To the popish argument (from these words) in favor of a showy and expensive worship, Calvin ingeniously and forcibly replies, that by applauding such an act 'as only practicable once,' our Lord implicitly forbids its repetition and condemns its habitual imitation, just as he would no doubt have rebuked this very woman for the same proceeding, if adopted as an ordinary token of affection."—J. A. ALEXANDER.

8. She hath done what she could, according to her ability and circumstances, her means and opportunities. This high praise, similar to that given to the poor widow (12 : 44), is recorded by Mark alone. **She is come aforehand to anoint my body;** rather, *She anointed beforehand my body.* She anointed by anticipation. It was an act, as Alford remarks, of *prospective* love. Although the evangelist had only spoken of anointing the head, his language here seems to imply that more than that had been anointed. See last paragraph on ver. 3. **To the burying,** *for the burial,* the whole preparation for burial. As there would be no time for this after his death, this anointing and embalming, as it were, for the sepulchre, took place, in the divine arrangement, while he was yet alive. This anointing was not only a symbol of what was about to take place, but was an act performed with definite reference to his death. The language seems to imply a *motive* on the part of Mary; she seems to have had a presentiment, a knowledge beyond his disciples of his approaching death. It also gave Jesus another opportunity of referring to his death. Her act of love and faith stands out in striking contrast to the avarice of Judas and the murmurings of the others.

9. Jesus proceeds to confer upon her one of the greatest honors ever bestowed upon a mortal. **Verily,** etc. A solemn and authoritative assertion. See on ch. 3 : 28. **This gospel.** *The glad tidings* of salvation through a dying and living Savior, which he commanded to be preached to every creature, ch. 16 : 15. **For a memorial of her..** Her deed shall be immortal; it shall be held in everlasting remembrance, and hence she shall, on account of it, be everywhere spoken of. It is remarkable that Matthew and Mark, who give this prophecy, do not give her name, but John, who gives her name, omits the prophecy. But her *deed* was the great thing; again, she was *one* in the world's history, the only one in regard to whom Jesus made such a promise; but her name, Mary, was common, and designated many. Yet John, in giving the account, and revealing the fact that the woman was Mary, the sister of Martha, still further contributes toward making the knowledge of her deed and person commensurate with the preaching of the gospel. How literally is this prophecy being fulfilled! Alford sees in it a distinct reference to the *written records* in which this event should be related.

10, 11. JUDAS ENGAGES WITH THE CHIEF PRIESTS TO BETRAY JESUS. Matt.

10 ᵏAnd Judas Iscariot, one of the twelve, went unto ᵏMt. 26. 14; Lk.
11 the chief priests, to betray him unto them. And   22. 3, 4.
when they heard *it*, they were glad, and promised
to give him money. And he sought how he might
conveniently betray him.

Jesus celebrates the Passover, and points out the traitor.

12 ˡAND the first day of unleavened bread, when   Mt. 26. 17; Lk.
they killed the passover, his disciples said unto 22. 7; Ex. 12. 6,
him, Where wilt thou that we go and prepare that   18-20.

26 : 14-16 ; Luke 22 : 3-6. Luke is the fullest, and, passing over the anointing, connects this account with the conspiring of the Jewish rulers to kill Jesus. Mark is the briefest; but, with Matthew, joins the account to that of the anointing, though less definitely.

10. **And.** Matthew says, with more definiteness, *Then,* connecting the act of Judas with what had just transpired. The continuous narrative of Mark confirms, however, the natural idea in Matthew. The words of Jesus were counter to those of Judas (John 12 : 4), and, in connection with the high honor bestowed upon Mary, were a severe reproof to him. He must have felt that, in the eyes of Jesus, and, indeed, of the others, he stood in insignificant contrast to the devoted Mary. Stung with the transactions and the words of the hour, his evil nature was aroused to thoughts both of abandoning the cause of Jesus, and of treachery. With a heart unrenewed, he had not only been captivated with an idea of an earthly kingdom, but a spiritual reign and a suffering Savior were also repulsive. He could not perceive spiritual truth. Hence the humiliation of Jesus, his prophecies concerning his death, his denunciation of the Jewish hierarchy, all ran counter to his feelings and spirit. He saw no prospect of worldly power, and his hopes of gain died with the anointing at Bethany, and the approving declaration of Jesus, that it was anticipatory of his burial. Turning away from Jesus and his cause with resentment and disappointment, he seeks to satisfy his avarice by selling him to his enemies. See Matt. 27 : 3. **Iscariot.** *Man of Karioth*, probably native of Karioth of Judah. See on ch. 3 : 19. Mark, as well as Matthew, makes prominent the idea that the betrayer was **one of the twelve.**

Went unto the chief priests. See on ch. 8 : 31. This occurred probably in the evening with which Thursday began. Yet if the supper took place in the daytime, Judas may have visited the chief priests on the afternoon of Wednesday. The latter supposition agrees well with Matt. 26 : 14, *From that time,* which seems to imply a longer time than part of a day. **To betray him.** To deliver him up to them, of course, treacherously.

11. **They were glad.** His proposal was received by the chief priests with joy ; it was an unexpected opportunity ; they thought that now they could apprehend him without delay, privately, and without causing a tumult among the people, Luke 22 : 6. **Promised to give him money,** or *silver,* silver money. Matthew (26 : 16) mentions the amount, thirty pieces of silver, that is, thirty silver shekels, the price of a slave's life (Exod. 21 : 32), commonly estimated at about fifteen dollars. From this it may be inferred that the money was paid him when he fulfilled his agreement.
He sought how, in what way and by what means. "He sought opportunity," says Matthew. **Conveniently betray him ;** that he might at a proper time, with safety to them and to himself, deliver him up into their hands; "in the absence of the multitude," Luke 22 : 6. The popular commotion was what they wished to avoid, ver. 2.

12-16. PREPARATION FOR THE PASSOVER. Matt. 26 : 17-19 ; Luke 22 : 17-13. Matthew's account is very brief. Mark and Luke enter more into details. Thursday, April 6.

12. **The first day of unleavened bread,** that is, of the feast of unleavened bread. The day is further designated, **when they killed the pass-**

13 thou mayest eat the passover? And he sendeth forth two of his disciples, and saith unto them, Go ye into the city, and there shall meet you a man
14 bearing a pitcher of water: follow him; and wheresoever he shall go in, say ye to the goodman of the house, The Master saith, Where is the guest-chamber, where I shall eat the passover with my disciples?
15 And he will show you a large upper room furnished *and* prepared: there make ready for us.

---

over, *the paschal lamb,* Luke 22 : 7. Hence the 14th of Nisan, occurring this year on Thursday, April 6th, Exod. 12 : 18. This in popular language was the first day of the Passover, although the feast did not strictly begin till the fifteenth. Hence Josephus speaks of the feast of unleavened bread lasting eight days. For fear of transgressing the law, the Jews were accustomed to cease from labor, and put away all leaven from their houses, at or before noon on this day, the fourteenth of Nisan. Compare Num. 28 : 16, 17. It is evident from this verse and the references given, that Jesus observed the Paschal Supper at the regular time, and not an anticipatory meal, as some suppose, twenty-four hours before the usual time. See a discussion of this question in the HARMONY OF THE GOSPELS, by the author, note on § 159. **Where,** etc. The point of this question refers to the *place* of the supper, and only incidentally to the preparation of the paschal lamb, Luke 22 : 9.

13. Sendeth forth two of his disciples. These were Peter and John, Luke 22 : 8. The names are here omitted by Mark, possibly through modesty, the Gospel being written under Peter's direction. **Go into the city.** From Bethany, where they now were, into Jerusalem, where only the paschal supper could be eaten. Hence, since the destruction of Jerusalem and of the temple, where only the paschal lamb was slain, the Jews omit eating the lamb, and confine themselves to the usual feast of unleavened bread, which followed the supper. **There shall meet you,** etc. In this Jesus showed his supernatural foresight. He gives the two disciples a sign similar to that which Samuel gave to Saul, 1 Sam. 10 : 2-7. **A pitcher;** an earthen vessel. **Follow him.** Jesus does not mention him by name, or if he does, his disciples do not know him; for his place is to be found by following a man bearing a pitcher of water, Luke 22 : 10. Compare Matt. 17 : 27. Some very plausibly suppose that Jesus concealed the place and the name of the individual, so as to prevent Judas from executing his purpose before the proper time.

14. Wheresoever he shall go in. *Where he shall enter.* **Goodman,** an old English word for *master* of the house. **The Master.** Very possibly this man was a disciple, since Jesus was known to him as *the Teacher.* However this may be, it is unnecessary to suppose any previous understanding between them, for it was common at that season to have rooms prepared in advance for any who might need them, and Jesus knew by his omniscience that this room was yet unengaged. It is said that rooms were furnished strangers at the Passover without pay, except the skins of the lambs sacrificed. **Where is the guest-chamber,** the lodging-room. According to some very ancient manuscripts, *my guest-chamber, my quarters.* **The passover.** The paschal supper.

15. A large upper room, a room above the first story, the most desirable part of an Oriental house, and still given to guests who are to be treated with honor. (THOMSON, *The Land and the Book,* vol. 1., p. 235.) **Furnished and prepared.** *Spread* or *furnished* with couches and tables, *ready* for the paschal supper. The man may have prepared it, and reserved it, under a deep divine impression. **There make ready,** or *prepare,* **for us.** Two preparations are brought to view in this verse. Of the room, by the master of the house; and of the lamb and other things necessary for the paschal supper, by the two disciples. On the latter see next verse.

16 And his disciples went forth, and came into the city, and found as he had said unto them: and they
17 made ready the passover. ᵐ And in the evening he
18 cometh with the twelve. And as they sat and did eat, Jesus said, Verily I say unto you, One of you

ᵐ Mt. 26. 20; Lk. 22. 14; John 13. 21.

16. Peter and John go as directed, and find the man and room as Jesus had said. **They made ready the passover,** the paschal supper. They slew the lamb, or had it slain, in the temple; its blood was sprinkled at the foot of the altar, and its fat burned thereon; and the bitter herbs, the bread and wine were prepared. The killing of the paschal lamb is thus described by Starke in Lange's Commentary: "A crowd of Israelites were received into the court, the gates were shut, the trumpets sounded. The householders slew their lambs. The priests formed a row which extended to the altar, received the blood in silver basins, which they passed on from one to another; and those who stood nearest the altar poured it out at its feet, whence it flowed subterraneously into the brook Kedron. The householder lifted the slain lamb to a hook on a pillar, took off its skin and removed the fat. This last the priest burned on the altar. The householder uttered a prayer, and carried the lamb to his house bound in its skin. The head of the house where the feast was held received the skin. When the first crowd departed another followed, and so forth."

17–21. THE CELEBRATION OF THE PASSOVER. JESUS FORETELLS HIS BETRAYAL, AND POINTS OUT THE TRAITOR. Matt. 26: 20–24; Luke 22: 14–18; 21–30; John 13.: 1–30. The accounts of Matthew and Mark are quite similar, with occasional differences, such as we would expect in independent narratives. Luke and John exhibit greater divergences, the former giving the contention of the disciples, the latter the washing of the disciples' feet. The time was Thursday evening, or, according to Jewish mode of beginning the day with sunset, Friday, April 6th.

17. **In the evening.** *Evening having come,* or at evening, which commenced Friday, the 15th of Nisan. The two having returned, and announced that all was ready.

18. **As they sat.** *As they reclined at table,* according to the custom of eating, with the left hand resting upon the couch, which was usually higher than the low table. The whole service was originally performed standing, the reclining was adopted after the Israelites possessed Canaan, symbolizing the rest God had given them. The standing posture (Exod. 12: 11) was appropriate and specially designed for the first observance. Sundry additions were afterward made. According to the Talmud, compiled in the third century from earlier traditions, four cups of the common red wine of the country, usually mingled with one-fourth part of water, were drunk during the meal, and marked its progress. The first, as they reclined at table, in connection with an invocation and blessing upon the day and the wine, corresponding with the cup mentioned in Luke 22: 17. Then followed washing of hands, the bringing in of unleavened bread, bitter herbs, the roasted lamb, and a sauce or fruit-paste. The master of the feast then blessed God for the fruit of the earth and gave the explanation respecting the Passover prescribed in Exod. 12: 26, 27. Psalms 113, 114 were then sung, and the second cup was drunk. Then each kind of food was blessed and eaten, the paschal lamb being eaten last. A third cup of thanksgiving, called the cup of blessing (compare 1 Cor. 10: 16), for deliverance from Egypt, was drunk. Psalms 115–118 were sung, and the fourth cup drunk, closing the celebration. Sometimes Psalms 120–137 were sung or repeated, followed by a fifth cup.

We may presume that Jesus observed the more ancient manner of celebrating the Passover, rather than that of the later Jewish traditions. We have no evidence that he used more than one cup at the Passover, Luke 22: 17, 18. Before the drinking of this cup, the contention among the twelve (Luke 22: 24–30) probably occurred, and the washing of the disciples' feet (John 13: 1–20) immediately after. The paschal supper is continued; the traitor is point-

19 which eateth with me shall betray me. And they began to be sorrowful, and to say unto him one by
20 one, *Is* it I? and another *said*, *Is* it I? And he answered and said unto them, *It is* one of the twelve,

ed out, who withdraws, and then the Lord's Supper is instituted.

The Passover was both commemorative and typical in its nature and design. It commemorated the deliverance from the destroying angel in Egypt, and typified the greater deliverance through Christ, "the lamb of God that taketh away the sin of the world." At this very feast "Christ our passover was sacrificed for us," 1 Cor. 5 : 7.

Did eat, the paschal supper. Luke (22 : 18-23) gives an account of the Lord's Supper, before that of pointing out the traitor; but the latter he only incidently notices, while he makes the former the central point in his narrative, and its position was probably decided by the mention of the first cup of wine. Both Matthew and Mark place the institution of the Lord's Supper afterward. **Verily I say unto you.** A solemn affirmation here introducing a declaration, which is both a solemn prediction and an expression of grief. **One of you which eateth with me,** etc., very expressive in the Greek: *One of you will betray me,* deliver me up into the power of my enemies, *the one that eateth with me.* These words with ver. 20 and John 13 : 26 have led some to suppose that Judas sat next to Jesus, and partook of the same dish. There may be a reference to Ps. 41 : 9, which is quoted by John (13 : 18), "He that eateth bread with me hath lifted up his heel against me."

19. **They began** at once **to be sorrowful,** distressed at this terrible announcement. **One by one.** One after another, in anxiety and amazement began to say, **Is it I?** This question is very striking in the original, and requires a negative answer, and is about equivalent to *It is not I, is it?* **And another said, Is it I?** These words are omitted in some of the oldest manuscripts and versions, probably because they were thought superfluous and the construction inadmissible. But the repetition really gives vividness to the narrative. One after another said, Is it I? Then another said, Is it I? till the question went the round, and even Judas with solemn hypocrisy asks it, Matt. 26 : 25. *Another* can hardly be a reference to Judas, but is merely thrown in in vivid description.

20. **It is one of the twelve,** etc. Very expressive language in the original, similar to that in ver. 18. *It is one of the twelve, one that dippeth with me.* **In the dish.** Of sauce prepared of dates, figs, and seasoning, which was of brick color, representing the clay and brick of Egypt. Into this they dipped their bread and bitter herbs. This pertained to the Passover, from which it is evident the Lord's Supper had not commenced. One dish may have been used, but more probably there were several. Judas was therefore probably near Jesus, using the same dish; and this answer amounted almost to a pointed designation of the traitor. Persons often expressed their affection to others by presenting them with dipped bread, etc. Dipping into the same dish was a mark of great friendliness and intimacy. Hence this answer, and the giving of the morsel to Judas (John 13 : 26) might easily be misunderstood. The right hand was used at the table, instead of spoons and forks; the hands being washed before and after eating. "The same is the case in modern Egypt. . . . To pick out a delicate morsel and hand it to a friend is esteemed a compliment, and to refuse such an offering is contrary to good manners."—HACKETT'S *Smith's Dict.*

From the full account of John, we learn that Peter beckoned to John, who was leaning on Jesus' breast, requesting him to ask privately who it was of whom he spoke. John did so, and Jesus gave him a sign by which he might know the traitor, namely, he to whom he should give a sop or morsel.

The answers of Jesus regarding the traitor may be harmonized as follows: The answer here given by Mark may be regarded as the first; then the sign to John, while several disciples con-

21 that dippeth with me in the dish. ⁿ The Son of man indeed goeth, as it is written of him: but woe to that man by whom the Son of man is betrayed! good were it for that man if he had never been born.

ⁿ Mt. 26. 24; Lk. 22, 22; Ac. 1. 25.

Jesus institutes the Lord's Supper.

22 ᵒ And as they did eat, Jesus took bread, and blessed, and brake *it*, and gave to them, and said,

ᵒ Mt. 26. 26; Lk. 22. 19; 1 Cor. 11. 23.

tinue to ask, *Is it I?* Then having dipped his hand into the dish with Judas, and given him the sop, he makes the reply recorded in Matthew (26:23), literally, *He that dipped his hand with me*, etc. Or the reply in Matthew may be regarded as the same as that in this verse, both being quoted according to sense. These replies of our Savior seem to have been better understood by Judas than by the others; for when Judas went out, no one appears to have understood the intent of our Lord's language to him, John 13:28, 29. The object of Jesus was not to expose the traitor, but to give him all necessary warning against committing so terrible a crime.

21. **Goeth as it is written.** The Messiah goeth in the path of humiliation and suffering to death, as it is written of him in such prophecies as Isa. 53:4–12; Dan. 9:26; Zech. 12:10; 13:7. **Woe unto that man.** Though his death was according to God's purpose, and foretold by ancient prophets, yet his betrayer and murderers were without excuse, Acts 2:22–24. God's purpose and foreknowledge are coexistent, and are in harmony with human freedom. Judas was not compelled to betray Jesus. His act was his own and freely committed. The woe upon the traitor points him out as an object both of pity and of wrath. The terrible consequences of his guilt are unutterable: it were good if he had never had an existence. His very being will be a curse to him. Our Savior's language points to a future miserable existence, and may be used as an argument against annihilation. The original is peculiar, *It were good for him, or Good for him, if that man had not been born.* As in the whole transaction, so here the language is pointed in respect to Judas, yet general and somewhat indefinite as to the other disciples.

At this point Matthew (26:25) records the question of Judas, "Rabbi, is it I?" and the reply of Jesus, "Thou hast said." The answer goes home to Judas' heart. His evil nature is thoroughly aroused when he finds that Jesus not only knows his treachery, but plainly tells him of it. Satan takes possession of the heart prepared to receive him, and Judas in bitterness hastens forth from the company where he can feel no longer at home into the congenial darkness without, to execute his treacherous plan, John 13:27–30. Hence he was not present at the institution of the Lord's Supper. See ver. 18.

22–26. INSTITUTION OF THE LORD'S SUPPER. Matt. 26:26–30; Luke 22:19, 20; compare 1 Cor. 11:23–26. Matthew's account is the fullest of the evangelists, though equaled by that of Paul. Luke's is briefest. Mark deviates but slightly from Matthew, but states the additional fact, regarding the cup, "They all drank of it." The supplemental character of John's Gospel explains his silence regarding the institution of this ordinance. The fourth account, though wanting in the fourth Gospel, is supplied by Paul.

22. **As they did eat.** This is in harmony with the supposition that Judas was not present at the supper. See on vers. 18, 21, and John 13:30. The time here indicated was probably very soon after.

These words show that the supper was instituted while they still reclined at the Passover table; but they do not teach that the Lord's Supper was grafted on the Passover, or sprang out from it. The supper was not instituted at the Passover because it was in any way connected with it, but because the Passover night immediately preceding his sufferings was the best and fittest time for its institution. It was entirely distinct, a new ordinance of the new

23 Take, eat: this is my body. And he took the cup, and when he had given thanks, he gave it to them:

dispensation. The Passover was sacrificial, the Lord's Supper is not; Christ has been offered once for all. The former was national and observed by families, the latter is intrusted to the church, and is emphatically a church ordinance. The one was commemorative of a temporal deliverance, yet pointing to the great Paschal Sacrifice of Christ; the other commemorates what Christ in his sufferings and death has done for his followers, yet points to him as a living Savior, absent for a time, but who will come again without sin unto salvation.

Took bread. *Taking a loaf* or thin cake of unleavened bread, which was before him. The *one loaf* points to the one body of Christ which has been offered up, and to the *oneness* of his followers with him, forming "one loaf, one body," 1 Cor. 10:16, 17. **Blessed.** He blessed God and invoked the divine blessing; Luke and Paul say, *he gave thanks.* The two verbs explain each other and amount to the same thing. The giving thanks was blessing God, and both were a blessing of the bread and a setting it apart to a sacred use. Compare ch. 6:41 and note, and John 6:11. **Brake.** This represented his body broken on the cross, the wounds and sufferings of death. Hence *breaking* of the bread is essential to the true idea. Cutting it is a perversion. The ordinance was even called "the breaking of bread," Acts 2:42. **Gave to the disciples.** The apostles were the representatives of that one body, the church; hence they alone partook, because it was an ordinance of that one body. The Lord's Supper is a church ordinance, 1 Cor. 11:20, 33. **Take, eat.** Simply, *Take it,* according to the oldest and best manuscripts. Matthew alone, according to the highest critical authorities, gives the full command *Take, eat.* In receiving the bread we signify our acceptance of Christ the living bread and the atonement he has made. We thus commune in this ordinance with Christ, and through Christ indirectly with one another, 1 Cor. 10:16, 17.

This is my body. Luke adds, "which is given for you; this do in remembrance of me." Not literally *my body ;* for Jesus was present in his body, and the broken bread was visibly not a part of it. So also in Paul's account, who declares that he received it from the Lord, and is therefore of the highest authority, Jesus says, "This cup is the New Testament in my blood," 1 Cor. 11:25; so also Luke 22:20. If this broken bread was literally Christ's body, then "This cup," etc., means, This material cup (not the wine in it) is the actual New Testament or covenant. The latter so evidently demands a figurative or symbolic meaning that Maldonatus, the Jesuit commentator, could meet the difficulty only by impiously setting himself up against the inspired penman, and declaring that Christ never uttered these words. The verb *is,* in the expression, *This is my body,* upon which papists have laid so much stress in advocating the doctrine of transubstantiation, belongs only to the Greek translation of our Savior's language, though it was implied in Aramaic, the language in which our Savior spoke. Similar expressions are, however, found in all languages, and with no doubtful meaning. Thus, Joseph, in explaining the dream of Pharaoh, says, "The seven good kine are seven years," Gen. 41:26. They signified or represented seven years. So also "The good seed are the children of the kingdom" (Matt. 13:38); "that rock was Christ" (1 Cor. 10:4); "Agar is Mount Sinai" (Gal. 4:25), and many similar expressions. So also Jesus calls himself a door (John 10:9), a vine (John 15:1), a star (Rev. 22:16). He also spoke of the temple of his body, John 2:19, 21. No one would for a moment take such language literally, but emblematically. So the bread represents his body, is an emblem of it. Or, turning our minds from the verb to the two things compared, we may say that as Christ is spiritually and figuratively a door, a star, a vine, or a temple, so his body is figuratively and spiritually the bread of life. Thus, in this part of the ordinance Christ is represented as the sustenance of his people. The doctrine of transubstantiation, therefore, finds no basis in this passage ; it is contrary to its plain meaning as well as to common sense.

23. **A cup.** Including the wine

24 and they all drank of it. And he said unto them, p This is my blood of the New q Testament, which is

p Ex. 24. 7, 8.
q Jer. 31. 31; Heb. 9. 14–22; 10. 4–14; 13. 20.

which it contained. Probably the wine mixed with water, used at the Passover. "The common wine of Palestine is of red color. Such was the wine used at the sacrament, as it would seem both from the nature of the case and from the declaration, This is my blood."— L. COLEMAN, D.D. Some hold that it was unfermented wine, since nothing fermented was permitted at the feast. But of this there is wanting proof. The Jews in Palestine now use fermented wine at the feast, but if any wine is found to be running into acetous fermentation, it is removed. Dr. C. V. A. Van Dyck, who has resided for more than a quarter of a century in Syria, says (*Bibliotheca Sacra*, vol. xxvi., p. 170): "In Syria, and as far as I can learn in all the East, there is no wine preserved unfermented; . . . they could not keep grape juice or raisin-water unfermented, if they would; it would become either wine or vinegar in a few days, or go into the putrefactive fermentation. . . . At the Passover, only fermented wine is used. As I said before, there is no other, and therefore they have no idea of any other." Dr. Van Dyck is decided in the opinion that such a thing as unfermented wine never has been known in Syria.

According to many high critical authorities, this should read *a cup*, implying that there were several cups on the table. We must beware of falling into the error of confounding it with one of the Passover cups. The wine was doubtless that used at the Passover; but it was a cup of a new ordinance and of a new dispensation. We must not suppose that Jesus slavishly followed the tradition of the elders in celebrating the Passover.

Had given thanks. The same act as performed over the bread. He praised God for it, set it apart to a sacred use, thereby blessing it. Hence it is called the *cup of blessing*, 1 Cor. 10 : 16. From the Greek verb, *eucharisteo*, to give thanks, the ordinance has been called *the eucharist*. So also it has been called *the communion*, because in it there is a communion or partaking emblematically of the body and blood of Christ, 1 Cor. 10 : 16, 17. The latter name is objectionable, because it conveys mere Christian fellowship too prominently to most minds. The former conveys too solely the idea of a thank-offering. Better call it by the names inspiration has given, either *The breaking of bread* (Acts 2 : 46), or, better still, the more comprehensive title, *The Lord's Supper* (1 Cor. 11 : 20), to which latter title the former seems to have given way. The Romish names *Mass*, and *High Mass*, the latter being sung or chanted, is without any Scriptural foundation or authority.

They all drank of it. The *all* is noticeable, as connected with the cup only; the fact may be used against the popish custom of withholding the cup from the people. The apostles were the representatives of the church; the entire membership of the church are, therefore, to drink of the cup. As has been remarked by Bengel, "If one kind were sufficient, it is the cup that should be used. The Scripture thus speaks, foreseeing (Gal. 3 : 8) what Rome would do." It was A.D. 1418 that the Church of Rome enacted that only the officiating priests should partake of the cup. In receiving the cup we signify our faith in the efficacy of that blood which cleanseth from all sin, the acceptance of the atonement made and the redemption procured. And as blood stood for life (Lev. 17 : 11, 14), so we by faith receive Christ as our life, his life as our life. For a beautiful illustration, see the language of our Savior in John 6 : 53–58.

24. **This is my blood.** This represents and is an emblem of my blood. **Of the New Testament.** According to the highest critical authorities this passage should read : *The blood of the covenant*, of the gospel dispensation (the conditions, promises and pledges of salvation), Jer. 31 : 31 ; Heb. 8 : 7–13. In contrast to the blood of the old dispensation, of which that of the Passover, of course, formed a part. The blood of the old covenant was the blood of lambs, calves, goats and bulls, Exod. 24 : 8; Heb. 9 : 18–22. The blood of the new covenant is the blood of Christ, of which the wine of the cup is an emblem, Heb. 9 : 11, 12, 24–26. As the former covenant was made, dedicated, and its blessings se-

25 shed ' for many. Verily I say unto you, I will drink no more of the fruit of the vine, until that day that I drink it new in the kingdom of God.

' Mt. 20. 28; Col. 1. 14, 20; 1 John 2. 2.

cured by the blood of beasts, so the latter was procured and established, and its blessings secured to all believers through the blood of Christ. The former by *types*, the latter by the *reality*; but both by the shedding of blood. In receiving the cup, therefore, we openly accept this covenant.
Which is shed. Though before his sufferings, yet Jesus, by anticipation, speaks of it as virtually accomplished.
For many. Great multitudes. In this place, in connection with the Lord's Supper, *many* are those to whom his blood is rendered efficacious through faith. The relation of Christ's atonement to all men is presented in 1 Tim. 2 : 6, and similar passages. See on ch. 10 : 45. Thus, the wine poured forth represents Christ's death as substitutionary *for many*, in their behalf, in their stead. Christ's sufferings were vicarious.

The simplicity of the ordinance is in striking contrast to that sacrificial ordinance which Romanists style the Mass. "The Council of Trent, Sept. 17, 1562, declared ' that in the eucharist a true propitiatory sacrifice was offered for sin, in the same way as when Christ offered up himself as a sacrifice on the cross,' and the council consigned all to damnation who should deny it. According to Romish authors, the bread or wafer is turned into God, and so the priests, by using the words of consecration, can *create* the Creator! Raising the consecrated wafer, that is, God, at the celebration of the mass, so high that all the people can see it, and worshiping it as *The Host*, that is, a victim (from the Latin *hostia*), was first ordered by the Pope Honorius. What 'damnable heresies' have an apostate church not brought in!"—N. M. WILLIAMS. This whole idea of the Lord's Supper being a sacrifice is opposed not only to its original institution, but also to Heb. 7 : 27; 9 : 25-28 : "Who needeth not daily, as those high priests, to offer up sacrifice, first for his own sins, and then for the people's : for this he did once, when he offered up himself."

25. I will drink no more. Emphatic, *I will in no wise, any more.* These words he had uttered at the Passover, Luke 22 : 16, 18. He repeats them at the supper. They are not inconsistent with the supposition that Jesus himself did not partake of the bread and wine of the supper. For so the language in Matt. 26 : 26, 27, *Take, eat*, as well as, *Drink ye all*, seems to imply. There really could be no significance in Jesus partaking of that which represented his own body and blood. They were offered for others; he himself needed no offering. Instead of saying definitely *this cup*, he says generally, *this* **fruit of the vine.** He had just previously, at the Passover, drank of it for the last time with them ; now he takes the cup, gives thanks, hands it to them, commanding all to drink, saying that from this time onward he will not drink it till he drinks it with them, fresh and of a different kind, in the kingdom of his Father. *This fruit of the vine*, however, includes the cup, and must have referred to the wine in it as a beverage. Hence it is worthy of notice that, though he had said, *This is my blood*, he yet speaks generally of the wine as *this fruit* of the vine. No change had taken place.

The phrase also affords an argument against the use of the various forms of domestic and adulterated wines at the Lord's Supper. It should be *the fruit of the vine*. Whether it should be fermented, or unfermented, is a question worthy of attention. Although there is no proof that unfermented wine was used at the Passover (see on ver 23), yet it was more in accordance with its spirit and nature, as the feast of *unleavened* bread. And in the Lord's Supper unfermented wine is in the truest and most literal sense *the fruit of the vine*, and answers to the idea of *freshness* implied in *new*, immediately following. Such considerations, together with the present state of society, and of the temperance question, incline me to prefer unfermented wine at the Lord's table.

New. The word in the original conveys not only the idea of *freshness*, but also of a *new kind*, and of *superior excellence*. Thus, *this fruit*, etc., and *new*, are in contrast. Jesus will not drink

26 And when they had sung an hymn, they went out into the mount of Olives.

of the earthly beverage, which is an emblem of his death, though also of the life of his people; but he will drink of that which is the result of his death, and which all his followers shall share with him; not of the earthly type, but of the heavenly reality. Thus, the new wine points to the felicity of the glorified state, the bliss of eternal life, which shall be enjoyed and celebrated at the marriage supper of the Lamb. The cup points to the life given for his people; the new wine, to that glorified life obtained for them, Rev. 19 : 6-9; 22 : 2. That is a tame interpretation indeed which makes this verse mean that the Jewish Passover is to be henceforth superseded by the Lord's Supper!

This verse also shows that the ordinance not only looks back to the death of Christ, but also forward to the establishment of his glorified kingdom. Paul more exactly defines its future limit and prospect by the words, *till he come*, 1 Cor. 11 : 26. The ordinance is thus confined to the church during the absence of the Lord. It is an ordinance of the earth, not of heaven. When he comes to be present with his glorified people, they will have the reality, and will not need the emblems, either to remind them or to aid their faith. Hence this verse cannot mean, that Jesus would unite with his disciples in this supper, in heaven. Jesus probably now utters that memorable discourse and prayer recorded by John in chs. 14-17.

26. **Sung an hymn.** A fitting close of the supper. This is the only recorded instance of singing by Jesus and his disciples. After an ordinance emblematical of his complete and perfect work, and after his consoling discourse and affectionate prayer, in all of which he seems to have viewed the work in its full accomplishment, he could well sing with his disciples a hymn of praise. Jesus sung and gave "songs in the night," Job 35 : 10. In the original, a single word is used, literally *having hymned, having sung hymns*, or *praise*, or *psalms*, the word by no means limiting it to a single hymn, or composition. It is very commonly supposed that they sung or chanted Psalms 115-118, which were said to be used at the close of the Passover. Of this, however, we have no means of determining. The ordinance is one of mingled solemnity and joy.

This is a fitting place to refer to the relation between the two ordinances Christ has intrusted to his church. In order of time, Baptism first, the Lord's Supper after. See on the various passages relating to baptism. In relation to individuals and churches, baptism is the initial rite; the Lord's Supper the memorial, covenanting and communing rite of those initiated by baptism. The former to individuals separately, and but once; the latter to individuals assembled in church relations, and oft repeated. The one is a profession of faith, a putting on Christ; the other the renewed vows and confession of the soul in Christ, and living on Christ. Again, baptism points to our burial into Christ's death; the Lord's Supper, to our living by Christ's life. The former is a symbol of our new birth; the latter, of the sustenance of our new life. The one shows how we are made one in Christ; the other, how we are continued one in him. Thus, in whatever way we may view these ordinances, the former precedes the latter. Baptism is in its nature and in its divine arrangement a prerequisite to the Lord's Supper. Faith, or a regenerate state, which is presupposed by baptism, and an orderly walk (2 Thess. 3 : 6) are also prerequisites. See on ch. 16 : 16.

The Mount of Olives. See on ch. 11 : 1. Jesus passes out of the city, down the deep gorge on the eastern side, crosses the Kedron, about where a small bridge now spans the dry channel, to a grove at the foot of the Mount of Olives, named Gethsemane, where he was wont to resort with his disciples, Luke 22 : 39; John 18 : 2. He goes thither to enter upon his sufferings, and to be betrayed to his enemies.

27-31. THE SCATTERING OF THE DISCIPLES AND PETER'S DENIAL FORETOLD. Matt. 31-35; Luke 22 : 39; John 18 : 1. Compare Luke 22 : 31-38 and John 13 : 31 -38. It is very commonly supposed that these four accounts refer to the same conversation. It seems very difficult

The scattering of the disciples, and Peter's denial foretold.

27 *And Jesus saith unto them, All ye shall be offended because of me this night: for it is written, ¹ I will smite the shepherd, and the sheep shall be scattered.' But ⁿ after that I am risen, I will go before you into Galilee.
28
29 ˣBut Peter said unto him, Although all shall be offended, yet *will* not I. And Jesus saith unto him, Verily I say unto thee, That this day, *even* in this night, before the cock crow twice, thou shalt deny
30

* Mt. 26. 31; Lk. 22. 31; John 13. 36.
ᶦ John 16. 32; Zech. 13. 7.
ⁿ ch. 16. 7.
ˣ Mt. 26. 33, 34; Lk. 22. 33, 31; John 13. 37, 38; 2 Ki. 8. 13; Jer. 10. 23; 17. 9.

to reduce them to any sort of harmony. The circumstances and time seem to be different. The scene in Matthew and Mark is on their going out to the Mount of Olives; that in Luke and John while they were still in the upper room. It seems more natural and in perfect harmony with the four narratives to suppose that Jesus twice intimated Peter's denial; the first after the departure of Judas, related by Luke and John, and the second an hour or two afterward, as they were going to the Mount of Olives, related by Matthew and Mark. See author's HARMONY, on § 169. The accounts of Matthew and Mark are given in almost the same language. Mark, however, excels in definiteness, vers. 30, 31.

27. **All ye shall be offended;** ye shall find cause of offense, of stumbling; so as to desert me, ver. 50. **Because of me this night;** these words are not found in most of the oldest and best manuscripts; they belong to Matt. 26:31. **For it is written.** In Zech. 13:7. The quotation which follows conforms quite closely to the Septuagint version of the Old Testament, and expresses the thought of the original Hebrew. Jesus quotes this prophecy, thereby intimating that a suffering Messiah was in accordance with the purposes of God, and that in connection with it his followers should be scattered. He quoted it also for their sake; doubtless they pondered it during those days of darkness. **I will smite.** God is said to smite Jesus, since he both permitted and purposed it; he gave him to be smitten, John 3:16; Acts 2:23. **The shepherd.** The Messiah, the great shepherd of the sheep (Heb. 13:20), spoken of immediately after as *my fellow* (Zech. 13:7), a fellow-ruler, the King of kings, and an equal, Phil. 2:6. In Zech. 11:8–13, it was foretold that he should be rejected and sold, and in 12:10, that he should be pierced. **Shall be scattered,** in all directions. A strong and authoritative assertion. Their scattering implied that they were offended in him, disaffected in their faith, discipleship, and thoughts of him, Luke 24:21.

28. **I will go before.** As a shepherd, John 10:4, 27. Jesus throws a beam of light on this dark picture. In accordance with the remainder of the verse in Zechariah, "And I will turn mine hand upon the little ones." It does not imply that he would not appear to them previous to meeting them in Galilee; but rather that, rising before their return thither, he would again collect the flock, and go before them to Galilee, ch. 16:7; Luke 24:33-36. For the fulfillment of this promise see ch. 16; Matt. 28:16; John 21:1; 1 Cor. 15:6.

29. **Peter said.** Impulsive and self-confident, Peter is the first to speak. He speaks not now, as frequently, as spokesman of the apostles, but for himself, arrogating a courage and devotion above his associates. **Though all.** Notice the strength of his self-reliant assertion, *Though all* (the rest), or even more strongly, *all* (every one) *should be offended,* **yet will not I.** Peter had been before warned of his defection and denial, Luke 22:31-34. The second warning arouses him to the strongest assertion. His self-sufficiency and arrogance found an antidote in his fall, and seem to have been alluded to by Jesus after his resurrection, at the Sea of Galilee, "Simon, son of Jonas, lovest thou me *more than these?*" John 21:15. He was permitted to fall lower than any of his brethren.

30. Jesus replies with the solemn and

31 me thrice. But he spake the more vehemently, If I should die with thee, I will not deny thee in any wise. Likewise also said they all.

Christ's agony in Gethsemane.

32 ʳAND they came to a place which was named Gethsemane. And he saith to his disciples, Sit ye here, while I shall pray.   ʳMt. 26. 36; Lk. 22. 39; John 18. 1.

authoritative beginning, "Verily I say unto you." **That this day** of twenty-four hours, which had begun at sunset. Literally, *That thou this day.* Notice that *thou* is emphatic, in striking contrast to, *yet will not I,* ver. 29. He more definitely marks the time, in **this night.** And still more definitely, **before the cock crow twice.** *A cock,* etc. So in the other Gospels the indefinite article is used, which is in harmony with the supposed scarcity of this fowl. Fowls are very abundant in the East at the present day. Later Jewish writers affirm, though not always consistent with themselves, that the inhabitants of Jerusalem, and the priests everywhere, were forbidden to keep fowls, because they scratched up unclean worms. But even if this were so, the Roman residents, over whom the Jews could exercise no power, might keep them. **Twice.** The first about midnight; the second about three o'clock. The former would be less noticed at a time when people were generally asleep. The latter was more commonly observed as the signal of approaching labors, and hence was called by way of eminence *the cock-crowing,* to which Matthew and the other evangelists refer. Mark records the very words of Jesus as they were indelibly impressed upon Peter's mind. Matthew gives the general sense. "The difference is the same as (similar to) that between saying *before the bell rings* and *before the second bell rings* (for church or dinner), the reference in both expressions being to the last and most important signal, to which the first is only preliminary. The existence or occurrence of the latter, though expressly mentioned only in the last phrase, is not excluded by the first, and, if previously known, may be considered as included in it."—J. A. ALEXANDER. **Deny me;** that I am your Lord and Teacher, and that you are, or ever have been, my disciple. **Disown me. Thrice.** Emphatic in the original, *Thrice deny me.* Thus he who exalted himself the highest should be abased the lowest.

31. This reply of Jesus leads Peter to make a still stronger assertion, that he would die with him rather than deny him. **He spake** or *talked* **the more vehemently,** uttering what is here said, and more beside, with the greatest earnestness. In this, Peter showed his strong self-will and self-confidence. The rest of the disciples catch his spirit and words, and join in like declarations. Such warnings should have put Peter and the other apostles on their guard, and led them to depend humbly on God; but they seem to have had the opposite effect of arousing their spiritual pride, and a dependence on their own will and strength.

32–42. THE AGONY OF JESUS IN GETHSEMANE. Matt. 26 : 36–46; Luke 22: 40–46; John 18:1. The accounts of Matthew and Mark are the fullest and very similar. Matthew mentions the three prayers of Jesus; Mark mentions two, but implies the third. Other differences will appear in the notes below. Luke's account is concise, but vivid. He indefinitely marks the different times of prayer, concentrates them in one description, and adds what the other evangelists omit, the appearance of the angel, the bloody sweat and sorrow, the psychological cause of their sorrow. John, in harmony with the supplemental character of his Gospel, refers merely to the fact that Jesus and his disciples entered a garden, without any account of the agony.

32. **And they came.** The incident just related occurred while they were on their way to the Mount of Olives, ver. 26. Mark uses the present, *And they come;* a vivid narrative. **A place.** A field, a possession. Compare John 4 : 5, where the same Greek word is

translated *a parcel of ground.* John calls it a garden, not in our sense, but in that of an orchard or olive-yard. Here Jesus was about to retire, Luke 22 : 39 ; John 18 : 1, 2.

Gethsemane means *"olive-press,"* a name seemingly prophetic of Christ's agony, where he trod the wine-press alone (Isa. 63 : 3), without the city, Rev. 14 : 20. It was just across the brook Kedron, about one half-mile east from Jerusalem, at the foot of the Mount of Olives. The modern garden without doubt occupies the same site, trees probably sprang from the roots of those standing in the days of our Lord. Thomson (*Land and Book,* ii. 284) thinks that the ancient Gethsemane was situated in a secluded vale, several hundred yards to the north-east of the modern one. There is much evidence, however, in support of the present locality.

"At the juncture of the three roads which lead to Bethany is the Garden of Gethsemane. It is an area of 120 feet east and west and 150 feet north and south. The entrance is through a low

GARDEN OF GETHSEMANE.

or a portion of it, possibly somewhat smaller, being an inclosure of about one-third of an acre, and surrounded by a low wall. In it are eight venerable olive-trees, still green and productive, but so decayed that heaps of stone are piled up against their trunks to keep them from being blown down. They were standing at the Saracenic conquest of Jerusalem, A.D. 636, since the sultan receives a tax on them, fixed at that time. But as all the trees around Jerusalem were cut down by Titus at the destruction of Jerusalem (Josephus, *Jewish War,* vi. 1. 1), these olive- iron gate on the western side, and the keeper is an old Franciscan monk. . . . With parental care he has nourished the eight remaining olive-trees, beneath which he thinks the fearful struggle occurred. They bear marks of great age ; their trunks are gnarled and hollow, their foliage scanty, and, true to their species in old age, their roots are far above the ground, but at present covered with an artificial soil. One more venerable than the rest is seven feet in circumference, and has separated into four parts from the roots upward to the branches ; a second is

33 And he taketh with him Peter and James and John, and began to be sore amazed, and to be very
34 heavy; and saith unto them, *My soul is exceeding sorrowful unto death: tarry ye here, and watch.
35 And he went forward a little, and fell on the ground, and prayed that, if it were possible, the

*John 12. 27.

twisted with age; a third is hollow. But the branches are strong, the leaf green, and from the aged roots young trees are sprouting."—Dr. J. P. Newman, *From Dan to Beersheba*, p. 118.

His disciples. Only eight, as the event showed, three being selected to go farther with him. **Sit ye here,** probably just within the inclosure. **Pray.** In regard to his sufferings, see on ver. 35. Matthew says "pray yonder," probably in a secluded and shady retreat. Luke says "about a stone's throw," that is, from a sling. It was now probably between eleven and twelve o'clock, and within two days of the full moon.

33. **Peter and James and John.** The same three who had witnessed his transfiguration (ch. 9:2) are selected to be witnesses of, and sympathizers in, his great humiliation and agony in the garden. The former scene was a preparative for the latter. He who had professed such an undying attachment to Jesus, and the two who would sit on his right and left hand, and said they were able to drink of his cup, ch. 10:39. **Began,** as here before, and continuing, as here described. **Sore amazed.** A very strong word in the original, *greatly distressed* with horror and amazement. **Very heavy.** Deeply dejected, burdened in spirit. According to some, the word expresses the sorrow of loneliness, which presses like a load of lead upon the soul.

34. The beginning of his anguish has just been stated. Another step in his overwhelming agony is now brought to view. **My soul.** Jesus had a human soul; and this was the scene of his agony. His emotional nature was overwhelmed with sorrow. **Exceeding sorrowful.** Literally, *environed with grief,* shut in, with sorrow on every side. This was in view of the connection of his sufferings and death with sin. **Even unto death.** The extremest intensity; deathly; a little more would be death itself. Compare Ps. 18:4, 5; 55:4; Jon. 4:9. Indeed,

he might have died had it not been for the angel who strengthened him, Luke 22:43. This language points to sufferings in his human nature. He had been before troubled in the anticipation of his sufferings (John 12:27), now he is overwhelmed with the sufferings themselves. A body and soul untainted, and unmarred by sin, must have been capable of endurance far beyond any of our sinful race. This endurance must have been greatly increased by the connection of the divine with the human. Hence the *sorrow unto death* was beyond anything that ever has, or could be, experienced in this world by any one of our fallen race. It was beyond all human conception. He was suffering for sinners, in their place. He made their case, as it were, his own. The horror and woe of the lost, and the pangs of hell, were taking hold upon him, so far as it was possible in his state of innocence. **Tarry ye here.** He would be alone with his Father. His sorrows are too great to be borne in the immediate presence of even these three favored disciples. **Watch.** Keep awake, to keep me company, and act as a guard. Yet his human nature craved their presence near at hand. He does not ask their prayers, but their attendance and watchfulness. In great dangers it is a comfort to know that friends are near us and vigilant, even though unable to help us.

35. **Went forward a little,** into the garden. Thus there were three companies: the eight, the three, and the one. As the high-priest entered the holy of holies alone, so Jesus must suffer alone. The disciples were probably as near to him as they could bear. The glory of the transfiguration doubtless fitted the three to be nearer than the rest. **Fell on the ground and prayed.** Luke says he "kneeled down." Doubtless he knelt first, and, as his agony increased, fell forward, as Matthew says "on his face." Compare Gen. 17:3. The posture was indicative of his extreme humiliation and an-

A.D. 30.   MARK XIV.   275

36 hour might pass from him. And he said, ^a Abba, Father, ^b all things *are* possible unto thee; take away this cup from me: ^c nevertheless not what I
37 will, but what thou wilt. And he cometh, and findeth them sleeping, and saith unto Peter, Simon, sleepest thou? Couldest not thou watch one hour?
38 Watch ye and pray, lest ye enter into temptation. ^d The spirit truly *is* ready, but the flesh *is* weak.

^a Ro. 8. 15; Gal. 4. 6.
^b Heb. 5. 7.
^c Ps. 40. 8; John 5. 30; 6. 38.

^d Ro. 7. 23; Gal. 5. 17, 24.

---

guish. **If it were possible;** that God's glory be respected and displayed, and the world's salvation be secured, without this suffering. **The hour might pass from me.** That hour or season of overwhelming anguish. See next verse, on **cup.** Mark alone gives the subject or substance of the prayer which follows.

36. **Abba,** the Aramaic word for **Father,** a word expressing a high degree of love and confidence and used from early childhood. Mark here, as in some other instances, preserves the very expression Jesus used, ch. 5 : 41; 7 : 11. This gives vividness to the narrative; and shows that Jesus used common language, and not mystic expressions on such occasions. He prayed as the Son. **All things are possible,** etc. He recognized the omnipotence of the Father. Compare "if it were possible," in the preceding verse. The meaning seems to be, All things consistent with thy perfections are possible unto thee. **This cup.** This bitter cup of anguish. *Cup* is a common figure of Scripture, sometimes representing joy (Ps. 16 : 5 ; 23 : 5; 116 : 13), and sometimes sorrow, Ps. 11 : 6; 75 : 8; Isa. 51 : 17; Jer. 25 : 15; Rev. 16 : 1. Not the cup of death, but of present overwhelming anguish, which he was suffering, as our substitute, Isa. 53 : 4, 5. To suppose him overwhelmed with the dread of death, and praying for its removal, is contrary to the spirit he had ever manifested toward it, and to all his declarations and prayers concerning it, John 12 : 27, 28; chs. 14–17. **Nevertheless,** etc. *But not what I will.* Not my will, but thine be done. Wonderful faith and resignation combined! The will of Jesus, who was both priest and victim, is swallowed up in the divine will. **But what thou wilt** was his rule, not only of action, but also of will. His will remained firm, and one with the Father's. The words of the prayer vary slightly in the different evangelists, but with the same import.

37. **Findeth them sleeping.** Most surprising, but explained by Luke ; they were sleeping for sorrow. Yet this did not relieve them of responsibility. **Saith unto Peter;** who had been foremost in his professions and promises; he is addressed in behalf of the others also. Mark's narrative is very vivid. He alone records that Jesus called him here *Simon,* which he, on several occasions, used when he would remind him of his weakness, Matt. 16 : 17; Luke 22 : 31; John 21 : 15. **Sleepest thou?** Is it possible that thou sleepest when I commanded thee to watch? **Couldest not thou watch?** Wast thou unable, not strong enough to watch? This whole address was one of mingled reproof and pity. **One hour.** An indefinite short time, ch. 13 : 11, 32; Matt. 9 : 22. Some find here an intimation of the length of the agony of Gethsemane.

38. Directing his address to all three, Jesus re-enjoins watchfulness, with the addition of prayer, with special reference to themselves, that they might not fall under the power of **temptation.** Their hour of *trial* was at hand, and they needed both to watch and also pray, for they needed strength and grace. The motive of the former injunction was sympathy with him ; that of this is their personal preservation and safety.

Spirit . . . flesh. Your higher spiritual nature is **ready** and *willing,* but your lower animal nature is feeble, worn and tired, yielding to the exhaustive weariness of anxiety and sorrow. This was a kind apology for their slumbering, yet, at the same time, an incentive for immediate watchfulness and prayer; for the weaker their flesh, the more they needed divine help, and to be on their guard. To suppose with

39 And again he went away, and prayed, and spake
40 the same words. And when he returned, he found them asleep again; for their eyes were heavy, neither wist they what to answer him.
41 And he cometh the third time, and saith unto them, Sleep on now, and take *your* rest: it is enough, ᵉthe hour is come; behold, the Son of man is be- 42 trayed into the hands of sinners. ᶠ Rise up, let us go; lo, he that betrayeth me is at hand.

ᵉ John 13. 1.
ᶠ Mt. 26. 46; John 18. 1, 2.

some that *spirit* and *flesh* mean simply *mind* and *body*, accords not so well with the usage of the terms, and fails in depth and fullness of meaning. The conditions of body and mind, of spiritual life and carnal weakness, are all taken into view; the one renewed and somewhat developed by divine grace, the other still suffering from sin and the effects of sin.

39. Jesus now goes away and prays again, and **spake the same words.** Matthew gives a brief summary of this prayer, in which submission is the chief idea. Compare Heb. 5 : 7-9.

40. Returning a second time, Jesus again finds them sleeping, **for their eyes were heavy,** weighed down and burdened with drowsiness. This expression implies that their sleep was not a deep, but a drowsy one. **Neither wist,** etc. *They knew not what to answer him;* they were confounded and ashamed. Compare ch. 9 : 6.

41. **He cometh the third time.** This implies a third season of prayer, which Matthew (26 : 44) definitely records, "and prayed the third time, saying the same words." The repetition shows the intensity and continuance of the agony. Luke vividly describes it: "His sweat was as great drops of blood falling down to the ground;" in large drops, probably mingled with blood. So Jesus suffered three assaults from Satan in the wilderness. Paul also prayed thrice, 2 Cor. 12 : 8. This has been erroneously called an unanswered prayer. But it was answered in the highest sense. The Father heard him always, John 11 : 42. The agony continued according to the Father's will; and the will of the Father was one with that of the Son. The angel appearing and strengthening him (Luke 22 : 43) was also in answer to his prayer; similar to the Lord's answer to Paul's repeated petition, 2 Cor. 12 :

9. This agony also did pass away, and in composure he gave himself up to his betrayer, and went calmly to the hall of judgment. This endurance and triumph over the agony of the garden was a pledge and foretaste of full and final victory.

Sleep on now. *Sleep the remaining time, and take your rest!* The exact meaning of these words has been much discussed. Some suppose they were spoken in mournful irony; but such a view is decidedly unnatural. Others suppose a question, *Do ye sleep,* etc. ? which is admissible. But it is better to take them as an exclamation of pain or grief, and to translate, *So then you are sleeping and taking rest!* The rendering, *so then* or *well then,* instead of *the remaining time,* is given in E. A. Sophocles' Lexicon of the later Greek. It is common in modern Greek, and traces of this meaning can be found as early as Plato. See on Matt. 26 : 45. Winer's view is worthy of consideration. He supposes the words uttered permissively by Jesus, in the gentle, resigned mood resulting from prayer: "*Sleep on then and take your rest.*" (GRAMMAR, Thayer's Revised Edition, § 43, 1.)

It is enough, that ye have slept, and remained here. This was probably spoken after a brief pause. **The hour of my sufferings by the hands of men is come. Behold.** At this moment he may have caught a glimpse of Judas and his band of soldiers. See next verse. **Is betrayed.** So far as the act of Judas was concerned, and to the mind of Jesus, who beheld the whole as actually accomplished. **Hands of sinners.** The Jews and the Gentiles. He was betrayed by Judas, and delivered up to the Jewish rulers, and by them betrayed and delivered up to the Roman authorities, ch. 10 : 33, 34.

42. **Rise.** Awake, arise. The word in the original includes the idea of rous-

Jesus betrayed and made prisoner.

43 *And immediately, while he yet spake, cometh Judas, one of the twelve, and with him a great multitude with swords and staves, from the chief priests

*Mt. 26. 47; Lk. 22. 47; John 18. 3.

ing from sleep. Not to escape danger, but to meet it. **Behold, he is at hand.** Look, see, he is at hand. The whole verse is a vivid picture of great earnestness and haste. "As I sat beneath the olives, and observed how very near the city was, with what perfect ease a person could survey at a glance the entire length of the eastern wall, and the slope of the hill toward the valley, I could not divest myself of the impression that this local peculiarity should be allowed to explain a passage in the account of our Savior's apprehension. Every one must have noticed something abrupt in his summons to the disciples : 'Arise, let us be going; see, he is at hand that doth betray me.' Matt. 26 : 46. It is not improbable that his watchful eye at that moment caught sight of Judas and his accomplices, as they issued from one of the eastern gates, or turned round the northern or southern corner of the walls, in order to descend into the valley. Even if the night was dark, he could have seen the torches which they carried," John 18 : 3.—Dr. Hackett, *Scripture Illustrations*, p. 266. If the night was clear he could have caught a view of the approaching company by the light of the moon then near its full.

43-52. JESUS IS BETRAYED AND MADE PRISONER. Matt. 26 : 47-56 ; Luke 22 : 47-53; John 18 : 2-11. The accounts of Matthew and Mark are the most extended, and of about equal length. John is fullest in narrating the first part of the betrayal. Luke is briefest. Matthew alone speaks of the twelve legions of angels, and that the Scripture must be fulfilled ; Mark alone relates concerning the youth who fled away naked ; Luke alone records that Jesus healed the servant's ear ; and John alone tells us of Jesus going forth to meet Judas and his band, and their going backward and falling on the ground. The variations in the several accounts are interesting in exhibiting variety in harmony, and are worthy of study. Compare author's HARMONY, § 171.

43. **Immediately.** Denotes a close succession of events. **While he yet spake,** or *was yet speaking*. He had probably roused the three disciples from their slumbers, and rejoined the remaining eight, possibly saying similar words to them ; but *immediately* cometh the betrayer. **Judas, one of the twelve.** Thus styled by Luke also, pointing him out not only as one of the apostles, but also as the apostolic criminal, whose crime and guilt were the more aggravated by the position he had held, and the knowledge and intimacy he had enjoyed with Jesus. Some of the oldest manuscripts add Iscariot after Judas. John (18 : 2) says that Judas knew the place, for Jesus often resorted thither. **A great multitude.** This consisted, first, of *the band* (John 18 : 3, 12), or Roman cohort, which, consisting of 300 to 600 men, was quartered in the tower of Antonia, overlooking the temple, and ever ready to put down any tumult or arrest any disturber. Probably so much of the band as could be spared was present. Then there were *the captains of the temple* (Luke 22 : 52), with their men, who guarded the temple and kept order. Also, some of the *chief priests and elders* (Luke 22 : 52) ; and finally their servants, such as Malchus (John 18 : 10), and others, who had been commissioned by the Jewish authorities. **With swords and staves.** Swords and *sticks,* or *clubs.* The swords were in the hands of the soldiers ; the staves, or clubs, were probably in the hands of the guards of the temple, and of others. According to John, they also had torches and lamps, which, notwithstanding the moonlight, they might need to search the shady retreats in the garden, and the dark caverns of the valley of the Kedron. **From the chief priests,** etc. The three classes of the Jewish Sanhedrim, who had obtained the soldiers, and sent them with their servants and others, under the leadership of Judas. The word translated *from* indicates that these persons were near servants and attendants of the Jewish leaders. Judas also held his commission from the Sanhedrim.

44 and the scribes and the elders. And he that betrayed him had given them a token, saying, ʰ Whomsoever I shall kiss, that same is he; take him, and lead *him* away safely. And as soon as he was come, he goeth straightway to him, and saith, Master,
45
46 master; and kissed him. And they laid their hands on him, and took him.
47 And one of them that stood by drew a sword, and smote a servant of the high priest, and cut off his ear.

ʰ Pro. 27. 6; Pa 55. 20, 21; 2 Sam. 20. 9, 10.

44. Had given them, the officers who accompanied Judas, **a token,** a concerted *signal,* which had been agreed upon. Matthew calls it simply *a sign.* **Whomsoever I shall kiss.** A common mode of affectionate salutation in the East. The kiss was used among early Christians as a symbol of love and brotherhood (Rom. 16 : 16; 1 Cor. 16 : 20; 2 Cor. 13 : 12; 1 Thess. 5 : 26; 1 Pet. 5 : 14), and very likely had often now been used among the disciples. **Take him.** A strong expression, *Lay hold of him,* seize him, secure him. **Lead him away safely** or *securely.* Judas was afraid that Jesus might escape, as he had done before, Luke 4 : 30; John 8 : 59; 10 : 39. He also might have feared that his disciples might attempt to rescue him, ver. 47.

45. As soon as he was come. Rather, *And coming* to the garden of Gethsemane. **He goeth straightway to him.** Probably a little in advance of the multitude. Jesus, a little in advance of his disciples, is met by Judas, leading his enemies; one at the head of a peaceful, the other of a warlike and inimical band. About at this point must come in the account of John 18 : 4–9. Jesus advances to meet them; in awe they start backward, and fall to the ground. Thus he shows that though he has power to retain his life, he willingly lays it down. At the same time he encourages the drooping hope of his disciples, and insures their safety from the public authorities.

Although Jesus discovered himself to them (John 18 :5–8), yet Judas must give the signal agreed upon in order that the officers might take him. It was night also; and many of them were probably not acquainted with Jesus, and none so well as Judas. **Master,**

Master; *Rabbi, Rabbi,* the honorary title of a Jewish teacher or doctor. Judas used the same title when he asked, Master (*Rabbi*), is it I? Matt. 26 : 25. **Kissed him.** *Kissed him tenderly.* The verb here is a compound of the one translated kiss in the preceding verse, and denotes that he not only gave the sign, but also that the act was performed in a tender and affectionate manner, thus adding to his guilt the sin of affectation and hypocrisy. What a contrast between Judas giving, and Jesus receiving the kiss. In the one we see the depth of baseness; in the other, the height of endurance. The one an object of contempt, the other of admiration.

At this point Matthew inserts the question, " Friend, wherefore art thou come?" And then Jesus adds (Luke 22 : 48), showing his full knowledge of the act, " Betrayest thou the Son of man with a kiss ?"

Some would insert John 18 : 4–9 here. It is admissible, but it seems more natural and more accordant with all the circumstances to place it as above.

46. Laid their hands on him. Laid hold of Jesus, so as to apprehend and secure him. **And took him.** Rather, *Secured him, held him fast.*

47. One of them. Peter, John 18 : 10. Prudence quite likely led the first three evangelists to omit the name of Peter, in order to shield him from any odium or violence which might arise from giving his name. As Jesus healed the ear (Luke 22 : 51), Peter was not then apprehended; and although he seems to have been recognized in the palace of the high-priest by a kinsman of the servant who received the injury (John 18 : 26), yet his name may have been unknown, and he was probably lost sight of as the perpetrator. But John, who wrote after the death of Peter, supple-

48 ¹And Jesus answered and said unto them, Are ye ⁱ Mt. 26. 55; Lk 22. 52.
come out, as against a thief, with swords and *with*
49 staves to take me? I was daily with you in the ʲ Ps. 22. 6; Is. 53. 7, etc.; Lk. 22. 37; 34. 44.
temple teaching, and ye took me not: but ᵏ the
Scriptures must be fulfilled. ˡ ver. 27; Ps. 88. 8; Is. 63. 3.
50, 51 ˡAnd they all forsook him, and fled. And there

ments the other accounts by giving his name.
Sword. Two swords were in the hands of the disciples (Luke 22 : 38), and more than one were proposing to resist (Luke 22 : 49); for they ask, "Lord, shall we smite with the sword?" And before the answer was given, Peter, in accordance with his impetuous nature, and doubtless emboldened by the supernatural awe which Jesus had just previously exerted on the multitude, drew his sword, and commenced the conflict, not doubting the power of Jesus to give the victory. **A servant of the high priest.** Rather, *the servant*, who was well known, namely, Malchus, John 18 : 10. The first three evangelists may have omitted his name, either because he was well known (and he may have become a disciple) or from prudential considerations. **Smote off his ear.** *Struck off, took off*, his right ear, Luke 22 : 50. The servant may have been stepping forward, as Dr. Hackett, in Smith's Dictionary, remarks, to handcuff or pinion Jesus. The blow was doubtless aimed at his head; the soldier may have thrown his head aside; perhaps the power of Jesus prevented a fatal stroke.
Matthew records the Savior's rebuke of Peter, with the interrogative declaration that twelve legions of angels were at his command, but that the Scripture must be fulfilled. John also gives Christ's rebuke, and, without referring to the angels or the Scriptures, adds that Jesus further said, "The cup that my Father hath given me, shall I not drink it?"
48. **Jesus answered.** Their acts were the occasion of his words. He replied to their thoughts and designs as carried out into action. See on ch. 9 : 5. **Unto them.** "To the multitude," Matt. 26 : 55, especially to their leaders, the captains of the temple, chief priest and elders, Luke 22 : 52. **Against a thief.** In the original *a robber*, a plunderer, one who is more than a thief. Such an array of force and weapons would be a becoming preparation against a notorious robber like Barabbas. **Staves.** See ver. 43. **Daily.** During that week, and at other times and previous festivals. He had often been with them, and among them, and that by *day;* their assault was secretly contrived and by *night.* **In the temple.** Within the courts of the sacred inclosure. **Teaching.** The farthest remote from the character of a robber. **Took me not;** did not seize me, arrest me. As they had opportunity. Your present violence is needless, and proves your malignity and moral weakness. Jesus then adds (Luke 22 : 53) the reason of their present success and of his quiet submission, "This is your hour and the power of darkness."
But the scriptures. This is a continuation of what Jesus says, and the idea is more clearly obtained from a more exact translation, *but that the scriptures*, etc. The ellipsis may be supplied thus: *But* this has come to pass (that is, your coming forth in the manner just described, ver. 48), in order that the Scriptures might be fulfilled. Isa. 53 : 7-12; Zach. 13 : 7; John 10 : 35.
But back of the Scriptures were the counsel and plan of God for the salvation of sinners, which find expression in his word, 1 Pet. 1 : 19, 20; Rev. 13 : 8; "Thus it must be," Matt. 26 : 54.
50. **All forsook him.** All his disciples left him to his enemies, when they saw him arrested and bound, and learned from his words that he did not intend to deliver himself. **And fled.** All, a little before, had declared their readiness to even die with him (ver. 31); but now all, panic-stricken, desert him. Peter and John, however, did not flee far, but follow at a safe distance, John 18 : 15.
51. More faithful and courageous than the eleven was a **young man,** probably between twenty and thirty years old, who now followed Jesus,

followed him a certain young man, having a linen cloth cast about his naked body; and the young men 52 laid hold on him: ᵐ and he left the linen cloth, and fled from them naked.

ᵐ ch. 13. 15, 16.

Jesus before the high-priest and the Sanhedrim.

53 ⁿ AND they led Jesus away to the high priest: and with him were assembled all the chief priests

ⁿ Mt. 26. 57; Lk. 22. 54; John 18. 13.

---

and barely escaped apprehension and violence. **A linen cloth,** etc. Fine linen, which is worn by the Orientals at night. Sheets or rather linen shirts, or night wrappers, were a part of the garments which Samson promised to the Philistines, if they should solve his riddle within seven days, Judges 14 : 12. It appears that this young man, being awaked from sleep by the commotion, had rushed out hastily with nothing but his linen wrapper or night-dress.

Who this young man was has been much conjectured. It could not have been one of the apostles, for they "all forsook him and fled." The most probable supposition is that it was Mark himself, who alone relates the incident as he vividly remembered it in his own experience, but modestly withheld his name. He was probably living at Jerusalem with his mother (Acts 12 : 12), and had been awakened out of sleep in the house at Gethsemane, or some house near at hand. That he was a friend of Jesus, and possibly a disciple, is most naturally inferred from the fact that he **followed him.** His demeanor was such also that some **laid hold on him,** attempted to arrest him, as if he was one of Christ's disciples. He seems to have manifested some peculiar interest in Jesus, or possibly opposed in some way his removal. **The young men.** Probably the attendants, or young persons who had joined the company. Compare Acts 5 : 6, 10. But some of the most ancient manuscripts and versions omit *the young men,* and read, *they laid hold on him.* It is possible that they seize him out of wantonness on account of his peculiar garb.

52. As they grasp the linen wrapper, he leaves it with them and escapes. Fear conquers the sense of shame. It may be added that the material, *linen,* rather indicates that whoever this young man was, he did not belong to the poorest class.

53–65. Jesus before Caiaphas and the Sanhedrim; tried and condemned. Matt. 26 : 57-68; Luke 22 : 54, 63–65 ; John 18 : 24. Matthew and Mark are similar in their account, with a few variations. Luke only alludes to this examination incidentally. John merely states that Jesus was sent to Caiaphas, after relating that they led him first to Annas, who, after having been high-priest for several years, had been deposed, but who was still the legitimate high-priest according to the law of Moses (the office being for life, Num. 20 : 28 ; 35 : 25), and may have been so regarded by the Jews. Before him he received an informal examination (John 18 : 12–14), and then, in order to have him officially tried and condemned in the eye of the Roman law, he is sent to Caiaphas. Annas appears to have possessed vast influence, and, as father-in-law to Caiaphas, doubtless exerted a very controlling influence over him. It is quite reasonable to suppose that they occupied a common official residence, and that Annas after his examination sent him across the court to the apartment occupied by Caiaphas.

53. **To the high priest,** who was the head of the priesthood and of all religious affairs. Aaron was the first high-priest (Exod. 28 : 1–38), and the office continued in his family about fifteen centuries; but Herod, and the Roman governors after him, changed the incumbents at pleasure, so much so that the office became almost annual. Matthew, writing for Jewish readers, says it was Caiaphas, a name familiar to them. It is noticeable that Mark never mentions him by name. Compare John 11 : 51, where it is said that Caiaphas was high-priest *that year.*

Joseph Caiaphas was high-priest about nine years, during the whole pro-

A.D. 30.   MARK XIV.   281

54 and the elders and the scribes. And Peter followed him afar off, even into the palace of the high priest: and he sat with the servants, and warmed himself at the fire.

55 °And the chief priests and all the council sought for witness against Jesus to put him to death; and

° Mt. 26. 59; Lk. 22. 63.

curatorship of Pontius Pilate, but was deposed by the Proconsul Vitellius soon after the removal of Pilate. He was son-in-law to Annas, who had been formerly the high-priest, and who is thought by some to have shared the office with him; the latter as actual high-priest, the former as president of the Sanhedrim, or else that Annas acted as the vicar or deputy of Caiaphas. Compare Luke 3 : 2 ; John 18 : 13, 19, 24; Acts 4 : 6.

With him; with Jesus. **Were assembled.** Rather, *assembled.* The three classes composing the Sanhedrim are mentioned who came together with Jesus. See on ver. 48. Some of these were with the band who arrested him, Luke 22 : 52. They assemble to receive their prisoner, and to make out a capital case against him. The dawn of day was drawing nigh, when the second cock-crowing would remind Peter of the Savior's prediction of his three denials. Jesus now undergoes a preliminary examination, preparatory to the regular meeting of the Sanhedrim in the morning (Luke 22 : 66), which should condemn him and hand him over to Pilate, ch. 15 : 1. See on ver. 64. The usual place of holding the Sanhedrim was at the council-room in the temple, called Gazeth, at the south-east corner of the court of Israel; but this meeting, being extraordinary and of a secret character, was held at the residence of the high-priest. They would make sure of their victim.

The early hour of this meeting was very much in keeping with the habits of the people. The habit of early rising has been noticed by modern travelers in Palestine. "During the greater part of the year, in Palestine," says Dr. Hackett, "the heat becomes so great a few hours after sunrise as to render any strenuous labor inconvenient. The early morning, therefore, is the proper time for work; midday is given, as far as may be possible, to rest or employments which do not require exposure to the sun. The arrangements of life adjust themselves to this character of the climate. . . . Men and women may be seen going forth to their labor in the field, or starting on journeys, at the earliest break of day. . . . Being anxious at Jerusalem to attend the services of a Jewish synagogue, I was summoned to rise for that purpose before it was light. In one instance I went thither at an early hour, as we should call it, but found myself too late."—*Scripture Illustrations,* p. 124.

54. **Afar off.** At a distance, and scarcely near enough for a mere spectator, much less a disciple. Yet he followed him, and he seems to show more courage than any of the eleven except John; he comes to the house of the high-priest, ventures to enter into the court, and sits with the servants to see the result, Matt. 26 : 58. **Palace.** The *court,* the inclosed square, under the open sky, around which the house was built. In the midst of it a fire had been kindled, Luke 22 : 55. Through the influence of John, who was acquainted with the family of the high-priest, Peter obtained access into this inner court, John 18 : 16. **Servants.** *Officers* and agents of the high-priest. Mark, with characteristic detail, adds that Peter *was warming himself at the fire.* The idea is that of a blazing fire. Hence Peter could be easily recognized. Jesus was probably now under examination in a room with an entrance from this court. Some houses in Cairo are said to have an apartment, open in front to the inner court, with two or more arches and a railing, and a pillar to support the wall above. The residence of Caiaphas may have had such a large apartment. (See HOUSE, *Smith's Dictionary*)

55. **All the council.** All of those present. Nicodemus, Joseph of Arimathea, and others (John 12 : 42) who did not approve of such proceedings, were doubtless absent. **The chief priests** are mentioned separately, it may be, because they were especially urgent for putting Jesus to death, ch. 15 : 3, 31.

56 found none. For many bare P false witness against   p Ps. 35. 11.
57 him, but their witness agreed not together. And there arose certain and bare false witness against
58 him, saying, We heard him say, q I will destroy this   q ch. 15. 29; John 2. 19.
    temple that is made with hands, and within three
59 days I will build another made without hands. But neither so did their witness agree together.
60   r And the high priest stood up in the midst, and   r Mt. 26. 62.
    asked Jesus, saying, Answerest thou nothing?
61 What *is it which* these witness against thee? But
   s he held his peace, and answered nothing.   s Is. 53. 7.
    t Again the high priest asked him, and said unto   t Mt. 26. 63.
    him, Art thou the Christ, the Son of the Blessed?

Sought for witness, *testimony.* They had determined to **put him to death,** right or wrong, and hence they seek for evidence to convict him of some capital crime. **Found none.** They found many false witnesses, but not the evidence they desired, namely, two witnesses agreed in sustaining a definite accusation, as required by the law of Moses, Deut. 17 : 6. And according to the Talmud "their testimony is not ratified in the council, until they both witness as one."

56. **For** introduces the reason and explanation of the last statement. **Many bare false witness.** Failing in obtaining true witnesses, they sought false ones, and obtained many, Matt. 26 : 59, 60. But these did not answer their purpose, for **their witness,** *their testimony,* **agreed not together;** they were not as one; no two of them agreed together, and hence the requisition of the law, that at least two witnesses must agree, was not met.

57. **There arose certain.** Matthew says, "At last came two." They appear to have come forward of their own accord, and were the nearest to agreement in their testimony. **Bare false witness.** They pervert one of the sayings of Jesus, and instead of an offer and a promise, they present it as a threat and a boast.

58. **I will destroy.** He had not said this. What he had said referred to his body, and not to the temple. They misquote and misapply what he did say three years before, John 2 : 19. "Destroy ye" and "I will destroy" are very different. **Made with hands** and **made without hands** are not found in Christ's declaration. Words against the temple were held to be of the nature of blasphemy, Acts 6 : 13. They would, if possible, convict him of blasphemy, which was punishable with death, Lev. 24 : 16. Yet even this language could hardly be considered as words against the temple, since he was to build it again; and besides, there was a tradition that when the Messiah came, he was to build a much more glorious temple than the one then existing. This testimony may also have suggested the question, whether he was the Christ, the Son of God, ver. 61.

59. Mark alone adds: **But neither so,** etc. *Not even thus,* although they testified regarding one of his sayings, did their **witness,** *testimony,* agree. The witnesses were probably not examined in the presence of each other. Matthew may give the testimony of one; Mark, of the other. This, however, need not be pressed. It is enough to know that their testimony did not sufficiently agree to answer the demands of the law.

60. **The high priest stood up.** Seeing that the evidence was insufficient, the high-priest, somewhat excited, and possibly with some affected indignation, rises from his seat, stands up **in the midst** of the Sanhedrim, and questions Jesus, in the hope that he may criminate himself. **Answerest thou nothing?** etc. Dost thou not explain, or tell us whether this testimony is true or false? The two questions were in harmony with the excited state of his mind, and give vividness to the narrative. It is therefore unnatural with some to so punctuate as to make only one question.

61. **Held his peace.** A solemn and

A.D. 30.   MARK XIV.   283

62 And Jesus said, I am: "and ye shall see the Son of man sitting on the right hand of power, and coming
63 in the clouds of heaven. Then the high priest rent his clothes, and saith, ʷWhat need we any further

ᵃ Mt. 24. 30; 26. 64; Lk. 22. 69.
ᵛ Is. 36. 22; 37. 1; 1 Ki. 29 9, 13; John 5. 18; 8. 59; 10. 33.

impressive silence, as Isaiah had foretold, Isa. 53 : 7. The evidence did not call for a defense. The high-priest by his conduct showed it was insufficient. **Again . . . asked him.** Mark simply states the question; but Matthew gives the additional fact, that the high-priest put him upon his oath, "I adjure thee by the living God." **Art thou the Christ?** The Messiah. As they had failed to convict him by witnesses, the high-priest seeks to draw from him some expression by which he would convict himself; something which they could construe into blasphemy. **The Son of the Blessed,** that is, Blessed God. The appellation, Son of God, was given to the Messiah from Ps. 2 : 7, making the question the more definite and expressive. The Jews did not, however, understand by it the full idea which Christ in his reply and the gospel reveals. It is also quite probable that the high-priest added this in hope that he would declare before the Sanhedrim what he had before said to the people, John 10 : 30, 33. In the final examination before the Sanhedrim (Luke 22 : 66-71), the high-priest divides the question, and uses the appellation *Son of God* in its more extended meaning. This was natural after the reply which Jesus now makes in this preparatory examination.
62. **I am.** I am the Christ, the Son of God. This is his first formal public declaration of his Messiahship and divinity. Matthew, writing for Jewish readers, uses their affirmative answer, "Thou hast said." **And ye shall see.** Jesus adds a declaration explanatory and prophetic. If he had simply confessed himself the Messiah, the high-priest would probably have asked him other questions, and if failing to elicit further confession, would then probably have condemned him to death as a false Messiah and false prophet, the latter being included in the former, Deut. 13 : 5 ; 18 : 20. But Jesus gave special prominence to the last portion of the question, using language which would remind him of the well-known passage in Dan. 7 : 13, and that he was Son of man as well as Son of God.
The Son of man, whom you now behold in humiliation, you shall see in exaltation. See on ch. 2 : 10. **Sitting on the right hand of power.** Now *standing* as a prisoner, but then sitting in his glory as Lord of lords, and King of kings, at the right hand of Omnipotence, sharing and exercising sovereign supremacy. **Coming in the clouds.** As Judge. Jesus thus answers the solemn question of the high-priest with a more solemn reference to his own judgment-seat, when the scene would be reversed—the prisoner the Judge, and the judge the prisoner.
63. **Rent his clothes.** Not his high-priestly robe, which was worn only in the temple ; but his under-garments. Sometimes two under-garments were worn, for ornament, comfort or luxury. Matthew speaks more generally, of his ordinary dress. This was to be done standing, and the rent was to be from the neck straight downward, about nine inches in length. The high-priest was forbidden to rend his clothes (Lev. 21 : 10); yet it seems to have been allowable in extraordinary cases of blasphemy and public calamity, 1 Macc. 2 : 14; 11 : 71 ; Josephus, *Jewish War*, ii. 15, 2, 4. The practice of rending the clothes at blasphemy was based on 2 Kings 18 : 37. The unexpected answer of Jesus, declaring his divine glory and judgeship, aroused the hatred, rage and horror of the high-priest to the utmost bounds, and he rends his garments as if too narrow to contain his exasperated emotions. This he does as if in holy indignation and horror. Terribly excited feelings and hypocrisy were doubtless mingled.
What need we, etc. The language of excited feeling. He takes for granted that the feelings of the Sanhedrim are the same as his own. Without considering the confession of Jesus, whether he had not spoken the truth, and in accordance with Scripture, he decides that they had no further need of witnesses. Prejudice, hatred, and haste unite in seeking the death of Jesus.

64 witnesses? Ye have heard the blasphemy: what think ye? And they all condemned him to be guilty of death.
65 ˣ And some began to spit on him, and to cover his face, and to buffet him, and to say unto him, Prophesy: and the servants did strike him with the palms of their hands.

ˣ Is. 50. 6.

64. Ye have heard the blasphemy. Impious language, which detracted from the honor of God, implying that he was the Son of God, the sharer in the power and glory of God, and the Judge of mankind. See on ch. 3 : 28. Thus Jesus confesses his true character, and for it is charged with blasphemy and condemned to death. **What think ye?** In hot haste he presses an immediate decision. **They all;** all present. See on ver. 55. **He is guilty of death.** He is justly liable to, deserving of death, or rather, his guilt requires death, according to the law, Lev. 24 : 16; Deut. 18 : 20. This was an informal expression or vote. It was necessary to assemble the Sanhedrim in the morning (ch. 15 : 1; Luke 22 : 66–71), when it was already day, to formally try and pass sentence; for, (1) they could not, according to Jewish law, investigate any capital crime during the night; and (2), according to Roman law, a sentence pronounced before the dawn of day was invalid. Yet in this examination, given by Matthew and Mark, Jesus was really tried and condemned; the one succeeding was but a formal repetition; the main thing then was the perfection of their plans to put him to death. It was, however, contrary to Jewish law to pronounce the sentence of death on the same day on which the investigation took place. If they thought to elude this law by the investigation in the night, it showed hot haste. But it was no elusion, for the Jewish day commenced in the evening. The truth is, the whole trial was but a form, a judicial sham; his death had been determined upon (ver. 1), and his conviction was a foregone conclusion.
65. Some began to spit on him. Expressive of the greatest contempt, Num. 12 : 14; Deut. 25 : 9. Thus a heathen would treat a slave only under the gravest provocation. When Aristides the Just was condemned to receive this indignity at Athens, it was with difficulty that a person was found willing to do it. Some of the Sanhedrim may have heaped upon Jesus these insults. Compare Acts 7 : 54, 57; 23 : 2. So will an Arab do at the present day, when filled with rage. Dr. H. C. Fish (1874) saw an instance in Egypt. Also in Palestine, one spitting in the face of an ass. A little later, when Pilate had delivered Jesus to be crucified, the soldiers heaped on him the same indignity, ch. 15 : 19. **Cover his face;** to prevent him from seeing; blindfold him. Criminals were often taken to punishment with their heads covered. **Buffet him;** to smite him with their fists. **Prophesy.** Speak through divine influence. Matthew and Luke give one of their taunts: "Who is he that smote thee?" Thus insult is added to insult, Isa. 52 : 14. They make his Messiahship the object of insult and mockery; and treat him as a base pretender and outlaw, mingling their revilings with deeds of violence. **The servants.** *The officers.* The mention of the officers last favors the view that members of the Sanhedrim had taken the lead in these insults. **Did strike**, etc. According to the highest critical authorities this should read, *With blows took him away*, or *took him in charge;* till the formal meeting of the Sanhedrim. The *blows* were with their open hands, or perhaps with their staves or rods, ver. 43.

66–72. JESUS IS THRICE DENIED BY PETER. Matt. 26 : 69–75; Luke 22 : 54–62; John 18 : 15–18, 25–27. With the exception of the second denial, on which Matthew is the fullest, Mark enters most into detail. The honesty and candor of Peter, under whose direction this Gospel was written, is seen in this full account. A comparison of the four narratives gives a fine illustration of their independence and of diversity of statement without contradiction. The following table is given for convenient comparison. See also author's HARMONY, § 173.

A.D. 30. MARK XIV. 285

First Denial.—Jesus before Annas.

	MATTHEW.	MARK.	LUKE.	JOHN.
Place.	The court.	Court, by the fire.	Court, by the fire.	The court.
Time.	Indefinite.	Indefinite.	Indefinite.	Soon after entering.
Interrogator.	A damsel.	A maid-servant.	A certain maid.	The damsel that kept the door.
Question.	"Thou also wast with Jesus of Galilee."	"Thou also wast with Jesus of Nazareth?"	"This man was also with him?"	"Art not thou also one of this man's disciples?"
Denial.	"I know not what thou sayest."	"I know not, neither understand I what thou sayest."	"Woman, I know him not."	"I am not."
		A cock crew.		

Second Denial.—Jesus before Caiaphas.

	MATTHEW.	MARK.	LUKE.	JOHN.
Place.	Porch.	Porch.	Indefinite.	Standing and warming himself.
Time.	Indefinite.	Indefinite.	After a little while.	After Jesus was sent to Caiaphas.
Interrogators.	Another maid.	The maid-servant.	Another.	They.
Question.	"This man was also with Jesus of Nazareth."	"This is one of them."	"Thou art also of them."	"Art not thou also one of his disciples?"
Denial.	With an oath, "I do not know the man."	He denied it again.	"Man, I am not."	"I am not."

Third Denial.—Jesus before Caiaphas.

	MATTHEW.	MARK.	LUKE.	JOHN.
Place.	Indefinite.	Indefinite.	Indefinite.	Indefinite.
Time.	After a while.	A little after.	About an hour after.	Indefinite.
Interrogators.	The by-standers.	The by-standers.	Another.	A servant of the high-priest, a kinsman of Malchus.
Question.	"Surely thou also art one of them; for thy speech betrayeth thee."	"Surely thou art one of them; for thou art a Galilean."	"Of a truth this man also was with him; for he is a Galilean."	"Did I not see thee in the garden with him?"
Denial.	He began to curse and swear: "I know not the man."	He began to curse and swear: "I know not this man of whom ye speak."	"Man, I know not what thou sayest."	Peter then denied again.
	Immediately a cock crew.	The second time a cock crew.	While he yet spake, a cock crew.	Immediately a cock crowed.

Jesus thrice denied by Peter.

66 ^y And as Peter was beneath in the palace, there
67 cometh one of the maids of the high priest: and
when she saw Peter warming himself, she looked
upon him, and said, And thou also wast with Jesus
68 of Nazareth. But he denied, saying, I know not,
neither understand I what thou sayest. And he

^y Mt. 26. 58. 69;
Lk. 22. 55; John
18. 16.

66, 67. **Peter was beneath,** *below,* **in the palace,** *in the court;* the interior court-yard, around which the house was built. See on ver. 54. This appears to have been lower than the room where Jesus stood on trial, which was probably on the ground-floor, in the side or rear, and was entered from this court by a step or steps. If, as

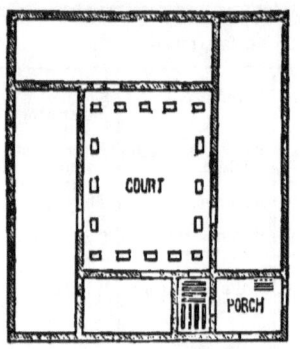

PLAN OF A HOUSE.

we have supposed, Annas and Caiaphas occupied a common official building, they quite likely occupied opposite side apartments. The doors being open from the court into the audience rooms, Peter could doubtless observe what was going on within.

The three denials, though occurring during the different stages of the preliminary examinations, are conveniently grouped together into one narrative by the first three evangelists. John alone notes the examination before Annas, and hence the first denial of Peter, as occurring during it.

One of the maids, or *maid-servants.* John speaks of her as the damsel who kept the door of the porch, or passage into the court. She probably observed Peter carefully when he entered with John, and afterward when he seated himself with the servants of the high-priest, **warming himself.** Something about his appearance or manner excites her suspicion. Then she thinks she remembers seeing him with Jesus. She approaches him, looks earnestly or intently upon him (Luke 22 : 56), and says, "This man was also with him." She tells him so (Matthew and Mark), and asks him (John) if he was not one of "this man's disciples." **Jesus of Nazareth.** Literally, *the Nazarene.* This was a contemptuous epithet among the Jews of Judea. See on ch. 1 : 24. She may have feared being blamed for admitting him. He seems to have been in no great danger, except as he might be recognized as the one who smote Malchus. **Thou also.** Some see in the word *also* a reference to John.

68. Peter's first denial. The precise words are differently reported by the different evangelists, but with the same meaning. This reply embraced all the forms given. The one here, **I know not, neither understand I what thou sayest,** what thou art talking about, is a strong expression, implying a denial of the charge itself. It would seem that Peter was taken by surprise, and, in his cowardice, not only denies, but pleads ignorance. He would have her suppose that he came in as a mere observer.

Went out into the porch. Into the passage-way, the fore-court. Disturbed by the question of the woman, Peter begins to think of retreat, yet not so hasty as to excite suspicion. He goes to the porch through which he had entered into the court.

At this time **the,** rather *a* **cock crew.** The article is indefinite, as in ver. 30. The exactness of the description is seen by this mention of the first crowing, which seems to have been impressed on Peter's mind and alone recorded by Mark. It was now probably between twelve and one,

A.D. 30. MARK XIV. 287

69 went out into the porch; and the cock crew. ᵃ And a maid saw him again, and began to say to them
70 that stood by, This is *one* of them. And he denied it again. ᵃ And a little after, they that stood by said again to Peter, Surely thou art *one* of them: ᵇ for thou art a Galilean, and thy speech agreeth
71 *thereto.* ᶜ But he began to curse and to swear, say-

ᵃ Mt. 26. 71; Lk. 22. 58; John 18. 25.
ᵃ Mt. 26. 73; Lk. 22. 59; John 18. 26.
ᵇ Ac. 2. 7.
ᶜ 1 Cor. 10. 12.

Very likely Peter's mind was so filled with anxiety and fear, that he was not reminded of the prediction of Jesus. But this clause is wanting in some of the oldest documents, and it may have been introduced by some one to harmonize the account. About this time also closed the informal examination before Annas, and Jesus is sent bound to the apartment of Caiaphas, John 18 : 24. The transfer would excite attention, and this may explain why Peter did not now leave the house.

69. Peter is still standing in the porch, probably in the door entering the court, with the blaze of the fire shining upon him, John 18 : 25. A little while (Luke 22 : 58) had intervened since the last denial. It is now between one and two o'clock. Another maid observes something about him which leads her to say, "This man was also with Jesus of Nazareth," Matt. 26 : 71. The **maid** servant who kept the door, seeing him again, joins in the charge. **This is one of them.** They therefore ask, "Art not thou also one of his disciples?" John 18 : 25. These several questions, by different persons, at this time, are perfectly natural, and, as recorded by the different evangelists, show how independent were their narrations. Yet how harmonious!

70. Peter's second denial. According to Mark, Luke and John, he denies that he is a disciple of Jesus. But Matthew tells us that he even denied knowing him, and that, too, with an oath, calling God to witness, and with the somewhat contemptuous form, "I know not the man." As if he had come from curiosity, to learn the cause of this gathering, without any interest in it, and possibly without knowing even the name of the one on trial. This denial is thus a step in advance on the first. That was when he was taken by surprise, possibly somewhat confused; this after he had had a little time to reflect, and hence more deliberate. The number now questioning him, doubtless, excited him to falsehood, a cowardly denial, and a rash and wicked oath. Sin does not go alone. Profanity is no sign of bravery. Yet even now no one appears to have intended him positive injury.

A little after. About one hour after, Luke 22 : 59. Peter was now probably in the court, Luke 22 : 61. **They that stood by.** They had, doubtless, discussed the matter among themselves, and, having observed his Galilean provincialisms, conclude that the charge of the maid-servant is true. They, therefore, say to him, **Surely, thou art one of them.** A strong affirmation, Thou certainly belongest to his disciples. The reason, **For thou art a Galilean,** as most of his disciples were Galileans. Compare Jud. 12 : 6. The pronunciation and accent of the Galileans were indistinct and less pure than those of the inhabitants of Judea. They confounded the gutturals and the two last letters of the Jewish alphabet. **And thy speech agreeth thereto.** This is omitted by the highest critical authorities. Matthew gives, "For thy speech betrayeth thee." At the same time a relative of Malchus, whose ear Peter had cut off, asked, "Did I not see thee in the garden with him?" John 18 : 26.

71. Peter's third denial. This was an advance upon his second. He not only, with an oath, repeats what he had said in the second, that he knew not of whom they spake, but he affirms it with imprecations of divine wrath on himself if he spake not the truth. **He began to curse, and to swear.** *He began to invoke curses* on himself, to take the most solemn oaths, in confirmation of the assertion, **I know not** (rather, *I do not know*) **this man of whom ye speak. Saying,** not in the original, gives a false sense to the preceding words, and destroys the connection. In this lowest point of Peter's fall he gives

72 *ing*, I know not this man of whom ye speak. ᵈ And the second time the cock crew. And Peter called to mind the word that Jesus said unto him, Before the cock crow twice, thou shalt deny me thrice. And when he thought thereon, he wept.

ᵈ Mt. 26. 75; Ps. 38. 18; Mt. 5. 4.

way to profanity, an old forsaken habit, as some suppose.

72. **The cock crew.** The article should be indefinite, as in vers. 30, 68. According to Matthew and Luke this occurred immediately. Mark alone records that it was *a* **second time.** This was at the opening of the fourth or morning watch, at about three o'clock. At this point also, "the Lord turned and looked upon Peter" (Luke 22 : 61), probably through the open door of the council-room of Caiaphas. **Peter called to mind** what Jesus had predicted concerning his denials and the cock-crowings, ver. 30. The look of Jesus doubtless helped to bring it to vivid remembrance. **And when he thought thereon.** The meaning of the verb, in the original, is doubtful. From among the several translations which have been suggested by scholars, the following are the most worthy of attention : 1. *Casting upon*, that is, his mind = *thinking upon*. 2. *Casting* his eyes *upon* Jesus = *looking upon*. 3. *Casting* his mantle *upon*, that is, *covering* his head, in shame and sorrow. Regarding the last it may be said, that as Peter desired concealment, he would hardly have covered himself, thereby making himself the more conspicuous. The second view probably states a fact, for doubtless Peter looked upon Jesus, inasmuch as Jesus looked upon him, and he was conscious of that look. But such a fact by no means settles the meaning of the verb. The first view has the most support on philological grounds, and commends itself as perfectly natural. He *cast it over in his mind*, going through the history of his denials, *reflected upon it*, until his whole soul was humiliated with shame and convulsed with sorrow. We have thus a glimpse of his inward experience. **He wept,** over his sins of lying, profanity, perjury and disloyalty to Christ.

It is needless to speculate here, whether Peter would have been lost if he had now died in this state. It was not Christ's will that he should either die or be lost, since Jesus had prayed for him that his strength fail not (Luke 22 : 32 ; John 17 : 12), and he had declared, "They shall never perish," John 10 : 28.

REMARKS.

1. Formal and worldly religious officials are often worse than the people under them, vers. 1, 2; ch. 11 : 18, 32; Matt. 23 : 13.

2. Men should fear lest God permit them to carry out their wicked designs sooner than they expect. *At the feast*, though they said, Not at the feast, ver. 2; Prov. 19 : 21. God overrules everything to his glory, Ps. 2 : 2–4; 76 : 10.

3. Love counts nothing too precious for Jesus, ver. 3; 2 Cor. 5 : 14.

4. A covetous and selfish spirit begrudges the gifts and sacrifices of love to Christ, ver. 4; 1 Tim. 6 : 10.

5. Many hypocritically plead the wants of the poor as an excuse for withholding their offerings to Christ and his cause, ver. 5.

6. It is God's plan that the poor should always be with his people to receive their sympathy and aid, ver. 7; Deut. 15 : 11; Prov. 22 : 2; Luke 18 : 22; Rom. 15 : 26, 27.

7. Whatever honors our Savior's death is pleasing to him. For example, baptism and the Lord's Supper, ver. 8.

8. Christians share in the honors of the gospel. Their deeds of love are held in everlasting remembrance, ver. 9; Ps. 112 : 6; Mal. 3 : 16; Acts 10 : 31.

9. Christian works are often undervalued and misunderstood by men; but Jesus puts upon them a proper estimate. And at the judgment he will acknowledge and defend his followers and what they did for him, vers. 1–9; Matt. 25 : 34–36, 40.

10. To what lengths a person may go in a false profession of religion! How many a false professor has turned against Jesus for the sake of worldly gain! Vers. 10, 11; 1 Tim. 6 : 9, 10; 2 Tim. 4 : 10; 2 Pet. 2 : 14, 15.

11. That Jesus should have been crucified on the day which was ushered

in by the paschal supper, is highly significant and instructive, ver. 12; 1 Cor. 5:7; Rom. 3:25; Heb. 9:14.

12. Jesus, in keeping the Passover, has taught us to attend faithfully to those ordinances which are now in force, vers. 12–17; 1 Cor. 11:2.

13. Jesus is the searcher of hearts, and knows all of the plans and purposes of his professed followers, ver. 18; Rev. 2:23.

14. The sins of God's people are the more aggravated on account of their relation to him, ver. 18; Zech. 13:6; Heb. 6:6.

15. The thought of dishonoring Jesus, or sinning against him, is sad to the renewed heart, ver. 19; ch. 14:72; 2 Cor. 7:8, 9.

16. The truly humble and pious heart is ever ready to suspect itself, rather than condemn others, ver. 19; 1 Sam. 24:17; 2 Sam. 24:17; Isa. 6:5.

17. Christ's death was in accordance with the eternal purpose of God, ver. 21; Luke 24:44; Acts 2:23; 1 Pet. 1:20.

18. The wicked act freely in sinning, even though in the divine arrangement they fulfill the divine purposes, ver. 21; Acts 4:25–28.

19. Self-examination should precede the reception of the Lord's Supper, vers. 18–21; 1 Cor. 5:8; 11:28.

20. The Lord's Supper reminds us of what Christ has done for us. It is adapted to produce humility, inspire gratitude and strengthen faith, vers. 22, 23; 1 Cor. 11:24, 25.

21. We must feed upon Christ as the bread of life, as well as trust in his atoning blood, vers. 22, 23; John 6:51, 54; 1 John 1:7.

22. The Lord's Supper is an ordinance of the new covenant, designed to continue till Christ's second coming, vers. 22–24; 1 Cor. 11:26.

23. It is our privilege at the Lord's table to look forward to the marriage supper of the Lamb, when the ordinance and the emblems will be no longer needed, since we shall be with Jesus and see him as he is, ver. 25; 1 John 3:2; Rev. 19:9; 21:3.

24. Singing is a fitting and divinely-appointed part of worship, ver. 26; Eph. 5:19; Col. 3:16; James 5:13.

25. Christians may greatly wander from Christ, and do great injury to themselves and his cause, vers. 27–30; Ps. 89:30–33; Rev. 2:4, 5.

26. To be forewarned of an evil is to be forearmed; but even then self-confidence is generally a precursor to a fall, ver. 27–31; Prov. 16:18; Rom. 12:3; 1 Cor. 10:12.

27. How much comfort is lost by not receiving the truth, and resting on the promises! Jesus foretold his resurrection, and promised to go before his disciples into Galilee; but all this was to them but as an idle tale, ver. 28; Luke 24:11.

28. Learn the weakness of human resolution and the folly of trusting thereon, vers. 29, 31, 68, 70; Prov. 28:26.

29. Christ has set us an example of prayer in enduring and overcoming suffering, vers. 32–36; Ps. 50:15; Isa. 26:16; James 5:13, 14.

30. They who go down into the deep valley of humiliation are generally privileged at other times to go up on the high mountain of enjoyment and blessing, ver. 33; ch. 9:2–5; Acts 2:14; 3:1, 4; Gal. 2:9; 1 Pet. 5:1.

31. Watchfulness and prayer are the best safeguards against temptation, ver. 38; Matt. 6:13; Eph. 6:18; 1 Pet. 4:7; Rev. 16:15.

32. If it was necessary for Christ to endure such agonies to save men, how hopeless the case of those who avail not themselves of his atonement! Vers. 33–39; Heb. 2:3.

33. What self-denial and self-sacrifice should we make for him who has endured so much for us! Vers. 33–39; Rom. 12:1; Gal. 6:14; 1 Pet. 4:1, 2.

34. Jesus has set us an example of entire submission to the will of God, vers. 36–39; Matt. 6:10; Phil. 2:6–8; James 4:7.

35. Earnest prayer and perfect resignation to the will of God are consistent with each other, vers. 35, 36.

36. Soul struggles and afflictions of various kinds are necessary, and should therefore be borne submissively, cheerfully, and with strong faith in Christ, vers. 36–39; Rom. 7:21–25; Gal. 5:17; Heb. 12:3–7.

37. Let us see to it that our spirits are willing, though our flesh be weak; thus shall we be objects of the divine compassion of Jesus, who will pity though he reproves, vers. 37, 38; Ps. 103:14; Gal. 5:16, 18; Heb. 4:15; 5:2, 5–9.

38. Let any beware how they sleep on when Christ is betrayed among his peo-

ple into the hands of sinners, vers. 37, 41; Rev. 3 : 15, 16.

39. The time will come when all who are in a religious sleep will be compelled to awake, vers. 41, 42; Isa. 33 : 14; Prov. 1 : 24–26; 6 : 9–11; Rev. 3 : 19.

40. If one of the twelve whom Jesus chose was a traitor, how unsafe to follow those who arrogate to themselves an apostolic succession! Ver. 43; Rev. 2 : 2.

41. Hypocritical discipleship and treacherous friendship are far more odious and injurious than open hostility. They who acknowledge Christ in word, but deny him in deed, seeking to make gain and merchandise of Christ, are fast following in the steps of Judas, vers. 43–45; Ps. 41 : 9; Prov. 27 : 6; Matt. 7 : 21.

42. Many now, like Christ's enemies and even friends, understand not the nature of his kingdom; and use carnal instead of spiritual weapons, vers. 43, 47, 48; John 18 : 36; 2 Cor. 10 : 4; Zech. 4 : 6.

43. When Christians have recourse to violence for Christ they most surely take off the ear, the spiritual hearing, from their opponents, ver. 47.

44. Let each one who comes to Jesus, in any way, ask himself, Wherefore am I come? Ver. 48; Ezek. 33 : 31.

45. Learn the certainty of the entire fulfillment of Scripture, ver. 49; Matt. 5 : 18; Luke 24 : 25; Rev. 22 : 7.

46. The wicked cannot afflict or persecute God's people except by divine permission, ver. 49; Job 1 : 5–12; 2 : 6; Ps. 31 : 15; 105 : 14, 15.

47. The persecutions of Christians have generally been characterized by secret designings, malignant cunning, and open violence, ver. 48; Acts 6 : 11–13; 23 : 20, 21.

48. Jesus, as a Savior, stood alone. As all human help failed him, so we must despair of all, and trust in his atonement alone, ver. 50; Isa. 63 : 3–5; Acts 4 : 12.

49. How frail is all human dependence! Even the best of men cannot trust themselves, ver. 50; Jer. 17 : 5; Prov. 28 : 26.

50. The youth who follows Jesus in his night garb, and then flees, is a striking picture of the pious resolutions of Christ's disciples, which are dissipated in the night of great temptation, vers. 51, 52; Gal. 6 : 1.

51. It is dangerous at any time to venture into temptation, especially in our own strength and when we are following Christ afar off, ver. 54; Matt. 6 : 13; Prov. 3 : 5.

52. Happy is he against whom his enemies can allege nothing, except falsely, vers. 55–59; 1 Kings 21 : 9–14; Ps. 27 : 12; 35 : 11; 64 : 5, 6; Matt. 5 : 11.

53. Evil men and false teachers commonly mingle some truth with error, ver. 58; Acts 6 : 14.

54. God hates lying lips. They were directed against Jesus; and they will not spare his followers, vers. 55–58; Ps. 31 : 2; 120 : 2; Prov. 12 : 19, 22.

55. There is a time for silence and a time to speak. Jesus treated frivolous and unjust charges with silence; but declared his character and mission, vers. 61, 62; Prov. 21 : 23; Isa. 53 : 7; 1 Pet. 2 : 23; Acts 4 : 20.

56. God gives the most wicked the light of his truth, so that their deeds are without excuse, ver. 62; John 15 : 22; Rom. 1 : 20.

57. He that charges others with blasphemy is sometimes himself the blasphemer, ver. 64; 1 Kings 21 : 13; Acts 6 : 13; 7 : 57.

58. They who jest at religion, make light of Christians, and strive to injure the cause of Christ, would have mocked him and spit upon him when upon earth, ver. 65; Acts 7 : 51–53.

59. Except when duty calls, we should avoid that company and place where our reputation may be injured, vers. 54, 66–68; Ps. 1 : 1; Prov. 2 : 12; 4 : 14; 1 Cor. 15 : 33.

60. If we go not forth in God's strength, but depend on ourselves, the smallest matter may overcome us. Peter fears and falls before a maid-servant, vers. 66, 69; Prov. 14 : 14; 28 : 14.

61. Sin is progressive. Beware of the beginning of sin, and especially of what are called little sins, vers. 54, 68, 71; James 1 : 15.

62. Little confidence can be placed in assertions abounding with profanity, ver. 71.

63. The smallest matter in God's hands may lead to repentance, and the feeblest means result in salvation. The crowing of a cock brought Peter to himself, ver. 72.

64. The fall of Peter should stand as a warning against a like sin; but his recovery should encourage those who

A.D. 30.   MARK XV.   291

Jesus finally condemned and delivered to Pilate.

XV. AND ᵃstraightway in the morning the chief priests held a consultation with the elders and scribes and the whole council, and bound Jesus, and carried him away, and delivered him to Pilate.

ᵃ Mt. 27. 1; Lk. 23. 1; John 18. 28; Ps. 2. 2; Ac. 3. 13; 4. 26.

have fallen to turn to God with humble repentance, ver. 72; Jer. 3 : 22. 65. Repentance has no merit, and can make no atonement for sin; but it should restore our confidence in those who truly exercise it, ver. 72; 2 Cor. 7 : 10. 66. How valuable is reflection! If sinners would but stop and think on their ways, many more would be led to repentance, ver. 72; Ps. 119 : 59; Hag. 1 : 5-7; Isa. 1 : 3; Ezek. 12 : 3.

CHAPTER XV.

Mark in this chapter continues the history of the sacrificial work of Jesus. He is formally and finally condemned by the Jewish rulers, and taken before Pilate, who examines him and at first proposes to release him. But the people, instigated by their rulers, demand the crucifixion of Jesus, and the release of Barabbas. Desirous of satisfying the people, Pilate grants their requests. Barabbas is released, and Jesus is scourged, mocked and led forth to Golgotha. One Simon, a Cyrenian, is compelled to bear his cross. The incidents of the crucifixion are described: the wine mingled with myrrh, the dividing of his garments, the inscription, the two robbers crucified with him, the supernatural darkness, the cry, the loud voice and the expiring of Jesus. The vail of the temple is rent, and the centurion utters his conviction that Jesus is the Son of God. Many women from Galilee stand watching from the distance. Joseph of Arimathea begs his body and lays it in a sepulchre near at hand. Although Mark gives some incidents not found in the other Gospels, yet his account of the events related in this chapter is the briefest of the four. This, together with the lack of detail, which so characterizes other portions of this Gospel, may be accounted for, perhaps, by Peter's state of mind and possible absence from the scenes of that day after his denials.

1. JESUS FINALLY CONDEMNED BY THE SANHEDRIM AND BROUGHT BEFORE PILATE. Matt. 27 : 1, 2; Luke 22 : 66–71; John 18 : 28. Matthew and Mark are very brief; but Luke, passing over the preliminary examination of Jesus, relates this meeting very fully. John, omitting all after the sending of Jesus from Annas to Caiaphas, goes at once with Jesus to Pilate's judgment-hall. Thus the four evangelists beautifully harmonize in giving us the different sides of the events connected with Jesus before the Jewish rulers. John relates the informal examination before Annas, implying his condemnation under Caiaphas (John 18 : 24, 28); Matthew and Mark record the preliminary examination before Caiaphas, at which Jesus was virtually condemned, implying a session in the morning; and Luke relates the regular and legal session when the condemnation of the night session was ratified.

1. **Straightway in the morning.** "As soon as it was day," Luke 22 : 66. About five or six o'clock of Friday, the 15th of Nisan, April 7th, in the seven hundred and eighty-third year from the founding of Rome. **The chief priests** are again presented as the leaders in this movement. See on ch. 14 : 55. **Held a consultation.** It was a meeting of the **whole council.** This meeting was also held, probably, at the house of Caiaphas, for John (18 : 28) says that they led Jesus from Caiaphas to the governor's palace. They met not only to ratify the action of the night session of the Sanhedrim, of which Luke gives a definite account and Matthew and Mark are confirmatory, but also to devise the best means of putting him to death. They doubtless fixed upon the twofold charge of blasphemy and treason, Luke 23 : 2; John 19 : 7. They could condemn to death, but could not put the sentence into execution without the sanction of the Roman governor, John 18 : 31. The Jews lost the power of life and death when Archelaus was deposed, A.D. 6. According to the Talmud this power was taken from the

2 'And Pilate asked him, Art thou the King of the ᶠMt. 27. 11.
Jews? And he answering said unto him, Thou

Sanhedrim about forty or more years before the destruction of Jerusalem.

Bound Jesus. They may have loosened or removed the bonds during trial (John 18 : 12); now they rebound him. **They carried him away.** It would seem that the whole Sanhedrim present went in a body to Pilate, who was now in his official residence in Herod's palace. Some suppose that they took him to the tower of Antonia, adjoining the temple area on the north. But from John 18 : 28 it seems evident that it was the governor's palace or prætorium, on Mount Zion, in the western part of the city. The governors generally resided at Cæsarea, but removed to Jerusalem during the great festivals to preserve order and exercise judicial functions. Hence Pilate would be occupying the governor's, that is, Herod's palace. Their coming thus early, with a prisoner bound in fetters, was adapted to produce the impression on the governor that Jesus was a great criminal. **Delivered him.** The same word as in ch. 26 : 2, 16, etc., translated *betrayed*. As Jesus is betrayed by Judas, one of his disciples, into the hands of the Jewish authorities, so is he betrayed by the latter, his own people, into the hands of the Gentiles.

Pilate. Matthew adds "the governor," or procurator. Matthew often styles him simply "the governor;" Mark, never.

After Archelaus was deposed, Judea and Samaria were annexed to the Roman province of Syria, and governed by procurators, of whom the sixth was Pontius Pilate. He was appointed A.D. 25, and held his office ten years during the reign of the Emperor Tiberius. He was noted for his severity and cruelty; and by several massacres, to one of which Luke refers (Luke 13 : 1), he rendered himself odious to both the Jews and Samaritans. The latter accused him of cruelty before Vitellius, the governor of Syria, by whom he was ordered to Rome to answer to the charge before the emperor. But Tiberius having died before he arrived, Pilate is said to have been banished by his successor, Caligula, to Vienna, in Gaul, and there to have committed suicide. The traveler who descends the Rhone, in the south of France, may see still standing the very tower from which, as tradition says, Pilate precipitated himself and died. The Roman historian Tacitus makes this important reference to Pilate and Christ : "The author of this name (Christian) was Christ, who was capitally punished in the reign of Tiberius by Pontius Pilate."

At the trial of Jesus, Pilate showed a lack of moral courage to do what he knew to be right. This led to his indecision, and to the various expedients to release Jesus, till at last he yields to the demands of the Jews, through fear of losing his standing as Cæsar's friend. Pilate doubtless made an official report of the crucifixion of Jesus to the Emperor Tiberius. So Justin Martyr and other early writers affirm; but the one that is now extant is spurious.

At this point Matthew relates the confession, remorse and suicide of Judas, Matt. 27 : 3–10 ; Acts 1 : 18, 19.

2–5. JESUS IS EXAMINED BY PILATE. THE FIRST TIME. Matt. 27 : 11-14 ; Luke 23 : 2–5 ; John 18 : 28-38. The accounts of Matthew and Mark are very similar. John is very full. Luke first gives the accusation against Jesus and then so arranges his narrative as to relate the sending of Jesus to Herod.

2. **Pilate asked him,** or *questioned him.* Mark takes us at once to the examination of Jesus by Pilate. John, however, relates that the Sanhedrim would not enter the governor's house, lest they should be defiled, and that therefore Pilate went out to them. They wish him to ratify and execute their sentence. This he refuses to do without knowing their accusation and the evidence. They therefore appear as his accusers, bringing the charge, not of blasphemy, on account of which he had been condemned by the Sanhedrim (ch. 14 : 63, 64), but of treason against Cæsar, as king of the Jews, John 18 : 28–32 ; Luke 23 : 2. They thought that the former charge, being religious, Pilate would not entertain, but that the latter he must entertain, relating as it did both to Cæsar and himself.

Art thou the King? etc. It is implied that this charge had been preferred against him. Accordingly Luke (23 :

3 sayest *it*. And the chief priests accused him of
4 many things: but he answered nothing. ᵍ And
Pilate asked him again, saying, Answerest thou
nothing? Behold how many things they witness
5 against thee. ʰ But Jesus yet answered nothing; so
that Pilate marvelled.

ᵍ Mt. 27. 13.

ʰ Is. 53. 7; John 19. 9.

Barabbas preferred to Jesus.
6 Now ⁱ at *that* feast he released unto them one

Mt. 27. 15; Lk. 23. 17; John 18. 39.

---

2), informs us that they charged him with seditious agitation, forbidding to pay the tribute money, and proclaiming himself Christ, a king. Before answering, Jesus brought out clearly before Pilate's mind the distinction between a civil and a spiritual kingdom, declaring that his was the latter, John 18 : 33-36. And then he answered, **Thou sayest;** a strong affirmative answer. The object of the verb, according to Hebrew idiom, is understood, *Thou sayest it*, it is as thou hast said.

3. Accused him of many things, in support of the charge that he proclaimed himself a king, and in addition to it. They would omit nothing which would blacken his character and make him appear a dangerous man in the eyes of Pilate. **But he answered nothing.** There are no words in the Greek text answering to these. Matthew (27 : 12) makes this statement, and it is implied by the question of Pilate in the next verse.

4. Answerest thou nothing? That is, to their charges. He had declared his Messiahship and the spiritual nature of his kingdom to Pilate. He had nothing more to add. Their malignant charges were unworthy an answer, and his silence a reaffirmation of what he had said. Compare 1 Pet. 2 : 23. **How many things.** Rather, *What great things*, or simply, *What things.* The reference is to the *magnitude* rather than the *number* of things. Pilate probably desired Jesus to deny the charges, in order to help him in declaring his innocence and his acquittal. But they needed no denial; Pilate knew his innocence (ver. 10), and that the Jewish rulers would not conspire against him because he would free them from Roman authority. Instead of **witness against,** some of the oldest manuscripts read *charge against* or *accuse*.

5. Pilate marvelled. He wondered that Jesus *no longer made* any reply, not even giving to him the cause of his silence. But Jesus was not under obligation to help Pilate to do his duty. He should have followed his own convictions and released him. The silence of Jesus continues till Pilate some time after referred to his power to crucify him or release him, John 19 : 10, 11.

Pilate now goes forth and declares the innocence of Jesus, Luke 23 : 4; John 18 : 28. The Jews are therefore the more violent, accusing him with stirring up the people throughout all Judea, beginning from Galilee. Learning that Jesus is a Galilean, Pilate sends him to Herod, the tetrarch of that country, who mocks him, and sends him back to Pilate, Luke 23 : 5-15. Mark omits this reference to Herod, which is recorded only by Luke, and passes to the next expedient of Pilate to release Jesus.

6-14. JESUS AGAIN BEFORE PILATE. BARABBAS PREFERRED TO JESUS. Matt. 26 : 15-23; Luke 23 : 13-23; John 18 : 39, 40. Mark and also Luke particularly describe the character of Barabbas. Matthew records the dream and message of Pilate's wife. The four accounts beautifully supplement one another. See author's HARMONY, § 180.

6. Luke relates that Pilate again called together the Jewish rulers, stating that neither he nor Herod found any fault in Jesus, and proposing to chastise and then release him, Luke 23 : 13-15.

At that feast. At every Passover; for such is the meaning of the words. **He released.** The idea "was wont to release," expressed by Matthew (27 : 15), is here implied in the original. The origin of this practice is unknown; it is not mentioned in history. The custom was probably established by the Romans to conciliate the Jews, since

MARK XV. A.D. 30.

7 prisoner, whomsoever they desired. And there was
one named Barabbas, *which lay* bound with them
that had made insurrection with him, who had com-
8 mitted murder in the insurrection. And the multitude crying aloud began to desire *him to do* as he
9 had ever done unto them. But Pilate answered
them, saying, Will ye that I release unto you the King
10 of the Jews? For he knew that the chief priests
had delivered him ᵏ for envy.
11 But ˡ the chief priests moved the people, that he

ᵏ 1 Sám. 18. 8, 9;
Pro. 27. 4; Is. 3.
14, 16.
ˡ Mt. 27. 20; Ac. 3.
14; Heb. 7. 26;
1 Pet. 1. 19.

persons would often be in prison whom the Jews would desire to liberate from Roman law. On the strength of this custom, Pilate tries to save Jesus without offending the Jews. Instead of boldly doing what he knew to be right, he weakly resorts to an expedient. **Whomsoever they desired** or *asked* as a favor to themselves.

7. Barabbas. The name means *son of his father.* Some think he was a son of a rabbi. "They rejected the true Son of his Father, and chose a robber, who bare the name of father's son, in his place."—WORDSWORTH. **Bound with them**, etc. *Bound with his fellow insurgents,* or *companions in sedition.* Mark alone records that he was one of a number engaged in insurrection and murder. Matthew styles him "a notable prisoner;" John, "a robber;" and Luke, that he "was cast into prison for a certain sedition made in the city, and for murder." As he is spoken of so prominently, he was quite likely a leader. The charge of insurrection would be offensive to Pilate. Barabbas may have been engaged in one of those popular movements which were the beginnings or germs of that political party called Zealots, whose excesses were so enormous during the last years of Jerusalem.—JOSEPHUS, *Jewish War,* iv. 3. Such a supposition will partly explain the popular clamor in his favor. **Who had committed murder.** In the plural referring to the insurgents, of whom Barabbas of course was one.

8. The multitude crying aloud. According to the highest critical authorities, *The multitude coming up;* to the place where Pilate was, outside of the governor's house, ver. 2. They were coming back from Herod. **Began to desire,** etc. *Began to entreat,* or *make request according as he always did for them.* This would seem to imply, although not necessarily, that Pilate was himself the author of this practice.

9. Will ye that I release, etc. Addressed to the multitude, the crowd, ver. 8. The question is the same in John 18 : 39. But Matthew brings out the fact that he also asked : "Barabbas, or Jesus who is called Christ?" Pilate hoped to get a popular expression from the multitude in favor of releasing Jesus, rather than Barabbas. The reason of this hope is stated in the next verse. And as he would put the case in the most taking light with the multitude, he ironically styles Jesus **King of the Jews.**

10. Envy. Pilate knew that the Jewish rulers were envious against Jesus on account of his popularity with the multitude, and because they regarded him as a formidable rival. He hoped the people would demand his release. Three times does he propose to release Jesus (Luke 23 : 22), but the people, persuaded by their rulers, to his surprise and mortification, demand Barabbas.

Notice that the **chief priests,** both in this verse and the next, are again presented as the instigators and leaders of the persecution against Jesus, ch. 14 : 10, 55; 15 : 1.

11. Moved. *Stirred up the multitude.* **Rather release Barabbas.** These sticklers for the law, deliberately violate their own law, in preferring to release a murderer and put to death the Messiah, Lev. 24 : 17 ; Num. 35 : 16-24. See how Peter puts the case in Acts 3 : 13-15. Just at this point Matthew brings in the message to Pilate from his wife, concerning her dream, warning him against having anything to do with that just man. It would seem that while Pilate was receiving this message, the Jewish rulers were active in counteracting the appeal

12 should rather release Barabbas unto them. And
Pilate answered and said again unto them, What
will ye then that I shall do *unto him* whom ye call
13 the King of the Jews ? And they cried out again,
14 Crucify him. Then Pilate said unto them, Why,
what evil hath he done ? And they cried out the

of Pilate in favor of Jesus. *The multitude* were those who had come together during the arrest and trial; doubtless composed very largely of the street rabble, who are now as ready to condemn him as they were a few days before to praise him. The disciples and friends of Jesus, who took the lead in his triumphal entry into Jerusalem, and whom the Jewish rulers so feared that they dare not to arrest him openly, were without doubt mostly absent, through fear or ignorance. Yet persuasion was necessary to induce even the rabble to ask for the discharge of such a notorious criminal as Barabbas, and the death of such a righteous one as Jesus.

12. **What will ye then that I shall do.** Pilate was taken by surprise that they should ask the release of Barabbas, the rebel, robber and murderer, rather than Jesus, who had committed no crime. He is left in doubt as to what they would have him do with Jesus. Here do we behold another step of Pilate in weakly yielding himself into the power of the Jews. At first, instead of acquitting Jesus, he adopts the expedient of having the people demand his release at the feast. This fails, and expediency leads to expediency. Instead of acting as a righteous and independent judge, he now asks those who had no jurisdiction over the case, "What will ye then that I shall do," etc. ? Though he desires to acquit him, and the question is adroitly put in a conciliatory manner, **whom ye call King of the Jews,** it is not his assumed title, but theirs ironically; yet the question implies and shows that his decision will be influenced by the demands of the people. He was doubtless also desirous of pleasing the people, because they might accuse him of disloyalty to Cæsar. The complaints of the Jews received particular attention at Rome. Archelaus had been deposed partly on account of the complaints of his subjects against him. A selfish motive, therefore, operated against his moral courage, and doubtless led him to desire to conciliate the Jews, to whom he was odious, by granting their request, at least in a modified form, as by scourging and mockery. See on ver. 15.

13. **They cried out again.** Not that they had uttered the same cry before, but simply that they shouted aloud again. **Crucify him.** How successful the chief priests had been in stirring up the people is evident from this and the next verse. They might have asked, Let him be stoned, which was the Jewish mode of execution and their penalty for blasphemy; or they might have simply said, Let him be put to death; but they demand crucifixion, the Roman punishment for sedition, since this was the crime they charge upon him. Thus also they gratify their hatred against Jesus. Moreover, as they demanded the release of Barabbas, who would, doubtless, have been crucified for his crimes, so they ask for Jesus the punishment which Barabbas would have received. Thus is Barabbas preferred to Jesus. Yet in this were the Scriptures and the predictions of Jesus being fulfilled, John 18 : 32, Matt. 20 : 19. He dies an ignominious death, his body is unmutilated and not a bone broken, and he is made a curse by hanging on the tree.

14. **Why, what evil,** etc. Literally, *For what evil*, etc., and well expressed in English, *What evil then hath he done?* Another step downward of the vacillating Pilate. Instead of acquitting Jesus, he had partially laid aside his rights as a judge, and asked the decision of the people, ver. 12. And now, having heard their decision, he accepts the situation, and strives to reason with them. If they insist on his death, they must show some crime meriting such a punishment; and certainly he had not done anything demanding crucifixion. Instead of stopping to reason, he should have retraced his steps and acted the part of a righteous judge. Luke (23 : 22) informs us

15 more exceedingly, Crucify him. ᵐAnd *so* Pilate, willing to content the people, released Barabbas unto them, and delivered Jesus, when he had scourged *him*, to be crucified.

ᵐ Mt. 27. 26; John 19. 1-16.

The insults of the soldiers.

16 ⁿAnd the soldiers led him away into the hall, called Prætorium. And they call together the whole

ⁿ Mt. 27. 27; Ps. 35. 15, 16; Is. 50. 6.

that though Pilate found no evil in him, yet on the principle of expediency he proposes to conciliate the Jews by the milder punishment of scourging. But the people saw their advantage and made the most of it. They cried **the more exceedingly,** the more vehemently, **Crucify him.** "You have given us the choice of the prisoner to be released, and the privilege of deciding what shall be done with Jesus. We have expressed our wishes; now do your part in executing them." From both Matthew and Luke we learn that the people were becoming tumultuous, taking the form and spirit of a mob.

15-19. PILATE RELEASES BARABBAS, AND SCOURGES JESUS. JESUS MOCKED BY THE SOLDIERS; DELIVERED TO BE CRUCIFIED. Matt. 27 : 24-30; Luke 23 : 24, 25; John 19 : 1-16.

Matthew and Mark record the release of Barabbas, the scourging and mocking of Jesus, and his being delivered up to be crucified. Luke simply relates the release of Barabbas and the delivering up of Jesus. John omits the release, but relates the rest with attending circumstances. Matthew is fullest upon the release of Barabbas and the mocking of Jesus. Mark resembles Matthew, but is briefer, though now and then peculiarly graphic.

15. **Willing to content the people.** *Wishing to satisfy the multitude,* or *crowd.* The Romans had found the Jews very difficult to manage, the emperors often conceding to their wishes. Hence Pilate was not merely *willing* but *desirous* of satisfying their wishes, and gaining the favor of both the leaders and the masses. See on ver. 12. We find the same disposition manifested respecting Paul, by Felix and Festus, Acts 24 : 27 ; 25 : 9. Thus we perceive that Pilate was actuated by a selfish motive. But on the other hand were the message of his wife, the voice of conscience, and the manifest innocence of Jesus. From Matt. 27 : 24, 25, we learn that Pilate vainly attempted to declare himself innocent of the blood of Jesus by washing his hands. An impressive act, doubtless; but one which could neither justify him in doing wrong, nor free him of his responsibility as a judge.

When he had scourged him. It was a Roman custom to scourge a criminal before crucifixion. Roman scourging was more severe than Jewish. The number of lashes was not limited to forty. The whips were armed with bones or lead, to render the blow the more fearful, and to lacerate the flesh. The criminal was generally bound to a low block, in a stooping posture, and received the fearful blows upon the naked back. The scourging before crucifixion was generally exceedingly cruel, and criminals frequently died under it. Jesus was probably scourged by soldiers appointed by Pilate for the purpose. It took place outside of the governor's house, and was a fulfillment of a prediction of Jesus, ch. 10 : 34; and of prophecy, Isa. 50 : 6; 53 : 5. Pilate seems to have been affected by the cruel scourging, and, thinking that what touched his heart might affect the hearts of others, he determines to make one more appeal to the Jewish people by showing him lacerated and bleeding, arrayed in a garb of mockery. But in vain. See John 19 : 1-16.

Delivered Jesus to be crucified. A summary statement, but in harmony with John, who places the delivering up of Jesus to crucifixion after the scourging, and the scourging before the mockery. After this statement, Mark passes to a brief description of the mockery.

16. **The soldiers;** "of the governor," Matt. 27 : 27. Probably his body-guard. **Led him away,** from near the judgment-seat, which was in front

17 band. And they clothed him with purple, and
platted a crown of thorns, and put it about his *head*,
18 and began to salute him, Hail, King of the Jews!
19 And they smote him on the head with a reed, and
did spit upon him, and bowing *their* knees wor-

---

of the house, John 18 : 28, 29. **The hall;** *the court*, the inner open court, around which the palace was built. Compare ch. 14 : 54. This large palace-court seems to have been the place where the guards were stationed. **Called Prætorium.** Rather, *which is Prætorium.* The head-quarters of the Roman military governor. This was the palace built by Herod, where Pilate resided when at Jerusalem. See on ver. 2. *Prætorium* is one of the many Latin words occurring in this Gospel, and indicating its character and design, as one for Gentile, and especially Roman readers. **Called together the whole band.** The whole Roman cohort, stationed at Jerusalem, which was a tenth part of a legion, and embraced from three to six hundred men or more. See on ch. 14 : 43. The whole band of soldiers were gathered to make sport with Jesus. Herod's guard had gone through the same cruel mockery, Luke 23 : 11. Luke, who alone relates that, omits this. The reason is apparent. For Luke to have also related the mockery under Pilate, or the other evangelist that under Herod, would have been a needless repetition.

17. **With purple.** So also John 19 : 2. Purple-red was a color worn by emperors. The ancient kings of Midian wore purple raiment, Jud. 8 : 26. In derision they clothe him in a royal dress and pay him royal honors. Matthew (27 : 28) says "a scarlet robe," most probably a crimson military cloak of a Roman officer. It was thus a mock imperial robe. Alford says that "purple is vaguely used to signify different shades of red, and is especially convertible with crimson." Similar colors intermingled, and the names were often indefinitely applied, and, in popular language, interchanged. Compare the prophetic utterance of David, Ps. 35 : 15, 16.

Platted. And having woven. **A crown of thorns.** The principal object was mockery; a derisive imitation of crowning kings and conquerors with wreaths of ivy, palm or laurel. It was, doubtless, a secondary object to make it a *painful* crown. So mean a plant as the thorn made it suitable for a mock crown, and well adapted to produce pain. It is a matter of dispute as to what species of thorn was used. Thorny plants and shrubs abound in Palestine. The *Spina Christi*, or *Christ's thorn*, is now common near Jerusalem, and is very generally pointed out as the species of thorn used on this occasion. Another plant (a *leguminous* flexile thorn) is preferred by others. Rev. E. P. Hammond, who was in Jerusalem in December, 1866, in referring to it says, "Before leaving, Mrs. Gobat presented me with a crown of thorns, which must be similar to the one which our blessed Savior wore; for all about Jerusalem the same kind of thorn grows as in the days of our Lord. . . . Each of the thorns upon the crown was, when it was given me, as sharp as a cambric needle." The latter plant is the more probable one. It is possible that this crown remained on his head during his crucifixion, since Matthew and Mark mention the removal of the purple robe, but not the crown.

18. **Began to salute him,** or pay him homage as to a king; or greet him as a sovereign. **Hail.** *Joy to thee.* Similar to the Hebrew phrase, Let the king live forever, Neh. 2 : 3; Dan. 2 : 4.

19. They add cruelty to mockery, and descend to the grossest insult and violence. **Smote him on the head.** The pain from the stroke was heightened by the sharp, thorny crown. **With a reed,** a plant with a hollow-jointed stock, a common product of the wilderness of Judea and of the banks of the Jordan, and sometimes used for walking-canes. This was probably the reed which, according to Matthew, had been placed "in his right hand" as a mock scepter. Compare Esth. 5 : 2. They also **spit upon** him, an act expressive of the deepest contempt, Isa. 53 : 3. See on ch. 14 : 65. **Bowing their knees.** Kneeling down. **Worshipped him.** *Did him reverence, paid him homage.* See on ch. 5 : 6. This mock-

20 shipped him. °And when they had mocked him, they took off the purple from him, and put his own clothes on him.

° Mt. 27. 31; Lk. 23. 26. John 19. 16.

Jesus led away to be crucified.

21 And [they] led him out to crucify him. ᵖAnd they compel one Simon a Cyrenian, who passed by, coming out of the country, (the father of Alexander and Rufus,) to bear his cross.

ᵖ Mt. 27. 32; Lk. 23. 26.

cry and violence was not required by law. It was the lawless sport of a coarse and brutal soldiery, who knew little of Jesus, except what they had heard from the Jews, and who, doubtless, regarded him as a religious fanatic. But all this Jesus bore meekly, submissively and silently, Isa. 53 : 7.

While Jesus still wore this mock attire, Pilate makes a final attempt to release him by appealing to the sympathy of the Jews, John 19 : 4-16. See on ver. 15.

20-23. JESUS IS LED FORTH TO CRUCIFIXION. Matt. 27 : 31-34; Luke 23 : 26-33; John 19 : 16, 17. Luke's account is the fullest. Mark describes Simon of Cyrene most particularly.

20. **Led him out,** of the city. Thus it became him to suffer without the gate, Heb. 13 : 12; Lev. 16 : 27. Criminals were executed outside the city, Lev. 24 : 14; Num. 15 : 35; 1 Kings 21 : 13; Acts 7 : 58. The four soldiers (John 19 : 23), headed by the centurion on horseback, who had charge of the crucifixion (ver. 39), led Jesus forth. A tradition, which has been traced no farther back than the fourteenth century, represents Jesus as passing along the *Via Dolorosa,* The Sorrowful Way, a narrow and crooked street from St. Stephen's gate to the church of the Holy Sepulchre. The tradition is unreliable. Jesus could not have passed along this way, if he was tried at the palace of Herod on Mount Zion.

21. **They compel.** The word thus translated is of Persian origin, and is found three times in the New Testament, here, Matt. 5 : 41 and 27 : 32, and means *impress, to press into service.* According to the postal arrangement of Cyrus, horses were provided, at certain distances along the principal roads of the empire, so that couriers could proceed without interruption both night and day. If the government arrangements failed at any point, the couriers had authority to press into their service men, horses or anything that came in their way which might serve to hasten their journey. A like authority was exercised over the Jews by the Roman governors. The word, originating in this custom, passed from the Persian into the Greek, and into rabbinical language, meaning *compulsory service* in forwarding royal messengers, and also *to press into service* for any purpose. Thus they did not arbitrarily assume power, but, under the direction of the centurion, who had the necessary authority under Roman law, they pressed this man into their service. The reason for selecting him was, probably, because he was a stranger and foreigner, and happened to meet them just at the time when some one was needed. He *was passing by,* and it was convenient to press him into service. It is not necessary to suppose him a disciple or a slave.

One Simon a Cyrenian. A native of Cyrene, an important city in northern Africa, between Egypt and the territory of Carthage. Many Jews resided there. They were accustomed to visit Jerusalem in large numbers at the great festivals, and had there a synagogue, Acts 2 : 10 ; 6 : 9. Simon may have taken up his residence at Jerusalem; but very probably he had recently come from Cyrene to attend the Passover. Mark very particularly designates him as the **father of Alexander and Rufus,** well-known disciples among the early Christians. A Simeon in Acts 13 : 1, Rufus in Rom. 16 : 13, and Alexander in Acts 19 : 33; 1 Tim. 1 : 20; 2 Tim. 4 : 14, are mentioned; but whether they are to be identified with Simon of Cyrene and his sons is conjectural. **Coming out**

22 ¹ And they bring him unto the place Golgotha, which is, being interpreted, The place of a skull. * Mt. 27. 33; Lk. 23. 33; John 19. 17.

of the country, literally, *coming from the field;* not necessarily where he had been at work, but with the general idea of coming from *the country* to the city, without regard to distance. Simon appears to have been just entering the city as Jesus was passing out bearing his own cross, John 19:17.
To bear his cross. The *cross* was of various forms. (1.) It was originally a simple stake. (2.) Afterward it was made of two pieces of wood, crossed like the letter X; or (3) like the letter X; or (4) the transverse beam crossed the perpendicular one at some distance from the top, as T. The latter was, doubtless, the one used on this occasion, since the title was placed over the head. The uniform tradition is, that this was the form of the Savior's cross. The cross which Constantine commanded to be placed on his standard represented the first two letters of the Greek *Christos* (*Christ*) ☧.
Jesus bore his cross to the gate, when he was relieved or aided by Simon. Compare Isaac carrying the wood in Gen. 22:6. It was usual for persons condemned to crucifixion to bear their own cross. A tradition says that Jesus sank to the ground under it. It is quite possible that, having fallen exhausted from great weariness and the loss of blood, it was put on Simon. Yet it is more in accordance with the language of Luke (23:26) to suppose that Simon bore only the part of the cross which was behind Jesus, and thus lightened the burden. As they pass along to the place of crucifixion, a great company of people, and of women, who also bewailed and lamented him, follow. This touching incident is related only by Luke (ch. 23:27-31).
22. **Golgotha.** The name in Hebrew, or, rather, Aramean, which Mark renders for his Gentile readers, **Place of skull.** According to Luke 23:33, correctly translated, it is "a place which is called *a skull.*" Calvary, in the common version, is from *Calvarium,* the Latin for skull. Some suppose that it was so called from the skulls of criminals executed or buried there. But these must have been buried according to Jewish law. Why, then, should the place be named from the skull rather than from any other part of the skeleton? Why in the singular and not in the plural? Others, therefore, suppose it so called because it was a rounded and skull-like knoll. But there is no intimation in the Scriptures that it was a hill. Still, the latter explanation is the best, unless we suppose it received the name from some skull which had been found there, or lain there exposed for a time contrary to Jewish usage. From the Gospels we learn it was nigh the city (John 19:20), near a thoroughfare (ver. 29), by a garden, where was the sepulchre hewn in the rock, ver. 46; John 19:41. Tradition places it north-west of the temple, where the Church of the Sepulchre is at present situated. But this is improbable, since the site of the church must have been within the city, and Golgotha was without the gate, Matt. 28:11; John 19:17. The present trend of opinion is to locate Calvary north of Jerusalem, near the Damascus gate, at the grotto of Jeremiah. This meets well all the conditions. Another site on the northeast of the city is thus described by one who knew well the modern city. "It would seem that the soldiers had not far to go from the palace to Golgotha. The gate of St. Stephen's (in the eastern wall) is about two hundred yards from the palace. Without the gate one road runs eastward across the Kidron, another northward along the narrow brow of the hill. Between these is an open space, rugged and rocky; just below it, in the shelving banks of the Kidron, are several rock tombs. This spot would seem to answer all the requirements of the narrative. The passers-by on both roads would be within a few yards of him; and his acquaintance could stand 'afar off' on the side of Olivet and see with the utmost distinctness the whole scene."—J. L. PORTER, in *Alexander's Kitto's Cyclop.*
Dr. J. P. Newman would place it toward the north-east corner of the city. He says, "There desolation is complete and the seclusion profound. The Kidron Valley winds around those rugged declivities, and the opposite sides of Olivet are barren and cheer-

23 ᵣAnd they gave him to drink wine mingled with   ᵣ Mt. 27. 34.
myrrh: but he received it not.

The crucifixion.

24   And when they had crucified him, *they parted   * Mt. 27. 35; Lk.
his garments, casting lots upon them, what every   23. 33, 34; John
man should take.   19. 18; Ps. 22. 18.

less. Midway the hill there is a projecting rock, not unlike in form a human skull. . . . Reading the four evangelists from the brow of this desolate rock, all the details appeared fulfilled with an exactitude not unworthy an intelligent faith. . . . It is nigh the city that had rejected him. Before him rose Olivet; beneath his eye Gethsemane; while the Mount of Ascension rose before him, crowned with the glory of his exaltation. Around the cross, both on the summit of Bezetha and on the slopes of Olivet beyond, is room for the multitude who had assembled to witness the melancholy spectacle, and for those women who, beholding afar off, 'bewailed and lamented him.' From the adjacent walls of the city the chief-priest, scribes, and elders beheld him, and mockingly said, 'He saved others, himself he cannot save.' On the road which passed beneath the cross came those Jewish travelers who, on reading Pilate's superscription, wagged their heads in disdain, saying, 'Thou that destroyest the Temple and buildest it in three days, save thyself.' Here the rocks are torn and riven. . . . In the hill-side are tombs. Down in the sequestered vale of the Kidron are gardens, where some old sepulchres still remain, any one of which answers the description of the Savior's tomb, John 19: 41."—*From Dan to Beersheba*, pp. 128-130.

23. **And they gave,** etc. *And they were giving,* or *they offered him wine.* **To drink** should be omitted, according to the best critical authorities. **Wine mingled,** drugged **with myrrh.** Myrrh is a bitter aromatic gum obtained from a low, thorny tree growing in Arabia, and was highly prized by the ancients and used in incense and perfumes. Matthew, with his eye ever upon prophecy, uses the general word "gall," denoting a very bitter substance, as wormwood, colocynth, myrrh and the like: "They gave him vinegar to drink mingled with gall." Thus the terms used agree with prophecy, "They gave me also gall for my meat, and in my thirst they gave me vinegar to drink," Ps. 69: 21. Mark, with his characteristic definiteness, states what the principal bitter substance was, namely, myrrh. The drink was probably the cheap sour wine used by soldiers, and but little better than vinegar, and being drugged with myrrh, wormwood, etc., was given to criminals, according to a Jewish usage, just before crucifixion, to stupefy and deaden the pain. Compare Prov. 31: 6. **Received it not.** He did not take it, since he would drink the cup of sufferings to its very dregs, without any alleviation, and retain his mind with all its powers clear and unimpaired unto the end.

24-41. THE CRUCIFIXION AND THE ATTENDING CIRCUMSTANCES. Matt. 27: 35-56; Luke 23: 33-49; John 19: 18-30. Matthew's account is, upon the whole, the fullest. That of Mark is similar, a little briefer, and sometimes more graphic. Luke alone records Christ's prayer for his enemies, "Father forgive," etc., and the account of the penitent robber. John more fully describes the parting of the raiment, and alone relates the dissatisfaction of the Jews with the superscription, and Christ's commendation of his mother to John.

24. **When they had crucified.** Nailed him to the cross, either before or after its erection; thus unconsciously fulfilling the prophetic words of David, "They pierced my hands and my feet," Ps. 22: 16.

Crucifixion was the severest and most ignominious punishment among the ancients. It was not a Jewish, but rather a Roman mode of execution, and was inflicted on slaves and the vilest criminals. "It is an outrage," said Cicero, "to *bind* a Roman; to *scourge* him is an atrocious crime; to *put him to death* is

25 And ¹it was the third hour, and they crucified him. ¹See Mt. 27. 45; Lk. 23. 44; John 19. 14.

almost parricide; but to CRUCIFY him, what shall I call it?" To a proud Roman, the cross was a symbol of infamy, and crucifixion an unspeakable disgrace.

The cross was generally first driven into the ground, and then the criminal was lifted up and fastened to it, by nails through the hands and feet, the latter being either separate or united, and about a foot or two above the ground. Sometimes the victim was first fastened to the cross, which was then sunk into the earth with a sudden shock, causing the most agonizing torture. Whether a single nail was driven through the feet of Jesus, or they were nailed separately, cannot be determined; but that they were *nailed* and not *tied*, as some have conjectured, is evident from Luke 24 : 39, and from the fact that nailing was usual in Roman crucifixion. Compare Hackett's *Smith's Dictionary of the Bible*, on CRUCIFIXION. In order that the hands might not be torn away, a large wooden pin was commonly inserted in the upright timber, passing between the legs, to support the weight of the body. The unnatural position and tension of the body, the laceration of the hands and feet, which are full of nerves and tendons, and the consequent inflammation; the pressure of the blood to the head and stomach, causing severe pain and terrible anxiety, and the burning and raging thirst; all these, with no vital part wounded, made crucifixion a most excruciating and lingering death. Sometimes the wretched victim would hang three days before death came to his relief. The unusual quickness of our Savior's death arose from his previous exhausting agonies and his deep mental anguish. This terrible mode of punishment continued till it was abolished by Constantine, the first Christian emperor.

While the soldiers were nailing him to the cross, he forgets, as it were, his own pains in his anxiety for their souls, and prays, Father, forgive them, for they know not what they do, Luke 23 : 34. This was the first of the *seven sayings* from the cross. See on ver. 37.

Parted his garments. Persons were crucified naked. It was an ancient belief and tradition that a linen cloth was bound about his loins. From John 19 : 23, 24, it appears that the four soldiers who were engaged in the crucifixion *divided* some of the garments among themselves, but cast lots for his coat, or tunic, being an inner garment, without a seam, and woven throughout. With more particularity than Matthew and Luke, it is here said, **What every man,** or *What any one* **should take.** Thus was fulfilled Ps. 22 : 18. The garments were the perquisites of the executioners.

25. **It was the third hour** of the day, nine o'clock in the morning, when they arrived at Golgotha, and fastened Jesus to the cross. John says (ch. 19 : 14) about the sixth hour. The discrepancy can be explained by supposing that some early transcriber mistook the sign for three for that of six, the two being very nearly alike (some manuscripts of John read *third* hour); or that the time of crucifixion was somewhere between the two broad divisions, the third and sixth hours, and that Mark designates the time by the beginning, and John by the ending of the period. But it is better to suppose that John uses the Roman mode of reckoning the day from midnight to midnight. He had long resided beyond the bounds of Palestine when he wrote his Gospel. His readers were largely composed of Gentiles, and the Jews were no longer a nation. To have used the Jewish mode of designating the hour of day would have misled the majority of his readers. Josephus, the Jewish historian, in his autobiography uses the Roman method. "About the sixth hour," in John, then may mean that it was between six and seven o'clock in the morning when Jesus stood before Pilate on the judgment-seat. This agrees with the fact that "it was early" (John 18 : 28) when the Jewish rulers led Jesus away to the governor, Matt. 27 : 1. Thus the time in John was when the trial was progressing; that in Mark when the sentence was put into execution. The intervening time could easily have been occupied with the closing of the trial, the preparation for crucifixion, and the going forth to Golgotha. Not only at this time, but on other occasions, does

26 And ᵘ the superscription of his accusation was written over, THE KING OF THE JEWS.
27 And ˣ with him they crucify two thieves; the one on his right hand, and the other on his left. And
28 the Scripture was fulfilled, which saith, ʸ 'And he was numbered with the transgressors.'

ᵘ Mt. 27. 37; John 19. 19.
ˣ Mt. 27. 38.
ʸ Is. 53. 12; Lk. 22. 37; 2 Cor. 5. 21.

John appear to use the Roman method of designating the hour. Thus, concerning his first interview with Jesus, he says, "it was about the tenth hour," i. e. ten o'clock in the morning, John 1 : 39. It was not a late and hurried visit, but one extending through the day, for the two disciples "abode with him that day." So also in John 1 : 35; 4 : 6; 4 : 52. Compare author's HARMONY on § 181.

26. **The superscription.** *The inscription.* Pilate appears to have written this himself, John 19 : 22. **Accusation.** The *reason* or *charge* for which he suffered. It was customary to publish in some way the crime for which a person was crucified. Sometimes a public crier announced it; sometimes it was written on a tablet, and hung about the neck of the criminal as he was led to execution; and very commonly it was, as in this case, written on a white tablet, and put above the criminal's head on the cross. It was **written over** him, Luke 23 : 38. In some cases, these three may have been combined.

The King of the Jews. Mark is the most concise. Matthew has, "This is Jesus the King of the Jews;" Luke, "This is the King of the Jews;" and John, "Jesus the Nazarene, the King of the Jews." The difference in these titles may be explained : (1.) That some of the evangelists, and even all of them, may have given the sense rather than the words. (2.) That the accusation was written in Hebrew, Greek, and Latin (John 19 : 20), and while the inscriptions were one in sense, they may have been very likely varied in expression, and hence the translation of them would vary. The Latin was the official language of the empire ; the Greek, the language of the cultivated classes, and very common in the province; the Hebrew, or Aramean, the vernacular language of the Jews and the common people. It is quite likely that John's inscription, containing the contemptuous phrase, "the Nazarene," was the one written in Hebrew, and which would be understood by the Jews of Palestine. Pilate purposely wrote the sarcastic title, purporting that the Jews were crucifying their king, and also that he was a Nazarene. The absurdity of the charge appeared upon its very face; yet when the Jews desired it changed, Pilate would not consent. They had pressed him to crucify Jesus, working on his fears, and saying, "If thou let this man go, thou art not Cæsar's friend;" and now he has the opportunity to return the taunt, and he does it, and perseveres in it, John 19 : 12, 20–22. Pilate at the same time unconsciously proclaimed him the King of the Jews (Matt. 2 : 2), the Messiah, whose claims they could not escape, and whose power they could not resist.

27. **With him they crucify two thieves;** *two robbers,* probably two associates of Barabbas, left to suffer while he was released. The Greek makes a distinction between the terms *thief* and *robber,* John 10 : 8. The governor was accustomed to crucify criminals at the passover. It was deemed a suitable time, as an impression might be made on the multitudes assembled at Jerusalem. Compare Deut. 17 : 13. Jesus is nailed to the cross; the superscription is put above his head. Then the two malefactors who were led out with Jesus (Luke 23 : 32) are also crucified, by the same soldiers, Luke 23 : 33; John 19 : 18. **The one on the right hand,** etc. Jesus is made the central sufferer, and by implication the greatest criminal.

28. This verse is wanting in the most ancient manuscripts, but found in ancient versions. It is possible, as Lange remarks, that it was early omitted, because it was thought to involve a discrepancy with Luke 22 : 37, where the quotation is applied to the apprehension of Jesus. The application of this prophecy is appropriate and striking in both Mark and Luke. In the latter it

Jesus mocked on the cross.

29 And ᵃ they that passed by railed on him, wagging their heads, and saying, Ah! ᵃ thou that destroyest
30 the temple, and buildest it in three days, save thy-
31 self, and come down from the cross. Likewise also the chief priests mocking said among themselves with the scribes, He saved others; himself he can-
32 not save. Let Christ the King of Israel descend now from the cross, that we may see and believe. And ᵇ they that were crucified with him reviled him.

ᵃ Mt. 27. 39; Lk. 23, 35; Ps. 22. 7.
ᵃ ch. 14. 58; John 2. 19.

ᵇ Mt. 27. 44; Lk. 23. 39.

---

is by Jesus himself, and looks forward to the fulfillment just at hand. In the former by the evangelist himself, at the point where the prediction found its most open fulfillment. **And he was numbered**, or *reckoned*. The prediction is from Isa. 53 : 12. **With the transgressors.** Rather, *among transgressors*.

29. In this and the three verses that follow, is the account of Jesus mocked on the cross. These indignities are related by the first three evangelists. **They that passed by.** The people going in and out of the city on the thoroughfare near the place of crucifixion. **Wagging their heads.** A contemptuous and scornful shaking of the head, fitting their words as they **railed on him,** or *blasphemed him*, for such is the word used in the original. And so it had been foretold in Ps. 22 : 7. See on ch. 3 : 29. They revile, or blaspheme his power and his Messiahship, as is shown by the next verses. The most atrocious criminal is hardly ever mocked and derided when undergoing execution. **Ah.** An exclamation here of derision, *Aha, vah!* **Thou that destroyest.** See ch. 14 : 58. Jesus had spoken not of *destroying*, but of *raising up* the temple of his body, John 2 : 19.

30. **Save thyself.** Connected with the preceding verse, Thou who possessest this power, save thyself. **Come down.** Shutting their eyes to all the manifestations and evidences of his divine power and Sonship, they prescribe this last test. Ever ready to applaud success (ch. 11 : 9) and denounce failure, they conclude that Jesus is an impostor, and revile him accordingly. Some, however, did it under greater light, and with more malicious intent than others.

31. **Chief priests . . . scribes.** The rulers, Luke 23 : 35. That the dignitaries of the Sanhedrim should thus mingle with the populace in their scoffs, shows how bitter their hatred and how terrible their malignity. **Mocking.** Held him up in derision, reviling his deeds of mercy and his royal Messiahship. Their mockery was even more blasphemous than that of the people. **He saved others.** They had been compelled to acknowledge his supernatural power. See, for example, ch. 3 : 22; John 12 : 10. They taunt him with having lost it now when he needs it for his own deliverance. They treat him as an impostor. **Himself** is put in derisive contrast to *others*. Compare Luke 4 : 23.

32. **Let Christ the King of Israel.** A challenge full of bitter sarcasm, *Let the Christ*, etc. The Sanhedrim had condemned him as a false Christ, and Pilate as the King of the Jews. To the Jewish mind a claim to Messiahship would also result in a claim to kingship. **That we may see and believe.** They deceived themselves; they who would not be convinced by his preaching and the raising of Lazarus, would not have believed though he had come down, Luke 16 : 31. Thus they fulfill their own Scriptures, Ps. 22 : 7, 8.

Luke (ch. 23 : 36) states that the soldiers also mocked him. Mark, as well as Matthew, records that the robbers **crucified with him** reviled him. But Luke speaks of the railing of only one, while he represents the other as reproving his companion, and seeking and obtaining mercy from Jesus. Some

The supernatural darkness.

33 And ᶜwhen the sixth hour was come, there was darkness over the whole land until the ninth hour. 34 And at the ninth hour Jesus cried with a loud voice, saying, Eloi ! Eloi ! lama sabachthani ? which is, being interpreted, "My God ! my God !

ᶜ Mt. 27. 45 ; Lk. 23. 44 ; John 19. 28 ; Amos 8. 9, 10.

suppose that Matthew and Mark, in general and popular language use the plural for the singular. Compare Matt. 9 : 8. But even this is not necessary. For both at first may have joined in reproaches; but one of them, being afterward convinced of the Messiahship of Jesus, repents, Luke 23 : 39–43. The climax of the picture is reached in the reproaches of his fellow-sufferers. Thus we have recorded by the evangelists two scoffs by the passing multitude, three by the rulers, one by the soldiers, and one by the malefactors; seven in all.

About this time probably occurred that interesting incident related in John 19 : 25-27: Jesus committing his widowed mother to the care of the beloved disciple.

33. In this and the three following verses Mark describes the extraordinary darkness, the desponding cry of Jesus, and the remarks of some of the bystanders. Mark is very similar to Matthew; Luke records only the darkness.

The sixth . . . until the ninth hour. From twelve o'clock to three in the afternoon. Jesus had hung about three hours upon the cross. **Darkness over the whole land.** Over all the land of Palestine, or over all the earth, that is, over that part of it where there was then day. The Greek word may have either the limited or the more extended sense. The *darkness* was supernatural. It could not have been an eclipse of the sun, for that occurs only at new moon, and it was then the Passover, which was observed at full moon. Nor was it the natural precursor of the earthquake, for that was miraculous, Matt. 27 : 51-53. Luke (23 : 45) adds, "The sun was darkened," after the darkening of the earth, which suggests a thickening of the atmosphere, or a dark gloom coming over the heavens, obscuring even the sun. This was evidently the first of the miraculous events attending the cruci-

fixion. "Yea, creation itself bewailed its Lord ; for the sun was darkened and the rocks were rent."—CYRIL ALEX. As the *night* of our Savior's birth was enlightened with the glory of the heavenly hosts (Luke 2 : 9), so now the *day* of his death is darkened with the gloom of a forsaken world. The darkness represented the eclipse of the Sun of Righteousness, the darkness and distress which overwhelmed his soul when the Father forsook him, and left him to meet alone the powers of death and hell.

Several heathen writers mention an extraordinary darkening of the sun about this time. Eusebius quotes the words of Phlegon, a chronicler under the reign of Hadrian : "There occurred the greatest darkening of the sun which had ever been known ; it became night at midday, so that the stars shone in the heavens. Also, a great earthquake in Bithynia, which destroyed a part of Nicæa." This language may apply to a darkening of the sun, either by an eclipse or by a supernatural power, and it is said to have occurred at about the time of our Savior's death. May it not be a heathen testimony to the wonderful phenomena of that event? Tertullian, Origen, and others also boldly appealed to the Roman archives for the proof of the eclipse of the sun, as it was called, at the time of our Savior's death.

34. **At the ninth hour.** For three hours had darkness prevailed, and Jesus continued the terrible conflict in silence. Amidst the gloom we may suppose the mockings around the cross had ceased. Into the mysterious agonies of these hours of darkness no mind on earth is permitted to penetrate. The evangelists let us not into its secrets, but simply record the length of the interval, and the bursting wail of agony at the close of the scene. **Eloi, Eloi**, Ps. 22 : 1. In the Aramean, the ordinary dialect of the day. The Aramean words are given to show more clearly

35 why hast thou forsaken me?' And some of them that stood by, when they heard it, said, Behold, he calleth Elias. ᵈ And one ran and filled a sponge full of vinegar, and put it on a reed, and ᵉ gave him to drink, saying, Let alone; let us see whether Elias will come to take him down.

ᵈ Mt. 27. 48; John 19. 29.
ᵉ Ps. 69. 21.

the reference to Elijah in the next verse. Matthew gives the corresponding and similar word, *Eli*. **My God! my God!** The cry, not of despair, but of extreme anguish, yet of resignation and holy confidence in God as his God. **Why hast thou forsaken me?** Rather, *why didst thou forsake me?* He was now just emerging from this terrible abandonment by the Father. We catch a glimpse of the incomprehensible height and depth of his sufferings, to which the agonies of Gethsemane were but a prelude. See on ch. 14 : 34. As he was made a curse for us and bore our sins, standing in the place of the sinner, the Father turned, as it were, his face from him. He who is of purer eyes than to behold evil (Habak. 1 : 13) turns away from his Son when the sins of a world were laid upon him, Isa. 53 : 4, 5, 10 ; Gal. 3 : 13 ; 2 Cor. 5 : 21 ; 1 Pet. 2 : 24. **Why?** The interrogative form gives intensity to the expression. It is not the cry of ignorance of the cause of this abandonment, but rather the strugglings of language in its weakness, to express the unfathomable woe and utter desolation of his vicarious sufferings. Yet the cry coming forth at the close of this abandonment, shows that he had endured all that was put upon him, and was coming forth victorious from the conflict. Though left to himself for a time, yet he did not forsake God. Personifying forsaken humanity under the wrath of God, he makes an atonement, cries unto God, and is heard in that he feared (Heb. 5 : 7)—the presence of the Father is restored, the darkness rolls away, and light returns to the land. This language also points to the twenty-second Psalm as fulfilled in him. David doubtless wrote the Psalm out of a deep experience; but he himself was a type of Christ, and his words find their profoundest meaning and fulfillment in Jesus his great Antitype. Compare especially verses 1, 7, 8, 16, 18.

35. **He calleth for Elias;** for Elijah, whose coming the Jewish people were expecting. Most commentators suppose this was said in jest. If so, it betrays the most terrible depravity, and insensibility and malignant hatred almost inconceivable. It hardly seems possible that after a supernatural darkness of about three hours, these attendants would have turned into derision this deathly wail of anguish. It is more natural to suppose that amid those hours of gloom, sadness and awe pervaded their minds, and that some of them really mistook the word Eli or *Eloi* for Elias, or, in their language, *Elia*. Their superstitious fears may have been so aroused in regard to the day of judgment, which they may have supposed the coming of Elijah would usher in (Mal. 4 : 5), as to seize instantly upon the word Eli, as the name of that old prophet. Or some, standing by the cross, might have been foreign Jews, who did not very readily understand the language, and therefore confounded the words. Or even some of the Roman soldiers, who, amid this wonderful phenomenon, had listened attentively to the conversation of the Jews about the coming of Elijah, might have thought Jesus calling for the prophet. It seems better to adopt any of these suppositions than to suppose mockery in the midst of supernatural occurrences. And it accords better with the confession of the centurion, and the conviction of the people soon after, related in Luke 23 : 47, 48.

36. Immediately after this cry, John informs us that Jesus, knowing that all things were now accomplished, and that the Scripture might be fulfilled (Ps. 69 : 21), said, "I thirst." Compare Ps. 22 : 15. Moved with sympathy, one, very probably a soldier, extends a sponge of vinegar to his parching lips. A feverish thirst was one of the greatest sufferings attending crucifixion. **Vinegar.** The sour wine of the soldiers. Possibly one of the guard-soldiers who

The death of Jesus and attendant circumstances.

37 *ᶠ* And Jesus cried with a loud voice, and gave up the ghost. ^{ᶠ Mt. 27. 50; Lk. 23. 46; John 19. 30.}

---

crucified him did this deed of compassion. This must not be confounded with the offering of vinegar in mockery by the soldiers, related in Luke 23 : 36, which took place before the season of darkness. **A reed.** A byssop-reed, or stalk, John 19 : 29. Jesus would not receive the drugged wine which was intended to stupefy and assuage the pain, nor the wine extended to him in mockery; but this, extended to him in sympathy, he receives. The great conflict, too, was over, and now he can drink it.
Let alone. *Wait, forbear.* Not desist from giving him the vinegar, for this was the utterance of the one giving it; but *wait*, let us see whether Elijah comes to his rescue. The language seems to be not in mockery, but in doubt and suspense. On the one hand was the supernatural darkness, but on the other Elijah does not immediately come. He is for waiting, and with some expectation, to see if there will be any divine interposition. It appears from John 19 : 29 that several assisted in filling the sponge and giving it to Jesus. Hence there is no real discrepancy in the language of Matthew, "The rest said." Several appear to have uttered about the same exclamation. And if necessary, it is possible to suppose that some may have uttered it in mockery, and others earnestly.
37. In this verse Mark relates the death of Jesus, and in the next verse the wonderful phenomena attending it.
Cried again, etc. When Jesus had received the vinegar, he said, "It is finished," John 19 : 30. Luke (23 : 46) states that Jesus, crying again with a loud voice, said, "Father, into thy hands I commend (commit) my spirit." The latter is doubtless the one here meant by Mark.
The most probable order of the seven sayings of Jesus from the cross is as follows : 1. Father, forgive them, for they know not what they do, Luke 23 : 34. 2. Verily I say unto thee, To-day shalt thou be with me in paradise, Luke 23 : 43. 3. Woman, behold thy son. . . . Behold thy mother, John 19 : 26, 27. 4. My God, my God, why hast (didst) thou forsaken me? Mark 15 : 34; Matt. 27 : 46. 5. I thirst, John 19 : 28. 6. It is finished, John 19 : 30. 7. Father, into thy hands I commend (commit) my spirit, Luke 23 : 46.
Gave up the ghost. Literally, *Breathed out, expired.* The expression is used by Luke 23 : 46; and in beautiful harmony with "yielded up his spirit," Matt. 27 : 50, and "gave up his spirit," John 19 : 30. Jesus died voluntarily (John 10 : 18), and so the language of all the evangelists indicates.
That Jesus should have died in six hours (ver. 44; John 19 : 33) instead of lingering two or three days upon the cross, was owing to the great mental agonies he endured, in comparison to which the physical pains of crucifixion were light. Intense anguish has itself been known to produce death. If the agonies of the garden caused a bloody sweat, and so affected him that an angel appeared to strengthen him, how must the greater agonies of the cross, when forsaken by the Father, have affected his already exhausted body?
Dr. Stroud, an eminent European physician, in the year 1847 advanced the theory that Jesus died of a broken or ruptured heart. It has been found that under violent and intensely excited emotions, the heart is sometimes rent or torn by the violence of its own action. The blood flows into the pericardium, the bag or sack which incloses the heart, and by its pressure gradually stops the beating. The blood then coagulates, and the watery matter is separated from the thicker substance. If the pericardium should be then pierced, there would flow out blood and water, which harmonizes with and best explains the singular phenomenon mentioned in John 19 : 34. This theory also strikingly harmonizes with the predictions in Ps. 22 : 14; 69 : 20. It also gives additional prominence to the *blood* of Christ, since then his death was literally caused by the flowing of his blood. Nor is it opposed to the Savior's declaration, "No man taketh my life from me; I lay it down of myself;" for he

38 And ᵍthe vail of the temple was rent in twain from the top to the bottom. ᵍ Mt. 27. 51; Lk. 23. 45.

39 And ʰwhen the centurion, which stood over against him, saw that he so cried out, and gave up the ghost, he said, Truly this man was the Son of God. ʰ Mt. 27. 54; Lk. 23. 47.

voluntarily took upon himself all this anguish, even unto death itself. The theory well deserves consideration.

38. **The vail of the temple.** A large, thick, inner curtain, which divided the holy place from the holy of holies, Exod. 26: 31–33; Heb. 9: 3. The Greek does not denote the whole sacred edifice, but the *temple* proper, or sanctuary. **Rent in twain.** Into two pieces. From Luke we learn that it was rent through the middle, Luke 23: 45. **From the top to the bottom.** Some sixty feet. This could not have been the result of an earthquake. It was rent by the same supernatural power that produced the earthquake and raised some of the dead.

This occurred at the ninth hour, about three in the afternoon, the time of offering the evening sacrifice, when the priest would be in the holy place burning incense, and the people praying without. Into the holy of holies the high-priest entered alone once a year to make an atonement, Exod. 30: 10; Lev. 16: 15–17; Heb. 9: 7. The rending of the vail symbolized the entering of Jesus, the great High-Priest of his people, into the holy of holies on high, there to present the atonement which he had made through his blood for their sins, Heb. 9: 12–14, 25, 26. The Aaronic priesthood and atonement were no longer needed. Each worshiper became himself a priest, a new and living way of access to God was opened, the middle wall of partition between Jews and Gentiles was broken down, Heb. 10: 12–14, 19–22; Eph. 2: 14; 1 Pet. 2: 5. The rent of the vail, seen by the priests, would very likely be known through rumor, and substantiated by the great company of priests who afterward became obedient to the faith, Acts 6: 7. Jesus himself may have revealed it to his disciples after his resurrection.

Matthew (27: 52, 53) adds other phenomena, the earthquake, the opening of tombs, and the coming forth of departed saints from the tombs after Christ's resurrection.

39. **The centurion** was a Roman officer, a commander of a hundred men. The one here mentioned had charge of the crucifixion. It is a peculiarity of Mark that he always uses the Latin word itself, *centurion*, while Matthew and Luke never use it, but a Greek translation. Such little points show the independence of Mark's Gospel and its design for Roman readers. With characteristic detail Mark specifies the position of the centurion: he **stood over against** Jesus, *stood near, opposite, in front of him*. **So cried out, and gave,** etc.; *and expired*. The best text reads, *that he so expired*. There was something in the manner of his death that impressed the centurion as superhuman. What seems to have specially arrested his attention was the strong voice of the expiring Jesus and his firm confidence in God. "The Lion of Judah is, even in his departing, a dying lion. The expression of a wonderful power of life and spirit in the last sign of life, the triumphant shout in death, was to the warrior, who had learned to know death from a totally different side upon the battle-fields, a new revelation." —LANGE. The centurion gives vent to his feelings, "Certainly this was a righteous man" (Luke 23: 47); he was not an impostor, but what he claimed to be. **Truly this man was the Son of God,** or more exactly, *God's Son*. The centurion does not mean *a son of a god* in a heathen sense, nor the Messiah, but that Jesus was indeed of a *divine* nature. He had doubtless heard something of what Jesus claimed to be, and the charge of the Jews against him, and the taunt, "If thou be the Son of God" (compare ch. 14: 61, 62 with Matt. 27: 40), and he now expresses his convictions that he was indeed divine. There was an impress of divinity on his death as well as on his life, which has been felt and recog-

40 ¹ There were also women looking on ᵏ afar off : ¹ Mt. 27. 55; Lk. 23. 49.
among whom was Mary Magdalene, and Mary the ᵏ Ps. 38. 11.
mother of James the less and of Joses, and Salome;
41 (who also, when he was in Galilee, ¹ followed him, ¹ Lk. 8. 2, 3.
and ministered unto him;) and many other women
which came up with him unto Jerusalem.

nized by the observing of every age. Even the infidel Rousseau exclaimed, If Socrates lived and died like a sage, Jesus of Nazareth lived and died like a god.

Luke also notices the effect in general: "All the people that came together to that sight, beholding the things which were done, smote their breasts and returned," Luke 23 : 48.

40. In this and the next verse Mark refers to the women of Galilee who witnessed his death.

Not only the centurion and soldiers stood beholding, but **also women looking on.** Dr. J. A. Alexander infers from the special mention of these two classes of spectators, that it is not improbable that they alone were present during the whole time of the crucifixion. In their devotion these women watched him to the last, and two of them (ver. 47) continued and saw where they buried him. They were, however, in less danger than the male followers of Jesus. Luke adds (ch. 23 : 49), "All his acquaintance." There may have been several groups. **Afar off.** Probably from the side of the Mount of Olives. See on ver. 22.

Mary Magdalene. *Mary the Magdalene,* from Magdala, now the village of Mejdel, on the west coast of the Sea of Galilee. From Luke 8 : 2, and Mark 16 : 9, we learn that Jesus had wrought a signal miracle upon her in casting out seven demons. She was a woman of some property, as is evident from her ministering to the wants of Jesus, and from the position of her name (Luke 8 : 2, 3); not only in connection with, but even before that of Joanna, the wife of Chuza, Herod's steward, who, from his official position, must have acquired considerable wealth. Tradition has confounded her with the sinner in Luke 7 : 37, but without evidence or reason. Naming charitable institutions for fallen women "Magdalene Hospitals," etc., is unwarranted by Scripture, and is little less than a libelous implication. Neither is she to be confounded with

Mary who anointed Jesus in Bethany, John 12 : 3. She was one of the two women who saw the burial of Jesus (ver. 47), and one of those who prepared spices and ointment to embalm him. She was early at the tomb on the first day of the week, and, lingering there after the other disciples had retired, she was the first to see her Lord, ch. 16 : 1 ; John 20 : 11–18.

Mary the mother of James the less and of Joses. Probably the wife of Cleopas, or Alpheus, John 19 : 25. She witnessed, with Mary Magdalene, the burial of Jesus, ver. 47. Mark designates James the **less,** literally, *the little,* but used in a comparative sense, meaning *the younger,* to distinguish him from James the son of Zebedee. The word is thus used in the Septuagint version, Gen. 25 : 23 ; Josh. 6 : 26 ; Jer. 42 : 1. See on chs. 3 : 17 and 6 : 3.

Salome. Supposed to be "the mother of Zebedee's children," mentioned by Matthew. Salome is also regarded by some as "his mother's sister" of John 19 : 25. Mary the mother of Jesus is not mentioned, as she had probably gone away with John, overwhelmed with sorrow (Luke 2 : 35), soon after she was committed to his care, John 19 : 25–27.

41. **Who also . . . ministered unto him.** To his wants from their own substance, Luke 8 : 3. Besides these, **many other women** were present, witnessing the scene, who had come up with him to Jerusalem.

42–47. THE BURIAL OF JESUS. Matt. 27 : 57–61; Luke 23 : 50–56; John 19 : 31–42. John's account is the fullest. He relates that the Jews requested the legs to be broken and the bodies removed, so that they might not remain upon the cross on the Sabbath. The request was granted, but the legs of Jesus were not broken, because he was already dead ; but one of the soldiers pierced his side, and thus two predictions of Scripture were fulfilled, John 19 : 31–37. He also relates that Nicodemus brought spices, and assisted in

A.D. 30. MARK XV. 309

The burial of Jesus.

42 ᵐ AND now when the even was come, because it
was the preparation, that is, the day before the sab-
43 bath, Joseph of Arimathaea, an honourable counsellor, which also ⁿ waited for the kingdom of God,
came, and went in boldly unto Pilate, and craved
44 the body of Jesus. And Pilate marvelled if he were
already dead: and calling *unto him* the centurion,
he asked him whether he had been any while dead.

ᵐ Mt. 27. 57; Lk. 23. 50; John 19. 38.

ⁿ Lk. 2. 25, 38; 19. 11.

the burial. Mark is next to John in fullness, and relates with minuteness the begging of the body of Jesus by Joseph of Arimathaea. The four accounts, though remarkably distinct and independent, harmonize beautifully and confirm one another.

42. **Now when the even was come.** The first evening, beginning with the decline of day, about three o'clock in the afternoon. See on ch. 6 : 35, 47. As the first evening had already come, we may suppose it to have been as late as four o'clock, or even later. The Romans were accustomed to let the bodies rot upon the cross and be devoured by birds. But the Jews were very careful to have the bodies of persons publicly executed taken down and buried in a common grave before sunset, Deut. 21 : 23. Hence it was common to hasten the death of those crucified, John 19 : 32. "So great care did the Jews take respecting the burial of men, that even the bodies of those condemned to be crucified they took down and buried before the going down of the sun."—JOSEPHUS, *Jewish War*, iv. 5. 2. A wonderful providence watches over the body of Jesus. He expires so quickly; so that not a bone is broken. A new tomb stands ready for his body, and distinguished individuals to attend to his burial.

The preparation, the day for making ready for the Sabbath, which would begin at sunset; and so explained, **the day before the Sabbath,** *the ante-Sabbath,* or *fore-Sabbath.* As the Jewish Sabbath was Saturday, the *preparation* was Friday. Such is the use of the term in Matt. 27 : 62; Luke 23 : 54; John 19 : 31, 42. From Josephus we learn that the preparation was strictly Friday afternoon from three o'clock until sunset (*Antiq.* xvi. 6. 2); but in popular usage it was applied to Friday, and is so translated in the Sy-

riac. "*The preparation* is the name by which Friday is now generally known in Asia and Greece."—WORDSWORTH.

43. **Joseph of,** *from* **Arimathaea.** Probably from Ramah, called Ramathaim Zophim, the birthplace of Samuel, 1 Sam. 1 : 19. The first book of Maccabees (11 : 34) speaks of it as transferred, together with Lydda, from Samaria to Judea, which may account for Luke's calling it "a city of the Jews," Luke 23 : 51. It has generally been located at the modern Lydda, about twenty-four miles north-west of Jerusalem. Its location, however, is uncertain. From the narrative in 1 Sam. 9 : 4-6; 10 : 2, it would seem that it lay south or south-west of Bethlehem. **An honorable counsellor.** A noble, honorable member of the Sanhedrim, "a good and just man who had not consented to the death of Jesus," Luke 23 : 51. **Waiting for the kingdom of God;** waiting with expectation for the Messiah's kingdom. See on ch. 1 : 15. He was a *disciple of Jesus,* but secretly, for fear of the Jews, John 19 : 38. Matthew states also that he was rich. Isa. 53 : 9.

Went in boldly unto Pilate; that is, dared, had the courage and confidence to go to Pilate, probably his official residence, and ask the body of Jesus. When Christ's own disciples are scattered and in dismay, two secret and timid followers are emboldened to attend to his burial. Joseph seems to have known what had occurred, that Jesus was dead, that the bones of the others had been broken, and that they were about to be taken down for burial.

44. **Pilate marvelled.** He had not yet heard of the death of Jesus from the centurion. He had given the order to break the bones to hasten death, but he wondered that Jesus was dead so soon, and calls for the centurion to as-

45 And when he knew *it* of the centurion, he gave the
46 body to Joseph. ⁰ And he bought fine linen, and took
him down, and wrapped him in the linen, and laid
him in a sepulchre which was hewn out of a rock, and

⁰ Mt. 27. 59, 60;
Lk. 23. 53; John
19. 40; Is. 22. 16;
53. 9.

certain the facts of the case. He wanted to act cautiously. The question, whether he had been **any while dead,** or *long dead,* with the implied answer, indicates that Jesus had then been some time dead.

45. Having learned that Jesus was really dead, Pilate **gave the body,** freely, as a present, without demanding money for it. Bodies under such circumstances were frequently sold, and as Joseph was rich, Pilate might have been expected to have extorted a price for it. The standing of Joseph as a member of the Sanhedrim, doubtless, had its weight; and Pilate's troubled conscience would naturally excite the desire to give Jesus a decent burial. We cannot but admire the providence which so ordered the circumstances of our Savior's crucifixion and burial that there could be no doubt about his death, and no deception in regard to his resurrection.

46. **Bought fine linen.** A winding-sheet, in which the body was wrapped.

BODY PREPARED FOR BURIAL.

The mummy-cloths of the Egyptians were universally linen. The *buying* here indicates that the Sabbath had not yet begun. John relates (19 : 39) that Nicodemus now joined Joseph, bringing a mixture of myrrh and aloes, about a hundred pounds weight. The sheet was wrapped about in such a way as to inclose the spices next to the body. This was hurriedly done, and preparatory to the more formal embalming by the women, after the Sabbath, for which there was not now time.

A sepulchre. Matthew and John state that it was a new tomb. It was fitting that Jesus should be laid in a tomb where no one had before been buried. It would also prevent the assertion, after his resurrection, that some one else had been raised. Matthew alone relates that it was Joseph's. John says it was in a garden, and in the place where he was crucified. The nearness of the place and of the Sabbath may have led Joseph to bury him in his own new tomb (John 19 : 42); but once laid there, we need not suppose that Joseph would have removed it, but rather, in his devotion, would have kept it there, had Jesus not risen. Thus was fulfilled Isa. 53 : 9, which may be translated, "And his grave was appointed with the wicked, but he was with the rich in his death."

Hewn out in the rock. The tombs of the Jews were generally cut out of the solid rock; sometimes below the level of the ground, but oftener above the ground, and on the sides of hills and mountains. They were generally large and commodious, with one or more apartments with cells for depositing the dead.

The tomb of Joseph was doubtless a family vault. **Rolled a stone unto the door.** This seems to imply that the tomb was excavated horizontally or nearly so. The stone was so heavy that the women, on going to the sepulchre, were perplexed to know how to obtain its removal. Dr. Hackett saw a

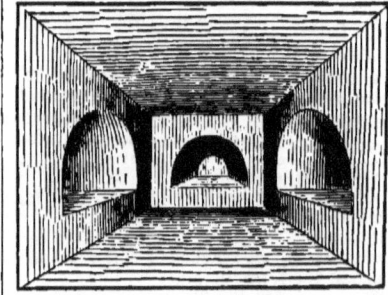

A TOMB.

tomb at Nazareth, cut in the rock, and a large stone rolled against its mouth. But most of the tombs he examined

47 rolled a stone unto the door of the sepulchre. And Mary Magdalene and Mary *the mother* of Joses beheld where he was laid.

near Jerusalem must have had doors, as is evident from the grooves and perforations for the hinges that still remain. "It is possible," he adds, "that the tomb used in the case of the Savior, which is said to have been new, was not entirely finished, and the placing of the stone at the entrance may have been a temporary expedient."—*Scripture Illustrations*, p. 108.

47. Mark closes the account of Christ's burial, by stating that the two Marys mentioned in ver. 40, **beheld where he was laid.** They staid to mark the spot of his burial, so that they might visit it, and anoint the body after the Sabbath. Matthew says they were "sitting over against the sepulchre," as if to watch it. Luke adds that "they returned, and prepared spices and ointment," which they took to the sepulchre after resting on the Sabbath.

Matthew (27 : 62–66) records the sealing and guarding the sepulchre. The chief priests and Pharisees beseech Pilate to make the sepulchre secure. He grants their request, seals the stone, and stations a watch.

THE DAY OF CHRIST'S CRUCIFIXION. As there is an occasional attempt to prove that Jesus was not crucified on Friday, a note on the subject will not at this point be out of place. Dr. Gustav Seyffarth, a learned Egyptologist, from astronomical calculations, fixes the death of Christ on Thursday, the 14th of Nisan, March 19th, A.D. 33; and also supposes that Jesus lay in the grave full three days and three nights till Sunday morning.

More recently a writer in the *Bibliotheca Sacra* (July, 1870, pp. 401–429) has endeavored to prove that Jesus was crucified on Thursday, not Friday. His reasons for adopting a view different from that generally held are the following: "1. If he was crucified on Friday, his body could not have lain *three days* and *three nights* in the grave, and in all probability he must have risen on the *second* and not the *third* day according to the Scriptures. 2. If he was crucified on Friday, there is a plain discrepancy between John and the other evangelists. 3. His crucifixion on Thursday removes both of these difficulties."

Following Townsend and Cudworth, but modifying their view, he supposes that Jesus observed the Passover a day before the Jews, yet both kept it on what might be regarded the proper day. His explanation may be thus briefly stated:

According to the Talmudists the commencement of the month was decided by the first appearance of the new moon; and in the later times of Jewish history, the Sanhedrim sat on the thirtieth of the month to receive the witnesses of the moon's appearance. When it was reported by competent witnesses, the beginning of the new month was officially announced, *It is consecrated*. If the announcement was made on the thirtieth before dark, the old month was considered as ended with the twenty-ninth day; but if it was not made before dark, then the old month ended with the thirtieth, and the ensuing day was regarded as the first of the new month. Yet in the latter case, if respectable witnesses came from far, and testified that they had seen the new moon on the thirtieth, the Sanhedrim was bound to alter their reckoning, and commence the month a day sooner. But they reluctantly received the testimony of such witnesses, and at length they made it a rule to continue their mistake throughout the month, and all were bound to order their feasts according to it. This Dr. Cudworth supposes actually took place at this Passover, Christ keeping it at the true time, and the Jews a day later, according to the erroneous proclamation of the Sanhedrim. Those adopting this theory have generally supposed that Jesus celebrated the Passover on the evening at the close of Thursday, and the Jews on the evening at the close of Friday. But the writer in the *Bibliotheca Sacra* supposes each a day earlier, namely, Wednesday evening and Thursday evening, and hence that Jesus was crucified on Thursday.

On this I remark:

1. The theory of two paschal suppers is as consistent with the view which

holds Friday to have been the day of crucifixion, as with that which holds Thursday to have been the day.

2. There is some uncertainty regarding the Jewish computation of months and the period of the Passover. The rabbinical mode of determining the commencement of the month relates to a period somewhat later than the time of Christ, though it may have been practiced in his time. A theory should not be built too confidently upon it. And the above theory, that the Jews had by mistake placed the Passover one day too late, is but a conjecture, unsupported by historical testimony.

3. The first three evangelists are most explicit in fixing the Savior's last paschal supper at the regular time, which was at the beginning of the 15th of Nisan, the evening after the sunset of Thursday, with which Friday, according to Jewish reckoning, began. Matt. 27 : 17; Mark 14 : 12; 15 : 42; Luke 22 : 7. According to Wieseler, the 15th of Nisan, A.D. 30, was Friday, April 7th. There is nothing in John demanding two observances of the paschal supper, or an observance before the regular time. Even John 18 : 39 implies that the Passover had already commenced. The difficulties would be increased by supposing the crucifixion to have been on Thursday, for John himself must be first harmonized with that view (John 19 : 31), and then the three other evangelists must be harmonized with him. Thus the supposed teaching and implications of John must be made the standard to which the apparently clear and positive declarations of the three others must bend. See author's HARMONY, note on § 159. But the testimony of Polycarp and of the Eastern Christians of the early churches favors the view that John himself in his Gospel places the last Supper on the evening following the fourteenth of Nisan, at the same time with the Jews.

4. The Jewish mode of reckoning a portion of a day as the whole has been long understood and acknowledged. See 1 Sam. 30 : 1, 12; Esther 4 : 16 and 5 : 1; Hos. 6 : 2. Josephus frequently reckons the extreme portions of two years as two years. The objection that Jesus would not have been "three days" in the grave, shows a want of familiarity with Hebrew usage.

That this principle of Jewish reckoning should be applied to the expression in Matt. 12 : 40, *three days and three nights in the heart of the earth*, is evident:

(*a*) From our Lord's language elsewhere. Thus in the first explicit prediction of his death and resurrection: *be raised again the third day* (Matt. 16 : 21), *and after three days rise again* (Mark 8 : 31); *and be raised the third day* (Luke 9 : 22). Again, in his second announcement: *the third day he shall rise again* (Matt. 17 : 22); *he shall rise the third day* (Mark 9 : 31). Again, a third time he declares: *the third day he shall rise again* (Matt. 20 : 19); *the third day he shall rise again* (Mark 10 : 34); *the third day he shall rise again* (Luke 18 : 33). Thus on these three occasions Jesus foretold that he should rise on the *third* day, which harmonizes with the view that he was crucified and buried on Friday. If it had been on Thursday, then Sunday would have been, according to Jewish reckoning, the *fourth day*. The above quotations are taken from what Jesus had said privately to his disciples. But Matt. 12 : 40 and John 2 : 19 were spoken more publicly. Judas also may have told the chief priests what Jesus had said.

Hence (*b*) we also argue the Jewish principle of reckoning in this instance (Matt. 12 : 40), from their own application of it to our Lord's language. They tell Pilate that Jesus had said, "*After three days I will rise again ;*" and there can be no doubt about what they understood by the language, for they wish *the sepulchre made sure until the third day*, Matt. 27 : 63, 64.

"The heart of the earth" in this passage (Matt. 12 : 40) may mean (Meyer, Alford and others) *Hades*, the place of departed spirits, in which case death had dominion over Jesus portions of three days, or until the third day, if we reckon from Friday afternoon about three o'clock (the time of his death) till Sunday morning. Or it may mean (Alexander and others) simply the *grave*, in which case we come to the same result. For it was when *even was come* (Matt. 27 : 57; Mark 15 : 42) the first evening (so the word is used in Matt. 14 : 15), which began about three o'clock, that Joseph went to Pilate and begged the body of Jesus. We need not suppose it later than four o'clock. About an hour longer would afford ample time for the burial and the preliminary circumstances. This agrees well with Luke (23 : 54), who concludes his account of the burial by saying, *the Sabbath drew on,* etc. This agrees also with the fact that the women remained awhile after the burial, and returned and rested the Sabbath which began at sunset, Friday, Matt. 27 : 61 ; Luke 23 : 55, 56. Thus, reckoning from Friday afternoon, the time of burial, the body of Jesus laid in the grave portions of three days, or until the third day.

5. The notes of time in the four evangelists point to Friday as the day of crucifixion. Mark (15 : 42) says *it was the preparation, that is, the day before the Sabbath.* The Jewish Sabbath being Saturday, the day before was therefore Friday. To suppose it not the regular Sabbath, but merely a ceremonial one, is forced and unnatural. So also Luke (23 : 54) says, in concluding his account of the burial, *that day was the preparation, and the Sabbath drew on.* Matt. 27 : 62 confirms it by calling the day of crucifixion *the day of preparation,* which appears to have been the usual title for Friday. John (19 : 31, 42) also designates the day *the preparation,* of what is evident from his mentioning *the Sabbath day* immediately after. Because he previously refers to it as *the preparation of the Passover* (John 19 : 14) should not lead us to upset his own clear language elsewhere, and the very plain language of the other evangelists. There is no clear proof that there was a special preparation day for the Passover. It is perfectly natural and reasonable to regard the *preparation of the Passover* as the Friday before the Sabbath of the Passover ; especially as the term preparation was applied to the day before the Sabbath, Mark 15 : 42.

6. The entire tradition of the Christian church has assigned Friday as the day of crucifixion. Even the Greek writers and others who have held that Christ died upon the fourteenth instead of the fifteenth of Nisan, have regarded Friday as the day of his death.

In conclusion, the theory which makes Thursday the day of crucifixion is entirely without an historical basis, and is in direct opposition to the positive statements of the first three evangelists, that Jesus ate the regular Passover with his disciples, and also to the plain teaching of all, that he died on the day preceding the Jewish Sabbath,

Matt. 27 : 62 ; Mark 15 : 42 ; 16 : 1 ; Luke 23 : 56 ; John 19 : 31, 42.

REMARKS.

1. The delivering of Jesus to Pilate by the Jewish rulers was an evidence that the Messiah had already come. The sceptre had departed from Judah, and the lawgiver from between his feet, ver. 1 ; Gen. 49 : 10.

2. Like Jesus we should have the courage to witness a good profession, ver. 2 ; ch. 8 : 34 ; 1 Tim. 6 : 13.

3. How should the meekness of Jesus before Pilate and his accusers engage our admiration ! Silence is often the best answer to the clamors and false accusations of our enemies, vers. 3–5 ; Ps. 39 : 1 ; Isa. 53 : 7 ; Heb. 12 : 3 ; 1 Pet. 2 : 21–23 ; 2 Pet. 3 : 3.

4. The case of Pilate illustrates how unsafe and unbecoming is mere expediency in matters of morals and religion, vers. 6–15.

5. The best of men must expect at times to be objects of envy, ver. 10 ; Matt. 10 : 24, 25 ; Gen. 4 : 4, 5 ; 37 : 11 ; Ps. 106 : 16 ; Acts 13 : 45.

6. How often is Barabbas preferred to Jesus : self, the world, and the devil to the Savior ! vers. 9, 11 ; Acts 3 : 14 ; 7 : 51, 52.

7. The ministers of a corrupt church are generally more corrupt than the people, and the leaders in their wickedness, ver. 11 ; Jer. 23 : 15 ; Mic. 3 : 5.

8. How many ask the world what they shall do with Jesus, instead of listening to God's messages, and following the dictates of their consciences ! They ask, and vacillate to their own destruction, vers. 12–14.

9. How fickle are they who make the popular current instead of truth their principle of action, crying out at one time, Hosanna to the Son of David ! and at another, Crucify him ! Vers. 13, 14 ; ch. 11 : 9 ; Acts 14 : 11, 19.

10. The release of Barabbas illustrates the plan of salvation. The guilty are set free ; the innocent suffers, ver. 15 ; Rom. 3 : 26 ; 5 : 6–8.

11. Jesus endured cruel scourging that we might be healed, ver. 15 ; Ps. 129 : 3 ; Isa. 50 : 6 ; 53 : 5.

12. Jesus was mocked and treated with the greatest indignity, in order that we might be raised with him to the highest glory, vers. 16–20 ; Phil. 2 :

9, 10; Heb. 2:10; 12:2; Rev. 5:8–14.

13. We must follow Christ, bearing his cross, if we would reign with him and share his glory, ver. 21; ch. 8:34–38; Phil. 3:10, 11; Heb. 13:13, 14.

14. We should willingly and patiently endure all that our Heavenly Father may put upon us, ver. 23; Acts 21:13; Heb. 12:3–5.

15. Jesus suffered the death of a slave, in order that he might give us true freedom, ver. 24; John 8:36; Gal. 5:1.

16. Jesus was stripped of his garments, pointing to the spiritual nakedness of the race, and to the white garments he has purchased to cover us, ver. 24; Gen. 3:7, 10; Phil. 3:9; Rev. 3:18.

17. In Jesus on the cross, suspended between heaven and the earth, we behold a mediator between God and man, vers. 24, 25; 1 Tim. 2:5.

18. Jesus was reckoned with transgressors, so that we might be reckoned innocent for his sake, vers. 27, 28; Isa. 53:12; Luke 22:37.

19. Jesus saved not himself, so that he might save others, vers. 29–32; Rom. 5:6; 1 Cor. 15:3; 2 Cor. 5:15; 1 Thess. 5:10.

20. Adversity is not a proof of God's displeasure, nor is a want of success always an indication of final failure, vers. 31, 32; Job 42:10; Ps. 3:2–4; 42:10, 11.

21. All classes, Jews, Gentiles, priests, rulers, people, soldiers and servants, were turned against Jesus, in order that he might be a Savior to all, vers. 29, 31; Luke 23:36; Gal. 3:28; 1 John 2:1, 2.

22. The darkness around the suffering and dying Jesus should remind us of the spiritual darkness of our world, and of Christ its true light, ver. 33; John 8:12.

23. In the darkest hour the Christian should imitate his Savior, and not lose confidence in God as his God, ver. 34, "*My* God;" Job 13:15; Ps. 43:5; Hab. 3:17, 18; Rom. 5:3–5; 2 Tim. 1:12.

24. We may for a time be forsaken by God, and yet be loved by him, ver. 34; Ps. 42:11; Isa. 50:10.

25. If the agony of the Savior when forsaken of God for sinners was so great, what shall be the misery of those who at last shall be forsaken forever to wrath and endless despair? Ver. 34; Jude 13.

26. As the soldiers around the cross failed to enter into the feelings and agonies of Jesus, so impenitent sinners of our day fail to be impressed with his sufferings and death, vers. 35, 36; 1 Cor. 2:14.

27. Jesus received drink from his enemies, suggestive of a complete atonement for sinners, and of peace and good-will to men, ver. 36; Dan. 9:24; Rom. 5:1; Eph. 2:14.

28. Christ in his death paid the ransom for sinners, made a full atonement for sin, and was made a curse for us, ver. 37; Gal. 3:13; Heb. 9:6–15; 1 Pet. 3:18.

29. Inasmuch as the way into the holiest of all has been opened through the rent vail of the Redeemer's flesh, let us draw near to God boldly, and in strong faith, ver. 38; Heb. 4:16; 9:12; 10:19–22.

30. In the death of Jesus we see evidences of his divinity. The centurion saw it. How much more should we, with our greater evidences! Ver. 39; Heb. 1:1–4.

31. How great the devotion of women, both at the cross and at the sepulchre; in his sufferings and death as well as in his life! Vers. 40, 41, 47; ch. 16:1.

32. God will at all times have a people in the world, vers. 43–46; Rom. 9:27; 11:5.

33. Jesus often has disciples who are but little known, ver. 43; 1 Kings 19:18.

34. Let us be suitably affected with the lifeless body of Jesus on the cross, and accept of the glorious fruits of his death, ver. 43; 2 Tim. 1:10; 1 Pet. 2:24.

35. God, who so wonderfully guarded the body of Jesus, will in like manner guard the dust of all them that sleep in Jesus, vers. 43–46; 1 Thess. 4:14.

36. In Joseph of Arimathæa we behold a man of wealth devoting his property to the Lord, vers. 43–46; 1 Kings 18:13; 1 Tim. 6:17–19.

37. The Christian should not fear the grave, since Jesus has been there before him, ver. 46; 1 Cor. 15:56, 57.

The women at the sepulchre.

XVI. AND ᵖ when the sabbath was past, Mary Magdalene, and Mary the *mother* of James, and Salome, ʳ had bought sweet spices, that they might come

ᵖ Mt. 28. 1; Lk. 24. 1; John 20. 1.
ʳ Lk. 23. 56.

CHAPTER XVI.

Mark closes his Gospel with a brief account of the resurrection and ascension of Jesus. The women come to the sepulchre. They find the stone rolled away, and see an angel who sends a message to the disciples. Jesus appears first to Mary Magdalene; afterward to two disciples on their way to Emmaus; then to the eleven apostles; the last commission is given. At length he is taken up to heaven; and his disciples go forth obedient to his command, and preach the gospel.

In comparing this chapter with the accounts of the resurrection as given by the other evangelists, the fact is at once apparent that they were independent narrators. On account of the great brevity of these narratives, especially those of Matthew and Mark, great difficulty has been experienced in bringing them into complete harmony. But a careful study of these records will convince any reasonable mind that the discrepancies are only apparent. They can all be so explained as to show at once that, if we were in possession of all the details, the difficulties would not exist. But God has wisely ordered difficulties here as well as in other things, in order to give his people the more opportunity to exercise their faith in his word, and the wicked their unbelief. See author's Harmony, introductory note to Part VIII. ; and on §§ 201, 202.

From a comparison of these four accounts, and of Paul (1 Cor. 15), we gather the following ten appearances after his resurrection : 1. To Mary Magdalene, Mark 16 : 9 ; John 20 : 11–18. 2. To the women, Matt. 28 : 9, 10. 3. To Peter, Luke 24 : 34; 1 Cor. 15 : 5. 4. To the two disciples, Mark 16 : 12; Luke 24 : 13–31. 5. To the apostles, except Thomas, Mark 16 : 14 ; Luke 24 : 36–49 ; John 20 : 19–23. 6. To the apostles, Thomas being present, John 20 : 26–29. 7. To some of his disciples on the shore of the lake of Tiberias, John 21 : 4–22. 8. To the apostles and others, comprising above five hundred brethren, on a mountain in Galilee, Matt. 28 : 16–20 ;

Mark 18 : 15–18; 1 Cor. 15 : 6. 9. To James, 1 Cor. 15 : 7. 10. To the eleven at Jerusalem, and on the Mount of Olives, near Bethany, just before his ascension, Luke 24 : 50, 51 ; Acts 1 : 4–9.

Jesus doubtless appeared at other times, since he showed himself to his apostles during forty days, speaking the things concerning the kingdom of God, Acts 1 : 3 ; compare John 20 : 30, 31.

1–8. THE WOMEN COMING TO THE SEPULCHRE ARE APPRISED AY AN ANGEL OF THE RESURRECTION OF JESUS. The spices, the open sepulchre, the angel and his message. The awe and wonder of the women, and their departure. Matt. 28 : 1–8; Luke 24 : 1–8; John 20 : 1, 2.

Mark is the most particular of the evangelists in naming the women who came to the sepulchre, and alone relates their anxiety in regard to rolling away the stone. With Luke he is fuller than Matthew in the account (John omitting it) of the angel in the sepulchre. Matthew (28 : 2–4), however, alone relates the resurrection, attended with a great earthquake, an angel descending and rolling back the stone, and the terror of the watch.

1. **When the Sabbath was past.** The Jewish Sabbath, ending Saturday at sunset. **Mary Magdalene,** etc. The three previously mentioned who witnessed the crucifixion, ch. 15 : 40. The two Marys also witnessed his burial, ch. 15 : 47. **Had bought.** Rather, *bought,* that is, after sunset on Saturday. It is possible that they bought spices on Friday before sunset, and prepared them after sunset on Saturday, Luke 23 : 56. But Mark here makes the more exact statement, and Luke, being somewhat indefinite, does not contradict it. The latter says nothing about purchasing : neither does he say when the women prepared their spices, but throws in the fact that they observed the Sabbath. Or, if the above explanation fails to satisfy, we may suppose that some of the women provided spices late Friday afternoon ; and others, after consultation, not being

2 **and anoint him.** **And very early in the morning the first** *day* **of the week, they came unto the sepul-** *Mt. 28. 2; Lk. 24. 1-3; John 20. 1, 2.*

satisfied, bought other spices on Saturday night. The two Marys very likely remained too long at the sepulchre to make purchases on Friday, ch. 15 : 47. **Sweet spices.** Simply, *spices.* Odorous perfumes and preventives of putrefaction, such as myrrh, aloes, etc. According to the Talmud there was a particular market for spices at Jerusalem. **Anoint him.** It was common to anoint and embalm dead bodies. Nicodemus had only hastily wrapped the body in the spices with the linen clothes. Embalming was rather the work of physicians, Gen. 50 : 2. The women probably intended to do an act somewhat similar to that which Mary the sister of Lazarus did while he was yet alive, ch. 14 : 8. Luke (23 : 56) speaks of "spices and ointments," which they may have mixed together.

2. **Very early in the morning.** The words were used to indicate the morning twilight, the period between daybreak and sunrising. With this agree the other evangelists. Matthew says, "As it began to dawn." Luke: "Very early." John: "When it was yet dark;" the light was struggling with darkness. **They came.** The women mentioned in the preceding verse. There is nothing here to limit the number to these three. The evangelists do not show a scrupulous exactness in giving just the number of persons who witnessed an event. Luke (23 : 55; 24 : 1, 10) relates that "the women of Galilee" prepared spices and visited the sepulchre; and that they were "Mary Magdalene, and Joanna, and Mary the mother of James, and other women with them." **At the rising of the sun.** *The sun having risen,* or *when the sun was risen.* Bishop Pearse guesses that Mark wrote "the sun having *not* risen." But this is not necessary. Mark must of course be consistent with himself, and he had just said " very early in the morning," and hence consistent with the other evangelists. Several explanations have been given, but the best is that which supposes Mark to have used the expression "rising of the sun" in a popular or general sense, to express his gradual approach, from the breaking of twilight to the ushering in of the full light of day, by his actual rising. Compare Judges 9 : 33. Several instances, parallel to this in Mark, are found in the Septuagint version of the Old Testament, where *rising of the sun* indicates *rising of the day,* or early dawn, 2 Kings 3 : 22; 2 Sam. 23 : 4. So also in Ps. 104 : 22, where the dawn is meant, at which time lions retire to their dens, not waiting for the appearance of the sun. Thus sunrise, from its beginning to its ending, embraced a considerable interval, just as the evening did from its beginning and ending.

It should, however, be added that the visit of the women to the sepulchre, which is so briefly described by the evangelists, may have occupied two or three hours from their first leaving their homes until they left the sepulchre. Mary Magdalene may have gone somewhat in advance of the rest. This is rendered quite possible from the fact that John mentions her, and her alone, and the other evangelists mention her first, as if peculiarly prominent in their visit to the sepulchre. So also there may have been different arrivals of the women. As one company came to the sepulchre the rising sun may have shed its first beams upon them. Or, if we suppose them all to have gone together, one evangelist may have in mind the time of starting, another of their going, and another of their arrival or of their stay at the sepulchre. There need, therefore, be no difficulty in harmonizing the evangelists in regard to the time of the visit.

The first day of the week. Sunday, the Lord's Day, Rev. 1 : 10. This day, on which Jesus rose from the dead, was ever afterward observed by the disciples as the day of Christian rest. And how appropriately! If the day when God rested from the work of creation was hallowed and observed, how much more the one when Christ rested from the greater work of redemption! Some have argued that the Lord's Day is but the restoration of the original Sabbath of creation, a change having been made at the reënactment of the Sabbath among the Jews (Deut. 5 : 15). This is a curious and interesting question. Certain it is that, as the original Sabbath was the first day of

A.D. 30. MARK XVI. 317

3 chre at the rising of the sun. And they said among themselves, Who shall roll us away the stone from
4 the door of the sepulchre? And when they looked, they saw that the stone was rolled away: for it was very great.

completed creation, so the Lord's Day was the first day of completed redemption. But, aside from conjectures, there was, in the nature of things, a reason for a change in the day. It was fitting that that day of unparalleled darkness, when Jesus lay in the grave, should be the last of Jewish Sabbaths, and that the birthday of immortality and of Christ's finished work should ever after be the day of the Christian's rest. How could those early disciples recall the former but with sorrow, and how could they remember the latter but with joy? It is enough to know that they ever after observed the first day of the week, and that it comes down to us with the sanction of apostolic authority and example, ver. 9; Acts 20:7; 1 Cor. 16:2; Rev. 1:10. Not only did Jesus meet his assembled disciples on the first day of the week (John 20:19, 26); but he also hallowed it by sending the Holy Spirit on the day of Pentecost, which that year occurred on the first day of the week. Lev. 23:15, 16; Acts 2:1.

The observance of the Lord's Day is confirmed by early Christian testimony. Ignatius, who was educated under the apostle John, and who was pastor of the church at Antioch for forty years, from about A. D. 70, testifies to the observance of the Lord's Day. See on Matt. 28:1. Barnabas, probably not the companion of Paul, but one bearing the same name, soon after the close of the first century, in his epistle says, "We keep the eighth day with joyfulness, the day on which Jesus rose from the dead." The first day of the week was often called the eighth day, and that it is so here is evident from the allusion to the resurrection. He also says that the Lord abolished Jewish sacrifices, new moons and Sabbaths, and represents Christ as saying, "Your Sabbaths are not acceptable to me." Pliny, in his letter to Trajan (about A. D. 112), speaks of Christians meeting on "a stated day," at "a promiscuous and harmless meal," doubtless referring to the custom of celebrating the Lord's Supper on the Lord's Day. Justin Martyr (about A. D. 140) says that "on the day called Sunday," Christians meet for reading the Scripture, prayer, celebration of the Lord's Supper and alms. Much testimony might be given, showing that while the Jewish Sabbath was observed more or less by early Jewish churches and Jewish converts, the Lord's Day was observed by all. Says Professor Stuart, "The zealots for the law wished the Jewish Sabbath to be observed as well as the Lord's Day; for about the latter there never appears to have been any question among any class of Christians, so far as I have been able to discover. The early Christians, one and all of them, held the first day of the week to be sacred."

The Lord's Day is an evidence of the resurrection of Christ. Its history and its observance can be satisfactorily explained only upon the fact that Jesus rose from the dead.

3. **Among themselves.** To one another. **Who shall roll us away,** etc. Mark alone records the question. They seem now to have thought of the difficulty for the first time; and not to have known that the stone was sealed, and that the sepulchre was guarded. *Rolling away* the stone, both in this and the next verse, is true to life. The stone, which had been rolled into the opening of the nearly horizontal tomb, must be rolled from this recess; literally, *out of* the door of the sepulchre. See on ch. 15:46.

4. **And when they looked.** Rather, *And looking up*. The expression appears to indicate that their eyes were somewhat downcast while absorbed in the subject of conversation, and also that the sepulchre was somewhat above them. See quotation from Dr. Newman, ch. 15:22. **They saw,** etc. Unexpectedly and with surprise. Mark relates this with his characteristic exactness, describing the scene as actually passing, which is exhibited by a more literal rendering, *They behold that*

5 ᵗ And entering into the sepulchre, they saw a young man sitting on the right side, clothed in a long white garment; and they were affrighted. ᵘ And he saith unto them, Be not affrighted: ye seek Jesus of Nazareth, which was crucified. ˣ He is risen; he is not here. Behold the place where they laid him.
7 But go your way, tell his disciples and Peter that he goeth before you into Galilee: there shall ye see

ᵗ Lk. 24. 3; John 20. 11, 12.

ᵘ Mt. 28. 5; Lk. 24. 4.

ˣ Ps. 71. 20.

---

the stone has been rolled away. **For it was very great,** and therefore could be seen at some distance that it was moved. Its size had also caused them anxiety, from which they are now instantly relieved.

But the sight of the stone rolled away appears to have produced a different impression upon Mary Magdalene. Quick to draw an inference of evil, she runs back to Jerusalem and tells Peter and John, "They have taken away the Lord out of the sepulchre, and we know not where they have laid him," John 20:2. The other women thus left by Mary Magdalene go on, and possibly tarry a little, in hesitation, at the entrance of the tomb. Then they enter and search, but find not the body of the Lord Jesus. They stand perplexed. While in this state they behold an angel (next verse).

5. **And entering into the sepulchre,** implying that it was a spacious tomb. **They saw a young man,** an angel in human form, Acts 1:10; Gen. 19:15, 16. Matthew speaks of the angel rolling away the stone and sitting upon it. He had now entered the sepulchre. Mark minutely describes the position, **on the right side;** and dress, **a long white garment,** rather, *a white robe,* the color being a radiant white. Compare ch. 9:3. Luke (24:3, 4) says, "*Two men stood* by them in shining garments." So also Mary Magdalene, on her return, saw two angels in white sitting, the one at the head and the other at the feet, where the body had lain, John 20:11, 12. That Matthew and Mark mention only one angel may be satisfactorily explained in various ways. They may speak only of the one who was the speaker on this occasion. Or, as the first one arose, the other may have suddenly appeared by his side to confirm his testimony. But see a similar instance in note on ch. 5:2. That Luke speaks of their standing, while Mark speaks of the one sitting, may also be variously explained. The former does not say that they had not been sitting, nor the latter that they did not afterward stand. The word translated *stood* in Luke 24:4 has reference, not so much to the *posture,* as the *suddenness* of their appearing, and may be translated, *came upon them, appeared suddenly.* Compare the use of the word in Luke 2:9; Acts 12:7. But Mark speaks of the posture which the angel may have immediately taken, that of *sitting,* the posture of one imparting instruction. Other possible explanations will occur to the thoughtful reader.

They were affrighted. Astonished, amazed with terror and awe at his presence; not expecting to see such a vision, but to find the body of Jesus. They were afraid and bowed down their faces to the earth, Luke 24:5.

6. The comforting and assuring language of the angel is vividly given. **Ye seek Jesus of Nazareth,** etc. *Ye seek Jesus the Nazarene, the crucified;* which may be taken as descriptive of his humiliation, as well as his person. He who was a resident of the despised city of Nazareth, the one who suffered an ignominious death by crucifixion. Then immediately follows the announcement, **He is risen. Behold the place,** etc. The *place* was, doubtless, a cell in the tomb, like a berth or shelf, so that the body lay parallel with the wall. See on ch. 15:46. John 20:12 seems to imply this, since Mary Magdalene saw two angels, one at the head and the other at the feet, where Jesus had lain. The appearance of this particular spot, where they laid the body, would corroborate his testimony. The orderly arrangement of the graveclothes showed that the body had not been stolen, but was confirmatory of his resurrection, John 20:6–8.

7. **His disciples.** The apostles in

8 him, ʸ as he said unto you. ᶻ And they went out quickly, and fled from the sepulchre; for they trembled and were amazed: ᵃ neither said they any thing to any *man;* for they were afraid.

ʸ ch. 14. 28; Mt. 26. 32.
ᶻ Mt. 28. 8.
ᵃ Lk. 24. 9.

particular. **And Peter,** especially. A gracious message to the one who had denied him, but who had deeply and truly repented. It would assure him of his Lord's forgiveness. Mark alone mentions the name of Peter in this connection, and it accords with the very common supposition that this Gospel was written under the direction of the latter. How the words, *and Peter,* must have been embalmed in his memory! The importance and prominence given to this appearance in Galilee, and the fact that Jesus did appear that day, and a week later, to his apostles and others, at Jerusalem, seem to indicate that the appearance here foretold was that to believers at large, and recorded in 1 Cor. 15 : 6. Hence, the message, which was to the apostles first in particular, may be regarded as through them to his whole discipleship. **Goeth before you into Galilee.** He would go, not as on former occasions, *journeying* with them, but as his resurrection body could go; he would be there on their return from the Passover, and would meet them gathered at the appointed place. He did not, however, go for more than a week, till the Paschal festival was over, and the disciples who came up to Jerusalem were ready to return, John 20 : 26. **There shall ye see him, as he said to you,** on your way from the upper chamber to the garden, ch. 14 : 28. The reference to a promise that Jesus had made to them in private would be a token and evidence of the truthfulness of the message. Luke (24 : 6) says that the angel reminded them that Jesus had foretold his crucifixion and resurrection; and that they remembered his words.

8. Terrified and amazed, the women flee from the sepulchre. **Went out quickly.** *Quickly* should be omitted according to the best manuscripts. **For they trembled and were amazed.** *For trembling and amazement seized them.* They were in a state of terror and confusion. And so great was their fear, that they did not even say **anything to any** one in their flight. But Matthew (28 : 8) says that "they departed quickly from the sepulchre, with fear and great joy, and did run to bring the disciples word." The accounts may be used to explain and supplement each other. They fled trembling with amazement, possibly away from the city toward Bethany, saying nothing to any one. Mark specially notices this, as he *emphasizes the unbelief and hesitation* of the disciples, here of the women; then of the disciples when they heard from Mary Magdalene that she had seen the Lord, ver. 11; and again when the two, who went to Emmaus, gave their testimony, ver. 12; till at length Jesus appears to the eleven, rebuking them for their unbelief. To return, the terrified women, recovering themselves a little, remember the words of Jesus quoted by the angel (Luke 24 : 8), and also the charge to go and tell his disciples and Peter of his resurrection and his promised appearance in Galilee. With changing feelings they turn their steps toward the city. And now Jesus appears to them, Matt. 28 : 9. This dispels their fears, and gives them utterance. Before his appearance, *fear* predominated; after it, *joy.* Before, they are silent; after, they hasten and tell his disciples. Mark, according to his plan, suggested above, relates only the former, omitting the appearance of Jesus to the women, and their going to report. But Matthew, briefly referring to all these, combines the two states of mind, without going into details.

For any who may not be satisfied with the above explanation, it may be added, that it is possible to refer these accounts to different parties of women. The company may have become separated, and thus our Lord may have appeared to one party, and not to the other. The one, therefore, with joy report the glad tidings to the disciples; while the other, not fully recovering from their state of terror, say nothing about it.

9–20. *General remarks upon the genuineness of this passage.* Some high critical authorities reject this whole passage as not genuine; others consider it a

Jesus appears to Mary Magdalene; then to two disciples; then to the eleven. The last commission.

9   NOW when *Jesus* was risen early the first *day* of the week, ᵇ he appeared first to Mary Magdalene,   ᵇ John 20. 14.

---

later addition made in very early times, but having the same claim to reception and reverence as the rest of the Gospel; while still others regard it as an original portion of Mark's Gospel.

It is now (1896) quite generally regarded as an authentic account. Doubtless some little thing in its history, if known, would clear away all mystery regarding it. Both from external and internal reasons I am led to accept it as the original ending of this Gospel. See Introduction, pp. viii-xii, xix.

9-11. JESUS APPEARS TO MARY MAGDALENE. Luke 24 : 9-11; John 20 : 11-18. John gives a full and detailed account. Luke makes no reference to this appearance, but relates the report of the women, among whom was Mary Magdalene, to the disciples.

9. **Now when Jesus was risen early.** Mark himself now records the fact of the resurrection, *And having risen early.* Before, he had only recorded the language of the angel, "He is risen," ver. 6. To make the phrase, *early,* etc., mark the time of the appearance to Mary, rather than of the resurrection of Jesus, seems to me unnatural, and a little forced. That he appeared to her early on that day is implied by the connection, and is confirmed by John's account. **The first,** rather, *on the first day of the week.* The original somewhat different from ver. 2 would be more intelligible to Roman or Gentile readers. The mention of the day a second time (see ver. 2) is significant, as if to emphasize that which ever after was to be a day of days. It is of the first importance that we maintain the sacredness of the Christian Sabbath. Albert Barnes has truthfully said : "There is one weapon which the enemy has employed to destroy Christianity, and to drive it from the world, which has never been employed but with signal success. It is the attempt to corrupt the Christian Sabbath, to make it a day of festivity, to cause Christians to feel that its sacred and rigid obligation has ceased, to induce them on that day to mingle in the scenes of pleasure, or the exciting plans of ambition, to make them feel that they may pursue their journeys by land and water, by the steamboat and the car, regardless of the command of God, and this has done, and will continue to do, what no argument, no sophistry, no imperial power, has been able to accomplish. The 'Book of Sports' did more to destroy Christianity than all the ten persecutions of the Roman emperors, and the views of the Second Charles and his court about the Lord's Day tended more to drive religion from the British nation than all the fires that were enkindled by Mary. Paris has no Sabbath, and that fact has done more to banish Christianity than all the writing of Voltaire; and Vienna has no Sabbath, and that fact does more to annihilate religion there than ever did the skepticism of Frederick. Turn the Sabbath into a day of sports and pastimes, of military reviews, and of pantomimes and theatrical exhibitions, and not an infidel anywhere would care a farthing about the tomes of Volney or Voltaire, about the skepticism of Hume, the sneers of Gibbon, or the scurrility of Paine."

He appeared first. Some take *first* in a relative sense, meaning, the *first* of the three appearances which Mark here records. But this is wholly uncalled for, and is the result of a supposition that the appearance to the other women (Matt. 28 : 9, 10) must have preceded that to Mary Magdalene. It is better to take the word in its most natural meaning, and to regard the appearance here related as absolutely the first one of our risen Lord, which is in accordance with a very natural arrangement of the several appearances of Jesus on that first day of the week. See author's HARMONY, § 191. **Out of whom he had cast seven devils.** This specification is remarkable, for Mary Magdalene had been mentioned but little before, ver. 1. It seems to have some close connection with this first appearance, as a reason or ex-

10 ᶜout of whom he had cast seven devils. ᵈ And she went and told them that had been with him, ᵉ as
11 they mourned and wept. ᶠ And they, when they had heard that he was alive, and had been seen of her, believed not.
12 After that he appeared in another form ᵍ unto two of them, as they walked, and went into the country.

ᶜ Lk. 8. 2.
ᵈ Lk. 24. 10; John 20. 18.
ᵉ Mt. 9. 15; Lk. 24. 17; John 16. 5, 6, 20.
ᶠ Lk. 24. 11.
ᵍ Lk. 24. 13.

planatory clause. The number *seven demons*, indicates, as *legion* in the Geresene demoniac (ch. 5 : 9), a possession of great malignity. We see a reason of her great devotion to the Savior (John 20 : 2, 11), which was honored with his first appearance to her. She who had been delivered from so great power of demons, with a heart filled with gratitude and love, was peculiarly fitted to believe and welcome him who came forth victorious over death and hell. See on ch. 15 : 40.

From a comparison of John 20 : 3-8, it appears that Peter and John arrived at the sepulchre about the time that the women fled, ver. 8, and that Mary Magdalene followed soon after. The two disciples soon depart, leaving Mary standing at the tomb, weeping. Here she sees the two angels sitting where the body of Jesus had lain; and then turning about she sees Jesus. Immediately after this we may suppose that Jesus appeared to the women (Matt. 28 : 9, 10) returning to the city. See on ver. 8.

10. **She went and told them,** *it to those*. She told the disciples that she had seen the Lord, and that he had said, "Go to my brethren and say to them, I ascend unto my Father and your Father, and to my God and your God," John 20 : 17, 18. **That had been with him.** Very expressive, suggesting the idea of their former close communion and companionship with him, and of their after desertion and present scattered and despairing condition.

Yet those who reject this whole passage, instance this expression as "foreign to this Gospel," and think that Mark would have used the word *disciples*. But the expression, "those with him," is not unusual with Mark (ch. 1 : 36; 2 : 25; 5 : 40), and was appropriate before his betrayal. And the full expression, *to those who had been with him*, was necessary, if used at all, and **equally** appropriate, on the morning of his resurrection. **As they mourned and wept.** One of the life-like strokes of Mark. They were overwhelmed with grief. They thought their loss irreparable. Hope and faith were eclipsed.

11. **Believed not.** That the disciples disbelieved Mary Magdalene, shows how completely they had given way to despair; and that, notwithstanding Jesus had foretold his resurrection, they did not expect it. Luke says (24 : 11), "Their words," that is, of Mary Magdalene and the other women, "seemed to them as idle tales."

12, 13. JESUS APPEARS TO TWO ON THEIR WAY TO EMMAUS. Luke 24 : 13-35, where is found the detailed account.

12. **After that;** his first appearance to Mary Magdalene; when, is not here stated. From Luke (24 : 13, 29) we learn that it was on the afternoon of the day of his resurrection. **He appeared in another form;** from what they had before seen him. His appearance was in some way changed. Compare John 20 : 14-16; 21 : 4. Luke states (24 : 16) that "their eyes were holden that they should not know him" —their eyes were kept from exercising their full power of recognition. The two evangelists state two sides of the incident: Jesus exercised his power over his own appearance, and also over their perception. The change in his appearance was not so great but that they would have known him if their eyes had not been holden. But Luke had occasion, and Mark no occasion, to speak of the latter fact. **Two of them;** not of the apostles (Luke 24 : 33), but of the disciples in the wider sense. The name of one of them was Cleopas, Luke 24 : 18. The most ancient tradition is that they were of the seventy. In the midst of great brevity the characteristic specifications of Mark are noticeable, "in another form;" **as they walked, and went** (*going*)

13 And they went and told *it* unto the residue: neither believed they them.

14 ʰAfterward he appeared unto the eleven as they sat at meat, and upbraided them with their unbelief and hardness of heart, because they believed not them which had seen him after he was risen.

ʰ Lk. 24. 36; John 20. 19.

into the country. Compare the last clause with similar ones in this Gospel, ch. 5 : 14 ; 6 : 36, 56 ; 13 : 16 ; 15 : 21. They were going to Emmaus, Luke 24 : 13.

13. To the residue. *To the rest,* those disciples who remained in Jerusalem, especially the eleven, Luke 24 : 33. **Neither believed they them.** Not only did they disbelieve Mary Magdalene, but also these two witnesses. From Luke 24 : 34 we learn that our Lord had appeared to Peter that afternoon, while these two disciples had been away to Emmaus, 1 Cor. 15 : 5. And here we meet with an apparent discrepancy between these two accounts. According to Luke the disciples believed Peter, that Jesus had risen ; but according to Mark they believed not the two who had returned from Emmaus. This may be explained : (1.) Some believed, for example, John (John 20 : 8); others, like Thomas, would not credit the report, but must have an ocular demonstration. (2.) Or, they were in that state of mind, not at all unnatural, in which they both believed and disbelieved. They were ready to tell whatever was remarkable within their own knowledge, but equally ready to discredit what others told to them.

Or (3), Peter, John and some others, believing that Jesus had risen, announced the fact to the two disciples, the rest giving assent by their silence ; but when the two relate how Jesus had been with them, and was known by the breaking of bread at Emmaus, they are filled with incredulity. They cannot conceive, it may be, how he should be here and there, and vanish from their sight ; they doubt, think it may have been an apparition, and thus most of those present believed them not, and were prepared to suppose Jesus a spirit when he appeared soon after, Luke 24 : 37. This explanation I think the best. The design of Mark is to make prominent their slowness to believe. The apostles were far from being credulous. But this unbelief was of short duration, Luke 24 : 36-39.

14-18. JESUS APPEARS TO THE APOSTLES. THE LAST COMMISSION. Matt. 28 : 16-20 ; Luke 24 : 29-49 ; John 20 : 19-29.

14. Afterward. Literally, *later*, and as an adverb well expressed by *Afterward*. There is a relation between the "*first* to Mary Magdalene" (ver. 9), "after that" (ver. 12), and "afterward" of this verse. Mark in his narrative traces briefly the way by which Jesus brought the evidences of his resurrection to his apostles :

First by Mary Magdalene. Matthew notices also by the other women. After this by two disciples, possibly of the seventy. At length, afterward, he appears to the apostles themselves. The women who had showed such devotion at the cross and sepulchre are honored with his first appearances. But the apostles, who had acted so unworthy of constant attendants and of their chosen and near relationship, are favored last. Jesus, too, would teach them the importance of believing upon evidence. Compare John 20 : 29.

Appeared unto the eleven, *themselves.* This was probably on the evening after our Lord's resurrection, Luke 24 : 13, 29, 33, 36 and John 20 : 19. The unbelief of the apostles mentioned here accords better with this appearance (Luke 24 : 37-42) than with that a week later, John 20 : 26. Although Thomas was absent (John 20 : 24), they are styled *the eleven* from their number as a body. Compare 1 Cor. 15 : 5, where Paul speaks of them as "the twelve" from their original number. **As they sat at meat.** *As they reclined at table* according to the Jewish custom at meals. See on ch. 2 : 15.

Upbraided . . . their unbelief. Chided, or sharply rebuked their want of faith respecting his resurrection. **Hardness of heart.** That obstinacy, that perversity of heart attending unbelief. Mark gives special prominence to their unbelief. Luke (24 : 38) gives but a glimpse of it. **Be-**

15 ¹And he said unto them, Go ye into all the world, ¹Mt. 28. 19; John 15. 16; Col. 1. 23.

cause they believed not, etc. The special ground of our Lord's rebuke, and the special direction of the apostles' unbelief. They disbelieved credible testimony, not only of one, but of several witnesses. Thomas is generally spoken of as the doubting disciple, John 20 : 24. But the rest of the eleven had the same unbelief in kind, though probably not so great in degree.

15. **And he said to them.** At that time when he first appeared to the apostles and others with them (Luke 24 : 33); or more probably, at a later appearance in Galilee (Matt. 28 : 16-20), when he was seen by over five hundred brethren, 1 Cor. 15 : 6. In his great brevity Mark records our Lord's rebuke, commission to the disciples, his ascension, and their going forth to preach after the day of Pentecost, as if they were immediately connected together in time. A comparison of the other Gospels shows that he observes the chronological sequence of events, but at a single glance touches several important points of evangelical history. A separation therefore between this and the preceding verse cannot be regarded as either severe or arbitrary. The command of Jesus, which immediately follows, harmonizes beautifully as a part of the last commission. First of all, Jesus declares that all power is given him in heaven and on earth, Matt. 28 : 18. This prepares the way for the command to preach the gospel to every creature, with the effect of believing and not believing (this and the next verse). Then he encourages them with the signs that shall attend them, vers. 17, 18. And finally, in view of all this, he says (Matt. 28 : 19, 20), "Go ye therefore, and teach all nations, baptizing them," etc., "and lo I am with you alway, even to the end of the world." It was fitting also that this great last commission should be publicly given and near the time of his ascension. When so fitting as at that gathering which Jesus himself had appointed in Galilee, and when over five hundred were assembled together? That no reference is made to any but the eleven, arises from the brevity of the account, and from the fact that the apostles were to be the witnesses of Christ's resurrection and first builders of the church.

All the world. Not merely the land of Israel, but every part of the habitable globe. The words "all nations" are similar, in Matt. 28 : 19. **Preach the gospel,** the *good news*, or *glad tidings* of salvation. "*Preach the gospel* without the addition 'of the kingdom' (Matthew), or 'of God' (Luke), is in Mark's *manner* (see ch. 1 : 15 ; 13 : 10)."—ALFORD. **Every creature,** to every intelligent inhabitant of "all the world;" to all mankind. There is no necessity of extending the meaning of *creature* or *creation* to every created thing, for the gospel is only intended for the human creation. Its influence indeed extends to the whole creation (Rom. 8 : 19-23), but unintelligent and inanimate creatures can neither hear nor receive it; and it cannot be said, in any proper sense, to be preached to them. Or to express ourselves differently: The most natural sense of the passage limits the meaning of *creature* to man. "The 'creature' is therefore put for humanity, but only in so far as humanity is the flower of the whole creation."—OLSHAUSEN. "By these words the missionary work is bound upon the church through all ages, till every part of the earth shall have been evangelized."—ALFORD.

The restriction in Matt. 10 : 5 was now removed. Beginning at Jerusalem, they were to preach the gospel in Judea, in Samaria, and unto the uttermost parts of the earth, Luke 24 : 47; Acts 8 : 1. How, then, did the apostles have any doubt in regard to going to the Gentiles with the gospel, and receiving them into the church? Acts 10 : 28. Their doubt was probably not in regard to the *fact*, but the *way* in which it should be accomplished. They were doubtless in much darkness about it, awaiting further developments and the guidance of the Spirit. They most probably expected the gospel would be preached to the Gentiles as they became proselytes to Israel, and were circumcised, Acts 2 : 10; 11 : 3. Hence they began to preach the gospel to the Jews among all nations, Acts 11 : 19. The spiritual nature of Christ's kingdom is here seen, that

16 and preach the gospel to every creature. ʲHe that believeth and is baptized shall be saved; but he

ʲ Ac. 2. 38; 16. 30; Rom. 10. 9; 1 Pet. 3. 21.

Christ commands them to use the sword of the Spirit, which is the word of God, leaving each one to the free exercise of his will.

16. The preaching of the gospel imposes duties and responsibilities upon those who hear, and will be attended with opposite results, according as it shall be accepted or rejected. **He that believeth;** receiveth the gospel as true and believeth with the heart, Rom. 10 : 10; accepts the gospel and in his feelings and conduct treats it as true. Believing is not a mere passive exercise, a bare assent, nor an intellectual belief, but an active exercise of the whole soul, including both mind and heart. **And is baptized;** expressing his belief in the gospel by this act of obedience to Christ. Notice the divine order: Preach; believe; be baptized. Baptism naturally follows faith, as a *symbol* of death to the world and life to God (Rom. 6 : 4), a *profession* of discipleship, a putting on Christ (Gal. 3 : 27), and as the *entrance* to the fellowship of a visible church, Acts 2: 41, 42. On the meaning of the word, see on ch. 1 : 4. Baptism is essential to obedience, and immersion is essential to baptism. See Remark 17. "Faith must precede baptism, as these words of Christ, and Scripture examples show; and such as have it, ought to make a profession of it, and be baptized; and in which way it is that faith discovers itself, and works by love to Christ; namely, in observing his commands, and this among the rest."— JOHN GILL. "Pædo-baptism is certainly not apostolic." — OLSHAUSEN. Faith before baptism, and baptism upon faith, are taught also by the last commission in Matthew (28 : 19), *Disciple all nations, baptizing them*, etc.; and by the uniform example of the early disciples in preaching the gospel and immediately baptizing those that believed. Such passages as Acts 2 : 37–41; 8 : 12, 34–39; 16 : 30–33, are the best comments on the intimate relation of faith and baptism. No instance can be found in the New Testament of baptizing before professed faith. Neither is there any instance, expressed or implied, of an infant baptized upon the faith of its parent. Nor is there an instance of partaking of the Lord's Supper or performing any act as a church member between faith and baptism.

Shall be saved; from the practice and consequences of sin, and to the practice of holiness with all its glorious results on earth and in heaven. Salvation has both its negative and its positive side, freedom from sin and conformity to Christ. **He that believeth not,** with all the heart, so as to love and obey Christ. Notice that it is not added, 'and is not baptized,' Baptized or unbaptized he shall perish, if he believes not, rejects the gospel in heart and life. Unbelievers would of course be unbaptized, and if any, like Simon Magus, should receive the ordinance without true faith, unbelief would be their ruin, Acts 8 : 21. **Shall be damned.** Rather, *Shall be condemned*, by the righteous judgment of God, to perish. They shall be "left in the love and practice of sin through time, and be miserable to eternity."

The language of the last commission implies that this was not the institution of the ordinance. It was the *extending* to all nations the preaching of the gospel, baptism, and the observance of Christ's commands. As well might it be said that here began gospel preaching, as that gospel baptism here had its origin or beginning. Baptism, as a gospel ordinance, was instituted by John at the dawn of the new dispensation, ch. 1 : 1–5; Matt. 11 : 12, 13. Jesus submitted to it as a gospel ordinance, and as an example, Matt. 3 : 15; the three persons of the Godhead were present to sanction it; pointing also to the fact that, after Christ had arisen and ascended, and the Holy Spirit had come, believers should be baptized, in reference to the name of the triune God, into an open allegiance and subjection to him. After the baptism of Jesus, his disciples baptized under his direction, John 4 : 1, 2. And now as he is about to leave the world and to send the Holy Spirit, which would complete a full manifestation of the Trinity, he enjoins upon his disciples the complete formula which would correspond to the completeness of revealed truth and to the full organization of his churches. Baptism, administered

A.D. 30.   MARK XVI.   325

17 that believeth not shall be damned. And these
signs shall follow them that believe; ᵏIn my name
shall they cast out devils; ˡthey shall speak with
18 new tongues; ᵐthey shall take up serpents; and if
they drink any deadly thing, it shall not hurt them;
ⁿthey shall lay hands on the sick, and they shall recover.

ᵏ Ac. 5. 16; 8. 7; 16. 18; 19. 12.
ˡ Ac. 2. 4; 10. 46; 13. 6; 1 Cor. 12. 10.
ᵐ Ac. 28. 5.
ⁿ Ac. 5. 15, 16; 9. 17, 34, 40, 41; 28. 8, 9.

by John, in view of the coming Messiah, or by the disciples of Jesus in his name as the Messiah, was valid, as it corresponded to the revelations of truth and to the development of Christ's kingdom. But after the full manifestation of the Son, and of the Holy Spirit, baptism, to be valid, must be administered in the name of the Father and of the Son and of the Holy Spirit.

17. **These signs,** as proofs of the gospel. See general remarks on Miracles, ch. 1 : 21-28. **Shall follow them,** *shall accompany them* and be done by them. **That believe;** that have believed. Notice how the faith of believers is made prominent in the words of Jesus at the end of this chapter, even as the unbelief of the apostles was made prominent at the beginning. The promise has reference to believers generally in the planting and early extension of Christianity in the world. "Jesus does not mean that each of these signs should manifest itself with each believer, but this miracle with one, and that with another."—MEYER. Nor does it necessarily mean that every believer should perform miracles. The promise is general, and, during the first age of Christianity, it found its fulfillment in the miraculous gifts which were exercised by persons from every class of believers, Acts 2 : 4; 10 : 36; 1 Cor. 12 : 4-11. How long these signs were continued with the early Christians, cannot be determined. They were probably withdrawn gradually soon after apostolic days. They were important and necessary as proofs of a new revelation from God. But when they had served this end their continuance was no longer necessary. They still exist, however, as facts of history, and thus have their place among the evidences of the truth of Christianity.

In my name. In all that my name imports and represents, as revealed in the gospel; not in your own, but in my divine authority, and in faith relying solely on my divine power, Acts 3 : 6. The use of his name without faith would avail nothing, Acts 19 : 13-16. **Cast out devils,** *demons,* ch. 1 : 34. See the fulfillment of this in Acts 5 : 16; 8 : 7; 16 : 18. Such exhibitions of power over the agents of the devil and the kingdom of darkness, were evidences of Christ's victory over Satan and his hosts, and pledges of the ultimate success of his kingdom over the mightiest of his foes. They are justly placed first among the signs which should accompany his followers. **New tongues.** In languages before unknown to them. *New* is emphatic. They should exercise a strange and wonderful power. The miraculous manifestation of the power and presence of the Holy Spirit, is fittingly placed second on the list. It was a sign to unbelievers, 1 Cor. 14 : 22. For the fulfillment of this, see Acts 2 : 4; 10 : 46; 19 : 6.

18. **Take up serpents,** poisonous reptiles, without injury. Fulfilled in Paul's experience, Acts 28 : 2-5. Giving the Greek verb the meaning of driving forth and exterminating, and applying the promise to such legends as that of expelling of noxious animals by St. Patrick from Ireland, is unnatural, and partakes of Popish superstition, rather than of sound exegesis. 'The taking up of serpents' immediately before 'drinking any deadly thing,' naturally point to a personal deliverance through the power of God. **Any deadly thing.** Any mortal poison. No instance of this is given in the Acts; but it doubtless occurred, as poisoning was very common at that period. The legends of John and also Barnabas drinking poison without injury, though uncertain and unreliable, may, notwithstanding, be suggestive of similar experiences among some early Christians. **Lay hands on the sick,** etc., Acts 28 : 8, 9. Compare Acts 5 : 12-16; 9 : 17; James 5 : 14.

The ascension; success of the gospel.

19 So then after the Lord had spoken unto them, he was º received up into heaven, and sat on the right hand of God.
20 And they went forth, and preached every where, the Lord working with *them*, ᵖ and confirming the word with signs following. Amen.

º Ps. 110. 1; Ac. 7. 55.

ᵖ Ac. 5. 12; 14. 3; Ro. 15. 19; 1 Cor. 2. 4, 5; Heb. 2. 4.

How completely this was fulfilled is shown by the fact that even the dead were raised to life, as Tabitha by Peter (Acts 9 : 40), and Eutychus by Paul, Acts 20 : 10-12. "Jesus Christ performed more than he promised."— BENGEL.

19, 20. THE ASCENSION. PREACHING EVERYWHERE THE GOSPEL. Luke 24 : 50-53; Acts 1 : 9-12. What is here so briefly stated by Mark, is fully related by Luke in his Gospel, and in the Acts of the Apostles.

19. **The Lord.** Those who regard the last twelve verses of this chapter as written by a later hand, say that the title, *the Lord*, applied to Christ in this and the next verse, is foreign to the diction of Mark. But it is not at all unnatural or strange. The title was peculiarly appropriate in the account of Jesus after the resurrection. It was fitting to speak of him as absolutely *the Lord*, when relating his ascension to heaven, and his carrying forward his kingdom through his disciples. It was fitting too to close the Gospel thus, which begins with announcing Jesus as "the Son of God," and with the prophecy, "Prepare the way of the Lord." Compare a similar use of the title in Matt. 28 : 6, after the resurrection. **After the Lord had spoken to them,** the last commission and the instruction, of which we have a brief summary in the preceding verses. Our Lord was on earth with his disciples forty days before his ascension, Acts 1 : 3. **Was received up into heaven.** *Taken up.* While he blessed them, Luke 24 : 51. He was borne up and a cloud received him out of sight (Acts 1 : 9), into the presence of the Father, Acts 1 : 11; John 20 : 17. This decides nothing respecting the locality of heaven. The direction that Jesus went was upward, and heaven is naturally and morally conceived as above us. Wherever heaven is, it is away from this earth; and *away* from this earth is

up. The verb in the original may also suggest the additional idea, that Jesus was taken up again from whence he came, Phil. 2 : 6. **Sat on the right hand of God.** Rather, *Sat down on*, etc. Denotes a position of great exaltation and honor, Acts 2 : 33; Phil. 2 : 10. He sat down as a king on his throne, and from thence he exercises his Messianic and royal power. The place of the ascension was the Mount of Olives near Bethany, Luke 24 : 50; Acts 1 : 12.

20. **And they went forth.** The apostles, whose unbelief is specially related in this chapter, and who witnessed his ascension (Acts 1 : 2-4), now believing and now obedient. **Preached everywhere;** in all parts of the known world, Rom. 10 : 18. The book of the Acts is here compressed into a single verse. **The Lord,** ascended and exalted (see preceding verse), **working with them.** Thus fulfilling his promise, "Lo, I am with you alway, unto the end of the world," Matt. 28 : 20. He co-operated with them; brought his divine power into co-operation with their human agency, 1 Cor. 3 : 9; 2 Cor. 6 : 1; Eph. 1 : 10. He worked with them by his Spirit, giving them unparalleled success. **And confirming the word,** which they preached, **with signs following;** the special miracles which had been promised in vers. 17, 18, accompanied them. A grand conclusion of a Gospel which specially records the deeds of Christ: Jesus exalted, the Lord, the Mighty Worker still with his people. **Amen.** So let it be and so it shall be. The word, however, should be omitted, according to the highest critical authorities. It was added by copyists.

REMARKS.

1. The women early at the sepulchre, patterns of love and devotion to Jesus, vers. 1, 2; Sol. Song 8 : 6, 7.

2. On the first day of the week we seek not a dead, but a risen and living Christ, vers. 2, 9; Ps. 118 : 24; Heb. 4 : 14–16; 12 : 2; Rev. 1 : 10.

3. The stone at the door of the sepulchre illustrates many hindrances in the Christian life. Men often make for themselves unnecessary anxiety. The difficulties they fear often disappear before they reach them, vers. 3, 4; Num. 14 : 2 and Josh. 6 : 20.

4. Seekers of Jesus have no reason to be afraid of angels, who are ministering spirits to the righteous, vers. 5, 6; Heb. 1 : 14.

5. "If we look with believing eyes into Christ's grave, all our anxiety falls into it; for Christ's resurrection is our resurrection."—STARKE. Ver. 6; Col. 3 : 1–4.

6. The empty grave of Jesus teaches his Messiahship, his death and resurrection, his humiliation and exaltation, the atonement fully made, and the salvation of believers sure. The believer should not, therefore, fear the grave, ver. 6; 1 Cor. 15 : 55–57.

7. How compassionate is Jesus toward his fallen yet penitent disciples! He sends a special message to Peter, who had denied him, and afterward wept bitterly, ver. 7; Heb. 5 : 2; Mic. 7 : 17, 18.

8. As all the previous appearances to the disciples were preparatory to the grand appearance to the collective body of disciples in Galilee, so are all of the manifestations of grace preparatory to the great gathering of all believers at last in glory, ver. 7; 1 Cor. 15 : 24–28.

9. Untimely and unbecoming fear often hinders the performance of duty, ver. 8; Matt. 25 : 25.

10. As woman was first to sin, so woman was first to seek and find a risen Savior, ver. 9; Gen. 3 : 6; 1 Tim. 2 : 14; Luke 7 : 47.

11. How unbelieving the human heart, and how kind the treatment of Jesus toward his unbelieving disciples! Vers. 10–14; Matt. 12 : 20; 14 : 31; John 20 : 27.

12. How strong and many the evidences of Christ's resurrection! Nothing but obstinate unbelief can reject it, vers. 9–14; 1 Cor. 15 : 3–8.

13. It is a great sin to reject competent evidence in religious matters, ver. 14; John 12 : 37–40; Acts 7 : 31; Heb. 11 : 6.

14. The grand mission of Christ's disciples is to convert the world. Each should in some way labor for this end, ver. 15; Matt. 5 : 16; Acts 1 : 8; 8 : 4.

15. Salvation through Christ is offered freely to all, ver. 15; John 3 : 16; Rev. 22 : 17.

16. A practical faith is absolutely necessary to salvation. Christ must be believed and obeyed, ver. 16; John 8 : 24; James 1 : 17, 18; Acts 16 : 31; 2 Thess. 1 : 8.

17. How important is baptism! The great importance that our Savior attached to baptism is manifest not only by the fact that he himself was baptized in the Jordan, and that his disciples baptized more disciples than John (John 4 : 1), but also that he included baptism in his last commission, placing it immediately after believing: "He that believeth and is baptized shall be saved." Had not Jesus considered it of great importance he would not have given it such a position. But that he considered faith of greater importance is evident, both from his demanding faith first, and also by referring only to faith in the last sentence of his command : "He that believeth not shall be damned." He thus intimated that baptism alone could not save, that outward religion would be unavailing without inward piety. How closely baptism may be connected with the salvation of certain individuals no one can certainly decide. As an act of obedience, as a way of confessing Christ, as a proof of love to him, we conceive it to be closely connected with salvation. Let no one carelessly or recklessly disregard it. I can therefore adopt the sentiment of Rev. Albert Barnes: "It is worthy of remark that Jesus has made *baptism* of so much importance. He did not say, indeed, that a man could not be saved without baptism, but he has strongly implied that where this is neglected, *knowing it to be a command of the Savior*, it endangers the salvation of the soul. *Faith* and *baptism* are the beginnings of a Christian life : the one the beginning of piety *in the soul*, the other of its manifestation *before men*, or a profession of religion. And every man endangers his eternal interest by being ashamed of Christ before men." Ver. 16; Rom. 10 : 9, 10 ; 1 Pet. 3 : 21.

18. As Christ, our supreme lawgiver and head, has fixed a regular order for his churches to follow in evangelizing the world, no one has a right to change

that order, as they do who put baptism before faith, or the Lord's Supper before baptism, vers. 15, 16; Lev. 10 : 1, 2; Isa. 1 : 12; Rev. 22 : 18, 19.

19. Christ will be with his people unto the end, giving them all necessary grace and help, vers. 17, 18; Isa. 59 : 19; Matt. 28 : 20; Acts 18 : 9, 10; 23 : 11; Phil. 4 : 13; 2 Tim. 4 : 17, 18; Rev. 2 : 10; 3 : 10.

20. Let us ever view Jesus, an exalted Savior, in heaven, at the right hand of God, ver. 19; John 14 : 2; Rom. 8 : 34; Heb. 7 : 25.

21. The preaching of the gospel has ever been attended with the evidences of its own divine origin, ver. 20; 2 Cor. 4 : 1–4; 1 Cor. 15 : 58. Whoever will do Christ's will shall know of the truth of his doctrine, John 7 ; 17.

LIST OF ILLUSTRATIONS.

	PAGE
Locusts,	25
Supposed Place of Christ's Baptism,	28
Uncovering the Roof,	46
Skin Bottle,	54
Show-bread,	56
Oriental Wheat,	85
Scrip, or Bag,	111
Sandals,	111
Dancing Girl,	117
Sea of Galilee,	150
Fig-leaves and Fruit,	212
Roman Denarius,	228
Reclining at Table,	237
Cruses and Vases,	260
Garden of Gethsemane,	273
Ground-plan of a House,	286
Body prepared for Burial,	310
A Tomb,	310

INDEX.

	PAGE
Abba	275
Abiathar	56
"Abomination of desolation"	248
Ahimelech	56
Alabaster	259
Allegories	76
Alpheus	50
Andrew, 33, 65, 123; call of	33
Angels, 31; at the sepulchre	318
Anger, in Jesus, in men	59
Annas	280
Anointing the sick, 113; by Roman Catholics, 113; at Bethany, 259; in the vicinity of Nain, 259; for burial	316
"Apostles," when only used by Mark	120
Apostles selected, 62, 63; why appointed, 63; catalogues of, 64; mission 112,	113
Arimathæa	309
Aramean expressions, xvi.; the colloquial language of Jesus,	103
Appearances of Jesus after his resurrection	315
Ass and colt	208
Ascension	326
Authority of Christ's teachings,	36
Baptism, 22–24; duty of, 327; of Christ, 27–29, 44; in the Holy Spirit, 26, 27; of suffering, 197; infant baptism, 203; relation to the Lord's Supper	324
Baptism of repentance	24
Baptist, as a name or title	118
Barabbas, 294; preferred to Jesus	293–296
Bartimæus 199,	200
Bartholomew	66
Baskets 124, 150,	153
Bed 46	83

	PAGE
Beelzebub	68
"Believe"	32
"Beside himself"	68
Bethany, 206; supper at	255
Bethphage	206
Bethsaida, two places of that name 125,	126
Betrayal of Jesus 277,	292
Blasphemy, 48, 69; different kinds of, 70; against the Holy Spirit, 70, 71; against the Son	72
"Bless"	123
Blind man healed at Bethsaida, 154,	155
Blind healed	155
Blindness in the East	155
Boanerges	65
Body prepared for burial	310
Bottles, skin bottles	54
Bread, loaves of	123
Brethren of Jesus	108
Burial of Jesus 308–	310
Burnt-offerings	234
Bush	231
Bushel	83
Butaiha	123
Cæsarea Philippi	156
Caiaphas 280,	281
Camel's hair	25
Canaan	141
Canaanite	67
Candle, candlestick	83
Capernaum	35
Carpenter	107
Centurion, how designated by Mark, 307; testimony of	307
Ceremonial practices of the Jews 134,	135
Chains	93
Charger	118

INDEX.

	PAGE
Chief estates of Galilee	117
Children, Christ's blessing little,	186, 187
Christ, meaning of	21
Christ's baptism, supposed place of, 28; temptation of,	30
Christ's knowledge, 48; ignorance of the time of his second coming, 254, 256; his power, 49; human nature, 109; his humanity and divinity, 236, 241; his coming with power, 162; his authority, 217–219; Son of David and David's Lord	236
Christ, the Lord of the Sabbath, 57; the corner-stone	225
Christ's mother and brethren, 72, 73, 74; his friends or relations	73, 108
Christ and our offerings	241
Christ's second coming, 252; time of	254
Christians and civil governments	240
Church and State	228
Clerical celibacy	39, 40
Cloth, new	53
Coasts	96, 97
Cock-crowing, first and second	272
Commandment, first and second, 233, 234; the distinctions made by the scribes	233
Compassion	148
"Compel"	298
Confession of Peter	157
Corban	137
Councils	246
Crosses	299
Crown of thorns	297
Crucifixion, 300, 301; day of Christ's	311
Cruses and vases	260
Cup of suffering, 197, 275; of joy	275
Decapolis	97, 98
Dalmanutha	151
Dancing, Oriental	117
Darkness at the crucifixion	304
David, father	209
Day of Christ's death	311–313
Dead	231, 232

	PAGE
Death a sleep	102
Death of Jesus, how caused, 306, 307	
Defilement, moral, 139, 140, ceremonial	132, 133
Demons 36; Jesus a torment to, 94; number of	94
Demoniacal possessions	36, 37, 40
Denials of Peter	285
Desert	43
Destruction of property through Christ's miracles	95, 96
Disciples, their obtuseness explained	128, 174
Discourse on the destruction of Jerusalem, etc.	241 ff.
Dish, eating out of the same	265
Divorces among the Jews, 183; why allowed, 183, 184; Christian law of	184, 185
Dogs, applied to Gentiles	142
Dove, 29; selling doves in the temple	214
Early rising in Palestine	281
Earthquakes preceding the destruction of Jerusalem	245
Elders	133
Elias, 114; the expectation of his coming, 114; how and when he came	167, 168
"Eloi"	304
Emmaus, Jesus on the way to	322
Ephphatha	145
Eras of John's imprisonment and death	120
Evening, first and second	122
Eventide	211
Executions on a birthday	118
Executioner	119
Extreme unction	113
Eye of a needle	191, 192
Fables	76
Faith, illustrated in healing, 60, 216; and prayer, 217; removing mountains	216, 217
False Christs	244, 245, 251
Famines preceding the destruction of Jerusalem	246
Fasts, Jewish	52
Fasting	53, 54, 58
Feast of Tabernacles, 181; of Dedication	181

INDEX. 331

	PAGE
Feeding the five thousand, 124; the four thousand, 148; two distinct miracles, 149; when performed	148
Fetters	93
Fevers at Capernaum	39
Fig-tree, 212; cursed, 211, 212, 216; time of figs, 212; barren fig-tree dried up, 216; its leaves a sign of summer	252
First last and last first	193, 194
Following Christ	159
Foot-stool	236
Forgiving sins	47
Friday the day of Christ's crucifixion	311–313
Funerals in the East	102
Gadara, 92; demoniacs of	92–95
Galilee, 27; beginning of Christ's ministry there, 31; why Mark begins his account of Christ's ministry there	31
Genuineness of Mark, vii., viii.; of Mark 16:9–20	viii.–xii
Galilee, Sea of	33, 150
Gemara	133
Gennesaret, land of	129
Gentiles, Mark's Gospel specially for	xv., xvi.
Geographical explanations	xvi.
Gerasa	92
Gergesa, 92; the steep at	95
Gestures and looks of Jesus	xv.
Gethsemane	273, 277
Gifts, Christ and our	241
Girdle	25
Golgotha, 299; where was it?	299, 300
Gospel, meaning of	21
Gospel, the Second	v.
Gospel, expansive power of, 87; where preached in apostolic days	246
Government, duty to	228
Gradual cure, 154; gradual conviction, etc.	161
Greatest in the kingdom	174, 175
Growth of spiritual life	86
Hearers, thoughtless, 80; superficial, 81; worldly, 81; good, 82; responsible	83, 84
Heart	233

	PAGE
"Heart of the earth"	312
Heaven	123
Hebrew or Aramean expressions	xvi.
Hedge	222
Hell	178
Herod Antipas, 113, 114; his birthday	116, 117
Herod Philip, 115; of Iturea	117
Herodians	60, 152, 226
Herodias	115
High captains	117
High-priests	280
Hosanna	209
Housetop	249
Horse	208
House, plan of	286
Husbandmen	222
Hypocrites	135
Idumea	61
Infant baptism	187
Infant communion	187, 188
Infant salvation	187
Inscriptions on the cross	302
Images on coins	228
Impediment of speech	144
Intermediate state	231, 241
"Into the mountain"	63
Jairus' daughter, 98; how designated	102
James, the less, son of Alpheus	66
James, son of Zebedee	34, 64, 65
James and John, ambitious request of	195, 196
Jericho	200
Jerusalem, 206; destruction of, 250, 251; sufferings during its siege, 250; Titus acknowledging the help of God in its capture	251
Jesus, meaning of, 21; temptation of, 29, 30; at prayer, 40; first general preaching tour, 40, 41; second preaching tour, 67; third preaching tour, 105–107, 109, 112, 113; final departure from Galilee, 181, 182; triumphant entry into Jerusalem, 208, 209; cleansing the temple, 213–215; sacrificial work, 257; agony in Geth-	

INDEX.

semane, 272-275; his prayer answered, 276; condemned to death, 284, 291; died on Friday............311-313
Jesus charged with madness... 67
Jesus asleep in the ship, 89; walking on the water, 127; sighing............145, 151, 152
Jesus a carpenter, 107; brethren of, 107-109; opinion of the people concerning him, 156; concerning his destruction of property, 213; death of, 308; resurrection of, 315; ascension of.................. 326
John, meaning of.............. 22
John the Baptist, 22, 113-118; Baptist as a surname, 118; and Jesus, 218, 219; disciples of John, 52; reasons for his beheading, 116; when and where beheaded, 119, 120; his burial, 120; era of his imprisonment and death......... 120
John, apostle, 34, 65; his mode of reckoning time........... 301
Jordan....................24, 29
Joseph...................... 107
Joseph of Arimathæa.......... 309
Judas Iscariot, 67, 262; not at the Lord's Supper, 266; the kiss of.................... 278
Judas not Iscariot............ 66
Judas the Gaulonite........... 227
Judea....................... 61

Kingdom of God.............. 32

Last commission.............. 323
Leaven...................... 152
Legion...................... 94
Leprosy, 41; modern, 41; emblem of sin, 41, 42; cleansing of..................... 43
Leper illustrating the repenting sinner....................42, 45
Levi........................ 50
Loaves...................... 123
Locusts..................... 25
Lords....................... 107
Lord's Day.............316, 317
Lord's Supper, 266, 270; its name, 268; its simplicity, 269;

its import, 270; relation to baptism................... 270
Lunatic whom the disciples could not heal............169 ff.

Machærus................... 120
Magdala.................... 151
Malchus.................... 279
Mark..............v., vi., 279, 280
Mark's Gospel, 21; the second Gospel, v.; the language of, vi., vii.; genuineness of, vii., viii.; of Mark 16: 9-20. viii.; external evidence, viii.-xi.; internal, xi., xii.; sources of, xii., xiii.; relation to the other Gospels, xiii., xiv.; peculiarities, xiv., xv.; for whom written, xv., xvi.; when written, xvii.; where written, xviii.; arrangement, xviii., xix.; how too often treated, iii.; Mark and the prophecies, 22; noting the weakness and unbelief of the disciples................90, 322
Market.................134, 237
Marriage, 203; and the future life.....................231, 232
Mary, the mother of Jesus..... 73
Mariolatry.................. 73
Mary, sister of Lazarus....259, 261
Mary, mother of James........ 308
Mary Magdalene, 308; Jesus appearing to her first......... 322
Matthew................50, 66
Messenger.................. 22
Millstone................... 177
Minister.................... 198
Mind....................... 233
Miracle, a gradual............ 154
Miracles, 34, 35; relation between bodily and spiritual, 47; Christ's miracles through his own divine power, 105; of feeding five thousand, 124; of four thousand.......... 148
Mishna..................... 133
Month, the beginning, how decided...................... 311
Mourning over the dead........ 102
Mount of Olives.............. 207
Mustard, 86, 87; a tree....... 87
Myrrh...................... 300

INDEX.

Nazareth, 27; first and second rejection at, 105-107; Christ leaving it forever........... 109
Needle's eye................191, 192
New dispensation began with John.......... 43
Nob........................ 55

Oath of Herod............118, 119
"Offend"..................... 177
"Offended"................... 108
Olives, Mount of.......... 207, 243
Our offerings to God.......... 241
Opposition to Jesus, beginning of, 45; taking an organized form....................... 60

Passover, how the word used, 258; feast of, 258, 263; how made ready, 264; how celebrated.................... 264
Palace....................... 281
Palestine, fertility of............ 78
Palsy........................ 45
Parables, 76; of Christ, 76, 77; designed for future use, 86; reasons for, 79, 80; design of, 91; interpretation of, 82, 83; of a sower, 77, 78; the seed growing secretly............. 85
Paying tribute to Cæsar....226, 228
Pella........................ 249
Penny....................... 122
Peter, 64; connection with Mark's Gospel, xiii.; ever at Rome.......................xviii.
Peter's wife's mother........... 39
Peter's confession, 157; rebuked, 158; his denial foretold, 271; following Christ afar off, 281; denials of..........285, 288
Peter, James, and John.....102, 274
Perea......................61, 182
Persecution of Christians, why? 247
Pharisees, 51; opposition to Jesus, 132, 135; new mode of opposition, 183; and Herodians........................ 226
Philip....................... 66
Phœnicia..................... 141
Pilate....................... 292
Pillow....................... 89
Plucking ears of grain......... 55

Prayer, Jesus answering, 97; posture in prayer........... 217
Prayer of Jesus always heard.. 276
Preparation day...........309, 313
Prætorium................... 297
Prophet in his own country, 108, 109
Proverbs.................... 76
Psalm cx.................... 236
Publicans.................50, 51
Purple, red, etc.............. 297
Purse....................... 111

Rabbi....................... 216
Rabboni..................... 202
Rapha....................... 231
Reed 297
Regeneration instantaneous.... 105
Rejection of Jesus by the Jewish people...............224, 225
Removing mountains......216, 217
Rending the clothes........... 283
Repentance, 32; joy and sorrow in......................... 91
Resurrection, 229, 231, 232, 241; time of Christ's.........315, 316
Retirement of Jesus, 120; with his disciples.............120, 121
Riches, trust in............... 191
Right hand and left, as positions of honor............... 196
Robber, 215; two robbers crucified with Jesus.........302-304

Sabbath, its observance, 55-57; for the race, 56, 58; what may be done on the, 59; Jewish and Christian 316, 317
Sacrifices, idea of all.......... 234
Sadducees................229, 231
Salome...................... 117
Salt losing its saltness......... 179
Salted with fire............... 179
Salutations.................. 237
Sandals..................26, 111
Sanhedrim................... 158
Satan, 30; Satan casting out Satan..................... 69
Scourging, Jewish and Roman.. 296
Scribes, 36; from Jerusalem, 68; their character and practices, 237, 238
Scrip 111
Scriptures fulfilled............ 279

INDEX.

	PAGE
Sea of Galilee, 33, 61; storm on,	89
Seaside, 75; teaching by	76
Second coming of Christ, 252; time of	254
Selfishness, 234; self-love	234
Sepulchre	310
Servant	199
Seven scoffs around the cross	304
Seven sayings on the cross	306
Shaking dust from the feet	112
Ship	34, 62
Shoes	26
Show-bread	56
Sidon, 61; Jesus passing through	143
Sign from heaven	151
Silence, why Jesus often prescribed	42, 62, 103
Simon	33
Simon the Canaanite	67
Simon, a Cyrenian	298
Sitting, Oriental posture of	50
Sleep applied to death	102
"Sleep on now"	276
Son of David	201
Son of God	21, 29, 282
Son of man	48, 49, 282
Sorrow unto death	274
Soul, 160, 233; losing the	160
Sower, parable of	80, 81–83
Sources of Mark's Gospel	xii., xiii.
Spikenard	259
Spirit or Ghost	127
"Spirit—flesh"	275
Spitting upon, the indignity	284
Stairs to housetop	46
Stilling the tempest illustrates what?	90, 92
Stone at the mouth of the sepulchre	317, 318
Stony ground	77
Superscription	228, 302
Straightway	29
Strength	233
Supper, 117; at Bethany	259
Surname	64
Swine	95
Synagogue, 35; ruler of, 98; chief seats in the, 237; scourging in the	246
Syrophœnician	141
Tabernacles	165

	PAGE
Talmud	133
Tempest on Sea of Galilee	127
Temple, 210, 243; house of prayer, 214; Titus tried to save it, 243; vail of	307
Temptation of Jesus, where, how, 30; lessons from	44
Tetrarch	113
Thaddeus	66
Thief, 215; the two thieves or robbers crucified with Jesus,	302–304
"Third hour, sixth hour"	301
"This generation"	254
Thomas	66
Thorns, crown of	297
"Thought thereon"	288
"Three days and three nights"	312
"Three hundred pence"	260
Thursday not the day of Christ's death	311–313
Tiberias	113
Time to speak	97
Time, Jewish mode of reckoning	312
Tombs	93, 120
Touch of faith	99, 100
Tradition of the elders	133, 134
Traditions against God's commands	136, 137
Transfiguration, 163 ff.; place of	164
Transubstantiation	267, 269
Treasury, 238; casting in offerings	238, 239, 241
Triumphal entry of Jesus	208, 209, 220
Truth and the Bible to be given to the people	83, 84
The Twelve, the number, 63; endowed with miraculous power, their mission	110
Tyre	61, 141
Unbelief, effects of	108
Unbelief of the apostles	322, 326
Understanding	234
Uncovering the roof	46, 47
Unwashen hands	132, 133
Uppermost rooms at feasts	237
Vail of the temple, 307; rent	307
Vases and cruses	260
Via Dolorosa	298

INDEX.

	PAGE		PAGE
Vineyard	222	Wine-fat	222
		Wine-press	222
Walking on the sea, 127; Peter's	128	Winter in Palestine	250
		Witnesses agreeing	282
Wars, etc., preceding the destruction of Jerusalem	245	Woman with issue of blood, 99, 100; her timidity and her faith	101
"Wash," 133, 134, 135; of hands,	133		
Washing of vessels	136	Women at the sepulchre	315
Watches of the night	127, 256	"Worm dieth not"	178
Watchfulness enforced	255, 256	Worship	93, 94
Wheat, Oriental	85		
Widow's mites	238, 239, 241		
Wilderness, meaning of	22	Young man at Christ's betrayal,	279, 280
Wind, contrary, on the Sea of Galilee	127	Young ruler seeks Jesus	189-191
Wine, fermented or unfermented, in Palestine, and at the Passover, 268; what should be used at the Lord's Supper, 269; withheld from the laity, 268		Zeal of John	176
		Zebedee	34

GENERAL CONTENTS.

	PAGE.
Preface	iii.
Introductory Remarks	v.
A few Works, etc	xx.
Explanatory Comments and Practical Remarks	21
List of Illustrations	328
Index	329
Table of Time, Festivals, Measures, and Money	336
Synoptical View of the Four Gospels	337
Suggestions on the Study of Mark	342

TABLE OF TIME, FESTIVALS, MEASURES, AND MONEY.

WATCHES.	DURATION.
1st, or Evening Watch,	From 6 P.M. to 9 P.M.
2d, or Midnight Watch,	9 " 12 "
3d, or Cock-crowing Watch,	12 " 3 A.M.
4th, or Dawn Watch,	3 A.M. 6 "

DAY.

"Third hour,"	9 o'clock, A.M.
"Sixth hour,"	12 o'clock, M.
"Ninth hour,"	3 o'clock, P.M.

FESTIVALS.

Name.	Time of beginning.	Duration.	Event commemorated.
PASSOVER,	14th evening of March and April moon,	8 days,	Deliverance from Egypt.
PENTECOST,	50th day after the 2d of Passover,	1 day,	Giving of the Law.
FEAST OF TABERNACLES,	15th evening of Sept. and Oct. moon,	8 days,	Harvest, and passing through the Wilderness.
FEAST OF DEDICATION,	25th evening of Nov. and Dec. moon,	8 days,	Consecration of the Second Temple, B.C. 164.

MEASURES.

	ft.	in.			
Cubit,	1.	7.	Sabbath day's journey,	Jewish,	2000 Jewish cubits, or six stadia.
Fathom,	6.				
Reed,	9.	6½			
Furlong,	606¾		Day's journey,		about 30 miles.

MONEY.

				cents.	mills.
Lepton, or Mite (Mk. 12 : 42),	Greek,	Copper,		.	2
Farthing, or Kodrantes (Mk. 12 : 42),	Roman,	"		.	4
" or Assarion (Mt. 10 : 29),	"	"		1	4
Denarius, or Penny (Mk. 6 : 37),	"	Silver,		15	.
Drachma (Lk. 15 : 8),	Greek,	"		15	.
Didrachma (Mt. 17 : 24),	"	"		30	.
Stater (Mt. 17 : 27),	"	"		60	.
Shekel,	Jewish,	"		60	.
Pound or Mina (Lk. 19 : 13),	Greek,	"	15	.	.
Talent (Mt. 18 : 24),	Jewish,	"	1500 +	.	.

SYNOPTICAL VIEW OF THE FOUR GOSPELS.

The chronology of the Gospels is in many respects undetermined. The duration of Christ's ministry is much disputed. It continued at least two and one half years; for John in his Gospel mentions three Passovers, John 2 : 13; 6 : 4; 13 : 1. If the feast (or "a feast of the Jews") mentioned in John 5 : 1 be also regarded as a Passover, then his public ministry continued about three years and a half. But if the feast was that of Purim (Esther 9 : 26), as many suppose, occurring a month before the Passover of John 6 : 4, then must we assign the shorter term to his public ministry. Although certainty may not be attained, yet the amount of labor that Jesus performed, and the time required for his three preaching tours throughout Galilee, before the Passover mentioned in John 6 : 4, incline us to regard the feast of John 5 : 1 as also a Passover. In accordance with this view the following table is arranged, and the probable chronological order and harmony given; but where either is quite doubtful, or beset with special difficulty, the references are printed in **heavy type**. The reasons for the arrangement are given by the author in his HARMONY OF THE GOSPELS.

I. EVENTS CONNECTED WITH THE BIRTH AND CHILDHOOD OF JESUS.

A period of about thirteen and a half years, from B.C. 6 to A.D. 8.

SECT.	SUBJECT	MATT.	MARK.	LUKE.	JOHN.
1.	Luke's Preface	....	....	1 : 1-4	....
2.	John's Introduction	....	....	....	1 : 1-14
3.	The Genealogies	1 : 1-17	....	3 : 23-38	....
4.	Annunciation of John's Birth	....	....	1 : 5-25	....
5.	Annunciation of the Birth of Jesus	....	....	1 : 26-38	....
6.	Mary visits Elizabeth	....	....	1 : 39-56	....
7.	The Birth of John the Baptist	....	....	1 : 57-80	....
8.	An Angel appears to Joseph	1 : 18-23	....	....	....
9.	Birth of Jesus	1 : 24, 25	....	2 : 1-7	....
10.	The Visit of the Shepherds	....	....	2 : 8-20	....
11.	The Circumcision	....	....	2 : 21	....
12.	Presentation in the Temple	....	....	2 : 22-38	....
13.	Temporary Return to Nazareth	....	....	2 : 39	....
14.	Again at Bethlehem ; Visit of the Magi.	2 : 1-12	....	....	....
15.	Flight into Egypt	2 : 13-15	....	....	....
16.	Herod's Massacre of the Children	2 : 16-18	....	....	....
17.	Return and Residence at Nazareth	2 : 19-23	....	2 : 40	....
18.	Childhood of Jesus	....	....	2 : 41-52	....

II. ANNOUNCEMENT AND INTRODUCTION OF CHRIST'S PUBLIC MINISTRY.

About one year, from the spring of A.D. 26 to that of A.D. 27.

19.	The Ministry of John the Baptist	3 : 1-12	1 : 1-8	3 : 1-18	....
20.	The Baptism of Jesus	3 : 13-17	1 : 9-11	3 : 21-23	....
21.	The Temptation	4 : 1-11	1 : 12, 13	4 : 1-13	....
22.	Testimony of John to Jesus	....	....	....	1 : 15-34

SYNOPTICAL VIEW OF THE GOSPELS.

SECT. SUBJECT.	MATT.	MARK.	LUKE.	JOHN.
23. Jesus gains Disciples; returns to Galilee..........	....	....	....	1 : 35–51
24. The Marriage at Cana.................	....	....	....	2 : 1–11
25. Visits Capernaum	....	....	....	2 : 12

III. FROM THE FIRST PASSOVER OF CHRIST'S PUBLIC MINISTRY UNTIL THE SECOND.

One year, from April, A.D. 27, to April, A.D. 28.

26. At the Passover; the Traders expelled.	....	....	....	2 : 13-25
27. Visit of Nicodemus.................	....	....	....	3 : 1–21
28. Jesus remains in Judea	....	....	....	3 : 22–24
29. Further Testimony of John the Baptist.	....	....	....	3 : 25–36
30. John Imprisoned	....	....	3 : 19, 20	
31. Jesus departs for Galilee.............	4 : 12	1 : 14	4 : 14	4 : 1–4
32. Discourses with the Woman of Sychar.	....	....	....	4 : 5–42
33. Teaches publicly in Galilee............	4 : 17	1 : 14, 15	4 : 14, 15	4 : 43–46
34. Heals a Nobleman's Son.............	....	....	....	4 : 46–54
35. Rejected at Nazareth.	4 : 13	....	4 : 16–30	
36. Makes Capernaum his Residence.....	4 : 13–16	....	4 : 31	
37. Four called as Constant Attendants...	4 : 18–22	1 : 16–20		
38. A Demoniac healed in the Synagogue..	....	1 : 21–28	4 : 31–37	... .
39. Heals Peter's Wife's Mother.	8 : 14–17	1 : 29–31	4 : 38–41	....
40. First Preaching Tour throughout Galilee........	4 : 23–25	1 : 35–39	4 : 42–44	....
41. The Miraculous Draught of Fishes....	....	....	5 : 1–11	....
42. Sermon on the Mount.................	5 : 1–7 : 29	....	....	....
43. A Leper healed.......................	8 : 1–4	1 : 40–45	5 : 12–16	....
44. Heals a Paralytic.................	9 : 2–8	2 : 1–12	5 : 17–26	....
45. The Call of Matthew.................	9 : 9	2 : 13, 14	5 : 27, 28	....

IV. FROM THE SECOND PASSOVER UNTIL THE THIRD.

From April, A.D. 28, to April, A.D. 29.

46. At the Passover; Heals the Impotent Man.....	....	....	....	5 : 1–47
47. Plucking the Ears of Grain...........	12 : 1–8	2 : 23–28	6 : 1–5	....
48. Healing the Withered Hand..........	12 : 9–14	3 : 1–6	6 : 6–11	....
49. Withdraws to the Sea of Galilee.....	12 : 15–21	3 : 7–12	....	....
50. The Twelve Apostles chosen..........	....	3 : 13–19	6 : 12–16	....
51. The Sermon in the Plain	....	....	6 : 17–49	....
52. Healing of the Centurion's Servant...	8 : 5–13	....	7 : 1–10	....
53. Raises a Widow's Son at Nain........	....	....	7 : 11–17	....
54. John's Message to Jesus.............	11 : 2–19	....	7 : 18–35	....
55. Upbraiding the Cities of Galilee......	11 : 20–30	....	....	....
56. Anointed by a Penitent Woman.....	....	....	7 : 36–50	....
57. Second Circuit of Galilee	....	....	8 : 1–3	....
58. A Blind and Dumb Demoniac healed..	12 : 22–37	3 : 19–30	....	....
59. A Sign demanded of Jesus...........	12 : 38–45	....	....	....
60. Christ's Mother and Brethren........	12 : 46–50	3 : 31–35	8 : 19–21	....
61. Parable of the Sower.................	13 : 1–23	4 : 1–25	8 : 4–18	....
62. Other Parables spoken to the Multitude	13 : 24–35	4 : 26–34	....	....
63. Wheat and Tares explained; and other Parables to the Disciples.....	13 : 36–53	....	....	....
64. The Tempest stilled	8 : 18, 23–27	4 : 35–41	8 : 22–25	....
65. The Two Demoniacs of Gadara.......	8 : 28–9 : 1	5 : 1–21	8 : 26–40	....
66. Matthew's Feast.....................	9 : 10–13	2 : 15–17	5 : 29–32	....
67. Discourse on Fasting.................	9 : 14–17	2 : 18–22	5 : 33–39	....
68. Jairus's Daughter; the Bloody Issue..	9 : 18–26	5 : 22–43	8 : 41–56	....
69. Healing of the Blind and Dumb......	9 : 27–34	....	....	....
70. Second Rejection at Nazareth........	13 : 54–58	6 : 1–6	....	....
71. Third Circuit of Galilee.............	9 : 35–38	....	....	....
72. The Twelve endowed and sent forth ..	10 : 1–42	6 : 7–11	9 : 1–5	....
73. They go forth; Third Tour continued..	11 : 1	6 : 12, 13	9 : 6	....
74. Herod's Opinion of Jesus; John's Beheadal........	14 : 1–12	6 : 14–29	9 : 7–9	....

SYNOPTICAL VIEW OF THE GOSPELS.

SECT.	SUBJECT.	MATT.	MARK.	LUKE.	JOHN.
75.	Return of the Twelve		6: 30, 31	9: 10	
76.	Feeding the Five Thousand	14: 13-21	6: 32-44	9: 10-17	6: 1-14
77.	Jesus walks on the Sea	14: 22-36	6: 45-56		6: 15-21
78.	Discourse at Capernaum				6: 22-71

V. FROM THE THIRD PASSOVER UNTIL THE ENSUING FEAST OF TABERNACLES.

Six months, from April to October, A.D. 29.

79.	Jesus continues in Galilee				7: 1
80.	Traditions of the Elders	15: 1-20	7: 1-23		
81.	The Canaanitish Woman	15: 21-28	7: 24-30		
82.	Deaf and Dumb Man, etc., healed	15: 29-31	7: 31-37		
83.	Feeds the Four Thousand	15: 32-39	8: 1-9		
84.	A Sign again demanded	15: 39-16: 4	8: 10-12		
85.	The Leaven of the Pharisees	16: 4-12	8: 13-21		
86.	Blind Man healed		8: 22-26		
87.	Visit to the region of Cæsarea Philippi	16: 13-20	8: 27-30	9: 18-21	
88.	Jesus foretells his Death	16: 21-28	8: 31-9: 1	9: 22-27	
89.	The Transfiguration	17: 1-13	9: 2-13	9: 28-36	
90.	Healing the Dumb Demoniac	17: 14-21	9: 14-29	9: 37-43	
91.	Jesus again foretells his Death	17: 22, 23	9: 30-32	9: 43-45	
92.	The Sacred Tribute	17: 24-27	9: 33		
93.	Contention among the Disciples	18: 1-14	9: 33-50	9: 46-50	
94.	Dealing with an Offended Brother, etc.	18: 15-20			
95.	On Forgiveness	18: 21-35			
96.	Still continues in Galilee				7: 2-9
97.	Goes to the Feast of Tabernacles			9: 51-56	7: 10
98.	Concerning following Jesus	8: 19-22		9: 57-62	

VI. FROM THE FEAST OF TABERNACLES TILL CHRIST'S ARRIVAL AT BETHANY, SIX DAYS BEFORE THE FOURTH PASSOVER.

Six months, less six days.

99.	Jesus at the Feast; teaches publicly				7: 11-8: 1
100.	The Woman taken in Adultery				8: 2-11
101.	Further Public Teaching				8: 12-59
102.	Seventy instructed and sent forth			10: 1-16	
103.	Return of the Seventy			10: 17-24	
104.	Reply to a Lawyer; Good Samaritan			10: 25-37	
105.	Jesus at the House of Martha and Mary			10: 38-42	
106.	How to pray			11: 1-13	
107.	Heals a Dumb Demoniac			11: 14-36	
108.	Jesus Dines with a Pharisee			12: 37-54	
109.	On Hypocrisy, Worldliness, etc.			12: 1-59	
110.	Slaughter of Certain Galileans			13: 1-9	
111.	A Blind Man healed on the Sabbath				9: 1-41
112.	The Good Shepherd				10: 1-21
113.	Jesus at the Feast of Dedication				10: 22-39
114.	Retires beyond Jordan				10: 40-42
115.	Heals an Infirm Woman on the Sabbath			13: 10-21	
116.	Journeying and Teaching; warned against Herod			13: 22-35	
117.	Jesus hears of Lazarus' Sickness				11: 1-6
118.	Dines with a Chief Pharisee			14: 1-24	
119.	Requirements of Discipleship			14: 25-35	
120.	Lost Sheep, Lost Silver, Prodigal Son			15: 1-32	
121.	Parable of the Unjust Judge			16: 1-13	
122.	The Rich Man and Lazarus			16: 14-31	
123.	Teaches Forbearance, Faith, etc.			17: 1-10	
124.	Goes to Bethany and Raises Lazarus				11: 7-46
125.	Retires to Ephraim				11: 47-54
126.	Passes through Samaria and Galilee			17: 11-19	
127.	On the Coming of the Kingdom of God			17: 20-37	
128.	The Importunate Widow, etc.			18: 1-14	
129.	Finally leaves Galilee; on Divorce	19: 1-12	10: 1-12		
130.	Blesses Little Children	19: 13-15	10: 13-16	18: 15-17	
131.	The Rich Young Ruler	19: 16-30	10: 17-31	18: 18-30	

SYNOPTICAL VIEW OF THE GOSPELS.

SECT. SUBJECT.	MATT.	MARK.	LUKE.	JOHN.
132. Laborers in the Vineyard...............	20 : 1-16	....	....	....
133. Third Time foretells his Death........	20 : 17-19	10 : 32-34	18 : 31-34	....
134. The Ambitious Request of James and John...	20 : 20-28	10 : 35-45	....	....
135. Healing Two Blind Men near Jericho..	20 : 29-34	10 : 46-52	18 : 35-43	....
136. Zaccheus; the Ten Pounds..............	....	....	19 : 1-28	....
137. Jesus sought at Jerusalem	....	....	....	11 : 55-57
138. Arrives at Bethany Six Days before the Passover..	....	....	19 : 28	12 : 1, 9-11

VII. THE LAST PASSOVER WEEK.
Seven days, April 2nd to April 8th, A.D. 30.

SECT. SUBJECT.	MATT.	MARK.	LUKE.	JOHN.
139. *First Day of the Week.* Public Entry into Jerusalem	21 : 1-11	11 : 1-11	19 : 29-44	12 : 12-19
140. Certain Greeks desire to see Jesus	21 : 17	11 : 11	....	12 : 20-36
141. *Second Day of the Week.* The Barren Fig-tree..	21 : 18, 19	11 : 12-14	....	....
142. The Temple Cleansed....................	21 : 12-16	11 : 15-19	19:45-46: 37, 38	....
143. *Third Day of the Week.* Withered Fig-tree...	21 : 20-22	11 : 20-26	....	....
144. In the Temple; the Two Sons..........	21 : 23-32	11 : 27-33	20 : 1-8	....
145. The Wicked Husbandmen	21 : 33-46	12 : 1-12	20 : 9-19	....
146. Marriage of the King's Son.............	22 : 1-14	....	....	....
147. Tribute to Cæsar..........................	22 : 15-22	12 : 13-17	20 : 20-26	....
148. Concerning the Resurrection...........	22 : 23-33	12 : 18-27	20 : 27-40	....
149. The Great Commandment..............	22 : 34-40	12 : 28-34	....	....
150. Christ the Son of David	22 : 41-46	12 : 35-37	20 : 41-44	....
151. Last Discourse to the Jews..............	23 : 1-39	12 : 38-40	20 : 45-47	....
152. The Widow's Mite........................	....	12 : 41-44	21 : 1-4	....
153. Reflections on the Unbelief of the Jews	....	....	....	12 : 37-50
154. Discourse on the Mount of Olives.....	24 : 1-51	13 : 1-37	21 : 5-36	....
155. The Ten Virgins; the Talents..........	25 : 1-30	....	....	....
156. Graphic Scene of the Judgment........	25 : 31-46	....	....	....
157. *Fourth Day of the Week.* The Rulers conspire..	26 : 1-5	14 : 1, 2	22 : 1, 2	....
158. The Supper and Anointing at Bethany	26 : 6-16	14 : 3-11	22 : 3-6	12 : 2-8
159. *Fifth Day of the Week.* Preparation for the Passover	26 : 17-19	14 : 12-16	22 : 7-13	....
160. *Sixth Day of the Week.* The Passover; Contention of the Twelve..................	26 : 20	14 : 17	22 : 14-18, 24-30	....
161. Washing the Disciples' Feet.............	....	....	....	13 : 1-20
162. The Traitor pointed out; Judas withdraws..	26 : 21-25	14 : 18-21	22 : 21-23	13 : 21-30
163. Jesus foretells the Fall of Peter........	....	....	22 : 31-38	13 : 31-38
164. Institutes the Lord's Supper (1 Cor. 11 : 23-26)...................................	26 : 26-29	14 : 22-25	22 : 19, 20	....
165. Valedictory Discourse	....	....	....	14 : 1-31
166. " " Continued....	....	....	....	15 : 1-27
167. " " Concluded....	....	....	....	16 : 1-33
168. Christ's Intercessory Prayer............	....	....	....	17 : 1-26
169. Again foretells the Fall of Peter.......	26 : 30-35	14 : 26-31	22 : 39	18 : 1
170. The Agony in Gethsemane..............	26 : 36-46	14 : 32-42	22 : 40-46	18 : 1
171. Betrayal and Apprehension.............	26 : 47-56	14 : 43-52	22 : 47-53	18 : 2-11
172. Jesus before Annas	....	....	....	18 : 12-14, 19-23
173. Peter thrice denies Christ	26:58,69-75	14:54,66-72	22 : 54-62	18 : 15-18, 25-27
174. Jesus before Caiaphas....................	26:57,59-68	14:53,55-65	22:54,63-65	18 : 24
175. The final Formal Examination.........	27 : 1	15 : 1	22 : 66-71	....
176. Jesus led to Pilate.........................	27 : 2	15 : 1	23 : 1	18 : 28
177. Remorse and Suicide of Judas (Acts 1 : 18, 19)....................................	27 : 3-10	....	....	....
178. Jesus before Pilate........................	27 : 11-14	15 : 2-5	23 : 2-5	18 : 28-38
179. Jesus before Herod.......................	....	....	23 : 6-12	....
180. Again before Pilate; Barabbas.........	27 : 15-26	15 : 6-15	23 : 13-25	18 : 39, 40

SYNOPTICAL VIEW OF THE GOSPELS.

SECT.	SUBJECT.	MATT.	MARK.	LUKE.	JOHN.
181.	Scourged and delivered to be crucified.	27 : 26-30	15 : 16-19	23 : 25	19 : 1-16
182.	Led away to be crucified	27 : 31-34	15 : 20-23	23 : 26-33	19 : 16, 17
183.	The Crucifixion	27 : 35-44	15 : 24-32	23 : 33-43	19 : 18-27
184.	Phenomena attending his Death	27 : 45-56	15 : 33-41	23 : 44-49	19 : 28-30
185.	The Burial	27 : 57-61	15 : 42-47	23 : 50-56	19 : 31-42
186.	The Seventh Day of the Week. Sepulchre sealed and guarded	27 : 62-66			

VIII. FROM CHRIST'S RESURRECTION TILL HIS ASCENSION.
Forty days, April to May, A.D. 30.

187.	The First Day of the Week. The Resurrection	28 : 2-4			
188.	Women visit the Sepulchre	28 : 1	16 : 1-4	24 : 1, 2	20 : 1, 2
189.	Vision of Angels	28 : 5-8	16 : 5-8	21 : 3-8	
190.	Peter and John at the Sepulchre			24 : 12	20 : 3-10
191.	Jesus appears to Mary Magdalene		16 : 9		20 : 11-11
192.	Meets the Other Women	28 : 9, 10			
193.	Report of the Women		16 : 10, 11	24 : 9-11	20 : 18
194.	Report of the Watch	28 : 11-15			
195.	Appears to Two Disciples and to Peter (1 Cor. 15 : 5)		16 : 12, 13	24 : 13-35	
196.	Evening at the Close of the First Day of the Week. Appears to Ten Apostles (1 Cor. 15 : 5)		16 : 14	24 : 36-49	20 : 19-25
197.	Evening at the Close of the First Day of the Next Week. Appears to Eleven Apostles				20 : 26-29
198.	Appears to Seven Apostles	28 : 16			21 : 1-23
199.	Appears to above Five Hundred (1 Cor. 15 : 6)	28 : 16-20	16 : 15-18		
200.	He is seen of James; then of all the Apostles, 1 Cor. 15 : 7; Acts 1 : 3-8				
201.	The Ascension (Acts 1 : 9-12)		16 : 19, 20	24 : 50-53	
202.	John's Conclusion of his Gospel				20 : 30, 31; 21 : 24, 25

NOTE TO THE REVISED EDITION.

In harmonizing the Gospels in the Common version the following should be said:

1. Our Common version was translated from later manuscripts. The oldest Greek manuscripts are acknowledged to be the purest and best; and they present the four Gospels in their greatest independence. The tendency among copyists, or transcribers, has been to introduce interpolations into the text in order to harmonize and assimilate the narratives. Assimilation was more often made by inserting from the longer text into the shorter; or by conforming a quotation more exactly to the Old Testament. Matthew appears to have frequently been assimilated to Luke, and Mark to one of the Gospels.

2. The translators of our Common version often used considerable variety in rendering the same Greek word. They increased the beauty of their style thereby, but sometimes sacrificed exactness. The Revised and the Improved versions are superior in both these respects. These notes on the Gospels have also sought to remedy these defects.

The author, in his *Revised Harmony of the Four Gospels*, has placed in foot-notes many corrections from the Revised version. Thus the student has the two-fold advantage of comparing the Gospels in both versions.

SUGGESTIONS ON THE STUDY OF MARK.

How rarely do we hear of a Sunday School or a Bible Class studying the Gospel of Mark? Yet no Gospel is more deserving of study. From none can we so soon get so good a view of our Savior's life. None is better suited for beginning the study of the Gospels. "There is something in its structure," says Dr. J. A. Alexander, "which makes it eminently fit to give the first impression of the Gospel History, and prepare the reader for the study of the other books." So also Webster and Wilkinson in their Greek Testament say, "We would suggest to those who put this work into the hands of their pupils at school, that there are reasons why the second Gospel should be read before any other, as the best introduction to the regular and systematic study of the New Testament." Such is also the opinion of many of our best educators; and in many Theological Seminaries, the Gospel of Mark is made the basis for the study of the Evangelists. But equally adapted is this Gospel to the various grades of Sabbath-school teachers and scholars. There is scarcely a reason for its critical study which is not also equally strong for its popular study.

In studying this Gospel I would suggest: First read it at a single sitting, if possible, so as to get a view of it as a whole. Then read it in order to note its general divisions, and then analyze each division. Familiarize yourself with these so as to be able to state from memory the analysis as a whole, and the contents of each chapter. Read the Introductory Remarks at the beginning of the volume. Refer frequently to the Synoptical View of the four Gospels. Familiarize yourself with the locality of places mentioned in the Gospel. Consult the comments so far as necessary, and read the practical remarks. Look out and fix in mind the Scripture references. You will thus become master of the Gospel, and prepared to study the others, either singly or in harmony.

www.ingramcontent.com/pod-product-compliance
Lightning Source LLC
Chambersburg PA
CBHW032048220426
43664CB00008B/911